René Verdon's
FRENCH COOKING FOR THE AMERICAN TABLE

RENÉ VERDON'S

French Cooking for the American Table

by RENÉ VERDON with CARL LYREN

Doubleday & Company, Inc., Garden City, New York   1974

ISBN: 0–385–08702–0
Library of Congress Catalog Card Number: 72–76217

TO THE PEOPLE OF AMERICA,
WHO HAVE MOST GRACIOUSLY SET A PLACE
FOR MY WIFE YVETTE AND ME
AT THE AMERICAN TABLE.

✳ Contents

COLOR PHOTOGRAPHS

✱ Preface

This book is about the fresh American foods at your supermarket, and how to cook them. Careful attention is given to the selection of fresh vegetables, meats, poultry, fish, and other basic foods. A few canned, frozen, and imported items are included, but they are mere embellishments.

The cooking procedures in this book are those developed by generations of French cooks, but they will be recognized as universal by good cooks everywhere. These procedures can be learned by rote, but they are better learned by understanding. The famous gastronomer Brillat-Savarin, reproving his cook for a badly fried sole, said, "Certain things that you do without attention, only because you have seen others do them, can nonetheless be traced to the highest principles of science." I will try to make known the principles behind these cooking procedures.

Of the recipes given in this book, some are ancient, some relatively new, but all are universally acknowledged to form part of the French cuisine. Thus in writing out these recipes, I do not invent. I report. I have given the names of these recipes both in English and in French. This will give you a certain degree of competence in deciphering French menus. It will also teach you that the frequently elaborate titles given various French dishes are often nothing more than helpful serving suggestions for very simply cooked foods.

To help you in preparing the recipes in this book, I have placed an asterisk (*) beside cooking procedures that are fully described elsewhere in these pages. Preparations or dishes for which a recipe exists are capitalized. In either case the most convenient way to find the dish or the cooking procedure is to consult the Index.

At first this book may seem overly demanding, and you may conclude that its use should be reserved only for special occasions. But if what is called for seems demanding, I have given the very good reasons that underlie these demands. If you hold to them, if you do not compromise, soon the all-important little things—the purity of taste in a little dish of carrots—will bring new interest to everyday eating. Little by little, as you follow these pages, something new will creep into your cooking.

Little by little your taste will awaken, until one day you will imperceptibly join that ancient fraternity of men and women who in every century have fallen under the spell of the good fruits of the earth. You will rejoice in nature's crispnesses and juicinesses, her tartnesses and tangs. You will find you are eating less, because you are tasting more. And your kitchen will become a happier place as you indulge in this most civilized and yet most innocent of vices.

René Verdon's
FRENCH COOKING FOR THE AMERICAN TABLE

1 *The Real French Cooking*

French cooking has been characterized in many ways. It is the exalted cooking of the great restaurants. Or it is the simple cooking of the French countryside. It is a glorious procession of warm, limpid, brilliant sauces. Or it is pot roast with a pretentious name. It is the cooking of pompous, high-strung chefs. It is cooking with butter and shallots and cream and wine. It is expensive cooking. It is frugal cooking.

Or French cooking, according to chef Louis Diat, is the cooking from his mother's kitchen.

Clearly, if we are going to cook in the French manner, we must understand what this manner is. We must go beyond what merely characterizes French cooking to arrive at its essence. We must push aside the leaves, penetrate the branches, and thump the trunk of this immense tree that was planted in the heart of Europe twenty centuries ago.

It has become customary to divide French cooking into two main branches —the *haute cuisine* of the restaurants and the *bourgeoise cuisine* of the home. I do not like this division. It emphasizes superficial differences. Remember, it was the leek-and-potato soup of his mother's kitchen that Louis Diat chilled and made into the elegant *vichyssoise*. It was a 1792 Paris restaurant that gave its name and fame to one of the most typical of French peasant dishes, *boeuf à la mode*.

The essence of true French cooking is found in its unity of purpose, a purpose that is pursued in restaurant and home kitchens alike. After all, the chef cooks at home, too. His facilities and ingredients may differ, but he does not change his way of cooking for that. What is the French chef up to? What grand design has he, however unconsciously, in mind? What is his purpose?

You must fully realize how important this statement of purpose is. It is the ultimate explanation of every culinary action you will be asked to perform in this book. It will also serve as a lifelong guide so that at every moment, whether you are slicing your carrots or stirring your sauces, you will know precisely what you are trying to achieve. Bear with me, then, if I take pains to make the purpose of French cooking clear.

Let me begin with the bare bones. The purpose of French cooking is to please the taste. Aha, you say, but is not all cooking concerned mainly with the taste of food? No, all cooking is not. Meat-and-potato cooking fills the stomach with warm food. Nutritional cooking pursues the elusive vitamin. Convenience cooking is mostly concerned with how quickly and easily it can be done with. Much of the famous cuisine of imperial Rome was devoted to conspicuous consumption. I am not saying that these kinds of cooking ignore taste entirely. But taste is secondary to quantity or nutrition or convenience. In French cooking, taste always comes first.

Taste, we know, is largely a matter of preference. What pleases the taste of one person may not please that of another. A cuisine develops to suit the taste of the people who eat it. The taste French cooking seeks to please is the collective taste of the French people. They have a taste all their own.

In remote times, when the French were still Gauls, they went beyond the simple joy of filling their stomachs and demonstrated their enjoyment of tasting. In their delight of taste for taste's sake, they drenched their meat with vivid sauces made with honey, vinegar, wine, pepper, broth, and a variety of pungent herbs—resinous, overpowering sauces that would horrify a French chef today.

Twenty centuries of simmering have mellowed these early sauces. Twenty centuries of cookery have tamed the French palate. Today the French delight, not in taste alone, but in a certain kind of taste. Today the French prize above all else *the natural taste* of foods. This glorification of the natural taste of foods is the *raison d'être* of real French cooking. And your abiding purpose, when you cook in the French manner, is to enhance the good natural tastes that nature has given us to enjoy.

Oh, the French make their little adjustments. They emphasize and complement and combine tastes in an endless and dedicated search for variety. But always they preserve and amplify the natural principle of the food—the beefiness of the beef, the fresh green asparagusness of the asparagus. Their haughty sauces, which may take days to prepare, are subservient to a single purpose—to glorify the natural taste of the simply-cooked foods they are served with. If you are going to cook in the French manner, you must learn to seek out this taste.

Your quest will require more than just skill and care in the cooking of foods. It requires a diligent search for the best that nature can provide. And most important, it requires the education of taste so that you can fully enjoy the fruits of your labors. Diligent marketing, careful cooking, appreciative eating—this is the threefold activity that true French cooking requires.

Let us trace this threefold activity with a bundle of asparagus. The French cook *knows* this asparagus. It is not just asparagus-in-general. It is a particular kind of asparagus, grown in a particular place. In fact, the French cook—chef or housewife—has at least five different kinds of asparagus from which to make a choice. It may be plump, ivory-stalked Argenteuil with pale purple tips, grown in the same fields outside Paris for five hundred years. It may be green Lauris from the South of France. It may be violet Genoa asparagus. Or pale Malines, fleshy and flavorful. Or tasty thin green Anglaise. Whichever asparagus is chosen, it will be chosen to fulfill a particular role, to supply a particular taste.

Before buying, the cook will pore over this asparagus. Are the tips tightly packed? Are the stalks free of ribs? Is the color the color this variety of asparagus ought to be? Is it tender and sweet? He will bite into a stalk to find out. Is it fresh enough? The nose—sniff, sniff—will tell him much about its freshness.

In the kitchen each stalk will be skinned, the woody base snapped off where it naturally breaks, and the stalks lined up at the tips and tied with soft string in single-serving bunches. One whack of the knife will trim the bases. Then into a bath of refreshing cool water to dislodge any sand or insects. The peelings and trimmings will be saved for soup.

He will cook the asparagus on its side in a flat pan of boiling water, first shaking out the cold water clinging to the stalks so the water in the pan may return more quickly to a gentle boil. The stalks, stripped of their skin, will cook quickly, keeping pace with the tender tips, and the natural creamy white or bright green color will be retained, even intensified. Cooking time—about 10 minutes. The asparagus, still slightly crisp (the stalks will not droop sadly when lifted from the pan), is then drained of all water and served on a snowy napkin.

When the final act is performed, when this asparagus is tasted, it will taste fresh as grass.

This, in microcosm, is French cooking. A respect for foods as nature made them. A passion for freshness. Painstaking preparation. Meticulous cooking. And a deep-felt appreciation of the natural taste of foods as they are. This is the way asparagus is bought, cooked, and eaten in the best restaurants of France. It differs not one whit from the way asparagus is bought, cooked, and eaten in the French home.

REAL FRENCH COOKING AT HOME

Now I can hear you muttering, "This René fellow is evading the facts. He takes as his illustration the simple asparagus. What about chicken in champagne sauce? What about filet of beef Montmorency? How is the cooking of these dishes similar to cooking at home? What is more, how can I hope to compete with the horde of restaurant chefs who specialize in roasting, grilling, sauce-making, and salad-making, who devote their full time to cooking, who do not have to take time to mingle with the guests or to serve them. How am I to amass the bases of cooking these chefs have ready at hand—the sparkling consommés, the gelatinous veal stocks, the rich brown sauces and meat glazes, the golden hollandaise kept warm in its water bath, all ready for instant use?"

To this I answer that the advantages often attributed to restaurant cooking have become a thing of the past. Today the French restaurant chef, who once served three or four diners, is now more likely to serve thirty or forty. As a result he has been denied one of his most valuable cooking ingredients —time. Lacking time, yet intent upon preserving the quality of the two dozen or more dishes of the menu, the chef inevitably simplifies. He learns to make do with fewer bases, fewer stocks and sauces. For example, instead of making his brown sauce from brown beef stock, he may use the more versatile brown veal stock, reducing it until it has the thickness of a sauce. The taste will be excellent, but it will not be authentic. It will not be the taste of brown sauce Louis XIV enjoyed.

For this and other reasons I believe classic French cooking is more easily produced in your kitchen than it is in the kitchens of many French restaurants today. At home you do not have the lengthy menu to contend with. You know the hour of dinner; you need not be ready to serve at a moment's notice. At home you can pace your efforts, cooking simply and quickly on some days, cooking as elaborately as you choose on others. At home you can leisurely plan for and prepare one meal at a time, as simple or elaborate as you choose, to be served to docile diners.

As for stocks, sauces, and other bases that are so characteristic of classic French cooking, these are easy for you to collect. The brown stock you make for one dish can be made in quantity, reduced to a meat glaze, and stored in the refrigerator for up to six months for use in a half-dozen other dishes. The brown sauce you make for a Sunday dinner can be made in quantity, put in one-cup receptacles, and frozen as a base for a half-dozen other delightful dinners. Almost anything at all a classic dish requires may be made in a greater quantity than needed and stored in the refrigerator or freezer for future use.

Stocking your home larder provides you with the most useful collection any hobbyist can make. With just a few items of this edible collection on hand, and a grasp of classic French cooking techniques, dozens of dishes you would pay dearly for in the restaurant become the work of thirty minutes. And you will *know* they are classic, authentic.

In the pages ahead you will learn the classic cooking methods as well as how to produce the important bases that make French cooking—both restaurant and bourgeoise cooking—a joy to perform at home. Indeed the real French cooking in America may find its future best secured in kitchens such as yours.

2 *The Foods and the Tastes*

The foods are unnumbered. It has been said there is nothing living in this world—neither plant nor animal, on land, in the sea, or in the air—that someone, sooner or later, will not devise a method for getting into the cooking pot.

In 1825 Jean Anthelme Brillat-Savarin, world's first professor of gastronomy, expressed his envious belief that the gourmets of the twentieth century would be feasting on the mineral kingdom. With all our scientific progress, we have failed him here.

Because only the plants can make food. Powered by energy from the sun, the plants transform chemical elements of the earth, air, and water into the substances we call foodstuffs. The plants themselves, the animals, the peoples of the earth, all subsist ultimately on these foodstuffs manufactured in the microscopic cells of the green plant.

In the search for nourishment there have been many attempts to create new foods by harnessing the plant's food-making abilities. The English have extracted foodstuffs from tree leaves, the Japanese have dined on cultures of green algae, and the Germans have sat down to vat-grown food yeasts. But all these foods taste terrible. It is still the foods closest to the way nature made them—the corn and asparagus, the heavy chops and plump fowl—that bring the most pleasure to our tables.

Gourmets have long considered my native France as the land God stocked most generously with good foods. With its happy climate, with its soil textured by centuries of careful farming, with its richly stocked fishponds —the Channel, Atlantic, and Mediterranean—with its sunny slopes where grapes grow so heavy and sweet the bees buzz hopefully around them, with its sweet rivers laden with crayfish, its cabbages big as pumpkins, its Norman butter-of-gold, its fat Bresse pullets (so exquisitely flavored one hesitates even to salt them) and Languedoc *cassoulets* (brimming with duck and mutton and sausages and snow white beans), with its *foie gras,* black truffles, and salt marsh lamb, its morels, brioches, and white asparagus, with a mustard served in every great restaurant on earth, with all of this to feast upon, France is indeed a great larder. But alongside America, France is like the corner grocery next to the supermarket.

Even before the first plow arrived the American pantry was richly stocked. Indian husbandry had already produced corn and beans, pumpkins, squashes, melons, and maple sugar. Deer ran free in the forests. Wild turkeys roosted in the branches. There were giant sturgeons in the rivers, ducks on the lakes, pigeons in the skies, fat nuts in the trees. There were persimmons, grapes, gooseberries, blueberries, and bogs of cranberries yet unheard of in Europe. The shores were encrusted with shellfish—lobsters, clams, mussels, and colossal American oysters. And this natural bounty lasted. In 1679 on Long Island, two Dutch missionaries dined "on a full pail of Gowanus oysters, some not less than a foot long; a roasted haunch of venison weighing thirty pounds, with a slightly salty, spicy flavor; turkey, fat and of good flavor; a wild goose . . ."

Old World livestock was brought in and the English cattle multiplied. Sheep fared less well, being an easy prey for American predators, and by the time safe pastures were assured the Americans had lost their taste for mutton. Most prolific of all, the pigs ran wild in the woods to stuff and fatten themselves on acorns and to be hunted as easy game. To the wild pigs of Jamestown we can credit the South's preference for pork and the magnificent Smithfield hams famous throughout the world.

The seeds of Europe, too, flourished in the new soil, throwing up joyous crops of wheat, rye, barley, and oats. Every farm had its orchard of apples, peaches, cherries, plums, and pears. Every kitchen has its garden of onions, carrots, cabbages, cauliflowers, turnips, and peas. Butter and milk filled cool crocks in the springhouse. Apple slices dried on strings in the sun. The savory smell of herbs was carried on the breeze. And the corn grew everywhere.

But this flow of milk and honey was not inexhaustible. The first colonists were neither hunters nor farmers, and the first flush of success was often followed by disappointment. Agricultural methods were crude, and improvements come slowly where labor is dear and the land is as free as the sky. The fertility of the land declined and the game, too, disappeared as the forests were cut and burned away. In search of fresh soils many Americans moved westward, where the same mistakes were made and repeated, again and again.

Those who stayed behind settled down to work the land with patience and humility. A period of consolidation began, lead by the careful farmers of Pennsylvania. They rotated their crops, fertilized their fields, pampered their cattle. They started an agricultural revolution. They made America bloom.

And then they feasted! The family room of the early American home was the rough wood-paneled kitchen with its red brick fireplace along one wall, five feet high and often ten feet long. During winter, maple logs popped and hissed in the flames, and the gentle heat radiating from the clay bricks warmed you to the bone. Slabs of beef and suet pudding bubbled in the big iron dinner pot, swinging from heavy pot chains. On a block of wood in front of the fireplace a row of cinnamon-sprinkled apples spluttered and fumed. Beside the fireplace hung the family's cherrywood salt box. Above the fireplace hung the famous American long rifle. And tunneled into the thick red brick walls of the fireplace—built in, you might say—was the American oven.

Through its creaking iron door came many of the great dishes of that day. Indian pudding, hot and rich with dark West Indies molasses and ginger, served with thick, cool cream. Golden crusted chicken-and-oyster pie, the fat oysters poached in their own salty liquor with a sprig of whole thyme. And north country beans, slow-baked in the bricks with lean-streaked salt pork and shaved maple sugar.

As these Americans settled down to eat, others moved restlessly on. In the forefront of this westward movement were the trappers and adventurers, dining on bear steaks and beaver tails. The homesteaders burned down the forests of Ohio and filled the potash-rich fields with corn and beans. The sodbusters turned the prairie into the world's richest granary, and the railroad builders—feasting on the tongues and the fat humps of the American bison— moved in to gather their harvests. Reaching out for the railroads and the Eastern meat markets, the cattlemen began their long drives to the north, and chuck-wagon cookery produced the world's first all-beef stew. The empire builders overran the Pacific coast, ousting the Russians from the banks of the salmon-choked rivers and appropriating the orange and lemon groves the Spaniards had planted a century before.

The fisheries, the farms, the ranges, the orchards, all were now united with a growing population in one colossal commonwealth. It could only be a matter of time before the first supermarket would appear.

In the pages ahead we will descend upon the supermarket to squeeze, poke, sniff, and selectively choose the good foods of America. Let us now discuss briefly what the taste of these foods is all about.

THE FLAVOR OF FOODS

A dish must delight the eye, but your reputation as a cook is founded mainly on the taste of the foods you prepare. Thus, the tasting spoon becomes your most necessary utensil, and increasing your taste perception is as important as perfecting your cooking technique.

The flavor of foods is determined mostly by taste- and odor-producing chemicals called flavor compounds. Although the subject of taste and flavor is little understood, it is believed there are tens of thousands of different flavor compounds in food. A single food—an orange for example, or a glass of beer—may contain several hundred *different* flavor compounds. Their quantity, proportion, and quality determine not only the taste of "orange" but how "good" the orange will taste.

What is more, these flavor compounds are altered by time, temperature, and other environmental factors. Fresh-picked asparagus has a different taste than old asparagus. Cooked carrot has a different taste than raw carrot, how different depending upon how and how long it is cooked.

Finally, the act of tasting is purely subjective. No food is really tasted until it finds itself in the mouth of a person, is chewed, and the flavor messages it contains are communicated to that person's brain. Every person reacts to these messages somewhat differently, and the total number of messages in every bite of food is dizzying to contemplate. How then can taste become a reliable instrument in the preparation of food?

Despite the complexity of flavor offerings and taste preferences, a certain consensus as to what is "bad" tasting has been reached by humankind. There is general distaste for rancid, soapy, sulfurous, medicinal, and excessively bitter tastes, and for some sour and metallic tastes. Unexpected flavors that do not seem to belong in a food are also generally rejected. We may like sweet potatoes, but we do not like our baking potatoes sweet. Unfamiliar tastes, unfortunately, are also frequently rejected out of hand.

What is "good" tasting is harder to arrive at. Fresh-tasting foods taste good to most people. Full-flavored foods are generally appreciated, and food processors usually strive to produce a fullness of flavor by incorporating into their products the four basic tastes of salt, sweet, sour, and bitter. Nevertheless these products are usually bland and characterless. Processors seem to be motivated more by the fear of offending the taste than by the desire to please it, and this strategy has been successful.

To cook well, we must demonstrate more daring than this. We must go beyond the mere avoidance of what tastes bad, beyond the merely full-flavored and bland. We will seek to please that higher consensus, arrived at by those people all over the world in every walk of life who have discovered the delights of tasting. These are people who, in castle or cottage, have regularly exposed their palates to a wide variety of fresh, carefully selected foods that have been cooked with knowledge and care. These are people who pay attention to what they are eating, who listen attentively for the flutes and piccolos above the violas and the brass. To discover what they are tasting, you must learn to taste yourself. Here is how tasting occurs.

Simple tasting begins in the mouth. Salt, sweet, sour, and bitter ingredients, when moistened with water or saliva, excite thousands of taste receptors in the taste buds that line portions of your tongue. These receptors telegraph an electrical signal to your brain, advising it of what they have discovered. Only salt, sweet, sour, and bitter flavors are registered. Salt and sweet flavors are best perceived at the tip of the tongue, bitterness at the back of the tongue, and sourness along the sides. Thus, to fully "taste" a food in your mouth, you must bathe your whole tongue in its juices. Many gourmets insist they have taste buds in their throats as well.

In addition to the taste receptors, other receptors in the mouth detect the temperature, moistness or dryness, smoothness, graininess and the lubricity of food as well as the prickly sensation of "pain" caused by carbonation. The chemical "heat" of substances like pepper and the chemical "cold" of mint are also detected. All of these impressions contribute to the sense of taste. But these are only the beginning.

When food is chewed, odor-bearing molecules escape from it and are carried up the nasopharyngeal passage at the back of the mouth. This passage functions like the flue of a chimney, creating a sort of draft that ensures the arrival of the odor-bearing molecules in the nose. There they are noted by the olfactory receptors, and the messages they bear are immediately transferred to the brain. (If you hold your nose while chewing, the nasopharyngeal draft is cut off and your sense of taste is seriously impaired.) Brillat-Savarin hails the nose as a sentinel, always on the alert, ready to cry, "Who's there?"

The olfactory receptors of the nose are amazingly sensitive. This is fortunate for gastronomy, for without them tasting would be a primitive experience. We would never be able to identify or appreciate the tens of thousands of different aromatics that occur in the foods. The tongue is Dr. Watson; the nose is Sherlock Holmes.

Now let us eat something and observe this wonderful mechanism in action. We will choose for this experiment a dish of deep-fried, that is French-fried, potatoes.

As this dish is placed before us our senses of sight, hearing, feeling, and smell are at once assailed by pleasant stimuli. The potatoes are beautifully golden, just the appetizing color deep-fried potatoes ought to be. Listen closely and you will hear a little singing sound, a little song of heat. Lean over the dish and the heat from the potatoes radiates to warm your face. It is all so very cheerful.

Now breathe in, and inhale the delicate volatiles emanating from the browned surfaces. Immediately the saliva starts to your mouth. Your stomach, waiting below, senses something extraordinarily fine is about to happen, and begins to produce the appropriate juices with which to cope with this fine thing.

Now impale a piece of potato on your fork and carry it to your mouth. There is a faint crunch as your teeth pass through the crisp golden surface and into the mealy interior. The fragrant steam is released in your mouth as you juggle the potato about to avoid being burned. Now the salt is melting and you perceive its taste enhancing the taste of potato. You chew and the subliminal flavors of sweet, sour, and bitter—present with salt in some degree in almost all natural foods and contributing to their fullness of flavor—are added to the impressions flooding your brain.

And now the odor-bearing molecules, the dozens of aromatics that together make up the fragrance of fried potato, are wafted upward to your nose. They superimpose new and more richly varied impressions upon those initial impressions supplied by the mouth. Thus the senses of sight, hearing, feeling, taste, and smell have all participated in this total experience that we call the "taste" of fried potato.

Many people feel inferior about their ability to taste. If you are one of them, an understanding of the mechanics of tasting should give you more confidence. While it is true some people seem to have more taste perception than others, it is not necessarily because their physical equipment is superior. Their secret is a simple one; they *pay attention* when they eat. By paying attention, by carefully taking note of taste impressions you receive many times a day, your ability to taste will markedly improve in a very short time.

The sense of smell, which is the most important of the "tasting" senses, is quite keen in all of us. Possessed of this delicate instrument, you can build a taste "library," which will allow you to recognize and pass judgment on thousands of simple and complex items of food. Among professional tasters, taste libraries of more than ten thousand flavor items are not uncommon.

Improving your ability to taste need not, indeed cannot, be laborious. Your sense of taste is quickly fatigued by the impressions it receives, and once this occurs only the passage of time can restore its keenness. But if you pay full attention, particularly seeking out all the nuances and subtleties present in the initial tasting of a dish, your ability to taste will soon become your greatest asset in the kitchen.

🌿 3   *The Ways of Cooking*

Food is complicated. We know more about our moon rocks than we do about our pot roasts. This lack of knowledge makes cooking a not very precise science. It is not so imprecise an art, however, for the cooks of this world have worked diligently at the problem for somewhat longer than the scientists.

But the scientists are busy. Probing into the composition of foods, they have come up with esters and aldehydes, amino acids and glycerides, sterols, polysaccharides, and hundreds of other strange substances. These esoteric discoveries would have mystified, perhaps even intimidated, the old chefs. But when the scientists begin *to cook,* when they put their thermometer-studded roasts into their precision ovens, when they remove these roasts to weigh them, to probe them for tenderness, and to squeeze out and measure their juices, and when, on the basis of this tomfoolery, they have the temerity to suggest that the best way to cook a roast is in a 325° oven from start to finish, I can hear peals of derisive laughter resounding from the old chefs' tombs.

The ancient Greco-Egyptian astronomer Ptolemy, after long study of the heavens, formulated a theory of the universe that precisely predicts the apparent motion of the sun, moon, and planets. Ptolemy erred in placing the earth in the center of the universe. Yet Ptolemy's theory, to this day, will tell you exactly when and where to find Venus.

If some of the old theories of classic cookery are being questioned today, the tangible results of these theories are still at hand for all to taste and enjoy. The proof of the pudding is in the eating, and although we will note what science tells us about the composition of foods, we will follow the classic cooking methods that have produced the feasts of kings. No pale, gray, sodden roasts for us! Together we shall follow the old paths. Together we shall find Venus.

Cooking is, mostly, the application of heat to foods. The heat can be at high or low temperature, moist or dry, and applied for long or short periods.

The foods are complicated mixtures of ingredients. There are different kinds of proteins, starch and sugar carbohydrates, fats, minerals, large amounts of water, and the all-important flavor compounds that are a prime concern of every good cook. Each of these ingredients reacts differently to heat.

Unless you learn how the different kinds of heat affect the different ingredients of foods, you will never really know how to cook. *Never*. Yes, you can follow recipes given to you by someone else. Yes, as a recipe-follower you can perfect a dish until it comes out right. But this is not cooking. Because this is not knowing how.

Learning how the different ingredients of foods behave when heated is not difficult. You already know that fat melts and water evaporates. In addition to these, most of cooking is concerned with three ingredients—proteins, starches, and flavor compounds. Once you understand how these ingredients react to heat, everything you cook will become a little cooking lesson. And everything you cook will taste better, and better, and better. We will begin with the proteins.

MEAT, AND THE COOKING OF PROTEINS

I can hear my chef friends exclaiming, "René, what nonsense. The cooking of proteins, indeed! One cooks roasts, not proteins. You must be pulling our legs!"

But if you think a moment, you will realize it is much more timesaving to describe the cooking of a few proteins found in all meat than to attempt to describe the cooking of hundreds of different cuts of meat. And once you know how these proteins react to heat, you can cook any cut of meat without looking up recipes. All you need know is which meat contains which proteins. And I will tell you that.

There are several proteins in meat that profoundly affect meat's tenderness. Those important to cooking may be divided into two groups—the muscle fiber proteins, and the connective tissue proteins.

The muscle fiber proteins, actin and myosin, are the "meaty" lean of meat. They are contained in individual cells one or two inches in length and one five-hundredth of an inch in diameter. Jellylike, they practically melt in your mouth. But when heated they quickly begin to toughen. When they reach 140° (the "rare" setting on meat thermometers), they coagulate. If cooked longer at this temperature, or if cooked at a higher temperature, they become increasingly tougher and dryer, even when cooked in water.

Connective tissues bind the protein-rich meat cells into bundles which you can see as the "grain" in the cut surface of meat. More connective tissues bind these bundles of cells into whole muscles, which we cut into steaks and roasts.

The connective tissues contain the proteins *collagen* and *elastin*. These proteins are quite the opposite of the muscle fiber proteins. Raw, they are tough. Tissues that have elastin as their predominant protein are yellow and elastic, and elastin remains tough throughout cooking. Tissues in which collagen predominates are tough and unstretchable. You see them in the meat as white fibers and glistening fibrous sheets. But collagen responds to heat in the presence of water (with which meat is amply supplied). Long, leisurely cooking will soften collagen and change it to gelatin. And gelatin adds juciness and succulence to meat, and desirable body to consommés and sauces.

Since these proteins are intermixed throughout the meat and must be cooked together, their contradictory behavior presents us with a dilemma. If we cook a piece of beef for a short time, the connective tissues remain tough. If we cook it for a long time, the meat fibers become tough.

The solution depends upon the piece of meat. If it has little connective tissue—such as porterhouse steak or a rib roast—we will cook it quickly to maximize the tenderness of the muscle fibers. The rarer we cook it, the more tender it will be. On the other hand, if the meat has a lot of connective tissue—such as chuck beef or veal—we must cook the meat slowly and long until the tissue has gelatinized. The muscle fibers will become well done, and therefore tough and dry, during the process. But if we cook with the moist heat of water, which speeds the changing of collagen to gelatin, the moisture will soften the hardened muscle fiber protein by the time the meat is done.

Another meat protein important to cooking is the pigment protein *myoglobin.* Myoglobin is contained in the muscle fibers and is responsible for the "red meat" color of beef and lamb. Subjected to heat, myoglobin turns brown, and is therefore a useful indicator of the degree of doneness of meat—that is, the condition of the muscle fiber proteins. The "white meats," such as veal and pork, contain less myoglobin and therefore turn gray or white when cooked.

In addition to the proteins of meat we must contend with meat's flavor compounds, some of which are proteins themselves. Mixed throughout the meat—in the juices, the lean, and the fat—they are responsible for meat's good taste and aroma. They also present us with another set of demands.

In general, the longer flavor compounds are cooked—up to about four hours—the richer their flavor. This requirement is no problem when cooking, for example, a pot roast, which itself requires long, slow cooking to soften connective tissues. But long, slow cooking cannot be used for the tenderer cuts of meat. Fortunately, flavor compounds also respond magnificently to high temperatures. This is apparent in the rich flavor of the browned bits left in the pan after the high-temperature browning of meat. Browning and searing in the pan and oven are two ways to develop flavor in tender meats.

Of course, there is more to meat than just flavor compounds and proteins. Excluding bone, beef contains an average of 67 percent water, 19 percent protein, 13 percent fat, and 1 percent minerals. Later on, we will learn more about what happens to the fat and juices of meat as they are cooked. We will also learn about the distribution of the different proteins, fats, and juices in the different meats, including fish and fowl. At this point it is enough to know that when the proteins and flavor compounds of meat are cooked properly, the other components of meat will take care of themselves.

You now have the significant facts required to cook any cut of beef. For muscle fibers, brief cooking to the rare stage to retain their tenderness. For connective tissues, long, slow cooking in the presence of water to make them tender. And for flavor compounds, long cooking or high temperatures (without actually burning, of course) to bring out their full flavor. Later on in this chapter we will put this information to work.

VEGETABLES, AND THE COOKING OF STARCHES

Just as the proteins dominate our attention in cooking meats, the starches dominate our attention in cooking vegetables. On the whole, vegetables contain mostly water, large amounts of starch, sugars, less protein, very little fat and important supplies of vitamins and minerals. But from vegetable to vegetable the differences are often great. For example, lettuce is 96 percent water and contains only 2 percent starch and 2 percent other solids, barely enough to hold it together. Potatoes contain 20 percent starch, and about 78 percent water. Still, the dry ingredients of vegetables are mostly starch, and an understanding of how it reacts to heat tells us much about vegetable cookery.

Like the proteins of meat, the starches of vegetables take different forms. Most of the digestible starch is clumped in large granules inside the vegetable cells along with the juices, vitamins, minerals, and vegetable flavor compounds. When heated in the presence of water (which is plentiful in the vegetable cell), the starch granules soften and swell enormously. Swelling begins at about 150° and is complete when the heat reaches 195°. This process, which makes the starch more digestible, is called *gelatinization*.

Another kind of starch, *cellulose,* forms the walls of the vegetable cells. These walls support the vegetable and are responsible for its hardness and shape. Cellulose softens when cooked, and although it cannot be digested by man it provides valuable bulk in the diet. A third starch, *protopectin,* cements the vegetable cells together. Protopectin dissolves when cooked. If it is overcooked, the vegetable will disintegrate.

The object of cooking vegetables is to soften the cellulose and gelatinize the starch granules inside the vegetable cells before the characteristic flavor, texture, and color of the vegetable are destroyed by heat. This is usually best accomplished by cooking the vegetable as little as possible. Most vegetables should be served crisp enough to offer some resistance to the teeth, and they should have that elusive "fresh" taste that is certainly lost by overcooking.

The flavor compounds of vegetables react to heat in a less predictable way than those of meat. Some can be developed with long, slow cooking. Vegetables containing stable flavor compounds—such as carrots and celery—can be used for stocks or sauces. The texture of the vegetable itself becomes unimportant, since it is either removed from or dissolved into the liquid. Other flavor compounds—including some found in the cabbage family—become decidedly unpleasant if cooked even a shade too long. Still others —such as the volatile compounds of the onion family—practically disappear with long cooking.

We will examine the cooking problems posed by the individual vegetables and their flavor compounds in Chapter 11. Let us now proceed to the different ways of cooking with moist and dry heat.

✷ COOKING WITH MOIST HEAT

Heat can be moist or dry. When we cook with moist heat we use water or steam as a vehicle for bringing heat to the food. This does not necessarily add moisture to the food. As we shall see, meat becomes actually *drier* the longer it is boiled. Sometimes we do not add moisture at all. Some foods may be steamed in their own juices. Moist heat cookery actually means cooking in a moist environment. The three basic methods of moist heat cookery are boiling, steaming, and braising.

BOILING

"But I can't even boil water!" This tearful confession, blurted out by many a young bride, suggests that the boiling of water is the simplest of culinary operations. Actually it is a more complicated process than most people imagine. Water progresses through several distinct stages from simmer to rolling boil. Each stage has its purpose. Each may be destructive if wrongly applied.

It is important that you fully understand the four stages of boiling, that is, cooking in water to cover. Let us therefore take this book to the kitchen, fill a heavy pot with cold water, and put it to boil with the heat turned up high.

First, the heat from the fire enters the metal bottom of the pan and begins to spread up the sides. Soon you will see tiny bubbles forming on the bottom. As the heat climbs the sides of the pan, the bubbles climb too. They reach the surface and the surface water pressing against the hot sides of the pan begins bubbling and singing. Steam begins to rise. The bottom and sides of the pan are thick with bubbles now. They continue to grow ever larger. Some break loose and struggle toward the surface, but they disappear before they can reach it. Then, suddenly, the surface of the water comes alive with shimmering dimples. The French have a name for it, "smiling water." The water temperature is 185°. The water is *simmering*.

Then one of the larger bubbles leaves the bottom and breaks the surface. Then another, and another, then hundreds. They grow fat, bubble up, burst, agitate the surface, froth at the sides of the pan. The water temperature is just about 212°. The water is at a *gentle boil*.

Larger bubbles rush up the sides, hit the surface, and careen toward the center of the pan. The water is moving swiftly now, up the sides, toward the center, down to the bottom, where it heats and rises again. The surface undulates. The water temperature is 212°. The water is at a *full boil*.

Finally the surface of the water heaves and churns and rolls violently in the pan. The bubbles burst noisily, the water sings louder and louder. The temperature is still at 212°. And the water is at a *rolling boil*.

By adjusting the fire you can quickly repeat this process, bringing the water from simmer to rolling boil and back again. Try holding the water for a minute or two at each stage. Fix the appearance of the water in your mind.

Cover the pot for a minute, thereby entrapping the heat, and notice how the water has moved to a higher degree of boiling.

Because the heat of uncovered boiling water can never exceed 212° no matter how furiously you boil it, boiling is a low-temperature method of cookery. It is quick, however, because water is very efficient in transferring heat to food.

USING THE FOUR STAGES OF BOILING

The *rolling boil* has limited but important applications in cookery. Although the water temperature will not rise above 212°, turning up the fire will cause the water to evaporate more quickly. The rolling boil is therefore useful for quickly evaporating liquids to concentrate their flavors. This is called *reducing*.

The rolling boil is also useful in cooking pasta. The violent action of the water *stirs* spaghetti, for example, to keep the strands from sticking together. Also, water should be at its rolling boil hottest when you first put pasta or vegetables or other foods into the pot. The foods immediately cool the water. By having the pot at its hottest, the water may thereby be brought more quickly to the proper degree of boiling again.

The *full boil* is frowned upon by knowledgeable cooks. The water is not significantly hotter, if at all, than water at the *gentle boil*. The food is unnecessarily agitated, fuel is wasted, heat and steam fill the kitchen and aggravate the cook. Do not use the full boil. ·

The *gentle boil* is used for most boiled vegetables. The vegetables receive all the heat water can deliver, and they are not bruised and battered in the process. Rice, dried peas and beans, sausages, and whole fruits are other candidates for gentle boiling. In fact, any food cooked in water that does not specifically require agitation or long, slow cooking may be boiled gently.

Simmering is the most delicate of all cooking methods. (Simmering and *poaching* are identical methods, poaching being simmering in shallower water to cover, usually in a flat pan.) The food lies almost motionless, submerged in the hot, gently moving liquid. But one must take care to achieve and maintain a perfect simmer. The fine line between simmer and gentle boil separates the good cooks from the bad ones.

Long, slow simmering performs four important functions. It cooks tough cuts of meat to melting tenderness. It cooks delicate foods such as fish without pounding them to pieces. It extracts and develops the flavors of meats and vegetables in order to make stock. And it melds and mellows the many individual flavors of sauces into a savory whole.

Between the 185° of simmering and the 212° of boiling is a useful range of temperatures for boiled foods that require neither long simmering nor quick cooking, boiled eggs for example. We will note these foods as we come to them.

We have examined boiling according to water temperature and divided it into four stages—simmer, gentle boil, full boil (which I have listed only so that you can avoid it), and rolling boil. Let us now see what happens when we cover the pot.

THE COVERED POT

A cover entraps heat. Water in a covered pot therefore boils more quickly. Also, it is quite possible for boiling water in a covered pot to exceed 212°. The heavier and tighter fitting the cover, the greater the pressure of the enclosed steam upon the surface of the water, and the hotter the water must be to force bubbles of vapor to the surface. This raises the boiling point, as in a pressure cooker. In practice, a heavy, tight-fitting cover can raise the boiling point of water by several degrees.

A cover also prevents the escape of volatile substances into the air. This allows us to control the flavor intensity of many foods. For example, if you crave the true flavor of onions, boil them in a covered pot to retard the escape of their flavorful oils. Uncovered, onions will give up their pungency and become quite mild tasting, actually sweet. Cabbage is almost always cooked uncovered to rid it of certain strong and unpleasant flavors.

Green vegetables are usually cooked uncovered to encourage the escape of volatile plant acids. In the raw vegetable, these acids are isolated from the green chlorophyll. Cooking releases them and they attack the chlorophyll, changing it to an unappetizing olive drab color. An uncovered pot allows much of this acid to escape, thereby preserving the fresh green look of the vegetable.

A covered pot also reduces evaporation. Steam, which would normally dissipate into the air, strikes the relatively cool cover, condenses back into water, and drips back into the pot. This saves us the trouble of continually replenishing the supply of water.

HOW BOILING COOKS MEAT

If you put a piece of beef in cold water, the water will gradually seep into it, soften the fibers, and dissolve the water-soluble ingredients. In a few hours, many muscle fiber proteins, minerals, and flavor compounds will have passed from the meat to the water, and the meat will appear white and doughy. This little experiment lets you see how water removes much of the goodness and flavor of meat.

If you plunge a piece of beef into boiling water, something quite different happens. First, the 212° heat of the water immediately attacks the muscle fibers at the surface of the meat and coagulates the muscle fiber proteins. Once coagulated, these proteins are fixed in the meat and will not dissolve into the water. As we have seen, the muscle fiber proteins shrink and become increasingly tougher and dryer when heated, and this surface layer of tough protein will to some degree resist the penetration of water into the meat. According to a theory of old cookery, this layer seals the meat against the loss of juices. In actuality the true juices of meat—those liquids that do not coagulate when heated—are progressively lost as boiling continues.

These juices are lost because now the heat and water begin working on the surface connective tissues between the bundles of coagulated meat fibers. As we know, the *collagen* in these tissues will soften and begin changing to gelatin. The gelatin dissolves into the water and opens up thousands of new waterways into the meat. As the water penetrates deeper, it carries away more and more of the flavor compounds that remain water soluble in the presence of heat. Meanwhile the heat—a step ahead of the water—has penetrated still deeper into the meat, coagulating more protein, shrinking it, and actually squeezing out the true meat juices.

The logical result of boiling is meat that is dry and flavorless. Although cooked in water, the meat shrinks and weighs considerably less after cooking. Some of this loss is melted fat, but most of it is the flavorful juices squeezed out by the shrinking meat fiber proteins. Also, at the boiling water temperature, these proteins will become very tough by the time the connective tissues at the center are tender enough to chew. Further cooking will dissolve the connective tissues completely, resulting in a piece of tough, dry, disintegrating, "stringy" beef, impossible to carve.

This extreme example illustrates the problems of boiling meat. Actually, we never boil meat in this barbarous manner. There are several steps we can take to minimize the ill effects of boiling and even turn them to our advantage.

First, we will cook the meat at a cool simmer to minimize the heat shock to the meat fibers at the same time we're giving the connective tissues the long, slow cooking they require. We will also cook the meat not in water but in stock, to restore to it some of its lost flavor. Toward the end of the cooking period we will further enrich the stock with flavorful vegetables. We will remove the meat from the pot just as soon as it is tender enough to eat. And finally, we will eat every bit of the good stock to which the meat has contributed both succulence and flavor. And in doing these things we will have created the famous *pot au feu,* or "pot on the fire," the boiled beef dinner the French have enjoyed for a thousand years.

You will find the recipe and directions for *pot au feu* in Chapter 6. Remember what you have read here, and the reasons behind the directions will be very clear to you. And your *pot au feu* boiled beef dinner will taste every bit as delicious as that of the most skilled of chefs.

There are other variations we make in basic boiling when we cook chicken, fish, and other meats, and we will discuss them in the appropriate chapters. Again, the basics of boiling you have learned here will make these variations easy to understand. Now let us apply these same basics to the boiling of vegetables.

HOW BOILING COOKS VEGETABLES

The water-soluble ingredients of vegetables are better protected against water than those of meat, partially by the skin of the vegetable and partially by its honeycombed cell structure. Consequently we sometimes soak vege· tables in cold water to "refresh" them, to clean them, or to expel tiny insects that may be skulking in the leaves. But this soaking should not be carried too far, because some interchange between the water and the vegetable does occur.

Some unscrupulous people, having limp and wilted leaves of lettuce on hand, will put them to soak in cold water. Miraculously, in an hour the leaves will become as crisp and crackly as if they were just picked. But this lettuce will have lost its original flavor. Its soluble (and flavorful) salts will have exuded through the thin skin and dispersed into the water. At the same time the flavorless water will have penetrated and plumped up the collapsed cells of the lettuce. Lettuce is an extreme example. But even the ruggedly built potato, when peeled and put into water to prevent its darkening, will lose Vitamin C to the water. And you can be sure it's losing some of its delicate flavor compounds, too.

In other words, water alone can rob you of some of the good flavor of vegetables. To free yourself of dependence upon recipes, you must understand precisely what is happening to vegetables cooked in water. Once you do, you will know why some recipes call for water to cover, and others call for a mere half cup. I will explain this phenomenon as briefly as I can.

In the language of physics, it is called osmotic pressure. Simply stated, pure water has an inner pressure that impels it to dilute any water that is less than pure, that is, water that has some substance dissolved in it. If you take a cup of pure water, and a cup of water in which you have dissolved a teaspoon of salt, and pour both of these cups of water into a bowl, separating them only by a permeable filter or membrane, the pure water will force its way through the membrane to dilute the salty water and make it more watery. At the same time, the salty water has its own inner pressure that impels it to dilute pure water, and its dissolved salt will force its way through the membrane in the opposite direction to dilute the pure water and make it more salty. In other words, salt and water move both ways through the membrane until both solutions are equally salty.

As we know, vegetables contain large amounts of water. This water is held inside the vegetable cells and surrounded by membranes. Dissolved in this vegetable water, or juice, are many flavor compounds and nutrients that are able to pass through the cells' membranes. If you put the vegetable with its flavor-rich water into pure water, the pure water will strive to dilute the vegetable's flavorful ingredients, and the vegetable will strive to share its flavorful ingredients with the surrounding water. This is enough to outrage any good cook.

Both the skin and inner structure of most vegetables resist this sharing process. The thin-skinned lettuce is vulnerable. The thick-skinned potato, when unpeeled, is relatively safe. Between the potato and the lettuce are the bulk of vegetables whose skins and cell structure resist, in varying degrees, the pressures of osmosis. Of course when a vegetable is peeled or cut up, its natural defenses are seriously impaired. But at the same time, the peeled and pared vegetable will cook more quickly and will be exposed to the leaching effect of water for less time.

We will weigh the alternatives open to us when we come to the different vegetables. For now, let us sum up by saying that when a vegetable is put in water there is a tendency for that vegetable to lose its soluble flavors to the water. To make vegetables taste milder, peel and cut them and cook them in large amounts of water. To keep vegetables more flavorful, minimize the peeling and cutting and cook in as little water as possible. Also cook the vegetables quickly to get them out of the water as quickly as possible. Heat greatly increases water's power to draw flavor out of vegetables.

When heat is added to water, the actual cooking of vegetables begins. As in the cooking of meat, the heat precedes the water into the vegetable, softening the cellulose and acting upon the protopectin that cements the vegetable cells together.

Needless to say, this loosening of the vegetable's structure makes it even more porous and susceptible to the pressures of osmosis, and long before the water can physically penetrate to the heart of the vegetable it is radiating its flavors into the surrounding water.

If we continue cooking (which we do when our object is to *extract* the flavor from vegetables), the cell-binding protopectin dissolves, allowing the water to freely penetrate and totally dilute the vegetable juices. Finally, the vegetable disintegrates.

It is clear, then, that when boiling vegetables we should boil them only until they have been made just tender enough for eating. The best test of this is made with your teeth. Vegetables should be served crisp.

MISCELLANEOUS THOUGHTS ON BOILING

A point to remember when boiling foods. As the liquid reduces in the pot, it continues to receive the same amount of heat. This lesser amount of liquid will therefore boil faster and reduce faster if you do not turn down the fire. This has been the undoing of many a poor cook trying to boil away all the water to preserve nutrients. The last quarter inch of water evaporates at a terrifying speed, leaving scorched food in its wake. Reduce the fire as the liquid reduces to retain the same degree of boil.

Several other cooking terms identify processes having to do with boiling. *Blanching* is briefly dipping fruits, vegetables, or nuts in boiling water to more easily remove their skins; or briefly cooking variety meats such as sweetbreads in boiling water in order to firm them up for further cooking; or boiling vegetables, bacon, or salt pork briefly in water to lessen strong flavors. *Parboiling,* which is also called blanching, is partially boiling foods as a first step in cooking that will be completed by another method. *Scalding,* applied to milk, is bringing milk almost to the boiling point.

POACHING

Poaching is a variation of boiling. It differs from boiling in that very little liquid is used and it is never allowed to reach the boiling point. The food cooks in a pot or skillet just large enough to hold it, barely covered with water or a flavorful poaching liquid maintained at about 185°. Poaching is an excellent method of cooking delicate foods such as chicken, fish, shellfish, and eggs. So-called boiled beef and lamb are also poached, as boiling at 212° would toughen them. Many so-called boiled dishes are actually poached. Poached food, like boiled food, is cooked only to the just-done stage.

In the nomenclature of cookery, boiling and poaching have become hopelessly entangled. Let me try to clarify. Any food cooked deeply immersed in water or a flavorful liquid at any temperature ranging from 185° to 212° is boiled food. After cooking, the liquid is usually discarded. On the other hand, any food cooked barely immersed in a flavorful liquid or stock at 185° is poached food. After cooking, the poaching liquid is usually reduced and made into a sauce. Thus, boiled salmon is a whole salmon cooked deeply immersed in salted water at 185°, because the tender flesh of fish requires that it be "boiled" at the "simmering" point. Poached salmon is salmon steaks cooked barely covered in a flavorful Court Bouillon at 185°, with the cooking liquid usually being made into a sauce. Although both methods cook the salmon in 185° liquid, the results will be quite different.

Poaching liquids include water, stock, wine, stock and wine, or Court Bouillons. The liquid is usually brought to a boil, and the food put into it. This immediately cools the liquid below the boiling point. It is then returned to a simmer, the pot is covered to prevent the liquid evaporating and falling below the level of the food, and the cooking is completed. (Sometimes, as in the case of whole fish and chicken, the boiling liquid is poured over the food to prevent the skin from splitting.)

The action of the hot liquid upon the food is the same as that of boiling. But the poaching liquid is usually highly flavored, and instead of the food's flavor being leached away, the flavors of food and liquid are mingled and shared. Gentle simmering helps keep the food tender and moist as these flavors intermingle. In time the proper temperature reaches the center of the food and the cooking is completed. The cooked food is then removed and kept warm, and the poaching liquid is quickly boiled down and made into a sauce as described in the particular recipe. Because of this reduction the poaching liquid is usually unsalted. Any food flavor lost during poaching is thus captured in the sauce.

Practical applications of poaching abound in the pages ahead. You will find chicken stuffed and poached, standing on end in a pot of rich chicken broth. Fish filets are excellent poached, and this is the best way to retain the flavor of filets that have been frozen. "Boiled" beef, as you will discover, is actually poached in beef stock flavored with aromatic herbs and vegetables. Poached eggs are in the appropriate chapter.

STEAMING

Steaming is cooking food completely surrounded by steam. The food is placed on a rack over boiling water, and the pot is tightly covered. In French cooking meat is rarely steamed, and every effort is made to prevent the accidental steaming of meat when it is cooked by other methods. (Pot roasts, for example, are regularly basted to keep the steam from their surface.) The French, however, steam many vegetables, and mussels are steamed to both open and cook them. The Chinese steam fish and rice, North Africans steam crushed grain to make couscous, and Americans steam shrimp, lobster, and crab in their shells.

Steam is not as efficient as water in transferring heat to foods. Consequently, the food to be steamed should not be too large in size. Potatoes, for example, should measure no more than about 1½ inches in diameter. For several reasons, steaming is an excellent method of cooking vegetables that have been cut or pared.

Steamed vegetables are more flavorful than boiled vegetables. When a vegetable is immersed in boiling water, the water is able to penetrate it, diluting and leaching away some of the vegetable's flavor. When a vegetable is steamed, steam continually condenses on the vegetable, making its surface very wet. This moisture drips back into the water, carrying with it some of the flavor, but less is lost than when the vegetable is boiled. Another advantage of steaming is that many steamed vegetables are cooked drier and taste less watery than boiled vegetables. Also, delicate vegetables such as broccoli are not jostled about during the cooking.

On the other hand, steamed vegetables must be cooked with a cover on the pot. Strong flavors of the onion and cabbage families, which you may or may not wish to get rid of, will be retained in the vegetable. Also because of the covered pot, green vegetables are likely to lose some of their fresh green color. And, of course, the cooking takes a little longer.

American nutritional cooking requires that vegetables be cooked in very little water, until the water is almost cooked entirely away. These vegetables, at least the upper layer in the pot, are cooked partly by boiling, partly by steaming. This is said to save more of the vitamins and minerals, which remain on the vegetables and on the sides of the pot when the water evaporates. The method is more or less successful, depending upon the vitamins and minerals involved. Cooking in half steam, half water takes longer than boiling the vegetables immersed, and some vitamins are harmed by the longer cooking.

BRAISING

Braising is a method of cooking partly in a gelatinous liquid, partly in aromatic steam, and partly in a rich sauce that is naturally produced during the cooking. The simplest definition of braising is "a simmering in sauce." The method is not often used in America.

Braising red meats—beef and mature lamb—is a lengthy, complicated procedure that can be simplified but never reduced in time. Once you have performed a proper braising, however, you will return to this method again and again. Veal, pork, poultry, and whole fish can be braised in much less time. All meats are succulent and delicious braised with or without their garnishing vegetables and dressed with their own sauce.

BRAISING RED MEATS

Beef and mature lamb are braised in two stages that we can call the first cooking and the second cooking. In preparation for the first cooking, the meat may be marinated. It is then dried and well browned to sear its surface and help retain its juices during the first stage of cooking. The meat is then placed on a bed of aromatic vegetables in a braising pan or casserole just large enough to hold it. Herbs are added and a boiling braising liquid, usually rich meat stock or part meat stock and part red wine, is added to just cover the meat. The pan is then covered and the meat is simmered very slowly, in the oven or on the stove.

During this cooking the heat slowly penetrates to the interior of the meat, coagulating the liquid protein in the meat fibers. The meat begins to shrink, and the juices squeezed from the meat fibers are concentrated in the center. Eventually the heat reaches the center of the meat, cooking it to the well-done stage, and the free juices and melting fat begin to emerge from the meat and mingle with the braising liquid. At this point, which requires about 3 hours of cooking for a 6-pound piece of beef, the first cooking is completed. The meat, when pricked deeply, will release a colorless juice. Also, the meat will be stiff and hard, much too tough to eat.

Now the meat is removed from the pan. The braising liquid, which should have reduced by about half, is skimmed of fat and strained. It should be rich and gelatinous, actually a thin sauce. The pan is cleaned and the meat is returned to it. The sauce is poured over the meat, and the meat rolled in the sauce to coat it thoroughly. The pan is then tightly covered and the second cooking begins.

During this second cooking, which is a slow simmering in sauce, the meat interchanges the remainder of its watery juices with the sauce surrounding it. As the connective tissues in the meat break down and dissolve into gelatin, the sauce impregnates the meat, softening it throughout and giving it an incredibly rich flavor and succulence. During this second cooking, which requires about 2 hours, the meat must be frequently basted or turned in its sauce to prevent any part of its surface from drying or being exposed to steam.

Also, during this period garnishing vegetables may be added to cook along with the meat.

Finally, the meat will become so tender that the point of a knife can be thrust into it without meeting any resistance at all, and the cooking is completed. The meat is removed to a hot serving platter, and the sauce receives a final skimming and straining. The sauce is then served as is, or cooked down to give it a thicker consistency, or finished in some other manner indicated in the particular recipe. Usually, the meat is put into the oven and coated with the sauce several times to lay down layers of shiny glaze on its surface.

Under the recipe for Braised Beef you will find a thorough discussion of the complete braising process and a somewhat less complicated method for achieving much the same result. Braising is very important in French cooking, and you must master this method if you intend to practice French cooking in depth. It is not at all difficult, and practically foolproof. Just remember to cook beef long enough, until it is very tender and soft to the touch. An hour's overcooking will not harm it in the least.

BRAISING WHITE MEATS

The white meats—very young lamb, veal, pork, and chicken—are excellent braised, but to cook them as long as you would cook beef or mature lamb would be disastrous. The white meats are naturally tender, and any cooking beyond the just-done stage can only dry and toughen them. Consequently, their braising is simpler. They are cooked in one stage only, and a 4-pound roasting chicken will take only about 1 hour.

Because their cooking time is much less, white meats are usually cooked only half covered with braising liquid, as it will have less time to reduce. The liquid is therefore cooked down in advance, so it will be rich and saucelike. In effect, you might say that the cooking of white meats begins where the first cooking of red meats leaves off. White meats are simply simmered in sauce.

Details for braising the white meats, poultry, and fish can be found in the appropriate chapters along with cooking times and ways to tell when they are done. The most important thing to remember is *do not overcook*.

BRAISING VEGETABLES

Vegetables are not always cooked quickly. Vegetables cooked very slowly in a moist environment are said to be braised. The taste and texture of these vegetables differ considerably from the same vegetables when they are boiled. Thus, braised vegetables serve the French penchant for variety. Carrots, cabbage, spinach, lettuce, endive, onions, leeks, Brussels sprouts, artichokes, the famous Peas à la Française, and other vegetables all have their classic braising recipes.

The vegetable, which often receives a preliminary blanching, is put into the braising liquid with a little butter and simmered very slowly with the cover on. (At this point, the method is similar to poaching.) As the cooking progresses the vegetable softens. The starch within its cells gelatinizes, the cellulose of the cell walls softens, and the protopectin binding the cells together begins to dissolve and make the vegetable more porous. Cooking continues until the liquid has almost entirely disappeared, part of it evaporating into the air, and the remainder being absorbed by the softened, porous vegetable. Obviously, the flavor of this concentrated liquid will affect the flavor of the cooked vegetable. In addition to water, the classic recipes include braising liquids made with various stocks, wine and stock, and cream. The addition of butter provides flavor and safeguards the vegetable against scorching.

Vegetables are also said to be braised when they are cooked very, very slowly in butter alone. This slow stewing or braising in butter in a tightly covered pan is what the French call cooking *à l'étuvée*. The vegetable is put into the pan with butter, rolled in it to prevent scorching, and cooked very slowly in the liquid supplied by its own juices. (When meat is cooked this way it is said to be pot-roasted.)

Recipes and detailed directions for braising vegetables can be found throughout Chapter 11, and they will add much variety and interest to your vegetable cookery. For example, the difference between cabbage boiled for 15 minutes until it is just-cooked, fresh-tasting, and crisp, and cabbage simmered slowly in red wine and brown stock for a good 5 hours, is remarkable. Both are delicious, yet cabbage cooked longer than 15 minutes and less than 5 hours is likely to prove disappointing.

STEWING

Stewing is the braising of food in small pieces. Thus, meat cut into 1½- or 2-inch cubes, or chicken parts, when slowly braised or "simmered in a sauce" are said to be stewed. Braised or braised-in-butter vegetables are also described as stewed. Very often, of course, the meat and vegetables are cooked together in what is called a "stew."

French cooking recognizes two basic kinds of stews, or *ragoûts*. A brown stew (*ragoût à brun*) is made with meat that is seared and browned before it is put into the braising liquid. A white stew (*ragoût à blanc*) is made with unseared, unbrowned meat. As in braising large pieces of meat, the liquid is reduced and enriched to form a sauce while the meat is cooking.

In general, as a result of the browning of the meat, a brown stew provides juicier meat, a characteristic "browned" taste, and a rich brown color. A white stew provides a more flavorful sauce; unbrowned meat gives up its flavor more readily. The degree to which this is evident, however, depends upon how long the meat is cooked. As in braising, red meats, white meats, poultry, and fish all have their own cooking times, and white meats must not be stewed too long. Meat responds to stewing exactly as it responds to braising, except of course the pieces are smaller and the cooking time is correspondingly reduced.

Stews belong to home cookery. You will find specific recipes for stews throughout the book, including ragouts, daubes, goulashes and carbonades of beef, navarins of lamb, blanquettes of veal, fricassees of chicken, and matelotes of fish.

POT ROASTING

Pot roasting is a method devised for cooking tough cuts of meat in a relatively dry atmosphere. The meat is cooked very slowly in a tightly covered casserole to which no liquid has been added. The meat, which is well browned, stews in its own juices and the juices of aromatic vegetables that are added to the pot. It is liberally basted with butter or fat throughout cooking to protect it from its own steam. At the end of cooking, stock or stock and wine may be added to dissolve coagulated juices in the casserole and to absorb the flavor of the basting fat and vegetables. This is then made into a sauce. As in braising, vegetables may be cooked along with the meat.

Pot roasting is a form of poëléing, adapted to tough cuts of meat. (Poëléing, discussed under dry heat cookery, is a method for cooking tender cuts of meat very quickly in a tightly covered casserole.) During the long, slow cooking the meat stiffens and becomes quite tough as it reaches the well-done stage. Then the meat softens as its connective tissues are gradually dissolved by the heat and the meat's own juices.

It is obvious that pot-roasted meat is quite different from braised meat, which is saturated with the flavor and the substance of its sauce. Pot-roasted meat is less rich but more natural tasting.

✻ COOKING WITH DRY HEAT

Dry heat cooking is cooking without the moderating influence of water. Water acts to keep foods soft, and also regulates the heat of cooking since it cannot under ordinary circumstances be heated beyond 212°. Dry heat cooking temperatures are considerably higher, and the cooking must be relatively swift to prevent moisture present in the food from drying out in this higher heat. The basic methods of dry heat cooking are roasting and baking, grilling or broiling, sautéing, and deep-frying. A modified form of roasting is poëléing.

ROASTING AND BAKING

Roasting and baking are identical methods of cooking food by surrounding it with hot, dry air. Whether a food is described as roasted or baked is purely a matter of custom. Usually, we say that meats are "roasted"; breads and vegetables are "baked."

ROASTING MEATS

The best of all roasts are spit roasts, succulent joints of beef or mutton revolving before a hot, open fire. An understanding of this ancient, original method of roasting will help you cook a better roast in the oven you use today. Four essential things happen to spit-roasted meat that you must reproduce in your oven.

First, the surface of a spit roast is well seared and browned by its proximity to a bright, clear fire. The meat does not burn, because it is continually revolving on its spit and, after a preliminary searing, it may be moved farther away from the fire. Second, the heat is high enough to quickly evaporate any juices emerging through the brown crust, thereby keeping the surface of the meat dry. Third, as the roast slowly turns, its own melting fat exudes and rolls over its crackling brown surface in a continuous self-basting operation. And fourth, steam developing from the roast's evaporating juices is quickly dissipated in the open air. Thus, a good searing, high heat, frequent basting, and a well-vented oven will give you oven roasts with a spit-roast taste. Let us cook an oven roast and see what happens.

HOW ROASTING COOKS MEATS

Take a 3- to 4-pound beef roast with a cylindrical shape and dry it carefully. Place it on a rack in a shallow baking pan and put it into a hot 450°

oven. We dry the roast so that it may begin to brown as quickly as possible. We place it on a rack to prevent the bottom of the beef from frying in its own fat, and to promote hot air circulation all around the meat. The shallow pan allows the dry heat to freely reach the sides of the meat and permits the steam escaping from the meat to dissipate quickly.

The high heat immediately attacks the surface of the meat, evaporating the surface moisture, which is quickly absorbed into the dry oven air. The surface of the meat dries. At the same time, the protein at the surface of the meat coagulates as its temperature reaches 140°. Coagulation proceeds layer by layer into the meat, as the heat from each succeeding layer is communicated to the layer beneath it, until eventually a brown surface crust is formed.

This brown crust that we have formed is nothing more than a coating of overcooked, dried-out meat protein which has shrunk considerably. Because it has shrunk, it squeezes the raw meat inside. You will find evidence of this by observing the ends of the cylindrically shaped roast. The ends bulge outward, responding to the greater inward pressure exerted by the greater area of shrunken protein on the sides of the roast. This protective crust, *to some degree,* seals in the juices of the meat and retards their escape. It does not seal in the juices entirely, but it *helps*. We can conserve the juices of the meat more effectively by reducing the heat of the oven after the crust has formed, thereby slowing the rate at which they evaporate.

The crisp, brown protective crust is formed in 20 to 30 minutes of cooking at 450°. For small roasts, this crust can be formed more quickly and effectively by browning in a skillet in very hot fat. Either way, as soon as the crust is formed the cooking proceeds at 350°.

At 350°, the heat continues to penetrate the roast, coagulating the meat fiber proteins and squeezing some of the water out of the meat fibers. Some of this water is driven inward. Some of it, bearing flavorful water-soluble flavor compounds, migrates outward to the surface of the roast. Its escape is retarded by the brown crust you have formed, but some of it gets through. At the surface it evaporates into the hot oven air and is carried away. But the flavor compounds it contains do not evaporate. They are deposited on the surface of the meat as solids. There, exposed to the 350° heat of the oven, their innate flavor is developed to its fullest, part of this developed flavor escaping as the good roast beef aroma that is now filling the kitchen.

While the roast is cooking you will baste it with fat. To do this, you either bard* the roast by tying a thin sheet of fat to its surface, or you frequently brush melted fat onto its surface. Fat on the surface of the meat *softens* the protective brown crust you have formed. It softens by retarding the passage of meat juices through it. (It works like a hand lotion. The oil in a hand lotion

32   FRENCH COOKING FOR THE AMERICAN TABLE

does not itself moisten or soften your skin; it retards the escape of inner moistures *through* your skin, thus making it moister and consequently softer.)

Some meats, notably duck and goose, are sometimes preferred with a crisp skin. If you like a crisp surface, baste the meat with liquid toward the end of the cooking period. This carries away protective fat exuding from the meat, thereby allowing the inner moisture to escape more easily. Consequently the surface will become dry and crisp.

During the cooking you must be sure that the heat is as hot as possible without unduly drying the meat. One way to tell if the oven is hot enough is to listen to the roast. You should be able to hear it sputtering as it cooks. Also, observe the cut ends of the roast. If you find little pearls of moisture appearing on the surface, watch out. French chefs call this "pearling" and say the meat is "boiling" inside. If pearling occurs, the temperature of the oven is too low, and the moisture appearing at the surface of the roast collects there instead of being immediately evaporated away. As a result, the roast steams. As the water changes slowly to steam, the surface of the roast is additionally cooled by the process of evaporation, and cooking is thereby slowed down even more. Many of the flavor extractives coming to the surface of the meat fall, with the accumulating water, into the pan. Those that do remain at the surface are insufficiently browned and their full flavor is not realized. Cheap restaurants cook roast beef at low temperatures to keep shrinkage and weight loss at a minimum, thereby getting more servings per pound of beef. But this beef is gray, flavorless, and watery, with none of the rich brown roasted taste we expect from roasted beef. Every piece of meat is individual, and I can only give you approximate temperatures for roasting. But if the meat "pearls" it is itself telling you what it requires. Turn up the heat!

Eventually the airborne heat of the oven reaches the center of the roast. As the protein coagulates at 140°, its juices are squeezed out and begin to migrate to the surface. Now, stop the cooking. At 140° the beef is fully cooked to the rare stage. A slice from this roast will give you the full range of roast beef flavor—the fresh taste of the just-cooked meat protein and naturally salty juices of the interior, and the fully developed flavor compounds concentrated at the surface.

To summarize, we have "overcooked" the surface of the roast to form a brown, tasty, protective crust. Then we have cooked the interior at a more leisurely pace until just-done, retaining most of the meat's natural juiciness.

How to tell when the roast is done. Ever since famous gastronomer Brillat-Savarin wrote that "a roast cook is born, not made," the roasting of meats has been made to seem more difficult than it is. There are five methods for determining the degrees of doneness of roasts, and if you are at all in doubt use all of them. Then, as your experience accumulates, you may reduce your testing to just one method—the one method used by French chefs and good roast cooks everywhere. Here are these five methods:

(1) You may obtain a rough idea of when a roast is done by calculating its cooking time in minutes per pound at a certain temperature. This is the most inexact method, as a beef roast (not to speak of other meat roasts) varies widely as to fat and bone content, size, shape, density, moisture content, aging, the part of the animal from which the meat was taken, and its temperature at the time it was put to roast. I hesitate even to tell you what to expect by this method, since it is bound to be wrong most of the time. However, the usual statement for rare beef is 15 minutes per pound at 350°, taking away a few minutes if the roast is large or elongated, adding a few minutes per pound if the roast is small or chunky.

(2) Heat is totally indifferent to the weight of a roast, but it cannot be indifferent to its size. Oven heat of 350° will penetrate meat at a certain speed with a "leading edge" of 140° heat moving at an average rate of 1 inch per 45 minutes. Thus, if you are cooking a cylindrical roast 4 inches thick, it will take 1½ hours for 350° of oven heat, penetrating the roast from all sides, to heat the center to 140° (the rare stage). However, if the meat contains a lot of fat, the heat will travel faster. If it contains a lot of bones, or the roast is rolled, the passage of the heat will be retarded. Also, if you begin by browning the meat at 450° for 25 minutes, 140° of heat will reach the center of the roast faster, at the rate of about 1 inch per 35 minutes of total cooking time.

The error inherent in these methods is apparent. According to the first, an 8-pound, 4-inch-thick roast will require 2 hours to cook. According to the second method, it will require only 1½ hours. Both of these methods cannot be right, and chances are neither of them will be.

(3) For the beginning roast cook, the above two methods may be considered to determine the approximate time the roast will be done. Then, by using a meat thermometer, it can be more precisely determined when the center of the roast reaches 140°. However, the meat thermometer has its faults too. It must be strategically placed in the center of the roast, away from fat or bone that may affect its reading of the lean meat temperature. (There is another fault of meat thermometers, which I will discuss in a moment.) Nevertheless, I recommend using the meat thermometer until you have become experienced in the use of the following two methods of testing for doneness.

(4) By thrusting a poultry skewer, or any other long needlelike object, into the center of the beef, you can quickly determine the color of the juices there. If the meat is insufficiently cooked, it is unlikely that much pressure has

been built up in the center, and little or no juice will emerge from the hole made by the probe. As the meat becomes cooked to the rare stage, red juices will emerge—even spurt—when the probe is withdrawn. At the medium stage, the juices will be pink. When the meat is well done, they will be clear and will dribble out very slowly. Then, when the meat is overcooked, no juices will emerge at all; the meat will be too dry. This is not a bad test if you do not overdo it; a small proportion of meat juices are lost when the probe is made, and if you puncture the meat like a pincushion you will be defeating the whole purpose of roasting. When we take up the different meats, I will tell you the colors of the juices you can expect at the various stages of their cooking.

(5) A chef tells when a roast is done by pressing and tapping it with his fingers. With a little practice, this will soon become for you the easiest and most reliable test of all. While you are gaining experience in the "feel" of a roast, I suggest you use all of the above four methods, and tap, press, and poke the roasts as they cook to teach your fingers the feel of a roast in the various stages of cooking. Press and tap the roast when it is raw, to determine its inherent tenderness and feel. When the roast is just browned, it will feel firm and stiff on the outside when tapped, but soft and squishy in the center when you press the browned surface firmly. As cooking progresses the roast becomes firmer to the feel, but you can still detect the soft center. Also, rap the roast sharply with your fingers or knuckles. You will be able to feel the soft insides shimmer and reverberate like jelly. Finally, when the roast is done to the rare stage, the jellylike protein in the center will have begun to coagulate, and the roast will "set" and feel firm (but springy) all the way through. Tap, poke, rap, and thump roasts as you would a watermelon every time you cook them, and in a surprisingly short time the confidence of a born roast cook will be coursing through your veins.

"Resting" roasts and anticipating their doneness. When a rare or medium rare roast is taken from the oven, its hot juices are concentrated in its center, and it must be allowed to rest for 20 to 30 minutes so that these free juices will be reabsorbed into the body of the meat. Otherwise, carving is difficult, and the juices will run freely from the cut surfaces, making the roast dry. At the same time that a roast is resting, *it will continue to cook in its own heat.* This is no great problem for small or elongated roasts, which will begin cooling the moment they are taken from the oven. But the temperature at the center of a large, chunky roast will *increase* while the roast is resting and the outside is cooling. Thus, if the center of the roast is 140° (rare), the higher temperatures in layers of meat closer to the surface will continue to move toward the center. Increases in center temperature by as much as 20° have been measured in a large roast. Obviously, this means that the roast you removed rare from

the oven will be almost well done when you carve it. To overcome this, re-move large, chunky roasts from the oven *before* they reach the stage of done-ness you desire. Thus, if you want to eat a 4-rib rib roast rare, remove it from the oven before the center has cooked, that is, when the meat thermometer registers about 120°. Unfortunately, many of the meat thermometers com-monly for sale do not read this low. You have to peer and squint anxiously, waiting for the little black column to appear above the edge of the metal probe, and by the time it is in sight, the meat is beyond all hope of eating rare.

To summarize, when roasting meats we "overcook" the surface of the roast to form a brown, tasty, protective crust. We keep the temperature high and the oven dry, so the meat will not steam. And we baste regularly with fat, to keep the roast moist and its surface tender. Details for roasting all meats, poultry, and fish will appear in the appropriate chapters.

BAKING VEGETABLES

Few vegetables are baked; they are mostly too delicate to survive long exposure to dry oven heat. Exceptions are firm-meated vegetables like po-tatoes, beets, squash, and eggplant, and sometimes onions and tomatoes. The heat penetrates these vegetables in layers, softening their structural carbohy-drates and gelatinizing their starch in the liquid obtained from their own juices. If not protected by their jackets, baked vegetables are liberally basted to prevent their drying out. For detailed treatment, see the vegetable in ques-tion in Chapter 11.

POËLÉING

Poëléing is a kind of roasting in butter. It is practically unknown in America, and few Americans have tasted poëléed meats except in those excep-tional cases when a true poëlé results from a casserole-cooking recipe. It is an excellent method of cooking and should be practiced more, particularly in America, where there is an abundant supply of the tender meats and poultry for which poëléing is most suited.

In olden times, meats to be poëléed were spread with a layer of minced, aromatic vegetables, wrapped in thin sheets of fat, wrapped again in buttered paper, and roasted quickly in the oven or on a spit. Today we poëlé meats in a close-fitting casserole.

The meat is lightly seared in butter and seasoned with salt and pepper. It is then placed in the casserole on a bed of raw chopped carrot, onion, and celery. Parsley, bay leaf, and thyme are added, and the meat is spread with butter and covered with buttered paper or foil. The casserole is then covered and put into a 350° to 400° oven, and the meat is *basted frequently* with butter until it is almost cooked. Ten minutes before cooking is completed, the casserole is uncovered, the paper or foil is removed, and the meat browned in the dry oven heat.

Poëléing, then, is similar to roasting in that the meat is cooked quickly at relatively high temperatures. It differs from roasting in that the moisture from the meat and the raw vegetables is trapped in the casserole. Nevertheless, the cooking is completed so quickly the juices have little time to escape, and those that do accumulate are dispelled during the final browning of the meat. Consequently, poëléed meat more closely resembles roast meat than braised meat, and it is a very juicy roast indeed.

After the meat is cooked and browned, the pan is deglazed* with stock or wine. The liquid is simmered with the butter, meat drippings, and vegetables in the casserole to absorb their flavors. This liquid is then strained, skimmed, and a sauce is prepared from it according to the recipe you are following.

Sometimes a larger casserole is used, and garnishing vegetables are put into it and poëléed along with the meat. This is cooking *en casserole*. The method is true poëléing because all the ingredients are cooked quickly in butter with no liquid added. (Recipes that call for cooking a variety of ingredients in a casserole with a liquid or a sauce are stews.)

Poëléing is best suited to small, tender roasts, such as loin roasts, and small poultry. It is an excellent way to cook chicken, as it keeps the juices and flavor in the bird while providing a rich roast chicken taste. You will find practical applications of basic poëléing and a number of recipes in Chapters 9 and 10.

GRILLING AND BROILING

Grilling and broiling are similar methods of cooking small, tender cuts of meat, poultry, fish, and vegetables with a combination of very hot, dry heats. Grilling usually means cooking over hot coals, whereas broiling suggests cooking under a gas flame. In either case, the heat is intense and the cooking is quick.

These cooking methods are a kind of roasting, the food being roasted one side at a time. They are more intense than roasting because three kinds of heat are assaulting the food at once. There is radiant heat beaming into the food from the glowing coals or the hot reflective metal of the broiler. There is convected heat borne by the hot air rising from the coals or filling the broiler section of the oven. And there is conducted heat, absorbed from the hot metal of the grill or broiler pan.

Although the composition of heat is the same, there are certain practical differences in the two methods. Meat grilled over wood or charcoal will absorb the flavor of the fuel; also it receives the heat from one side only. Meat broiled under a gas flame receives some of its heat from the metal on which it rests, as well as from the flame above it, and will cook a little faster. Of the two methods, grilling over charcoal gives the best results, if only because an open grill permits quick dissipation of steam.

GRILLING AND BROILING MEAT

The objective of grilling and broiling is to cook the meat very quickly so it will be done before it can dry out. To help achieve this end, the meat is brought to room temperature so that it may more quickly reach the desired interior temperature. It is well dried and rubbed with melted fat so that the surface may be quickly seared without burning, thereby helping seal in the juices. The grill or broiler pan is greased and heated very hot so that the meat will not stick and will begin cooking instantly.

HOW GRILLING AND BROILING COOK MEAT

When meat is grilled, it is instantly attacked by the very hot wires or bars of the grill, the hot air rising from the coals, and the radiant heat of the embers. Very quickly, the protein at the surface of the meat coagulates and begins to shrink and brown. The juices just beneath this surface flee the heat, taking the path of least resistance into the soft, uncooked parts of the meat. As the heat continues to penetrate the meat, these juices become concentrated on the far, cool side. Eventually, they emerge from the surface as little droplets. At this moment, the meat is turned over and the cooking of the other side begins. Again the protein at the surface of the meat coagulates, shrinks, and browns. Again the juices fleet the heat, rushing toward the relatively soft center. The heat pursues them, coagulating protein as it penetrates, freeing more and more juices, and partially melting the marbling fat that bastes the inside of the meat. Eventually the pressure becomes so great that the juices penetrate the brown crust on the opposite side of the meat. Their appearance on the surface is a signal to you that the meat is, at that instant, cooked medium rare.

Much the same thing happens when you broil meat, except that the juices are driven downward rather than upward, and the hot broiling pan effects some coagulation of protein at the bottom surface of the meat. Nevertheless, when juices begin escaping from the bottom surface, it is your signal to turn the meat over and expose the second side to the hot flame.

Although the appearance of juices on the second side is a reliable test of doneness, they are difficult to detect in the broiler, and their appearance indicates that the meat is already cooked medium rare. If you like your meat rare, you must stop the cooking before the juices appear a second time, and your best test is poking the meat with your fingers. The meat is cooked rare the moment it loses its "soft" feeling in the center and becomes springy and resilient to the touch.

Other facts about grilling and broiling will be found in Chapters 8, 9, and 10. In general, mature lamb is grilled and broiled like beef. Thicker cuts are first browned on both sides close to the flame, and then moved farther away to complete their cooking at a more leisurely pace. This prevents burning and charring the surface before the center is cooked. Pork, which must be well done, is cooked at a lower heat farther from the flame so that its interior will become cooked simultaneously with the browning of its surface. Chicken, which is a very dry and delicate meat, can be grilled and broiled more safely if it is first precooked in the oven for 20 to 30 minutes. Small fish or fish filets that are broiled are usually not turned, for fear they will break; the heat of the broiling pan is sufficient to complete their cooking. All broiled foods should be well basted with fat, or additionally protected with breadcrumbs, to protect them from the fierce heat.

GRILLING AND BROILING VEGETABLES

Because of the honeycomb cell structure of most vegetables the juices in them cannot migrate about as freely as the juices in meat. Consequently, they dry and burn on the outside while the inside is still quite raw. It is best, therefore, to partially cook most vegetables and baste them well with fat before exposing them to the fire. On the other hand, slices of eggplant and juicy tomatoes can be successfully grilled and broiled if they are well basted. See Chapter 11 for details on grilling and broiling vegetables.

SAUTÉING

Sautéing is cooking food over a hot flame in an open pan with just enough fat or oil to keep the food from sticking. It is suitable only for flat, tender pieces of food that will cook through quickly.

Any heavy-bottomed, low-sided skillet or frying pan can be used for sautéing, but it must be heavy to spread the heat evenly and prevent the food from sticking. An ideal sauté pan has flared, sloping sides that quickly dissipate any steam that might collect about the food during cooking. Also, if you "throw" the food against the far sloped side, briskly manipulating the pan as if it were an airplane doing a loop-the-loop, the pieces of food will jump into the air and fall back into the pan on their uncooked sides. Sautéing takes its name from the French verb *sauter,* "to jump." (Practice this action in a clean pan with a book of matches; you will become expert in no time at all.)

Generally only 2 or 3 tablespoons of fat are used in the pan. The most delicate fat is butter, but it must be clarified to prevent it from burning at the high temperatures sautéing requires. Sometimes a mixture of half vegetable oil and half unclarified butter is used, which can be heated to a higher temperature than the butter alone. Fresh beef and pork fat can be heated even hotter, as can packaged lard. Goose fat, also, is excellent for sautéing. Olive oil is the preferred fat for many southern French dishes.

SAUTÉING MEAT

Meats for sautéing should be no more than 1 inch thick, usually less. Beefsteaks, lamb, pork and veal chops, *escalopes* of veal, hamburger, calf's liver, sweetbreads, small fish and fish filets are all ideal for sautéing. Chicken parts also are sautéed, but because of their thickness and irregular shape they require special treatment. The object of sautéing all these foods is to obtain a crisp, flavorful brown coating on the outside, and a juicy, perfectly cooked interior.

Meats for sautéing are prepared so they will lie flat in the pan. Pound steaks and chops lightly to flatten them. Trim away all but about ¼ inch of fat on the edges, and slash through this fat every inch or so, cutting just through the membrane that lies between the fat and the lean. This prevents the meat from curling under the effects of high heat. Slices of liver and fish filets lie flat without special treatment, and sweetbreads are pressed flat after the precooking they always undergo. Whatever meat you use, it should be no more than 1 inch thick, and it must be carefully dried with paper towels before placing it in the hot pan.

HOW SAUTÉING COOKS MEAT

When a piece of steak strikes the pan, its bottom side is immediately seared by the hot metal and fat. The protein at the surface coagulates and begins to brown, and the heat travels upward layer by layer through the meat.

The process is identical with grilling, except only one kind of heat—the heat of conduction—is passing into the meat. Conduction transfers heat very efficiently (as you would discover if you touched the pan), and sautéed meats cook more quickly than grilled meats.

As the heat travels upward through the meat, the juices freed from the coagulating protein move upward. The hard marbling fat distributed throughout the meat melts and bastes the drying meat fibers. In 3 to 5 minutes ruby droplets of juice emerge at the surface of the meat, driven out by the advancing heat. It is time to turn the meat over.

As the second side strikes the hot pan, the process is repeated. The droplets of juice are instantly vaporized, the protein coagulates and browns, the juices flee upward awway from the heat, and the interior fat melts and bastes the inside of the meat. Eventually the interior pressure on the juices becomes so great that they again emerge on the upper, browned surface. At this point, the meat is cooked medium rare. As in grilling and broiling, if you want your meat rare you must test for doneness by pressing with your fingers. The meat is cooked rare as soon as it loses its interior softness and becomes slightly resilient to the touch.

During the whole of cooking make certain the heat of the pan is high enough. You should hear the meat sizzling at all times. If the heat is too low, you will see juices leaking from the meat into the pan and these will cool the pan even more.

Details for sautéing all meats, fish, and poultry will be found in the appropriate chapters. In general, the thinner and juicier the meat the higher the heat. Also, beef and mature lamb that are cooked rare receive the highest heat. Pork chops, which must be cooked well-done, are sautéed at lower temperatures so that the inside is well cooked before the outside is charred. Fish are floured and cooked in Clarified Butter made as hot as possible without burning. Chicken is first browned, and then cooked more slowly.

SAUTÉING VEGETABLES

Potatoes, onions, eggplant, and mushrooms are frequently sautéed. They are cut in suitable sizes, carefully dried, and usually cooked in a little more fat than is allowed for meat, in as much as they have no fat of their own. Also, the fire need not be so hot, as vegetables will brown and develop a good flavor at lower temperatures than meat. The usual fat used is butter. Sautéing is also commonly used to brown and develop the flavor of the aromatic vegetables—onions and carrots. Minced, chopped, and sautéed, these vegetables add a good round flavor and color to stocks, sauces, and stews.

DEEP-FRYING

Deep-frying (or just frying, as the French call it) is cooking food completely immersed in very hot fat or oil. It is used only for small, tender pieces of food that will cook through very quickly, or larger portions of precooked food (such as croquettes) that need little further cooking.

Although deep-frying is the fastest method of cooking there is, it is not much used in the home. A large amount of good quality fat or oil is required, which must be heated until it is very, very hot, and a bumbling approach to this method can be very dangerous. Also, improperly fried foods are fattening, indigestible, and an abomination to eat. Nevertheless, a perfectly turned-out basket of *pommes frites* and a golden encrusted fish with flesh moist as cream makes the effort well worth your while. The calorie count is lower than you think. And the kids love crisp-fried foods.

For equipment, you will need a large heavy pot or saucepan. The pan must be heavy to hold a large amount of heat in its metal, because extreme loss of temperature when food is put into the fat will lead to a bad result. Also, the pan should be so heavy that it shows no tendency to tip, even when empty, and it should sit firmly on the burner. You will need a frying basket to fit the pan, so that the food may be immersed in the fat all at once, and so it may be as quickly removed if the fat begins to bubble over. You will need a deep-frying thermometer. Judging the temperature of fat by the time it takes to brown a cube of bread is too imprecise; breads differ. Finally, you should have a wide pot lid at hand with which to smother the flame if the fat catches fire. Thermostatically controlled deep-fat fryers are available, but be sure that any you buy is stable, firm-footed, and made with heavy metal.

The best fats for deep-frying are rendered beef kidney fat, rendered pork fat or packaged lard (preferably leaf lard), and the widely available vegetable shortenings or oils (salad oils).

Many foods are deep-fried. Deep-fried potatoes are famous. Onion, eggplant, cauliflower are other vegetables that are commonly deep-fried. Parsley is deep-fried as a garnish. Eggs are also treated in this manner, "poached" very quickly in hot oil. Of the meats, chicken, variety meats, and fish are often deep-fried. Croquette mixtures, which are combinations of meat and other ingredients bound with a sauce, are also deep-fried.

Foods are prepared for deep-frying in different ways. Some foods, like sliced potatoes or parsley, are simply dried and put into the fat as they are. Other foods receive some kind of coating. Fish may be simply dipped in milk and flour. Chicken may be coated *à l'Anglaise*—dipped in flour, then in a mixture of egg, milk, and oil, and finally rolled in breadcrumbs. Or it may be dipped in batter. The purpose of these coatings is to quickly seal the surface and to create an impenetrable crust that keeps the juices in the food as it keeps the fat out. The fat must be very hot to form this protective crust instantly.

HOW DEEP-FRYING COOKS MEATS

Deep-frying is like a terribly swift roasting. Instead of thin air, the heat-bearing medium is the dense, liquid fat that slams at least 370° of solid heat into the food all at once on every surface. (As an example of the intensity of this heat, you can put your hand into a 370° oven with impunity, but even a single drop of this hot fat falling on your skin would raise a blister.) What is more, this fat is much dryer than oven air; it contains absolutely no temporizing moisture. Compared to roasting, this method of cooking is incredibly quick.

As soon as the meat is plunged into the oil, a great bubbling arises. This is the surface moisture of the meat or its coating vaporizing as the water (which boils at 212°) boils away in the heat. Almost instantly the coating solidifies, as does the protein at the surface of the meat. The juices flee inward as the protein cooks and shrinks. Eventually the juices reach the center, where they become superheated. As their own pressure begins to surpass the surrounding pressure, they begin to migrate outward again. But now, the center has heated enough; the meat is cooked. Remove it, drain it, and eat it, crisp brown surface, tender cooked center, hot flavorful juices, all.

DEEP-FRYING VEGETABLES

Aside from potatoes, vegetables to be deep-fried are dipped into flour or a mixed coating before cooking. The object in all cases is to retard the escape of juices from the vegetables while they are cooking, and to provide a delicious brown crunchy crust. The cooking is quick, and the vegetables must be drained and served promptly if they are not to grow soggy in their own steam. Recipes for deep-fried vegetables will be found in Chapter 11.

✲ 71 COOKING PROCEDURES DESCRIBED

In addition to understanding and applying the basic methods of cooking with moist and dry heat, there are a number of other little actions you must understand and become deft at performing. Some of these actions are a necessary part of the cooking process itself. Others have to do with the preparation of food for cooking, or final touches after the food has been cooked. Many are seldom used in America, which is a shame. Good American cooks, who thoroughly understand basic cooking, thereby fail to take advantage of golden opportunities to elevate their dishes to the level of the best French restaurant cooking.

Throughout this book, you will find numerous references to such things as larding,* glazing,* and swirling in.* All these little actions are explained and named here, in alphabetical order. They are part and parcel of the French ways of cooking.

À L'ANGLAISE, COATING

When food to be fried is dipped in a mixture of egg, oil, and milk, and then in breadcrumbs, it is said to be coated or treated *à l'anglaise.* You will find the recipe for this frequently used French coating in Chapter 4.

À L'ANGLAISE, COOKING

Food cooked *à l'anglaise* is simply boiled in salted water and served with butter. In this manner the French summarize English cooking.

EN BAIN MARIE, COOKING

Food placed in a small dish or cocotte, which is then placed in a pan of hot water to cook (usually in the oven), is said to be cooked *en bain marie.* This gentle method of cooking is used for delicate foods, such as custards. Foods and sauces are also kept warm in a *bain marie,* or water bath.

BARDING

Barding is covering roasting meat with thin sheets of fat to prevent it from drying out in the dry heat of the oven or spit. As the cooking progresses, the fat melts and bastes the meat, keeping it moist. The fat is either tied in place with string, or simply draped over the meat. The sheet of fat is called a Bard.

BASTING

Basting is brushing or pouring melted fat or liquid over food to prevent it from drying out while cooking. Foods cooked by dry heat—roasted, grilled, or broiled—are basted with melted fat. Baste with fat only—do not allow juices from the roasting pan or any other liquid to come into contact with the surface of the meat or it will cool, become dry and hard, and develop a "steamy" taste. Foods cooked by moist heat—pot roasted or braised—are basted with liquid, either their cooking juices or the sauce in which they are cooked.

BEATING

Beating is the brisk mixing of liquid or semisolid foods with fork, spoon, wire whisk, or a mechanical beater. To make this task easier, beat with a loose wrist and turn the mixing bowl so the entire mass is beaten evenly.

BINDING

Binding is the "holding together" of various ingredients in a preparation. Binding includes the thickening of liquids by blending them with such starch thickeners as flour. cornstarch, arrowroot, or egg yolks and cooking them, as in the making of a sauce. Binding also includes the "holding together" of small pieces of food by blending them with thickeners or with a thickening sauce, such as in the making of Forcemeats, Salpicons, and Croquette mixtures. Binding also includes the "holding together" of small pieces of vegetable or purées with starch, butter, or cream.

AU BLANC, COOKING

This is cooking—specifically boiling or poaching—in such a manner as to maintain the whiteness of the food being cooked. Sweetbreads, for example, are cooked in water and vinegar. Cauliflower is cooked in water and milk. Mushrooms are cooked in water and lemon juice. The liquid in which the food is cooked is itself called a *Blanc*.

BLANCHING

Blanching is the partial cooking of food in boiling water. Foods are blanched for different purposes. Vegetables—such as cabbage or old carrots—are sometimes blanched to rid them of strong flavors. Bacon and salt pork are blanched to rid them of their salty or smoked taste. Variety meats are blanched to whiten and stiffen them. Some fruits and vegetables are blanched so that they can be peeled more easily. When foods are blanched, they are usually plunged into cold water immediately afterward to stop the cooking process. See parboiling.*

BLENDING

Blending is an easy mixing of liquid or solid foods with a fork, spoon, or spatula. The action need not be brisk and should be more or less thorough according to the recipe.

BREADING

Breading is the coating of food with breadcrumbs to protect it from dry heat and to provide a tasty, dry surface. The food is usually first dipped in liquid so that the breadcrumbs will adhere, and it is then deep-fried, grilled, broiled, or baked. Both soft and dry breadcrumbs are used.

EN BROCHETTE, COOKING

This is simply cooking food that has been impaled on a skewer, usually by grilling, broiling, or deep-frying.

BROWNING

This is an extremely important preliminary process widely used in both moist and dry cooking. Briefly, browning is the subjecting of food to high, dry heat until its surface has become brown. It is applied both to meat and vegetables.

When meat is browned a crust is formed at its surface that helps retard the escape of juices during subsequent cooking. This crust, consisting of coagulated protein, also contains the solidified residue of meat juices that have evaporated from it. Much of the flavor of meat is contained in this residue, and high heat further develops its flavor to give the meat a characteristic "browned" taste. Also, this brown crust gives an appetizing color to the meat, and if the meat is then cooked in liquid, it will transfer some of this good color to the liquid in which it is cooked.

To brown meat, first dry it carefully with paper towels to prevent excess moisture at the surface from interfering with the browning process. Small pieces—such as stewing beef—are briskly sautéed in very hot fat, usually beef fat, lard, or oil. A skillet is best for this purpose, as its low sides allow steam to be easily dissipated. Large pieces of meat—such as beef roasts—are browned in a hot 450° to 500° oven for 20 to 30 minutes, basting all the while with melted fat. Grilled and broiled meats may be first browned by placing them close to the flame, or they may be browned as part of their cooking. They are usually basted with Clarified Butter. Sautéed meats, also, may be first browned over a high flame and their cooking completed at a more moderate temperature. They are usually sautéed in clarified butter.

Vegetables, too, are frequently browned as a preliminary to cooking. Browning develops their flavor and rids them of some of their watery juices, and their brown color will be transferred in part to the liquid they are cooked in. Vegetables can be browned in the oven after basting with melted fat, or they may be browned in a skillet. Vegetables brown at lower temperatures than meat, and unclarified butter can be used.

CARAMELIZING

This is the melting and cooking of sugar until it assumes a rich red-brown color. Water is then added and the mixture is boiled for several minutes. Caramelized sugar is used, when necessary, to add color to sauces, soups, and stews.

EN CASSEROLE, COOKING

This is simply cooking in a heavy pot with a tight-fitting lid (a casserole), either in the oven or on top of the stove. Pot roasts, braised beef, and poëléed chicken are all cooked *en casserole.*

CHOPPING

Foods are chopped more or less finely with a chef's knife. Pieces of coarsely chopped foods may measure up to 1 inch. Very finely chopped foods, with pieces no more than 1/16 inch at their greatest dimension, are said to be minced.

CLARIFYING

This is the process by which all microscopic bits of food are removed from a stock so that it might be perfectly transparent and sparkling clear. For full details of this procedure, see Clarified Beef Consommé. Stocks and sauces are also clarified by straining them through a filtering cloth.

Butter, also, is clarified so that it can be heated to a higher temperature without burning. To clarify butter, cut it in small pieces and melt it very slowly in a heavy saucepan. When the butter is melted, carefully skim away the white froth that has risen to the top. Then carefully pour off the clear butter fat, leaving the milky residue at the bottom of the pan. This residue and the milky froth are quick to burn, blacken, and become bitter-tasting at sautéing temperatures. Clarification increases the burning temperature high enough to sauté beefsteak. Store clarified butter, covered, in the refrigerator.

COATING

Foods are coated by dipping them in various Batters, in Villeroi Sauce, in an *à l'Anglaise* coating, or in breadcrumbs. These coatings help seal the food and protect it from the dry heat of grilling, broiling, baking, sautéing, and deep-frying. The coatings also provide a good taste and texture of their own.

Hot foods can be coated with sauces and cold foods can be coated with Aspics and Chaud-Froid Sauces, which are brushed or spooned on the surface. These coatings add flavor, a fine appearance, and they keep the food moist by protecting it from the air.

EN COCOTTE, COOKING

This is just about the same as cooking *en casserole,** except that cooking *en cocotte* suggests that both the meat and its vegetable garnish are cooked and served in the casserole.

CREAMING

This refers to the vigorous working of soft butter or another food that has been reduced to a paste until it becomes light in consistency. This is done by a brisk stirring with a spatula or wooden spoon to incorporate some air into the mixture.

CRISPING

Lettuce and other leafy green vegetables are crisped by plunging in cold water, briefly, to plump up the vegetable cells and give the vegetables a more crispy texture. Hard rolls and crusty bread are crisped by placing them in a moderate oven for about 5 minutes.

EN CROÛTE, COOKING

This means, literally, cooking in a crust. The food so cooked is wrapped in a dough or batter that contains all the food's juices and provides an edible golden crust.

CUBING

Cubing is the cutting of meat into very large dice, that is, 1- to 2-inch cubes.

EN DAUBE, COOKING

This is cooking very, very slowly in a tightly closed casserole. Frequently the lid of the casserole is sealed with a flour and water paste (leaving only a small hole for the steam to escape). Cooking *en daube* is usually reserved for stews cooked in the oven.

DEGLAZING

To liquefy the solidified meat juices adhering to the bottom of a skillet or pan in which meat has been browned or cooked. To deglaze the pan, add water, stock, or wine. Bring the liquid to a boil while scraping the bottom of the pan with a wooden spoon or spatula. The solidified, concentrated juices "melt" and disperse into the liquid, adding both color and flavor to it. The liquid is then used as a base for making pan sauces.

DICING

Vegetables or other foods cut into cube shapes are said to be diced. Large dice are about ½ inch square; very fine dice about ⅛ inch square. To obtain professional uniform dice, first cut the food into square sticks. Bundle the sticks together and cut them all at once into dice.

DREDGING

To coat a food thinly with flour. The purpose of dredging is to dry the surface of the food, especially fish and meat, so it will brown more readily and more appetizingly. Dredging also seals the surface of the food to some degree, and dredged food is less likely to stick to the pan.

To dredge food, first dry it carefully. Roll it in the flour to coat it all over. Avoid excess flour, which will come loose and burn in the pan, by slapping the food sharply over the sink to dislodge loose flour particles. Dredge food just before cooking, or moisture will begin to seep through and make the flour pasty. Flour for dredging may be seasoned, although it is best to salt the food after it is cooked. (Salt draws moisture to the surface, which interferes with the cooking and browning.)

Meat for a "white" stew that is not browned is sometimes dredged in flour, but the purpose of this dredging is only to distribute flour evenly throughout the stew so that it may thicken the sauce during cooking.

ÉMINCER

To slice food very thinly. Very thin slices of leftover meats are frequently used in leftover dishes called *émincés*.

ENRICHING

To add an ingredient or ingredients to a sauce that enriches its taste and usually thickens it as well. The usual enriching ingredients are cream, egg yolks, and butter, and they are added at the last moment. Cream is simply stirred in and heated until the sauce is the proper temperature. Beaten egg yolks are stirred in off the fire, and the sauce is then cooked over a moderate flame, stirring, until it thickens. Small pieces of butter are added to the hot sauce off the fire, and the saucepan is "swirled" with a circular motion until the butter melts. The butter adds flavor, richness, texture, and a slight degree of thickening to the sauce. Once the butter is added, the sauce is not reheated.

À L'ÉTUVÉE, COOKING

To cook meat or vegetables very, very slowly in a tightly closed casserole or pot with little or no added liquid. This is the same as pot roasting, except the meat is usually cut in small pieces.

FINISHING

This is the name given the final actions in preparing a sauce or other food. Thus, we say "finish the sauce by swirling in 3 tablespoons butter" or "finish the sauce with egg yolks and cream."

FLAMBÉING

To pour brandy over a food or dish and set it aflame. To burn readily, the brandy should first be warmed on the fire. Stand back when you ignite it, as the rising fumes will burst into a towering flame. Meats, fruits, and desserts are all flamed or *flambéed,* of times mainly for show. Flaming brandy is also an important agent in the kitchen, where it adds an appropriate flavor to such dishes as Lobster à l'Américaine.

FOLDING

Folding is the very delicate mingling of light and heavy ingredients. An important application of folding is in the making of a soufflé mixture. The beaten egg yolk and purée mixture is placed in the bottom of a mixing bowl, and the light, beaten egg white is placed on top. Using a spatula, carefully cut down in the middle of the bowl and draw the spatula across the bottom and up the side, gently spilling the heavier mixture over the egg white. Turn the bowl, repeating the process, until the egg yolk and egg white are somewhat intermixed. A thorough mixing is not possible, as much of the air trapped in the egg white would escape and the soufflé would be sodden and heavy.

GARNISHING

Garnishing, in America, refers to the ornamental edible that is used to decorate a dish. Thus, slices of lemon or a sprig of parsley placed on a fish dish is its garnish. In French cooking this meaning is widened to include all the foods served with the main food at a single course, whether these foods are placed on the platter with the main food or not.

These garnishes or *garnitures* have been devised over the centuries as happy assemblages of foods that have a nice affinity for each other. Some are appropriate to only certain meats, or meats cooked in a particular way. For example, the *financière* garnish for chicken and sweetbreads includes cockscombs, kidneys, *quenelles,* slices of truffle, mushroom caps, and pitted olives. The Rossini garnish, used mainly for small steaks cut from the filet and sautéed, includes slices of *foie gras* sautéed in butter, slices of truffle, and a pan sauce made with Madeira and meat glaze. This is the way the famous Italian composer Gioacchino Rossini liked his tournedos, and when we serve the dish properly we honor him to this day.

Many of the classic French dishes take their names from the garnish. *Suprême de volaille financière* is chicken breast with a *financière* garnish. Thus, the classic garnish is nothing other than a serving suggestion that suggests to you what to serve with what.

Garnishes take their names from persons, places, things, special occasions, and sometimes from the name of the chef who invented them. Many have been suggested; only a small percentage have survived.

Most of the recipes in this book include their garnishes and sauce suggestions, and directions for making them. Thus, under Sautéed Breast of Chicken you will find listed and described eleven different ways to serve it, that is, garnish it.

GLAZING

This term includes a number of different operations, the common purpose of which is to create an attractive shine or "glaze" on the surface of the food being treated.

Braised meats such as *Boeuf à la Mode* are glazed by repeatedly spooning their own gelatinous sauce over them, and repeatedly placing them in a hot oven to allow the sauce to "set" in layers. This glaze coats the meat with a rich, brown, semitransparent coating.

Entire dishes, already sauced and garnished, are glazed by placing them in a hot oven or under the broiler flame for a few minutes before serving. Thus, poached fish in a Mornay Sauce may be placed in the broiler until the sauce begins to bubble and turn brown.

Vegetables are glazed by cooking them in water to which a little sugar and butter are added. The quantity of water used is just enough to assure that the vegetable will be done when the water is cooked entirely away. The remaining melted sugar and butter give the cooked vegetables—notably carrots and onions—their characteristic glazed appearance.

The term glazing is also applied to the act of coating cold meats with layers of Aspic or Chaud-Froid Sauce, and to painting breads with a mixture of beaten egg and water and allowing this "glaze" to set in a hot oven to form a transparent shine.

AU GRATIN

To sprinkle food with melted butter or oil and with breadcrumbs or grated dry cheese, and to place it in a hot oven or under the broiler until a flavorful brown crust is formed.

JULIENNE

To cut vegetables into matchstick shapes about ⅛ inch in diameter and in any length you prefer. For example, to julienne a carrot, cut it lengthwise in ⅛-inch slices, then cut a stack of these slices into ⅛-inch-square sticks. The sticks are then cut to the desired length.

AU JUS

To serve a meat with its own natural juices.

KNEADING

The rigorous working of dough by pressing, turning, and gouging with the heels of your hands until it is smooth and springy.

LARDING

Larding includes several methods of introducing fat into lean meat to give it more flavor and apparent juiciness. Special tools are required.

The best fat for larding is fresh pork fat, which is flavorful and soft enough so that it will not crumble. Fat from salt pork or bacon can also be used after it is parboiled. The fat is cut in strips of the desired length, from ¼- to ⅜-inch square. These strips are called lardoons. Before using, lardoons are usually marinated in a little cognac, then seasoned with salt and pepper and rolled in finely minced parsley or another herb.

One type of larding needle resembles a long, hollow cone with a sharp tip and an open end. The larding fat is inserted into the hollow end of this needle, which is then threaded in and out of the meat as if "sewing" in a basting stitch. As the tip of the needle emerges, the lardoon is grasped with one hand. The hollow needle is then pulled on through, leaving the lardoon inside the meat. The ends of the lardoon are then trimmed, leaving about ¾ inch on either end to aid in basting the outside of the meat as it cooks.

Another type of larding needle is a long, sharp-pointed steel cylinder with a wooden handle. Sometimes called a larding spike, it is used to place lardoons entirely through a roast from end to end. The spike contains a slot, about ⅜ inch in diameter, into which the lardoon is seated. The lardoons are placed parallel with the grain of the meat. When the meat is sliced across the grain, each slice contains a slice of each of the lardoons, displayed in a patterned arrangement.

MACERATING

To place fruit in a flavorful liquid, frequently a liqueur or brandy, until it has absorbed some of the flavor and substance of the liquid.

MARINATING

To place meat or vegetables in a flavorful, acid liquid until it has absorbed some of the flavor and substance of the liquid.

Meat can be marinated for as little as a few hours at room temperature, or for 4 days or more in the refrigerator. Meat marinated for several days assumes a "game" taste, and the longer it is marinated the more it is tenderized by the acid in the marinating liquid. For a basic marinade recipe, see Chapter 4.

MASKING

To cover a food completely with a sauce.

MIJOTER

To simmer or stew food very slowly over gentle heat.

MINCING

To chop food very finely, in fact, just about as finely as you can.

NAPPING

To coat a food completely with a sauce, as in masking.

AU NATUREL, COOKING

To cook food in the simplest possible manner.

EN PAPILLOTE, COOKING

This is cooking in paper cases. The food or foods, which are partially or wholly cooked, are placed on heart-shaped pieces of buttered parchment paper. A sauce or basting is spooned onto the food, and half of the paper "heart" is folded over it and the edges of the paper are sealed by rolling and pressing. The paper cases are then put into a hot oven until they puff up and the cooking is completed. Each paper case contains an individual serving. This is an excellent way of cooking delicate foods, such as fish. All the flavor and juices are sealed into the case.

PARBOILING

To boil a food, especially a vegetable, until it is partly cooked as a preparation for further cooking. The vegetable is drained and, if not used immediately, plunged into cold water so that its cooking will be stopped. When the vegetable has cooled, it is again drained, and it may be stored in the refrigerator. Vegetables prepared in this manner can be cooked in a very few minutes, and they will be as delicious and fresh-tasting as when just-cooked from first to last. See blanching.*

POUNDING

To press and pound food in a mortar with a pestle until it is reduced to a paste, such as when shrimp meat trimmings and shells are pounded to make a paste for Shrimp Butter. Today the blender can sometimes be enlisted to do big pounding jobs.

PURÉEING

To divide, mash, and strain a food until it assumes a pulpy or semiliquid consistency. The food—either meat or vegetable—is first cooked and then rubbed through a sieve or put through a food mill, grinder, or blender. Purées for garnishing are thick, and if the puréed food is too watery it may be thickened by incorporating a bland starchy food, such as rice or potatoes, into it, or by adding thick cream or a sauce. Soup purées are made to a thinner consistency.

REDUCING

To reduce the volume of a liquid by simmering or boiling, thereby evaporating a portion of it. The purpose of reduction is to concentrate the flavor of a liquid or sauce, and to increase its body or thickness.

Reductions can be made quickly or slowly. When making a pan sauce, for example, wine or stock is added to deglaze* the pan and then is boiled down very quickly. The food is cooked and waiting; you must hurry to finish the job.

On the other hand, classic sauces are reduced very slowly. Boiling would trap fat and other impurities in the body of the sauce and cloud it beyond redemption. Also, the sauce requires long simmering to mellow its flavor, to establish its texture, and to give it a brilliant appearance.

In cooking terminology, "reduce by ⅓" means to simmer or boil the liquid until it is ⅓ less than its original quantity. This is the exact same quantity that would result if you were to "reduce to ⅔." Pay attention to the "by" and the "to" given in recipes.

REFRESHING

This is the act of plunging parboiled or blanched food into cold water to stop the cooking process.

RENDERING

This is nothing more than the slow melting of animal fats to transform them into a liquid. The simplest rendering is to heat the fat trimmings from a pork chop or beefsteak in a sautéing pan until the liquid fat has run out, the water is cooked out of the fat, and only the crisp brown "cracklings" of the fat remain. These are discarded, and the chop or steak is then sautéed in its own fat.

When rendering large amounts of fat for storage or deep-frying, the hard animal fat is put into a saucepan with water and simmered until it liquefies and rises to the top. It is then skimmed off, strained, and stored.

Beef kidney fat (suet) and pork kidney fat (leaf lard) are the best. (The 1-pound boxes of lard you buy at the supermarket are rendered pork fat; look for those labeled "Leaf Lard.")

Stock fat is that fat which is rendered as a by-product of making stocks. It is skimmed from the top of chicken or beef stock and strained.

RICING

To press cooked foods, especially potatoes, through a colander or a ricer. The food comes through in little cylinder shapes resembling rice.

RISSOLÉING

To fry foods in deep fat until they are crisp.

SCALDING

To heat a liquid until it is just below the boiling point.

SEARING

To seal and stiffen the surface of a food by subjecting it to intense dry heat. See browning.*

SEASONING

To add spices, herbs, or other condiments to a food. Usually, "season to taste" or just "season" calls for the addition of salt and pepper only. Seasonings other than salt and pepper are specifically stated in the recipe.

SHREDDING

When lettuce, sorrel, or various other leafy plants are cut in julienne, the result is known as a chiffonade. When this process is applied to herbs, the result is known as a *pluche*. In America this process is called shredding.

SIEVING

To pass food through a sieve. Liquid foods are simply strained by this process. More solid foods must be "pressed through a sieve" or "rubbed through a sieve"; that is, they are placed in the sieve and worked with a wooden spoon, emerging at the bottom as a purée.

SKIMMING

To remove fat or impurities from the surface of a liquid or sauce by dipping it up with a ladle, a spoon, or a long-handled, flat-bowled skimmer. Unless this action is carefully and regularly performed, you cannot expect clear stocks or transparent sauces.

STIRRING

Liquids and semiliquids are stirred to mingle their various components, to spread heat evenly throughout their mass, and to prevent them from scorching by allowing a portion of the mass to remain too long in contact with the bottom of a hot pot. Also, the frequent stirring of white sauces improves their texture. When stirring, be certain to reach into the corners at the bottom of the pan to displace the mass that tends to stick there. A "figure 8" motion—clockwise around half the saucepan, across the diameter, and counterclockwise around the remainder—is effective. Use a wooden spoon and dig into the corners. Obviously, a round-cornered saucepan is best.

STRAINING

To pass a stock or sauce through a fine sieve. The sieve may be lined with several thicknesses of cheesecloth that has been washed in water. Washing removes any loose fibers and causes the remaining fibers to swell, making the cloth a more effective filter. Liquids are also strained through muslin or linen cloths. (To accomplish this, you will need two beefy chefs—one at each end of the cloth—twisting mightily to squeeze the liquid through.)

STUDDING

To embellish the surface of a food by pressing or inserting various ingredients into it. Thus, meat may be studded with slivers of truffle or tongue tucked into small surface incisions. Or a ham may be studded with cloves that pierce its surface.

SWIRLING IN

To finish a sauce by adding, off the fire, small pieces of butter. The pan is then "swirled" with a circular motion until the butter melts and blends with the sauce to both enrich and slightly thicken it.

THICKENING

To give more body or thickness to a liquid or sauce. Thickening is attained by reducing* the liquid or by adding a thickening ingredient that will cause it to emulsify or jell. Egg yolks, cream, flour, Roux, starches such as arrowroot and cornstarch, gelatin, and already-thickened stocks and sauces are some of the thickeners used.

TOMATOING

To give sauces a tomato flavor by adding a Tomato Sauce or Purée to them.

TOSSING

To finish foods, usually vegetables, by rolling them about in a pan with melted butter. The cooked vegetables are first drained and then heated in the pan until they are dried. Tossing also refers to the turning over and over of salad greens in dressing so that they may be evenly coated.

TRUSSING

To tie poultry with string in such a way that the legs and wings of the bird are held tightly against its back and sides. For a simple way to truss, see Chapter 9.

WHIPPING

To thoroughly aerate liquid or semiliquid foods by beating them vigorously with a wire whisk or a mechanical beater or mixer. The food, such as egg whites or cream, expands in volume and becomes very light and frothy as a result of the air entrapped within it. This process is also called whisking.

✄ 4 The Bases of Cooking

Perhaps this has happened to you. You work carefully and conscientiously to prepare a classic French meal. The guests arrive, they taste, they smile, they exclaim, "How delicious!" and politely, if rather vaguely, inquire about your recipe. But the dish—perhaps it is a Beef Bourguignonne or a *Coq au Vin*—bears no resemblance to the delicious food you were served in France or in a good French restaurant. You are disappointed and discouraged. You fear you do not have the touch. Never again, you say.

Take heart. The fault is not yours. What is more likely, you found your recipe in a popular magazine alongside a magnificent two-page color photograph of the dish in question. "Here," suggests the photograph, "is how your dish will look. And here," says the print, "is a quick and easy way to make it."

In place of the Brown Stock you should have used, you will find listed a few cubes of beef bouillon. In place of an important Meat Glaze you will find a few tablespoons of cornstarch for thickening. In other words, in place of the rich, flavorful ingredients that are as important as the meat itself, you are given tasteless substitutes. No wonder the guests smile vaguely. No wonder your own palate tells you something is missing, something is wrong.

The ingredients missing from these quick-and-easy recipes are the *bases* of cooking, the *fonds de cuisine*. Some, like the aromatic mixture of vegetables called *Mirepoix,* can be made right along with the dish. Others, like many of the sauces, must be prepared in advance. And these sauces are mostly dependent upon stocks that are made in advance of the sauces. "Indeed," master chef Escoffier tells us, "stock is everything in cooking, at least in French cooking. Without it, nothing can be done." Now, if Escoffier could not cook without good stock, how in the world can you?

You might ask, "Is the making of these bases so difficult or tedious as to prevent me from cooking French?" Not at all. Stocks and sauces simmer unattended for most of their cooking time. They may be put into 1-cup or 1-quart containers and stored in the freezer for months. A Meat Glaze, which is nothing more than a stock simmered until it is thick as syrup, will keep in your refrigerator for six months or more, handy for use in dozens of recipes.

If you keep some of these bases on hand, and get into the habit of using them, you will absolutely revolutionize your cooking. You will become a *great* cook. You will actually *save* time, preparing more delicious dishes more quickly and with less fuss than you can in any other way. You will be able to perform as the chefs do in the finest restaurants, because you will have overcome the biggest difference between home and classic restaurant cooking— the availability of bases for instant use.

The best known bases are stocks and sauces. Also, in this chapter I will include those other preparations which may be prepared in advance, or sometimes bought, and used as ingredients in cooking. These preparations, which I might loosely translate as "things at hand" (*mise en place*), include such things as Clarified Butter, *Bouquets Garnis* (herb bunches tied in cheesecloth), and *Duxelles* (a cooked mushroom flavoring). Many of these are prepared just before cooking and need not be stored. We will begin with the stocks.

✳ STOCKS

Stock is the flavorful liquid made by simmering meat, bones, vegetables, and seasonings in water to extract their flavors. A good stock has enough flavor to provide a full and satisfying taste of its own. Any stock you make should be flavorful enough to drink as a clear soup, adding only the necessary salt to complete its flavor.

Stock is variously called broth, bouillon, or consommé. These terms are no longer precise, and I hesitate to make firm definitions that might mislead you when reading other books about cooking. However, the term "stock" usually denotes a flavorful liquid that you have deliberately extracted from meat, bones, and vegetables, and that you keep "on hand" in order to make something else. The term "broth" usually refers to the flavorful liquid that incidentally results when you boil or poach a food in water or stock, such as the "broth" obtained from boiling a chicken. "Bouillon" usually means a clear stock made from beef. "Consommé" is a very clear beef bouillon or chicken stock that has been specially clarified to be exceptionally clear and sparkling. All are flavorful liquids; all should be transparent and clear.

Stocks are made to be brown or white. In the making of white stock, the meat and other ingredients are raw when put into the liquid. In the making of brown stock, the meat, bones, and vegetables are browned before they are simmered. As a result, "white" stock is pale and relatively colorless, or golden. "Brown" stock has a rich, warm, burnt-amber color and what I can only describe as a richer "brown" taste that results when meat is seared and browned at high temperatures.

Following are most of the important stocks of classic French cooking. They are all made in much the same manner, and I will teach you how to make them in detail so that you can be assured of a clear, flavorful, perfect stock the first time you try. You need not have all these stocks on hand. Actually, it is unlikely that even one French restaurant in the United States has all these stocks in the kitchen. The hectic pace at which a chef works today has made this quite improbable. Instead, the chef works with fewer stocks, adapting as wisely as he can to meet demands much more severe than yours. (This, again, is why I say that the preservation and future of classic cooking lies in your own kitchen, where you can leisurely select and cook these classic dishes, freezing the leftover stock to be just as leisurely thawed and used another day.)

THE CONSOMMÉS

BEEF CONSOMMÉ (*Fonds Blanc Ordinaires*). A very clear, golden (white) stock made from beef. Used for thick soups, for boiling beef, and for making French boiled dinners such as *Pot-au-Feu* and *Poule-au-Pot*.

CLARIFIED BEEF CONSOMMÉ (*Fonds Blanc Clarifiés*). This is the above beef consommé enriched with beef and clarified to be sparkling clear. It is used for making the classic clear soups (consommés).

CHICKEN CONSOMMÉ (*Fonds de Volaille*). A very clear, golden (white) stock made from beef and chicken. Used for thick soups, white sauces, and for poaching poultry.

CLARIFIED CHICKEN CONSOMMÉ (*Fonds de Volaille Clarifiés*). This is the above chicken consommé enriched with beef, chicken meat, and bones and clarified to be sparkling clear. Used for making classic clear soups (consommés).

THE BROWN STOCKS

BROWN STOCK or ESTOUFFADE (*Fonds Brun ou Estouffade*). A clear, burnt-amber (brown) stock made from browned beef and browned veal. Used for making Brown Sauces, Meat Glazes, and as a braising liquid for beef and lamb.

BROWN VEAL STOCK (*Fonds de Veau Brun*). A clear, burnt-amber (brown) stock made with browned veal. It is gelatinous and neutral in flavor, combining well with other flavors with which it may be blended. Boiled down and thickened with arrowroot or cornstarch, it becomes Starch-Thickened Brown Veal Stock, which is widely used in making quick pan sauces. Also used as a braising liquid for beef and lamb, and for making Aspic. (This adaptable stock is now frequently supplanting Brown Stock as the base for Brown Sauces, but it does not have the full flavor of brown stock and the resulting sauces are milder.)

THE WHITE STOCKS

WHITE VEAL STOCK (*Fonds de Veau Blanc*). A clear, relatively colorless, pale (white) stock made from unbrowned veal. Like Brown Veal Stock, it is gelatinous and neutral in flavor. Used as a braising liquid for veal and poultry, for making white sauces and aspic jellies, and for making a pale Meat Glaze.

WHITE CHICKEN STOCK (*Fonds de Volaille Blanc*). Similar to White Veal Stock, above, except that it is golden in color and has a chicken flavor. It is made from unbrowned veal and chicken. Used as a braising liquid for veal and poultry, for making white sauces and aspic jellies, and for making a chicken Meat Glaze.

FISH STOCKS

WHITE FISH STOCK or FISH FUMET (*Fumet Blanc de Poisson*). A clear, almost colorless stock made from the trimmings and bones of lean fish and white wine. Used for poaching fish and making fish sauces.

FISH STOCK WITH RED WINE (*Fumet de Poisson au Vin Rouge*). This is similar to the above White Fish Stock except that it is made with red wine. Used for poaching fish and making fish sauces.

COURT BOUILLONS

These meatless stocks for boiling fish and shellfish are very quickly made, hence the name "short bouillons." They are usually made as part of the recipe and are not stored.

WHITE COURT BOUILLON (*Court-Bouillon Ordinaire*). This is no more than salt water, milk, and lemon. It is used for boiling flavorful white fish.

COURT BOUILLON WITH VINEGAR (*Court-Bouillon au Vinaigre*). This is made with water, vinegar, aromatic vegetables, and spices. Used for boiling fat fish, such as trout and salmon, and shellfish.

COURT BOUILLON WITH WHITE WINE (*Court-Bouillon au Vin Blanc*). Made with water, white wine, and seasonings. For boiling or poaching fish.

COURT BOUILLON WITH RED WINE (*Court-Bouillon au Vin Rouge*). This is similar to the above, except it is made with red wine. For poaching and boiling fish, particularly fresh-water fish.

ASPIC JELLIES

Aspics are sparkling clear, specially flavored, naturally gelatinous stocks firm enough to hold their shape when chilled, yet soft enough to become a melting jelly the instant they arrive in your mouth. They are used as a flavorful embellishment for dishes of cold meat, fish, and other foods. Aspics may be used to coat the meat or to cover it entirely in a mold. They are also chopped and used as a sparkling bed for meat and are cut in fancy shapes and used as a decorative garnish.

MEAT ASPIC (*Gelée de Viande*). This can be made using beef or veal stock.

CHICKEN ASPIC (*Gelée de Volaille*). Can be made with Chicken Consommé or a clarified White Chicken Stock.

FISH ASPIC (*Gelée de Poisson*). Can be made with a clarified White Fish Stock (Fumet), or with a clarified Court Bouillon with Wine in which a fish has been cooked.

THE COOKING OF STOCKS

Before we begin to make stock, let me impress upon you the need for using only the finest and freshest ingredients. The meats must be from the tougher, more flavorful cuts. The bones and the vegetables must be absolutely fresh. Even the water you use must be pure and free of off-flavors. I say this because the stock you make may leave its imprint on a dozen meals. It should be perfect.

In general, for each quart of stock you should use about 1 pound of lean meat, 1 pound of meaty bones, ½ pound of aromatic vegetables, a pinch or two of herbs and spices, and about 1⅓ quarts of water. The meat and bones are put into the cold water and simmered until their albuminous scum is expelled. The vegetables and seasonings are added, and the whole simmered very slowly for 4 to 5 hours. The liquid is then strained, cooled, and skimmed of all fat. This is stock—the clear, fat-free, flavorful liquid that is the foundation of classic French cooking.

To understand the method, read the following recipe for beef consommé closely. The same method, with little variation, applies in all the other stock recipes given. The detailed directions for clarifying stock will also be given under beef consommé.

THE CONSOMMÉS

BEEF CONSOMMÉ
(*Fonds Blanc Ordinaires*)

Lean beef, 4 pounds—chuck, brisket, or round

Beef bones, 4 pounds, well meated —from the shin, plate, or neck

Chicken bones, 1½ pounds, or 1½ pounds chicken backs, necks, wings

Water, about 5 quarts

Salt, 2 teaspoons

Carrots, 8 medium

Onion, 1 medium

Leeks, 4, or 4 medium onions

Turnips, 3 small

Parsnip, a 3-inch piece

Bouquet garni—1 rib celery, 3 sprigs parsley, 1 bay leaf, and 1 sprig or pinch of thyme, all tied in cheesecloth

A 10- to 12-quart soup kettle

Our objective is to obtain 4 quarts of clear, golden, full-flavored stock. The dominant flavor will be that of beef, rounded out by the flavors of the vegetables and herbs. The body of the stock will come from the gelatin that is extracted from the bones. The procedures given are designed to extract the most flavor and gelatin from the ingredients without clouding the stock.

The meat may be in one or several pieces. The meaty bones should be broken up or sawed in small pieces; if they are not very meaty add a little more beef. Place the beef, bones, and chicken bones or parts in the soup kettle. Cover them with 5 quarts of cold water and add 2 teaspoons salt. Place over a medium fire and bring slowly to a simmer.

The objective of cooking at this point is to expel the albumin (which appears as a grayish scum) from the meat and bones to prevent it from clouding the stock. Skim away this natural scum as it rises to the surface of the water. To promote this cleansing process, retard the speed at which the water heats by adding ½ cup of cold water from time to time and stirring up the meat and bones, thereby releasing more of their albumin. Do this 3 or 4 times, skimming regularly, until the scum ceases to rise to the surface and the water is simmering gently.

Now add the carrots, whole or cut in half crosswise; onion; well-washed leeks; turnips (parboiled for 5 minutes if they are old or strong); parsnip; and the *bouquet garni*. Return the water to a simmer, skimming away the white froth that rises from the vegetables. Partially cover the kettle, leaving a 1- or 2-inch opening for the steam to escape (thereby allowing the stock to reduce while cooking), and simmer over very low heat for 4 to 5 hours. The water should move gently without bubbling, except for a wayward bubble that breaks the surface now and then.

During this long simmering, the water will penetrate the meat and vegetables, extracting their flavors. From time to time you may skim away the stock fat rising to the surface, but do not disturb the ingredients. They should remain covered by about 1 inch of liquid. If the liquid evaporates too quickly, add a little more water, gently, to avoid stirring up sediment in the bottom of the kettle.

When the cooking is completed, turn off the heat and allow the stock to rest for 5 or 10 minutes. This will settle many of the small particles floating in the stock. Next, carefully skim away most of the fat floating atop the stock. And finally, strain the stock through a strainer lined with several thicknesses of washed cheesecloth into cool, wide-mouthed bowls. Use a ladle to take the stock from the pot a little at a time, working carefully to avoid stirring up sediments at the bottom. You will have to remove some of the ingredients to get the bowl of the ladle to the bottom of the pot; do so carefully. Add 1 cup cold water, wait a few minutes for the stirred-up sediment to settle, and ladle off most of the remaining stock. Leave the dregs of stock in the kettle. The vegetables are tasteless and useless. The meat, also relatively tasteless, may be used to make hash or sliced and served with a piquant sauce.

Allow the stock to cool until it reaches room temperature. Do not cover the bowls before this time, or off-flavors of fermentation will result. When the stock is cooled, cover it and chill it in the refrigerator. The fat will rise to the surface and form a protective coating as the stock jellifies. This fat is easily removed when the stock is ready for use.

This beef consommé is used, as is, as the liquid for making *Pot-au-Feu, Petite Marmite,* and *Poule-au-Pot,* the famous French boiled dinners that provide soup and main course from a single pot. It also provides stock for thick soups, and is an excellent braising liquid for beef. Most important, beef consommé is used for making the classic clear soups (consommés) after it has been further enriched and clarified. We will perform this operation next.

NOTE: Beef consommé can be made more gelatinous, that is, with greater body, by simmering the bones for a longer period than the 5 hours required to extract the flavor from the meat. To do this, put the bones into the pot with the salt and water and simmer them for 5 hours, taking all precautions for keeping the liquid clear. At the end of this period, strain the stock, cool it, and use it in place of water as the liquid for making beef consommé. Wash the bones and put them in the kettle with the meat. They will continue to exude gelatin all during the time the stock is simmering. The resulting stock will jellify more firmly than the stock obtained from the preceding method.

CLARIFIED BEEF CONSOMMÉ
(*Fonds Blanc Clarifiés*)

Lean beef, 1 pound	Celery, 1 rib (optional)
Egg white, 1	Beef Consommé, 4 quarts
Carrot, 1 medium (optional)	
Onion, 1 medium (optional), or 1 leek	

Scrupulously remove any fat from the beef and cut it up finely. Put the beef through a grinder with the egg white. You may also put into the grinder the carrot, onion or leek, and celery. These vegetables are not necessary if the beef consommé is well made and well rounded in flavor. Put all through the grinder twice if necessary to cut the ingredients finely. They will appear rather like a paste.

Put this paste into a saucepan or soup kettle and add 4 quarts of fat-free, cold beef consommé. Mix thoroughly and heat the mixture, stirring, until it reaches the simmer. Simmer slowly for about 1 hour.

Here is what is happening. The cold stock quickly penetrates the finely chopped beef, extracting its albuminous protein. This protein and the similar protein of the egg white begin to coagulate under the influence of the heat. Meanwhile, you are stirring. Stirring brings the coagulating protein into contact with the millions of microscopic particles in the stock which have caused it to be less than perfectly clear. These particles become entangled in the protein, from whence they can no longer escape. As the stock simmers, you will see grayish clumps of protein moving through the liquid, blotting up even more of the impurities suspended in it. (Once the stock has reached a simmer, you may stop stirring and allow the protein to do its scouring work unaided.)

Also, while the stock is simmering, flavor is extracted from the beef (and the vegetables if you used them), thereby further enriching the stock. This extra measure of flavor more than makes up for the scouring action of the protein, which, while it is removing microscopic impurities, is robbing the stock of some of its flavor as well. For this reason, never use more than 1 egg white for 4 quarts of stock.

After the stock has simmered for 1 hour, you may carefully ladle out the liquid, straining it through several layers of washed cheesecloth into a cool, wide-mouthed bowl. The liquid should be sparkling clear, golden in flavor, and giving off a heady, delicious steam. This is clarified beef consommé, an elegant clear soup that may be served as it is or quickly garnished to become one of the dozens of classic consommés of *haute cuisine,* soups regularly served to financiers and kings. For these garnishes, see Chapter 6.

CHICKEN CONSOMMÉ
(*Fonds de Volaille*)

To make chicken consommé, follow the recipe and directions for Beef Consommé, substituting a 3- to 4-pound stewing chicken for half (that is, 4 pounds) of the beef and bones. Before putting the chicken in the pot, brown it lightly in the oven to give the consommé a more golden color.

CLARIFIED CHICKEN CONSOMMÉ
(*Fonds de Volaille Clarifiés*)

Clarify chicken consommé exactly as you clarified Beef Consommé.* Instead of the beef, you may use 1 pound of lean chicken meat.

THE BROWN STOCKS

BROWN STOCK or ESTOUFFADE
(*Fonds Brun ou Estouffade*)

This stock is made less and less today, being replaced by Brown Veal Stock, which can be made to serve more general purposes. If, however, you demand the authentic flavor of the French brown sauces, you must begin with the full, authoritative flavor of this classic stock. You can store it in clean, covered containers in the refrigerator for about 1 week. If you wish to refrigerate it longer, bring it to the boil, simmer for 10 to 15 minutes, cool it, and store it for another week. Or, you may freeze it for several months. If you have little space, you can reduce 4 quarts of this stock to little more than 1 cup of concentrated syrupy liquid, which will cool to form a thick, rich, flavorful paste called Meat Glaze. This will keep in your refrigerator for six months or more. One tablespoon of this glaze added to 1 cup of hot water will give you 1 cup of brown stock.

Lean beef, 2 pounds—shin, chuck, brisket, or round
Veal, 2 pounds
Beef bones, 2 pounds
Veal bones, 2 pounds—shin or knuckle
Butter or fat, ¼ cup
Carrots, 6 medium, minced
Onions, 4 medium, minced
Raw ham, ½ pound, diced

Pork rind, fresh, ½ pound (or ½ pound cured bacon rind, parboiled 5 minutes)
Water, about 5 quarts
Bouquet Garni—1 rib celery, 3 sprigs parsley, 1 bay leaf, and 1 sprig or pinch of thyme, all tied in cheesecloth
No salt!
A 12-quart soup kettle

This stock is made exactly like Beef Consommé except that the beef, bones, and vegetables are browned prior to simmering. Place beef and veal in a baking pan and brush with melted fat or butter. The meat should be in large pieces (or tied together if in small pieces). Also place beef bones and veal bones in a baking pan and sprinkle with fat. The bones should be well broken up or sawed. Brown meat and bones in a 450° oven for about 30 minutes, turning them now and then until they are richly browned on all sides.

The carrots and onions can be browned along with the meat and bones, adding them after 15 minutes so they will not burn. But it is perhaps best to brown these separately. Sauté them in butter until they are nicely browned.

Put the browned beef and bones into a 12-quart soup kettle and add the ham and the fresh pork rind or bacon rind. Pour off the fat from the baking pans, add 1 cup water to each, put them over a low flame, and scrape them with a wooden spoon, dissolving the drippings in the bottom of the pan and scraping up all the flavorful brown bits. Pour this liquid over the meat and bones, and add 4½ quarts of water. Bring the water slowly to a simmer, *observing all precautions* and procedures listed under Beef Consommé for keeping the stock clear. This will take even more care, because the veal in the pot will expel large quantities of albumin.

When the scum ceases to rise, add the browned vegetables and the bouquet garni. Do not add salt. Brown stock is frequently greatly reduced for some of the uses to which it is put, and the flavor of the salt would become too concentrated.

Partly cover the kettle and simmer the stock gently for 5 hours, occasionally skimming away the fat that rises to the surface. Remove, strain, and cool the stock as described for beef consommé.

NOTE: Brown stock can be made more full bodied and gelatinous by simmering the bones in advance of the meat to extract more of their gelatin. See Beef Consommé for details.

BROWN VEAL STOCK
(*Fonds de Veau Brun*)

This rich brown, gelatinous, neutral-flavored stock is widely used in making sauces from pan juices and the drippings of roasts. (Remember, a properly cooked roast will have few drippings, the juices being retained in the meat itself.) Brown veal stock extends these juices and drippings, providing a greater volume of full-bodied sauce without dominating the flavor of the drippings. It also thickens them, being itself first reduced or, more often, being thickened with arrowroot to provide a rich brown, transparent base. Browned veal stock is also an excellent braising liquid for beef and lamb.

Veal, 4 pounds
Veal bones, 4 pounds—shin or knuckle
Fat or butter, ¼ cup
Water, about 5 quarts
Carrots, 6 medium
Onions, 2 medium

Leeks, 2, or 2 medium onions
Bouquet Garni—1 rib celery, 3 sprigs parsley, 1 bay leaf, and 1 sprig or pinch of thyme, all tied in cheesecloth
A 12-quart soup kettle

Brush veal and veal bones with melted fat or butter, and brown in a 450° oven for about 30 minutes, turning them so that they are browned on all sides.

Veal contains large amounts of albumin and produces large amounts of grayish scum. As a result, veal stock cannot be as clear as beef or chicken stock. To make it as clear as possible, you may first blanch the browned meat and bones by simmering them in water for 5 minutes. Then wash them under running water and proceed with the cooking.

This stock must be very gelatinous, so you may simmer the bones in advance of the meat to more fully extract their gelatin. Put browned, parboiled bones in a kettle with 5 quarts of cold water and bring to the simmer, observing all precautions and procedures listed under Beef Consommé for keeping the stock clear. Simmer the bones for 5 hours. Strain the stock, cool it (if you have time), and return it to the pot with the bones and the browned, parboiled veal. Again bring the liquid slowly to the boil, skimming carefully, until the scum from the meat is thoroughly expelled.

Meanwhile, finely chop carrots, onions, and leeks and sauté them in butter until they are browned. Add these to the pot, along with the bouquet garni. Partly cover and simmer for 3 to 4 hours more. Remove, strain, and cool the stock as described for beef consommé.

THE WHITE STOCKS

WHITE VEAL STOCK
(*Fonds de Veau Blanc*)

Prepare this exactly as Brown Veal Stock, but do not brown the ingredients. This stock is used for braising white meats and for making white sauces. Greatly reduced, it becomes a pale Meat Glaze. Colored and flavored with wine, it becomes a natural aspic jelly.

WHITE CHICKEN STOCK
(*Fonds de Volaille Blanc*)

Prepare this exactly as White Veal Stock, but add 1 or 2 stewing chickens to the pot when you add the meat. The uses of this stock are similar to those of white veal stock, being preferred when these uses are applied to poultry.

GIBLET STOCK
(*Fonds d'Abatis*)

This is a casually made stock—brown or white—that is very useful in home cookery. It is made from the neck, wing tips, heart, and gizzard of chickens, turkeys, ducks, or geese. Also, if the poultry is cut up, the backs may go into this stock. If the poultry is wholly or partially boned, the bones go into it as well. The stock simmers unattended while the poultry is cooking and provides a flavorful liquid for pan sauces.

Roughly chop the giblets and brown them or not, depending on the color of the sauce you intend to make. Put them in a saucepan with 1 medium carrot and 1 medium onion, both chopped (and browned if you prefer), 2 sprigs of parsley, ½ bay leaf, a pinch of thyme, a pinch of salt, and a few peppercorns. Cover with cold water, bring to the simmer, skim, partially cover the pan, and simmer for 1 to 3 hours, adding a little water if necessary. When you are ready to use the stock, skim the fat from its surface, strain it, and reduce it to the quantity of liquid you need.

FISH STOCK

FISH FUMET (WHITE FISH STOCK)
(*Fumet Blanc de Poisson*)

This stock is quickly and easily prepared from the bones and trimmings of lean fish. It is the basis of fish sauces and is the correct liquid to use for poaching fish when the liquor is to be made into a sauce.

Onions, 3 medium	White wine, dry, 2 cups
Parsley, 8 sprigs	Water, about 4 quarts
Bay leaf, 1	An 8-quart saucepan
Lemon, 1	
Lean white fish trimmings and bones, 4 pounds	

Lightly butter the bottom of the saucepan. Add onions, which you have sliced and blanched,* in 1 quart simmering water for 3 minutes. Also add parsley, bay leaf, the juice of 1 lemon, and trimmings and bones of fish. Cover and stew gently over a low fire for 10 minutes, stirring occasionally to prevent the ingredients from scorching. Add wine and reduce rapidly until 1 cup remains. Add 4 quarts of cold water, bring to the simmer, skim, and allow to simmer for 20 to 30 minutes. Strain through several thicknesses of washed cheesecloth into a wide-mouthed bowl and cool uncovered.

FISH STOCK WITH RED WINE
(*Fumet de Poisson au Vin Rouge*)

This stock is prepared as for Fish Fumet, except for the liquid use 6 cups dry red wine and 8 cups water and omit the lemon juice.

COURT BOUILLON

These preparations are used for "boiling" fish and shellfish, that is, cooking fish completely immersed in simmering liquid. They may also be used for poaching fish—cooking fish in barely enough liquid to cover. Court bouillons subtly flavor the delicate flesh, restoring some of the taste necessarily lost when fish is cooked in liquid. They also help to efface the sometimes "muddy" flavor of some fresh-water fish.

WHITE COURT BOUILLON
(*Court-Bouillon Blanc*)

Salt, 1 tablespoon	Milk, 1 cup
Lemon, 2 peeled slices	Water, 2 quarts

Add all ingredients to the water. This stock needs no advance cooking; it is ready for use when mixed. Used especially for white fish, it helps keep their flesh white and preserves their natural flavor.

COURT BOUILLON WITH VINEGAR
(*Court-Bouillon au Vinaigre*)

Carrots, 2 medium, chopped	Parsley, 8 sprigs
Onions, 2 medium, chopped	Bay leaf, 1
Salt, 1 tablespoon	Thyme, 1 sprig or a pinch
Peppercorns, 8	Water, 2 quarts
Vinegar, ½ cup	

Add all ingredients to the water. Bring to the simmer and simmer for 1 hour. Allow the ingredients to remain in the stock while it cools. Then strain it through several layers of washed cheesecloth. This is an excellent stock for cooking fat fish like trout and salmon, and shellfish.

COURT BOUILLON WITH WHITE WINE
(*Court-Bouillon au Vin Blanc*)

White wine, dry, 1 quart	Parsley, 3 sprigs
Onion, 1, chopped	Bay leaf, 1
Salt, 2 teaspoons	Thyme, 1 sprig or a pinch
Peppercorns, 4	Water, 1 quart

Add all ingredients to the water. Bring to a simmer, and simmer ½ hour. Strain the stock through several thicknesses of washed cheesecloth into a wide-mouthed bowl and cool it. Use for boiling and poaching fish, particularly fresh-water fish.

COURT BOUILLON WITH RED WINE
(*Court-Bouillon au Vin Rouge*)

Prepare as for Court Bouillon with White Wine, but use dry red wine and add to the ingredients 2 finely chopped carrots. Use for boiling and poaching fish, particularly fresh-water fish. Also, this court bouillon may be used for making a Fish Aspic after the fish has been cooked in it, using 1 quart of gelatinous Fish Fumet in place of the water in the recipe.

ASPIC
(*Gelée*)

The most tender, melting aspics are those that jellify naturally as a result of the gelatin in the stock they are made from. Most of the stocks listed here will jellify naturally. Those containing relatively large amounts of veal bones—such as Veal Stock and White Chicken Stock—will set more firmly because of the large amount of gelatin contained in these bones. In addition to veal bones, calf's feet, fresh pork rind, and well-blanched bacon rind all supply generous amounts of gelatin to stock.

If, however, your stock will not set firmly enough when chilled, you may add unflavored commercial gelatin to it. Soften 1 tablespoon of gelatin in a little cold stock and dissolve this in about 1 quart of hot stock. Cool the stock and test it by pouring a little into a cold saucer and chilling it. If it does not set stiffly enough for your purpose, add a little more gelatin. Be careful not to add too much; a rubbery aspic is an abomination.

When the stock is sufficiently gelatinous, clarify it as you would Beef

Consommé. Then strain the aspic into a bowl and cool it in the refrigerator or on a bed of cracked ice, stirring frequently to prevent it from setting unevenly.

When the aspic is still barely warm, you may flavor it with wine. When flavoring with dessert wines, such as port, sherry, Marsala, or Madeira, add ⅓ cup of wine for each quart of aspic. When flavoring with other wines, including champagne, add ½ cup of wine to each quart of aspic. Do not add the wines until the aspic is just barely warm or their delicate bouquet will be lost.

To line a mold with aspic, chill the aspic until it is almost at the point of setting, and pour a little of it into a chilled mold. Turn the mold in your hands, to coat the inside evenly with the aspic, which should set as it comes into contact with the cold surface of the mold. By chilling the mold after each application, several layers of aspic can be built up in this way. Hard-cooked egg white and vegetables cut in fancy shapes may be affixed to the aspic lining and secured in place with another layer of aspic.

To mold food, first line the mold with aspic to the depth you want, decorating it or not as you choose. Chill the food so that it is quite cold. Center it in the mold, pour the remaining aspic over it, and chill.

To unmold aspic, free the aspic from the edges of the mold with a thin, sharp-pointed knife. Dip the mold quickly in hot water, place the serving platter over it, and invert quickly onto the platter. If at first you don't succeed, try again, but dip the mold in hot water only very briefly between trials.

To coat with aspic, be sure the food to be coated is very cold and the aspic chilled to the point where it is just about to congeal. Pour or spoon a coating of aspic over the food and chill. Pour another layer of aspic over the food and chill again. Continue with succeeding layers until you have obtained the depth you want. You may decorate the food while coating it, with cutouts of different foods and herb leaves, affixing them to the aspic and covering them with the succeeding layer.

To garnish with aspic, pour the liquid aspic into a shallow dish and chill until it is firmly set. You may then cut it into decorative shapes with a knife or fancy-shape cutters, or you may simply mince the aspic until it forms a sparkling mass that looks like a bed of crushed jewels.

MEAT ASPIC
(*Gelée de Viande*)

Make this aspic by adding veal bones, calf's feet, fresh pork rind, or blanched bacon rind when making meat stock. Beef Consommé will give you a golden aspic; White Veal Stock gives you a pale aspic; Brown Stock and Brown Veal Stock will give you a beautiful burnt-amber-colored aspic.

CHICKEN ASPIC
(*Gelée de Volaille*)

Make this aspic by adding veal bones, calf's feet, fresh pork rind, or blanched bacon rind when making Chicken Consommé or White Chicken Stock. It will be golden in color.

FISH ASPIC
(*Gelée de Poisson*)

You will need packaged gelatin for making this aspic from Fish Fumet or from a Court Bouillon with Wine in which a fish has been cooked.

For clarification, use egg white alone or egg white and chopped or ground lean white fish. For 1 quart of stock, 1 egg white and ½ pound fish are sufficient. (At one time fish stocks were clarified with fresh caviar, but those elegant days are long past.) Observe the procedures for clarifying listed under Beef Consommé, but reduce the simmering time to 20 minutes.

Fish aspics made with fish fumet or with a court bouillon with white wine are relatively colorless. The aspic made with a court bouillon with red wine is a rosy pink. A little food coloring may be added if necessary to obtain this traditional color.

❋ THE SAUCES

"I would eat my own father with such a sauce!"
GRIMOD DE LA REYNIÈRE

French sauce making began about two thousand years ago. At this remote period the French were Gauls and had already been largely lead astray by the Romans. They dined lying on couches, ate dormice, and regaled themselves with great quantities of meat which they drenched with resinous sauces made from honey, vinegar, wine, pepper, oil, broth, and a variety of pungent herbs.

By the time the Franks arrived, the bad habits of the Gauls were firmly established. The Franks, being a rude people with no cuisine of their own, took to the Gallic diet with gusto. In all of Western Europe there was hardly anything to be found to eat that did not taste of honey, vinegar, wine, pepper, oil, broth, and pungent herbs, all mixed up together. I only mention these ancient matters to prove the early advent of sauces in French cookery. Bad as they were, they were a prologue. Today there are more than two hundred sauces in the repertory.

What are these sauces that have become a mainstay of French cooking? They can be simply described as liquid or semiliquid seasonings for food. They include mayonnaise, hollandaise, vinaigrette, butter sauces, compound butters, dessert sauces, and pan sauces. But mostly when we consider classic French sauce making, we think of the warm, cooked *sauces mères*, the mother sauces of the French cuisine.

The mother sauces differ from mayonnaise, hollandaise, vinaigrette, and others in that they are never served as they are, but undergo additional treatment to become finished sauces. These finished sauces are called the compound sauces. With the mother sauces in your possession, dozens of traditional French compound sauces can be quickly and easily made.

There are five mother sauces—three brown and two white. All five are traditionally based on a Roux of flour and butter, to which you add some flavorful liquid. If you cook 1 tablespoon of flour in 1 tablespoon of butter for a few minutes, and then stir in 1 cup of milk, you have the essential basis of *Sauce Béchamel*. If in place of the milk you stir in 1 cup of white stock, you have *Sauce Velouté*. These are the basic white sauces. Nothing could be easier.

The brown mother sauces are Tomato Sauce, *Demi-Glace,* and *Sauce Espagnole,* or Brown Sauce. You are familiar with tomato sauce, which is widely available in cans. *Demi-Glace* is no more (and no less!) than *Sauce Espagnole* cooked down with brown stock and flavored with a little sherry or Madeira wine. It takes little more than an hour to make if you have *Sauce Espagnole* on hand. And I strongly recommend that you make and store a quart or two of this legendary brown sauce of the French cuisine. *Sauce Espagnole* can be your introduction to heights of good cooking that will render your family and guests speechless.

Centuries of cooking have gone into the creation of the classic sauces. Millions of palates have tasted and tested their worth. Many sauces of old have disappeared. Sometimes they were not worthy. Other times they were debased by incompetent cooks and the debasement has ruined the sauce's reputation. This shameful attrition continues today, affecting sauces and other classic dishes as well.

This is why we must strive to maintain the purity of our sauces. I do not oppose new methods. We should simplify wherever possible. But we must never compromise the quality of our work. And we should carefully review the ever-changing ingredients produced by our farms and food industries to see that they perform as well as the less sophisticated ingredients of old. If they do not, we must devise ways to make them do so.

A classic sauce, faithfully made, is an excellent thing. It is perfectly adjusted to the flavor, texture, and temperature of the food it sauces. It never dominates the food, nor is it itself dominated. There is an engaging interchange, more or less subtle, between the natural taste of the food and the created taste of the sauce. And just as the taste of the food is unique and well defined, the taste of the sauce is unique and well defined—the combined result of all the flavors of all its ingredients.

In addition to taste, a classic brown or white sauce has clingability (*nappe*), velvety smoothness (*velouté*), and body (*corps*). You can feel the body when you stir it, a light, liquid density that tugs lightly at your wooden spoon. You can feel its velvety texture in the smooth glide of spoon through the body of the sauce. You can see its clingability when you lift the spoon, a lingering honeylike coating that is neither syrupy nor sticky.

And finally, the classic sauce is infinitely beautiful. Whether it is white or ivory, lemon, golden, transparent amber, or rich warm brown, it delights the eye with the purity of its color, its glossiness and brilliance. I swear to you before all the world, a classic sauce *glows!*

Smooth, light without being liquid, glossy to the eye, and decided in taste—this is what Escoffier insisted that any sauce whatsoever should be. So let us gather the materials to make this perfect sauce. The flavorful liquids. The ingredients that thicken. The aromatic vegetables and meats. A squeeze of this. A pinch of that. Heavy saucepans. Utensils to whip and stir and strain with. A little heat. A lot of care. And knowing what we are doing.

In this chapter you will learn to make all the mother sauces, some of their variations, and all other sauces needed to make all the dishes listed in this book.

ROUX

This is a mixture of fat and starch cooked together and used as a thickener for sauces.

Butter is the preferred fat for making a roux, and in good home cooking there is no reason why you should use any other. Flour is the usual starch, but pure starches such as arrowroot and cornstarch are also used. In either case, the blend consists of equal weights of butter and flour or starch. These are mixed and cooked together, stirring, so that each particle of starch or flour is coated with butter so it cannot clump up.

Although the thickening power of flour varies, it is usually calculated that 1 tablespoon of flour will thicken 1 cup of liquid to the consistency of medium cream or a thin sauce. Only 1½ teaspoons of arrowroot or cornstarch provides about the same amount of thickening.

There are three kinds of roux. Brown roux is used to thicken the basic brown sauces, Brown Sauce and Demi-Glace Sauce. Blond roux is used to thicken Velouté Sauce. White roux is used to thicken Béchamel Sauce and other sauces that must be kept very white.

The making of a roux is so easy one tends to be careless about it. Avoid this carelessness, as a well-made roux is extremely important to the success of a sauce. Take your time and do not allow the flour or starch to become the least bit burned, or it will lose its thickening power and give the sauce a horrible taste.

To make a brown roux (roux brun): Heat Clarified Butter and sprinkle in, while stirring, an equal weight of flour (or starch). Flour weighs half as much as butter, so you should have 2 tablespoons of flour to 1 tablespoon of butter. Cook slowly, stirring frequently, until the mixture takes on a light brown color and sends forth a nutty aroma. Depending upon the heat, this will take about 20 minutes. During this time the starch will be partially cooked, any water remaining in the butter will be evaporated, and the roux will take on a grainy appearance. Take care that the starch does not begin to burn or the roux will become bitter.

To make a blond roux (roux blond): Proceed exactly as for brown roux, but remove the roux from the fire just as soon as it exhibits a pale gold color.

To make a white roux (roux blanc): Proceed exactly as for brown roux, but do not allow the roux to color at all. About 3 to 5 minutes cooking is all that is required to overcome the raw taste of the flour.

A roux made with a purer starch, such as arrowroot or cornstarch, will produce a clearer sauce, and only about half as much roux will be required to achieve the desired amount of thickening.

THE BROWN SAUCES

The brown sauces *Espagnole* and *Demi-Glace* are used as a base for finished sauces. They are also used as cooking sauces for braising, as a thickening and flavoring for pan sauces, and as a coating for meats glazed in the oven.

The velvety texture of these brown sauces is attributed mostly to the long simmering they traditionally get. A good amount of stock is required because during this long simmering more than half of the original liquid is evaporated away. Long simmering also contributes to the body of the sauce, and to the concentration and blending of its many flavors into a distinctive whole.

A heavy pan is required to prevent scorching of the thickening liquid. The bottom of the pan should be rounded where it meets the sides to prevent the sauce from hiding and scorching in corners. Also, as the sauce cooks down, it should be strained into successively smaller saucepans so that less and less heat is required to keep the sauce at a gentle simmer.

The cooking must be very, very slow. If the sauce boils, it will become choked up with starch and fat and other impurities that come naturally to the surface when the sauce is just simmering. These, of course, are regularly skimmed away.

Once a brown sauce is well under way, it is best not to stir it. While stirring improves the texture of white sauces, it lightens brown sauces without helping their texture. If you fear a brown sauce will scorch at the bottom, move a wooden spatula gently over the bottom and in the corners. Or swirl the pan gently to move the sauce around.

Finally, I cannot overestimate the importance of working with good stock and a good roux. You can make a stock of sorts with trimmings and cooked bones, but a first rate stock should be based on fresh meat as well as fresh bones, and fresh, sound vegetables. A good roux can be made with fresh beef fat, but the best and most delicately flavored is made with fresh, flavorful Clarified Butter.

BROWN SAUCE OR ESPAGNOLE
(*Sauce Espagnole*)

The curious name given this famous French sauce is said to have been in honor of the Italian cooks brought to France by Catherine de Médicis at the end of the sixteenth century. These cooks flavored the French brown sauce of that period with tomato. The French liked the taste. Much of Italy, at that time, was under Spanish rule. Hence, *sauce espagnole*.

There are four ways to make *sauce espagnole*, and good results are obtained from each. Beginning with the raw meat and vegetables (without a stock), a classic *espagnole* will take days of cooking to make. On the other hand, if you have an excellent brown stock, *espagnole* can be made in 1 hour. In as much as the sauce simmers mostly unattended, you may want to make at least one classic *espagnole* in your life. Do it if only to satisfy yourself as to how an *espagnole* should taste. Your handiwork will keep for months in the freezer, rewarding you for your pluckiness again and again.

CLASSIC BROWN SAUCE, THICKENED WITH FLOUR
(4 Quarts)

Flour, 2 cups
Claried butter, 1 cup (½ pound)
Brown Stock, 8 quarts
Mirepoix, about 1 pound (see below)

Tomatoes, 2½ pounds, chopped, or 2 cups Tomato Purée
A deep, heavy, 8-quart saucepan
No salt!

Stir flour into melted butter and cook very slowly for about 15 minutes, stirring constantly, until the flour becomes light brown in color. This is a Brown Roux (read the remarks on roux in this chapter). Take great pains not to heat the roux too quickly or to allow the flour to scorch in the bottom of the pan. A well-made roux is absolutely vital to a clear, brilliant sauce.

When the roux is brown and smells of baked flour, add 6 quarts of hot brown stock to the pan, constantly stirring with a wire whisk to evenly dissolve the roux into it. The quality of this stock is as important as the quality of the roux. It should be rich in meat flavor, gelatinous, well skimmed and strained, and free of impurities and fat. Continue stirring with a wooden spatula until the sauce returns to the simmer. Then lower the heat until the bubbles can barely struggle to the surface. Simmer, skimming regularly, for at least 6 hours. During this time you should strain the sauce twice, returning it to a clean saucepan, and adding more brown stock to keep the sauce at 6 quarts. *Take care never to allow the sauce to boil or it will cloud up irrevocably.*

After 6 hours of simmering you will notice the sauce will become somewhat lighter in color. Now add to it about 1 pound of *mirepoix,* consisting of, 2 medium carrots, 2 medium onions, 2 small celery ribs, ¼ cup diced fresh ham or blanched salt pork or bacon, ½ bay leaf, and a pinch of thyme—the vegetables cut in fine dice, all browned in butter and finished with 2 tablespoons of Madeira wine. Also add tomatoes or tomatoe purée. Simmer, skimming, for 2 hours or a little longer to reduce the sauce to 4 quarts. Strain the sauce into a cold, wide-mouthed bowl and allow it to cool uncovered.

This is a classic *sauce espagnole,* as made in the great restaurants of Europe in the days of wine and roses. You need not do all the cooking in one day. You may stop at any time, cool the partly finished sauce uncovered, and store it in the refrigerator until you resume sauce making. The finished sauce will keep for weeks in the refrigerator if you simmer it occasionally. Or you can pour it into handy 1-cup freezer jars and keep it frozen for months. It will, however, lose flavor if kept frozen for too long a time.

BROWN SAUCE, THICKENED WITH STARCH
(4 Quarts)

There is an easier, faster, and some say better way to make *Brown Sauce*. It is made in one operation, it is finished in one hour, and it can produce a clearer and more brilliant sauce than the long-simmered classic method above.

This method employs pure starch in place of flour in the making of the roux. Flour is only partly starch. Therefore more of it is required than pure starch to obtain a desired thickening; this extra burden chokes up the stock and prevents it from clearing itself of its impurities. Long cooking and much skimming are therefore necessary. A pure starch—such as arrowroot, potato starch, or cornstarch—allows the stock to purge itself in just one hour. During this brief period of simmering the stock has not the time to reduce and concentrate sufficiently. We therefore reduce and concentrate it in advance.

Starch, arrowroot or cornstarch, 1 cup
Clarified Butter, ½ cup (¼ pound)
Brown Stock, 8 quarts reduced to 5 quarts
Mirepoix, about 1 pound (see below)
Tomatoes, 2½ pounds, chopped, or 2 cups Tomato Purée
A deep, heavy, 6-quart saucepan
No salt!

Stir arrowroot or cornstarch into melted butter. Cook very slowly for about 15 minutes, stirring, until the starch browns and forms a Brown Roux. Heat very, very slowly so that the starch expands evenly. Do not allow it to scorch.

When the roux is light brown add the brown stock. Stir constantly with a wire whisk to dissolve the roux evenly. As soon as it is well mixed, add the *mirepoix,* consisting of 2 medium carrots, 2 medium onions, 2 small celery ribs, all finely diced; ¼ cup raw ham or blanched salt pork or blanched bacon, diced; ½ bay leaf; a pinch of thyme—all well browned in butter and moistened with 2 tablespoons of Madeira wine. Also add the tomatoes or tomato purée. Simmer, skimming, for 1 hour, or until the sauce is reduced to 4 quarts. Strain the sauce into a cold, wide-mouthed bowl and allow it to cool uncovered. Who says French sauces are difficult?

BROWN SAUCE, THICKENED BY REDUCTION

The restaurant kitchen of today is a more hectic place than it was in former times, when there was one chef for every three or four diners. Today a chef is expected to administer to ten times as many people. He must devise short-cuts to free his busy hands. To simplify the making of Brown Sauce, he has resorted to reduction.

The method is excellent, and based firmly in classical cookery. Meat Glazes have long played an important role in the French cuisine. The chef simply follows the procedure for making glazes, stopping when the brown stock has achieved the thickness and consistency of brown sauce.

This method requires a great deal of brown stock, which a good restaurant will have on hand. The stock must be well flavored and made with lots of veal and veal bones to supply the gelatin necessary to bring about the thickening. Tomatoes are added to the stock to give the sauce their necessary flavor. It is a long, slow, continuous process, but it requires only occasional skimming and transfer of the sauce, as it cooks down, to smaller and smaller pans. The sauce is finished when it nicely coats a wooden spoon and is full of flavor.

BROWN SAUCE, MADE WITHOUT STOCK
(2 Quarts)

The preceding three recipes for brown sauce all required a well-made, flavorful brown stock as their base. In this recipe, stock and sauce are made simultaneously in one pot.

Beef, 2½ pounds of chuck, brisket, rump, or other flavorful cut, in stewing-size chunks	Flour, ½ cup
	Water, 2 quarts
	White wine, dry, 1 bottle
Veal bones, 2½ pounds, with some meat attached	Tomato paste, 4 tablespoons
	Parsley, 3 sprigs
Onion, 1 large, quartered	Bay leaves, 3
Carrots, 3 medium, peeled and quartered	Thyme, 2 sprigs or ½ teaspoon
	Salt, 1 tablespoon
Celery, 2 ribs with leaves, coarsely chopped	Peppercorns, 1 teaspoon, crushed

Put beef and veal bones in a roasting pan, sprinkle them with fat, and place them in a preheated 475° oven to brown. Turn them in their own melting fat to prevent them from burning, or reduce heat slightly as browning progresses. After 20 minutes add: onion, carrots, and celery. Turn the vegetables in the fat and leave meat, bones, and vegetables to brown for another 20 minutes. (We add the vegetables later because they brown more quickly and burn more easily than the meat and bones.) Sprinkle flour into the pan and continue baking for 15 minutes more to brown the flour.

When meat, bones, and vegetables are well browned, transfer them to a heavy saucepan. To the roasting pan add 2 cups of water and cook on the burner over low heat, stirring to dissolve brown bits in the bottom of the pan. Pour this into the saucepan, add 1½ quarts of cold water, wine, tomato paste, parsley, bay leaves, thyme, salt, and peppercorns. Bring to a simmer and simmer slowly, skimming off fat and foam as they rise to the surface. Add more hot water if necessary to keep liquid at the same level. Continue simmering for at least 2 hours, preferably 5 hours or more.

To keep the sauce clear, carefully ladle out as much as you can without disturbing other ingredients in the saucepan. Strain through 2 layers of cheesecloth (rinsed in water and wrung out) into a wide-mouthed bowl. Remove the other ingredients from the pan (you may save the beef for another use), allow the sauce to settle, then pour it through the cheesecloth into the bowl. Cool, uncovered, to prevent off-flavors from developing.

DEMI-GLACE SAUCE
(1 Quart)

Demi-Glace, or Half-Glaze, Sauce is Brown Sauce further reduced and flavored with wine. Traditionally, it is the form in which brown sauce is usually used. Any of the preceding four recipes for brown sauce may, and should, receive this treatment. *Demi-glace* can be used in place of the brown sauce called for in any traditional recipe.

Brown Sauce, 1 quart	Sherry wine, ½ cup
Brown Stock, 1 quart	A heavy, 2½-quart saucepan

Combine brown sauce and brown stock and simmer without boiling, skimming, until the sauce is reduced to about 3½ cups. Strain the sauce off the fire and stir in sherry wine. To prevent a skin from forming, either butter the top of the sauce, or float a little stock on it.

Demi-glace sauce, which is a reduction of brown sauce, should not be confused with Meat Glaze, which is a greatly reduced stock.

TOMATO SAUCE
(*Sauce Tomate*—2 Quarts)

The ready availability of tomato sauce in cans and the difficulty of obtaining good tomatoes have made the making of this sauce an anachronism. In as much as the canners have better material to work with—they get their tomatoes vine-ripened—it is perhaps best to use their product. If, however, you want to experience an authentic *sauce tomate,* here is the recipe. You may use fresh, vine-ripened tomatoes, which you will have to get from a farmer or from your own or your neighbor's garden. Or you may use canned tomatoes, American or imported.

Salt pork, a 2-ounce slice	Sugar, 3 tablespoons
Clarified Butter, 2 tablespoons	Salt, 1½ tablespoons
Carrot, 1 medium, diced	Pepper, a pinch
Onion, 1 medium, diced	Garlic, 1 clove, crushed
Flour, ⅔ cup	Bay leaf, ½
Tomatoes, 5 pounds fresh or	Thyme, a pinch
2 quarts canned	A heavy 4-quart saucepan with cover
White Stock, 1 quart	

Cook salt pork in butter in a heavy saucepan. When the pork fat is well melted, add carrot and onion. Lightly brown the vegetables. Sprinkle in flour, stirring, until the flour browns and forms a Roux with the fat. To the pan, add: fresh tomatoes, roughly chopped, or canned tomatoes with their juice, white stock, sugar, salt, pepper, garlic, bay leaf, and thyme. Cover the saucepan, place it in a 325° oven, and cook for 1½ hours. (The weight of the tomatoes is so great that the sauce might scorch if cooked on the burner. If you do choose to cook on the burner, stir the sauce frequently.) Press the sauce through a sieve and simmer it, stirring, for 10 minutes or until it is as thick as a tomato sauce should be. Cool it in a wide-mouthed bowl, coating the surface with butter to prevent a skin from forming.

TOMATO PUREE

Make this in exactly the same way you make Tomato Sauce, except omit the flour and use only 1 cup of White Stock.

THE WHITE SAUCES

The two white *sauces mères*—*velouté* and *béchamel*—are made with a light-colored Roux and light-colored liquids. Consequently, they are creamy in color and care is taken to keep them free of specks. White pepper is used in place of black pepper, and a whole sprig of fresh or dried thyme is preferred to powdered thyme.

These sauces are used as a base for compound sauces, as a binding for stuffings and other preparations, for thick soups and purées, as cooking sauces, and for both hot and cold glazings. In as much as they may be subsequently thinned with pan juices or thickened by the addition of egg yolks or cheese, they are originally made thick or thin to suit their destiny. Their thickness is adjusted by the amount of roux used per cup of liquid—1 tablespoon of flour for a thin sauce, 4 tablespoons of flour for a very thick sauce.

Like the brown sauces, the white sauces are cooked very slowly over low heat. Unlike the brown sauces, their cooking takes much less time and they are much less reduced in volume. Also, they are regularly stirred to prevent scorching and to give them their characteristic velvety smoothness.

It is best to cook white sauces in heavy enameled iron, stainless steel, or tin-lined copper saucepans. Egg yolks and wine are frequently used in their finishing, and aluminum tends to darken the sauce to an unappetizing grayish color.

Generally, less white sauce is made at a time than brown sauce, because white sauces are quick to make and they keep less well. *Velouté* will keep in the refrigerator for several days. *Béchamel* should be used within a day or two.

VELOUTÉ SAUCE
(*Sauce Velouté*—1 Quart)

Flour, ½ cup	White pepper, a pinch
Clarified Butter, ¼ cup	Mushrooms, chopped, ½ cup (optional)
White Veal Stock, 5 cups	
Salt, 2 teaspoons	A heavy 2-quart saucepan
Nutmeg, a pinch	

Add flour to melted butter and cook over heat for about 5 minutes, stirring constantly to form a Blond Roux. Remove from heat the instant the roux shows evidence of changing color, and continue stirring until the pan has cooled somewhat.

Dissolve into the roux 4 cups hot white veal stock, reserving 1 cup for later use. Add salt, nutmeg, white pepper, and chopped mushrooms, which you have kept white in lemon water. Bring this to the simmer and simmer very slowly, skimming, for 1½ hours. Strain through 2 thicknesses of washed and wrung-out cheesecloth into a smaller saucepan, add the remaining 1 cup of white veal stock, simmer for a few minutes, then allow to partially cool and settle. Strain the sauce into a wide-mouthed bowl and cool, stirring occasionally to prevent a skin from forming. Or float a little melted butter on top of the sauce.

CHICKEN VELOUTÉ

This is a frequently used Velouté Sauce, made exactly as above, except that White Chicken Stock is used in place of the White Veal Stock. It is the basis of most white sauces served with chicken.

FISH VELOUTÉ

This is made exactly the same as ordinary Velouté Sauce, except the liquid used is a Fish Fumet. Also, it is simmered for only 15 minutes. Obviously, this is the base of white sauces served with fish.

Velouté Sauce (a short form). If necessary, a *velouté* of sorts can be made in just a few minutes. For 1¼ cups, make a Blond Roux with 1 tablespoon of butter and 2 tablespoons of flour. Add 1 cup of White Stock, stirring with a whisk to dissolve the roux into it. Simmer, stirring with a spatula, for 5 minutes or until the sauce thickens and becomes smooth. Add ¼ cup heavy cream and return to the simmer, stirring to blend the cream in evenly. Season to taste with salt and white pepper. The cream adds smoothness and finish to the sauce, normally obtained by simmering.

BÉCHAMEL SAUCE
(*Sauce Béchamel*—1 Quart)

Flour, ½ cup	Salt, ½ teaspoon
Clarified Butter, ¼ cup	White pepper, a pinch
Milk, 5 cups	Nutmeg, a pinch
Veal, lean, ¼ cup diced (optional)	Thyme, 1 sprig fresh or dry, or a
Butter, 1 tablespoon	pinch of powdered thyme
Onion, ¼ cup minced	A heavy 2-quart saucepan

Add flour to melted clarified butter. Cook over low heat, stirring constantly with a wooden spatula, for 2 or 3 minutes to form a White Roux. Remove from the heat and continue stirring until the pan has cooled. There should be absolutely no trace of a change in color. You are cooking only to remove the raw taste of the flour, and to prepare it to receive the liquid.

Bring milk to the boiling point, pour it into the roux, and whisk briskly to blend smoothly. Bring to the simmer and simmer slowly. Put the veal in a sauté pan with the butter and onion and sear over moderate heat without browning. Add the veal and onion to the saucepan. Also add salt, white pepper, nutmeg, and thyme. (If you have a whole sprig of fresh or dried thyme, use this in preference to powdered thyme.)

Simmer the sauce for one hour, stirring now and then to prevent scorching at the bottom of the pan, and skimming occasionally. Strain the sauce into a wide-mouthed bowl, and butter the top to prevent a skin from forming.

The veal in this recipe adds a nice body and flavor to the sauce, but it may be omitted. In this case, cook the onion in the clarified butter to develop flavor. Then add the flour to the butter and onion and make the roux.

If you omit the veal, you can add more flavor to the basic béchamel by using half White Stock and half milk as the liquid.

Béchamel Sauce (a short form). If you must, you can also make this sauce in a hurry. For 1¼ cups, make a White Roux with 1 tablespoon butter and 2 tablespoons flour. Whisk in 1 cup of boiling milk. Simmer for 5 minutes, adding more milk if the sauce seems too thick. Add ¼ cup cream and return to the simmer, stirring to blend the cream in evenly. Simmer for a few minutes and season to taste with salt, white pepper, and a tiny pinch of nutmeg. The addition of cream enriches and velvetizes the sauce, thereby creating an illusion of long-simmering.

THE OIL, BUTTER, AND EGG SAUCES

Mayonnaise and hollandaise are based upon the thickening power of egg yolk protein. They are not really cooked. Mayonnaise is made cold, and hollandaise need not be warmed much beyond the melting point of butter. A little gentle heat, however, aids in thickening and saves a bit of beating.

These sauces are finished sauces in that they are used without further treatment. They are also used as a base for a number of compound sauces, which you will find in this chapter.

MAYONNAISE
(*Sauce Mayonnaise*—about 5 cups)

Egg yolks, 6	Dijon mustard, 1 tablespoon
Salt, 1½ teaspoons	Vegetable oil, 1 quart
Cayenne pepper or white pepper, a pinch	Boiling water, 3 tablespoons
Wine vinegar, red or white, 4 tablespoons	

Bring egg yolks to room temperature. Put them into a warm bowl with salt and pepper. Beat the yolks briskly, gradually adding to them, little by little, the vinegar and the mustard. Next add the oil, which should be at room temperature, dribbling it out of a tablespoon a few drops at a time at first, then in a very thin stream, constantly beating to permit the egg yolk protein to encapsulate the pinpoint droplets of oil and hold them in suspension. When the oil is all absorbed and the sauce is creamy, beat in the boiling water to make the sauce more stable. The sauce will thicken as it cools.

Blender Mayonnaise. Mayonnaise is easily made fresh in small quantities by use of the blender. Room temperature ingredients, hot vinegar, and hot water aid in the formation and stability of the sauce. For 1 cup of mayonnaise, put into the blender container 1 whole egg, 1 teaspoon prepared mustard, ½ teaspoon salt, and ⅛ teaspoon white pepper. Cover and run on low speed. When the yolks are well beaten, slowly add 1 cup of vegetable oil, a few drops at a time at first, then in a very thin stream. Increase the speed of the blender as the sauce thickens and more power is needed. When all the oil is incorporated, add 1 tablespoon of boiling vinegar and 1 tablespoon of boiling water, and blend at high speed until just mixed in.

HOLLANDAISE SAUCE
(*Sauce Hollandaise*—about 2 cups)

Wine vinegar, red or white, 1½ tablespoons
Water, 2½ tablespoons
Salt, ½ teaspoon
White pepper, a pinch
Egg yolks, 4
Butter, 1½ cups (¾ pound)
Lemon, ½

Combine vinegar, 1½ tablespoons of water, salt, and white pepper in a small saucepan and simmer until the liquid has reduced by ½. Cool the mixture with 1 tablespoon of cold water, pour it into a glass mixing bowl, and place the bowl atop a saucepan of barely simmering water. Add egg yolks and beat with a wire whisk until the mixture is thick and creamy. Turn off the heat. To the thickened egg yolk mixture add melted butter, at first just a few drops at a time, then in a thin stream, beating all the while until the sauce is thick and firm. If it is too thick, thin it with a little water. The sauce should be able to just pour, and it should be fluffy and yellow. Finish the sauce with a squeeze of lemon.

Blender Hollandaise. For 2½ cups, put 4 egg yolks into the blender container and run on low speed for 1 minute, or until the yolks are creamy. Continue on low speed while slowly adding: 3 tablespoons boiling water; 1 pound Clarified Butter* in a thin stream; 2 tablespoons lemon juice; ¼ teaspoon white pepper. As sauce thickens and more power is required, increase blender speed. Blend until just mixed.

VINAIGRETTE OR FRENCH DRESSING
(*Sauce Vinaigrette*—1 Cup)

This is simply French dressing—the familiar oil-and-vinegar dressing used so frequently on green salads and both hot and cold vegetables. Basically it is microscopic droplets of seasoned vinegar swimming in a sea of oil.

Olive oil gives the dressing more taste than other salad oils. Vinegars vary widely in the intensity of their taste and flavor, but American vinegars are generally stronger than French vinegars, and the usual proportion of 3 parts oil to 1 part vinegar can be changed to 4 parts oil. You must taste to tell. The dressing should have a little sass to it, without scratching your throat, however.

There is nothing to making vinaigrette, and you can make it up as you need it instead of taking up valuable space in your refrigerator. It's more interesting to experiment with this dressing each time you make it—trying different wine vinegars or herb-flavored vinegars or lemon juice in place of all or part of the vinegar. The addition of mustard is common in France. It can be omitted.

Red wine vinegar, ¼ cup	Olive oil, ¾ to 1 cup
Prepared mustard, 2 teaspoons	A glass mixing bowl and a wire
Salt, ½ teaspoon	whisk
Pepper, ¼ teaspoon	

Put vinegar into a mixing bowl with mustard, salt, and freshly ground pepper. Stir with a wire whisk to dissolve the salt into the vinegar (it will not dissolve in the oil). Add oil slowly at first, whisking it heartily to blend with the vinegar. On standing this sauce will separate. Just whisk it up again. For variations on basic vinaigrette, see Chapter 12.

BUTTER SAUCES

Good butter itself is a wonderful sauce, melting on hot vegetables, just-melted and flavored with chopped egg and herbs, or clarified and cooked until brown and nutty in flavor, and you will find a number of butter-based sauces at the end of this chapter. Here I will discuss basic butter sauce, and two kinds of creamed butters—hot and cold.

BUTTER SAUCE
(*Sauce au Beurre*—about 3 cups)

Flour, 2 tablespoons	Cream, 4 tablespoons
Butter, 7 tablespoons	Lemon, ½
Boiling water, 2 cups	A 1-quart enameled iron, stainless
Salt, ½ teaspoon	steel, or tin-lined copper sauce-
Egg yolks, 3	pan

In a nonaluminum saucepan, mix flour into 2 tablespoons melted butter and cook a few minutes over very low heat to form a White Roux. Add boiling water and salt, and stir to dissolve the roux thoroughly. Lower heat so the thickening mixture does not boil, and simmer for 10 minutes. Lightly beat egg yolks with cream and the juice of the ½ lemon. Remove the saucepan from the heat and let it cool for a few minutes. Spoon some of the hot sauce into the egg yolk mixture, stirring, to warm it. Then pour all the egg yolk mixture into the saucepan, stirring vigorously with a wire whisk until the sauce thickens again. Strain the sauce and finish it by beating in, little by little, 5 tablespoons soft butter.

WHITE BUTTER SAUCE
(*Beurre Blanc*—1½ cups)

This sauce contains no flour or egg yolk thickening whatsoever. The thickening is actually a creaming of the butter with acid. Unlike butter that is simply creamed (that is, has air beaten into it), butter creamed with acid will remain creamy at a temperature above the melting point of butter and may therefore be served warm (not hot, however). This sauce is not as golden as the preceding *Sauce au Beurre,* but it is infinitely smoother and creamier.

White wine vinegar, ¼ cup	Butter, 1 pound
White wine, dry, ¼ cup	Lemon, ½
Shallots, 1 tablespoon minced	A 2-quart enameled iron, stainless
Salt, ¼ teaspoon	steel, or tin-lined copper saucepan
White pepper, ⅛ teaspoon	

Put into a nonaluminum saucepan the vinegar, white wine, shallots, salt, and white pepper. Reduce over brisk heat until you have 1 tablespoon of liquid remaining, and remove from heat. Begin beating in tablespoon-size pieces of cold butter one at a time. After 3 or 4 pieces are beaten in and the butter is creaming, return the saucepan to very low heat and continue beating in pieces of cold butter one piece at a time. When all the butter is beaten in and creamy, transfer the sauce to a bowl set in a pan of lukewarm water so that the butter cannot solidify. On the other hand, the sauce will separate if you try to reheat it or place it in hot water. It is all very touchy, but worth it. Pike with White Butter is a famous dish originating in Nantes (see Chapter 8).

COMPOUND BUTTERS

These are nothing more than butter that has been creamed and flavored in various ways and allowed to cool. They provide wonderful variety, the flavorful little pieces melting over roasted or broiled meats and fish. They may also be used as a flavorful enrichment for soups and sauces, particularly those based on Velouté and Béchamel.

To make a compound butter, begin with the butter, working it in a bowl with a spoon until it is soft enough to beat but not melting soft. Beat briskly with a heavy wire whisk, incorporating tiny bubbles of air into the butter. Do not allow the butter to melt or become oily-looking. If it does, chill it for a few minutes in the refrigerator. When the butter is light and creamy throughout, beat in the seasonings and the particular flavoring that gives the butter its name.

Flavorings include herbs, spices, aromatic vegetables, wine, lemon juice, purées, meat glazes, and other flavorful liquids greatly reduced. If the flavoring is liquid, it must be beaten in very slowly. Solids such as parsley are finely minced. Shellfish and anchovies are first pounded to a paste. Recipes for all of these are in this chapter.

Do not refrigerate the finished compound butter. The liquid in it may separate, and the butter loses its creamy quality and becomes hard. Keep it in a cool place.

PAN SAUCES

These excellent sauces are essentially products of the roasting, sautéing, poëléing, and stewing pans—skimmed of fat, flavored, extended with liquid, and then thickened in some manner. These sauces do not command names of their own in *haute cuisine*. Instead they form part of the recipe of the meat being cooked, and directions for their making are given with the recipe. These sauces are also sometimes described as being sauces made *à la ménagère,* housewife style, or prepared with whatever materials are at hand. Invariably they are based upon juices derived from the meat with which they are served, and this unifying element contributes mightily to their excellence.

To make a pan sauce, remove from the pan the meat and any garnishing vegetables cooked along with the meat. Leave flavoring vegetables in the pan. Roughly skim or pour off the fat floating atop the pan juices. Place the pan on a low fire and scrape the bottom with a wooden spatula, loosening and dissolving the solidified pan juices into the liquid juices.

Frequently, when roasts and sautées are properly cooked, there is little or no liquid juice at all remaining in the bottom of the pan. To remedy this (and to increase the volume of the finished sauce) add water or stock or wine to the pan. Heat the liquid to simmering, and scrape the bottom with a wooden spatula to dissolve into the added liquid the solidified pan juices.

It is obvious that the addition of water will not add flavor. The use of stock compatible to the meat cooked will fortify the flavor of the sauce. Thus, if you are making a pan sauce for sautéed chicken, you will add Chicken Stock, frequently made with the giblets and trimmings of the chicken you have sautéed. Veal stock, being neutral in flavor, can be used for most anything.

Wine is also frequently used to flavor pan sauces. In many recipes a particular wine is specified for the deglazing of the pan, providing a specific flavor characteristic of the dish. Other flavoring ingredients—spices, herbs, and aromatic vegetables—are also specified in the recipes.

The next step in making a pan sauce is to give it the right thickness. This is done in several ways, alone or in combination. Begin by straining the sauce to remove the flavoring vegetables, herbs, and other bits and pieces. You can press the vegetables through a sieve to extract their flavor (the resulting purée also helps thicken the sauce). Simmer the sauce for a few minutes and skim away additional fat rising to the surface. Then proceed in one or more of the following ways:

1. Thicken the sauce by cooking it down until it reaches the consistency you want. This can result, however, in the sauce becoming too strong-flavored.

2. Thicken the sauce by adding to it arrowroot or cornstarch dissolved in a little liquid. (Arrowroot produces a clearer sauce than cornstarch; sometimes this degree of clarity is not important.) About 1 tablespoon of starch dissolved in 2 tablespoons of cold liquid (water, wine, or stock) is about right for thickening 1 cup of sauce. Keep the starch well dispersed in the liquid (it tries to settle to the bottom quickly) and pour the mixture little by little into the simmering sauce, whipping with a wire whisk to mix it in thoroughly. The starch will expend all its thickening power when the sauce returns to the simmer. When the consistency is right (generally, when the sauce just coats a wooden spoon), stop.

3. Thicken the sauce by adding *Beurre Manié* to the pan. *Beurre manié* is flour and butter creamed together in equal amounts, tablespoonful for tablespoonful. Cream it well so that the butter gets in among the individual grains of flour. Roll this mixture into balls the size of large peas, and add them to the pan 2 or 3 at a time. Mix them in vigorously with a wire whisk or mash them against the side of the pan, and cook until they have fully dissolved in the liquid before adding more. Simmer the sauce, stirring, for at least 5 minutes to realize the full thickening power of the flour and to overcome its raw taste.

4. Thicken the sauce by adding the sauce to a Roux of flour or starch in butter, which you have prepared in advance. Return to the simmer and cook until the sauce thickens.

5. Thicken the sauce by adding to it another thick sauce, such as Brown Sauce, Demi-Glace, or Velouté. The added sauce will also contribute its flavor.

6. Thicken the sauce by adding to it a Starch-Thickened Stock appropriate to the dish. This also adds flavor.

7. Thicken the sauce by adding an appropriate Meat Glaze. This also adds flavor. Taste carefully as you add 1 teaspoon at a time.

8. Thicken the sauce by adding to it small pieces of cold butter and swirling the pan until the butter has just mixed in and melted. This also flavors and enriches the sauce.

9. Thicken the sauce by adding beaten raw egg yolks and cooking these lightly without boiling. This thickening is for white sauces. The yolks are beaten in a separate bowl with some of the warm sauce. This mixture is then returned to the saucepan. Cook over gentle heat, stirring constantly, until the sauce has thickened.

This completes the methods of thickening pan sauces. Because the sauce is cooking, it always thickens somewhat by reduction. One or more of the other methods are usually applied. Enriching with butter to finish the sauce is an often-used fine and final adjustment. Starch-in-liquid, which acts immediately, is also a commonly used final adjustment of the sauce's consistency.

You will note that thickening with flour and water is not among the recommended methods. If you do resort to this thickening—which is common in American gravies—add it slowly and cook the sauce thoroughly to remove the pasty taste of uncooked flour. To my mind, it is a needless risk.

With a final taste for the correctness of the seasoning, the sauce is finished. We shall meet sauces made this way again and again in the pages ahead.

STARCH-THICKENED STOCKS OR GRAVIES

In home cookery, when there are no *sauces mères* on hand to provide a base for sauces, you can resort to what the French call a thickened juice (*jus lié*) or gravy. This preparation refers to one of two things.

It is the juice of roasted, sautéed, braised, or poëléed meat, poultry, or fish that has oozed out during cooking, thickened with starch to become the base of a pan sauce for that meat.

It is also a separate stock obtained by simmering meat, poultry, or fish and flavorings in water, reduced to concentrate its flavor, and thickened with starch. In this case the thickened stock is independently obtained. As such, it is a cooking ingredient (part of the kitchen supply) that can be put to many uses. This is the ingredient I mean, throughout this book, when I refer to a Starch-Thickened Stock.

It is obvious that any starch-thickened stock can be no better than the stock from which it is made. The stock, which is full flavored to begin with, is reduced by half to further concentrate its flavor and its body. It is then given the desired thickness by stirring in arrowroot or cornstarch. If the starch is added to a hot stock, it must first be dispersed in a little cold liquid. As soon as the stock has returned to a simmer, the starch will have expended all its thickening power. If you need more thickening, you must reduce the stock further or add more starch.

All stocks can be concentrated and thickened in this manner. Thickened White Veal Stock, which is quite neutral in taste and therefore combines well with other flavoring liquids, is very useful to have on hand. Thickened White Chicken Stock can be used with pan sauces for sautéed chicken and as a cooking sauce for braised chicken and chicken stews. Thickened Fish Fumet is a base of sauces for fish.

Thickened Brown Veal Stock and Thickened Brown Stock are used as a replacement for Brown Sauce and Demi-Glace when these are unavailable.

These preparations are easily and quickly made if you have the stock on hand. Various flavorings can be added to the stock while it is reducing. Tomato purée added to brown stock, for example, will bring you closer to Brown Sauce. Arrowroot will produce a clearer result than cornstarch if clarity is required. Here is the basic recipe:

STARCH-THICKENED STOCK
(*Jus Lié*—1 cup)

Stock, 2 cups, reduced to 1 cup
Arrowroot or cornstarch, 1 tablespoon
Cold stock, wine, or water, 2 tablespoons

Salt, pepper, other seasonings to taste
A heavy 1-quart saucepan

If the stock is cold, stir arrowroot or cornstarch into reduced stock and continue stirring, keeping the starch from settling, until the stock comes to a simmer and thickens.

If the stock is hot, stir arrowroot or cornstarch into cold stock, wine, or water. Add this mixture, a little at a time, to reduced stock and whisk until the mixture thickens.

Season the thickened stock to taste. For use directly as a sauce, add 1 tablespoon cold butter for each cup of hot thickened stock and swirl the pan, off heat, until the butter just melts.

In this section I list all the sauces and butters in alphabetical order based on their names in English. Consequently, whenever you see a sauce listed in a recipe in this book, you can refer to this section and quickly find it, without having to know whether it is white or brown, warm or cold, or anything else about it. After you locate the sauce by name, you can quickly tell from the ingredients and directions what kind of sauce it is. I will tell you what it is commonly used for.

The recipes and directions are simply put, but they are also as authentic as I can make them. It is possible to make substitutions—Starch-Thickened Stock in place of Brown Sauce, for example—which can be more or less satisfactory. But remember, the taste of a classic sauce is the taste you get from the ingredients and methods specified for that sauce. Departures from these specifics may have good results, but they can only be different, more or less, from the authentic taste and texture.

The foundation ingredients of these sauces—the stocks and mother sauces—have been fully discussed. Most other ingredients are readily available fresh or canned. You should use fresh ingredients whenever possible, and there is no adequate substitute for such items as fresh lemons and fresh garlic.

Fresh herbs are more difficult to come by, although fresh parsley is available everywhere throughout the year, and chives can be grown in your kitchen or purchased frozen. All other herbs listed in the following recipes are given as teaspoon or tablespoon measures of the dried herb. If you are fortunate enough to have fresh herbs on hand, multiply these measured amounts by three. Also, when a chopped dried herb is a final addition to a sauce, I suggest you cover it with a little boiling hot water, allow it to steep for 3 or 4 minutes, and drain before adding it to the sauce. This softens the herb so it is not gritty to the teeth, releases its aromatic flavors, and gives it a fresh green color. An easy way to do this is to tie the dried chopped herb in a double thickness of cheesecloth, dip it in the boiling water, cool in cold water, and squeeze dry.

Finally, when seasoning to taste at the end of sauce making with final additions of salt, pepper, and spices or herbs, give the sauce a minute or two to take on the new flavor before you taste and make any further adjustments. These final moments are all important, and taste is your only reliable guide.

In general, you will find the 1-cup results are usually for flavorful sauces that require no more than a few tablespoonfuls per serving. The 2-cup results are for sauces that are used more liberally. By reading the recipe you can judge how much sauce you are likely to get. Of course you can double the recipes, which should also make the cooking of them easier.

The recipes are not as abbreviated as those you would find in a chef's handbook. But they are economical of words, and include such semitechnical terms as "reduce by ⅔" and "swirl in" and "finish the sauce with . . ." These actions, and the reasons for them, have been explained in Chapter 3. It is really a very simple language, and the little time you take to learn it will save you hours of time in just reading recipes. Besides, since they are definite directions, they will bring precision, confidence, and professionalism to your cooking.

Let us begin. Our first compound sauce is *Sauce Aioli*. It is actually a garlic-flavored mayonnaise. The French often call it Provence butter. Don't let any of this confuse or discourage you. If in doubt, reread the recipe for Mayonnaise, and you will know exactly what you are doing and why.

AIOLI SAUCE (*Sauce Aioli*). This is a garlicky mayonnaise. In a mortar or bowl mash 5 cloves garlic to a paste with 1 raw egg yolk and a pinch of salt. Add 1 cup olive oil, little by little, as in making mayonnaise, beating it in with a wire whisk. Also add, a few drops at a time, 1 tablespoon lemon juice and 1 tablespoon cold water to stabilize the sauce. This sauce has the same consistency as mayonnaise and is sometimes called Provence butter, *beurre de Provence*. (For cold entrees.)

ALBERT SAUCE (*Sauce Albert*). Simmer 4 tablespoons grated horseradish in 4 tablespoons White Stock for 15 minutes. Add ½ cup Butter Sauce, ½ cup cream, and ¼ cup fresh breadcrumbs. Boil briskly for 5 minutes, stirring. Rub through a fine sieve, cool slightly, and thicken with 1 beaten egg yolk. Season with a pinch of salt and white pepper, ½ teaspoon of dry mustard, and 1 teaspoon vinegar. (For braised or boiled beef.)

ALBUFÉRA SAUCE (*Sauce Albuféra,* also called Ivory Sauce or *Sauce Ivoire*). To 1 cup of Supreme Sauce add 1 tablespoon melted veal Meat Glaze or 3 tablespoons reduced Veal Stock. Stir to blend and give the sauce its characteristic ivory color. (For poultry and poached sweetbreads.)

ALLEMANDE SAUCE (*Sauce Allemande*). Thoroughly mix 2 cups White Stock and 2 cups Velouté Sauce. Cook gently, stirring frequently, until the sauce reduces to about ½ and is thick enough to coat a spoon. Allow the sauce to cool a little and thicken it by stirring in the yolks of 2 eggs beaten with 2 tablespoons heavy cream and a little of the hot sauce. Heat gently, stirring, to the simmering point. Remove from the fire, swirl in* 3 tablespoons cold butter, and strain. You may further season the sauce with a squeeze of lemon, a pinch of nutmeg, and with salt and white pepper if necessary. (For sweetbreads, vegetables, eggs, poached chicken.) For fish, make the sauce with a Fish Velouté. For dishes with mushrooms, add 2 tablespoons Mushroom Essence.

AMERICAN SAUCE (*Sauce Américaine*). This sauce is the natural result of cooking Lobster American. When used for dishes other than lobster American itself, the lobster meat is used to garnish the dish. For the recipe see Chapter 8. (For fish, eggs.)

ANCHOVY BUTTER (*Beurre d'Anchois*). To ½ cup creamed butter add 1 tablespoon anchovy paste, or 6 filets of anchovy pounded to paste in a mortar. (For flavoring sauces, and for grilled and sautéed fish and meat.)

ANCHOVY SAUCE (*Sauce Anchois*). To 1 cup Normandy Sauce, add 3 tablespoons Anchovy Butter and 1 tablespoon finely chopped anchovy filets. This sauce can also be made using Butter Sauce or Béchamel Sauce as a base. (For fish.)

ANDALOUSE SAUCE (*Sauce Andalouse*). To 1 cup Mayonnaise add ¼ cup very rich Tomato Purée and 2 tablespoons finely shredded pimento. (For eggs, fish, and poultry.)

AURORA SAUCE (*Sauce Aurore*). Mix 1 cup Velouté Sauce with ¼ cup Tomato Purée. Simmer for a few minutes, strain, and finish with 3 tablespoons butter. (For eggs, poultry, and sweetbreads.)

BÉARNAISE SAUCE (*Sauce Béarnaise*). In a saucepan combine 1 tablespoon chopped shallots, 1 tablespoon tarragon, 1 tablespoon chervil, a pinch each of salt and white pepper, 4 tablespoons white wine vinegar, and 4 tablespoons dry white wine. Cook until the liquid is reduced to about 2 tablespoons, and cool slightly. In a bowl, lightly beat 4 egg yolks with 1 tablespoon water and the cooled mixture from the pan. Place the bowl over simmering water and gradually beat in ¾ cup melted butter, a few drops at a time at first, and then in a thin stream as in making Hollandaise Sauce. Finish the sauce with ½ teaspoon each of chervil and tarragon steeped in boiling water and drained, a pinch of cayenne, and a squeeze of lemon. Do not allow the sauce to become more than just warm, for fear of separation. (For broiled and sautéed meats, broiled fish.)

BEAUHARNAIS SAUCE (*Sauce Beauharnais*). To 1 cup Béarnaise Sauce add 2 tablespoons Tarragon Butter. (For broiled and sautéed meat and broiled fish.)

BÉCHAMEL SAUCE (*Sauce Béchamel*). See White Sauces.

BERCY BUTTER (*Beurre Bercy*). Simmer 2 tablespoons finely chopped shallots in ½ cup dry white wine until the wine is reduced by ½. Cool the mixture, add 1 teaspoon finely chopped parsley and 4 tablespoons cubed beef marrow (poached and well drained), and beat it all into ¾ cup soft butter, creaming the butter. Season with salt and white pepper and a squeeze of lemon juice. (For grilled meat, fish.)

BERCY SAUCE (*Sauce Bercy*). Simmer without browning 2 tablespoons chopped shallots in butter. Add ½ cup dry white wine and ½ cup Fish Fumet and reduce by ⅔. Add ⅔ cup fish Velouté Sauce and simmer for 10 minutes. Remove from the fire and finish the sauce by swirling in* 2 tablespoons butter until it just melts, 1 tablespoon chopped parsley, and a squeeze of lemon. (For fish.)

BIGARADE SAUCE or **ORANGE SAUCE** (*Sauce Bigarade*). This sauce is reserved for duck and is made according to the method by which the duck was cooked. It is a pan sauce.

For braised duck: Strain the braising sauce, skim off all the fat, and reduce it until it is quite thick. Now, thin the sauce by adding orange juice and an occasional squeeze of lemon to taste until the sauce coats a spoon. Finish by adding 2 tablespoons of a very fine julienne* of orange and lemon rind that has been parboiled for 5 minutes, and swirl in* 2 tablespoons butter.

For poêléed duck: Strain the pan juices and skim off all the fat. Prepare Caramel by cooking 1 tablespoon sugar in 1 tablespoon vinegar. Dissolve the caramel in ½ cup of the pan juices, and return to the pan along with 1 cup Starch-Thickened Brown Veal Stock. Cook until the sauce is quite thick. Then, as above, add the orange juice, the lemon juice, and the julienne of rind. Finish by swirling in* 2 tablespoons butter.

BLACK BUTTER (*Beurre Noir*). Clarify* the butter and brown it slowly, swirling it in the pan so that it cooks evenly. When it is dark brown (the butter should not actually become black), and at the moment it begins to smoke, remove from the fire and cool with a sprinkle of fresh-chopped parsley, and serve immediately. You can also add capers or boiled-down wine vinegar to the butter. (For fish, brains, and boiled vegetables.)

BOHEMIAN SAUCE (*Sauce Bohémienne*). In a bowl, combine 4 tablespoons cold Béchamel Sauce with a little salt and white pepper and the yolks of 2 raw eggs. Beat lightly, and add 2 cups olive oil, a few drops at a time at first, and then in a thin stream as in making Mayonnaise, beating constantly. Also add 4 teaspoons tarragon vinegar, a sprinkle at a time, from time to time during the beating in of the oil. Finally beat in 1 tablespoon dry mustard. (For cold meats.)

BONNEFOY SAUCE (*Sauce Bonnefoy*). In a saucepan, cook 4 tablespoons minced shallots, a pinch each of white pepper and thyme, and ¼ bay leaf in 1 cup dry white Bordeaux wine. When the wine is almost entirely reduced, add ½ cup Velouté Sauce. Simmer for 20 minutes, strain the sauce, and swirl in* 4 tablespoons butter and ½ teaspoon tarragon steeped in boiling water and drained. (For broiled white meats and broiled fish.)

BONTEMPS SAUCE (*Sauce Bontemps*). Lightly cook 1 tablespoon chopped onion in 1 tablespoon butter. Season with a pinch of salt and a little paprika, add 1 cup cider, and reduce by ⅔. Add 1 cup Velouté Sauce and bring to the boil, stirring until the sauce is well blended. Off the fire swirl in* 3 tablespoons butter in small pieces and 1 teaspoon dry mustard. Strain and serve. (For broiled meat and broiled poultry.)

BORDELAISE SAUCE (*Sauce Bordelaise*). In a saucepan, cook 4 tablespoons minced shallots, a pinch each of white pepper and thyme, and ¼ bay leaf in 1 cup dry red wine. When the wine is almost entirely reduced, add 1 cup Demi-Glace Sauce. Simmer the sauce, skimming, for 30 minutes. Remove from the fire, swirl in* 2 tablespoons butter in small pieces, and strain the sauce. When ready to serve, add 4 tablespoons cubed beef marrow (poached and well drained) and 2 teaspoons chopped parsley. (For broiled meats.)

BREAD SAUCE (*Sauce de Pain*). To 2 cups boiling milk add 1 cup fresh, soft white breadcrumbs, a pinch of salt, 2 tablespoons butter, and 1 onion pierced with 1 clove. Simmer for 15 minutes. Remove the onion, beat the sauce with a wire whisk, and finish with 4 tablespoons heavy cream. (For roasted poultry.)

BRETON SAUCE (*Sauce à la Bretonne*). Thinly slice 6 onions and simmer them in butter until they become soft and lightly golden. Rub the onions through a sieve, and add to them 2 tablespoons Brown Stock, 2 tablespoons Brown Sauce, a sprinkle of sugar, and 2 tablespoons chicken Meat Glaze. Cook this purée for a few moments, stirring, and rub again through a fine sieve.

BROWN BUTTER or **NOISETTE BUTTER** (*Beurre Noisette*). Clarify* the butter and cook it slowly, swirling it in the pan to prevent its scorching, until it becomes a light, warm brown color and smells nutty. Serve immediately, sizzling. (For variety meats, eggs, fish, vegetables.)

BURGUNDY or **BOURGUIGNONNE SAUCE** (*Sauce Bourguignonne*).
Lightly brown in butter 2 tablespoons chopped shallots. Add 2 cups red
Burgundy wine, a little salt and pepper, 3 sprigs parsley, 1 bay leaf, 1 sprig
or pinch of thyme, and 2 tablespoons mushroom trimmings. Cook until the
wine is reduced to ⅓ its volume, and add 1½ cups Brown Sauce. Cook
again, until the liquid is reduced by ½. Off the fire, swirl in* 4 tablespoons
butter. (For meat, poultry, eggs.)

For eggs and snails: Burgundy Sauce can also be made without brown
sauce. Proceed as above, using 3 cups of wine, and reducing the wine by ½.
Strain the sauce and thicken it with *Beurre Manié.* Just before serving, swirl
in* 8 tablespoons butter cut in small pieces, and a pinch of cayenne.

BUTTER SAUCE* (*Sauce au Beurre*). See Oil, Butter, and Egg Sauces.

CAMBRIDGE SAUCE (*Sauce Cambridge*). In a mortar or bowl, mash and
pound together 6 cooked egg yolks, 4 anchovy filets, 1 teaspoon capers, 1
tablespoon prepared English mustard, 1 tablespoon vinegar, 1 teaspoon
chopped chives, and ½ teaspoon each of chervil and tarragon steeped in
boiling water and drained. Into this paste beat, little by little, 6 tablespoons
oil. Season with a pinch of cayenne, rub through a fine sieve, and finish with
1 teaspoon chopped parsley. (For cold meats.)

CAPER SAUCE (*Sauce aux Capres*). Add 1 tablespoon drained capers to
1 cup Butter Sauce. (For boiled fish.)

CARDINAL SAUCE (*Sauce Cardinal*). To 1 cup fish Velouté Sauce or
Béchamel Sauce add ½ cup Fish Fumet. Cook down by ½ and add 4 tablespoons heavy cream. Simmer this for a few minutes, remove from heat, add
a pinch of cayenne pepper, and swirl in* 3 tablespoons Lobster Butter in
small pieces. Finish the sauce with 1 tablespoon chopped truffles. (For fish.)

CELERY SAUCE (*Sauce Céleri*). Simmer 3 hearts of celery in White Stock
with 1 onion and a *Bouquet Garni* until tender. Drain the celery, grind it,
and press it through a sieve. To the resulting purée, add an equal amount of
Cream Sauce mixed with some of the reduced stock in which the celery was
cooked. (For boiled or braised poultry.)

CHAMPAGNE SAUCE (*Sauce au Champagne*). Prepare as for White Wine
Sauce, using White Chicken Stock in place of the Fish Fumet, and using
champagne as the wine. (For chicken.)

CHANTILLY SAUCE (*Sauce Chantilly*). To 1 cup extra-thick Supreme
Sauce add ½ cup whipped cream. (For poultry, white variety meats, and
fish.)

CHARCUTIÈRE SAUCE (*Sauce Charcutière*). To 1 cup Robert Sauce add ¼ cup minced pickles. (For grilled and sautéed pork.)

CHASSEUR SAUCE (*Sauce Chasseur*). Briskly sauté 1 cup minced mushrooms in Clarified Butter until lightly browned. Season lightly with salt, add 1 tablespoon minced shallots, and cook for a few minutes more. To the pan, add ½ cup dry white wine, quickly reduce this by ½, and add ¾ cup Demi-Glace Sauce and ½ cup Tomato Sauce. Bring to the boil and cook for about 5 minutes, stirring to blend the sauces. Finish the sauce by swirling in* 2 tablespoons butter and add 1 tablespoon chopped parsley. (For small cuts of meat and poultry.)

CHATEAUBRIAND SAUCE (*Sauce Chateaubriand*). Combine 2 tablespoons chopped shallots, 2 tablespoons chopped mushrooms, 1 sprig or pinch of thyme, and ¼ bay leaf with ½ cup dry white wine, and boil until the wine is almost entirely reduced. Add 1 cup Starch-Thickened Veal Stock and reduce by ½. Strain the sauce and add ½ teaspoon tarragon steeped in boiling water and drained. Finish by swirling in* 6 tablespoons Maître d'Hôtel Butter. (For grilled filet steaks, especially the Chateaubriand.)

WHITE CHAUD-FROID SAUCE (*Sauce Chaud-Froid Blanche*). To 2 cups White Velouté Sauce add 1½ cups white Chicken Aspic and reduce, stirring, by ⅓. Gradually add 1 cup light cream, stirring to blend the mixture smoothly, and simmer until the sauce nicely coats a spoon. Cool, stirring frequently to prevent a skin from forming. When the sauce becomes cool enough, it will congeal to a jellylike consistency, and at this point it is used to coat cold foods.

There are many variations for chaud-froid sauce, too many to attempt to list here. For example, when making a chaud-froid sauce for fish, use Fish Velouté and Fish Aspic. For a rosy chaud-froid sauce, add a few tablespoons of Tomato Purée. For a green-tinted chaud-froid sauce, add a few tablespoons of fresh green herbs that you have blanched, dried, and rubbed through a fine sieve. Also, the sauce may be flavored with wines such as port, sherry, or Madeira, which are added to the sauce after it has cooled so they will retain their fragrance.

In a pinch, you may replace the aspic called for in the above recipe with 2 tablespoons gelatin softened in 1½ cups Chicken Stock or Chicken Consommé.

CHIVRY SAUCE (*Sauce Chivry*). To 1 cup boiling White Chicken Stock add 1 teaspoon chervil, 1 teaspoon tarragon, 1 tablespoon chopped parsley, and 1 teaspoon chopped chives. Cover and simmer for 10 minutes. Strain the liquid into 2 cups of chicken Velouté Sauce, and reduce by ⅓. Finish the sauce by swirling in* 4 tablespoons Printanier Butter. (For boiled or poached poultry and eggs.)

CHORON SAUCE (*Sauce Choron*). Prepare as for Béarnaise Sauce, but in place of the final addition of chervil and tarragon, stir in ¼ cup Tomato Purée per cup of Sauce. (For grilled and sautéed meat.)

COLBERT BUTTER (*Beurre Colbert*). Beat into ½ cup Maître d'Hôtel Butter 4 teaspoons melted pale Meat Glaze and ½ teaspoon finely chopped tarragon which you have steeped in boiling water and drained. (For grilled and fried fish and meat.)

COLLIOURE SAUCE (*Sauce Collioure*). See Chapter 10.

CRANBERRY SAUCE (*Sauce aux Airelles*). Cook 2 cups cranberries in water until they are tender and the berries split. Drain them, reserving the liquid, and rub them through a sieve. Thin this purée with the cooking liquid until it has the consistency of a thick sauce. Add sugar to taste, cook for a few minutes, and chill. (For roasted poultry.)

CRAYFISH BUTTER (*Beurre d'Écrevisses*). Pound the shells and remains of crayfish cooked in a *Mirepoix,* or put them through a blender. Add an equal weight of butter and rub through a sieve. Pass the butter again through a very fine sieve to remove every trace of shell. Season to taste with salt and white pepper. (For cold fish and hors d'oeuvres, and for flavoring soups and sauces.)

CREAM SAUCE (*Sauce à la Crème*). To 1 cup Béchamel Sauce add ½ cup light cream and reduce by ⅓. Remove from heat, and finish the sauce with 3 tablespoons butter and 3 tablespoons heavy cream, or enough cream to give the sauce the desired consistency. Season to taste with salt, white pepper, and lemon juice (if desired), and strain through a fine sieve. (For fish, poultry, eggs, and vegetables.)

CURRY SAUCE (*Sauce au Currie*). Mince 2 medium onions and slightly brown them in butter with 1 rib celery, minced, 1 sprig or pinch of thyme, ¼ bay leaf, and a pinch of mace. When the onions are slightly brown, sprinkle with 4 tablespoons flour and 1 to 3 tablespoons curry powder. Cook for a few minutes more, add 1½ cups White Stock, stir, and simmer for 45 minutes. Strain the sauce, reheat it, skim away the fat, and stir in ¼ to ½ cup of cream. Season to taste with salt, white pepper, and lemon juice. (For fish, lamb, shellfish, poultry, eggs, vegetables.)

DEMI-GLACE SAUCE (*Sauce Demi-Glace*). See Brown Sauces.

DEVIL SAUCE (*Sauce Diable*). Cook ¼ cup chopped shallots, 1 sprig or pinch of thyme, and ¼ bay leaf in ¾ cup dry white wine and 1 tablespoon vinegar until the wine is reduced by ⅓. Add 1 cup Demi-Glace Sauce and reduce again by ⅓. Season liberally with cayenne pepper, strain, swirl in* 2 tablespoons butter, and add 1 tablespoon chopped parsley. (For grilled poultry and leftover meats.)

DIJONNAISE SAUCE (*Sauce Dijonnaise*). See Chapter 12.

DIPLOMAT SAUCE (*Sauce Diplomate*). To 1 cup Normandy Sauce add 2 tablespoons Lobster Butter, 1 tablespoon finely diced lobster meat, and 1 tablespoon finely diced truffle. This sauce may be flavored with a little brandy and cayenne. (For fish.)

DUXELLES SAUCE (*Sauce Duxelles*). To ½ cup dry white wine add 1 tablespoon minced, sautéed shallot and 1 cup minced, sautéed mushrooms and cook until the wine is almost entirely reduced. Add ¾ cup Demi-Glace Sauce and ½ cup Tomato Purée, cook for a few minutes more, and season with salt and pepper. Just before serving, swirl in* 2 tablespoons butter and add 1 tablespoon chopped parsley. (For small cuts of meat, chicken, fish, eggs.)

ÉCOSSAISE SAUCE (*Sauce Écossaise*). To 2 cups hot Béchamel Sauce add the chopped white of 4 hot hard-cooked eggs and their yolks pressed through a coarse sieve. Season to taste with salt and white pepper. (For boiled fish, particularly fresh and salt cod.)

EGG SAUCE WITH BUTTER (*Sauce aux Oeufs au Beurre*). Season ½ cup melted butter to taste with salt, pepper, and lemon juice. Add 3 hot hard-cooked eggs, cut in large dice, and finish the sauce with 1 teaspoon chopped, blanched parsley. (For boiled fish.)

ESPAGNOLE SAUCE (*Sauce Espagnole*). See Brown Sauces.

FINES HERBES SAUCE (*Sauce aux Fines Herbes*). To ½ cup dry white wine add 1 tablespoon chopped parsley, 1 tablespoon chopped chives, and 1 teaspoon each of chervil and tarragon. Cook until the wine is almost entirely reduced. Add 1 cup Demi-Glace Sauce, cook for a few minutes more, and strain. Finish with a squeeze of lemon juice and 1 teaspoon tarragon steeped in boiling water and drained, or 1 tablespoon chopped parsley.

GENEVOISE SAUCE (*Sauce Genevoise*). Dice 1 medium carrot, 1 medium onion, and 1 rib of celery and cook this *Mirepoix* without bacon in butter until it is lightly browned. Add 1 pound fishbones and trimmings (particularly a head of salmon cut in pieces), 3 sprigs parsley, ½ bay leaf, and 1 sprig or pinch of thyme. Cover and simmer for 15 minutes. Pour off the fat from the pan, add 2 cups dry red wine, and reduce the wine by ½. Add 1 cup Brown Sauce and simmer for 30 minutes. Strain the sauce, allow it to cool a little, and skim away all of its fat (using a paper towel to blot up the last little globules). Add ½ cup red wine and ½ cup Fish Fumet and simmer for 1½ hours, skimming regularly to rid the sauce of all impurities. Strain again, and finish the sauce with a little anchovy paste to taste and 4 tablespoons butter. (For fish.)

GLOUCESTER SAUCE (*Sauce Gloucester*). To 2 cups thick Mayonnaise Sauce add ½ cup sour cream flavored with 4 tablespoons lemon juice, 1 teaspoon bottled Worcestershire sauce, and 1 teaspoon chopped fennel. (For cold meats.)

GODARD SAUCE (*Sauce Godard*). To ¼ cup *Mirepoix* add 1 cup champagne and reduce the wine by ½. Add 1 cup Demi-Glace Sauce and ½ cup Mushroom Essence. Reduce by ⅓, season with salt and pepper, and strain. (For poultry and sweetbreads.)

GOOSEBERRY SAUCE (*Sauce aux Groseilles*). Parboil ½ pound green gooseberries for 5 minutes. Drain them, put them in a saucepan with ½ cup dry white wine and 4 tablespoons powdered sugar. Simmer gently until the berries are soft, and rub them through a fine sieve. Blend this purée with 1 cup Butter Sauce. Season to taste with nutmeg. (For mackerel and other fat fish.)

GREEK SAUCE (*Sauce à la Grecque*). Lightly brown 2 tablespoons chopped onions and 2 tablespoons chopped celery in butter. Add ¼ teaspoon fennel seeds, ¼ coriander seeds, 1 sprig or pinch of thyme, 1 bay leaf, and ½ cup dry white wine. Reduce the wine to ⅓ and add ½ cup Fish Velouté Sauce and ½ cup light cream. Reduce by ⅓, season to taste with salt and pepper, strain, and swirl in* 2 tablespoons butter. (For fish.)

GRIBICHE SAUCE (*Sauce Gribiche*). Mash 6 hard-cooked egg yolks with 1 tablespoon Dijon Mustard until a smooth paste is formed. Little by little beat in 2 cups olive oil as in making Mayonnaise. Season to taste with salt and pepper and vinegar. Add 1 teaspoon chopped parsley, ½ teaspoon each of chervil and tarragon steeped in boiling water and drained, 1 teaspoon capers, 2 tablespoons chopped gherkins, and the whites of 3 hard-cooked eggs cut in thin julienne.* (For cold fish and shellfish.)

HOLLANDAISE SAUCE (*Sauce Hollandaise*). See Oil, Butter, and Egg Sauces.

HORSERADISH SAUCE, COLD (*Sauce au Raifort*). Mix ½ cup grated horseradish with 1½ cups soft breadcrumbs soaked in milk, drained and pressed. Beat well. Season with 1 tablespoon powdered sugar, salt and vinegar to taste, and bring to the desired consistency with 4 to 6 tablespoons heavy cream. (For cold meats.)

HORSERADISH SAUCE, HOT. (See Albert Sauce.)

HUNGARIAN SAUCE (*Sauce Hongroise*). Cook 2 tablespoons chopped onions in butter until they are transparent. Sprinkle with 1 to 2 tablespoons paprika and a pinch of salt. Add 1 sprig parsley, ½ bay leaf, a pinch of thyme, and ½ cup dry white wine, and reduce the wine by ⅔. Add 2 cups Velouté Sauce and cook for a few minutes more. Rub the sauce through a sieve and swirl in* 4 tablespoons butter. (For meat, poultry, fish, and eggs.)

INDIENNE SAUCE (*Sauce Indienne*). See Curry Sauce.

ITALIAN SAUCE (*Sauce Italienne*). To ½ cup *Duxelles,* add ¼ cup lean cooked ham cut in small dice, ¾ cup Demi-Glace Sauce, and ⅓ cup Tomato Purée. Simmer for 10 minutes, and just before serving add 1 teaspoon chopped parsley and ½ teaspoon each of chervil and tarragon steeped in boiling water and drained. (For poultry and small cuts of meat.)

IVORY SAUCE (*Sauce Ivoire*). See Albuféra Sauce.

JOINVILLE SAUCE (*Sauce Joinville*). Stir into 1 cup of hot Normandy Sauce ½ cup of Shrimp Butter or ½ cup of Crayfish Butter or ¼ cup of each. Just before serving, add 1 tablespoon truffles cut in fine julienne. (For boiled fish.)

LOBSTER BUTTER (*Beurre de Homard*). Pound the shells, unused meat, and creamy parts of cooked lobster in a mortar with an equal weight of creamed butter, and rub through a sieve. Pass the butter again through a very fine sieve to remove every trace of shell. Or you may put the lobster remains in a blender with hot, melted butter, remelting the mixture and returning it to the blender until the shellfish is thoroughly pulverized. Then strain several times. Season to taste with salt and pepper. (For flavoring soups and sauces, for fish and hors d'oeuvres.)

LOBSTER SAUCE (*Sauce Homard à l'Anglaise*). To 1 cup Béchamel Sauce add 2 tablespoons diced lobster meat, ½ teaspoon anchovy paste, and a pinch of cayenne pepper. (For fish.)

LYONNAISE SAUCE (*Sauce Lyonnaise*). Lightly brown ½ cup finely minced onions in 4 tablespoons butter. Add ½ cup dry white wine and ½ cup wine vinegar. Reduce by ⅓ and add 3 cups Demi-Glace Sauce. Simmer for 30 minutes, season to taste with salt and pepper, and serve strained or unstrained. (For small cuts of meat and cold meats.)

MADEIRA SAUCE (*Sauce Madère*). Reduce 1½ cups Demi-Glace Sauce by ⅓. Restore the sauce to its original consistency with 3 or 4 tablespoons Madeira wine, and strain. Do not allow this sauce to boil after the wine is added, or its flavor will be lost. (For meat.)

MAÎTRE D'HÔTEL BUTTER (*Beurre à la Maître d'Hôtel*). To ½ cup softened butter add 1 tablespoon chopped parsley, and salt and lemon juice to taste. (For grilled meats, poultry, fish; sautéed fish; boiled vegetables.)

MALTAISE SAUCE (*Sauce Maltaise*). Flavor 1 cup Hollandaise Sauce with ½ teaspoon grated fresh peel of orange and 3 tablespoons orange juice. (For boiled vegetables, especially asparagus.)

MARCHAND DE VINS BUTTER or **WINE MERCHANT'S BUTTER** (*Beurre Marchand de Vin*). Cook 4 tablespoons finely chopped shallots in ½ cup dry red wine until the liquid is almost entirely reduced. Add 1 tablespoon Meat Glaze, stir to dissolve, and allow the mixture to cool. (Instead of the meat glaze, you may add ½ cup Brown Stock at the beginning and allow it to cook down with the wine.) Cream ½ cup butter with 1 teaspoon parsley and a squeeze of lemon juice. Little by little, beat in the shallot and wine mixture. Season to taste with salt and pepper. (For broiled meats.)

MARINIÈRE SAUCE (*Sauce Marinière*). To 1 cup Bercy Sauce add ¼ cup of the liquid in which mussels have been cooked. Thicken the sauce, off the fire, with 2 egg yolks. Bring barely to the simmer. (For mussels and poached fish.)

MARROW SAUCE (*Sauce à la Moelle*). Prepare as for Bordelaise Sauce, using white wine in place of red wine. (For grilled meats, vegetables.)

MAYONNAISE SAUCE (*Sauce Mayonnaise*). See Oil, Butter, and Egg Sauces. For variations, see Chapter 12.

MEUNIÈRE BUTTER (*Beurre Meunière*). To Brown Butter, add a squeeze of fresh lemon juice and a little parsley. (For grilled and sautéed fish.)

MINT SAUCE (*Sauce de Menthe*). Pour ¼ cup boiling water over 1 cup finely shredded mint leaves. Add 2 tablespoons powdered sugar, ½ cup vinegar, and salt to taste. (For hot or cold lamb.)

MONTPELLIER BUTTER (*Beurre Montpellier*). Parboil in salted water for 2 minutes: ¼ cup each of parsley, chives, and watercress leaves; 1 cup spinach leaves; and 3 tablespoons finely chopped shallots. Quickly cool these ingredients in cold water, drain, and press in a towel to squeeze out their water. Put them into a mortar with 1 tablespoon each of chervil and tarragon steeped in boiling water and drained, and pound to a paste. Add ½ cup finely chopped gherkins, 1 tablespoon well-drained capers, 4 anchovy filets, 1 chopped clove of garlic, 3 hard-cooked egg yolks, mashed, and 2 raw egg yolks, and pound again to a paste. Cream ¼ pound of butter and work it into the paste. Then, little by little, add ½ to 1 cup olive oil. Strain the butter through a fine sieve, season with salt and a little cayenne pepper, and stir until smooth. (For hot or cold fish.)

MORNAY SAUCE (*Sauce Mornay*). To 2 cups hot Béchamel Sauce add ½ cup cream and reduce by ¼. (If this sauce is intended for fish, you may use Fish Fumet in place of the cream; if intended for chicken, use White Chicken Stock.) To the reduced sauce, add ¼ cup each of grated Parmesan and grated Swiss (Gruyère) cheese, and stir over low heat until the cheese is fully melted. Season to taste with salt and white pepper, and finish the sauce off the fire with 4 tablespoons butter added little by little. (For eggs, vegetables, fish, poultry.)

MOUSQUETAIRE SAUCE (*Sauce Mousquetaire*). Cook 2 tablespoons finely chopped shallots in ½ cup dry white wine until the liquid is almost entirely reduced. Add 1 tablespoon Meat Glaze, stir to dissolve, and allow the mixture to cool. Little by little, beat this mixture into 2 cups Mayonnaise. Season with cayenne pepper. (For cold meats, vegetables.)

MOUSSELINE SAUCE (*Sauce Mousseline*). To 2 cups Hollandaise Sauce add 1 cup stiffly whipped cream just before serving. (For fish, boiled vegetables.)

MOUSSEUSE SAUCE (*Sauce Mousseuse*). Soften 1 cup butter, flavor it with a squeeze of lemon juice, and beat into it, little by little, ¾ cup cold water. At the last moment, add 2 tablespoons whipped cream. (For boiled fish, boiled vegetables.)

MUSHROOM SAUCE (*Sauce aux Champignons*). This versatile sauce can be made in a number of ways, using a white or brown sauce base. For all of the following variations, begin by lightly sautéing ½ pound mushroom caps (or 3 cups diced or sliced mushrooms) in 3 tablespoons butter. Also, cook mushroom stems and trimmings in water with a squeeze of lemon juice to obtain ½ cup of mushroom cooking liquid.

(1) Add ½ pound sautéed mushrooms and ½ cup mushroom cooking liquid to 2 cups thick Allemande Sauce. (For fish, poultry.)

(2) Add ½ pound sautéed mushrooms and ½ cup mushroom cooking liquid to 2 cups Chicken Velouté Sauce thickened with the yolks of 4 eggs. (For poultry.)

(3) Add ½ pound sautéed mushrooms and ½ cup mushroom cooking liquid to 2 cups Fish Velouté Sauce thickened with the yolks of 4 eggs. (For fish.)

(4) Add ½ pound sautéed mushrooms and ½ cup mushroom cooking liquid to 2 cups Demi-Glace Sauce. Simmer until the sauce returns to the desired consistency. At the last moment, stir in 1 tablespoon Madeira wine. (For small cuts of meat.)

MUSTARD SAUCE (*Sauce Moutarde*). This sauce, like mushroom sauce, can be made in a number of ways. (For grilled meats, cold meats, grilled fish.)

(1) To 1 cup Butter Sauce add 1 tablespoon prepared Dijon Mustard.

(2) To 1 cup sour cream add 1 tablespoon prepared Dijon Mustard.

(3) To 1 cup Cream Sauce add 1 teaspoon dry English mustard moistened with 1 tablespoon water.

(4) To 1 cup Hollandaise Sauce add 1 teaspoon dry English mustard moistened with 1 tablespoon water.

(5) Simmer until soft 4 tablespoons chopped onions in 1 tablespoon butter with salt, pepper, and a pinch of powdered bay leaf and thyme. Add I cup white wine and reduce by ⅔. Add ¾ cup Demi-Glace Sauce and reduce by ⅓. Finish the sauce with 1 tablespoon prepared Dijon Mustard, a squeeze of lemon, and 1 tablespoon butter. Strain or serve as is.

MUSTARD CREAM SAUCE (*Sauce Moutarde à la Crème*). See Chapter 12.

NANTUA SAUCE (*Sauce Nantua*). To 1 cup Béchamel Sauce add ¼ cup cream and reduce by ⅓. Finish the sauce by swirling in* 3 tablespoons Crayfish Butter, 1 tablespoon fresh cream, a pinch of cayenne, and a dash of brandy. (For fish, shellfish, eggs.)

NIÇOISE SAUCE (*Sauce Niçoise*). See Chapter 12.

NOISETTE BUTTER (*Beurre Noisette*). See Brown Butter.

NOISETTE SAUCE (*Sauce Noisette*). To 1 cup Hollandaise Sauce add 1 tablespoon Noisette Butter. (For fish, vegetables.)

NORMANDY SAUCE (*Sauce Normande*). To 1 cup Fish Velouté Sauce add ½ cup Fish Fumet and ½ cup mushroom cooking liquid, and reduce by

⅓. Beat 2 egg yolks with ¼ cup cream, and blend this into the sauce mixture, stirring until the sauce has thickened. Strain the sauce, season with a little cayenne pepper, and swirl in 2 tablespoons butter and about 2 tablespoons heavy cream. (For fish.)

OYSTER SAUCE (*Sauce aux Huîtres*). To 1 cup Normandy Sauce add ¼ cup concentrated oyster liquor (which you have reduced from ½ cup and strained) and 6 poached oysters. This sauce can also be made using White Wine Sauce in place of Normandy Sauce. (For fish.)

PARISIAN SAUCE (*Sauce Parisienne*). See Chapter 12.

PARSLEY SAUCE (*Sauce Persil*). To 1 cup Butter Sauce add 2 teaspoons chopped parsley. You may also add a squeeze of lemon juice if desired. (For boiled poultry and braised veal.)

PEPPER SAUCE (*Sauce Poivrade*). Chop 2 medium carrots, 2 medium onions, and 2 ribs celery and cook in 4 tablespoons butter until browned. Add 3 sprigs parsley, 1 crumbled bay leaf, 1 sprig or pinch of thyme, ½ cup wine vinegar, and ½ cup dry red wine (or the meat's own marinade) and reduce the liquid by ½. Add 2 cups Brown Sauce and simmer for 30 minutes, skimming as needed. Add 5 crushed peppercorns and simmer for 10 minutes more. Strain the sauce, pressing to extract the liquid from the vegetables. Return to the cleaned saucepan, add 1 cup Brown Stock (or 1 cup of the meat's marinade), and simmer, skimming, for 15 minutes more. Season to taste with salt, strain, and finish the sauce by swirling in* 4 tablespoons butter. (For meat.)

PÉRIGUEUX SAUCE (*Sauce Périgueux*). Gently simmer 2 to 3 tablespoons finely diced truffle in butter for 3 or 4 minutes. Remove and reserve the truffles, deglaze the pan with 1 tablespoon Madeira wine, add 1 cup Demi-Glace Sauce, and simmer for 2 or 3 minutes. Strain and skim the sauce, season with salt and pepper, and return the truffles to it with 1 tablespoon Madeira wine. Do not allow the sauce to boil after the truffles and wine have been added. (For small cuts of meat, poultry, *Timbales,* hot pâtés.)

PIQUANT SAUCE (*Sauce Piquante*). To ½ cup minced shallots add ½ cup dry white wine and ½ cup wine vinegar, and reduce by half. Add 2 cups Demi-Glace Sauce and simmer, skimming, for 30 minutes. Season to taste with salt and pepper. Off the fire, stir in ¼ cup finely chopped gherkins, 2 tablespoons capers, 1 teaspoon finely chopped parsley, and 1 teaspoon each of chervil and tarragon steeped in boiling water and drained. (For small cuts of meat and cold meats.)

PORTUGUESE SAUCE (*Sauce Portugaise*). Simmer 2 tablespoons minced onions in 1 tablespoon olive oil until soft. Add 4 tomatoes, peeled, seeded, squeezed, and chopped (about 1½ cups), 1 clove finely minced garlic, salt, and pepper. Cook uncovered, for 10 minutes, to reduce the liquid in the tomatoes. Then cover and simmer for 30 minutes, stirring occasionally. Add ½ cup Demi-Glace Sauce, stir a few minutes, and finish the sauce with 1 tablespoon chopped parsley. (For meat, poultry, fish, eggs.)

POULETTE SAUCE (*Sauce Poulette*). To 1 cup boiling Allemande Sauce add 3 tablespoons Mushroom Essence. Remove from the fire, and add a squeeze of lemon juice, a good pinch of chopped parsley, and 2 tablespoons butter. (For vegetables, fish, and poached variety meats.)

PRINCESS SAUCE (*Sauce Princesse*). To 1 cup boiling Allemande Sauce add 2 tablespoons chicken Meat Glaze. Remove from the fire and add a squeeze of lemon juice, a good pinch of blanched, chopped parsley, a pinch of nutmeg, and 2 tablespoons butter. (For chicken, fish, vegetables.)

PRINTANIER BUTTER (*Beurre Printanier*). Pound in a mortar early-season green vegetables (peas, green beans, asparagus) that you have boiled, drained, dried, and cooled. Add an equal quantity of butter and cream the butter and vegetables together. Season to taste with salt and pepper, and press through a fine sieve. (For flavoring soups, sauces, and for hors d'oeuvres.)

PRINTANIÈRE SAUCE (*Sauce Printanière*). To 1 cup boiling Allemande Sauce add 3 tablespoons Printanier Butter. Strain and serve. (For poultry and eggs.)

PROVENÇAL SAUCE (*Sauce Provençale*). To ¼ cup hot olive oil add 6 medium tomatoes (about 1½ pounds), peeled, seeded, and chopped; 1 clove of garlic, crushed; ½ teaspoon powdered sugar; 1 teaspoon chopped parsley; and a little salt and pepper. Simmer for 30 minutes. (For small cuts of meat, poultry, fish, eggs, vegetables.)

RAVIGOTE SAUCE, COLD (*Sauce Ravigote, Froid*). To ½ cup olive oil, add 2 tablespoons wine vinegar. Also add 2 tablespoons capers, 1 tablespoon minced onion, 2 teaspoons finely chopped parsley, 2 teaspoons of finely chopped chives, and ½ teaspoon each of chervil and tarragon steeped in boiling water and drained. Season to taste with salt and pepper. You may also add 1 chopped, hard-cooked egg. (For cold meats and cold fish.)

RAVIGOTE SAUCE, HOT (*Sauce Ravigote, Chaud*). To ¼ cup dry white wine add 2 tablespoons wine vinegar and reduce by ½. Add 1 cup Velouté Sauce and cook, stirring, a few minutes more. Off the fire, add 2 tablespoons

Shallot Butter 1 teaspoon chopped chives, and ½ teaspoon each of chervil and tarragon steeped in boiling water and drained. (For poached poultry, fish, variety meats.)

RED WINE SAUCE (*Sauce au Vin Rouge*). To 2 cups Court Bouillon with Red Wine in which a fish has been poached, add 2 tablespoons mushroom trimmings. Reduce by ½, and thicken to the desired consistency with *Beurre Manié*. Strain and flavor to taste with salt and a pinch of cayenne. Finish the sauce by swirling in* 2 tablespoons butter. (For fish.)

RÉMOULADE SAUCE (*Sauce Rémoulade*). To 1 cup Mayonnaise* add 1 teaspoon Dijon Mustard; 2 teaspoons chopped gherkins; 2 teaspoons capers; 2 teaspoons of chopped parsley; ½ teaspoon each of chervil and tarragon steeped in boiling water and drained, and ½ teaspoon anchovy paste. (For cold meat, poultry, fish, shellfish.)

RICHE SAUCE (*Sauce Riche*). See Diplomat Sauce.

ROBERT SAUCE (*Sauce Robert*). Cook 1 cup finely minced onions in 2 tablespoons butter until transparent and soft. Add ½ cup dry white wine and reduce by ⅓. Add 1 cup Demi-Glace Sauce and simmer for 15 minutes. At the last moment add 1 teaspoon dry mustard, a pinch of powdered sugar, and 2 teaspoons Meat Glaze. This sauce may be strained or not, as you choose. (For hot and cold meats, especially pork.)

RUSSIAN SAUCE (*Sauce Russe*). Mix the cooked coral and tomalley of a lobster with 1 tablespoon caviar and rub the mixture through a fine sieve. Add this purée to 1 cup Mayonnaise along with 1 teaspoon prepared mustard. You may also add 1 teapsoon finely chopped chives or parsley. (For cold shellfish.)

SCOTTISH SAUCE (*Sauce Écossaise*). See Écossaise Sauce.

SHALLOT BUTTER (*Beurre d'Échalote*). Chop 8 shallots, blanch them for 2 minutes in boiling water, drain and dry them by pressing in a towel, and allow them to cool. Pound very finely in a mortar and cream in 8 tablespoons butter. Press through a fine sieve. (For flavoring sauces, and for grilled meats, poultry, and fish.)

SHRIMP BUTTER (*Beurre de Crevettes*). Pound cooked shrimp meat and shells in a mortar with an equal weight of creamed butter. Rub several times through a fine sieve and season to taste with salt and pepper. Or prepare in a blender as described for Lobster Butter. (For flavoring sauces, and for fish.)

SOUBISE SAUCE (*Sauce Soubise*). Finely chop 1 pound of onions (about 4 cups). Parboil for 3 minutes, drain and dry. Sauté the chopped onion in 4 tablespoons butter until soft and transparent. Add 2 cups Béchamel Sauce,

1 teaspoon powdered sugar, and a pinch of salt. Simmer for 30 minutes and rub through a fine sieve. Reheat the sauce adding, while stirring, ½ cup heavy cream. Off the fire, finish the sauce with 2 tablespoons butter. (For lamb, veal, variety meats, fish, chicken.)

SOUBISE SAUCE, TOMATOED (*Sauce Soubise Tomatée*). To 2 cups Soubise Sauce add ⅔ cup Tomato Purée.

SUPREME SAUCE (*Sauce Suprême*). To 2 cups White Chicken Stock add 1 cup chopped mushrooms (or ¼ cup Mushroom Essence), and reduce by ½. Add 1 cup Chicken Velouté Sauce and simmer until the liquid is again reduced by ½. Gradually add 1 cup heavy cream, stirring constantly. Season to taste with salt and white pepper, strain, and swirl in* 3 tablespoons butter. Keep warm in a double boiler. (For poultry, variety meats, eggs, vegetables.)

TARRAGON BUTTER (*Beurre d'Estragon*). Steep 2 tablespoons tarragon in boiling water for 3 minutes. Drain, dry, pound in a mortar, and cream with ½ cup butter. For a smoother butter, rub through a fine sieve. (For flavoring sauces, for broiled meats, poultry, and fish, and for cold hors d'oeuvres.)

TARRAGON SAUCE (*Sauce à l'Estragon*). Add 1 tablespoon tarragon to ½ cup dry white wine and reduce by ½. Add 1 cup Demi-Glace Sauce (or Starch-Thickened Brown Stock), and simmer for a few minutes more. Strain, and finish the sauce with 1 teaspoon tarragon steeped in boiling water and drained. This sauce can also be made right in the pan in which chicken has been sautéed. You may use Chicken Stock in place of Demi-Glace Sauce and thicken the sauce with *Beurre Manié*. (For chicken, small cuts of meat, eggs.)

TARTAR SAUCE (*Sauce Tartare*). To 1 cup Mayonnaise add the chopped yolks of 2 hard-cooked eggs and 1 teaspoon chopped chives. (For fish.)

TOMATO SAUCE (*Sauce Tomate*). See Brown Sauces.

LA VARENNE SAUCE (*Sauce La Varenne*). To 1 cup Mayonnaise add ⅓ cup *Duxelles* cooked in oil, and ½ teaspoon each of parsley and chervil steeped in boiling water and drained. (For hors d'oeuvres, eggs, fish.)

VELOUTÉ SAUCE* (*Sauce Velouté*). See White Sauces.

VENETIAN SAUCE (*Sauce Vénitienne*). To ¼ cup dry white wine add ¼ cup tarragon vinegar, 1 tablespoon chopped shallots, 1 tablespoon chopped parsley, and 1 teaspoon chervil, and reduce the liquid to ⅓. Add 1 cup White Wine Sauce and simmer together for a few minutes. Strain the sauce and add 3 tablespoons Montpellier Butter and ½ teaspoon each of chervil and tarragon steeped in boiling water and drained. (For poultry, eggs, fish.)

VILLEROI SAUCE (*Sauce Villeroi*). This sauce is used only to coat foods that are then coated *à l'anglaise* and deep-fried. It is nothing more than Allemande Sauce reduced until it will easily coat a spoon. It may be flavored with 1 tablespoon Truffle Essence and 1 tablespoon Ham Essence per cup. According to the food it is to coat, Villeroi sauce may be additionally flavored by adding ⅓ of its volume of onion or tomato purée. Chopped truffles or mushrooms may also be added to it. When used for fish, Villeroi sauce should have as its base an Allemande Sauce made with Fish Velouté. (For deep-fried foods.)

VINAIGRETTE SAUCE (*Sauce Vinaigrette*). See Oil, Butter, and Egg Sauces. For variations, See Chapter 12.

VINCENT SAUCE (*Sauce Vincent*). Take ½ cup each of parsley, chives, chervil, tarragon, sorrel, and 1 cup each of watercress and spinach. Parboil for 2 minutes, plunge into cold water, drain, and dry. Chop the herbs with the yolks of 4 hard-cooked eggs, and add 1 tablespoon each of chervil and tarragon steeped in boiling water and drained. Rub the mixture through a sieve. Blend with 1 cup thick Mayonnaise and 1 teaspoon bottled Worcestershire sauce. (For fish and shellfish.)

WHITE BUTTER SAUCE (*Beurre Blanc*). See preceding section on Basic Sauces.

WHITE WINE SAUCE (*Sauce au Vin Blanc*). Boil down ½ cup Fish Fumet made with white wine until it is reduced by half. Allow the concentrated fumet to cool a little, and add 4 beaten egg yolks. Beat with a whisk over very low heat until the mixture begins to thicken. Then, little by little, beat in 2 cups melted butter as in making a Hollandaise Sauce. Season to taste with salt, white pepper, and a little lemon juice. This sauce may also be made by cooking ½ cup fish fumet with 2 cups Velouté Sauce until reduced by half. The sauce is then finished off the fire with lemon juice and 8 tablespoons butter. (For fish.)

❋ THE MISE EN PLACE

The culinary term *mise en place* refers to a number of preparations that are assembled just before the cooking of a meal. Some of these preparations may be made or purchased long in advance and kept on hand as part of the kitchen stock. Others are made up just before cooking begins. Frequently, in home cooking, these preparations are integrated into a recipe.

I am using the term *mise en place* loosely here to summarize in one place and in alphabetical order all the ingredients, preparations, and garnishes that are called for to create the classic dishes discussed in this book. Thus you will find here such things as canned anchovies and *foie gras*, cooking wines and croutons, fried parsley and marinades. I will include buying information for those items that are purchased, and recipes for those that are made. Frequently a preparation may be made in quantity for one dish and stored in your refrigerator or freezer to serve on other occasions.

ANCHOVIES (*Anchois*)

Used as an hors d'oeuvre, a garnish, and a flavoring, filets of this tiny fish are widely available packed in oil. Six of these filets, drained and mashed, equal about 1 tablespoon of anchovy paste. They are very salty, so make allowances when salting a dish to which you add anchovy paste as a flavoring. Anchovy paste is also available in tubes.

A L'ANGLAISE COATING

Beat 1 whole egg with 2 tablespoons milk, 1 tablespoon salad oil, and ½ teaspoon salt. Dry the food to be coated, dip it in flour, and slap it sharply to remove loose flour. Dip the food in the egg mixture, drain it, and roll it in fine white dry breadcrumbs. This constitutes a coating *à l'anglaise* for food that is sautéed or deep-fried.

AROMATICS (*Aromates*)

Certain vegetables and herbs are invariably used in French cooking to give their flavor to stocks, consommés, and sauces, and to poached, braised, and poëléd meats. They provide an aromatic flavor base, pervading yet subtle, that adds fullness of flavor to a dish as it enhances the particular flavor of the food featured in the dish.

The indispensable vegetables are carrots, onions, and usually celery. These vegetables constitute what is called a *Mirepoix*. Even when meat is roasted, these vegetables are frequently added to the drippings pan so that they might add their characteristic flavor to the pan juices. Leeks are considered indispensable by many, and shallot, garlic, turnip, parsnip, and tomato are other vegetables utilized for their aromatic qualities.

The customary herbs used as aromatics are parsley, bay leaf, and thyme. Tied in cheesecloth, with or without a rib or two of celery, these herbs are known as a *Bouquet Garni*, herb bunch, or faggot, and they appear in almost every recipe calling for flavorful liquids or moist-cooked meats.

Other herbs used as aromatics are chosen more specifically to suit particular foods. These include basil, marjoram, rosemary, sage, chervil, savory, and tarragon. Basil has a particular affinity for tomatoes, rosemary for lamb, sage for pork, and tarragon for chicken.

Obviously, a broad interpretation of the term would have to include aromatic spices, such as pepper, in this classification.

ARROWROOT

This is a fine white powder starch used for thickening liquids. It has twice the thickening power of flour, and you may therefore substitute 1½ teaspoons of arrowroot for 1 tablespoon of flour.

Arrowroot contains fewer impurities than flour, and a clear liquid thickened with arrowroot will remain perfectly limpid and clear, whereas sauces thickened with flour require long simmering to attain a lesser degree of clarity. Also, arrowroot will thicken a liquid at a mere 150°, whereas a liquid must be brought to 200° before flour will thicken it.

Arrowroot can be used as the basic thickening for a sauce, when made into a Roux consisting of arrowroot and butter. Or it may be used as a final fine-adjustment thickening, by mixing it into a little cold stock, wine, or water and stirring this mixture into the hot sauce 1 teaspoon at a time.

Packed in little bottles by spice companies, arrowroot is unduly expensive. Look for it packed in volume, in 1-pound cans.

BARDS (*Bardes*)

These are thin sheets of fresh pork fat used for tying around or draping over meat while it is cooking. The fat acts as a solid basting substance that slowly melts and bastes the meat to prevent it from drying out. Sheets of pork fat are also used to line Terrines and Pâté crusts.

To make a bard: slice the fat in ¼-inch-thick sheets, place these between 2 pieces of wax paper, and pound with a mallet until the sheets are about ⅛ inch thick. This will make the sheets larger. Also, by overlapping the edges of small sheets and pounding them you can form them into larger sheets.

The best fat for barding is firm, fresh pork-back fat. This is often difficult to get, and you may use the softer pork fat taken from the loin or leg. Lacking fresh pork fat, you may use salt pork or fat bacon, simmering it in water for 3 or 4 minutes after you have pounded out the sheets. You may also use sheets of beef fat, but this tends to shrink during cooking.

BARQUETTES

These are small, boat-shaped pastry cases with plain or fluted sides, filled with sweet fillings for a dessert or with savory Purées or *Salpicons* for hors d'oeuvres, small entrees, or garnishes.

To make barquettes: line barquette molds with Short Paste or Puff Paste. Prick the bottoms all over with a fork and allow the pastry to rest for an hour. (You may freeze it in the mold if you care to.) Bake the barquettes with their filling in a 425° oven for 15 to 20 minutes, or until the pastry has browned lightly and withdrawn from the sides of the mold.

To retain the crispness of barquettes for cold fillings and for hot, moist fillings, you may cook them empty (blind), their inner shape being retained by a foil lining filled with dried beans, peas, or rice placed inside them. For cold fillings, bake the barquettes in a 425° oven for 7 to 10 minutes, remove the foil and beans, and return to the oven to dry the interior and complete the cooking. To waterproof them, brush with beaten egg. For hot fillings, bake the barquettes only partially, completing their cooking in the oven or under the broiler along with the hot filling they will contain. If appropriate, the filling may be sprinkled with butter and crumbs or grated Parmesan cheese.

Metal barquette molds with plain and fluted sides are available at kitchen specialty shops. Those with fluted sides are more interesting. Tartlets are identical to barquettes except they are round.

BATONNETS
These are little sticks of food, usually a vegetable, used as a garnish. They are 1 to 2 inches long, and their square ends may measure from ¼ to ½ inch across.

BATTERS FOR DEEP-FRYING (*Pâtes à Frire*)
Batters are used to envelope in a protective coating a food that is to be deep-fried. They should be tasty in themselves, tender when fried, and they should color appetizingly. Most important, a batter must be instantaneously impervious to the penetration of fat; it must congeal the instant it strikes the hot fat to prevent the fat from penetrating the food and to keep the juices inside.

Food dipped in batter should first be thoroughly dried, then dipped in flour, and slapped sharply to remove the excess. It must be thoroughly coated with the batter. To achieve a good coating, allow the batter to rest for 2 hours or more before it is used. This relaxes the gluten in the flour, excited by stirring, and allows the batter to cling more closely to the food. Always stir batter gently; vigorous mixing makes it tough. If you must use a batter immediately, stir it minimally.

The consistency of the following batters can be adjusted by adding more or less liquid to the basic recipe. Irregularly shaped foods, such as chicken parts, should have a relatively thin batter that will infiltrate into every crevice and cranny. Soft, moist foods, such as Croquettes, should have a relatively thick batter to keep them intact in the fat.

To make a batter for deep-frying meat, chicken, fish, Fritters, and Kromeskies: to 1 cup flour add 2 tablespoons melted butter, ¼ teaspoon salt, 2 beaten egg yolks, and 1 cup warm water. Mix gently but well. Just before using, stir in 2 egg whites that you have beaten until slightly stiff. (You may replace ½ or all of the water with flat beer. You may also add 1 tablespoon of brandy.)

To make a batter for deep-frying vegetables: to 1 cup flour add 2 tablespoons melted butter, ¼ teaspoon salt, 2 beaten whole eggs, and enough warm water to make a batter with the consistency of heavy cream.

BEIGNETS

These are sweet or savory mixtures that are dipped in batter and deep-fried. See Fritters.

BEURRE MANIÉ

This floured butter is used as a final thickening for stews and sauces. It can be made just before use, or may be stored, covered, in the refrigerator. It is essentially an uncooked Roux.

To make beurre manié: for every 1 tablespoon of softened butter add 2 to 3 tablespoons of flour and work the flour into the butter until the two are thoroughly blended.

To use beurre manié: drop one or two pea-sized pieces of this floured butter into liquid just below the boiling point. Stir the pieces until they dissolve, mashing them against the sides of the pan if necessary. The butter, which coats each particle of flour, permits the flour to disperse evenly and swell in the heat, thickening the liquid without lumping. Add the pieces, one or two at a time, waiting until they are dissolved before adding more to obtain the desired thickness. Liquids thickened with *beurre manié* should be simmered for 5 to 10 minutes to overcome the raw taste of the flour.

BLANCHED VEGETABLES (*Légumes Blanchis*)

Many vegetables can be partially prepared in advance to simplify cooking them at the last minute. By following this technique you will avoid the mushiness and discoloration that inevitably result when, because of the vagaries of cooking times, a vegetable must be held before serving.

Green vegetables, especially, benefit from this technique of partial cooking. Asparagus, broccoli, Brussels sprouts, green beans, peas, and spinach all can be depended upon to come to the table well colored and full of fresh flavor.

To partially cook a vegetable by blanching: trim or cut the vegetable in the form in which you intend to serve it. Drop it into a large quantity of boiling salted water, a few pieces at a time, so that the water remains at the boil. Boil until the vegetable is barely tender. Then refresh the vegetable by plunging it into a large bowl of cold water. This stops the cooking, retains the crispness, and fixes the color of the vegetable. When it is thoroughly cooled, drain and dry the vegetable and store it in the refrigerator. Vegetables can be prepared in this manner a day in advance of final cooking.

Vegetables that are to be braised are also blanched as above as a preliminary to braising.

Strong-tasting vegetables, such as cabbage, chicory, and endive, and some root vegetables that have become unavoidably strong in storage, such as carrots and turnips, can be blanched to ameliorate their strong flavors.

To lessen the flavor of a vegetable by blanching: trim or cut the vegetable to the desired shape, cover it with several inches of salted water, bring the water to a boil, and boil for about 5 minutes. Refresh the vegetable by plunging it in cold water, allow it to cool, and drain it in preparation for further cooking.

BLANCS

A *blanc,* which is made just prior to using, is simply salted water to which a little flour, lemon juice or milk is added. This helps retain a desirable white color in certain foods cooked in the blanc. Blancs appropriate for various foods are included in recipes throughout this book.

Do not confuse with *fonds blanc,* which is white stock, or *blanc de volaille,* which is the white breast meat of poached chicken.

BOUCHÉES

A *bouchée* is an individual-serving-size patty shell made with Puff Paste and filled with a *Salpicon* or Purée of meat, poultry, fish, shellfish, or vegetables, bound with a sauce. It is served as an hors d'oeuvre or small entree.

To make bouchées: roll out puff paste ¼ inch thick. Using a 3- to 4-inch-diameter cooky cutter, stamp twice as many rounds in the paste as you will need bouchées. Using a smaller cooky cutter, stamp circles into half of these rounds to make rings with ¾-inch-wide rims. Place the rounds top side down on a baking sheet moistened with water, brush a ¾-inch border of cold water on the surface of the rounds, and press a ring of dough top side down upon each. With the back of a knife, make diagonal scores all around the outside of each bouchée case, thereby decorating it and helping lock the two pieces of dough together. Using the smaller cooky cutter, reach down inside the rings of dough and press down halfway through the bottom rounds. Prick the bottoms all over with a fork, and chill the cases in the refrigerator for 30 minutes or more.

When you are ready to bake the bouchée cases, brush the *tops only* with egg yolk and water. Bake in a 425° oven for 20 to 30 minutes, or until they are puffed up, crisp, and brown. While cooling on a rack, reach down inside each case with a knife and pry up the little cover you stamped in the bottom round of dough. Scrape out any uncooked dough beneath the cover.

The cases can be kept warm in a very low oven for several hours. Fill them just before serving. Or you may cover and freeze the cases, warming and crisping them in a hot oven for a few minutes just before you fill them. The sooner the bouchées are served after baking, the lighter they will be.

Little bite-size bouchées (*petites bouchées*) are made with puff pastry rolled out ½ inch thick. They are stamped in about 2-inch rounds, and the centers of these rounds are stamped halfway through with a 1-inch-diameter cooky cutter. Rest the dough for about 30 minutes, brush the *tops only* of the cases with egg yolk and water, and bake in a 425° oven for 10 to 15 minutes until brown and crisp. Remove the little cover and scrape out any of the interior left uncooked.

BOUQUET GARNI

Also called an herb bunch, the *bouquet garni* is a bundle of aromatic herbs tied in cheesecloth so that the herbs are not in jeopardy of being skimmed from the top of a stock or stew, and so that they can be easily found and removed when cooking is completed.

To make a bouquet garni: tie in cheesecloth 3 sprigs of parsley, ½ bay leaf, and 1 sprig of fresh or dried thyme, or a pinch of powdered thyme. Sometimes 1 rib of celery is included in the bouquet garni. In this case, you can make a faggot.

To make a faggot: cut an 8-inch rib of celery in 2 pieces, crosswise. In the curve of the smaller piece, stuff 3 sprigs parsley, ½ bay leaf, and 1 sprig of thyme or a pinch of powdered thyme. Enclose the smaller piece of celery in the curve of the larger piece and tie securely by winding soft string around its entire length.

BRANDY

Brandy for cooking should be of excellent quality, as its results are notable and far-reaching. I suggest you keep a bottle of Cognac on hand, the finest of the French brandies.

Many French recipes call for brandy. It is used as a flavoring in many creations from soups to sauces, stuffings and desserts. It is called for in batters and marinades, and the Lardoons that add flavor and juiciness to meat should receive a preliminary soaking in brandy.

Brandy is also the spirit mostly used for the flaming of dishes described as *flambé*. Flaming brandy adds a delightful flavor to those dishes for which it is traditional and appropriate, but the indiscriminate setting afire of all manner of dishes is to be regretted.

To flame brandy: warm it a little in a small flameproof receptacle, light it with a match, and pour it over the dish. Be careful.

BREADCRUMBS (*Mis de Pain*)

In order to make breadcrumbs a loose-textured bread should be used. Use the white portion of French or Italian bread of good quality, or the best quality firm white sandwich breads.

For fresh breadcrumbs: crumble the white part of day-old bread between your fingers. If it is too doughy, slice it and allow the slices to dry a little. Crumbling bread can be tedious if you need a lot of crumbs. If you have a blender, it will make short work of this task. Use these crumbs immediately, or they will either dry out or become moldy. To make these crumbs finer, rub them through a sieve.

For dry breadcrumbs: cut the crusts from dry white bread, break the white part into pieces, place them between two sheets of foil, lightly pound them with a rolling pin, and then roll and crush the crumbs in the foil until they are quite fine. Pass the crumbs through a fine sieve and store them in a sealed container. Fresh bread may be dried in the oven to make dry crumbs.

For golden dry breadcrumbs: treat the dry, golden crusts of bread as for dry breadcrumbs. These crumbs, called *chapelure,* are used mainly for sprinkling over dishes that are finished *au gratin.**

BRUNOISE

This is the name given to finely diced or shredded vegetables stewed slowly in butter and used as a garnish, or in soups, or as an ingredient in sauces, stuffings, and other mixtures, or as a flavoring element. One or more vegetables may be included in the brunoise. (Also see *Mirepoix, Matignon,* and *Macédoine.*)

BUTTER (*Beurre*)

Butterfat is the natural fat of milk. Butter contains 80 percent butterfat, 18 percent water, and about 2 percent protein. It is the most delicate of all the fats.

French and American butters differ in that French butter is made with mature cream and all American butters, both "sweet" and "lightly salted," are made with fresh cream.

Most butter for sale at stores carries the Grade AA seal, the highest given by the Department of Agriculture. It is worth while, however, to find a good source of butter, since much can happen to it after it has been graded. It must be kept chilled until used, and its flavor suffers the older it is. Some cheese stores and specialty food stores offer tub butters of which they are, sometimes justifiably, proud. A very special butter, made from unpasteurized cream obtained from certified cows—that is, made the way all butter used to be made—can sometimes be found in specialty stores at three times the price of ordinary butter. A taste of this will make you long for the good old days.

Most of our butter contains about 1 teaspoon of salt per pound, and the package is marked "lightly salted." Unsalted "sweet" butter is used for pastries and cakes and is preferred as a spread by many. Be certain you buy sweet butter at a store with a good turnover. It does not keep as well as salted butter and develops a cheesy odor and taste. Smell it when you buy it.

Butter is, of course, a standby of the kitchen. It is used to make the flour-and-butter Roux that thickens the finest sauces. It also becomes a final flavoring and enrichment for sauces, and when it is dropped into the sauce a few pieces at a time, and swirled around in the pan gently without stirring, it performs a slight amount of final thickening. And butter is a fine sauce in its own right, melted directly on steaks or vegetables, or first browned and poured over them.

Butter is also the preferred fat for sautéing. Delicate foods that cook at low temperatures, such as eggs, may be sautéed in butter just as soon as the hot butter in the pan ceases bubbling. Most foods, however, must be cooked at higher temperatures in order to brown properly. For this purpose the butter must first be clarified to remove the 2 percent of milky solids that burn at about 250°, a temperature too low for most sautéing.

To clarify butter: cut the butter in small pieces and melt it slowly in a heavy saucepan. When the butter is melted, carefully skim away the white froth that has risen to the top. Then pour off and reserve the clear butter, leaving the milky residue at the bottom of the pan.

This clarified butter will still contain much of its original water. When heated in the sauté pan it will bubble and froth until the water has completely evaporated. When the bubbling subsides, the pure butterfat remaining will begin to absorb the full heat of the pan. Watch it carefully and add the food to be sautéed just as soon as the butterfat begins to brown. Adjust the flame to prevent the butterfat from smoking and burning.

Butter, clarified or unclarified, can be heated to a hotter temperature without burning if it is mixed with an equal amount of oil.

Butter is also used for basting meats and vegetables. Unsalted butter is best for this purpose; salt tends to draw moisture from the food. Also, if the oven or broiler is very hot, it is best that the butter be clarified.

CAPERS (*Capres*)

These are the flower buds of the caper bush, pickled in vinegar. They are olive-green in color and about the size of a small pea. They are used for seasoning and as a condiment. You can buy them anywhere.

CARAMEL

Aside from its use as a candy, caramel may be kept as part of the kitchen stock for coloring soups, stews, sauces, and aspics when this is required. Very little is used, and the sugar flavor is not detected.

To make caramel: heat granulated sugar without water in a heavy pan for 15 to 20 minutes until it melts and becomes a rich red-brown. Add about the same amount of water and boil rapidly for a few minutes. Store in a small covered bottle in the refrigerator.

CASSOLETTES

These are individual casserole dishes, single-portion servings of *Salpicons,* Purées, or other mixtures in various ovenproof containers. They are used as hors d'oeuvres or small entrees.

The cassolettes may be sprinkled with fine white dry breadcrumbs, butter, and grated Parmesan, and browned in the oven. They may receive a border of Puff Pastry, or of Duchess Potatoes piped through a pastry bag. They may also be completed covered with the pastry or the potato mixture. The cover is brushed with beaten egg and the cassolette is browned in the oven.

CAVIAR

Not many years ago the United States exported fine quality caviar to Europe. Today we import caviar from Russia and Iran. The supply is dwindling and caviar is very expensive.

Caviar is the roe or eggs of three fishes from the sturgeon family, the beluga, the ocietrova, and the sevruga. Beluga caviar is the largest and most expensive, and it ranges in color from dark steel-gray to blue-white. Ocietrova caviar may be golden-brown, green, or steel-gray. Sevruga caviar, the least expensive, is dark green or black.

Caviar comes fresh or canned; fresh caviar, of course, is the most prized.

It is traditionally brought to the table in its original can set in a bed of ice. It is served with a crystal spoon.

Caviar is packed with the eggs loose and separate, or pressed into a more or less solid mass.

Also, caviar comes more or less salted. In general, caviar containing the least salt is the most prized. This caviar is called *malossol*.

Thus, caviar is not just caviar. It ranges from fresh, large, loose, steel-gray beluga malossol, to canned, small, pressed black sevruga.

It is considered one of the most elegant of hors d'oeuvres, served on thin slices of buttered rye with lemon and chopped chives.

CHAPONS

A *chapon* is a crust of bread rubbed with garlic and sometimes sprinkled with oil and vinegar. Chapons are tossed with salads to add a very subtle garlic flavor. These chapons are removed before the salad is served, and are usually eaten by the chef.

Croûtes and *croûtons* (see below), which are used for garnishing, are something else again.

CHEESE (*Fromage*)

The two cheeses that are indispensable to French cooking are Swiss and Parmesan (see Chapter 13 on cheese). Wrapped tightly, both of these cheeses will keep in your refrigerator for a hundred years. They should be always on hand.

CHESTNUTS (*Marrons*)

Fresh chestnuts in America are mostly imported from Italy. They have many uses as a vegetable, a purée, an ingredient in stuffings and desserts, and as a garnish. To shell chestnuts, cut an "X" in the flat side of the shell, brush with oil, and bake them in a hot 450° oven for 6 or 8 minutes or until the shells are loosened.

To shell and bake chestnuts: leave them in the oven for 20 or 30 mintes, or until they are soft. Peel away the shells and the inside skin as soon as they are cool enough to handle.

To boil chestnuts: cover peeled and skinned nuts with stock or water, add a few ribs of celery and a pinch of salt, and simmer for 30 minutes until the nuts are soft. Serve them hot as a vegetable. If used in a stuffing, allow them to cool in the stock.

To braise chestnuts: place peeled and skinned nuts in a single layer in a fireproof baking dish or skillet. Cover the nuts with Starch-Thickened Brown

Veal Stock or Starch-Thickened Brown Stock, bring to the boil, and add 1 to 2 tablespoons butter per dozen nuts. Bring to a simmer, cover, and cook very slowly on the stove or in a 325° oven for up to 60 minutes, occasionally rolling the chestnuts gently in the stock. The chestnuts are cooked when they are soft and their stock is reduced to a glaze.

CHIFFONADES

This is a green, such as lettuce or sorrel, cut in fine strips and used as a garnish for soups and consommés.

To make a chiffonade: separate the leaves of the green, cut out the coarse ribs, wash and dry the pieces, press them flat and cut them in thin strips with a stainless steel knife.

For a consommé, the *chiffonade* may be simmered in the consommé for 20 or 30 minutes before serving. For a thick soup, the chiffonade is usually first cooked until soft in a little butter, and then simmered in stock for about 10 minutes.

CHIPOLATA SAUSAGES (*Saucissons Chipolata*)

These are small, fresh pork sausage links frequently used as a garnish. The links are about ½ inch in diameter and 2 inches long. Chipolata sausages are Italian in origin and traditionally flavored with chives. They are grilled or baked, after having been pricked a few times with a fine skewer.

CHOUX

These are round puffs of pastry filled with sweet or savory mixtures and served hot or cold. For these and other pastries made with Cream Puff Paste see Chapter 15.

CLARIFIED BUTTER (*Beurre Clarifié*)

This is melted butter from which the white froth and the milky protein sediment have been removed. It can be brought to a higher temperature than ordinary butter without burning. See Butter.

CORNICHONS

These are tiny, inch-long, very sour pickles made from immature cucumbers. They are eaten as an hors d'oeuvre or a garnish, or chopped and added as a condiment to sauces and combination dishes, which are then described as *charcutière*. Cornichons are imported from Orleans, France, and are available in glass jars in specialty food stores and many supermarkets. They can be kept in the refrigerator for a very long time.

CORNSTARCH

This is a fine white powder starch, similar to arrowroot. It is used for thickening sauces and puddings.

Like arrowroot, cornstarch has twice the thickening power of flour. When used to thicken a clear stock, the resulting Starch-Thickened Stock will be clearer than if thickened with flour, but less clear than if thickened with arrowroot.

CREAM (*Crème*)

American cream differs from French cream. French cream, although not sour, is mature cream and it is quite thick. The best French cream is *crème double,* containing 30 percent butterfat.

American cream and cream products range from Half and Half, about 11 percent butterfat; sour cream and light cream, 18 percent butterfat; whipping cream and medium cream, both 30 percent butterfat; and heavy cream, which is 36 percent or more butterfat.

American heavy cream can be given the thickness of French *crème double,* and a similar flavor, by adding 1 tablespoon of buttermilk to 1 cup of heavy cream, heating it until lukewarm, and allowing it to stand in a warm place until it has thickened. There is not much purpose in doing this, however, as fresh American heavy cream is usable in French recipes.

Depending upon the recipe, cream can be used at both the beginning and the end of sauce making. When cream is called for at the beginning, use light cream. When it is added at the end as a final enrichment, use heavy cream.

The heavier the cream, the better it will whip. Thus, cream labeled "whipping cream" that sells for less than "heavy cream" is neither as rich nor as good for whipping as the heavier cream.

To whip cream: beat very cold heavy cream in a cold bowl until it has doubled in volume. When used as a dessert topping, finish the cream by beating in 2 tablespoons powdered sugar and ½ teaspoon vanilla extract per cup of unwhipped cream. This is called *crème chantilly.*

CROQUETTES

Croquettes consist of finely diced or minced cooked food, flavored with other ingredients, seasoned, mixed with a thick sauce to which whole egg or egg yolks are added, coated *à l'anglaise,** and deep-fried. Croquettes are frequently made with poultry and fish. They are served as an hors d'oeuvre, a small entree, or a garnish.

A croquette mixture is basically a *Salpicon* to which eggs are added as a binding ingredient.

As a rule, the finest croquettes are made from the softest croquette mixtures. Fine croquettes have crunchy golden coatings and centers that are soft, creamy, and delicious. Soft croquette mixtures are difficult to shape unless they are thoroughly chilled. Also, soft croquettes should receive two coatings *à l'anglaise,* the crumbs should be pressed firmly into the croquettes, and they should be chilled again for at least one hour after coating. This will assure that the croquettes will not burst in the hot fat.

Croquettes are sometimes made with uncooked diced meat or fish, and are sometimes coated with a Batter for Deep Frying.

To make croquettes: to 2 cups finely diced or minced cooked meat, poultry, variety meat, fish, or shellfish, add 1 cup cooked minced mushrooms and a few tablespoons of finely diced truffles if you have them. You may also add ¼ to ½ cup finely diced cooked ham or tongue and 2 to 4 tablespoons Madeira wine.

To this mixture add 1½ to 2 cups of thick *Velouté* or Béchamel Sauce and heat the mixture, stirring, until it achieves sufficient thickness so that it can be shaped by hand. Off the fire, beat in 4 egg yolks, spread the mixture on a buttered platter, brush it with melted butter, and chill thoroughly.

Working on a floured board, shape the croquette mixture into squares, cylinders, balls, olive shapes, patties, sticks, cutlet shapes, or anything else you fancy. Dredge the croquettes with flour, coat them *à l'anglaise,** and deep-fry them in 390° hot fat until they are golden.

For an entree, separately serve peas, green beans, mixed vegetables, or most any vegetable Purée, and a sauce appropriate to the meat in the croquettes.

CROUSTADES

These are pastry or bread cases filled with *Salpicons,* Ragouts, Purées of meat or vegetables, or buttered or creamed vegetables. Large *croustades* serve as entrees; small croustades are used as an hors d'oeuvre.

Croustades made with flaky pastry (Puff Paste) are made like Tartlets or *Timbales,* for which croustade is a generic name. Croustades are also made from stale bread and from potatoes.

To make bread croustades: cut stale sandwich bread in slices up to 4 inches thick, trim the slice to the desired shape, and carve the sides decoratively. To make a lid, make a 1-inch-deep cut all around the top of the croustade case, about ½ inch inside the rim. Cook the case in deep fat until it is golden brown. Drain it, remove the lid, and scrape out the inside of the case to provide room for the filling.

Stale bread rolls make excellent croustade cases. The lid is marked, they are deep fried, drained, and scooped out in the usual manner. Or they may be scooped out, brushed with beaten egg, and browned in the oven.

To make potato croustades: roll Duchess Potato mixture out on a floured board to a thickness of about 1½ inches. Use a round cutter to cut the mixture in rounds of about 2 inches. Coat the rounds twice *à l'anglaise** and make a circular cut on top to mark the lid. Deep-fry the rounds, drain them, remove the cover, and scoop them out.

CROÛTES AND CROÛTONS

Croûtes (crusts) are pieces of stale French bread which have been brushed with butter and baked in the oven or sautéed in Clarified Butter or oil until they are a rich, golden-brown color. They may be served floating on a bowl of thick family soup or passed separately.

Croûtes for *Croûte au Pot* traditionally consist of the bread crusts alone. Cut the bread in 2-inch slices, cut the slices in half, and scrape out the white interior. The crusts may then be sprinkled with stock fat, browned in the oven, and served in the soup. Or they may be browned, spread with cooked bone marrow, and served separately.

Croûtes are also used as bases for other foods. A croûte made from one slice of bread is used as a base for creamed fish or mushrooms or other similar dishes. In this case, some of the white interior is scooped from the inside of the slice before browning to provide a saucerlike crust to contain the food.

Large croûtes, made from bread sliced horizontally, are used as a base for chickens and other entrees, thus raising the *pièce* above the level of its surrounding garnish.

Croûtons are little *croûtes*. For soups, especially cream soups, the croûtons are made from bread cut in ¼-inch dice. These may also be added to scrambled eggs.

Croûtons are also used as a garnish for meat, fish, poultry, creamed dishes, fricassees, *blanquettes,* and vegetable purées. For these purposes the bread is cut in ornamental shapes—hearts, triangles, diamonds, squares or circles, and artfully arranged around the dish. Crescent-shaped croûtons are used to separate the various garnishes on a platter from one another.

DIABLOTINS

These are a kind of *croûte* served separately with soup. Cover ¼-inch-thick slices of French bread with thick Béchamel Sauce to which you have added 2 to 4 tablespoons of grated Parmesan cheese per cup, and a pinch of cayenne. Sprinkle with more grated Parmesan and brown in a 450° oven or under the broiler.

DIJON MUSTARD
See Mustard.

DORURE

A beaten egg, whole or the yolk only, sometimes with a little water added, is a *dorure*. A very light brush is used to apply the dorure to pastry or Duchess Potatoes so they will become beautifully golden. If the oven is very hot and a light color is desired, beat one whole egg with 1 tablespoon of water. If the oven is moderate and a darker color is desired, use only the yolk with a few drops of water. It is nice to have a name for everything.

DRIPPINGS (*Gouttes*)

The fat and juices that fall from a roast into the roasting pan are rich in flavor. Much of the liquid in the juices is evaporated in the heat of the oven, and the remaining juices and brown encrustation on the bottom of the pan are concentrated essences of the original liquid drippings.

In as much as drippings are valuable to have, take care that they do not burn. Use a pan only large enough to catch the drops falling from the roast; too large a pan will become too hot, receiving insufficient drippings to cool it. If the juices in the pan still show signs of smoking and burning, add a little water or wine to the pan from time to time to lower the temperature.

To retrieve the natural meat juices from drippings: pour or skim off the fat from the roasting pan and reserve it. Place the pan on a medium fire, add a little water, wine, or stock, and scrape the bottom of the pan with a wooden spoon or spatula, dissolving the solidified juices and thus deglazing* the pan. Strain this rich, flavorful liquid and pass it in a sauceboat for serving meat *au jus,* or thicken it into a sauce.

To purify the fat from drippings: put the fat into a bowl, pour boiling water over it, and stir to wash impurities from the fat so that they will settle to the bottom with the water. Refrigerate until hard, poke a few holes in the fat, and drain off the liquid and sediment trapped underneath. Heat the remaining fat until the moisture it contains is completely boiled out of it. When the bubbling ceases, immediately remove the fat from the fire. Cool it a little, strain it through a fine sieve or several thicknesses of cheesecloth, and store it, covered, in the refrigerator. Thus purified, it will keep for months.

DUXELLES

This is a mushroom hash widely used as a flavoring for sauces and stuffings, and as a garnish ingredient. Correctly made, it will keep for weeks in the refrigerator, and it may be frozen.

To make about 1 cup of basic dry duxelles: in 2 tablespoons butter and 2 tablespoons olive oil (or 4 tablespoons Clarified Butter), cook 4 tablespoons minced onions until lightly browned, adding 2 tablespoons minced shallots for the last few minutes of cooking. Mince 1 pound of mushrooms, using only stems if you prefer. You should have about 5 cups. Place the minced mushrooms in a towel and squeeze out all the moisture you can. Add the mushrooms to the pan with the minced onions and shallots, and cook together until the mushrooms have given up some of their remaining liquid and are browned. Use a brisk heat, but be careful not to overcook and burn the mushrooms. Season to taste with salt, pepper, and nutmeg. You may now cool, cover, and store this dry duxelles in the refrigerator, using it in the following ways:

As a flavoring for sauces: use dry duxelles as is.

As an ingredient in stuffings: to 1 cup of dry duxelles add 1 tablespoon finely chopped parsley. For added flavor, before adding the parsley, you may add ¼ cup Madeira wine and ¼ cup Brown Stock and boil this down completely.

As a filling for garnishing vegetables: to 1 cup of dry duxelles add ½ cup of tomatoed Demi-Glace Sauce or Starch-Thickened Brown Stock, ¼ cup dry wine, and ½ clove garlic. Simmer until the duxelles can be heaped up, thickening it if necessary with fresh bread crumbs. Remove the garlic and mix in 1 tablespoon finely chopped parsley. Use as a filling for broiled tomato shells or boiled artichoke bottoms.

ÉCLAIRS

Éclairs, filled with custard and topped with chocolate sauce, have long been popular in America. For these and other pastries made with Cream Puff Paste see Chapter 15.

ESSENCES AND EXTRACTS (*Essences et Extraits*)

These are concentrated flavorings in ready-to-use form. They are employed to make up for deficiencies in stocks, soups, sauces, and stews that have not quite attained the full flavor they ought to have.

Essences are a welcome expedient when a sauce or a stew is lacking in flavor. Meat essences, especially, are used quite properly to enhance the quickly prepared pan sauces, giving these sauces the roundness and fullness of flavor only long simmering can ordinarily supply. On the other hand we are cooks, not chemists, and it is incumbent upon us, whenever possible, to incorporate the fresh flavoring ingredient into the stock or stew as it is cooking. In this way the best results are obtained.

Among the most useful essences, one kind consists of the commercially extracted oils of such flavorful foods as vanilla and almonds. These extracts are available in supermarkets.

Another kind of valuable essence is that obtained from meat, poultry, and fish. These essences are discussed under the heading of Meat Glaze in this chapter. These you must make yourself.

A third kind of essence is obtained from aromatic herbs and vegetables. Most of these strike me as being superfluous, since it is simple enough to add these ingredients to the dish as it is cooking. One exception, perhaps, is Mushroom Essence, which is described in this chapter.

FATS AND OILS (*Graisses et Huiles*)
Cooking fats and oils are obtained from both the animal and vegetable kingdoms. A supply of various kinds of fats and oils, each of which is more or less suitable for a particular purpose, should be kept on hand in the refrigerator.

Fats are used as a shortening for dough and as an ingredient in many dishes. Here I will consider them only for their performance as a cooking medium in sautéing and deep frying.

Crucial to a fat's cooking qualities is its flavor, in as much as a good deal of the flavor of meat is contained in its fat portion. Also crucial is the fat's smoke point, the temperature at which the fat begins to smoke, decompose, burn, and ruin the food being cooked in it.

Deep-frying temperatures range from 350° for chicken to 395° for French fried potatoes. Obviously, a fat for deep-frying should provide a comfortable margin beyond these temperatures.

Fats and oils used in deep frying "wear out" with prolonged use. They begin to smoke at lower and lower temperatures until they can no longer properly cook the food and must be discarded. A deep-fat thermometer will cost you less than a dollar and is an invaluable tool.

For reuse strain the fat through a fine sieve lined with cheesecloth to remove bits of food and particles of burned flour, cover, and store in the refrigerator. Fats will absorb some of the flavor from food, and fats or oils used for deep-frying fish and shellfish should be kept separate from that used for frying other foods.

Butterfat is widely used in French cooking for its delicate yet distinctive flavor. Its disadvantage is that it burns at low temperature and cannot be used for high-heat sautéing. Butter is 80 percent butterfat. To clarify the butter and isolate the butterfat, see Butter in this chapter.

Chicken fat is a characteristically flavored fat used for enriching poultry dishes and stuffings. It burns at low temperature and therefore cannot be used for deep-frying or high-heat sautéing.

Goose fat is a fine-flavored, excellent fat for frying, flavoring, and preserving foods. Its delicacy is equaled only by butter. It can be brought to quite high temperatures without burning, and it will keep in the refrigerator for months. Be sure to save and purify all the fat drippings from the very next goose you cook.

Duck fat is similar to goose fat. It is not considered to be quite as choice.

Lard is the rendered fat of pork, usually obtained from the back (fat back) or from the area surrounding the kidney. Pork kidney fat, the finest and most delicate, is called *leaf lard*. Lard can be heated to temperatures as high as 400° without burning.

Bacon fat has a pronounced smoked bacon flavor, delicious in some dishes, undesirable in others.

Beef kidney fat or *suet,* taken from the area of the kidney, is the best obtainable from the beef animal. Because of its good characteristics and relatively low cost, it is the traditional fat for deep-frying.

Stock fat is the fat skimmed from the top of stock made with veal or beef. It should not be wasted, and it is purified in the same way as the fat of roasts (see Drippings in this chapter).

Vegetable oils come from a number of sources including peanuts, corn, soybeans, flaxseed, cottonseed, and safflower seed. They can be heated to a high temperature (about 450°) before they will burn, and are therefore most suitable for deep-fat frying, which requires temperatures ranging from about 350° to 395°. After use, carefully strain the oil and refrigerate for future use.

Olive oil is a preferred cooking oil in the South of France, and foods sautéed in or basted with olive oil are typical of this region. You should always have fine quality olive oil on hand for salads, and, to achieve the authentic flavor of Mediterranean recipes, you should use it for sautéing, alone or mixed with Clarified Butter.

Butter and oil, in equal proportions, are used for sautéing. The butter provides its fine flavor and the combination of butter and oil can be heated to higher temperatures without burning.

Shortening can be used for deep-fat frying if it contains no emulsifiers. Shortening containing monoglyceride emulsifiers will burn at a temperature as low as 300° and is useless for this purpose. Read the label.

FINES HERBES
This is a mixture of finely chopped herbs which is added to a dish such as scrambled eggs. The herbs should be fresh, and traditionally they consist of equal amounts of parsley, chervil, tarragon, and chives.

These are small fluted ovals or crescents of Puff Paste made with leftover paste. They are affixed to the top of pastry cases as a decoration, or glazed* with beaten egg and baked separately as a garnish for elegant entrees.

FLOUR (*Farine*)

Apart from its use in making breads, Pastry Doughs, and Batters, flour is kept always on hand for thickening liquids and dredging foods.

To thicken liquids with flour: combine the flour with the liquid and heat the liquid, stirring constantly, to the boiling point. Take care that the flour is cooked so that its raw taste is overcome.

To combine flour with a warm liquid without clumping, it must first be dispersed by mixing it with butter (see *Beurre Manié*), by mixing and cooking it with butter (see Roux), or by mixing it with a little cold liquid, such as water, wine, or stock.

American pan gravies are usually made by stirring spoonfuls of flour and water, little by little, into simmering pan juices from which the fat has been skimmed. Once the flour is added, the gravy should be simmered for at least 10 minutes to eliminate the raw taste of the flour. Liquids thickened in this manner will be very opaque, due to the protein content of the flour.

The thickening power of flour may vary considerably from bag to bag, with 1 tablespoon sometimes doing the work of 2 tablespoons. Usually 1 tablespoon of flour will thicken 1 cup of liquid to the consistency of medium cream or a thin sauce.

To dredge foods with flour: roll the food in the flour and slap it smartly over the sink to remove any loose flour that would assuredly burn in the pan.

Flour aids in browning foods by blotting up the moisture on the surface that would inhibit browning. Also, the cooked flour itself contributes to the brown color.

Foods that are dipped in a batter or coated *à l'anglaise** are also dredged with flour; the batter will adhere more closely to the floured surface.

When stewing meat is first dredged with flour and browned, the flour combines with the fat in the pan to form a roux, which tends to thicken the liquid in which the stew is simmered.

FOIE GRAS

Foie gras is the fat liver of an overfed duck or goose. Goose liver is preferred, and it may weigh 2 pounds or more. The best quality livers are cream-colored with a tinge of pink, and they are one of the great delicacies of the Western world. Foie gras is cooked whole in Terrines or baked in a crust, or cut in slices, sautéed in butter, and used in a number of rarely encountered dishes.

In America, foie gras is available in *pâté* form—a mixture of goose liver and pork liver paste flavored with truffles. It may be packed in tunnel-shaped cans for slicing (*bloc tunnel de foie gras truffé*) or packed in decorated terrines for scooping (*terrines de foie gras truffé*) or coated with a wine jelly, baked in an edible crust, and canned (*pâtés de foie gras truffé en croûte*).

Cans or terrines labeled *pâté de foie* are not foie gras. Their major ingredient is pork liver. Read the ingredients, which must appear on the label.

Foie gras is the hors d'oeuvre *par excellence,* served in slices from the *bloc* or in little balls or shell-shaped scoops from the terrine. It is also used as an elegant garnish. Taken from the terrine, it may be used to make foie gras *Quenelles*. Sliced from the bloc, it may be sautéed in butter and used in such dishes as Tournedos Rossini.

It is very expensive.

FONDANTS

A *fondant* is a small croquette, made with a Purée of meat, poultry, fish, shellfish, or vegetables bound by an appropriate thick sauce.

To make fondants: combine 2 or 3 parts Purée with 1 part thick sauce. Shape 2-ounce (¼ cup) portions of the chilled fondant mixture in egg shapes, roll in flour, coat *à l'anglaise,** and deep-fry just before serving. See Croquettes.

FORCEMEATS OR STUFFINGS (*Farces*)

These preparations are diverse and unnumbered, but I shall do my best to present them in an orderly fashion.

Forcemeats or stuffings are mixtures of ingredients, frequently pounded or ground to a paste, seasoned, and bound together with eggs. More often, but not always, the principal ingredient of a forcemeat is the raw meat of veal, pork, chicken, fish, or shellfish. It also contains a good proportion of butter or another fat. Forcemeats stiffen when cooked, although they should be tender and light.

Forcemeats are used for stuffing meats, poultry, fish and vegetables; as a filling for Pâtés, Terrines, and Galantines; and as a garnish. When used as a garnish the forcemeat is usually shaped and poached in salted water to form *Quenelles*. When poached in molds, the forcemeat forms *Mousselines*.

As you will discover in the following recipes, the major meat paste ingredient of a forcemeat is bound with other ingredients in various ways. Panada-based forcemeats are given substance by the addition of a flour or bread panada. The most delicate of all forcemeats, mousseline forcemeat, is bound with egg whites and cold heavy cream. Some forcemeats, such as pork sausage, contain only meat, fat, eggs and seasonings.

FORCEMEAT WITH BREAD PANADA
(*Farce à la Panade au Pain*)

Prepare a bread panada by putting 2½ cups soft white bread crumbs in a pan with ¾ cup boiling milk. The milk will be absorbed almost instantly. Cook over a hot fire, stirring with a wooden spoon, until the panada leaves the sides of the pan and forms a ball. Spread the panada on a buttered baking tin or platter, brush it with butter, and chill it.

While the panada is cooling, cube 1 pound of raw chicken, veal, pork, fish, or shellfish, removing gristle and connective tissue. Grind the meat finely, putting it through the grinder at least twice. Pound it in a mortar or mash it in a bowl until it assumes a pastelike consistency, and season with 1½ teaspoons salt, ¼ teaspoon pepper, and a dash of nutmeg.

Blend the cold panada thoroughly with ½ pound of softened butter. Then mix the meat paste and the panada-and-butter mixture together, blending them thoroughly. Little by little, add 2 whole eggs and 4 egg yolks, stirring vigorously to thoroughly blend the mass. When it is smooth and homogeneous, rub it through a sieve, butter its surface, and chill it until it is quite cold.

Finally, test the cold forcemeat by dropping an olive-sized ball into boiling salted water and poaching it for a few minutes until it stiffens and is cooked. You may now taste it and correct the seasoning if necessary. If the test ball disintegrates or cooks too soft, beat a little more egg white into the forcemeat. If it is too tough, beat in a little more butter.

FORCEMEAT WITH FLOUR PANADA
(*Farce à la Panade à la Farine*)

Prepare a flour panada by putting ½ cup plus 2 tablespoons of water in a pan with 3 tablespoons butter and ½ teaspoon salt. Bring to a boil, melting the butter, and add ¾ cup of flour all at once. Cook over a hot fire, stirring with a wooden spoon until the panada leaves the sides of the pan and forms a ball. Spread the panada on a buttered baking tin or platter, brush it with butter, and chill it.

Proceed as for the preceding recipe, Forcemeat with Bread Panada.

FORCEMEAT WITH CREAM PUFF PASTE
(*Farce à la Panade Pâte à Choux*)

By using Cream Puff Paste as a panada, you can make a very light forcemeat for *Quenelles*. Make the paste according to the recipe in Chapter 15. Blend it thoroughly with an equal amount of seasoned meat paste, and chill. Just before using, you may beat in 3 or 4 tablespoons of cold heavy cream.

MOUSSELINE FORCEMEAT
(Farce à la Mousseline)

This preparation, which is essentially a richly creamed meat paste, is the most delicate and elegant of the forcemeats. It can be used in every forcemeat application—as a filling, as a stuffing, and for the finest *Quenelles*. It is especially suitable for the sweet flesh of shellfish.

Cube 1 pound of raw chicken, veal, pork, fish, or shellfish, removing gristle and connective tissue. Grind the meat finely, passing it through the grinder at least twice. Pound it in a mortar or mash it in a bowl until it assumes a pastelike consistency, and season it with 2 teaspoons salt, ½ teaspoon white pepper (for white meats), and ¼ teaspoon nutmeg.

Little by little add 2 egg whites (3 egg whites for fish and shellfish), stirring vigorously to thoroughly blend the mass, and rub it through a sieve into a chilled bowl. Place the mixture in the refrigerator until thoroughly chilled, gradually beat in 2 cups of cold heavy cream, and chill again.

Test the forcemeat for flavor and texture as suggested in the preceding recipe for Forcemeat with Bread Panada. Beat in a little more egg white if it is too soft, or a little more cream if it is too firm.

VEAL FORCEMEAT OR GODIVEAU
(Farce de Veau ou Godiveau)

This is one of the most ancient preparations in French cookery. It is used especially for making *Quenelles,* and the neutral flavor of veal makes it an excellent garnish for meats and poultry. Godiveau quenelles are also used as a filling for *Pâtés* and *Vol-au-Vents*.

Cube 1 pound of fine raw veal and 2 pounds of beef kidney fat (suet), removing gristle and connective tissue. Grind these finely, passing them through the grinder at least twice, season with 2 teaspoons salt, ½ teaspoon pepper, and ¼ teaspoon nutmeg, and pound the veal and fat in a mortar or mash them in a bowl until they assume a pastelike consistency. Little by little add 4 whole eggs, stirring vigorously to blend the mass, rub it through a sieve, cover, and chill it thoroughly all the way through.

When the mixture is quite cold, add to it little by little 1¾ cups ice water or the same weight (14 ounces) of crushed ice, beating thoroughly all the while. Test the godiveau for flavor and texture as suggested in the preceding recipe for Forcemeat with Bread Panada. Beat in a little more egg white if it is too soft, or a little more ice or ice water if it is too firm.

VEAL FORCEMEAT OR GODIVEAU WITH CREAM
(*Farce de Veau ou Godiveau à la Crème*)

The finest *godiveau* is made with cream. Proceed as in the preceding recipe for Veal Forcemeat or Godiveau, using 1 pound of fine white veal, 1 pound of fine beef kidney fat, 2 teaspoons salt, ½ teaspoon pepper, ¼ teaspoon nutmeg, 2 whole eggs, and 2 egg yolks. Chill thoroughly and beat in, little by little, 3 cups cold heavy cream.

PORK FORCEMEAT
(*Farce de Porc*)

This is nothing other than pork sausage meat. It is used for making sausages and for filling Pâtés and vegetables. It is also used for stuffing poultry and meats, with chopped parsley, sautéed onion, and breadcrumbs added to it.

Cube 1 pound of raw pork and 1 pound of fresh pork fat, removing gristle and connective tissue. Grind these as finely as you please, season with 1 tablespoon Spiced Salt and 1 tablespoon cognac, and beat in 1 or 2 whole eggs.

This sausage meat can be made smoother by pounding it in a mortar or mashing it in a bowl until it assumes a pastelike consistency. It is then called *farce fine de porc*.

CHICKEN FORCEMEAT FOR PÂTÉS
(*Farce de Volaille pour Pâtés*)

Cube 1 pound raw chicken, ½ pound raw veal, ½ pound raw pork, and 2 pounds fresh pork fat, removing gristle and connective tissue. Grind these finely, season with 2 tablespoons Spiced Salt, and work the meats and fat thoroughly in a mortar or in a bowl until they assume a pastelike consistency. Little by little add 5 whole eggs, stirring vigorously to blend the mass, add 6 tablespoons brandy, and rub the forcemeat through a sieve.

PORK AND VEAL FORCEMEAT FOR PÂTÉS
(*Farce de Porc et Veau pour Pâtés*)

Cube 1 pound raw veal, 1 pound raw pork, and 2 pounds fresh pork fat, removing gristle and connective tissue. Grind these finely, season with 2 tablespoons Spiced Salt, and work the meats and fat thoroughly in a mortar or mash in a bowl until they assume a pastelike consistency. Little by little, add 3 whole eggs, stirring vigorously to blend the mass, mix in 3 tablespoons brandy, and rub through a sieve.

FORCEMEAT FOR FISH
(*Farce pour Poisson*)

This forcemeat, based on soft breadcrumbs, is especially suitable for stuffing fat fish.

Soak 2 cups soft breadcrumbs in 1 cup milk for 10 minutes, drain and press out the milk, and toss the crumbs with a fork to loosen them. To the crumbs add: 1 tablespoon minced onions and 1 tablespoon minced shallots, both simmered in butter for 2 or 3 minutes; 4 tablespoons mushrooms, minced and pressed dry; 1 tablespoon chopped parsley; ½ clove garlic, minced; ½ teaspoon salt; a dash of pepper and nutmeg; and 2 beaten whole eggs. Toss these ingredients to mix them thoroughly.

MUSHROOM STUFFING
(*Farce de Champignons*)

This forcemeat is used especially for stuffing poultry. For an interesting flavor, use for half of the common field mushrooms one or another of the imported, dried mushrooms, which you have moistened in a little water or white wine and squeezed dry.

Put ½-pound chopped mushrooms (about 2½ cups) and 2 teaspoons Spiced Salt into a saucepan with ½ cup butter and simmer gently for about 5 minutes. Drain the mushrooms, reserving the butter, and chill them. Pound the chilled mushrooms, the butter, and ½ cup of bread panada (see the preceding recipe for Forcemeat with Bread Panada) in a mortar until they assume a pastelike consistency. Finish by beating in 4 egg yolks.

For other stuffings based on mushrooms see *Duxelles*.

SAGE AND ONION STUFFING
(*Farce à la Sauge*)

This traditional English stuffing for turkeys, ducks, and geese has won its way into the French repertoire.

Finely chop 4 onions (about 1 pound) and simmer them in 6 tablespoons butter until they are soft. Soak 9 cups (about 1 pound) soft breadcrumbs in milk, press them dry, and fluff them with a fork. Add the breadcrumbs to the onions along with 1½ tablespoons sage, 2 teaspoons salt, and ½ teaspoon pepper. Mix these ingredients and taste to be certain you have the right amount of seasoning. Finally, add 1 cup (about ½ pound) chopped veal or beef fat and mix thoroughly.

FRIED BREAD

To form a base for other foods, bread is cut into whatever shape desired and deep-fried for a few minutes until it is golden brown. If you do not have a quantity of deep hot fat on hand, sauté the slices quickly in very hot Clarified Butter. Or brush them with butter and put them in the oven to brown.

FRIED PARSLEY (*Persil Frit*)

Whole sprigs of parsley are deep-fried for use as a garnish with deep-fried or sautéed foods.

To fry parsley: remove most of the stem, wash, and carefully dry the parsley. Plunge it into very hot fat for 1 or 2 minutes, until the parsley is crisp and floats to the top. Deep-fried parsley crunches in your mouth and rewards you with an unusual flavor. Perhaps we should be deep-frying other herbs as well.

FRITTERS (*Beignets*)

Fritters include simple doughs that are deep-fried, such as American doughnuts. Also called *beignets* are sweet or savory mixtures that are dipped in batter and deep-fried.

Savory fritters include bite-size pieces of cooked meat, poultry, fish, shellfish, and vegetables. These are usually marinated before they are dipped in batter and deep-fried.

Sweet fritters include fresh and cooked fruits, which may or may not be macerated.

See Batters for Deep-Frying in this chapter.

GALANTINES

A galantine is a dish of cold, boned, stuffed meat, usually poultry, that has been poached in a gelatinous stock.

As an example, a chicken is boned and stuffed with a Forcemeat and with slices of its own marinated meat, ham, tongue, truffles, mushrooms, and seasonings. The skin is sewed up to form a pouch for this mixture, wrapped in pork fat and tied tightly in a cloth, and poached. The galantine is then cooled in its stock, pressed to form a compact shape, and thoroughly chilled. It is served in slices. See *Pâtés* and Terrines.

GELATIN

When the connective tissues, skin, and bones of animals are cooked in moist heat, the collagen they contain in large proportion is converted to gelatin and tough cuts of meat are made tender. If the meat is surrounded by a liquid, the gelatin will be dissolved in it. This gives the warm liquid a desirable succulence—a gelatinous body—that can be detected in your mouth and on your lips. If the liquid is cooled, the gelatin it contains converts it into a jelly or gel. Thus, gelatin contributes to the succulence and body of hot consommés and sauces, as well as to the cold aspic jellies in which its presence is more apparent.

Powdered gelatin, which is colorless and odorless, may also be used to supplement natural gelatin in consommés and aspic jellies. It comes in envelopes containing 1 tablespoon of powder that must first be softened in a little cold stock or water for about 3 minutes. A firm jelly is obtained from 1 tablespoon of powdered gelatin in 2 cups of liquid, but if a stock already contains natural gelatin it is difficult to tell how much supplementary gelatin to use. Your only recourse is to test the jelly.

To test aspic jelly: pour the gelatin mixture into a saucer and chill in the refrigerator, cut the jelly in pieces, and allow it to stand at room temperature for about 10 minutes. If the jelly is for a consommé, the pieces should be meltingly soft with rounded edges. If the jelly is for coating meats or a decorative garnish, the pieces should remain firm with sharp edges. Use no more gelatin than you need to get the desired result; it can make hot soups too sticky and cold aspics too rubbery (see Aspic).

GNOCCHI

This is a sort of dumpling served as an hors d'oeuvre or garnish. It is Italian in origin.

To make gnocchi: prepare Cream Puff Paste (see Chapter 15), substituting milk for the water in the recipe. Also, after beating in the eggs, blend in ½ cup grated Parmesan cheese. Using a pastry bag, pipe this dough in walnut-sized pieces into simmering salted water and poach. When the gnocchi rise to the surface and are firm to the touch, drain them on paper towels.

To make gnocchi au gratin: place cooked and drained gnocchi in an ovenproof dish on a layer of Mornay Sauce. Cover with more sauce, sprinkle with grated Parmesan cheese and butter, and brown in the oven.

HERBS

The only herbs commonly found fresh in American supermarkets are parsley and, occasionally, chives growing in little pots. Other herbs used fresh in French cooking are savory, chervil, and tarragon. All of these you can grow yourself. Tarragon, especially, is called for in many French recipes; it must be grown from roots, as it does not form seeds. Dry herbs can be substituted and are available everywhere. You will find whole dried herbs imported from France in many specialty food stores.

Although fresh herbs are preferred, many dried herbs are used in French kitchens. These commonly include thyme, basil, rosemary, sage, sweet marjoram, and bay leaf, and should be kept always at hand.

Herbs and spices are used with caution in French cooking. They are usually more suggested than tasted.

KROMESKIES

The original *kromeskie,* prepared *à la russe,* is a small 2- to 3-ounce portion of Croquette mixture, shaped like a cork, wrapped in thin pig's caul (membrane covering the stomach), dipped in batter, and deep-fried.

Kromeskies made *à la polonaise* substitute a wrapping of thin pancake (crêpe) for the pig's caul.

Kromeskies made *à la française* are shaped like corks or rectangles, dipped in batter, and deep-fried without any wrapping.

Kromeskies are served as an hors d'oeuvre or small entree.

LARDOONS

This name (French, *lardons*) refers to pork fat used in two separate applications.

For one application, fresh pork fat or blanched salt pork or bacon is cut into small sticks about ¼ inch square and 1 inch long. These are partially rendered* and their rendered fat is used to brown the meat in country stews such as Chicken à la Bonne Femme. The browned lardoons are then incorporated into the stews to give them additional flavor and richness.

The name lardoons also refers to strips of pork fat used for larding* meats. Preferably, these lardoons are cut from fresh, firm pork back fat, but you can also use salt pork that has been parboiled for a few minutes to relieve it of excess salt. The strips, which are of any size and length to suit the meat, are inserted into it with long larding spikes or threaded into its surface with larding needles. Before using, lardoons are seasoned with salt (if not made from salt pork), pepper, and nutmeg, and they are marinated in brandy for 15 to 20 minutes. They are then rolled in finely chopped parsley and inserted into the meat. See larding,* studding.*

LEMONS (*Limons*)

These happy little fruits are constantly needed in the kitchen. Use a cut half of lemon to scrub a chicken or to remove onion odors from your hands. Use the juice of lemon in water in which you cook mushrooms or artichoke bottoms to keep them white. Squeeze fresh lemon to taste into white sauces to give them a final dash of piquancy. Squeeze lemon into salad dressings. Pass lemon quarters for squeezing onto fish or fruit, and garnish fish platters with lemon slices and parsley. Use only fresh lemon juice; there is no substitute for it.

MACÉDOINE

A hot *macédoine* of vegetables is a mixture of vegetables that have been regularly shaped in balls, dice, diamond or other shapes, boiled separately, then mixed together and tossed in hot butter or boiling cream. The usual vegetables of a macédoine are carrots, turnip, green beans, asparagus tips, and peas (which of course are left whole). For a cold macédoine of vegetables, the cooked vegetables are covered with an Aspic jelly. Macédoines are served as a garnish or as hors d'oeuvres. (See also *Brunoise.*)

A macédoine of fruits is a mixture of fresh fruits, sliced, diced, or cut into balls, sprinkled with fine sugar or sugar syrup and with a liqueur such as kirsch, and left to steep (macerate*) for a few hours. It is served as a fruit salad or dessert.

MARINADE

A marinade is a liquid, usually containing wine, vinegar, oil, aromatic vegetables and seasonings, in which meats and sometimes poultry and fish are steeped. The purpose is to impregnate the meat with the flavors of the marinade. Also, the wine or other acid liquid softens tough meat fibers. The oil prevents the meat, which sometimes projects above the surface of the marinade, from drying. At room temperature, marinades are very active and 5 or 6 hours should be sufficient for a 5-pound piece of beef. At refrigerator temperature, the meat may remain in the liquid up to 4 days. The longer it remains in the marinade, the more its flavor is changed. Carried to the extreme, the meat takes on the taste of game. Marinades are prepared just before using. Following is a commonly used marinade.

To marinate meat: rub the meat with salt and pepper and place it in a bowl just large enough to hold it and the aromatic vegetables. Add 1 chopped carrot, 1 chopped onion, 3 sprigs of parsley, 1 bay leaf, 1 sprig or pinch of thyme, and 1 peeled clove of garlic. Then pour ¼ cup olive oil over the meat, and add 2 or 3 cups of dry red wine or enough to almost cover it. You may also add a sprinkle of brandy. Turn the meat periodically in this marinade, so that it may be thoroughly treated.

When marinated meat is braised, the marinade vegetables are browned and added to the braising pan, and the marinade liquid is poured into the pan as part of the braising liquid.

MARROW (*Moelle*)

Marrow is the tasty fat substance inhabiting the center of large beef bones. At room temperature it has the consistency of frozen butter, but it melts partially and becomes soft when heated. It is used to flavor and enrich many French dishes, notably cabbage, soups, and Bordelaise Sauce. It is delicious spread on crusts of bread.

Marrow is a by-product of stock making and should be retrieved from the marrow bones. Although good, marrow from the stock pot is overcooked. In order to fully appreciate marrow it should receive a cooking of its own.

To cook marrow: have big beef marrow bones sawed in 2- or 3-inch lengths. (If you can, soak the bones in several changes of cold water for 24 hours. This improves the color of the cooked marrow, changing it from a gray to a creamy color.) Place the bones in cold salted water, bring the water to a simmer, simmer for 15 minutes, and scoop the cooked marrow from the bones with whatever implement that can reach inside.

To cook marrow another way: have the butcher split 5- or 6-inch lengths of beef marrow bone lengthwise. Use a flexible knife to remove the raw marrow in one piece if possible, and slice in ½-inch-thick pieces or dice it with a hot knife. Drop the raw marrow into boiling salted water or stock and cook for 1 minute. Remove and drain.

MATIGNON

Matignon is a flavorful pulp used as an aromatic coating for meats or as a garnish. It consists of the same ingredients as *Mirepoix,* but the ingredients are finely minced instead of diced, and they are cooked in butter and wine until they have a pulpy consistency.

To prepare about 1 pound of matignon: finely mince 2 medium carrots, 2 medium onions, and 2 small ribs of celery. Add to these vegetables ¼ to ½ cup of minced raw ham or blanched lean bacon, ½ crumbled bay leaf, and a pinch of thyme. Stew slowly in 2 tablespoons butter until the vegetables are soft. Add ¼ to ½ cup Madeira wine, shake the pan to mix it thoroughly with the vegetables, and boil down until the liquid has disappeared. The ham may be omitted.

MAZAGRANS

These are various savory fillings contained in a case of Duchess Potato mixture.

To make small mazagrans for hors d'oeuvres or garnish: line Tartlet molds with a thin layer of rolled duchess potatoes, fill with a Purée, *Salpicon,* or other savory filling, cover with a round of duchess potatoes, brush with beaten egg, and brown in the oven.

To make large mazagrans for entrees, prepare as for a *Timbale* using duchess potato mixture in place of the pastry.

MEAT GLAZE (*Glace de Viande*)

Meat glaze, or *glace de viande,* is a greatly reduced meat or poultry stock. No adequate substitute is available commercially, so you will have to make meat glazes yourself. They are easily made, however, and will keep in the refrigerator for many months.

Glazes of meat and poultry have many uses. By adding 1 tablespoon or more to 1 cup of hot water, you will get 1 cup of flavorful stock. Mixed with a little Madeira wine, meat glaze becomes an excellent substitute for Demi-Glace Sauce. Meat glaze is invaluable for adding final flavor and body to pan sauces, soups, and stews. It is also brushed on cooked meats to give them a handsome glazed look.

To make meat or poultry glaze: make Brown Stock, Veal Stock, or Chicken Stock in the usual manner, but do not use any salt. The meat or poultry can be simmered with the aromatic vegetables and herbs for up to 24 hours. When a clear stock is obtained, skim it of all fat and slowly reduce it by simmering, straining it from time to time into successively smaller saucepans, until it will coat a spoon. In the refrigerator this liquid will stiffen to the consistency of rubber. Cover it tightly and it will keep for many months. It melts readily when heated.

Fish Stock or *Fumet,* similarly reduced, is called an Essence.

MEDAILLONS

These are croquettes of a specified shape, namely a small, flat patty or cake. They are prepared from a croquette mixture, coated and deep-fried exactly like croquettes. They may be served as an hors d'oeuvre with an appropriate sauce and Fried Parsley, or as a garnish. See Croquettes.

MIREPOIX

This is a classic base of aromatic vegetables and herbs. Like the stocks of which it forms an indispensable part, it is one of the foundation stones of French cooking.

If you read French recipes attentively, you will find the *mirepoix* included in them with astonishing regularity. It appears in the stocks. It reappears in the sauces made from these stocks. It forms an aromatic bed for pot roasts, braised beef, and poëléed chicken. It flavors stews. It is, in essence, the flavorful background against which other flavors perform.

To prepare about 1 pound of mirepoix: cut 2 medium carrots, 2 medium onions, and 2 small ribs of celery in small dice. Add to these vegetables ¼ to ½ cup diced raw ham or blanched lean bacon, ½ crumbled bay leaf, and a sprig or pinch of thyme. Cook together in 2 tablespoons butter for about 15 minutes until the vegetables have given up their water and are slightly browned.

The ham may be omitted. Also, mirepoix may be used uncooked to supply a small amount of moisture to poëléed meats and pot roasts.

MOUSSELINES

These are molded *Quenelles*. The quenelle Forcemeat is pressed into buttered *mousseline* molds, and the molds are covered with boiling salted water. As the mousselines cook they will leave the molds and rise to the surface of the water. They have a flat bottom and domed top, ideal for garnishing.

MUSHROOM ESSENCE

This liquid is simply the liquid in which mushrooms have been cooked, reduced to ¼ its original quantity. The cooking liquid is made in the following proportions: to ¼ cup water, add 1 teaspoon lemon juice, 1 tablespoon butter, and a pinch of salt. The reduced and strained essence may be stored in the refrigerator or freezer.

MUSTARD (*Moutarde*)

French recipes call for Dijon mustard, made in the ancient *haute cuisine* capital of Burgundy. It comes prepared and is available almost everywhere in the United States. Traditionally it is mixed with the juice of unripened grapes, and the plain mustard is often varied with other aromatic ingredients, especially tarragon. Dijon mustard is rather sharp-tasting and salty in flavor. When used in cooking, such as when coating grilled meats, it may seem that too much mustard is called for, but cooking ameliorates much of its piquancy.

English mustard, also widely used in French cooking, comes in powder form and contains turmeric, which gives it its bright yellow color and a pleasantly bitter taste. It is much hotter than Dijon mustard.

American prepared mustards vary enormously, and those made simply with ground mustard seed, vinegar, and spices can be very good. The brilliant yellow mustards taste least like mustard is expected to taste.

PANADA (*Panade*)

This is a stiff paste made with flour, fresh breadcrumbs, potato, or rice, used to give substance to Forcemeats and *Quenelles*. Cream Puff Paste is also used as a panada.

Recipes for bread and flour panadas can be found in this chapter under forcemeats.

PARMESAN CHEESE
A hard, dry Italian grating cheese of which the French are extraordinarily fond. It is a mainstay of French cookery. It keeps for a hundred years, so you have no excuse not to have it on hand. The best Parmesan comes from Italy. (See Chapter 13.)

PARSLEY (*Persil*)
Parsley is the only fresh herb that can always be found at the supermarket, usually the curly-leaved variety. It is widely used as a decorative garnish and is indispensable as a flavoring in stocks, soups, sauces and braising liquids. It keeps well, up to 2 weeks when tightly covered in the refrigerator, and is the indispensable fresh herb in a *Bouquet Garni*.

Parsley should be washed and pressed in a towel to dry it before chopping. The knife must be very sharp, so as not to crush the parsley and cause it to stick together. Only the tiny leaves are chopped; the stems, which are somewhat bitter, may be used to flavor stocks and sauces. When finely chopping parsley in advance, place the chopped parsley in the corner of a towel and twist it tightly. This will dry the parsley so that it can be easily scattered over a dish.

Parsley sprigs, used as a garnish for fried foods, are often deep-fried.

PASTRY DOUGH
The mastery of just a few of these doughs is the key to literally thousands of characteristic French dishes, ranging from delectable bite-sized hors d'oeuvres made with leftover meats to magnificent entrees serving a dozen guests. The necessary pastry doughs are of three kinds.

Short Paste gives us a tender, flaky crust for enclosing *Pâtés* and for lining pie plates, tart rings, and *Timbale* molds.

Puff Paste gives us incredibly light, crisp, flaky, puffed-up cases for *Bouchées* and *Vol-au-Vents*.

Cream Puff Paste gives us puffed-up hollow cases for *Choux, Profiteroles,* and Éclairs.

Directions for making these pastry doughs are in Chapter 15.

PÂTE
Pâte, without an accent on the *e,* is the French word for dough and pastry. *Pâté* is a meat pie.

PÂTÉS

A *pâté* is a meat pie, a smooth mixture of meat baked in a pastry crust. It is served hot or cold, as an hors d'oeuvre or entree.

The meat mixture is a well-seasoned Forcemeat, recipes for which can be found in this chapter. This forcemeat sometimes contains strips of marinated meat and other garnishes, which provide a decorative effect in the center of the pâté slices. The pastry crust is made with Short Paste, the recipes for which can be found in Chapter 15.

Metal pâté molds are bottomless and rectangular, with a hinge and locking pin that allows you to easily remove the mold from around the baked pâté. These molds are available at many kitchen specialty stores. You may also use a bread loaf pan.

To make a cold pâté (pâté froid): line a buttered pâté mold placed on a buttered baking sheet with Short Paste (see Chapter 15). Line the paste with sheets of pork fat (see Bards). Fill the mold with a forcemeat of your choice or one suggested below.

In the center of the forcemeat you can imbed strips of meat cut in ½-inch-square julienne* and marinated in a few tablespoons of Madeira with salt, pepper, parsley, bay leaf, thyme, shallots, or other flavorings, adding the drained marinade to the forcemeat.

Cover the forcemeat with a sheet of pork fat. Fold the overhanging lining paste over the fat, moisten it, and cover with another piece of lining paste cut to fit the top of the mold. Crimp the edges and seal them tightly.

You may now decorate the top of the crust with pastry embellishments that are moistened and affixed to the surface. Brush the top of the crust with 1 whole egg heated with 1 tablespoon water. Finally, make a small cone of heavy buttered paper and insert this improvised funnel into the crust.

Place the pâté in a 400° oven for 15 minutes, and then reduce the heat to 375°. Continue cooking, allowing about 30 minutes per pound in all, until the fat you can see percolating in the paper funnel has become absolutely clear.

Remove the pâté from the oven and allow it to cool for 30 minutes. To fill air holes and firm up the slices, pour in enough of an appropriate Aspic jelly into the paper funnel to fill the pâté. Allow it to cool to room temperature and chill overnight in the refrigerator.

To make a hot pâté (pâté chaud): proceed as for making cold pâté, but omit the lining of pork fat. When the pâté is baked, plump it out by adding a few tablespoons of an appropriate sauce through the paper funnel.

By a tasteful calculation of forcemeats, garnishing meats, and seasonings you can create excellent pâtés of your own invention, your own *pâté maison*.

PLUCHES

These are the leaves only of herbs, such as tarragon, parsley, chervil, and mint, used unchopped. If the central vein of the leaf is substantial, it should be removed. Pluches are to herbs what Chiffonades are to greens. They are used in soups and salads. Tarragon leaves are frequently blanched and used as a flavorful decoration.

POLENTA

This is a sort of corn meal mush flavored with Parmesan cheese and prepared as a vegetable or garnish.

To make polenta: to 6 cups salted water add 1½ cups yellow corn meal, stirring to break up any lumps. Cook for 20 to 30 minutes, stirring occasionally, until the mixture is thick and smooth. Add 4 tablespoons butter and ¼ to ½ cup grated Parmesan, stirring until the cheese has melted and the mixture thoroughly blended. The polenta may now be served hot, or you may prepare it for further cooking as follows:

Spread the polenta evenly in a ¼- to ⅜-inch layer on a buttered tin, brush the surface with butter to prevent it from drying, and allow it to cool. When it is cold, cut it in squares, rectangles, or diamond shapes. Sauté the pieces in Clarified Butter until golden brown, sprinkle with grated Parmesan or Parmesan and Brown Butter, and serve as a garnish for meats and fish, or as an hors d'oeuvre.

PROFITEROLES

These are small round puffs of pastry filled with sweet or savory mixtures and served hot or cold. For these and other pastries made with Cream Puff Paste see Chapter 15.

PURÉES

Food that is cooked and then run through a food mill, forced through a sieve, or otherwise reduced to a soft, homogeneous consistency is known as a purée. Meat, poultry, fish, vegetables, and fruits all can be puréed.

There are two kinds of purées, thick purées and soup purées. Soup purées are used as a base for all the classic thick soups. They are discussed in Chapter 6.

Thick purées are used as a vegetable, as a garnish, as a filling for pastry or stuffed vegetables, as a stuffing for meat and poultry, and as an hors d'oeuvre. Specific recipes for making various purées appear throughout the book, and I will state here only the general procedures for making them.

To make purées of starchy vegetables: cook the vegetable, drain it, rub it through a sieve or purée it in the blender. Put it in a saucepan with 1½ tablespoons butter per cup of purée and cook it for 3 to 5 minutes, stirring, until it gives up its excess liquid. Stir in milk or cream, a little at a time, until the purée reaches the desired degree of thickness, and simmer for a few minutes more.

To make purées of watery vegetables: proceed as above but add to each cup of puréed vegetable ¼ cup mashed potatoes, boiled rice, or thick Béchamel Sauce.

To make purées of white meats, fish, or shellfish: poach the meat, drain it, pound it very finely, mix it with heavy cream or Béchamel Sauce or Velouté Sauce, and rub it through a sieve. If you are using a blender, chop the meat finely and purée it in the blender along with the cream or the sauce. Cook for a few minutes, adjusting the consistency by adding more cream or sauce if needed.

To make purées of red meats: proceed as above except mix the puréed meat with Brown Sauce, Demi-Glace Sauce, or Starch-Thickened Brown Stock.

QUENELLES

Quenelles are simply a Forcemeat of meat, poultry, fish or shellfish, formed into balls or other shapes and poached in salted water. They may be described as a meat dumpling. They are served as an hors d'oeuvre, an entree, and as a garnish, and are usually covered with an appropriate sauce. Most of the forcemeats described in this chapter can be used to make quenelles.

Quenelles can be molded by hand, piped through a pastry bag, or shaped with two spoons. They can assume many sizes and shapes. Frequently they are made in the size and shape of olives or eggs, and in cylinders about 3 inches long.

The character of a quenelle depends upon the delicacy of the forcemeat from which it is made. If the forcemeat is stiff, the quenelle is easily molded and shaped with your lightly floured hands. If the forcemeat is very soft, it must be piped through a pastry bag or shaped with two spoons. One of these spoons is kept immersed in hot water. A spoonful of the soft forcemeat is lifted, and the top smoothed and shaped with the hot bowl of the other spoon. The spoons are then inverted and the quenelle is eased out. It will slip easily from this spoon into the pan.

In as much as this may take a little time, the quenelles are placed one by one in a buttered skillet. When they are all in place, boiling salted water is carefully added and the quenelles are poached for 8 to 12 minutes or until they have plumped up to almost twice their volume, feel firm, and turn over easily in the water.

The softest quenelle mixtures are used for the most elegant and delicate quenelles. These soft mixtures, made with egg whites and cream (see Mousseline Forcemeat), should be tested to make certain they will not disintegrate when cooked. Add a small, olive-shaped quenelle to simmering water and cook for a few minutes. If it tends to fall apart, you must beat another egg white or two into the mousseline mixture.

RICE (*Riz*)

Although any rice may be cooked in any rice dish, some varieties of rice are more appropriate to a given result than others.

For desserts, puddings, and thickening Purées, a soft, short-grained rice such as Italian *risotto* is preferred. For use as a vegetable, where it is imperative that the grains of rice be distinct and separate, the firmer American long-grained (Carolina) or Indian long-grained (Patna) rice is the proper choice.

Converted rice is rice that has been partially cooked in a vacuum. Any converted rice is preferred when the grains must stand separate. Because converted rice cannot be reduced to a creamy consistency, it should not be used for desserts or thickening. For these purposes, use raw white rice.

For recipes using rice as a vegetable, see Chapter 11.

RISSOLES

Rissoles are savory mixtures wrapped in pastry and deep-fried.

To make rissoles: cut Short Paste or Puff Paste in small circles. Fill the center of these circles with a spoonful or two of a Croquette mixture or *Salpicon*. Fold the circle in half and crimp the edge, thereby sealing the mixture inside a half-moon shape. Deep-fry in 360° fat until crisp and golden-brown, drain, and serve on a paper napkin.

Rissoles can also be made in other shapes—square, rectangular, or oval. Also, instead of folding the dough over, they may consist of two pieces of dough, the edges brushed with water, crimped and sealed. Rissoles are sometimes baked in a 450° oven.

In America, rissoles are often called fried pies.

ROYALE

A *royale* is a savory custard used mainly to garnish consommés. It may have as its base a rich stock, cream, puréed chicken or fish, or puréed vegetables. Into this are mixed egg and egg yolks. The mixture is cooked *en bain marie,** in the oven in buttered molds or pans that are placed in another pan of boiling water. When the custard has set, it is allowed to cool and then is cut in decorative shapes.

To make a royale: to 1 cup clear Brown or White Stock add 2 sprigs chopped fresh chervil or 1 teaspoon dried chervil. Bring to a boil, remove from the fire, cover, and allow to cool. In a bowl, beat 1 egg and 3 yolks. Strain the cooled stock into the bowl, season with salt and pepper, and beat to mix thoroughly. Strain the custard mixture into a buttered baking pan or deep cylindrical mold, and skim off any froth that has formed on the top. Place the pan or mold in a larger pan of boiling water and bake in a 300° oven for 20 to 30 minutes, without allowing the water to boil, until the custard has set. A knife thrust into the center of the custard should come out perfectly clean. Allow the custard to cool in the pan or mold, and cut it into fancy shapes. If you are using a deep mold, you will have to first slice the custard in ½-inch-thick slices.

To make chicken royale: pound ¼ pound cooked white meat of chicken and add ¼ cup Béchamel Sauce, mixing to form a paste. Season with salt, white pepper, and a little nutmeg, add ½ cup heavy cream, and strain. In a bowl, beat 1 egg and 3 yolks. Strain the mixture into the bowl and proceed as described above.

To make vegetable royale: to ½ cup vegetable Purée add ¼ cup Béchamel Sauce, ¼ cup scalded heavy cream, salt, pepper, and other flavorings appropriate to the vegetable. In a bowl, beat 1 egg and 3 yolks. Strain the purée mixture into the bowl and proceed as described above.

To make cream royale: in a bowl beat 1 egg and 3 yolks. Strain into the bowl 1 cup scalded heavy cream and mix well. Season with salt and nutmeg, and proceed as described above.

SALPICONS

A *salpicon* is cooked food that has been cut into dice and bound together with a thick sauce appropriate to the food.

Salpicons have innumerable uses, and once you get in the habit of making them, leftover foods will disappear from your refrigerator. They are used as a filling for large or small pastry cases served as entrees and hors d'oeuvres. They are used as a garnish. And with the addition of an egg or two to their sauce, they become Croquette mixtures.

Salpicons of meat, poultry, fish, shellfish, and vegetables are commonly made. The size of the dice and the thickness of the sauce are governed by the purpose for which the salpicon is intended. A salpicon that is to become a croquette mixture is rather finely diced. A salpicon intended to fill a large *Timbale* case may be cut into bite-sized dice. The sauce should be thick enough to hold these dice in a mass.

A simple salpicon contains only the food named, plus an appropriate sauce. Thus we have salpicons of chicken in Velouté Sauce, chicken livers in Madeira Sauce, fish in Normandy Sauce or Béchamel Sauce, lobster in

American Sauce, brains in Allemande Sauce, ham in Demi-Glace Sauce, and veal in either a white or brown sauce, to name a few. Salpicons of artichoke bottoms, asparagus, carrots, eggplant, green beans, mushrooms, and onions may be bound with Béchamel, Cream, Velouté, or Supreme Sauce. We also have cold salpicons, such as artichoke bottoms, asparagus, beets, cucumbers, or potatoes in thick Mayonnaise.

Compound salpicons contain 2 or more cooked, diced ingredients bound by a sauce. The different ingredients should be cut in the same size dice. Compound salpicons are often awarded a name of their own; thus we have:

Salpicon Chasseur: sautéed chicken livers and mushrooms in Chasseur Sauce.

Salpicon à la Reine: chicken breast, mushrooms, and truffles in Allemande or Chicken Velouté Sauce.

Salpicon Cussy: sweetbreads, mushrooms, and truffles in Madeira Sauce.

Salpicon Financière: chicken, sweetbreads, mushrooms, truffles, and pitted olives in Madeira Sauce.

Salpicon Cancalaise: poached oysters and mushrooms in Normandy or Fish Velouté Sauce.

Salpicon Cardinal: lobster, mushrooms, and truffles in Cardinal Sauce.

Salpicon Dieppoise: mussels, crayfish (or shrimp) and mushrooms with White Wine Sauce.

Salpicon à la Périgourdine: foie gras and truffles in Madeira Sauce.

Salpicon à la Montglas: foie gras, pickled tongue, mushrooms, and truffles in Madeira Sauce.

The list could go on and on.

SALT

This mineral is used ubiquitously in cooking, not only for its seasoning, but for other duties it performs as well.

It is known that our blood contains salt in the same proportion as sea water, not the sea water of today, but sea water as it is reliably estimated to have been when the first creature lumbered up out of the sea to seek its fortune on dry land. We both crave and need salt.

Salt as seasoning is familiar to all. Some people like more salt than others. Salt provokes thirst.

Salt is also a flavor enhancer, and the merest pinch added to a dish or a sauce gives point and emphasis to other flavors in the dish or sauce. Also, even when present below the level of detection, salt contributes to fullness of flavor by subliminally activating the salt taste receptors in the mouth.

Salt attracts water. When sprinkled on the surface of meat, it draws moisture from the meat, thus drying and preserving it. Sprinkled on slices of eggplant or cucumber, it draws bitter liquids out of these vegetables.

Salt dissolves entirely in water. It is used in cooking water, not only for its seasoning, but for its tendency to equalize the osmotic pressure between the water and the food being cooked in it. Cooking water is usually salted with 1½ teaspoons of salt per quart, or about 1 percent. Too salty water (a brine) will draw moisture from the food and dry it. Pure water tends to penetrate the food and dilute its juices and flavor.

The salt most commonly available is the highly refined, free-pouring salt. Preferred for good cooking is sea salt. It comes in coarse crystals (*gros sel*) for grinding in your own salt mill. Both mills and sea salt are available in specialty food stores.

SALT PORK (*Porc Salé*)

Salt pork is frequently mentioned in this book because fresh pork back fat, from which salt pork is made, is usually unavailable. When using salt pork be certain it is not old. Smell it; it must not be rancid. Blanch* the salt pork in fresh water for 5 minutes or more to freshen it and remove the salt.

SPICED SALT

This is a combination of salt, pepper, and spices used especially for seasoning Forcemeats.

To make spiced salt: thoroughly mix ¼ teaspoon each of powdered bay leaf, thyme, cloves, cinnamon, nutmeg, ginger, mace, and coriander; ¾ teaspoon mixed black and white pepper; a pinch of cayenne; and 3 tablespoons salt. Seal tightly and keep dry.

This small quantity will allow you to adjust the recipe to suit your taste. You may wish to add more or less salt, or you may wish to leave out the ginger and add more herbs, such as sage, rosemary, or sweet marjoram. To retain authenticity, however, this seasoning should be kept characteristically warm with pepper and the allspice flavoring of cinnamon, nutmeg, and cloves. Its taste can be properly appreciated only when cooked with a forcemeat, adding from 1 to 2 teaspoons per pound.

STUFFINGS

Stuffings and dressings for meat and poultry are called forcemeats (*farces*) in the French language of cooking, whether or not they contain meat. For stuffings with and without meat, see Forcemeats in this chapter.

SUBRICS

Subrics are various *Salpicons,* bound with egg as for a Croquette mixture, and sautéed in Clarified Butter or butter and oil. They are not coated. They are spooned into the pan and shaped while they are cooking into small, regular patties.

TAPIOCA

Tapioca is a white starch product available in tiny round balls (pearl tapioca) or granules (minute tapioca). It is used for thickening consommés and puddings.

Consommés are often thickened with minute tapioca because the tapioca, being partially cooked during processing, requires a minimum of additional cooking. Also, its flavor is very bland and the thickened consommé remains clear.

Tapioca has about 1½ times the thickening power of flour. Thus, you will obtain equal thickening from 1 tablespoon flour, or 2 teaspoons minute tapioca, or 1½ teaspoons arrowroot or cornstarch.

TART (*Tarte*)

This is an open-faced pastry usually filled with fruit. Tarts, large and small, are baked in rings about ¾-inch high, placed on flat baking sheets. Tarts are also called *flans* and may be filled with savory mixtures. *Quiche Lorraine*, for example, is a custard tart or flan with bacon and sometimes Gruyère cheese.

TARTLETS (*Tartelettes*)

These are small, round pastry cases with plain or fluted sides, filled with sweet fillings for a dessert or with savory Purées or *Salpicons* for a garnish, small entree, or as hors d'oeuvres. They are made and filled exactly like *Barquettes,* from which they differ only in shape. Tartlet molds are available at kitchen specialty shops.

TERRINES

A terrine is a *pâté* without a crust, baked in an oval or rectangular pottery dish called a terrine. Terrines are always served cold, as an hors d'oeuvre or luncheon entree.

To make a terrine: prepare a meat mixture exactly as you would for a *Pâté.* Use a heavy pottery dish or casserole with vertical sides and a cover. Line the dish with thin sheets of pork fat (see Bards). Arrange the meat mixture inside and cover with a sheet of pork fat. Cover tightly and bake the terrine *en bain marie,** set in a pan of boiling water in a 350° oven. Allow about 30 minutes per pound of meat mixture. The terrine is cooked when the fat puddling on its top has become perfectly clear.

Uncover the terrine, place a weight on it to compress the mixture, and allow it to cool to room temperature and reabsorb its own fat. Then chill it, still weighted, for about 12 hours.

You may serve the terrine as is, cutting slices right from the dish. Or you may remove its shell of pork fat and replace it with Aspic jelly. To accomplish this, unmold the terrine by first dipping the dish in hot water. Clean the dish, cover the bottom with a layer of aspic, and chill it. Remove the pork fat from the meat, return it to the dish, cover with aspic, and chill.

TIMBALES

Timbales are pastry shells with a savory filling. Timbales are also Purées mixed with egg, put into straight-sided molds, and cooked *en bain marie.* And timbales are deep serving dishes, both large and small (single-serving size), in which soft, rather liquid foods are served, such as creamed vegetables. Edible timbales are of course preferred. Timbales are named for Arab drums that they resemble in shape, the classic timbale being in the shape of a cylinder that is taller than it is broad. Large timbales usually come with a cover. Small timbales are usually open, like Tartlets, and their surface is garnished. They are filled with *Salpicons* and other mixtures, are made from Short Paste, may be elaborately decorated, and are usually baked empty (blind) and filled just before serving.

To form a timbale: on a floured board, roll out a ¼-inch-thick circle of Short Paste of sufficient size to completely cover the mold you are using. You may use a charlotte, *dariole,* or timbale mold or any other straight-sided mold. Dust the circle of pastry with flour, lightly fold it in half, then fold it again in quarters. Gently stretch the center of the dough (where the folds meet), so as to give it a bowl shape. Liberally butter the sides and bottom of the mold and fit the dough into it, pressing it into the bottom first and then up the sides until it lines the mold snugly. (Prior to lining the sides, you may stick small cutouts of pastry to the sides of the mold as decoration. Leaf shapes are popular because they are easy to make. The pastry dough is then pressed over the decorations, which will show when the pastry case is unmolded.)

Trim the overhanging dough with scissors, allowing about 1 inch to overhang the sides. Decorate this with a pastry wheel, or by adroit pinching or dazzling knife work.

Now, line the mold with waxed or buttered paper and fill it with dried peas or beans so that it will hold its shape. If you desire a cover, roll out another circle of dough, cut it to fit the top of the mold, heap the peas or beans into a dome, cover them with a circle of buttered paper, and lay the cover on top. The rim of the cover is decorated with a pastry wheel or by pinching, and its surface is embellished with artful pastry cutouts. Also, cut 3 or 4 circles of pastry, each slightly larger than the other, moisten their surfaces to fix them together, and afix them to the top of the cover to form a knob.

Paint the cover and rim with egg beaten with water and bake the case in a 400° oven until it is a good golden-brown. Remove the beans from the case, paint the inside with egg-and-water, and allow it to dry in the turned-off oven.

Just before serving, unmold the timbale and fill it with an excellent *Salpicon.*

Large timbales are entrees for several people. Small timbales are served as hot hors d'oeuvres, and they may be covered with an appropriate sauce.

Small timbales are also made without pastry. The buttered molds are lined with Forcemeat, soft cooked rice, or a spiral layer of cooked macaroni, which is then spread with forcemeat. Before lining the molds, they may be decorated with tongue or truffles, sliced or finely diced. The molds are filled, then placed in a pan of boiling water and baked in a 350° oven for 15 to 20 minutes.

Timbales are always served unmolded.

TONGUE (*Langue*)

Pickled or scarlet tongue (*langue d'écarlate*), soaked in brine and saltpeter to preserve it and give it its handsome red color, is a frequently used garnish both edible and decorative. It can be purchased cooked in specialty food stores and delicatessens and is frequently available pickled but uncooked at the supermarket. To cook pickled tongue, simply poach in water. For cooking fresh tongue see Chapter 10.

TOURTE

A *tourte* is a double crust pie, such as American apple pie, made with flaky Short Paste.

TRUFFLES (*Truffes*)

This highly aromatic fungus is found only in parts of France and Italy. Its flavor and perfume are exceptional; it has a taste all its own.

Truffles grow underground and are sniffed out by specially trained pigs and dogs. Unfortunately, they lose their fragrance soon after they are removed from their native earth, and they must be consumed quickly or canned.

The French black truffle of Périgord is considered the finest of truffles.

It is available here canned and it is very expensive. The Italian white truffle, or Piedmont truffle, is usually eaten raw. It has a slight garlic flavor.

It is sometimes suggested that mushrooms be used in place of truffles when these are unavailable. This is all right, but the flavor of the dish will have no resemblance to that which is intended. If you have recourse to this expedient, you may more closely approximate the eerie flavor of truffle by using imported mushrooms.

TURNOVERS (*Chaussons*)

These are pastries made with round or square pieces of Puff Pastry, which are folded over to encase a filling and baked. Turnovers are usually filled with fruit, but savory fillings are also used.

VINEGAR (*Vinaigre*)

Good vinegar is really necessary, and you should make it a point to evaluate the flavor of all the vinegars available to you. For cooking and salads, the preferred vinegar is wine vinegar—red or white—rather than the malt or cider vinegars.

To help you in evaluating vinegars, I strongly suggest you try red and white wine vinegars imported from Orléans, France.

Vinegar may be flavored by steeping a fresh herb in it, frequently tarragon.

VOL-AU-VENTS

These are large pastry cases made with Puff Paste, baked free-standing and empty, filled with a *Salpicon,* and served as an elegant entree.

To make a vol-au-vent: roll out puff paste ¾ inch thick. Cut out an 8-inch round of paste and place it top side down on a baking sheet moistened with water. (You may use pot covers as guides to give you these approximate dimensions.) Cut out another 8-inch round of paste, and remove a 6-inch circle from its center, giving you a ring of paste with a 1-inch-wide rim. Brush a 1-inch border of cold water on the surface of the round, and press the ring of dough onto it, top side down. With the back of a knife, make diagonal scores all around the outside of the vol-au-vent case, thereby decorating it and helping lock the two pieces of dough together. Using a sharp knife, reach down inside the case and trace a circle around the inside ring, cutting halfway through the bottom round of dough. Prick the bottom all over with a fork and chill the case in the refrigerator for 30 minutes or more.

You may use the cover formed in the bottom of the case. Or you may bake a separate cover, using an 8-inch round of paste rolled out ¼ inch thick. Decoratively scallop the edges, prick all over with a fork, affix scraps of dough cut in fancy shapes to its top, and chill in the refrigerator for 30 minutes or more.

To bake, brush the *top edge only* of the case and *top only* of the cover with 1 whole egg beaten with 1 tablespoon water. Bake in a 425° oven for 10 or 15 minutes, until the shell is puffed and lightly browned. Lower the heat to 375° and bake for 20 to 30 minutes more, until the case is fully puffed, crisp, and golden brown. While cooling on a rack, reach down inside the case and remove any uncooked dough at the bottom of the case.

You may keep the case warm in a low oven for several hours, to be filled just before serving. Or you may wrap the case in foil and freeze it, warming and crisping it in a hot oven for a few minutes just before you fill it.

Fill the case with an elegant *Salpicon,* and serve it crisp and steaming with its cover set artistically askew.

WINE

Use only good dry wines for cooking. Of the imported French wines, the most substantial are the reds and whites of Burgundy. The red and whites of Bordeaux are lighter, longer-lived, and less expensive. The best California wines are given the varietal names of the grapes from which they are made. Thus, in place of a red Burgundy choose Pinot Noir; in place of white Burgundy choose Pinot Chardonnay or Pinot Blanc. In place of red Bordeaux choose Cabernet Sauvignon; in place of white Bordeaux choose a dry Semillon or Sauvignon Blanc.

Also in cooking you will need aromatic fortified wines, which are used as a final flavoring for many soups and sauces. You should have on hand imported Madeira, from the Madeira Islands; port, from the Douro Valley of Portugal; and a dry sherry from Spain. These wines are used in small amounts.

Finally, keep on hand a bottle of good brandy, preferably French cognac.

❦ 5 *Appetizers*

Not too long ago the appetizer for all well-ordered dinners was soup, a sparkling consommé or smooth cream soup, the character of which prepared the palate for the courses to follow. This pre-eminent position was assailed by the hors d'oeuvre, the dish "outside the main work." As a first course, the hors d'oeuvre, both hot and cold, was admitted to light luncheon menus readily enough. But when the vulgar suggested that hors d'oeuvres might become the first course of a dinner, all hell broke loose.

For a while the issue was in doubt. Admitted to dinner were certain elegant cold hors d'oeuvres, namely caviar, *foie gras,* oysters, or smoked salmon, *but only if the soup were omitted*. The purists insisted that anything, anything at all, taken first would spoil the flavor of the soup. And, of course, they were absolutely right. They lost their battle, nevertheless.

I recount all this only to emphasize what a dinner hors d'oeuvre must do. To stand in place of a soup, it must perform like a soup. It must stimulate the appetite without filling, and must therefore be small, light, well seasoned, and not rich. It must reflect the nature of the dinner to follow, and therefore must be in character with it. Finally, it must be eaten at the table with a fork.

Today, if a dinner hors d'oeuvre does not replace the soup, it may precede or follow it. This last is a happy solution, since it allows the flavor of the soup to stand unsullied. It also provides a *petite entrée,* thus entering into the spirit of traditional dinners in which a greater number of courses were offered.

Larousse Gastronomique lists more than six hundred hors d'oeuvres, so it is not difficult to observe the few rules regarding their use. Do not use in an hors d'oeuvre any food that is served during the meal; do not serve stuffed tomatoes if tomatoes are used as a garnish. Also, do not anticipate any flavor that will be used during the meal; do not set out with a curry of shrimp if you are to arrive at curried lamb. Keep the portions small and the foods well seasoned but light, particularly at dinners. Choose the hors d'oeuvre in keeping with the character of the meal; you do not serve a caviar before a *pot-au-feu.* Finally, no matter how simple the hors d'oeuvre, take as much care in its preparation as you would in preparing a perfect consommé.

Luncheon hors d'oeuvres, which are a first course, are similar to dinner hors d'oeuvres. However, they may be several in number and somewhat more substantial if the main luncheon dish itself is light. If you are serving a variety of appetizers (*hors-d'oeuvres variés*), it is traditional to include something fresh, something meaty, something salty, and something moist and smooth, such as raw vegetables, ham, anchovies, and eggs in a smooth white sauce. Luncheon hors d'oeuvres are served hot or cold to vary the menu; if the main dish is cold, you would serve at least one hot hors d'oeuvre. It, also, is eaten at the table with a fork.

Other kinds of hors d'oeuvres are those one gets with cocktails. Canapés, dips, olives, celery sticks with cheese, marinated mushrooms, raw or broiled, and other foods eaten with the fingers or skewers are characteristic of this kind of appetizer. Many of these preparations are smaller versions of dinner and luncheon hors d'oeuvres, adapted to eating with the fingers.

Hors d'oeuvres are an essential part of French family meals. These small extra pleasures, at luncheon or dinner, contribute to the variety of tastes the French so much enjoy. The hors d'oeuvre may be something picked up at the sausage shop and served with a slice of melon. It may be a little leftover fish, warmed in cream sauce and served in a tartlet crust. Or it may be yesterday's leftover vegetables, marinated. Hors d'oeuvres like these are delightful to eat and equally delightful to make. Most likely, right now in your refrigerator there is the wherewithal to make a half-dozen perfect hors d'oeuvre dishes.

Hors d'oeuvres embrace the entire range of foods and cooking, and dozens of recipes throughout this book may be used to create them. You may invent an infinite number of hors d'oeuvres of your own, being limited only by the few general rules regarding them. Here are a few of the most popular hor d'oeuvres taken from the classic cuisine.

(Curiously enough, it is traditional to bring to the table the container in which a "bought" hors d'oeuvre is packed. Thus, at an elegant dinner, you may find among the china and the silver the tin can in which the caviar or foie gras came, complete with brand name and handsomely bedded in crushed ice.)

✳ COLD HORS D'OEUVRES

A great many table hors d'oeuvres consist simply of cold vegetables, meats, or fish, flavorfully cooked and garnished. Many of these call for Mayonnaise, and I strongly recommend that you make this fresh.

VEGETABLES À LA GRECQUE (*Légumes à la Grecque*). Artichoke hearts, and whole onions, pieces of carrot, celery, cucumber, leek, asparagus, zucchini, cauliflower, and mushroom caps are often prepared *à la grecque*. Parboil the vegetables a few minutes. Drain and cook in a Court Bouillon consisting of 2 cups water, ½ cup olive oil, the juice of 2 lemons (or 2 tablespoons vinegar), ½ teaspoon salt, 1 bay leaf, 1 sprig or pinch of thyme, a pinch of coriander seeds, a pinch of fennel seeds, and 6 peppercorns. When the vegetables are barely cooked, allow them to cool in the liquid. Chill and serve very cold, moistened with a few tablespoons of cooking liquid.

GREEN BEANS (*Haricots Verts*). Cook in salt water, drain, and cut in dice. Season with Mayonnaise or Vinaigrette.

MUSHROOMS (*Champignons*). Cut cooked mushrooms in dice. Season with Mayonnaise or Vinaigrette.

SWEET PEPPERS (*Piments Doux*). Peel the peppers. (To do this you must first put them under the broiler, turning them frequently until the skin is blistered and lightly browned.) Clean out the seeds and thick ribs, and cut the peppers into thin strips (julienne*). Season with Vinaigrette, sprinkle with chopped parsley, and garnish with thin raw onion rings.

TOMATOES À L'AMÉRICANE (*Tomates à l'Américaine*). Peel and thinly slice firm tomatoes. Sprinkle with Vinaigrette and let them stand for at least 20 minutes. Garnish with thin raw onion rings.

TOMATOES À LA VINAIGRETTE (*Tomates à la Vinaigrette*). Peel and seed the tomatoes, coring and squeezing the jelly out of them. Cut in quarters, sprinkle with salt, and allow the salt to draw out their moisture for 1 hour. Drain the tomatoes, and sprinkle them with oil, vinegar, pepper, chopped parsley, chopped chervil, and chopped tarragon. Garnish with thin raw onion slices.

CELERY À LA BONNE FEMME (*Céleri à la Bonne Femme*). Finely mince equal amounts of celery and peeled apples. To a few tablespoons of prepared mustard, add a little salt, pepper, and lemon juice. Beat in fresh cream—little by little—until the sauce is light. Mix this sauce into the celery and apple mixture.

MARINATED MUSHROOMS (*Champignons Marinés*). Parboil small white mushrooms. Prepare a marinade with 2 cups vinegar; ½ cup olive oil; 2 cloves garlic, crushed; 3 sprigs parsley; ½ bay leaf; a sprig or pinch of thyme; 1 teaspoon coriander; a pinch of fennel; and a few peppercorns. Bring this marinade to the boil, pour over the mushrooms, and marinate for at least 6 hours, or better yet, 5 or 6 days.

MARINATED RED CABBAGE (*Chou Rouge*). Cut cabbage in fine strips and pour boiling vinegar over it. Let it marinate in the vinegar for 5 or 6 hours, drain, and season with olive oil, salt, and pepper.

TOMATOES AU NATUREL (*Tomates au Naturel*). Use small cherry tomatoes, or make small walnut-sized tomatoes from larger ones (see Tomatoes). Peel the tomatoes and twist them in a towel to squeeze out their moisture. Marinate for ½ hour in Vinaigrette. Fashion a stem and leaves with a parsley stalk and Montpellier Butter applied with a pastry bag.

SMOKED MEAT (*Viande Fumée*). Slice the meat very thinly. Trim the slices in a triangular shape, roll into cones, and garnish with parsley.

HAM (*Jambon*). Slice fine ham very thinly, trim the slices in a triangular shape, roll into cones, and garnish with parsley.

PICKLED OR SMOKED TONGUE (*Lange Écarlate ou Fumée*). Slice thinly and serve, garnished with parsley.

SALAMI. Cut in thin slices and garnish with parsley.

SAUSAGES (*Saucissons*). Slice delicatessen sausages into thin rounds and serve garnished with parsley.

CHICKEN REINE (*Salade de Volaille à la Reine*). Cut breast of poached chicken, mushrooms and truffles into dice. Season with Mayonnaise or Vinaigrette.

PÂTÉ. Serve in slices with parsley and crusty bread. In addition to a fork, provide a knife for spreading.

FOIE GRAS. An elegant hors d'oeuvre, served very simply. Either slice or shape in little balls.

OYSTERS (*Huîtres*). An elegant hors d'oeuvre, served on the half shell.

OYSTERS WITH CAVIAR (*Huîtres au Caviar*). Serve the oysters in their shells, rimmed with very black caviar. Place a slice of serrated lemon atop each oyster, and separately serve finely chopped parsley.

SMOKED SALMON. This classic and elegant hors d'oeuvre exploits the striking beauty of red salmon meat. Slice the salmon thinly and serve flat, or trim the slices in triangular shapes and serve rolled into cones. Garnish with parsley.

LOBSTER OR SHRIMP (*Homard ou Crevette*). Cut the cooked meat in dice. Season with Mayonnaise or Vinaigrette.

SHRIMP SALAD (*Salade de Crevettes*). Poach and shell the shrimp, leaving the tips of the tails on, and chill them. Dip the shrimp in Mayonnaise and arrange in a circle on a deep dish. Garnish the dish with lettuce and slices of hard-cooked egg.

TUNA FISH (*Thon*). Use fine white canned albacore packed in olive oil. Cut into dice and season with Vinaigrette or Mayonnaise.

ANCHOVIES AND HARD-COOKED EGGS (*Anchois et Oeufs Durs*). Dice filets of anchovies and mix with twice their amount of chopped hard-cooked eggs. Season with Mayonnaise or with vinegar, pepper, and chopped herbs.

CUCUMBERS STUFFED WITH VEGETABLES (*Concombres Farcis à la Printanière*). Cut peeled cucumber into 3-inch pieces, blanch a few minutes in salted water, drain, and hollow out the pieces at one end to form a small receptacle. Fill the cucumber cases with a variety of cooked diced vegetables and peas, blended in Mayonnaise. Sprinkle with oil and vinegar.

STUFFED TOMATOES (*Tomates Farcies*). Peel the tomatoes, cut a slice from their tops, and carefully empty them of their seeds and jelly. Marinate for 1 hour in Vinaigrette. Drain and fill the tomatoes with a Purée or a *Salpicon*.

STUFFED EGGS (*Oeufs Durs*). Cut hard-cooked eggs in half lengthwise. Remove the yolk and replace it with a heaped-up Purée or *Salpicon* to which you have added the mashed yolk. Cut a thin slice from the bottom of the egg halves so they will stand without rolling. Garnish with curly parsley.

EGG SALAD (*Salade d'Oeufs Durs*). Overlap sliced rounds of hard-cooked eggs in rows alternating with rows of sliced vegetables—cucumbers, tomatoes, cooked potatoes, or cooked beets. Sprinkle with Vinaigrette.

BARQUETTES AND TARTLETS (*Barquettes et Tartelettes*). These are baked pastry shells made with flaky pastry or pie dough. They are identical except for their shape, tartlets being round and barquettes being boat-shaped. They are filled with *Salpicons* of fish, chicken, or vegetables; with Purées; with marinated fish or vegetables; with poached shrimp, mussels, or oysters; with sausages; with caviar or *foie gras;* or with any other cold hors d'oeuvre preparation. Decorate the tops of filled barquettes or tartlets with capers, diced aspic, chopped herbs, chopped hard-cooked eggs, or thin strips of lettuce. (See Barquettes, Tartlets.)

SMALL GARNISHED BRIOCHES (*Brioches Mignonnes Garnies*). Cut the top from a small brioche or soft dinner roll and scoop it out. Fill as you would a Barquette or Tartlet.

CAROLINES. These are unsweetened Éclairs filled with Purées of fish, shell-fish, poultry, game, or *foie gras.* Coat with Chaud-Froid Sauce and glaze* with Aspic.

PROFITEROLES. These are unsweetened round Éclairs and may be prepared as for Carolines (above). Also, the top may be cut from the *profiterole.* It may then be filled, and the rim decorated with finely chopped hard-cooked egg or parsley. The cover is then replaced so it only half covers the contents of the profiterole and its decorative border.

MELON WITH PORT (*Melon au Porto*). Cut a round plug from the stem end of a sweet, ripe melon and remove the seeds. Put 1 cup port wine into the melon, replace the plug, and chill thoroughly. Usually, the melon is brought to the table whole, and the flesh of the melon scooped out in shell-like pieces. The pieces are served with a few tablespoons of the wine spooned over them.

✳ HOT HORS D'OEUVRES

ATTEREAUX. These dishes are cooked on skewers. Small pieces of cooked food are impaled on skewers, coated with a thick sauce, chilled, coated *à l'anglaise,** and deep-fried. They are then drained and served on or off the skewers.

ATTEREAUX OF BRAIN À LA MIREPOIX (*Attereaux de Cervelle à la Mirepoix*). Alternate on the skewer pieces of poached brain and cubes of ham. Coat with a fine *Mirepoix* blended with Villeroi Sauce.

ATTEREAUX OF CHICKEN LIVERS À LA DUXELLES (*Attereaux de Foies de Volaille à la Duxelles*). Alternate on the skewer sautéed chicken livers with mushrooms. Coat with Duxelles Sauce.

ATTEREAUX OF OYSTERS (*Attereaux d'Huîtres*). Alternate on the skewer poached oysters and mushrooms. Coat with Villeroi Sauce made with Fish Fumet.

ATTEREAUX OF VEGETABLES (*Attereaux de Légumes*). Impale on the skewer one or more cooked vegetables—artichokes, potatoes, carrots, squash, etc. Coat with Béchamel Sauce.

INDIVIDUAL CASSEROLES or CASSOLETTES (*Cassolettes*). These are small, ovenproof dishes filled with hot *Salpicons* or Purées or other mixtures suitable for Barquettes and Tartlets. They are usually decorated with a border of Duchess Potatoes, sprinkled with butter and grated cheese or breadcrumbs, and glazed* in the oven.

OYSTERS CASINO. For 12 oysters, finely chop ¼ green bell pepper and 1 small shallot. Simmer gently in 2 tablespoons dry white wine until tender, and cool. Meanwhile, cut bacon slices into 12 1-inch squares and parboil for 5 minutes. To the cooled mixture add ¼ pound room-temperature butter, 1 tablespoon finely chopped red pimento, white pepper and salt to taste, and mix. (Take care in adding the salt, because oysters are already more or less salty.) Open 12 oysters and place them in their deep shells on a bed of coarse salt in an ovenproof serving dish. Spoon a little of the butter mixture over each oyster, and top with a square of parboiled bacon. Bake in a 450° oven for 5 to 10 minutes, until the bacon is crisp. Serve with wedges of lemon.

GRILLED OYSTERS. Open the oysters, place them in their deep shells, and put the shells on a bed of coarse salt in an ovenproof serving dish. Sprinkle with lemon juice and fresh-ground pepper, and bake in a 400° oven for 8 to 10 minutes or until the oysters are cooked through.

GARNISHED SCALLOP SHELLS (*Coquilles Garnies*). These are scallop shells (or similarly sized and shaped dishes), rimmed with a border of Duchess Potatoes piped through a pastry bag and brushed with egg, and filled with hot *Salpicons* or other cooked foods in sauce. They are frequently glazed.*

SCALLOP SHELLS OF EGGS AU GRATIN (*Coquilles d'Oeufs au Gratin*). Border the shells with Duchess Potatoes brushed with egg. Fill with hard-cooked eggs cut in large dice and Mornay Sauce, sprinkle with grated Parmesan cheese and melted butter, and glaze.*

SCALLOP SHELLS OF POULTRY À L'ALLEMANDE (*Coquilles de Volaille à l'Allemande*). Border the shells with Duchess Potatoes brushed with egg. Fill with slices of cooked breast of chicken and Allemande Sauce. Sprinkle with grated Parmesan cheese and melted butter, and glaze.*

SCALLOP SHELLS OF SHRIMP (*Coquilles de Crevettes*). Border the shells with Duchess Potatoes brushed with egg. Fill with shrimp in Béchamel or Velouté Sauce. Sprinkle with grated Parmesan cheese and melted butter, and glaze.*

BARQUETTES AND TARTLETS (*Barquettes et Tartelettes*). These are the same preparations as discussed under cold hors d'oeuvres. They are, of course, served hot, and are usually glazed* in the oven.

BARQUETTES WITH MIXED VEGETABLES (*Barquettes à la Bouquetière*). Fill the barquettes with mixed vegetables in Velouté or Béchamel Sauce. Decorate with asparagus tips.

BARQUETTES WITH OYSTERS (*Barquettes d'Huîtres*). Fill the barquettes with poached oysters in Oyster Sauce and glaze* in the oven.

BARQUETTES WITH SHRIMPS (*Barquettes de Crevettes*). Fill the barquettes with cooked shrimp meats in Mornay Sauce, sprinkle with grated Parmesan cheese and melted butter, and glaze* in the oven.

QUICHES. These are savory custards of cream and eggs, mixed with a flavoring food and baked in a tartlet shell. These can be made in large sizes, or small single-serving sizes. The dough, which is the same dough used for Barquettes and Tartlets, is filled when only half baked. Its baking is completed along with the ingredients of the *quiche*.

QUICHE LORRAINE. Cut 3 or 4 slices of lean bacon in short strips ¼ inch wide. Parboil for 2 minutes, sauté lightly, and put in the bottom of a half-baked 9-inch pastry shell. Beat 3 eggs with 1½ cups heavy cream, ½ teaspoon of salt, ¼ teaspoon of white pepper, and a pinch of nutmeg. Pour into the pastry shell, dot with butter, and bake in a 350° oven for 30 minutes, or until the *quiche* is cooked and brown.

LITTLE QUICHES WITH HAM (*Petites Quiches au Jambon*). Follow the recipe for Quiche Lorraine (above), using single-serving sized pastry shells and replacing the bacon with ham.

LITTLE QUICHES WITH CHEESE (*Petites Quiches au Fromage*). Follow the recipe for Quiche Lorraine (above), using single-serving pastry shells and replacing the bacon with small strips of Gruyère (Swiss) cheese.

SMALL GARNISHED BRIOCHES (*Brioches Mignonnes Garnies*). Cut the top from a small brioche or soft dinner roll and scoop it out. Fill with a hot *Salpicon* of poultry, fish, or vegetables, as you would a Barquette or Tartlet. Reheat in the oven.

PUFFS (*Choux*). These are puffs made with ordinary Puff Paste, filled with Purées or *Salpicons,* and reheated briefly in the oven.

PUFFS WITH CHEESE (*Choux au Fromage*). Fill the puffs with thick Béchamel Sauce blended with Gruyère, Parmesan, or another cheese.

PUFFS À LA MARAÎCHÈRE (*Choux à la Maraîchère*). Fill the puffs with a *Salpicon* of carrots, celery, and the white part of leeks, simmered in butter and blended with a thick Béchamel Sauce.

PUFFS À LA STRASBOURGEOISE (*Choux à la Strasbourgeoise*). Fill the puffs with a *Salpicon* of *foie gras* and truffles in thick Demi-Glace Sauce.

PUFFS AU VERT-PRÉ (*Coux au Vert-Pré*). Fill the puffs with a Purée of green beans mixed with cooked peas, asparagus tips, and cream.

LITTLE CROQUETTES (*Petits Croquettes*). These consist of a *Salpicon* or Croquette mixture, chilled, shaped in a variety of forms, dipped in flour, egg, and breadcrumbs, and deep-fried until golden brown.

KROMESKIES (*Cromesquis*). These are Croquette mixtures, Forcemeats or Mousseline Forcemeats, chilled, formed in the shape of bottle corks or small loaves, dipped in flour and a Batter, and deep-fried. They are garnished with Fried Parsley.

FRITTERS (*Beignets*). These are bite-size pieces of cooked meat, fish, poultry, or vegetables, marinated in oil and vinegar or lemon juice, dipped in a Batter, and deep-fried.

SOUFFLÉ FRITTERS (*Beignets Soufflés*). These are little balls or olive-shaped nuggets of Cream Puff Paste which are deep-fried. Flavoring foods such as chopped ham, anchovy, or onion are added to the dough, or a pastry bag is used to stuff the puffs with a flavorful filling.

SOUFFLÉ FRITTERS WITH CHEESE (*Beignets Soufflés au Fromage*). For every 1 cup of Puff Paste mix in ⅓ cup grated Parmesan cheese.

SUBRICS. These consist of diced meat or fish or vegetables, mixed with beaten egg and Béchamel Sauce, and sautéed in butter. They are not dipped in bread-crumbs.

BEEF SUBRICS À LA MÉNAGÈRE (*Subrics de Boeuf à la Ménagère*). To 1½ cups diced boiled beef, add 2 eggs beaten with ½ cup grated Gruyère (Swiss) cheese, 1 tablespoon flour, salt, and pepper. Mix well. Sauté the subrics in Clarified Butter, spooning them into the pan and shaping them, and turning them to cook on both sides. Serve with Tomato Sauce.

SPINACH SUBRICS (*Subrics à la Florentine*). Combine cooked, chopped, and dried spinach with Béchamel Sauce and grated Parmesan cheese. Sauté in butter.

LITTLE SOUFFLÉS (*Petits Soufflés*). Bake individual serving-size soufflés. (See Chapter 7).

6 *Soups Polite and Raucous*

"France is one great soup tureen."
ALEXANDRE DUMAS

France is a land of soups both polite and raucous, both thick and thin. Whether the soup is a small cup of clear consommé, a flavor with which to stage a meal, or whether the soup is a great feast in itself, it is always carefully made. Only the finest and freshest ingredients to be had are put into the pot and balanced to achieve a planned taste. Far from being a haphazard process, soup making is the *highest* expression of culinary art. For when we make soups, we make *new* tastes from the fresh, natural tastes of foods as they are. Discovering these tastes is the great reward of making your own soup.

THE ORDER OF SOUPS

There are three kinds of French soups, classified according to the way they are made and the way they appear in the soup plate. This little outline will help you to place them all in your mind.

1. Clear Soups (Consommés)
2. Thick Soups
    (a) Purées, including:
        (1) Purées of vegetables
        (2) Cullises of poultry, fish, or game
        (3) Bisques of shellfish
    (b) Veloutés
    (c) Creams
3. Family Soups

The first two kinds of soup are aristocrats and are regularly invited to great dinners. Family soups, although proudly served at many *haut monde* restaurants, and with a lineage centuries older than the others, are never admitted to great affairs. They are none the less excellent for that.

The making of all these soups embraces two contradictory goals of cooking in liquid. Is the flavor to be retained in the food being cooked? Or should the flavor of the food be transferred to the liquid it is cooked in? In making stock for clear soups, we simmer slowly and lengthily to extract as much flavor as possible from the meat and vegetables being cooked.

Thick soups, on the other hand, are a blend of both the food and the liquid it is cooked in. Consequently the cooking time for thick soups depends upon the nature of the food itself. (Texture doesn't matter since the food is puréed.) Potatoes, peas, cucumbers, fish, shellfish, and chicken are cooked briefly to retain the freshness or delicacy of their flavor. Stronger-flavored or acid foods, such as tomatoes, carrots, cauliflower, Brussels sprouts, green beans, and celery, are simmered slowly to mellow them and develop their maximum cooked flavor.

Family soups, which are usually both meat and drink, are cooked in a variety of ways according to their content and the method of their assembly. For a student of cookery, they are perhaps the most fascinating food of all.

✳ CLEAR SOUPS OR CONSOMMÉS
(Les Potages Clairs)

At one time, consommé was a white stock made from unbrowned beef, poultry, fish, or game. This stock, clarified, was the basis of all clear soups served with or without garnishes. Consequently, clear soups are themselves called consommés. The clarified consommés or clear soups were flavorful, transparent, and almost colorless.

Today, consommé has come to mean any stock that is clarified, whether it is browned or not. The liquid is flavorful and transparent, but it may have color. In fact, the skins of shallots are sometimes added to white stock to give the finished consommé a color as rich and golden as a field of North Dakota wheat. Consommé also has body, obtained from the gelatin in the bones that are one of its ingredients. In Chapter 4, you will find the recipes for Beef Consommé and Chicken Consommé and their clarification, as well as recipes for Brown Stock, Veal Stock, and Chicken Stock, which are, as I have said, also clarified to become consommé.

Consommés, or clear soups, are served in cups or in bowls. Cups of consommé (for light suppers) are drunk at the table and usually contain no garnish. Bowls of consommé (for dinners) are variously garnished and are eaten with a spoon. When served hot these soups should be served very, very hot in heated cups or bowls. When served cold, they should have the consistency of a tender jelly that is just about to melt and does melt almost instantly in the mouth.

CONSOMMÉS WITH GARNISHES
(*Consommés Garnis*)

A cup or bowl of well-made consommé is a fine way to begin a dinner. It is very simple, very good. However, this limpid, flavorful liquid is a great temptation for the creative chef. "How empty, how forlorn that little bowl looks," he mutters to himself. "It is wanting something, and I must discover what it is." Prompted by natural instincts, urged on by the jaded diners of the *haut monde,* adding a spoonful of this and a sprinkle of that, chefs have filled the little bowl with a bewildering variety of garnishes.

These garnishes range from a simple handful of pasta cooked in the consommé to elaborate additions calling for a spoonful of eight or ten different preparations. These elaborate garnishes belong to old-time restaurant cooking; the sheer work that goes into them can be put to better uses in the home kitchen. Also, *consommé aux paillettes d'or* is best left to the restaurant. It calls for a sheet of gold leaf to be cut into spangles and added to the consommé.

There are, however, many traditional garnishes that can be made with little fuss and that add variety to a simple consommé. They are usually cooked separately. They include pasta; grains; fine strips of meat and vegetables; diced vegetables; shredded greens; shredded herbs; custards cut in fancy shapes (*royales*); small pastry puffs with a savory filling (*profiteroles*); French pancakes cut in strips; egg white cut in fancy shapes; *quenelles;* or just a spoonful of fresh green peas.

The quantity of consommé served to each person is from ¾ to 1 cup, and the quantity of garnish required for each serving ranges from 2 to about 6 tablespoonfuls. The lesser amount is usual for the heavier garnishes, such as a julienne of chicken breast; the greater amount is usual for lighter garnishes such as diced custard. If both light and heavy garnishes are included in the consommé, the volume of the light garnish is usually twice that of the heavy garnish. It is all a matter of balance.

If the garnish is very hot it may be added to the hot consommé in the bowl. Usually it is safer to mix the garnish into the consommé and boil it briefly to heat it through. Whichever method is used, be certain to rinse the garnish under hot running water to free it of any fat or butter used in cooking it.

Finally, consommés are sometimes thickened with tapioca or with arrowroot starch to give them greater body without stickiness. About 3 teaspoons of minute tapioca or about 2 teaspoons arrowroot added to 4 cups of consommé will give the very light consistency required. When using tapioca, as soon as the thickening has occurred, the consommé should be strained through a very fine sieve.

Here is a selection of classic clear soups from the more than two hundred available.

Consommé aux Cheveux d'Ange. Garnish the consummé with very fine poached vermicelli. Serve with grated Parmesan cheese.

Consommé à l'Orge Perle. Garnish the consommé with pearl barley.

Consommé au Riz. Garnish the consommé with rice. Serve with grated Parmesan cheese.

Consommé au Tapioca. Garnish the consommé with cooked tapioca. Serve with grated Parmesan cheese.

Consommé aux Nouilles. Garnish the consommé with noodles. Serve with grated Parmesan cheese.

Consommé aux Oeufs Pochés. Garnish the consommé with one very small poached egg per serving.

Consommé Balzac. Garnish the consommé with a dice of shrimp, small turnip balls, and green peas.

Consommé Vert-Pré. Thicken the consommé with tapioca. Garnish with asparagus tips, green beans cut in bits, peas, poached shredded lettuce and sorrel, and shreds of chervil.

Consommé Rachel. Thicken chicken consommé with topioca. Garnish with a julienne* of artichoke hearts. Separately serves slices of poached beef Marrow on rounds of crustless bread sautéed in butter.

Consommé Olga. Flavor consommé with ½ cup port wine per quart. Garnish with a julienne* of celeriac, carrots, the white part of leeks, and salted gherkins.

Consommé Aurore. Thicken consommé with tapioca and Tomato Purée. Garnish with julienne* of chicken breast.

Consommé Belle Fermière. Garnish the consommé with cut green beans, julienne* of cabbage, and pasta cut in small pieces.

Consommé Bouquetière. Thicken chicken consommé with tapioca. Garnish with carrot and turnip balls, sliced green beans, asparagus tips, and green peas.

Consommé Brunoise. Garnish the consommé with carrots, turnips, leeks, celery, onions, and green beans cut in small dice; and green peas. Sprinkle with shredded chervil.

Consommé Favori. Thicken chicken consommé with tapioca. Garnish with small potato balls, julienne* of mushrooms and artichoke hearts, and shredded chervil.

Consommé à la Crécy. Thicken chicken consommé with tapioca. Garnish with shredded cooked carrots and chervil.

Consommé Princess Alice. Thicken chicken consommé with tapioca. Garnish with shredded lettuce, julienne* of artichoke hearts, vermicelli cooked in stock, and shredded chervil.

Consommé Printanière. Garnish the consommé with carrot and turnip cut into tiny ½-inch sticks, string beans cut into bits, peas, asparagus tips, and shredded lettuce, sorrel, and chervil.

Consommé à la Basquaise. Garnish chicken consommé with cooked diced tomatoes, julienne* of sweet pimentos, rice, and shredded chervil.

Consommé Dalayrac. Thicken chicken consommé with tapioca. Garnish with a julienne* of chicken breast, mushrooms, and truffles.

Consommé Florette. Thicken chicken consommé with tapioca. Garnish with a julienne* of leeks cooked in butter and with rice. Serve with whipped cream and grated Parmesan cheese.

Consommé Niçoise. Flavor consommé during clarification with 1 tablespoon Tomato Purée per cup. Garnish with diced potatoes, diced tomatoes, sliced green beans, and shreds of chervil.

Consommé à la Colbert. Garnish chicken consommé with a variety of cooked, shredded spring vegetables and a very small poached egg per serving. Sprinkle with a little shredded chervil.

Consommé aux Quenelles. Garnish the consommé with small Quenelles of chicken or other forcemeat.

Consommé Sévigné. Garnish chicken consommé with chicken Quenelles, small slices of braised lettuce, peas, and shreds of chervil.

Consommé Montmorency. Thicken chicken consommé with tapioca. Garnish with chicken Quenelles, asparagus tips, rice, and shreds of chervil.

Consommé Grande Duchesse. Garnish chicken consommé with julienne* of chicken breast, chicken Quenelles, julienne* of tongue, and asparagus tips.

Consommé Francillon. Garnish chicken consommé with chicken Quenelles and one very small poached egg per serving.

Consommé Alexandra. Thicken chicken consommé with tapioca. Garnish with chicken Quenelles, julienne* of chicken breast,. and shredded lettuce.

Consommé Princesse. Thicken chicken consommé with tapioca. Garnish with small chicken Quenelles, asparagus tips, and shredded chervil.

Consommé à la Royale. Thicken chicken consommé with tapioca. Garnish with Royales cut in interesting shapes, and shredded chervil.

Consommé Du Barry. Thicken the consommé with tapioca. Garnish with rounds of Royale, cauliflowerets, and shredded chervil.

Consommé à la Reine. Thicken chicken consommé with tapioca. Garnish with diced Royale made with chicken Purée and julienne* of chicken.

Consommé Grimaldi. Flavor consommé during clarification with 1 tablespoon Tomato Purée per cup. Garnish with Royale cut in dice and julienne* of celery.

Consommé à la Flamande. Garnish the consommé with diced Royale made with a Purée of Brussels sprouts, green peas, and shredded chervil.

Consommé Leverrier. Thicken chicken consommé with tapioca. Garnish with a variety of Royales cut in star shapes, and shredded chervil.

Onion Soups, clockwise from the top, au Porto, à l'Oignon, Soufflé, and Gratinée

Le Soufflé

Lobster à la Nage

Consommé à l'Infante. Thicken chicken consommé with tapioca. Garnish with julienne* of sweet pepper. Separately serve warmed Profiteroles that you have filled with a Purée of foie gras.

Consommé Blanc-Manger. Garnish chicken consommé with fresh green peas and shredded chervil. Separately serve small tartlet cases filled with minced chicken.

Consommé Florentine. Garnish chicken consommé with spun eggs (*oeufs filés*), rice, and shredded chervil. (To make spun egg threads for 1 quart of consommé: Break up but do not beat 1 egg. Strain the egg through a fine strainer directly into the boiling consommé, stirring vigorously.)

Consommé Celestine. Thicken chicken consommé with tapioca. Garnish with rounds of rolled herbed crepes stuffed with chicken forcemeat. Sprinkle with shredded chervil.

Consommé Ambassadrice. Garnish chicken consommé with diced black Royale of truffle, red Royale of tomato, and green Royale of green peas; julienne* of chicken breast; and finely minced mushrooms. This one's a beauty.

Consommé à la Madrilène. During the clarification, add 1¼ cups raw tomato chopped and sieved to 6 cups consommé. Strain and chill the consommé until it jells.

❋ THICK SOUPS
(*Potages Liés*)

Thick soups have as their flavor base specially prepared *soup purées* of vegetables, poultry, fish, shellfish, and game. This base is brought to the desired consistency (liquidity) and finished in one of three ways. Whichever way is used determines whether the soup is a purée, a velouté, or a cream soup. Many soup purées, but not all, can be finished in all three ways.

To purée a food is to divide it very finely, usually by cooking it and then forcing it through a fine sieve or processing it in a blender. In order to make soup of a purée it must be thinned with a liquid. However, the finely divided particles of a purée have a tendency to sink to the bottom of the liquid. To prevent this, we suspend these particles by thickening (binding) the purée-in-liquid mixture.

The liquids used for thinning, and the method of thickening, are the keys to understanding these soups.

You will notice that these soups present their flavors quite forthrightly. There is something about their smooth, succulent consistency that bathes the mouth with flavor, throwing it in bold relief. Thick soups provide good practice for your taste, so taste with attention and mind your seasonings.

(There is a simplified method of thick soup making, which calls for cooking or mixing the meat or vegetables of the soup in prepared bases of potato purée, split pea purée, or Chicken Velouté. The advantage is that the bases can be made in quantity and stored, and that a number of different soups can be quickly made from them. These soups are usually called "cream of . . ." whatever the main flavor is. They are usually excellent. But they are not authentic cream soups, and in most cases are either a velouté or a mixture of purée and velouté. The disadvantage of this standardized method is that a sameness may steal over all your soups—you may tire of the cream of chicken taste—and you are denied the opportunity of appreciating the differences between true creams, purées, and veloutés. I do not think a thick celery soup should necessarily have a chicken flavor, and I think the differences between these soups is the very essence of fine cookery.)

THE PURÉES

Purée soups are purées of vegetables, poultry, fish or shellfish cooked in water or stock. They are thickened by their own starch or other starchy foods combined with them. They are thinned with stock and finished with butter.

Dried beans or potatoes need no additional starch. Less starchy vegetables, such as carrots, celery, green beans, or herbs, are thickened with rice, potato, or soft bread that is cooked along with the vegetables. The food to be puréed is seasoned and cooked in the stock that is the liquid or thinning element of the soup. Food and liquid are put through a food mill or sieve together or puréed in the blender.

The purée is then thinned with stock if necessary to achieve the desired consistency, which should be that of medium cream. It is then simmered for about 20 minutes, and any froth rising to the surface is skimmed away. Just before serving, remove the soup from the fire and stir in 6 tablespoons butter per quart of soup to smooth, flavor, enrich, and give it a final bit of thickening.

Haute cuisine recognizes three kinds of purée soups. When vegetables are the flavor base, the soup is called a *purée*. When poultry, fish, or game is the flavor base, the soup is called a *cullis* (French: *coulis*). When shellfish are the flavor base, the soup is called a *bisque*. All are purée soups, thinned with stock and thickened by their own starch or other starchy foods cooked with them.

PURÉE OF TOMATO SOUP (*Potage Purée de Tomates* or *Potage Portugaise*). Prepare a *Mirepoix* of 2 tablespoons finely diced blanched bacon, ½ finely diced carrot, ½ finely diced onion, a pinch of thyme, and ¼ bay leaf, sautéed in 2 tablespoons butter until golden. Squeeze the seeds and jelly from 8 tomatoes (about 2 pounds), chop them, and add them to the mirepoix. Also add ¼ cup raw rice, a pinch of sugar, and 2 cups White Stock. Simmer for 20 to 30 minutes or until the rice is soft. Rub through a sieve or purée in the blender. Return the purée to the cleaned saucepan and add white stock if necessary to obtain a medium-cream consistency. Cover the soup and simmer, skimming occasionally, for 15 minutes more. Season to taste with salt and pepper. Off the fire, stir in ½ cup butter in pieces. Garnish with a little poached rice and diced tomatoes sautéed in butter.

PURÉE OF FRESH PEA SOUP (*Potage Purée de Pois Frais* or *Potage Saint-Germaine*). Cook 3 cups fresh green peas (or frozen peas) in boiling salted water until they are just tender (you may add a few leaves of fresh mint to the peas if this sounds good to you). Drain the peas, mash them, and mix them with 2 cups White Stock. Rub through a sieve or purée in the blender. Return the purée to the cleaned saucepan, add white stock if necessary to obtain a medium-cream consistency, and heat just until the soup boils. Season to taste with salt and pepper. Remove from the fire and stir in 6 tablespoons butter. Garnish with green peas and shredded chervil.

PURÉE OF POTATO SOUP (*Potage Purée de Pommes de Terre* or *Potage Parmentier*). Mince the white part of 2 leeks and lightly sauté them in 2 tablespoons butter. Add 3 peeled and quartered potatoes (about ¾ pound) and 2 cups White Stock. Cover and boil for 15 minutes, or until the potatoes just become soft. Rub through a sieve or purée in the blender. Return the purée to the cleaned saucepan, add milk if necessary to obtain the consistency of medium cream, and heat to boiling. Season to taste with salt and white pepper. Remove from the fire and stir in 8 tablespoons butter. Garnish with croutons sautéed in butter, and shredded chervil.

PURÉE OF BRUSSELS SPROUTS SOUP (*Potage Purée de Choux de Bruxelles* or *Potage Flamande*). Parboil 1 pound Brussels sprouts for 5 minutes and drain them. Put them in a saucepan with 6 tablespoons butter, partially cover, and simmer for 15 minutes. Add 2 medium potatoes, peeled and quartered; ½ onion, thinly sliced; ½ bay leaf; 3 sprigs parsley; and 2 cups White Stock. Cover and simmer for 20 minutes, or until the vegetables are soft. Rub through a sieve or purée in the blender. Return the purée to the cleaned saucepan, add milk (an exception to the usual addition of stock) if necessary to obtain a medium-cream consistency, simmer and skim the soup for 15 minutes more. Season to taste with salt and white pepper. Remove from the fire and stir in ½ cup butter. Garnish with croutons sautéed in butter.

LOBSTER BISQUE (*Bisque d'Homard*). Finely dice ⅓ carrot and ⅓ onion. Put the dice into a saucepan with 1 bay leaf and a pinch of thyme, and sauté until golden in 4 tablespoons butter. Cut a 3-pound live lobster (or 2 1½-pound lobsters) in small pieces, discarding the inedible parts but retaining all of the shell. Add the lobster to the saucepan and turn in the butter until the shells are bright red. Sprinkle the meat with 2 tablespoons brandy, ignite it, add ½ cup dry white wine and 2 sprigs parsley, season with salt and pepper, and cook over low heat until the liquid has almost entirely disappeared. Then add ½ cup White Stock or Fish Stock and simmer for 10 minutes. Meanwhile, cook 6 tablespoons raw rice in 3 cups white stock.

Drain the lobster pieces and vegetables, reserving the liquid. Remove and reserve the claw meat for garnishing the finished soup. Grind and pound together the remaining lobster meat, the shells (which are very flavorful and add color), and the vegetables, reducing them to a paste. Add the reserved cooking liquid and the soft-cooked rice. Rub this mixture through a fine sieve, or purée it in the blender.

Strain the purée to remove every trace of shell. Place in a clean saucepan and add enough of the white stock in which the rice was cooked to bring the bisque to the consistency of medium cream. Bring to the simmer, season to taste with salt and white pepper, and stir for a few minutes to thoroughly blend the flavors. Remove from the fire and finish the bisque with 6 tablespoons butter and 3 tablespoons thick cream. Garnish with the claw meat cut in dice, and sprinkle with a little cayenne.

SHRIMP BISQUE (*Bisque de Crevettes*). Prepare this exactly like Lobster Bisque, using 2 pounds of raw shrimp.

CULLIS OF CHICKEN or **CHICKEN SOUP À LA REINE** (*Coulis de Volaille* or *Potage Purée de Volaille à la Reine*). Poach a 3-pound chicken in 4 cups White Stock with the white part of 2 leeks, 1 celery rib, and 4 tablespoons blanched rice. When the chicken is cooked (in about 45 minutes), discard the leeks and the celery, and remove the chicken and bone it. Reserve the breasts for a garnish, and finely grind the remaining chicken meat. Combine the ground meat with the cooked rice and pound it in a mortar to reduce it to a paste. Mix with some of the white stock from the pot, and rub the mixture through a sieve or purée it in the blender. Put the purée into a saucepan and add enough white stock to give it the consistency of thin cream.

Bring the cullis almost to the boil. Thicken with the yolks of 3 eggs and ¼ cup cream (an exception for purée soups), and finish with 6 tablespoons butter. Garnish the cullis with finely diced chicken breast meat.

THE VELOUTÉS

Velouté soups are soup purées of vegetables, poultry, fish, or shellfish cooked in a thin Velouté Sauce. They are thinned with White Stock and thickened by the velouté, egg yolks, and cream, and they are finished with butter.

The Velouté used is one appropriate to the food being puréed. For vegetable purées, the velouté is made with a White Stock. For chicken purées it is made with White Chicken Stock. For fish and shellfish purées, the velouté is made with Fish Fumet. The velouté sauce is thickened with a White Roux made with 4 tablespoons flour and 2 tablespoons butter per quart of liquid. Thus it is quite thin.

To enhance their flavor, many vegetables are braised in butter until just cooked before they are puréed. Poultry and fish are poached in the velouté sauce, removed, boned, ground, returned to the sauce, and the whole is rubbed through a sieve or puréed in the blender. Shellfish are cooked in a *Mirepoix* (as in the making of a bisque), then pounded or ground with their shells and their mirepoix, put into the velouté sauce, rubbed through a sieve or puréed in the blender, and strained.

The velouté sauce and purée mixture is then diluted with the same kind of stock that was used in the sauce, until it is of the desired consistency. This mixture is brought almost to the boiling point while stirring. It is then removed from the fire, its surface is buttered to prevent a skin from forming, and it is kept warm in a pan of hot water (a *bain marie*). Just before serving, additionally thicken the soup with 3 egg yolks and 6 tablespoons cream per quart of soup, bring almost to the boil, stirring constantly, and finish off the fire with 4 tablespoons butter.

Velouté soups are very rich and elegant and the final addition of egg yolks, cream, and butter gives them a very velvety texture. This final enrichment tends to mildly supplant the seasoning of the soup, so before your velouté goes to the table a final tasting is advised.

TOMATO VELOUTÉ SOUP (*Potage Velouté aux Tomates*). Prepare a *Mirepoix* of 2 tablespoons finely diced blanched bacon, ½ finely diced carrot, ½ finely diced onion, a pinch of thyme, and ¼ bay leaf, sautéed in 2 tablespoons butter until browned. Squeeze the seeds and jelly from 8 tomatoes (about 2 pounds), chop them, and add them to the mirepoix. (Up to this point, the treatment is exactly as for Purée of Tomato Soup.) Add 3 cups thin Velouté Sauce made with White Stock, and a pinch of sugar, cover, and simmer for 20 to 25 minutes or until the tomatoes are very soft. Rub through a sieve or purée in the blender. Return the purée to the cleaned saucepan, add white stock if necessary to obtain the consistency of thin cream. Cover and simmer the soup for 15 minutes, skimming occasionally. Thicken the soup with the yolks of 4 eggs beaten with ⅓ cup heavy cream. Bring almost to the boil, stirring constantly. Season to taste with salt and pepper. Off the fire, stir in 6 tablespoons butter. Garnish with a little boiled rice and diced tomatoes sautéed in butter.

CELERY VELOUTÉ SOUP (*Potage Velouté de Céleri*). Parboil 1 pound white celery for 5 minutes and drain it. Slice it and put it in a saucepan with 2 tablespoons butter, cover, and simmer for 15 minutes or until the celery is soft. Add 2½ cups thin Velouté Sauce made with White Stock, cover, and simmer for 15 minutes more or until the celery is well cooked. Rub through a sieve or purée in the blender. Return the purée to the cleaned saucepan, add white stock if necessary to obtain the consistency of thin cream, and bring almost to the boil. Thicken the soup with the yolks of 3 eggs beaten with ¼ cup heavy cream. Bring almost to the boil, stirring constantly. Season to taste with salt and white pepper. Off the fire, stir in 4 tablespoons butter. Garnish with finely chopped celery simmered in butter.

CARROT VELOUTÉ SOUP (*Potage Velouté aux Carottes* or *Potage Niver-naise*). Thinly slice 6 medium carrots and 1 medium onion. Put them in a saucepan with ½ teaspoon salt, 1 teaspoon sugar, and 2 tablespoons butter. Cover and cook slowly for 20 minutes or until the carrots are soft. Set aside 8 slices of carrot. Add 2 cups thin Velouté Sauce made with White Stock, cover, and cook for 20 minutes more or until the carrots are well cooked. Rub through a sieve or purée in the blender. Thin the purée with white stock if necessary to obtain the consistency of thin cream, and bring almost to the boil. Thicken the soup with the yolks of 3 eggs beaten with ¼ cup heavy cream. Bring almost to the boil, stirring constantly. Season to taste with salt and pepper. Off the fire, stir in 4 tablespoons butter. Garnish with the reserved carrot slices.

SHRIMP VELOUTÉ SOUP (*Potage Velouté de Crevettes*). Finely dice ¼ carrot and ⅓ onion. Put the dice into a saucepan with 1 bay leaf and a pinch of thyme, and sauté until golden in 4 tablespoons butter. Add 2 pounds raw shrimp and turn in the butter until the shells are red. Sprinkle the shrimp with

2 tablespoons brandy, ignite it, add ½ cup dry white wine and 2 sprigs parsley, season with salt and pepper, and cook over low heat until the liquid has almost entirely disappeared. Then add ½ cup White Stock or Fish Fumet and simmer for 10 minutes. (To this point the treatment is exactly the same as for Shrimp Bisque.)

Drain the shrimp and the vegetables, reserving the liquid. Peel and devein the shrimp, reserving the meat of 6 shrimp for garnishing the finished soup. Grind and pound together the remaining shrimp meat, the shells (which are very flavorful and add color), and the vegetables, reducing them to a paste. Rub this mixture through a fine sieve, or purée it in the blender.

Strain the purée to remove every trace of shell. Place in a clean saucepan and add 3 cups Velouté Sauce made with white stock or fish fumet. The soup should have the consistency of medium cream; add a little stock if necessary to thin it. Bring to the simmer and stir for 10 minutes to thoroughly blend the flavors. Season to taste with salt and pepper. Do not thicken with egg yolks (this is an exception to the rule). Off the fire, stir in 6 tablespoons Shrimp Butter. Garnish with the reserved shrimp meat cut in dice, and sprinkle with a little cayenne pepper.

LOBSTER VELOUTÉ SOUP (*Potage Velouté de Homard* or *Homard Cardinal*). Prepare this exactly like Shrimp Velouté Soup, using a 3-pound lobster (or 2 1½-pound lobsters) cut in pieces. Finish the soup with 6 tablespoons Lobster Butter, and garnish with Royale of lobster, cut in the shape of a cross.

THE CREAMS

Cream soups are soup purées of vegetables, poultry, fish, or shellfish cooked in a thin Béchamel Sauce. They are thinned with milk and finished with fresh heavy cream.

Cream soups are made exactly like Velouté Soups, except that they contain no egg yolks, they are thinned with milk instead of stock, and they are not buttered. Just before serving they are finished with ½ to ¾ cup of thick cream per quart of soup.

CREAM OF TOMATO SOUP (*Potage Crème de Tomates*). Prepare this like Tomato Velouté Soup, using Béchamel Sauce in place of the Velouté, thinning with milk, and finishing the soup with ¾ to 1 cup heavy cream.

CREAM OF ASPARAGUS SOUP (*Potage Crème d'Asperges*). Parboil 1½ pounds of asparagus for 5 minutes and drain it. Cut in pieces, put it in a saucepan with 2½ cups thin Béchamel Sauce, and simmer for 20 to 25 minutes or until the asparagus is soft. Reserve asparagus tips for a garnish, and rub through a sieve or purée in the blender. Return the purée to the cleaned saucepan, adding milk if necessary to obtain the consistency of medium cream, and bring to the boil. Season to taste with salt and white pepper, and finish the soup with ½ cup heavy cream. Garnish with asparagus tips and shredded chervil.

(In a French restaurant you might be served a cream of asparagus soup made with white asparagus. This appears on the menu as *Potage Crème d'Asperges Argenteuil*.)

CREAM OF SPINACH SOUP (*Potage Crème d'Épinards* or *Potage Florentine*). Parboil 1 pound shredded spinach, drain it and squeeze out the water, and put it in a saucepan with 3 cups thin Béchamel Sauce. Simmer for 15 minutes. Rub through a sieve or purée in the blender. Return the purée to the cleaned saucepan, adding milk if necessary to obtain the consistency of medium cream, and bring to the boil. Season to taste with salt and white pepper, and finish the soup with ½ to ¾ cup heavy cream. Garnish with parboiled shredded spinach simmered in butter.

CREAM OF LETTUCE SOUP (*Potage Crème de Laitues*). Parboil 1 pound shredded white leaves of lettuce, drain, and simmer in 4 tablespoons butter for 10 minutes. Add 3 cups thin Béchamel Sauce and rub through a sieve or purée in the blender. Put the purée in a saucepan, adding milk if necessary to obtain the consistency of medium cream, and bring to the boil. Season to taste with salt and white pepper, and finish the soup with ½ to ¾ cup heavy cream.

CREAM OF CORN SOUP (*Potage Crème de Maïs* or *Potage Washington*). Briskly boil 6 ears of fresh corn (or 3 cups frozen corn kernels) in salted water. Strip the kernels from the cob, reserving 6 tablespoons choice kernels for the garnish, add the remainder to 3 cups thin Béchamel Sauce, and rub through a sieve or purée in the blender. Put the purée in a saucepan, adding milk if necessary to obtain the consistency of medium cream, and bring to the boil. Season to taste with salt and white pepper, and finish the soup with ½ to ¾ cup heavy cream. Garnish with choice cooked kernels.

CREAM OF CHICKEN SOUP (*Potage Crème de Volaille Princesse*). Mix 2 cups chicken Purée into 3 cups thin Béchamel Sauce. Put the purée in a saucepan, adding milk if necessary to obtain the consistency of medium cream, and bring almost to the boil. Season to taste with salt and white pepper, and finish the soup with ½ to ¾ heavy cream. Garnish with small, thin slices of chicken breast, asparagus tips, and shredded chervil.

This selection of thick soups should be sufficient to demonstrate how they are put together. Many more kinds can be made, to suit any dinner. Some meats and vegetables that can be prepared in all three ways—as purées, veloutés, and creams—are chicken, shrimp, lobster, crab, carrots, celery, green beans, lettuce, peas, potatoes, sweet potatoes, and tomatoes. You may freely experiment, using the final thinning with liquid or extra egg yolks to adjust the consistency of the soup.

✳ FAMILY SOUPS

At this very instant, across the length and breadth of France, the *marmites* are on the fire. In the kitchens of every province you will hear their hot gurgles and the tap, tap, tap of their covers. Breathe deep and you can *taste* the flavors forming within them; pork and vinegar flavors in the north, tomato and garlic flavors in the south, the tang of iodine on the seacoasts, butter, onions, and wine everywhere. Look inside and you will see the foods of the province and of the season, the very essence of time and place distilled before your eyes. Twenty-five generations of Frenchwomen have fed and stirred these pots. Twenty-five generations of Frenchmen have argued over what goes into them.

The marmites of France are richly supplied by the seas and slopes and countryside. Peer into the bubbling broth and you will see great lumps of beef, fish, and pickled goose, whole cabbages and jolly potatoes, plump red tomatoes disintegrating in shreds, beans bursting with fat and broth, green-and-white leeks a foot long, stocky red-meat carrots, crisp green beans, turnips white as snowballs, onions like giant pearls, a sprinkle of spring peas, sprigs of thyme and chervil bobbing at the top, perhaps an orange peel (bright as a goldfish) darting underneath, and all churning and revolving tirelessly in a wheat- or wine- or saffron-colored broth.

From these kettles are ladled the soup feasts of men who live the good life, the farmers, foresters, fishermen, shepherds, and mountaineers who have the good fortune to eat what is close at hand. A perfect consommé is a beautiful thing, and to be sipped with a silver spoon. But it is in the marmites simmering on the stove that you will find the Great Soups of France.

One day a Texan demonstrated to me the thickness of his chili by standing a soup ladle in it. "Hah!" I cried. "Come with me to Brittany and I will show you a soup to make that ladle *quiver!*"

SOUPE BONNE FEMME
(Leek and Potato Soup)

Joined together and freshened with milk, the gentle leek and the mild potato produce a taste that is admired in every nook and cranny of France. It is a quiet, unassuming taste, but one you can never quite forget. Of everything I know, this shy little soup offers the most convincing proof that "less is more." Here, made simply as it should be made, is one of the Great Soups of France.

Leeks, 4	Potatoes, 4 medium, diced
Butter, 2 tablespoons	Milk, 2 cups
Water, 4 cups	A heavy 2½-quart saucepan
Salt, 2 teaspoons	

Finely dice the white and a little of the tender green of the leeks. Simmer in a covered saucepan in 1 tablespoon butter for a few minutes until soft but not brown. Add water, salt, potatoes, and cook slowly for 35 minutes. Add hot milk and stir in 1 tablespoon butter. It is ready.

VICHYSSOISE
(Cold Cream of Leek and Potato Soup)

In the enormous kitchens of the Ritz-Carlton in New York, Chef Louis Diat was deep in thoughtful search for a new cold soup. His mind wandered back to his mother's kitchen. He remembered how his mother used to cool his breakfast *soupe bonne femme* by adding cold milk to it. And he created vichyssoise, now served in every great restaurant in the Western world.

Leeks, 4	Light cream, 2 cups
Water, 4 cups	Heavy cream, 1 cup
Salt, 2 teaspoons	Chives, chopped
Potatoes, 4 medium, diced	A heavy 2½-quart saucepan
Milk, 2 cups	

Finely dice the white part only of the leeks, so that the finished soup may be snowy white. (The leeks are not simmered in butter, as the butter may congeal in the cold soup.) Put the leeks into a saucepan and add water, salt and potatoes. Cook slowly for 35 minutes. Put the soup through a sieve, or purée it in the blender. Return it to the saucepan, add hot milk and hot light cream, bring almost to the boil, and cook for a few minutes to marry the flavors, stirring to prevent scorching. Strain the soup through a fine sieve, cool it, stir it, and strain it again. Taste the soup for seasoning. It should be slightly oversalted to overcome the inhibiting effect of cold on the flavor of salt. Then stir in heavy cream and chill in the coldest part of the refrigerator. Serve the vichyssoise sprinkled with finely chopped chives.

SOUPE À L'OIGNON
(Onion Soup)

When I inhale the fragrance of onion soup, I am reminded of the whole-sale food markets of France, to which I paid many a predawn visit as apprentice and young chef. In early-hour restaurants surrounding these markets the onion soup ladle was always busy. Early risers and night people alike shared this hot breakfast of soup and cheese and crusty bread, which is as quick and easy to make as porridge but has so much more taste.

Onions, 6 small or 4 medium, thinly sliced	Salt to taste
Butter, 2 tablespoons	Pepper, freshly ground, to taste
Flour, 1 teaspoon	Bread, day old, 6 slices
Brown Stock, 6 cups	Cheese, Swiss, 3 tablespoons grated
Dry white wine (optional), ½ cup	A heavy 2½-quart saucepan

Brown the onions lightly in butter. Sprinkle with flour and continue to cook for a few minutes, stirring to mix in the flour and cook it. Add boiling Brown Stock, wine if you like, salt and pepper. Simmer the soup for 15 minutes.

Sauté bread slices in butter until crisp, or brown in the oven, or toast. Put them in a soup tureen or in individual soup bowls and pour the soup over them. Sprinkle with cheese, and put into a hot oven or under the broiler until the cheese is bubbling and brown and exuding a tantalizing fragrance. Serve the soup very hot.

The above soup is also called Onion Soup Gratinée (*Soupe à l'Oignon Gratinée*) or Cheese Soup (*Soupe au Fromage*) to distinguish it from onion soup served without the sprinkling of grated cheese (*Soupe à l'Oignon*). Here are some other delicious variations:

Soupe à l'Oignon Soufflé. For 1 quart (4 bowls), make a soufflé mixture (see Soufflé) with 1 teaspoon butter, 1 teaspoon flour, ¼ cup milk, 1 tablespoon grated Swiss cheese, salt and white pepper to taste, 2 egg yolks, and 2 beaten egg whites. Float this mixture on top of the onion soup in the soup tureen or in individual bowls in which you have already placed slices of toasted bread. Put in a 375° oven for 10 minutes or until the soufflé cake rises and is golden brown.

Soupe à l'Oignon au Porto (with port wine). For 1 quart (4 bowls), beat 2 egg yolks with ¼ cup port wine. Ladle 1 cup of the hot soup into this mixture, stirring it in little by little to prevent the yolks from curdling. Just before serving, blend this mixture into the onion soup.

Soupe à l'Oignon Thourins. Make onion soup with milk in place of Brown Stock. For 1 quart (4 bowls), beat 2 egg yolks with ¼ cup heavy cream. Ladle 1 cup of the hot soup into this mixture, stirring it in little by little to prevent the yolks from curdling. Just before serving blend this mixture into the onion soup. Separately serve toasted bread sprinkled with grated Swiss and browned in the oven.

GARBURE

Garbure is mountaineer's soup, originating in Béarn in the Pyrenees, and a dish of it is enough to fuel a smuggler to Spain and back. The Béarnaise insist that this soup be fiercely boiled from start to finish. Considering the altitude of Béarn, where water boils at a mere 205°, this is not a bad suggestion. Those of us at sea level, however, can cook this soup at a lively simmer.

Beans, dry white or lima, 1 cup
Water, 4 quarts
Meat, 1½ pounds lightly cured ham, or lean bacon, or lean salt pork, or pork sausage
Pepper, 6 peppercorns or a pinch of red pepper
Garlic, 4 cloves, mashed
Parsley, 4 sprigs
Marjoram, ½ teaspoon
Thyme, ½ teaspoon
Green beans, 1 cup, cut in 1½-inch lengths

Potatoes, 4 medium (about 1 pound) of the waxy, "boiling" type, thickly sliced
Cabbage, 3 quarts finely shredded (about 2 pounds)
Peas, 1 cup
Salt, if necessary, to taste
Bread, stale slices for the bottom of the soup plates
An 8- to 10-quart soup kettle

Separately cook beans until they are half-cooked. Bring 4 quarts of water to boiling in the soup kettle. Into this plunge the meat in one piece. Do not salt the water; the meat will do it.

(The traditional meat for this dish is salt goose (*confit d'oie*), which is added about ½ hour before the soup is finished cooking. Although the Béarnaise will accept the meats I have listed, which are more readily available here, they do insist that you add a big lump of goose fat to the pot. If you have it, add it. The beans will love you.)

As soon as the water returns to the boil, add the half-cooked beans, drained of their cooking liquor. Also add peppercorns or red pepper; garlic cloves, parsley, marjoram, and thyme. Then add green beans and potatoes. Dry these vegetables and add them to the pot a little at a time so that the water in the pot does not cool too much. It should not cease to bubble. Cover the pot, adjust the heat so that the water is just above the simmer, and allow the cooking to proceed until 45 minutes have elapsed from the time you put the meat into the pot.

Now, turn up the heat until the water is boiling. Add cabbage with heavy ribs removed and the leaves shredded into fine strips, and peas. Again, dry these vegetables and add them slowly so that the water does not cease to bubble. If more water is needed to cover the contents, add boiling water to the pot.

Continue to boil gently for 5 minutes with the pot uncovered to release the heavy odors of the cabbage. Then partially cover the pot (leaving a 1-inch opening) and adjust the heat so that the water is just above the simmer. Continue cooking for another 45 minutes, or until the meat is tender and the vegetables are done. The soup should be thick. Season to taste with salt if necessary.

To serve, place a slice of stale bread in the bottom of a soup plate and ladle the broth and the vegetables over it, reserving the meat for a second course. Or you may reserve the meat and most of the vegetables and begin with the bread and broth alone. Either way you eat garbure, add a glass of wine to the last few spoonfuls of broth in the bottom of the plate, and drink it. This interesting liquid is called a *goudale,* and the Béarnaise say it will "keep a coin from the doctor's pocket."

SOUPE AUX POISSONS
(Fish Soup)

This is a rich, aromatic, saffron-flavored soup of fish, strained and served with a sauce. There are no pieces of fish in it; these have been pressed and strained out. This soup is made all along the Mediterranean, using a variety of fish and trimmings from the day's catch, and is a very close cousin to bouillabaisse. In fact, by cooking the appropriate fish in *soupe aux poissons* a very rich bouillabaisse is made.

Fish soup making differs from other fish cookery in that the fish is boiled, not poached. It is found to taste better that way. In fact, bouillabaisse and other fish soups containing olive oil are boiled furiously throughout, the purpose being not only to thicken the liquid by reduction, but to additionally thicken it by amalgamating the olive oil with the water to form a mayonnaise-like emulsion. This fish, although battered about somewhat, is removed *just as soon* as it is cooked.

Onion, 1 medium, chopped

Leeks, 2, chopped (or 1 medium onion)

Olive oil, ½ cup

Flour, 1 tablespoon

Tomatoes, 3 large, chopped (or ½ cup Tomato Purée)

Garlic, 4 cloves, crushed

Water, 3 quarts

Fish, the meat of lean fish, bones, and trimmings, all chopped, 6 pounds

Salt, 2 teaspoons

Pepper, a good pinch

Parsley, 3 sprigs, crushed

Bay leaf, ½, crumbled

Thyme or basil, a good pinch

Fennel seed, ⅛ teaspoon

Orange peel, dried, 1 strip (or ½ teaspoon)

Saffron, 2 good pinches

Vermicelli, 4 tablespoons

Bread, toasted

Parsley, 1 tablespoon, chopped

Cheese, grated Parmesan, 1 cup

Sauce (see below)

A heavy-bottomed, 4- to 6-quart saucepan

Sauté onion and leeks in olive oil for a few minutes until soft but not brown. Sprinkle with flour and cook for a few minutes more, stirring to blend in the flour. Add tomatoes and garlic, cook for a few minutes more. Then add cold water and fish. Also add salt, pepper, parsley, bay leaf, thyme or basil, fennel, orange peel, and saffron. Cook at a furious boil for 20 minutes.

Strain the soup, pressing the ingredients with a wooden spoon to extract all the good juices. Correct the seasoning, adding more saffron if necessary to create a beautiful rich saffron color. Bring the soup to boiling, add vermicelli, and boil furiously for 8 minutes or until the pasta is just done. Pour the soup over toasted bread rounds and sprinkle with chopped parsley. With the soup serve fresh-grated Parmesan cheese. For mixing with the soup, pass a sauceboat of Aioli Sauce or the following *rouille*.

Rouille

Hot red chili peppers, 2 mature Fresno, Serrano, or jalapeño peppers (available in cans)

Mild red pepper, 1 mature bell or Ancho pepper, or ½ cup pimentos (available canned)

Garlic, 6 cloves

Breadcrumbs, soft, 1½ cups

Soupe aux Poissons (above), 8 tablespoons

Basil, 1 teaspoon

Olive oil, 8 tablespoons

Salt and fresh-ground pepper

Tabasco sauce, a few drops (optional)

A mortar and pestle and a mixing bowl

Boil hot red chili peppers until tender (or use canned peppers). Chop and boil mild red pepper until tender (or use canned pimentos). Pound the peppers in a mortar with garlic, breadcrumbs moistened with 2 to 4 tablespoons of *soupe aux poissons,* and basil. When this is reduced to a paste, rub it through a fine sieve and beat in the olive oil little by little. Season with salt and fresh-ground pepper to taste. To make the sauce hotter (it is diluted in the soup) add a few drops of Tabasco sauce. Just before serving, beat in 4 or more tablespoons hot *soupe aux poissons* until the sauce has the consistency of heavy cream.

BOUILLABAISSE

There is a long-standing controversy as to which of the cities and towns along the French Mediterranean coast make the true bouillabaisse, hinging upon whether or not lobster or such and such a fish is included in the soup. This need not trouble us here, in as much as the indispensable fish, the *rascasse,* is not available anyway. I think, therefore, that we can go ahead and make bouillabaisse if we want to. And I think you will find it very good indeed.

Fish, 8 pounds lean fish and shell-fish (crabs and lobsters only), about 8 different kinds	Bread rounds
	Parsley, 1 tablespoon chopped
	A 6-quart soup kettle
Soupe aux Poissons, 3 quarts	

Cut in uniform pieces (about 2 inches at the largest dimension) lean salt water fish of as many different kinds as possible, including both tender and firm-fleshed fish and an eel if you have one. Also clean and cut in pieces crabs and lobsters. In the kettle, bring to a boil 3 quarts of *soupe aux poissons* without the vermicelli (see above recipe). Add the crab, lobster, and firm-fleshed fish, a few pieces at a time to keep the water at the boil, and boil furiously for 5 minutes. Add the tender-fleshed fish, a few pieces at a time, and boil furiously for another 5 minutes.

Test the fish for doneness with a fork, and if necessary boil for a few minutes more. The fish is done *as soon as* it flakes easily. Arrange the fish on a platter and pour over it a ladle of hot soup. Pour the soup into a tureen over untoasted rounds of bread. Sprinkle the soup and fish with chopped parsley. Serve the soup as a first course, or serve soup and fish together. Pass a sauceboat of Aioli Sauce or *Rouille.*

Bouillabaisse à la Parisienne. They make bouillabaisse in Paris, too, although Riviera chefs refuse to recognize it. The Parisians start out just about the way the southern cooks do, using any fish they can get their hands on and substituting 3 cups of dry white wine for 3 cups of the water (in *Soupe aux Poissons*), which is innocent enough. But then, horror of horrors, they do two things that are universally condemned in the south. They pile well-scrubbed mussels on top of the fish, and they thicken the broth with a few tablespoons of butter.

SOUPE AIGO-SAOU

Fish cooks so quickly it is possible to prepare a fish soup meal, from start to finish, in 20 to 30 minutes. Here's how it's done in the kitchens of Provence.

Water, 2 quarts	Bay leaf, ½, crumbled
Potatoes, 4, cut in quarters	Thyme, a pinch
Onion, 1 medium, chopped	Salt, 1 tablespoon
Tomatoes, 3 large, chopped	Pepper, a pinch
Garlic, 2 cloves, crushed	White fish, 2 pounds
Celery, 1 rib, chopped	Bread, day-old, sliced and toasted
Parsley, 3 sprigs, crushed	A heavy-bottomed 4-quart saucepan

Bring water to a rolling boil. Add potatoes, onion, tomatoes, garlic, celery, parsley, bay leaf, thyme, salt, and pepper. Return the water to the boil and add any white fish cut in 2-inch pieces. Continue boiling until the fish and potatoes are cooked, about 15 minutes. Place fish and potatoes on a platter. Strain the soup into a soup tureen over toast. Serve soup and fish and potatoes together with Aioli Sauce or *Rouille*.

SOUPE AIGO À LA MÉNAGÈRE

This soup starts out like bouillabaisse without the fish and gets a last-minute surprise addition. I often wonder if this soup got its start when some fisherman husband came home empty-handed.

Onion, 1 medium	Thyme, a pinch
Leeks, 3	Fennel seed, ½ teaspoon
Olive oil, ¼ cup	Orange peel, dried, 1 strip (or ½
Tomatoes, 2, chopped	teaspoon ground)
Garlic, 4 cloves, crushed	Saffron, a pinch
Water, 2 quarts	Potatoes, 4 large, thickly sliced
Salt, 2 teaspoons	Eggs, 6 to 8
Pepper, a good pinch	Bread, day-old slices, toasted
Parsley, 3 sprigs, crushed	A heavy-bottomed 4-quart saucepan
Bay leaf, ½, crumbled	

Chop onion and the white part of leeks (or another onion) and sauté in olive oil for a few minutes until soft but not brown. Add tomatoes and garlic, and cook for a few minutes more. Then add hot water, salt, pepper, parsley, bay leaf, thyme, fennel seed, orange peel, and saffron. Bring the water to a boil, add potatoes, and boil for 15 minutes.

When the potatoes are just about cooked, poach eggs in the soup, allowing 1 per serving. Remove the cooked potatoes, and arrange them on a dish with the drained poached eggs. Strain the soup over slices of toast. Serve the soup along with the eggs and potatoes.

POTAGE CULTIVATEUR
(Farmer's Soup)

This simple soup, flavored with bacon, is eaten all over France.

Onion, ½ small, diced	Beef Consommé, 6 cups
Leeks, 2 (white part only), diced	Potato, 1 medium, thinly sliced
Turnip, 1 small, diced	(about ¾ cup)
Carrots, 2, diced	Bacon, 6 tablespoons, diced and
Salt, 1 teaspoon	blanched
Sugar, a pinch	A heavy-bottomed 2½-quart sauce-
Butter, 3 tablespoons	pan

Sprinkle the diced vegetables with salt and sugar, and simmer them for 5 minutes in butter in a covered saucepan. Add beef consommé, cover, and simmer for 50 minutes. Add potato and bacon. Simmer for 20 minutes more, or until the potatoes are done.

POTAGE PAYSANNE
(Country Soup)

This is an all-vegetable soup, containing no meat except the essence found in the stock it is cooked in. And if you have no stock on hand, you can make the soup with water.

Onion, ½ small, minced	Butter, 3 tablespoons
Leek, 1 minced (white part only)	White Stock or water, 6 cups
Turnip, 1 small, finely chopped	Potato, 1 small, thinly sliced (about
Carrot, 1, finely chopped	½ cup)
Celery, 2 tablespoons, finely chopped	Peas, 2 tablespoons
Cabbage, ¼ cup shredded	Chervil, 1 tablespoon chopped
Salt, 1 teaspoon	A heavy-bottomed 2½-quart sauce-
Sugar, a pinch	pan

Sprinkle onion, leek, turnip, carrot, celery and shredded, tender, inside cabbage leaves with salt and sugar. Simmer these vegetables for 5 minutes in butter in a covered saucepan. Add white stock, cover, and simmer for 50 minutes. Add potato and fresh green peas and simmer for 20 minutes more, or until the potato is done. Serve sprinkled with chopped chervil. (If the soup is made with water instead of stock, stir in 4 tablespoons butter before serving.)

SOUPE À L'AIL À LA PROVENÇALE
(Garlic Soup à la Provençale)

As you might guess, this soup is spicy and full of flavor. I like it with plenty of fresh-ground pepper. You may soften the flavor of the garlic by simmering the soup for a longer time.

Garlic, 18 to 24 cloves	Salt, 1 tablespoon
Water, 2 quarts	Pepper, a pinch
Thyme, 1 sprig or a pinch	Bread slices
Bay leaf, 1	Parmesan or Swiss Cheese, grated
Sage, a good pinch	Olive oil, 2 to 4 tablespoons
Clove, 1	

Put garlic into a saucepan with the water. Add thyme, bay leaf, sage, clove, salt, and pepper. Bring the water to the boil and simmer for 25 minutes. Sprinkle small slices of bread with grated Parmesan or Swiss cheese and olive oil, put them into a hot oven until the cheese melts, and then put them in the bottom of a soup tureen. Pour the boiling soup over the bread. (And take bets on who gets the lone clove!)

POT-AU-FEU
(Pot-on-the-Fire)

This soup of beef and bones and vegetables surprises most Americans who taste it. Since the beef and vegetables are in plain sight, they suspect some trickery has gone into the broth. "René, what is your secret?" they demand. "There is more to this than meets the eye."

There is no secret to the *pot-au-feu* that has not been known for a thousand years. But there is more to it than just boiling beef and vegetables together. This is a case where the whole appears to exceed the sum of its parts. The beef and vegetables are good, yes, but the broth tastes like something more. Like a consommé, the broth of a pot-au-feu has savor, body, and limpidity. It tastes of fresh beef, not vegetables. And it has the peculiar, mellow succulence that is the product of slow careful cooking. If there is any secret to pot-au-feu, that secret is taking care.

Pot-au-feu is not difficult to make, but it has its pitfalls. If you avoid these, there is no reason why your first pot-au-feu cannot be the best there is. Regarding the beef and the aromatic vegetables, the cooking principle is exactly the same as in making a stock; their flavor is transferred to the broth. The beef (or *bouilli,* as it is called) is then served with piquant seasonings to bolster its taste. On the other hand, the vegetables for eating are put into the pot last, and served just-cooked with their flavors intact.

Pot-au-feus in different parts of France vary in their ingredients, depending upon the season and local food supplies. Although there is no one recipe, the one I give you here is to me the most traditional. There is a reason for every ingredient, and I strongly suggest you cook this pot-au-feu according to the recipe, omitting nothing. It will give you an accepted standard of how this dish should taste. Then, if you choose, you can make little adjustments in the ingredients of succeeding pot-au-feus. In no time the method will become second nature to you. Do not vary the method if you want a real pot-au-feu.

Ingredients for the Pot-au-Feu

Beef, 2 pounds lean beef—rump or round—in one compact chunk

Beef, 2 pounds fatty beef—chuck, plate, or brisket—in one compact chunk or rolled and tied tightly

Veal knuckle, 1, sawed in 3 pieces; or veal bones, 2 pounds

Brown Stock, 4 quarts

Carrots, 6 medium

Onions, 4 medium

Leeks, 3

Celery, 1 rib

Turnips, 2 small

Parsnip, ½ small

Bouquet Garni—3 sprigs parsley, 1 bay leaf, and 1 sprig or pinch of thyme, all tied in cheesecloth

Salt, 1½ tablespoons

GARNISHING VEGETABLES: The amounts of the following vegetables will depend upon the number of people served. Allow about ½ cup of each vegetable per person

Celery, hearts only

Carrots, cut in the shape of large olives

Turnips, cut in the shape of large olives

Onions, medium

Leeks, white part only

Cabbage, sliced in wedges and *cooked separately*

Chicken giblets, 2 sets—necks, wings, gizzards, hearts; or chicken backs, to weigh about ¾ pound

Marrowbone, 1, about 6 inches long, split or sawed in 3 pieces

Bread slices, lightly buttered and browned in the oven

Seasonings for the beef: mustard, horseradish, pickles, coarse salt, or any piquant sauce

A 12-quart soup kettle

Let us undertake this recipe in a leisurely fashion, so that the reason behind every action is clear and memorable. Some of these explanations I have already given in Chapter 4. But it will not hurt to repeat them, for the lessons learned in making a perfect pot-au-feu are applicable to much of cooking.

What is left over from a pot-au-feu dinner is every bit as good as the dinner itself, so we will make enough to be worth while. You will need 4 pounds of beef in compact 2-pound chunks. One of these chunks should be rump or round, as the leanness of these cuts makes them ideal for slicing and eating. The other chunk should be from the chuck or plate (brisket). These fattier pieces are very juicy and flavorful (much of the flavor of meat is contained in the fat). Tie these pieces with butcher's twine so they are as compact as possible.

Next, get a beef marrowbone about 6 inches long. Have it split in two lengthwise, or sawed into 3 pieces. Wrap these together in cheesecloth and tie them.

Now add to your collection a veal knuckle sawed in 3 pieces, or sawed veal bones to weigh about 2 pounds. The veal is needed for the high proportion of gelatin it contains and contributes to the body of the broth.

Finally, from the meat department, you will need 2 sets of chicken giblets (that is, the wings, necks, and gizzards of two chickens), or enough chicken backs, wings, etc., to weigh about ¾ pound.

The aromatic vegetables—carrot, onion, leek, celery, turnip and parsnip —are mostly left whole. Their flavor will easily be extracted during the long cooking, and if they are cut up they tend to disintegrate and cloud the broth. You may cut the carrots and celery in 2 pieces to fit more easily into the pot. Leave the skin on the onion if it is clean; it will give a good color to the broth. Slit the leeks and flush out the sand they always contain, and tie them together with twine, as they fall apart easily. If the turnips and parsnip are not very young and small, use ½ of a larger turnip and a piece of parsnip, and parboil these vegetables for 5 minutes to remove their strong flavors. (These two vegetables, although present in small amounts, contribute importantly to the full flavor of the broth.) The aromatic vegetables are completed by a *Bouquet Garni* of parsley, bay leaf, and thyme, all tied in cheesecloth.

The liquid for the pot-au-feu is Brown Stock. This stock will become very richly flavored during the cooking of the meat and vegetables; nevertheless it is obvious that the better this stock, the better the pot-au-feu.

If you do not have brown stock on hand, proceed as follows: brown the veal knuckle (or veal bones) in hot fat in a skillet, along with slices of

3 carrots and 3 onions. Also brown in the oven 2 pounds or more of beef bones, which you have sprinkled with melted fat. The browning of these ingredients will add both flavor and color to the liquid. Cover the browned ingredients well with water, salt lightly, add the same bouquet garni as you will add to the soup, and simmer for 2 to 6 hours in advance. The broth obtained from this simmering, carefully skimmed and strained, is used as the liquid for the pot-au-feu. The simmered veal knuckle is also added to the pot, as it has much more gelatin to contribute. If you have no time to simmer bones, brown the veal knuckle, onions and carrots, and use water as the liquid. The broth will not be as rich, but it will be flavorful nevertheless. Do not use canned bouillon until you have tasted a fresh-made pot-au-feu.

Eating vegetables for the pot-au-feu are carrots and turnips cut in olive shapes, medium onions, the white part of leeks, and halved or quartered celery hearts. A good trick is to tie these vegetables separately in cheesecloth rinsed to remove any loose fibers. You may then retrieve them easily from the pot, and have them ready and clean for garnishing the meat. The quantity of these vegetables depends on the number of persons to be served, allowing 3 or 4 carrot pieces, 3 or 4 turnip pieces, 1 leek, 1 onion, and a piece of celery per person.

Cabbage for the pot-au-feu is cooked separately so that its strong flavors will not dominate the broth. You can cook it in water or a little of the broth and some of the fat that rises to its surface. The cabbage, cut in wedges, joins the dish only at the time of garnishing the meat.

Cooking the Pot-au-Feu

Our first concern is to make sure the stock is perfectly clear. Put the beef and bones (all but the marrowbone) into the pot and cover with 4 quarts of cold brown stock. Bring this slowly to the boil, and simmer for about 15 minutes, stirring occasionally and skimming assiduously, until the gray scum ceases to rise to the surface and nothing is produced but a little bubbly white froth. Now, add all the aromatic vegetables, the bouquet garni, and the salt. Return the liquid to a very gentle simmer, and partially cover the pot, leaving a 1-inch opening to release some of the steam. Watch the pot carefully at this point as the cover will raise the heat of the liquid. You must finely adjust the heat so that the liquid just shimmers in the center, with perhaps an occasional bubble breaking the surface now and then. (From this point, total cooking time will be about 4 hours.) Simmer the beef and bones for 2½ hours, skimming occasionally to remove the fat rising to the surface.

After 2½ hours (that is, 1½ hours before the dish is to be ready), begin adding the garnishing vegetables, a few at a time, so that the stock will not be overly cooled and will remain at the simmering point. First add the celery hearts, then the carrots, turnips, and onions. The leeks, which are the quickest to cook, are added last. If the liquid does not cover the vegetables, add boiling brown stock or water.

When all the vegetables except cabbage have been leisurely added, add the chicken giblets. (They are added late because they release their flavor quickly, and are also likely to fall apart and clutter up the broth if cooked too long.) There should now be about 1 hour of cooking time remaining. Simmer for ½ hour and add, finally, the marrowbone in its cheesecloth wrapping.

At this time, also, you can cook the wedges of cabbage. Plunge them into boiling salted water or stock containing a few tablespoons of fat skimmed from the pot.

Serving the Pot-au-Feu

When the cooking is completed, add 1 cup cold water or stock to the pot and leave it to rest for 5 minutes. This allows any sediment buoyed up by the simmering stock to settle at the bottom. With tongs, carefully lift out the chicken giblets and discard them. Lift out the cheesecloh bags containing the marrowbone and the garnishing vegetables, and keep them warm. Then ladle out enough broth for immediate serving, taking it from the top of the pot, where it is most clear, and putting it through a fine strainer lined with cheesecloth and into a bowl. Finally, remove the beef and veal knuckle.

Slice the beef and the meat from the veal knuckle and arrange the slices on a hot serving platter. Surround with the garnishing carrots, turnips, onions, leeks, celery hearts, and cabbage wedges. Sprinkle a little hot broth over the beef and keep it warm.

Roughly skim away the fat at the top of the broth in the bowl (it is traditional that a few globules or "eyes" should remain floating on the surface). Pour the broth into a clean pot, and heat it to boiling.

Scoop or press the marrow from the marrow bones. Spread the marrow on slices of hot toasted bread and serve it with the clear, boiling broth as the first course of the pot-au-feu. As the second course, serve the meat and vegetables. Separately serve a bowl of boiling broth as a sauce, along with piquant seasonings such as horseradish, mustard, pickles, and coarse sea salt.

Next week, having finished the leftovers and remembering the taste, you will be ready to make pot-au-feu all over again.

PETITE MARMITE

This is Pot-au-Feu brought to the table in its cooking pot (or earthenware marmite), with the meat and vegetables already sliced and returned to the perfectly clear, strained broth. Slices of meat are put into each soup plate, and the broth and vegetables ladled over them. The dish is, therefore, but a single course served with bread. (The small marmites brought to restaurant tables are of a size to contain quantities for from 2 to 6 persons, hence the name *petite marmite*.)

POTÉE NORMANDE

Here is a Pot-au-Feu that literally overflows with the goodness and bounty of the land. Make it according to the recipe for pot-au-feu (above), omitting half the beef and the chicken giblets. One hour after the beef and bones have been purged of scum and settled to simmer, add 2 pounds of pork butt or pork shoulder, and a 3- to 4-pound stewing hen. Skim until the stock is clean. After 2½ hours (30 minutes before the end of cooking), add 2 pounds of mildly seasoned, cured sausage, such as Polish sausage (*kielbasy*). Serve the broth first, and then the meats, which are served with a variety of sauces.

CROÛTE AU POT

This soup is one of the things that can happen to Pot-au-Feu on the second day. Take the carrots, turnips, and leeks of the flavoring vegetables, and any of the leftover eating vegetables, and cut them into 1-inch pieces. Take leftover marrow (or boil more marrowbones) and spread it on crusts of French bread. Strain the pot-au-feu broth, heat it, and warm the vegetables in it. Serve the crusts of bread separately or drop them in the soup.

POT-AU-FEU À LA BÉARNAISE
also called **PETITE MARMITE HENRI IV**
also called **POULE-AU-POT HENRI IV**

Whatever it is called, this version of Pot-au-Feu contains chicken. These names all honor King Henry IV, who was a Béarnaise, and who promised the people of France a chicken in every pot. In its simplest form, this dish is the pot-au-feu omitting half the beef and the chicken giblets, and adding a whole stewing chicken. In another form, the chicken is stuffed with a Forcemeat of pork, ham, chicken livers, onion, garlic, and parsley.

In its most sublime form, usually called *petite marmite Henri IV*, the pot-au-feu is *made all over again* using the pot-au-feu broth as its liquid and including cut-up chicken legs and oxtail as well as beef and marrowbone. Thus the original water of this soup may have been flavored four times over —once during the simmering of bones, once while making the brown stock, again while making pot-au-feu, and finally during the cooking of the petite marmite Henri IV. It is remarkably rich in flavor and served in one course, as a soup.

POULE-AU-POT
(Chicken-in-the-Pot)

Chicken, a 5-pound stewing chicken (fowl)
White Chicken Stock, 4 quarts
Salt, 1 tablespoon
Carrots, 2
Onion, 1
Leeks, 2
Celery, 3 ribs
Parsley, 3 sprigs

GARNISHING VEGETABLES: The amounts of the following vegetables will depend upon the number of people served. Figure on 2 of each vegetable per person
Carrots, cut in the shape of large olives
Celery, sliced in 1-inch pieces
Leeks, white part only, sliced in 1-inch pieces
Rice, boiled
An 8-quart soup kettle

Truss the chicken, bring it slowly to a boil in water, and simmer for 5 minutes. Remove the chicken and clean the kettle. Return it to the kettle with White Chicken Stock, and add salt if the stock is unsalted. Simmer the chicken for 1 hour, and add carrots, onion, leeks, celery, and parsley. Cover and simmer for 1 hour more. Remove the chicken and keep it warm. Strain the stock so that it is very clear, and skim off the fat. Put it in a clean pan, add the garnishing vegetables, and cook them at a gentle boil until tender. Slice the chicken and serve in the broth with the vegetables and boiled rice. Or serve the clear broth as a first course, followed by the chicken and vegetables, rice, and a cream sauce for chicken.

7 *The Busy Egg*

Some animals have babies by having eggs instead. Let us rejoice at this, because much of cookery would be undone without the egg. Certainly we would be thoroughly confounded without egg's thickening, binding, coating, blending, leavening, coloring, enriching, and clarifying of foods. And certainly we would miss the good taste of egg.

For good cooking, eggs *must* be fresh. To tell if an egg is fresh, break it onto a flat white plate and observe its profile. A fresh egg's yolk stands high and round. A trembling jelly of transparent egg white is heaped up, huddled tightly around the yolk. A ring of thinner, watery white surrounds the jellied white, moored at opposite ends by two small white "knots." The yolk ranges in color from lemon yellow to dark orange, but this tells you nothing about freshness or flavor. The egg white is clear, with perhaps a slight greenish cast (which indicates it is rich in Vitamin B_3). The egg smells fresh and clean.

This freshness is very perishable. Once out of the hen an egg at room temperature may show evidence of becoming stale in just eight hours. As eggs grow stale, the white becomes watery. The yolk soaks up some of this water, swells, and weakens the membrane containing the yolk so that it breaks easily. Out of its shell the egg spreads out on the plate like a puddle. This egg is not worth having.

Government inspectors and other professionals determine the freshness of eggs in the shell by candling them. The egg is held up to a strong beam of light. The inspector rotates the egg and observes the shadow cast by the yolk inside. In a fresh egg, the thick white will hold the yolk firmly in the center of the shell. In a stale egg, the thinner, more watery white will allow the yolk to travel around, casting a sharper shadow as it nears the shell. The thinner the white, the staler the egg.

Another way to test the freshness of an egg in the shell is to measure the air bubble it contains. This air bubble is formed in the broad end of an egg as soon as it is laid (the eggs you buy at the store are always packed with their broad ends upward to keep the air bubble from migrating). As the egg ages, and the jellied egg white becomes more watery, the water evaporates through the porous eggshell and the air bubble grows larger. The larger the air bubble, the staler the egg.

The French are very fussy about the freshness of foods, and in the November 1, 1913, issue of *Le Cordon Bleu* magazine there appears a method for testing the freshness of eggs based on the size of their air bubbles. Place the suspect egg in water. If it is fresh, it will rest horizontally on its side. If it is 3 or 4 days old, the broad end of the egg (containing the air bubble) will rise and the egg will assume a 45° angle. An 8-day-old egg will rise to 55°, a 15-day-old egg will achieve 60°, and a 3-week-old egg 70°. A month-old egg will stand on end. Older eggs will begin to rise to the surface.

There are 2 ways to estimate the freshness of eggs that have already been hard-boiled or soft-cooked in the shell. When you crack the egg at its broad end, you will see the gouge scooped out of the white by the air bubble. If this gouge is more than 3/16-inch deep, the egg is stale. Also, an off-center yolk indicates a stale egg. The watery white cannot hold the yolk in the center of the egg.

In addition to staleness, the good taste of eggs can also be spoiled by odors. The porous shell absorbs them greedily, giving the egg an off flavor. In Paris, eggs that had been packed in straw to protect them from breaking on their way to market were sometimes offered for sale. We called these "straw eggs" and would have none of them. (On the other hand, eggs stored in close proximity to truffles will take on their heady fragrance and taste perfectly delightful.)

The freshest eggs, in all sizes, are graded U.S. Grade AA. U.S. Grade A is less fresh. Eggs receive these grades *before* they are shipped or stored, and grading therefore provides no real guarantee of how fresh the eggs actually are. Buy eggs only as you need them. Store them in the refrigerator, covered, in the carton, to keep them free from odors. And if, on the day you buy them, these eggs do not exhibit the characteristics of freshness I have described, find yourself another egg man. Remember, for good cooking eggs *must* be fresh.

Eggs are sorted into 6 sizes, based on weight. There are peewee, small, medium, large, extra large, and jumbo eggs. The eggs you have in the refrigerator are likely to be medium (weighing 1¾ ounces, shell and all), large (weighing 2 ounces), or extra large (weighing 2¼ ounces). The recipes in this book are based on the large (2-ounce) egg. It contains about 1 tablespoon of yolk and 2 tablespoons of white. Whether the shell is white or brown matters not one whit.

Eggs are very important in the French cuisine, but they are rarely eaten at breakfast. (When I was chef on the S.S. *Liberté,* we could judge the number of Americans we had aboard at each crossing by the number of breakfast egg orders.) Among the recipes that follow are many that can be cooked up quickly for breakfast.

✳ *11 WAYS TO COOK EGGS*

Egg cookery is protein cookery at its most delicate. Both the egg white and the egg yolk are rich in protein. The egg white proteins begin to solidify at about 135°, become jellylike at about 140°, and completely coagulate at about 150°. The corresponding temperatures for egg yolk proteins run about 10° higher. If heated much beyond the coagulation temperature, or if held at this temperature for too long a period, the proteins will shrink and exude water and the egg will become tough and dry. Egg cookery, then, demands a very light touch and great restraint in the use of heat. You must be kind to your eggs. Cooked with kindness, even a "hard-boiled" egg will be wonderfully tender.

One of the kindliest things you can do for eggs is to remove them from the refrigerator at least one half hour before cooking them. Starting at room temperature, eggs will take less time to reach the desired degree of doneness. Eggs cooked in their shells particularly benefit when there is no icy yolk at their center to inhibit cooking. If you do cook chilled eggs, add a half to 1 minute to their cooking time. Better yet, hold the chilled eggs under running warm water for a few minutes before cooking.

SOFT-BOILED EGGS
(Oeufs à la Coque)

Like many other so-called boiled foods, soft-boiled eggs are never actually boiled. The 212° temperature of boiling water is much too high for them and would make the outside of the white tough and rubbery in less than a minute of cooking.

The best and most precise way to soft boil an egg is to bring it to room temperature and then to lower it into simmering water to cover. (The bubbles of simmering water barely reach the surface; the temperature is about 185°.) If the egg cools the water below the simmering point, turn up the heat to return the water to the simmer. When the water begins to simmer again, adjust the heat to keep it at the simmer and begin timing the egg.

Once in simmering water, the timing of soft-boiled eggs depends upon the temperature of the egg, the size of the egg, the freshness of the egg, and the degree of doneness you want. Eggs at room temperature cook more quickly than cold eggs. Small eggs cook more quickly than large eggs. Fresh eggs cook more quickly than stale eggs.

A large (2-ounce size), fresh, room-temperature egg will be cooked very soft in about 3 minutes. The white will have turned milky and the yolk will be warmed throughout. In 3¾ minutes the white is turning jellylike while the yolk is still soft and runny. In 4½ minutes the white is jellied and the yolk is thickening, but still liquid. In 5½ minutes the white is almost solid and the outside of the yolk has set. In 6½ minutes, only a tiny liquid core remains in the yolk. Beyond this point the egg is hard-boiled. Of course all these times will be shortened if you allow the temperature of the water to creep upward toward the boiling point.

However firm you like them, soft-boiled eggs are best served steaming in the shell, with salt, pepper, and flavorful bits of butter melting and bathing their little insides. Serve them in egg cups with their broad ends up. Their shells will crack more readily and they will be easier to scoop out.

CODDLED EGGS
(Oeufs Mollets)

Coddled eggs are 5½-minute soft-boiled eggs that have been shelled after cooking. Thus prepared, they can be used in various recipes interchangeably with poached eggs. Coddled eggs have a white that is just firm enough to be peeled and handled, and a runny liquid yolk. Unsupported, the coddled egg will sag under the weight of its golden liquid center, but it will still retain its egg shape.

It is important that the white of coddled eggs be kept very tender. When eaten, the egg is cut with the edge of a fork. If the surface of the white is tough and rubbery, the egg will compress under the fork and burst when cut, splattering yolk all over the place. You must therefore never allow a coddled egg to be cooked anywhere near the boiling point.

To cook, bring the egg first to room temperature. Lower it into simmering water, return the water to the simmer, and cook for 5½ minutes. Then plunge the egg into cold water to stop the cooking and loosen the shell. Crack the broad end of the shell and carefully peel it away, supporting the whole egg with the palm of your hand. Coddled eggs may be kept warm or reheated in hot salted water (about 140°).

Another way to cook coddled eggs is to plunge them all at once into boiling water and remove the pan from the fire. The eggs immediately cool the water below the boiling point, and the eggs are left to stand, covered, for about 8 minutes. This method is not quite so precise, in that varying amounts of water will cool at varying rates. Also, since water boils at 2° lower temperature for every thousand feet above sea level, a cook in Denver may lose most of her cooking heat at the moment the eggs go in.

Coddled eggs may be used in any of the recipes given for poached eggs. You will find, however, that peeling these eggs is both tricky and time-consuming. You will save yourself a great deal of bother by learning how to poach eggs perfectly.

HARD-BOILED EGGS
(Oeufs Durs)

Hard-boiled eggs are cooked in exactly the same way as soft-boiled eggs, only longer. By this I mean to emphasize that the water should not be allowed to boil. During the longer time it takes to hard-cook an egg, water at 212° is certain to make the white rubbery and tough. Eggs that are hard-cooked in boiling water are difficult to slice without crushing the yolk.

To cook, place room temperature eggs in simmering water to cover. Return the water to the simmer and cook for 10 to 12 minutes. During this time the white becomes solid but remains tender throughout. The yolk cooks all the way through (no waxy center) and becomes dry and mealy.

As soon as 10 minutes are up, plunge the eggs into cold water to stop the cooking and chill them thoroughly. This shrinks the egg and helps loosen the shell. You can speed this process by reaching into the water and cracking each egg against the side of the bowl. Rapid chilling helps prevent the formation of ferrous sulfide—an unsightly green discoloration that forms on the surface of the hard-cooked yolk when eggs are cooked too long or at too high temperatures.

To peel the eggs, crack them lightly all over and roll them on the counter, pressing lightly with the palm of your hand. Open the shell at its broad end and peel the egg under running tap water, letting the water help you strip away the surface membrane. (Remember, if the air bubble at the broad end is more than 3/16 inch deep, your eggs are on the stale side.

Hard-boiled eggs are used cold as an ingredient (potato salad), as an appetizer (stuffed), and as a garnish or decoration. Following are some recipes for hot hard-boiled eggs and egg mixtures. Reheat hard-boiled eggs in hot salted water (about 140°). They will slice more easily if you dip the knife in water.

Oeufs Durs à la Soubise. Arrange hot hard-boiled eggs on a bed of Onion Purée. Cover the eggs with Cream Sauce.

Oeufs Durs à la Cressonière. Place hot whole hard-boiled eggs on a bed of watercress Purée. Cover the eggs with Cream Sauce.

Oeufs Durs à la Bretonne. Cut hot hard-boiled eggs in half lengthwise. Place them on a dish coated with Béchamel Sauce to which you have added chopped onions, chopped leeks, and sliced mushrooms, all sautéed in butter. Pour more of this sauce over the eggs.

Oeufs Durs Granville. Cut hot hard-boiled eggs in quarters. Dress them with Bordelaise Sauce.

Oeufs Durs sur Macédoine de Légumes. Arrange hot hard-boiled eggs on a *Macédoine* of vegetables that you have tossed with hot melted butter or cream. They can also be served cold with Mayonnaise.

Oeufs Durs sur Purées. Arrange hot hard-boiled eggs, whole or cut in half, on a Purée of mushrooms, spinach, asparagus, carrots, sweet potatoes, or peas, etc.

Oeufs Durs Farcis à l'Aurore. Cut hard-boiled eggs in half lengthwise. Remove the yolks. Reserve ⅓ of the yolks and mix the remaining ⅔ with very thick Béchamel Sauce, mashing to form a thick paste. Flavor this mixture to taste with salt and pepper, and nutmeg or powdered basil or thyme, and stuff the eggs, heaping the mixture in the form of a dome. Place the stuffed eggs on a baking dish coated with Mornay Sauce, sprinkle them with grated cheese and melted butter, and brown in a hot oven or under the broiler. Sprinkle the remaining ⅓ chopped egg yolks over the eggs and surround the dish with a ribbon of Tomato Sauce.

Oeufs Durs Farcis Chimay. Cut hard-boiled eggs in half lengthwise. Remove the yolks, mash them, and mix them with an equal amount of dry *Duxelles*. Stuff the eggs with this mixture, heaping it in the form of a dome. Place them on a buttered dish, cover them with Mornay Sauce, and sprinkle them with grated cheese and melted butter. Brown in a hot oven or under the broiler.

Oeufs Durs en Côtelettes. Cut the whole hard-boiled eggs into small dice. Blend this dice into thick Béchamel Sauce to which you have added several raw egg yolks. Chill this mixture. When chilled, divide the mixture into whole egg-sized pieces and shape these pieces in the form of cutlets, such as small lamb chops. Dip these cutlets into egg and breadcrumbs and deep-fry until golden brown, or sauté them in Clarified Butter. Thoroughly drain the cutlets, arrange them on a round dish in the form of a crown, and fasten a tiny frill to the tail of each one. Garnish the dish with Fried Parsley and serve with Tomato Sauce.

Oeufs en Cromesquis. Cut the whole hard-boiled eggs into small dice. Add to this dice some diced mushrooms and truffles. Blend into an Allemande Sauce and chill the mixture. When chilled, form the mixture into small oval or cork-shaped cakes. Dip these into a light frying Batter and deep-fry until golden brown. Drain and serve with Fried Parsley and Tomato Sauce.

POACHED EGGS
(*Oeufs Pochés*)

One day almost two centuries ago, on the road to Melun, the Father of Gastronomy, Brillat-Savarin, stopped at an inn to appease his hunger. But, alas, the inn had had a very busy day. Aside from a few eggs there was no food at all, excepting a fine leg of mutton that three Englishmen had brought with them. Eying the mutton turning on the spit, Brillat-Savarin prevailed upon the cook to poach the eggs in the gravy dripping from the roast. Then, when the cook was not looking, he crept up upon the leg of mutton and, using his pocket knife, slashed it deeply in a dozen places so that the gravy ran out to the last drop. Thus the good professor dined enjoyably on his poached eggs in gravy, delighting in the thought that he was enjoying the very essence of the roast leg of mutton, while the Englishmen were left only the bother of masticating its empty remains.

Eggs poached in gravy or just plain water are the basis of many delightful dishes. A little dexterity is required, but you can get the hang of poaching after just a few trials.

The eggs *must* be fresh. The object of poaching an egg is to wrap the liquid yolk in the soft jellied white. The white must remain intact, and it must congeal quickly. If the white is stale and watery, it will dissipate through the water in shreds. It simply will not wrap around and seal the yolk.

As an aid to quickly congealing the white, you may add 1 tablespoon vinegar and 1 teaspoon salt to each quart of water in which the eggs are poached. This helps but sometimes gives the egg a wrinkled, shriveled look. Poached eggs should look like translucent pearls. Let us then try to poach our eggs without the aid of vinegar.

Fill a skillet or flat pan with water about 2 inches deep. Bring the water almost to the boil. Move the pan to the side of the fire so that the bubbles concentrate at one side. At this point the water will be welling up from the bottom, rolling slightly at the surface, and sinking down to the bottom again.

Just before cooking, break the egg (which should be at room temperature) into a saucer or shallow bowl. With a wooden spoon in one hand, gently slide the egg from the dish into the gently bubbling water. As it revolves in the current, use the wooden spoon to shape the congealing white around the yolk. When the white has begun to set, push the egg to the side of the pan and slide in another. *Do not allow the water to boil.*

Continue in this manner until all the eggs are cooking. Cook for about 4 minutes. Then, with a slotted spoon, remove the poached eggs from the water, beginning with the first, and plunge them into cold water to stop the cooking.

There are usually a few ragged edges, so trim these off while the eggs are in the water. The eggs may now be drained thoroughly and served still warm. Or you may store them in the water. You may reheat the eggs by placing them in hot salted water for a minute or two, until they are warmed through. Remove them with a slotted spoon, drain *thoroughly* on a towel, and serve according to the recipe.

Oeufs à l'Américaine. Poach the eggs. Place them on Fried Bread on in *Croustades* and garnish with pieces or dice of lobster. Pour over American Sauce.

Oeufs Pochés Bénédictine. Poach the eggs. On toasted English muffins place slices of broiled ham. Put a hot poached egg on each slice of ham and pour over Hollandaise Sauce. Slices of truffle are optional.

Oeufs Pochés Henri IV. Poach the eggs. Place them in *Croustades* and coat them with Béarnaise Sauce. Glaze* quickly under the broiler.

Oeufs Pochés Sévigné. Poach the eggs. Place them on bread *Croustades* that you have stuffed with Braised Lettuce and arranged in a circle on a round dish. Pour over Supreme Sauce and decorate each egg with a slice of truffle.

Oeufs Pochés à l'Aurore. Poach the eggs. Place them on rounds of Fried Bread arranged in a circle on a round dish. Coat the eggs with Aurora Sauce and sprinkle them with chopped egg yolk.

Oeufs Pochés à la Chivry. Poach the eggs. Place them on rounds of Fried Bread arranged in a circle on a round dish. Garnish with asparagus tips cooked in butter and pour over Chivry Sauce.

Oeufs Pochés à la Duchesse. Poach the eggs. Place them on oval cakes of Duchess Potatoes that you have baked until they are golden. Pour over the eggs Starch-Thickened Veal Stock enriched with butter.

Oeufs Pochés à la Cressonière. Poach the eggs. Place them on a bed of watercress Purée and cover them with Cream Sauce.

Oeufs Pochés aux Crevettes. Poach the eggs. Place them on top of Tartlet shells that you have filled with shrimp and Shrimp Sauce, and pour shrimp sauce over all.

Oeufs Pochés d'Orsay. Poach the eggs Place them on rounds of Fried Bread arranged in a circle on a round dish. Coat the eggs with Chateaubriand Sauce.

Oeufs Pochés Suzette. Bake medium potatoes. Cut a circle in their tops large enough to hold an egg. Scoop out the potato, mash the pulp with butter and season it with salt and pepper. Return the pulp to the potato shell, leaving enough space to hold an egg. Poach the eggs, place them in the space provided, coat with Mornay Sauce, and sprinkle with grated Parmesan cheese. Brown quickly under the broiler or in a hot oven.

Oeufs Pochés Toupinel. Proceed as for *Oeufs Pochés Suzette* (above) but use Celery Purée in place of the Mornay Sauce.

Oeufs Pochés Normande. Poach the eggs. Place them on top of Tartlet shells that you have filled with poached oysters bound with Normandy Sauce. Coat the eggs with Normandy sauce.

Oeufs Pochés Rossini. Poach the eggs. Place them on top of Tartlet shells into which you have put a slice or some dice of sautéed Foie Gras. Pour over the eggs Starch-Thickened Veal Stock flavored with Madeira and place on top of each egg a slice of truffle.

Oeufs Pochés à la Bourguignonne. Put 3 cups of dry red wine into a saucepan and turn on the fire. To the wine add 1 clove garlic, crushed; 3 sprigs of parsley; ½ bay leaf; a pinch of thyme; a pinch each of salt and pepper. Bring to the simmer, simmer 10 minutes, and strain out the seasonings. Return the wine to the saucepan, bring it almost to the boil, and poach 6 or 8 eggs in it. Remove the eggs and keep them warm in hot salted water. To the wine in the saucepan add *Beurre Manié* to make a sauce. Place the eggs on rounds of Fried Bread, garnish them with tiny Glazed Onions and button mushroom caps sautéed in butter, and pour the sauce over all.

SHIRRED EGGS
(*Oeufs sur le Plat*)

Shirred, or baked, eggs are very popular in France. They are called eggs-on-the-plate (*oeufs sur le plat*) or looking-glass eggs (*oeufs miroir*) because of the shiny white film that forms on the yolk during cooking. They are perhaps the easiest of all eggs to cook, whether you are cooking just one egg or a dozen, but they do require careful watching and must be whisked out of the oven as soon as they are done.

To cook, break the eggs into a flat ovenproof dish that you have thoroughly buttered. The usual choice is a shallow earthenware ramekin or a shallow, oval, enameled cast iron gratin dish, or *plat*, of a size to comfortably accommodate 2 eggs and whatever garnish the recipe demands for a single serving. The eggs, of course, are served on the dish, *sur le plat*.

Place the plat of eggs on a low fire for 1 minute to warm it. Brush the eggs with a little melted butter and place them in a 300° oven to bake for 10 to 12 minutes. The eggs are done when the whites are set but quite soft, and the yolks still liquid but with a shiny white transparent glaze that is described as mirrorlike. Do not salt the eggs until after cooking, or they will become unattractively speckled.

To accentuate this glaze, or to glaze or brown other foods being cooked on the same dish, the eggs may be started in the oven and finished close to the broiler flame. Give the eggs an extra basting with melted butter before exposing them to the flame.

Oeufs Bercy. Bake the eggs. Garnish them with small grilled or fried sausages, and surround with a ribbon of Tomato Sauce.

Oeufs au Beurre Noir. Bake the eggs. Pour over them a little Brown Butter followed by a few drops of vinegar.

Oeufs Clamart. Bake the eggs on a bed of Peas à la Française.

Oeufs Lyonnaise. Bake the eggs on a bed of onions sautéed in butter. Surround the dish with a ribbon of Lyonnaise Sauce.

Oeufs à la Crécy. Bake the eggs on a thin bed of Carrot Purée, and surround them with a ribbon of Cream Sauce.

Oeufs à la Bretonne. Bake the eggs and surround them with a ribbon of Breton Sauce.

Oeufs à l'Italienne. Bake the eggs on a bed of lean chopped ham and surround with a ribbon of Italian Sauce.

Oeufs Chasseur. Bake the eggs and garnish them with sautéed sliced chicken livers dressed with Chasseur Sauce. Sprinkle with chopped parsley.

Oeufs Mornay. Bake the eggs, which you have coated with Mornay Sauce and sprinkled with grated cheese and melted butter, on a thin bed of Mornay sauce. If necessary to get a good brown glaze,* finish quickly under the broiler.

Oeufs à la Florentine. Bake the eggs, which you have coated with Mornay Sauce and sprinkled with grated cheese and melted butter, on a bed of spinach simmered in butter. If necessary, to get a good brown glaze,* finish quickly under the broiler.

Oeufs Metternich. Bake the eggs, which you have sprinkled with grated cheese and melted butter, on a bed of minced mushrooms sautéed in butter.

Oeufs à la Chevreuse. Using a pastry bag, pipe a ribbon of very thick Green Bean Purée around the edge of the baking dish. Break the eggs into the center of the dish, sprinkle them with grated cheese, and bake them.

Oeufs à la Lorraine. Bake the eggs, with 1 tablespoon cream surrounding each yolk, on a bed of thin slices of grilled bacon and Gruyère cheese.

Oeufs Opéra. Bake the eggs. Garnish them with sautéed chicken livers in Madeira Sauce on one side, and asparagus tips on the other.

Oeufs à la Provençale. Before buttering the baking dish, rub it with a cut clove of garlic. Bake the eggs on a bed of eggplant slices fried in olive oil. Surround each egg yolk with a ring of Provençal Sauce.

Oeufs Grand-Duc. Bake the eggs, which you have coated with Mornay Sauce and sprinkled with grated cheese and melted butter. If necessary to get a good brown glaze,* finish them quickly under the broiler. Garnish with asparagus tips in butter.

Oeufs Carmen. Bake the eggs and trim them so that only a ½-inch ribbon of white remains surrounding the yolk. On rounds of Fried Bread place round slices of sautéed ham. Place a trimmed egg on top of each ham slice and coat each egg with Tomato Sauce flavored with paprika and enriched with butter.

EGGS EN COCOTTE
(*Oeufs en Cocotte*)

These are very soft, fine-textured, unbeaten eggs cooked slowly in their own steam. They are cooked in ovenproof cocottes with tight-fitting covers, which may be of a size to hold just one egg or a number of eggs and their garnish.

To cook a single egg in a small cocotte, brush the inside of the cocotte with melted butter, add 1 tablespoon heavy cream, and heat the cocotte in a shallow pan of boiling water. When the cocotte is hot to the touch, carefully break a whole egg into it. Dot the egg with a few bits of butter. Cover the cocotte tightly and continue cooking in the gently boiling water, or place the pan in a 350° oven. Cooking time is 10 to 12 minutes. The egg is done when the white is almost set (jellylike) and the yolk is bright and glossy. This basic dish is called *oeufs en cocotte à la crème*.

Oeufs en Cocotte au Chambertin. Fill the cocottes one-third full with a boiling Red Wine Sauce made with Chambertin wine. Break the eggs into the sauce, salt lightly, and place the cocottes in gently boiling water. When the eggs are almost cooked, uncover the cocottes and glaze* the eggs briefly.

Oeufs en Cocotte à la Lorraine. Heat and butter the cocottes. Place in the bottom of each 1 teaspoon diced and fried bacon, 2 or 3 thin slices of Gruyère cheese, and 1 tablespoon heavy cream. Break the eggs into the cocottes, season with salt and pepper, cover and place the cocottes in gently boiling water.

Oeufs en Cocotte Montrouge. Heat the cocottes and line them with a thick Mushroom Purée. Break the eggs into the cocottes, season with salt and pepper, and add 1 tablespoon cream. Cover and place the cocottes in gently boiling water.

Oeufs en Cocotte à la Jeannette. Heat and butter the cocottes and cover the bottom with a layer of chicken Quenelle mixture. Break the eggs into the cocottes, season with salt and pepper, cover and place the cocottes in gently boiling water. When cooked, pour a ring of Velouté Sauce around the eggs and garnish with asparagus tips.

Oeufs en Cocotte à la Tartare. Heat and butter the cocottes. Line them with finely minced raw beef to which you have added chopped chives, salt, and pepper. Break the eggs into the cocottes and add 1 tablespoon heavy cream. Cover and place the cocottes in gently boiling water.

Oeufs Ambassadrice en Cocotte. This is very elegant. Heat and butter the cocottes. Line them with a purée of Foie Gras sprinkled with chopped truffles. Break the eggs into the cocottes, cover, and place the cocottes in gently boiling water. When the eggs are cooked, surround them with a ring of Supreme Sauce flavored with sherry, and garnish with asparagus tips.

SAUTÉED EGGS
(Oeufs Sautés)

Sautéed eggs are eggs fried very slowly in just enough butter to keep them from sticking to the bottom of the pan. (American fried eggs are sautéed eggs, except that I have noticed that often more fat is used than called for by a true sauté.)

To cook, melt a little butter in a heavy skillet, keeping the heat very low to prevent the egg from toughening on the bottom before the top is cooked. To speed cooking, you may cover the pan to trap the heat and cook the top of the egg in its own steam, adding 1 tablespoon water if you want to create more steam and keep the edges of the egg very soft. Or you may flip the egg over when the bottom has set firm. (Spooning fat over the egg to speed cooking will make it greasy in appearance and in fact.) When cooked, the white will be set but soft with no brown, lacy edges. Season with salt and fresh-ground pepper and serve the egg at once.

Oeufs au Bacon Poêlés. Here is a dish every American knows. I put it here to show that the French know it too, although they rarely would have it for breakfast. Sauté the eggs. Serve with grilled or sautéed bacon.

Oeufs à la Diable. Sauté the eggs, turning them over part way through cooking. Sprinkle them with very hot Brown Butter and heated vinegar.

Oeufs à l'Italienne. Sauté the eggs in olive oil. Garnish with thin slices of sautéed ham and pour Italian Sauce over the eggs.

Oeufs à la Catalane. Sauté the eggs. Serve them on a bed of sautéed eggplant and tomato slices, seasoned with salt, pepper, and garlic, and sprinkled with chopped parsley.

Oeufs à la Romaine. Sauté the eggs. Serve them on a bed of chopped spinach simmered in Noisette Butter and mixed with chopped anchovy filets. Sprinkle the eggs with noisette butter.

DEEP-FRIED EGGS
(Oeufs Frits)

Deep-fried eggs are an exception to the rule that eggs must be cooked at moderate temperatures. The fat must be quite hot and 2 to 3 inches deep. The eggs must be very fresh. Just before cooking, break them into a saucer, season with salt and pepper, and carefully slide them into the hot fat, shaping the egg with a wooden spoon to wrap the solidifying white around the yolk. This procedure is similar to poaching, except that you must work much more swiftly. The egg is cooked in less than a minute, with a golden brown exterior and a hot, liquid yolk.

Oeufs Frits à la Bordelaise. Prepare halved Sautéed Tomatoes à la Provençale, adding a little chopped shallot. Arrange the tomato halves on a round dish in the form of a crown and garnish with finely minced *cèpes* (see Mushrooms) or mushrooms sautéed in olive oil and sprinkled with a little lemon juice and chopped parsley. Place a deep-fried egg on each tomato half, and fill the center of the crown with Fried Parsley.

Oeufs Frits à l'Alsacienne. Deep-fry the eggs. Arrange them on a bed of braised sauerkraut with alternating slices of ham. Surround the dish with a ribbon of Demi-Glace Sauce.

Oeufs Frits à la Provençale. Season and dredge in flour thick slices of eggplant. Deep-fry the slices and arrange them on a dish in the form of a crown. On top of each slice put a Grilled Tomato half. On top of each tomato half place a deep-fried egg. Fill the center of the crown with Fried Parsley.

Oeufs Frits aux Anchois. Deep-fry the eggs. Place them on ovals of Fried Bread garnished with crisscrossed strips of filets of anchovy. Sprinkle with Brown Butter.

Oeufs Frits à la Créole. Broil buttered zucchini halves and place them on a dish in a ring. Deep-fry the eggs and place one on each zucchini half. Fill the center of the ring with Rice à la Créole. Sprinkle the eggs with Brown Butter.

Oeufs Frits Moissonneur. Arrange blanched and fried bacon slices on a round dish in a ring. Between the slices of bacon place deep-fried eggs. In the center of the ring put a mound of large green peas that you have cooked with shredded lettuce and thin slices of potato.

SCRAMBLED EGGS
(Oeufs Brouillés)

When it comes to scrambled eggs, everyone indulges their own taste. Some like them dry, some moist, some fluffy, some chewy, some undercooked and jellylike, some so overcooked the moisture is actually draining out of them onto the plate. But if you have never tasted French scrambled eggs, a golden mound of soft moist curds enriched with cream and butter, you owe it to yourself to try them as your very next scrambled egg dish.

In order to cook scrambled eggs the heat must be very, very low. You can use a heavy skillet or a double boiler. Either way, butter the pan with ½ tablespoon butter and place it over very low heat. Lightly beat 2 eggs with 1 tablespoon heavy cream or milk and a seasoning of salt and fresh-ground pepper until they are well mixed but not foamy. Pour them into the warm pan and cook very slowly, stirring constantly with a wooden spoon (eggs may discolor if stirred with a metal spoon in an aluminum pan). Keep the heat very low and keep stirring the eggs over the entire bottom of the pan, as they take on a custardlike consistency. If the mixture begins to lump, remove the pan from the fire and stir it vigorously. When the eggs are just thick enough to please you, remove from the fire and stir in ½ tablespoon butter and 1 tablespoon heavy cream. This enriches the eggs and stops the cooking. Serve immediately. Scrambled eggs won't wait.

There are many delicious variations on basic scrambled eggs. Herbs and grated cheese can be added to the eggs before scrambling. Meats and vegetables must be cooked and heated before they go into the eggs. Firm foods, such as diced ham or mushrooms, are first sautéed in the pan. The heat is then lowered and the eggs poured over them. Delicate foods, such as asparagus tips and peas, are cooked separately and mixed into the eggs when they are finished cooking. Very watery foods, such as tomatoes, should have some of their water cooked out of them before they are mixed with the eggs.

Finally, do not underestimate the place of scrambled eggs in fine cookery. Escoffier rated them as undoubtedly the finest of all egg preparations.

Oeufs Brouillés à l'Américaine. Scramble the eggs with diced and sautéed bacon. Garnish the eggs with grilled bacon and Grilled Tomato halves.

Oeufs Brouillés aux Champignons. Scramble the eggs with minced mushrooms sautéed in butter. Serve in a deep serving dish with a large cooked mushroom head in the middle surrounded with sliced mushrooms sautéed in butter.

Oeufs Brouillés au Fromage. Scramble the eggs with grated cheese, half Parmesan and half Gruyère (about 4 tablespoons of cheese for every 2 eggs).

Oeufs Brouillés à la Bercy. Scramble the eggs. Place them in a deep dish and garnish with grilled or sautéed Chipolata Sausages. Surround the dish with a ribbon of Tomato Sauce.

Oeufs Brouillés à la Romaine. Place a bed of spinach, simmered in butter and mixed with chopped anchovy filets, in the bottom of a flat ovenproof dish.

Scramble the eggs with grated Parmesan cheese and spread them on top of the spinach. Sprinkle with grated Parmesan cheese and melted butter and brown quickly under the broiler.

Oeufs Brouillés Clamart. Scramble the eggs. Mix them with Peas à la Française. Garnish the top of the eggs with a little mound of the peas.

Oeufs Brouillés aux Pointes d'Asperges. Scramble the eggs. Mix them with asparagus tips finished in butter. Garnish the top of the eggs with a little mound of the asparagus tips.

Oeufs Brouillés Panetière. Scramble the eggs. Mix them with diced mushrooms and diced ham, both sautéed in butter. Spoon the eggs into a *Croustade* made from a round loaf of bread, hollowed out and lightly browned in the oven. Sprinkle the top of the eggs with grated Parmesan cheese and melted butter and brown quickly in the broiler.

Oeufs Brouillés à l'Espagnole. Scramble the eggs. Place them in hollowed half tomatoes sautèed in olive oil. Garnish the top of the eggs with a julienne* of pimentos.

Oeufs Brouillés Grand'mère. Scramble the eggs. Mix them with fine diced Croutons of Fried Bread, and garnish the eggs with more of these croutons. Sprinkle with chopped parsley.

Oeufs Brouillés aux Fines Herbes. Scramble the eggs with minced fresh herbs —chervil, parsley, tarragon, thyme, alone or in combination, or with other herbs you think go well with eggs. Just before serving, sprinkle a little of the fresh herbs over the eggs.

OMELETS
(*Omelettes*)

A French omelet is a soft, moist French scrambled egg enclosed in a tender coating of coagulated egg. The omelet is folded in an oval shape and filled with something good (*omelette fourrée*). Or it is cooked flat like a thick, light pancake with a filling incorporated inside its body (*omelette plat*). In either case, the omelet has a soft, moist center.

Unlike most egg cookery, omelets are cooked very quickly at high heat. Because of this, it is not at all difficult to make frightful errors. Tough, leathery omelets, dried-out omelets, brown omelets (smelling horribly of burned egg), and "grandmother" omelets with wizened skins are the lot in life of the unwary cook. Yet, if omelets are easy to spoil, they are also easy to cook properly.

All the fuss that is made about omelet pans is perfectly justified. The purpose of the pan is to cook the omelet quickly without allowing it to stick. The best pan for this purpose is a French omelet pan of ⅛-inch-thick sheet iron with wide, curved, sloping sides and a long handle. It responds quickly to heat, allowing you to cook omelets in rapid succession (2 a minute, when you become proficient). Another good choice is a cast iron skillet with curved, sloping sides. These pans should have a bottom diameter of about 7 inches, which is the correct size for a 2- to 3-egg omelet. (Larger omelets, up to the 6-egg size, are possible but not recommended.) Either the French iron or American cast iron pan is quite inexpensive, and you should reserve it for cooking omelets alone. For all I know, these pans, properly cared for, will last forever. You can bequeath them to your grandchildren. And the more and longer they are used, the better omelets they will turn out.

Before you use either of these pans for the first time, it must be cured. Scrub the pan smooth with soap pads or with steel wool and cleanser. Pour about ¼-inch of oil into the pan and heat very slowly until the oil is quite hot. Remove the pan from the fire and let stand overnight. Pour off the oil, wipe the pan dry, and it is ready for its maiden omelet. From this time on, you should never wash the pan or even dip it in water. Simply wipe it dry with paper towels. If some food does stick to the pan, scrub it off with paper towels and dry salt. If sticking becomes a problem, scrub the whole pan with salt and cure the pan again. Sooner or later you will have a fine kitchen instrument on which you can absolutely rely.

Now let us cook a plain and simple omelet. Place 1 tablespoon butter in the pan and heat slowly until the butter turns light brown and smells nutty. This indicates the pan is at the right temperature and produces a delicious taste as well. Meanwhile, beat 3 eggs with a scant ½ teaspoon salt and 3 tablespoons milk or light cream. (The liquid enriches the eggs; it also retards their cooking slightly, giving you a little more time to work with the eggs in the pan.) Beat the eggs lightly. Too much beating makes the omelet heavy and watery.

Remove the pan from the fire and tilt it all around to coat the sloping sides part way up with the hot butter. Return the pan to the heat and pour in the eggs. Immediately thrust the pan in a forward and backward motion, keeping it flat on the burner over a moderate flame. At the same time stir the eggs with a fork, keeping the flat of the tines on the bottom of the pan, stirring with broad, circular sweeps and moving the thickening egg mass at the sides toward the center of the pan. The object is to get the whole mass to thicken evenly, without allowing it or any portion of it to become overly firm. Consequently, the fork must stroke the entire bottom and sides of the pan, displacing any of the egg that may be congealing there. In about 30 seconds the egg mass will have been heated and thickened evenly throughout. It should look like a fluffy custard, very soft and moist. (It *must* have a very soft consistency because it will continue to cook in its own heat after being folded.)

Now, stop stirring and shaking the pan and allow the bottom of the omelet to congeal lightly for 4 or 5 seconds. (At this point, you would add the hot filling for a filled omelet, laying it in a broad thick ribbon across the center of the omelet at a right angle to the handle of the pan.)

When the bottom has set, depress the handle of the pan slightly so that the omelet slides toward you. Use your fork to loosen edges if necessary to allow the omelet to slide. As the edge of the omelet slides up the slope of the pan, use your fork to flip ⅓ of it over on top of its middle.

Now, lift the handle of the pan to about a 45° angle, so that the partially folded omelet slides away from you. As it slides up the slope of the opposite side of the pan, lift the pan from the burner (still at a 45° angle) and sharply strike the handle several times with the heel of your free hand. Lo and behold, the far side of the omelet will rise up and curl over upon itself to complete the folding.

Replace the pan on the burner, still holding it at a 45° angle, and quickly shape the omelet with your fork if necessary to obtain a more perfect oval shape. (Omelets are cooked to be just golden or a light golden brown. If you prefer your omelet with some color, let the pan remain in its 45° position for a few seconds.) Then, grasping the handle of the pan with your palm upwards, hold a heated plate to the outside edge of the pan and invert the pan, flipping the omelet plop into the center of the plate.

Finally, draw a piece of butter over the surface of the omelet and serve it wreathed in its own steam.

Flat omelets are cooked like folded omelets, except they are flipped over in the pan instead of folded. The egg mass is kept moving until it thickens to the custardy stage, and then is allowed to set for several seconds until the bottom is firm but not tough. If the filling has not already been incorporated into the egg mixture, it is distributed over the top at this time and pressed in lightly with the fork so that it is bound by the moist egg. The omelet is then carefully lifted with a spatula and flipped over onto its other side. Carefully cooked, a flat omelet is just as soft and moist inside as the folded variety.

There is another omelet-type egg preparation that is half omelet, half soufflé. The egg mixture is prepared by beating the whites separately and folding them into the beaten egg yolks. The "omelet" is then cooked over a slow fire without stirring. It will rise like a very thick pancake. It may be folded over once. If served flat, it may be covered with a lid to set the top, or finished in a moderate oven. This preparation is called *omelette mousseline*.

All the following variations are based on 3 eggs (or 9 tablespoons of lightly beaten egg) and a scant ½ teaspoon of salt.

Omelette aux Croutons. Combine the egg mixture with 2 tablespoons bread crusts cut in dice and sautéed in Clarified Butter.

Omelette aux Fines Herbes. Combine the egg mixture with 1 tablespoon *fines herbes*—equal parts of fresh parsley, chives, chervil, and tarragon, finely chopped. The omelet will take on a fresh green color.

Omelette aux Champignons. Combine the egg mixture with 2 tablespoons sliced and sautéed mushrooms. Garnish the top of the omelet with sautéed mushroom slices, or 3 sautéed mushroom caps.

Omelette à la Clamart. Fill the omelet with Peas à la Française. Cut a lengthwise slit in the finished omelet and fill with 1 tablespoon peas.

Omelette à la Crécy. Combine the egg mixture with 2 tablespoons Carrots à la Vichy. This omelet is also called *omelette à la Vichy.*

Omelette aux Artichauts. Combine the egg mixture with 2 tablespoons sliced and sautéed artichoke hearts. Garnish the top of the omelet with a row of sliced, sautéed artichoke hearts and surround it with a ribbon of buttered Starch-Thickened Veal Stock.

Omelette aux Pointes d'Asperges. Fill the omelet with 2 tablespoons asparagus tips finished in butter. Cut a lengthwise slit in the finished omelet and fill with asparagus tips.

Omelette aux Aubergines. Combine the egg mixture with 2 tablespoons diced sautéed eggplant. Garnish the top of the omelet with a slice of sautéed eggplant, sprinkle with chopped parsley, and surround it with a ribbon of Demi-Glace Sauce.

Omelette au Maïs à la Crème. Fill the omelet with Corn in Cream and surround it with a ribbon of Cream Sauce.

Omelette à la Provençale. Combine the egg mixture with lightly sautéed tomato that you have peeled, seeded, squeezed, chopped, and mixed with a little chopped parsley and minced garlic.

Omelette à la Lyonnaise. Combine the egg mixture with 3 tablespoons minced onion lightly browned in butter and ½ teaspoon chopped parsley.

Omelette au Bacon. Combine the egg mixture with 4 tablespoons bacon, diced and lightly sautéed in butter. Garnish the top of the omelet with slices of sautéed bacon.

Omelette au Jambon. Combine the egg mixture with 4 tablespoons ham, diced and slightly sautéed in butter. Garnish the top of the omelet with strips of sautéed ham.

Omelette à la Duxelles. Fill the omelet with 2 tablespoons Duxelles mixed with diced ham sautéed in butter. Surround it with a ribbon of Demi-Glace Sauce flavored with Tomato Sauce.

Omelette Chasseur. Fill the omelet with 2 tablespoons chicken livers and mushrooms, sliced and sautéed in butter. Garnish the top of the omelet with slices of sautéed chicken livers and mushrooms, and sprinkle with chopped parsley. Surround it with a ribbon of Chasseur Sauce.

Omelette aux Crevettes. Fill the omelet with 2 tablespoons sliced cooked shrimp mixed with Shrimp Sauce. Surround it with a ribbon of shrimp sauce.

Omelette à la Florentine. Fill the omelet with 2 tablespoons Spinach in Cream. Coat the finished omelet with Mornay Sauce, sprinkle with grated Parmesan cheese and melted butter, and brown quickly under the broiler.

Omelette à la Princesse. Combine the egg mixture with 2 tablespoons asparagus tips finished in butter. Garnish the top of the omelet with a row of truffle slices warmed in butter. Surround it with a ribbon of Supreme Sauce.

Omelette à la Normande. Fill the omelet with 2 or 3 poached oysters mixed with Normandy Sauce.

Omelette à la Prélats. Fill the omelet with a *Salpicon* of poached fish roes, shrimp, and julienne* of truffle, mixed with Normandy Sauce that you have blended with Crayfish Butter. Coat the finished omelet with this sauce and sprinkle it with chopped truffle. (Why not whip this up for breakfast tomorrow?)

SOUFFLÉS
(Soufflés)

There are two kinds of soufflés, sweet and savory. Sweet soufflés contain sugar and have as their flavoring ingredients fruits, nuts, liqueurs, or chocolate. They are in the category of desserts.

Savory soufflés are served as small entrees or hors d'oeuvres. They have as their flavoring ingredients meat, fish, or vegetable purées, or cheese. The flavoring ingredient is mixed into a white sauce blended with egg yolk. This mixture is then aerated with beaten egg white and baked until it puffs up and becomes golden brown on top. (The French word *soufflé* means "puffed.")

There is a generally accepted formula for soufflés that is easy to memorize, and that you can use as a point of departure for devising soufflés of your own. For a standard 6-cup soufflé dish, use 1 cup of the flavoring ingredient, 1 cup of thick Béchamel Sauce, 4 egg yolks, and 5 beaten egg whites. This will produce about one quart of soufflé mixture, which will puff up nicely over the top of the dish to serve 4 or 5 persons. I do not recommend making soufflés larger than this, as the heat must penetrate the mixture quickly. At most, you can increase the above proportions by one-half. It is better to make 2 soufflés.

There are exceptions to the basic formula, depending upon the nature of the flavoring ingredient. Is it too mild in flavor? You must add more of it. Is it watery? You must use more or thicker white sauce. Is it heavy? Add an extra egg white. Is it starchy and thick of itself? Perhaps you can dispense with the white sauce and the egg yolks entirely! In the following recipes you will find these little adjustments, which are no more than common sense.

In addition to the formula, there is also a certain order in which the ingredients are usually assembled. (1) Make the white sauce. (2) Add the flavoring ingredient. (3) Add the egg yolks. (4) Fold in the beaten egg whites. This procedure, too, is subject to change.

Do not be overawed by this exception-making or by the soufflé's reputation as a kitchen troublemaker. Soufflés are quite easy and even fun to make. Just be sure you are ready to eat when the soufflé is ready to be eaten. Soufflés won't wait.

Now let us make a soufflé. We will illustrate the procedure with a spinach soufflé, or *soufflé d'épinards.*

(1) *Make the white sauce.* Melt 2 tablespoons butter in a saucepan, sprinkle and stir in 3 tablespoons flour, and cook, gently stirring, for a few minutes until golden. Add 1¼ cups almost boiling milk, and beat with a wire whisk until the sauce is thick and smooth. Season with ½ teaspoon salt, a good dash of white pepper, and a generous pinch of nutmeg (these seasonings are widely dissipated in the finished soufflé, so they should be quite strong). Cook the sauce over low heat, stirring, for about 10 minutes. It will have reduced to about 1 cup. This is béchamel sauce.

(2) *Add the flavoring ingredient.* Make 1 cup Spinach Purée. Properly made, this purée is too moist for use in a soufflé. Therefore, simmer it over low heat in 1 tablespoon butter until it gives up some of its moisture. It should not stick to your hand when you touch it. Mix the purée into the béchamel sauce, and remove the mixture from the fire.

(3) *Add the egg yolks.* Beat 5 egg yolks with a wire whisk until they become light and take on a lemon color. To guard against curdling the yolk,

add ½ cup of the hot sauce to the yolks, 1 tablespoon at a time, mixing thoroughly. Then pour the yolks into the sauce and purée mixture, beating until well blended and smooth. Taste for seasoning. Remember, the flavor must be strong.

(4) *Fold in the beaten egg whites.* Beat 5 egg whites. Be sure that the bowl and beaters are scrupulously clean—even a speck of fat or egg yolk in the whites will seriously impair results. For fastest beating, the egg whites must be at room temperature. Use a big balloon whip or a hand mixer that will allow you to move freely through the entire mass of white. After the whites begin to froth, add a pinch of salt. Also add ¼ teaspoon cream of tartar for its acidity, which helps stabilize the beaten whites. (If you are using a copper bowl, which itself creates the desired acidity, you can leave out the cream of tartar.) Continue to beat only until you get glistening, moist peaks when you lift the beater from the whites. (A moment too long and you will have a dry meringue.)

Now, pour the soufflé mixture (which should be warm but not hot) into a round-bottomed bowl and carefully but thoroughly mix in one-fourth of the egg whites to lighten the mixture. Then pour the rest of the egg whites on top and lightly fold them in, using a rubber spatula to pull the heavier mixture up the sides from the bottom of the bowl and spill it over the egg white. Don't overdo it—a minute's folding is enough. Some patches of egg white will remain. Ignore them. The soufflé is ready for baking.

The classic soufflé dish is the metal charlotte mold. In America the white, straight-sided casserole is more popular. For spectacular effect, a stiff paper collar, buttered, may be tied around the outside of the casserole to guide the soufflé upward to greater heights. Butter the bottom and sides of the casserole thickly, and dust the inside with breadcrumbs or grated cheese, discarding the excess. Pour in the soufflé mixture, smoothing the top with a knife. Finally, run your finger around the inside of the casserole about ½ inch deep in the soufflé mixture to wipe the sides of the casserole clean.

Place the soufflé on the lowest rack in a 375° oven. (The bottom of the oven is its hottest part, giving the bottom of the soufflé a delicious brown crust and heating the interior so that the soufflé begins to rise before a crust forms on the top.) Bake the soufflé for 25 to 35 minutes, but do not open the oven door during the first 20 minutes or the soufflé may become chilled and collapse. The soufflé is fully cooked when it ceases to shimmer like jelly in the center, and a skewer thrust into it is perfectly clean when withdrawn. Or you may want to withdraw the soufflé 5 minutes earlier and serve it in the French manner, just barely cooked, frothy and light on top and around the edges, with a soft, golden, creamy center as runny as warm Camembert cheese.

Soufflé au Fromage. Season 1 cup thick, hot Béchamel Sauce with ½ teaspoon salt, a pinch each of cayenne pepper and nutmeg. Stir in 4 well-beaten egg yolks. Add ¾ cup finely grated Swiss, Parmesan, or dry Cheddar cheese. Fold in 5 beaten egg whites and bake.

Soufflé aux Champignons. Cook 1 minced shallot (or 1 teaspoon minced onion) in 1 tablespoon butter until soft. Add ½ pound finely chopped mushrooms and cook until they give up their moisture. Add 1¼ cups thick Béchamel Sauce and simmer for 5 minutes, stirring, until the sauce is reduced to about 1 cup. Season the mixture, including a little cayenne pepper and nutmeg. Stir in 4 well-beaten egg yolks, fold in 5 beaten egg whites, and bake.

Soufflé d'Épinards. To 1 cup seasoned thick Béchamel Sauce add 1 cup Spinach Purée, simmered in butter to remove excess moisture. Season the mixture, including a pinch of nutmeg. Stir in 5 well-beaten egg yolks, fold in 5 beaten egg whites, and bake.

Soufflé d'Épinards à la Florentine. Prepare as above, adding ½ cup grated Parmesan cheese to the hot mixture before folding in the egg whites.

Soufflé de Laitues. Proceed as for *Soufflé d'Épinards* (above) using 1 cup Lettuce Purée simmered in butter to remove excess moisture.

Soufflé de Tomates. To 1 cup thick seasoned Béchamel Sauce add 1 cup Tomato Purée and 2 tablespoons grated Parmesan or Swiss cheese (or chopped tarragon). Season the mixture, stir in 4 well-beaten egg yolks, fold in 4 beaten egg whites, and bake.

Soufflé de Maïs. To ¾ cup thick seasoned Béchamel Sauce add 1 cup Corn Purée. Season the mixture, stir in 4 well-beaten egg yolks, fold in 4 beaten egg whites, and bake.

Soufflé aux Pommes de Terre. To 2 cups Potato Purée add ¼ cup heavy cream, 1 teaspoon salt, and a pinch of nutmeg. Stir in 3 well-beaten egg yolks, fold in 4 beaten egg whites, and bake.

Soufflé de Pommes de Terre au Fromage. Proceed as above, but add to the very hot Potato Purée ½ cup grated Gruyère or Parmesan cheese.

Soufflé de Patates. Prepare as for *Soufflé de Pommes de Terre* (above), using sweet potatoes.

Soufflé de Légumes. Purées of artichokes, asparagus, eggplant, carrots, celery, mushrooms, cauliflower, or turnips all may be used as flavor bases for soufflés. Be sure to dry out these purées by simmering them in butter.

Soufflé de Homard. To ¾ cup thick Béchamel Sauce add 1¼ cups Lobster Purée. Season the mixture, stir in 3 well-beaten egg yolks, fold in 4 well-beaten egg whites, and bake.

Soufflé de Crevettes. Proceed as above, using 1¼ cups Shrimp Purée.

Soufflé d'Huîtres. Make 1 cup thick Velouté Sauce, cooked down from ¾ cup oyster liquor and ¾ cup milk. Season, and stir in 4 well-beaten egg yolks. Add 1 cup poached medium oysters, cut in half. Fold in 5 egg whites, and bake.

Soufflé de Poisson. To ¾ cup thick Béchamel Sauce add 1¼ cups fish Purée made by cooking ½ pound boneless fish in ¼ cup dry white wine and a little butter, and rubbing it through a sieve (or use puréed leftover fish). Season the mixture, stir in 3 well-beaten egg yolks, fold in 4 beaten egg whites, and bake.

Soufflé de Volaille. To 1 cup thick Béchamel Sauce add 1½ cups chicken Purée. Season the mixture, stir in 4 well-beaten egg yolks, fold in 4 beaten egg whites, and bake.

Soufflé de Viandes. To ½ cup thick seasoned Béchamel Sauce add 1 cup meat Purée made from boiled or braised meat. Season the mixture, stir in 3 well-beaten egg yolks, fold in 4 beaten egg whites, and bake.

Soufflé de Jambon. To 1 cup seasoned Béchamel Sauce add 1½ cups ham Purée. Season the mixture, stir in 4 well-beaten egg yolks, fold in 5 beaten egg whites, and bake.

Soufflé de Jambon à la Strasbourgeoise. To 1 cup thick seasoned Béchamel Sauce add 1 cup ham Purée mixed with ⅓ cup *Pâté de Foie Gras* and 1 tablespoon chopped truffles. Season the mixture, stir in 4 well-beaten egg yolks, fold in 5 beaten egg whites, and bake.

Soufflé à la Royale. To ¾ cup thick Béchamel Sauce (flavored with truffle Essence) add 5 ounces truffle Purée. Season the mixture, stir in 3 well-beaten egg yolks, fold in 3 beaten egg whites, and bake.

✳ THE DUTIFUL EGG

In addition to providing us with many delightful dishes, eggs perform eight specific duties in the kitchen. Sometimes several of these duties are performed in a single dish. In a soufflé, for example, eggs thicken the sauce, aerate the soufflé mixture, and flavor and color the soufflé.

THICKENING

Eggs become solid when heated because their proteins coagulate. But coagulation is a gradual process. Under the influence of heat, and before coagulation is complete, the proteins of egg demonstrate an amazing ability to attract water and bind it to themselves. Thus, when suspended in liquid, the individual protein molecules act like tiny magnets, forming relatively large water "balls" around themselves. These balls of water, distributed evenly, *thicken* or *bind* the mixture. When you stir a sauce over gentle heat, you are mechanically rolling these balls around, enabling them thereby to collect more loose water and grow larger until the sauce is fully thickened. However, when egg protein reaches about 150°, it coagulates, losing its ability to attract and hold water. The balls of water "melt" and you are left with a leaky custard or a curdled sauce that is nothing more than scrambled eggs in water.

BINDING

Eggs mixed into chopped solid food will hold the food together by binding it. This binding is caused by the full coagulation of the egg protein, which performs as a wholesome "glue." Quenelles and Croquettes are bound in this manner.

CLARIFYING

Eggs in liquid will clarify the liquid, cleansing it of microscopic particles that cloud it. This clarification is caused by the gradual and full coagulation of the egg protein. Only the white is used, and it is used in very dilute form. For example, the white of one egg is usually sufficient to cleanse 4 quarts of stock. The protein is heated slowly in the liquid, which is constantly stirred. Stirring brings the protein in contact with more of the particles. These particles stick to the coagulating protein and are removed in clumps when the fully coagulated egg white is strained out. (Egg white must be used sparingly, as it blots up not only impurities but some of the stock's flavor as well. For a practical application of the clarification process see Clarified Beef Consommé.)

COATING

Foods coated with egg and dipped in hot fat are instantly packaged in a protective coating that resists the penetration of fat from without and the escape of juices from within. This coating is caused by the instant coagulation of the egg protein. It is wholesome, delicious, and beautiful to behold. It may be flavored and texturized with breadcrumbs, grated cheese, or other ingredients.

BLENDING

Eggs mixed into oil and water will blend these liquids together and prevent their natural tendency to separate. When you beat this mixture you break up the oil into tiny globules. The protein of egg surrounds these globules, forming a kind of "skin" that prevents them from joining other oil globules. At the same time, the outer surface of the protein skin attracts and holds water. This is called an oil-in-water emulsion. The oil is evenly suspended in the water and will not separate. This mixture can be further thickened by beating. (Beating as well as heating coagulates protein. The more you beat, the thicker the mixture will become. For a practical application of the process, see Hollandaise Sauce.)

LEAVENING

Semiliquid foods containing beaten egg white will puff up when heated. When egg white is beaten, tiny bubbles of air are incorporated into it. At the same time, the proteins of egg white begin to coagulate just as if they were heated. The protein forms an elastic "skin" around the bubbles. Just as in blending, this skin prevents the air bubbles from joining other air bubbles, and at the same time the outer surface of the skin attracts and holds the free water existing in the white. This is called an air-in-water dispersion, or a foam. When this foam is carefully folded into a semiliquid mixture, it lightens the mixture with the millions of air bubbles it contains. When the mixture is heated, these air bubbles expand and the mixture puffs as it cooks. (For a practical application of this process, see Soufflés.)

ENRICHING AND FLAVORING

The incorporation of egg into a food enriches the food with flavorful fats. Cakes and custards are examples.

COLORING

Eggs add a rich golden color to many foods and dishes. Orange yolks will produce more coloring than lemon-colored yolks.

8   *The Fishes*

Fish are the last great natural food we have in good supply. Meat, poultry, fruits, vegetables, cereals, all have been altered by man's domination of the land. But fish live in the boundless waters. Fish are as God intended them. Fish are wild. Fish are hunted. Most fish, still today, are *game*.

The fish differ greatly. Some are of monstrous size, some tiny. Some are lean, some fat. Some flavorful, some bland. Some fine-grained, some coarse. Some firm, some soft. Some live in fresh water, some live in the sea, and some share both of these environments. Yet most fish are enough alike that with knowledgeable cooking these natural differences can be overcome and practically every fish can be broiled, baked, fried, poached, or stewed to suit your taste. And we have lots to choose from.

There are more than 350 whole families of edible fish and shellfish, and 240 of these are sold in the United States. Yet we eat little more than 10 pounds of fish per person a year, 4 pounds of this canned. We are not a fish-eating nation, but we can do better than this.

There are two good reasons for not eating fish, and both have to do with its taste. On the one hand the fish is tasteless; on the other hand the fish tastes too "fishy." I think tasteless fish are the result of poor cooking, and that "fishy" tasting fish are the result of poor buying. In this chapter we will attempt to overcome both of these calamities.

BUYING FRESH AND FROZEN FISH

A good fish market is indispensable to outstanding fish cookery. If you live in the center of the country, it will provide you with fresh fish of the season from both fresh and salt waters, as well as local fish caught that very morning. The market will receive its fish packed in crushed ice and will display it in crushed ice. There is nothing old-fashioned in this; it is still the best way to keep fresh fish in moist, prime condition. (As a rule, I will not buy a fish unless I see it packed in ice.) A good fish market will also provide the fish heads and bones you need to make fish stocks, soups, and stews.

A fresh fish proclaims its freshness with clear, bright, bulging eyes; with red gills; with tight, shining scales; with a clean, fresh odor; and with a firm body and elastic flesh that springs back when you press it. (If a fish exhibits all these characteristics except the last, and indentations are left in the flesh when you press it, the fish has been frozen and thawed.) Have nothing to do with fish having sunken, cloudy eyes; brown or gray gills; loose scales; slimy bodies; mushy flesh; or a fish odor.

Fresh fish today, in most supermarkets, are sold already fileted or cut into steaks. They will be put up in little packages and they will not be packed in ice. Observe the edges of the cut flesh closely. If they show evidence of drying, or a yellow color, the fish was fileted too long ago. Also the flesh should be translucent and springy to the touch, not mushy. Most important, smell the fish. Odor is the most reliable test of all. Fresh fish smells fresh and clean, not fishy. (In France an argument rages as to whether fresh-caught smelt smell more like violets or cucumbers. I am of the cucumber persuasion.)

Fish is frozen whole, in pieces, and in filets. It loses its flavor when frozen more rapidly than other frozen foods, and can spoil even when it is frozen hard as a rock. There is little you can do to judge the fish before buying it, except that if you can see the fish its flesh should not be yellowed. Also, frozen fish keeps best if the package it is frozen in has no air pockets. At home, when you begin to thaw the flesh, the smell will quickly tell you if the fish has been frozen too long.

THE COOKING OF FISH

Fish is protein cooking of a very delicate nature. In cooking a fish, you should exercise as much care as in cooking an egg.

The flesh of fish, like beef and chicken, contains about 20 percent protein, about 1 percent minerals, 1 percent to 20 percent fat, and the rest water. This flesh is very tender and its connective tissue easily dissolved. Fish is therefore not cooked to tenderize it, but only to develop its flavor and make it palatable. In fact, lean raw fish can actually be "cooked" by marinating for one or two hours in lime juice (in Mexico this dish is called *seviche*). The liquid protein coagulates, and the flesh losses its translucency and becomes opaque, firm, and white, just as if it were subjected to heat.

The first rule of fish cookery, then, is to cook very lightly. You may use high temperatures briefly, but never overcook. Fish will never become tough, but it will become dry and tasteless and will easily fall apart.

The second rule of fish cookery is concerned with the fat content of the flesh. Fat fish are considered best for broiling and baking because their interior fat protects them from the dry heat; if poached in liquid, their flesh tends to slip, flake, and fall apart too readily. Lean fish hang together better when poached; when baked or broiled they are liberally basted with butter to make up for their lack of interior fat.

A third rule of fish cookery is concerned with the natural flavor of the fish. Fat fish are usually more flavorful than lean fish and need little supplementary flavoring. Many lean fish, but not all, are very delicate in flavor. If you prize the flavor of a delicately flavored fish, it must be just as delicately cooked to preserve its natural taste. Many fish that are good-tasting have a certain sameness to their flavor. You can vary this sameness by cooking the fish in a flavorful medium, or by saucing it, or by deep-frying it and developing a flavorful crust.

A fourth rule of fish cookery has to do with frozen fish, about which I must first say a few words.

Freezing brings the good tastes of the sea to the interior of America, as it brings the good tastes of our lakes and streams to American tables on both coasts. Also, freezing brings to us from abroad new and distinguished tastes of fish we have never seen before. And most important, it brings these fish at low cost to areas where ice-packed fresh fish are not available. This is a good thing for gastronomy, and to be taken advantage of by cooking in a manner that will preserve every bit of savor the frozen fish contains. But there are problems.

Even frozen fish that are in good condition are never as juicy and tasty as when they were fresh. The act of freezing crushes the delicate tissues of fish. In fact, the flesh of fish is so very delicate that freezing actually *cooks* it somewhat. As ice crystals form in the flesh, the natural salts of the fish are concentrated in the tissues. This concentration of salts partially coagulates the liquid protein of the flesh. (You can often tell when raw fish has been frozen by its opaque, slightly cooked look.)

The fish meat contained in convenient, one-pound frozen packages can be perfectly delicious. If you gnawed it raw in its frozen state (Vilhjalmur Stefansson, the great arctic explorer, calls this Eskimo ice cream), you would have no problems. But as soon as you *thaw* this meat, damage is done. The juices, which are only tenuously held in the delicate flesh, pour out like a Niagara. (As an experiment, heat these juices in a pan. They will coagulate like the white of an egg.) This meat can *never* be as succulent as the meat of fresh fish.

The lame alternative we sometimes have with frozen meats, of starting their cooking while they are still frozen (and thereby coagulating their liquid protein before it has a chance to leak out), does not work well with fish. The flesh is too delicate, too quickly cooked. The outside will become dry and tasteless while the center is still icy and raw.

It is grim to think of all those blocks of frozen fish that—at this very minute—are thawing out in the kitchens of America, their flavorful juices draining out. As one admittedly biased fresh fish dealer at New York's Fulton Street fish market put it, "You should drink the juice and throw the fish away."

We can do better than this by poaching or stewing frozen fish and serving it sauced with the essence of its thawed juices. Any of the recipes for poaching and stewing can be applied to frozen fish. You just thaw the fish gradually in a bowl in the refrigerator. Put it with its juices in a well-buttered skillet, pour over it a flavorful boiling liquid, and cook until the fish is done. Remove the fish, boil down the flavorful liquid in the pan, thicken it, finish the sauce with butter or cream, and pour it over the fish. When cooked in this manner, it is difficult to tell if the fish has been frozen for weeks or just caught. And endless variety is possible.

Some of the fresh fish recipes that follow violate the second and third of these general rules. For example, the favorite French way of cooking salmon, a fat fish, is by boiling it. The first rule, however, is never violated. Fish must never be overcooked.

Some fish cook more quickly than others, and to guard against overcooking always test the fish well before you expect the cooking to be done. Rely on observation, not on thermostats or minutes-per-pound (a thick fish will need more minutes-per-pound than a slender fish of the same weight).

Use a sharp knife to make a short cut along the backbone at the thickest part of the fish to expose the flesh. When the surface flakes the fish is almost done. Carefully separate two of these flakes and peer deep into the flesh. Use a flashlight if you have to. When the flesh has lost its translucency and become opaque all the way into the fish, it is done. The flesh should still be moist. If it is dry, the fish is overcooked and will be relatively tasteless.

I have said that most fish are enough alike that the methods for cooking one can be used for any other. Knowledgeable cooking overcomes differences of fatness, texture, and firmness to deliver a moist, tender dish to the table. If we want to broil a lean fish, we protect it with a blanket of crumbs and butter. If we want to poach a soft fat fish, we will wrap it in cheesecloth and cook it very quickly. But the different *tastes* of different varieties of fish pose quite another matter. French recipes are painstakingly constructed to enhance these unique tastes. When it comes to taste, the French chef joyfully cries, *"Vive la différence!"*

✳ THE TASTES OF FISH

Fish range in taste from the very delicate to the decidedly flavored. In addition to tasting like fish, fish may taste meaty, chickenlike, buttery, sweet, or nutty. One fish, the grayling, tastes like thyme. Also contributing to the sensation of taste are the varying fatness, juiciness, and gelatinous qualities of fish. All of this makes cooking and eating fish an exciting gastronomic adventure.

Some delicately flavored fish have a unique, sought-after taste, and this is best preserved by simply poaching them in salt water or sautéing the fish and serving them with butter. Other delicately flavored fish are quite nondescript, and we fortify their bland flavor by cooking them in a well-seasoned liquid, by saucing them, or by frying them to develop a flavorful crust. Sometimes we smoke them.

Fish of decided flavor are approached more boldly. We may choose to pit a sauce against them to throw their flavors into bold relief. For example, an oily-tasting fish may be enhanced with a tart and tangy sauce.

French cooking takes close account of these more or less subtle differences in the taste of fish, and hundreds of years of trying and tasting have produced recipes to exploit these differences. Following are some of the fishes available to us. They account for almost all of the fish eaten in the United States.

SALT-WATER FISH

Marine waters offer us the greatest variety of fish tastes and textures. Taken mostly from the open sea over continental shelves, salt-water fish must have remained unchanged throughout all of history. Thus, when we read how much the Romans enjoyed a certain Mediterranean tuna fish, we can still taste for ourselves the flavors they enjoyed.

All fish contain fat, but the fish we call lean-fleshed either contain less fat or have their oils concentrated in their heads or livers. Fat-fleshed fish have their oils distributed throughout the flesh, and usually have a more pronounced flavor. A lean fish contains less than 2 percent fat in its flesh; a fat fish, like the salmon, may contain more than 20 percent fat.

The firmness and flakiness of a fish's flesh also contributes to that complex of sensory impressions that produces taste. I will attempt to describe all these factors for the fish commonly available, as well as for exceptionally good, if harder to come by, American fish. I will also describe a few of the gastronomically famous fish from European waters, which are sometimes available frozen.

ANCHOVY

These small fish from the Channel and the Mediterranean are delicious fresh, but they must be eaten immediately after they are caught. Preserved anchovies, salted and packed in oil, are widely used in French cooking as a flavoring, as a garnish, and as an hors d'oeuvre. (The large anchovy catch developed in California in recent years is used almost entirely to produce fish meal and oil.)

BLUEFISH

A fine, fat, juicy fish, the bluefish has a distinctive flavor needing no more seasoning than pepper, salt, and the butter it is basted with. Its large-flaked, soft purplish flesh cooks to a creamy color. Weighing from 1 to 6 pounds, bluefish are most plentiful in May and somewhat plentiful in August, September, and October. Small fish are called "baby blues." Generally eaten from New York City southwards.

BRILL

Brill is a European flatfish somewhat similar to the European turbot. Neither fish is available here, except as an expensive import. I only mention this fish because there are many excellent recipes for brill in the French cuisine. You can apply these recipes to American flounders, of which the gray sole resembles brill the most.

BUTTERFISH (HARVEST FISH, DOLLARFISH, PUMPKIN SEED)

This soft, fat little fish melts in your mouth, hence the name. Sold whole, weighing from ¼ to 1 pound, they are excellent for cooking *en papillote*. They are in good supply throughout the year, except May and December, and are eaten with relish from New York north.

CALIFORNIA KINGFISH

This good-tasting fish is a whiting, and is also known as a corbina. It weighs about 1 pound. It is available in every month, most plentiful in November, and somewhat plentiful in March, April, May, and June. It is eaten mostly in California.

COD

One of the most famous of food fishes, the cod stimulated the growth of New England by attracting people there who might have wintered more comfortably in the south. In fresh form it is available in steaks and filets and whole, weighing from 1½ to 10 pounds. The smaller fish are known as scrod. Cod is an extremely flaky-fleshed, lean fish, the considerable amount of fat it contains being concentrated in the liver. Its flavor is quite mild, and cod is much appreciated simply boiled and served with melted butter. It is also excellent smoked and salted. The French, reversing their habitual demands for fresh foods, prefer salt cod to fresh cod and have developed a number of fine recipes for it. Cod is dry and fluffy when cooked, and its flesh is very white.

CUSK

This tasty fish is eaten whole mostly in New England, and eaten elsewhere on the East Coast as filets of something or other. It is not very handsome and therefore not very likely to become known south of Boston for itself alone. It is available throughout the year fileted, cut into steaks, or whole, weighing from 1½ to 10 pounds.

DRUMFISH

The black drum or spot is a favorite food in Virginia, and is marketed at about one pound. The red drum, also called redfish and channel bass, is caught around Florida and the Gulf and is eaten mostly in Texas and Louisiana.

EELS

Eels are a fat and deliciously rich-flavored fish. The American colonists regarded them highly, as do Europeans and some Americans today. The supply of eels is low, however, because of large exports to Scandinavia. Smoked eel is a great delicacy and can be had in most specialty shops. In large seacoast markets they are sometimes found live in tanks throughout the year, and they are at their best when purchased this way.

FLOUNDERS OF THE ATLANTIC COAST

The most numerous Atlantic flounder is the yellowtail (or rusty dab). The thickest, meatiest, and best-tasting are the gray sole, the dab (sea dab or American plaice), and the winter flounder (or blackback flounder). Other Atlantic flounders you are likely to find in the market are the summer flounder (or fluke), and the similar Southern flounder. Lemon sole from the Georges Bank is also available fresh in the East; it resembles the winter flounder. Some of these flounders are discussed in more detail in this section. About 90 percent of these fish are sold in filet form, fresh or frozen.

FLOUNDERS OF THE PACIFIC COAST

Of the Pacific flounders, the petrale, the sand dab, and the rex sole are considered the best. Other Pacific flounders are the Dover sole and the English sole (no relation to the famous European sole), the starry flounder and the California halibut.

GRAY SOLE

This is an exceptionally fine Atlantic Coast flounder, with fine-grained, lean white flesh. It is firmer than other flounders, but not so firm as true sole. The taste is very delicate, somewhat reminiscent of shrimp. It is taken mostly in northern waters and weighs from ¾ to 4 pounds.

GROUPER

This lean southern fish is a member of the sea bass family. It is available in steaks and filets and whole, weighing from 5 to 12 pounds. Among the groupers, the Nassau grouper and the red grouper are perhaps the tastiest.

GRUNION

These tiny fish fling themselves upon California beaches to lay their eggs, whereupon they are picked up by hungry Californians, fried, and eaten on the spot. They are 5 to 8 inches long and resemble smelt in flavor.

HADDOCK

This close relative of the cod can be distinguished from it by the black lateral line along its sides and the dark patch above each pectoral fin. It is a very important food fish, caught in North Atlantic waters. It usually weighs from 1½ to 7 pounds, available whole or cut into filets. Much of the catch is frozen. The flesh is lean, firm, and white, with a decided meaty flavor, and it is well liked in America. Haddock is smoked by Scotsmen and called finnan haddie. It is delicious.

HAKE

Hakes are codlike fish from the North and Middle Atlantic. Their flesh is lean, soft, flaky, and white and it has a delicate, neutral flavor. Much of the catch is fileted and frozen, and sold as "deep sea filets." On some French menus the hake is called "white salmon," but this is absurd.

HALIBUT

A giant flounder, the halibut grows as large as 8 feet long and weighs up to 600 pounds. Its market weight begins at 5 pounds, these smaller fishes being called chicken halibut. The halibut is greatly prized in America for its steaks, which are firm, flavorful, and white. It is the closest fish to European turbot, but turbot is firmer. Atlantic halibut is in season from March to September; Pacific halibut from May to September. Another halibut, the California halibut, is considered less choice.

HERRING

Herring is the most abundant of all food fishes, but it is rarely eaten fresh because of its numerous bones. (The American shad, which is a herring, is an exception.) Herrings are smoked, pickled, salted, and are perhaps best known as sardines. The huge California sardine catch of a few years back consisted of pilchard, which is a small herring. The English greatly enjoy their herring lightly salted and smoked (bloaters) or lightly smoked, slit, and opened (kippers). Schmaltz are very fat Icelandic herring. Matjes are herring in a wine sauce. Bismarcks are filets of herring in a vinegar sauce. Rollmops are Bismarcks rolled around a pickle.

KING MACKEREL (CERO, KINGFISH)

Weighing from 5 to 20 pounds, this excellent fish is sold whole or cut into steaks. It is a fat fish, with oily, pinkish flesh and a distinctive and delicious flavor. It is caught around Florida and in the Gulf, and is mostly available during the winter.

KING WHITING (KINGFISH)

This fish has lean, firm, flavorful white flesh with few bones. It weighs from 1 to 3 pounds and is taken mostly along the middle Atlantic coast in winter months. Related fish are caught in the Gulf year round.

LING COD (LONG COD)

This Pacific Coast fish is a good food fish, although it is not a cod. Weighing from 5 to 20 pounds, it is available whole or cut into steaks. This is a lean fish and can be prepared like cod. The flesh has a greenish tint (in young fish the flesh is *alarmingly* green), but the color disappears with cooking.

MACKEREL

This is a fat, savory fish with a decided, distinctive, and satisfying flavor. The fish are available whole, weighing from ½ to 4 pounds. The flesh is firm, dark, and rich. Among the mackerels—Atlantic, chub, king, Pacific, wahoo, and Spanish—the Spanish mackerel of Florida and the Gulf has the richest flavor. All these fat fish are excellent broiled or baked and piquantly sauced. This fish spoils very quickly and should be eaten very fresh.

MULLET

Mostly available in the South, striped mullet (called black mullet in Florida), is Florida's favorite food fish. It weighs from ½ to 3 pounds, and the flesh of the mullet is fat and firm and contains a mild oil with a distinct, nutty flavor. The American mullet is not related to the red mullet (*rouget*), considered to be the Mediterranean's best food fish.

OCEAN CATFISH (WOLFFISH)

This New England fish is frequently fileted and frozen and distributed across America. It is a lean, mean fish, weighing about 8 pounds, and has attacked bathers.

OCEAN PERCH

This is also called rosefish. The filets of this small rockfish have the blandness of flavor that many people enjoy.

PACIFIC POMPANO

This is no pompano, although it wears the same dumb expression. It is a scion of the Eastern butterfish family, very delicate, buttery, and good-tasting, weighing from ¼ to 1 pound. It pops in and out of the market, being most plentiful in March, April, October, January, and November, in that order. It is reserved mostly for California palates.

POLLOCK

Weighing from 1½ to 12 pounds, this cousin of the cod has firm, lean white meat with a good fish flavor. Much of the frozen blocks of fish labeled "deep sea filets" are pollock.

POMPANO

This fat, white-fleshed, fine-flavored fish contains flavorful oils in the head and is consequently sold whole. The fish weighs up to about 4 pounds and is caught in Florida and Gulf waters. What is not consumed on the scene is sold to Northern restaurants at outrageous prices.

PORGY (SCUP)

Weighing up to 2 pounds, this East Coast fish is usually sold fresh and whole. Its lean, tender, flaky white flesh has a hearty flavor.

RED SNAPPER

This handsome fish is a photographer's favorite, the skin retaining its fresh red color through baking. The lean flesh is juicy and sweetly flavored. The fish weighs from 2 to 20 pounds. Smaller fish are cooked whole, and the larger cut into steaks and filets. Smaller snappers—gray, muttonfish, and yellowtail—are equally good eating.

ROCKFISHES

These large-headed fish, which include over 50 varieties on the Pacific Coast, are characterized by a bony plate under the eye. They are often sold fresh as rock cod. The important East Coast rockfish is the rosefish. When fileted and frozen these fish are sold under the name of ocean perch. Their meat varies from white to pink, becoming white and flaky when cooked. They are a lean, mild-flavored fish that few tastes can quarrel with.

SABLEFISH

For a fat fish, the sablefish has an unusually delicate flavor. The rich white flesh (14 percent fat) has a soft, almost buttery texture reminiscent of a ripe avocado. It is a Pacific Coast fish, weighing from 5 to 15 pounds, and is sold whole or fileted. It is frequently smoked. Sablefish is also called black cod and butterfish.

SALMON

Salmon, I believe, is the best-liked of all fishes, and for many generations of Americans, a boiled salmon dinner was traditional on the Fourth of July. It is a rich, fat fish with very fine-textured flesh, ranging in color from pale pink to orangish to red. The raw flesh of the sockeye salmon is one of the most breath-taking sights in all gastronomy, looking for all the world like a piece of very fine crimson velvet. Salmon are excellent cooked in any manner, and smoked salmon is considered one of the most elegant of all hors d'oeuvres.

There are two main kinds of salmon—the Atlantic salmon and the Pacific salmon (which marine biologists tell us is not really a salmon at all). The fresh fish are available mostly from July through November.

The Atlantic Salmon (also called the Kennebec salmon because of the huge runs that once occurred in that Maine river) has all but disappeared from United States waters. Most of this variety is taken by Canada, Greenland, Scotland, and Norway. Its flesh is orange-pink and very delicious. Market weight is usually from 5 to 10 pounds. Smoked Nova Scotia salmon is highly prized in New York. Some Atlantic salmon have become landlocked. They are called Sebago salmon, but they are no longer commercially important.

The Pacific Salmon. There are five species of Pacific salmon, and we catch and eat more of these fish than any other kind.

Sockeye, or red salmon, has the richest, reddest meat and is the most expensive to buy. Practically all of it is canned.

Chinook, or king, salmon is the largest salmon, weighing over 100 pounds and averaging 25 pounds. Its meat is usually deep salmon-red.

Silver, or coho, salmon is smaller, averaging 5 to 8 pounds. Its flesh is salmon-red to pink. Its eggs are used to make salmon caviar.

Pink, or humpback, salmon is the smallest of the five species, averaging 3 to 6 pounds. It is usually the most abundant. Its flesh is more pink.

Chum, or dog, salmon has pale pink flesh that turns yellowish when canned. It is the poorest of the salmons, and the least expensive.

When buying fresh salmon, look for meat that is firm, moist, and red. The meat of stale salmon turns pale and orangish, becomes soft, and is relatively tasteless.

SAND DAB
This fine, lean, delicately flavored flatfish is restricted mostly to California. It is a small flounder, weighing 2 pounds at most, and one of the best of the Pacific Coast flatfishes.

SARDINES
Sardines are any small fish that are caught in quantity and canned, usually in oil. California once was a major producer of sardines, packing great quantities of pilchard at John Steinbeck's Cannery Row, but this fish has virtually disappeared. Maine sardines consist of young herring. Sardines are named for the island of Sardinia, where little fish were first preserved in this way.

SEA BASS

This is a large family of firm, flavorful, white-meated fishes that abound on both coasts and come in all sizes. Included are the black sea bass of the East Coast, weighing from 1 to 4 pounds; the rock hind of Florida waters, averaging 2 pounds; the Florida giant sea bass or jewfish, weighing more than 600 pounds, and the California giant sea bass that often grows as large as the Florida variety. Also included in the family is the famous striped bass.

SEA DAB (PLAICE)

Also called the sand dab or American plaice, this thick-meated, lean, relatively boneless flatfish has a sweet, distinctive flavor. Weighing ¾ to 2½ pounds, it is caught in northern waters. It is one of the finest of the American flounders.

SEA SQUAB (BLOWFISH)

This small fish tastes like frogs' legs. Its firm, fine-grained flesh is sweet-smelling and pinkish when raw, and it cooks to a creamy color. The fish is a new arrival at the American table; a few years ago it was thrown away. Only the back meat is eaten, and the fish comes skinned with the backbone in, looking like a skinned chicken drumstick and weighing about ¼ pound. Most sea squab is eaten in the East.

SHAD

A member of the herring family, the shad has long been praised on both sides of the Atlantic for its good-tasting flesh and magnificent roe. For a fat fish, it has an exceptionally delicate, meatlike flavor. It is bony, containing rows of tiny bones that make the fish almost impossible to filet (only highly experienced and highly paid professional shad boners can do it), but the taste of shad makes it well worth your patience in stripping the meat from the bones. Shad has been transplanted to the Pacific Coast, where it is available in May. Peak season on the East Coast is March and April. Whole shad weigh from 1½ to 5 pounds.

SHAD ROE

This is the eggs of the shad, which are enclosed in a thin membrane. They are parboiled for 20 minutes to firm them, cooled, and then deep-fried or sautéed in butter. Shad roe is one of the great delicacies of the world.

SHEEPSHEAD

These delicious porgies are so well liked that intensive fishing has drastically reduced their numbers. They are a lean fish, weighing from 1 to 10 pounds, and are taken mostly on the South Atlantic coast and in the Gulf.

SMELT (SALT WATER AND FRESH WATER)

These small fish look and behave like salmon, to which they are related. They seek fresh water in which to spawn, or lay their eggs on the beaches like grunion. They have been transplanted to fresh water and have multiplied there, and have provided many a fine feast for Americans living around the Great Lakes. Smelt are fat little fishes. Indians along the Columbia River used to dry them and burn them as candles, and Columbia River smelt are still called candlefish. Smelt weigh 1 or 2 ounces and have a rich, distinctive, and delicious flavor that will remind you of trout.

SOLE (ENGLISH SOLE, DOVER SOLE, CHANNEL SOLE)

This is the sole that has achieved gastronomic fame as the finest of all the flatfishes. Its flesh is very fine, white, firm, delicately flavored, and easily boned. Unhappily, this fish is not found in American waters. The small amount of sole available here is flown in, fresh or frozen, from Europe. Unhappily also, it has become traditional in American restaurants to call all fileted flounder "filet of sole," thereby withholding the rather important fact of just which flounder one is getting to eat. True sole is unlike any flounder, the flesh being firmer, more delicate and delicious in flavor. The best American substitutes for sole are the gray sole, the winter flounder, and the sea dab (American plaice) on the East Coast, and petrale, sand dab, and rex sole on the West Coast. These are all fine fish, although their meat is softer than that of true sole.

SPOT

This small panfish, weighing from ¼ to 1¼ pounds, is much enjoyed in Virginia. The flavorful flesh is at its best in autumn.

STRIPED BASS

The lean flesh of this sportsman's fish is mild in flavor, and when fresh it is one of the greatest delicacies the United States has to offer. The flesh is flaky and white. Market weight ranges from 2 to 25 pounds, and the fish is usually available whole or cut into steaks. This is an East Coast fish. It has been transplanted to Pacific Coast waters but may not be taken by commercial fishermen.

STURGEON (FRESH WATER AND SALT WATER)

At one time our rivers and Great Lakes held an abundance of these ancient fishes, the source of that most costly of delicacies, caviar. As soon as its value was fully perceived, the fish was wantonly slain. Little remains of this great natural resource. Today we import caviar from Russia and Iran, and fresh sturgeon is rarely seen, although the number of fish has increased in the Columbia River in recent years. The flesh is lean but rich in flavor, and you will find the compact meat mostly smoked and canned as an expensive delicacy. This is the largest of the American fresh-water fishes, the record fish, taken in the Columbia River in 1917, being 12½ feet long and 1,285 pounds.

SUMMER FLOUNDER (FLUKE)

This is a relatively large, deep-water flounder with a market weight of from 2 to 12 pounds. The meat is lean, white, and delicately textured, but it is not so fine as winter flounder or the flounder called gray sole. The fish is taken from waters off the northern and mid-Atlantic coast.

SWORDFISH

Swordfish steaks are well liked by Americans. The white meat is moderately fat, firmer and oilier than halibut, but it is considered a lean fish. Fresh swordfish has a rich, distinctive, meatlike flavor and is in greatest supply during July and August.

TAUTOG (BLACKFISH)

This fish is found from Maine to South Carolina. It weighs from 2 to 3 pounds, and its juicy white flesh has a fine flavor.

TUNA

Most tuna is sold canned, after having been frozen at sea. They are fat fish, related to the mackerel. There are several varieties of tuna, mainly albacore, bluefin, skipjack, yellowfin, and little tuna, their flesh color ranging from white to hazelnut to a purplish red. The whitest, firmest, and finest is albacore; it resembles fine veal. Pacific bonito, a tunalike fish, is darker and more decidedly flavored, and it is wise to cut away dark flesh on both sides of the fish before cooking it.

TURBOT

This is one of the *haute cuisine* fishes of Europe. It is a flatfish with firm white, savory flesh and is most like the American halibut, although much smaller in size, from 1½ to 3 feet long. In France, small turbot is known as *turbotin* or chicken turbot. French recipes for turbotin can be applied to America's small halibut, called chicken halibut.

WEAKFISH (SEA TROUT)

Weakfish are named for the tenderness of their flesh and their mouths. The largest is the gray sea trout, weighing from 1 to 6 pounds. The spotted sea trout weighs from 1 to 4 pounds, and the white sea trout from ½ to 1½ pounds. These lean-fleshed fish are taken from the Mid-Atlantic coast to the Gulf.

WINTER FLOUNDER

Taken along the northern and mid-Atlantic coast, the winter flounder, or blackback flounder, has thick, lean, white, delicious meat. One of the finest of the American flounders, it weighs from ¾ to 2 pounds. It is the second most plentiful of the Eastern flounders.

WHITEBAIT

These small, minnowlike fish are eaten whole without cleaning. They are usually the small fry of herring and smelt. The French call this food *blanchaille*. The fish are floured and deep-fried.

WHITING (SILVER HAKE)

This fish comes from the northern and mid-Atlantic coast. Its flesh is lean, white, and well flavored, and much of the catch is frozen and sold in fish-and-chip establishments.

FRESH-WATER FISH

Fresh-water fishes supply us with less variety than marine fishes, but they do give us a range of tastes and they are both fat and lean. The flavor of fresh-water fishes is often delicious (and the trout is one of the most important fishes in *haute cuisine*), but due to the fact that many live in contained, quiet, tideless waters, their flavor is sometimes muddy. If we suspect a muddy taste, we can overcome this by cooking the fish in a special Court Bouillon.

BASS

Largemouth, smallmouth, calico and rock bass, and sunfish, blue gills, and crappies are all members of the fresh-water bass family. In general they are thick-bodied, firm-fleshed, meaty fish, living mostly in the rivers and lakes of the Mississippi watershed. These fish have been introduced to Eastern lakes and rivers and have obtained a good foothold there.

BUFFALO FISH

Taken from inland rivers, this lean fish is sold whole or cut into steaks. It weighs from 3 to 25 pounds. Buffalo fish is often smoked.

CARP

This fish is thoroughly disliked by many, partly because its spread has eliminated other more desirable fishes; partly because of its muddy flavor; and partly because of its ability to survive in polluted waters. Carp are highly regarded in other countries where they are raised in clean water and grain-fed to make their flesh finer. Carp are usually sold whole, and, to give carp a try, select a silvery carp, which indicates it was taken from clear, clean waters. Yellow, olive-colored carp from muddy waters will have a muddy taste. Much of American carp is produced in Iowa, Michigan, and Wisconsin.

CATFISH

Catfish is suspect by many Americans because it survives in murky waters and will readily seize "high" baits. But it is the favorite fish of many people, and inland America consumes surprising quantities of blue cats, channel cats, spotted cats, yellow cats, and the similar-appearing bullheads. Their flesh is firm, white, flaky, sweet, and flavorful. Today, large numbers of pond-raised, soybean-fed catfish are becoming available in the Middle West and Western states (mainly Missouri, Mississippi, and Arkansas), and in time we will find these hygienic, special-diet fish on tables throughout America.

CHUB

This is a small, fat, soft-fleshed fish taken in the Great Lakes. It weighs from 2 ounces to ¼ pound and is frequently smoked.

GRAYLING

The grayling is a relative of the trouts and salmons. Its flesh is quite delicate, and it tastes of thyme. Unfortunately, this fish has become rare.

LAKE HERRING (CISCO)

Related to the whitefish, these small lean fish weigh from ⅓ to 1 pound. They are excellent smoked.

LAKE TROUT

Once plentiful in the Great Lakes, this fish was seriously decimated by the lamprey, which fastens itself to the body of the trout and sucks it dry. (The catch in Lake Michigan, for example, declined from 5 million pounds in 1945 to 400 pounds in 1953!) Although control of the lamprey is slowly returning this large trout to the Great Lakes, most of what we receive is from Canadian lakes. Lake trout is a member of the salmon family, and their meat is fat, sweet, and delicately flavored, similar to brook and mountain trout. The flesh varies in color from white to deep reddish-orange. One variety of lake trout, the siscowet of Lake Superior, is perhaps the fattest of all fish, ranging up to 70 percent fat in large adults. Lake trout are also called Mackinaw, togue, and gray trout. Usual market weight is from 1½ to 10 pounds.

MULLET (WHITE SUCKER)

This fat fish, taken from clean, cold waters, is notable for its dark, firm, sweet flesh. It weighs from 1½ to 6 pounds.

PANFISH

These are more often caught than bought, and they include many of the bass family—bluegill, crappie, sunfish, rock bass, calico bass, and yellow perch. Taken from clean, clear waters these small pan-sized fish are highly prized in America. A good portion of their appeal must lie in the fact that these fish, being caught by the diner himself, are usually very fresh when eaten.

PERCH

Izaak Walton, the famous fisherman, tells us that the river perch is "so wholesome that physicians allow him to be eaten by wounded men." The flesh is lean and delicately sweet. The perches include the yellow perch, blue pike, and sauger, which weigh around 1 pound; and the walleye or walleye pike, which weighs from 1½ to 4 pounds.

PIKE

The sweet, white, lean, firm flesh of the pike, although rather dry and bony, has made it an important gastronomical fish, and many excellent recipes have been developed for it. Some of these fish grow very large, but market weight is usually from 1½ to 10 pounds. The pikes include muskellunge, northern pike, eastern or jack or chain pickerel, and the small grass pickerel. The walleye pike is a perch. Much of our commercial pike is imported from Canada.

SHEEPSHEAD

This is a fresh-water drum, sometimes called white perch and gaspergou. Its fine-flavored meat is lean and white. Market fish weigh from 1½ to 8 pounds.

TROUT

This is the ultimate fresh-water fish for *haute cuisine*. The scales of trout are very small, and the fish should not be scaled. Trout is a member of the salmon family, and its flesh is firm, meaty, and sweet, but it is not quite so fat as salmon and has a more delicate flavor. It is very tender-meated; the bones lift out easily after cooking. Unless you catch your own, the only trout available for cooking are small brook or rainbow trout that have been specially raised for market. They are tender and delicate-tasting but do not have the full flavor of wild trout. Trout are farmed in Idaho, and frozen farm trout are also imported from Denmark and Japan.

WHITEFISH

Whitefish, like the lake trout, has suffered the attacks of the lamprey in the Great Lakes. Today much of our fresh whitefish comes from Canada. It is a fat, delicious-tasting fish weighing from 1½ to 6 pounds. It is sometimes called whiting.

✳ BOILED FISH
(Poissons Bouillis)

Fish that is completely immersed in liquid and simmered until cooked is said to be boiled. The liquid never actually boils, however, or the fish would fall apart.

This method is generally confined to large whole fish weighing 3 pounds or more, large pieces of fish weighing several pounds, and sometimes fish steaks (*darnes*) of 1-inch thickness or more. It is also the method to use if fish is to be served cold.

The liquid used is salted water or Court Bouillon. Salted water is the best medium for retaining the pure, natural flavor of the fish. Use 1½ teaspoons of salt, preferably sea salt, per quart of water.

There are three kinds of court bouillon for boiling fish, all containing some kind of acid. White Court Bouillon contains 2 or 3 slices of peeled fresh lemon and ½ cup milk per quart of salted water. The purpose of this liquid is to keep the flesh of white fish very white. Court Bouillon with Vinegar contains vinegar and is used for trout or salmon. Court Bouillon with Wine contains white or red wine (rarely) and is used mostly for fresh-water fish. You will find the recipes for the court bouillons in Chapter 4.

The most popular fish for boiling is the salmon. Its delicate, distinctive flavor is well retained by this method, and boiled salmon is also delicious cold. Also boiled are other large meaty fishes—cod and salt cod, haddock, pollock, hake, turbot, *turbotin,* chicken halibut, mackerel, striped bass, red snapper, sea bass, whitefish, and grouper. (A small fish that is boiled in a special way is the trout. The recipe for *Truite au Bleu* is given a few pages ahead.) Now let us roll up our sleeves and boil one of these fish.

To boil a whole fish, place the fish on the tray of a fish boiler or on a rack in a deep roasting pan. If the fish is large, make a few slits in the flesh where it is thickest so it will cook more evenly. It is wise to wrap the fish in cheesecloth to facilitate moving it after it is cooked. (Also, to assure that the fish does not curl during cooking, you may tie the fish flat to a thin board with strips of cheesecloth.)

Pour into the pan enough cold salted water or court bouillon to cover the fish. Bring the liquid to the simmering point and complete the cooking at the simmer. By starting in cold liquid, the flavorings are given time to penetrate the unskinned fish. Also, plunging the fish into boiling salted water would cause its skin to split. Do not allow the liquid to boil. The cooking time for fish is about 6 minutes per pound; under 4 pounds takes about 10 minutes of cooking. But be sure to test for doneness early to avoid over-cooking.

To boil large pieces of fish or thick fish steaks, place the fish on the boiler tray or on a rack. Bring the liquid to a full boil and plunge the tray and the fish into it. The liquid will immediately be cooled below the boiling point. Return it to a simmer, and simmer until the fish is done. By plunging the cut fish in boiling water you are partially coagulating its protein juices at the cut surfaces, thereby retarding their escape. Pieces or steaks of 1½-inch thickness will cook in about 15 minutes, but test for doneness early.

When the fish is cooked, turn off the heat and allow it to cool for 3 or 4 minutes to firm the flesh. (If the fish is to be served cold, turn off the heat as soon as it begins to show signs of doneness, so it will not overcook. Allow it to cool completely in the liquid with the pan uncovered.) Lift the fish from the liquid, allowing it to drain, and place it on a napkin on a hot serving platter. If the fish is whole, it is traditional that the head of the fish be to the left when the belly is facing toward you. Strip the skin from the top side of the fish, and with a thin, sharp knife pare away the darkened strip of flesh just below the skin. This strip of flesh, which runs along the lateral line of the fish, contains blood vessels and is unpleasant-tasting. If the fish is in pieces, strip away all the skin and the darkened flesh beneath it.

Boiled fish is plainly served in keeping with the intent of boiling, that is, to present the natural flavor of the fish unadorned. Garnished the platter with parsley. Separately serve fine boiled potatoes and a hot fish sauce.

HOT BOILED SALMON (*Saumon Bouilli, Chaud*). Cook the salmon, whole or sliced, in Court Bouillon made with vinegar. Serve with plain boiled potatoes. Separately serve any sauce appropriate for fish, such as Mousseline,

Ravigote, Anchovy, Hollandaise, Nantua, Shrimp, Caper, White Wine Sauce, or melted butter.

HOT BOILED COD (*Cabillaud Bouilli, Chaud*). Cook the cod, whole or sliced, in White Court Bouillon made with milk and lemon. Serve on a dish covered with a napkin, and garnish with parsley and plain boiled potatoes. Separately serve any sauce appropriate for fish, especially Hollandaise, Oyster Sauce, or melted butter.

Hot boiled haddock, hake, pollock, turbot, halibut, sea bass, whiting, cusk, tuna, and flounder are also prepared in this manner.

BLUE TROUT (*Truite au Bleu*). For this famous dish, the trout must be alive and swimming up to the very moment of cooking. Quickly kill and clean a fresh-water trout, dip it in vinegar, and plunge it into a rapidly boiling Court Bouillon made with a double portion of vinegar. The skin, which will immediately shrivel and shred, will turn light blue. Serve on a dish covered with a napkin, garnished with parsley. Separately serve Hollandaise Sauce or melted butter.

Pike may be prepared in the same manner.

PIKE WITH WHITE BUTTER (*Brochet au Beurre Blanc*). This is a famous dish from Nantes on the Loire River, based on a most unusual and delicious sauce for which you will find full directions in the section on sauces. Boil a whole pike in Court Bouillon made with white wine. Meanwhile, prepare White Butter Sauce. When the pike is cooked, drain and dry it. Put it on a platter, slit the skin along the bone, cut through and carefully remove the backbone, and reshape the fish. Cover the pike with white butter sauce and sprinkle with chopped parsley.

Shad is also prepared in this manner.

CREAMED COD AU GRATIN (*Cabillaud Crème Gratin*). Cook cod or pieces of cod in White Court Bouillon made with milk and lemon. Drain the cod and cut it in small pieces. Place the cod on a heatproof platter on top of a thin layer of Mornay Sauce. Surround the platter with a fancy border of Duchess Potatoes piped through a pastry bag, and brush the potatoes with beaten egg yolk. Pour Mornay sauce over the cod, keeping it ½ inch below the rim of the platter so it will not bubble over. Sprinkle with melted butter and Parmesan cheese, and glaze* in a hot oven.

Hot boiled haddock, hake, pollock, turbot, halibut, sea bass, whiting, cusk, tuna, and flounder can be prepared in this manner.

BOILED MACKEREL WITH GOOSEBERRY SAUCE (*Maquereau Bouilli, Sauce aux Groseilles*). Cut the mackerel in thick slices, and cook in Court Bouillon made with vinegar and seasoned with a little fennel. Drain and skin the mackerel pieces, put them on a platter, and surround with parsley. Separately serve green Gooseberry Sauce.

BOILED SALT COD (*Morue Bouillie*). The salt is hard to remove. Soak filets of salt cod 24 hours in several changes of cold water. Cut them in pieces of equal size, roll them up, and tie them. Boil the rolls in unsalted water until they are half cooked. Drain the rolls, and finish their cooking in fresh unsalted water. Untie them and serve on a dish covered with a napkin. Garnish with parsley. Separately serve boiled potatoes and a sauce appropriate for fish, such as Cream, Curry, Parsley, Caper, or Hollandaise.

SALT COD À LA PARISIENNE (*Morue à la Parisienne*). Soak slices of salt cod for 24 hours in several changes of cold water. Cook them in White Court Bouillon made with milk and lemon. Drain and put them on a hot serving platter. Cover the cod with chopped hard-cooked egg, capers, and chopped parsley. Sprinkle with fresh lemon juice. Just before serving, pour on a little Brown Butter with fried breadcrumbs minced in.

COLD BOILED SALMON (*Saumon Bouilli, Froid*). Boil the salmon, whole or in one large piece, in Court Bouillon made with vinegar and allow it to cool in the liquid. Drain it and dry it, taking care not to break the skin. Put it on a platter and garnish it with hearts of lettuce and quartered hard-cooked eggs. Serve cold sauce appropriate for fish, such as Chantilly, Vinaigrette, Gribiche, Mayonnaise, Rémoulade, Vincent. Separately serve various *Salpicons,* Mousses, Purées, and *Macédoines* of vegetables in Tartlet crusts, Barquettes, cucumbers formed into Timbales, artichoke bottoms, and scooped-out tomatoes.

COLD BOILED CODFISH (*Cabillaud Bouilli, Froid*). Prepare as for Cold Boiled Salmon, except cook the fish in White Court Bouillon made with milk and lemon.

GLAZED SALMON BELLEVUE IN ASPIC (*Saumon Glacé Bellevue, en Aspic*). Boil a whole salmon in Fish Aspic and allow it to cool in the liquid. Drain the salmon, skin it carefully, dry it, and chill it in the refrigerator. Clarify* the fish aspic in which the salmon was cooked. Chill the clarified aspic until it is half-set, and glaze the salmon with several layers of aspic (see Aspic). Place the salmon upright on a platter on a bed of firmly set aspic, and surround it with chopped aspic or aspic cut in decorative shapes. Place the platter on a larger dish and surround it with cracked ice.

✻ POACHED FISH
(*Poissons Pochés*)

Poached fish are barely covered with a flavorful liquid and simmered until cooked. The poaching liquid is then made into a sauce. Poached fish are always served with their sauce poured over them. Many elegant dishes are quickly and effortlessly made in this manner.

The traditional fish for poaching are Dover sole and *turbotins,* both whole and cut into filets. These fish are not available here, but the European sole can be replaced with the softer American gray sole or flounder, and the turbot can be replaced with small halibut (if you can find one) or halibut filets. Ideally the fish should be lean, white-meated, fine-textured, and firm-fleshed. Soft-fleshed fish are more easily poached if the pieces are spatula-sized for easy handling. Use filets of fluke, flounder, halibut, haddock, pollock, hake, whiting, whitefish, and walleyed pike. Poaching is also the very best method of preparing frozen filets of fish, which are apt to be dry. The fish is cooked in a moist environment, and every drop of the juice that thaws from it is incorporated into its sauce.

To poach filets of fish, remove any membrane on the flesh to prevent them from curling in the heat, and trim them nicely. Liberally butter a sauté pan or skillet large enough to hold the filets side by side. Poach whole fish with the skin left on, with or without heads and tails. Add whatever ingredients the recipe calls for, such as shallots, mushrooms, tomatoes. Season the fish with salt and white pepper and place it in the pan on top of the bed of ingredients. Barely cover with the poaching liquid called for in the recipe. Place fishbones, if you have them, on top of the fish and cover with waxed or parchment paper in which you have cut a little hole to allow the steam to escape. (The fishbones will add their flavor and gelatin to the sauce.) Bring the poaching liquid to the simmer, cover the pan, and complete the cooking at a simmer. Begin testing for doneness in 8 minutes.

(Very delicate fish, like flounder, are sometimes poached in a minimum of liquid, sometimes with juicy chopped vegetables that provide liquid of their own (see *Sole Duglére*). In as much as a good portion of the fish is above the liquid, fish "poached" in this manner are essentially steamed. When using minimum liquid, dot the surface of the fish with bits of butter, and be sure to cover it with waxed or parchment paper.)

Remove the cooked fish with a slotted spatula, drain them, put them on a warm serving platter and keep warm. Quickly boil down the poaching liquor and use it to make the sauce as described in each of the following recipes. Finally, drain or blot up the liquid that has collected on the fish platter and pour the sauce over the fish. The dish may then be put under the broiler or in a hot oven to glaze* if the recipe so requires. Glazing must be done quickly to prevent the fish from drying.

FILETS OF MACKEREL À LA VENETIAN (*Filets de Maquereau à la Vénitienne*). Poach the filets, seasoned with salt and pepper, in dry white wine flavored with chopped shallots and chervil. Drain the filets, put them on a hot platter, and reduce the poaching liquid by ⅔ or more. Strain the reduced liquid, blend it with Venetian Sauce, and pour over the fish. (This dish can also be made with mullet.)

MACKEREL À LA BOULONNAISE (*Maquereau à la Boulonnaise*). Poach thick slices of mackerel, seasoned with salt and pepper, in Court Bouillon made with vinegar. Drain them, put them on a hot, long platter, and reduce the poaching liquid by ⅔ or more. Strain the reduced liquid and blend it with Butter Sauce. Surround the fish slices with poached mussel meats, and pour the sauce over all. (This dish can also be made with mullet.)

EEL À LA BONNE FEMME (*Anguille à la Bonne Femme*). Lightly sauté in butter ½ onion chopped, in a sauté pan. Put an eel, either cut in pieces or whole and rolled in a ring, onto this bed of onions. Season with salt and pepper and poach in dry white wine. Drain the eel, dry it, and put it on a platter on a bed of bread Croutons sautéed in butter, and garnish with potatoes cut in large dice and sautéed in butter. Reduce the poaching liquid by ½, strain it, thicken it with *Beurre Manié,* and pour it over the dish. Sprinkle with chopped parsley.

COD FLEMISH STYLE (*Cabillaud à la Flamande*). Poach 1-inch-thick slices of cod, seasoned with salt, pepper, and nutmeg, in dry white wine to which you have added chopped shallots; a few sprigs or pinches of parsley, chervil, and tarragon; and a few slices of peeled and seeded lemon. Drain the cod slices, dry them, and arrange them on a hot platter. Boil down the poaching liquor by ½, strain it, thicken it with crushed toast (rusk), and pour it over the cod slices.

SALMON À LA PRINCESSE (*Darne de Saumon Princesse*). Season with salt and pepper a cross section cut of salmon 6 inches or more in length. Poach it in Fish Fumet. Drain it, dry it, and place it on a hot platter. Reduce the poaching liquid by ½, strain it, blend it with Fish Velouté Sauce, and finish it with butter and cream. Coat the salmon with this sauce, place on top of the salmon a row of truffle slices warmed in butter, and garnish it with asparagus tips in butter. Lay a border of fish glaze (fish fumet reduced to a syrupy consistency) around the edge of the platter.

CÔTELETTES OF SALMON À LA FLORENTINE (*Côtelettes de Saumon à la Florentine*). Cut 1-inch thick salmon steaks in half to form cutlet-shaped pieces. Season them with salt and pepper, and poach them in Fish Fumet. Drain and dry them, and place them on a fireproof dish on top of a bed of chopped, cooked, seasoned spinach that you have dried and simmered in butter. Coat the salmon with Mornay Sauce, sprinkle with grated Parmesan cheese and melted butter, and brown in a hot oven or under the broiler.

POACHING SOLE AND OTHER FLATFISHES

The European sole, brill, and *turbotin* are replaced in America by any of the American flounders or small halibut. American gray sole (a flounder), winter flounder, California sand dab, and rex sole (a flounder) are particularly fine. However, the flesh of flounder is not quite as firm as the flesh of sole, so you must handle it carefully.

When a flatfish is poached whole, it is usually presented with its eyeless, white side uppermost. The fish is skinned on the dark side. The sauce is poured over the fish, with only the tip of the trimmed tail peeking out. The fins running the length of the top and bottom of the fish are usually trimmed off.

Sometimes a whole fish is partially fileted. A slit is cut along the backbone, and a knife worked in to partially detach the two filets. Butter is put into this opening, and the fish cooked as directed. This facilitates removing the filets of the fish at the table. (One reason for the popularity of European sole is that its flesh is exceptionally easy to detach from the bones.)

Flatfish have a tendency to curl when cooked whole. To prevent this, bend the whole fish to crack the backbone in one or two places. Or sever the backbone with a knife.

Certainly the most convenient way to cook and serve flatfish is in filet form. There are dozens of elegant, traditional recipes for poached filets of flatfish in the French repertoire. These dishes take only minutes to prepare, and their sauce is made as part of their cooking.

The following recipes are given using the name of the traditional European flatfish. Just remember, for sole or brill substitute flounder. For turbot or *turbotin,* substitute halibut.

CHICKEN TURBOT FERMIÈRE (*Turbotin Fermière*). Poach a whole turbot or flounder (about 2 pounds), seasoned with salt and pepper, in dry red wine to which you have added 1 tablespoon butter, 2 minced shallots, 1 tablespoon minced carrot, 1 tablespoon minced onion, a sprig of parsley, a pinch of thyme, and ½ bay leaf. Also, sauté ¾ cup minced mushrooms in 6 tablespoons butter. Drain the turbot, dry it, put it on a platter, surround it with the minced mushrooms, and keep warm. Reduce the poaching liquid by ½, strain it, and thicken it with *Beurre Manié*. Swirl in 6 tablespoons butter, pour the sauce over the fish and mushrooms, and glaze* in a hot oven. (This dish may also be made with halibut.)

BRILL À LA MÉNAGÈRE (*Barbue à la Ménagère*). Poach a whole brill or gray sole or other flounder (about 2 pounds), seasoned with salt and pepper, in dry red wine to which you have added ½ cup chopped onions lightly sautéed in butter, a pinch of thyme, and ½ bay leaf. Drain the fish, dry it, and put it on a hot platter. Reduce the poaching liquid by ½, strain it, and thicken it with *Beurre Manié*. Swirl in* 6 tablespoons butter and pour the sauce over the fish.

BRILL À LA BOURGUIGNONNE (*Barbue à la Bourguignonne*). Poach a whole brill or gray sole or other flounder (about 2 pounds), seasoned with salt and pepper, in dry red wine to which you have added small Glazed Onions and small mushrooms, a sprig of parsley, a pinch of thyme, and ½ bay leaf. Drain the brill and the vegetables, dry them, and arrange them on a hot platter. Reduce the poaching liquid by ½, strain it, and thicken it with *Beurre Manié*. Swirl in* 6 tablespoons butter and pour the sauce over the fish and vegetables.

BRILL À LA DIEPPOISE (*Barbue à la Dieppoise*). Poach a brill or gray sole or other flounder, whole or fileted, and seasoned with salt and pepper, in dry white wine. Drain the fish, dry it, put it on a platter, surround it with poached mussel meats, shrimp, and mushrooms, and keep warm. Boil down the fish poaching liquid by ½, strain it, and blend it with White Wine Sauce. Pour this sauce over the dish.

SOLE MORNAY (*Sole Mornay*). Season a whole sole or flounder with salt and pepper. Dot the fish with butter and poach it in a buttered pan in Fish Fumet. Drain and place the fish on a fireproof platter on a thin layer of Mornay Sauce. Pour Mornay sauce over the fish, sprinkle with grated Parmesan and Gruyère cheese, and glaze* it.

SOLE MORNAY DES PROVENÇAUX (*Sole Mornay des Provençaux*). Proceed as in the above recipe, except use White Wine Sauce in place of Mornay sauce.

SOLE DUGLÉRÉ (*Sole Dugléré*). Season a whole sole or flounder with salt and pepper. Put the fish in a buttered pan on a bed consisting of 2 tomatoes, peeled and chopped; ½ medium onion, chopped; and 1 tablespoon chopped parsley. Poach the fish, covered with buttered paper, in a minimum amount (about ½ cup) of dry white wine. Drain the fish, put it on a platter, and keep it warm. Reduce the poaching liquid by ½ and thicken it by mixing with a little Fish Velouté Sauce. Finish the sauce with butter and lemon juice, and pour it over the fish.

Filets and steaks of many other fish are also cooked *Dugléré*.

SOLE À LA FERMIÈRE (*Sole à la Fermière*). Season a whole sole or flounder with salt and pepper. Poach it in a buttered pan in dry red wine. Drain and place the fish on a hot platter. Reduce the poaching liquid by ½, strain it, thicken it with *Beurre Manié,* and finish it by swirling in* a few tablespoons of butter. Surround the fish with a border of sliced mushrooms lightly sautéed in butter. Pour the sauce over the fish and glaze* it.

SOLE WITH FINE WINES (*Soles aux Grands Vins*). (By cooking the sole in various Bordeaux and Burgundy wines, a number of differently flavored dishes are prepared, each named according to the wine it is cooked in. Thus we have *Sole au Chambertin, Sole au Saint-Émilion,* etc.) Season a whole fish with salt and pepper. Poach it in a buttered pan in ⅔ cup of fine dry red wine. Drain the sole and place it on a hot platter. Reduce the poaching wine by ½, add a few turns of fresh-ground pepper from the mill, squeeze in a few drops of fresh lemon juice, thicken with *Beurre Manié,* and finish the sauce by swirling in* 3 tablespoons butter. Pour the sauce over the fish.

SOLE IN WHITE WINE (*Sole au Vin Blanc*). Season a whole sole or flounder with salt and pepper. Put the sole in a buttered pan with ½ onion, chopped, and poach it in ½ dry white wine, ½ Fish Fumet, and a few tablespoons of Mushroom Essence. Drain the fish and put it on a hot platter. Reduce the poaching liquid by ½, thicken it with Fish Velouté Sauce, and finish it by swirling in* a few tablespoons of butter. Pour the sauce over the fish, and glaze* it or not, as you choose. (This dish may also be prepared using a fine white wine, in which case it takes the name of the wine. Thus, made with Chablis it becomes *Sole au Chablis,* made with Château-Yquem it becomes *Sole au Château-Yquem.*)

SOLE BONNE FEMME (*Sole Bonne Femme*). Season a whole sole or flounder with salt and pepper and place it in a fireproof serving dish with 2 shallots, chopped, ½ cup minced mushrooms, and a little chopped parsley. Poach the sole in ½ dry white wine, ½ Fish Fumet. Drain the cooking liquor and juices into a saucepan, reduce by ½, thicken with Fish Velouté

Sauce, and finish it by swirling in* 4 tablespoons butter. Pour this sauce over the sole and glaze* it.

SOLE IN CHAMPAGNE (*Sole au Champagne*). Season a whole sole or flounder with salt and pepper. Poach it in a buttered dish in 1 cup of champagne. Drain the fish and put it on a hot platter. Reduce the wine by ½, thicken it with ⅓ cup Fish Velouté Sauce, and finish the sauce by swirling in* 3 tablespoons butter. Pour this sauce over the sole and glaze* it. Garnish each end of the platter with little mounds of julienne* of fileted sole, seasoned with salt and pepper, dredged in flour, and sautéed in Clarified Butter. (Substitute other white wines in this recipe to create *Sole au Sauterne, Sole au Chablis,* etc.)

SOLE À LA FLORENTINE (*Sole à la Florentine*). Season a whole sole or flounder with salt and pepper. Poach it in a buttered dish in Fish Fumet. Drain the fish, and place it on an ovenproof platter on top of a bed of chopped, cooked, seasoned spinach that you have dried and simmered in butter. Cover the fish with Mornay Sauce, sprinkle it with grated Parmesan cheese and melted butter, and glaze* it.

SOLE MONTREUIL (*Sole Montreuil*). Season a whole sole or flounder with salt and pepper. Poach it in a buttered pan with ½ dry white wine, ½ Fish Fumet. Drain the fish and put it on a hot platter. Reduce the poaching liquid by ½, thicken it with Fish Velouté Sauce, and finish it by swirling in* 4 to 6 tablespoons butter. Surround the sole with boiled potato balls. Pour the sauce over the sole, and lay down a ribbon of Shrimp Sauce over the potatoes.

SOLE WITH OYSTERS (*Sole aux Huîtres*). Poach 6 or 12 oysters in their own liquor. Season a whole sole or flounder with salt and pepper, and poach it in a buttered pan in the oyster liquor. Drain the fish, place it on a hot platter, and surround it with the oyster meats. Reduce the poaching liquid by ½, blend it with White Wine Sauce and pour this sauce over the sole and the oysters. Glaze* very quickly.

SOLE À LA PROVENÇALE (*Sole à la Provençale*). Season a whole sole or flounder with salt and pepper. Poach it in ⅓ cup Fish Fumet and 2 tablespoons olive oil to which you have added 1 crushed clove of garlic. Drain the fish and put it on a hot platter. Reduce the poaching liquid by ½, and mix it with Provençale Sauce. Pour the sauce over the sole, and sprinkle with chopped parsley. Garnish the dish with Grilled Mushroom caps stuffed with garlic-flavored *Duxelles* and small Grilled Tomatoes.

SOLE À LA MARINIÈRE (*Sole à la Marinière*). Season a whole sole or flounder with salt and pepper. Poach it in a buttered dish in ⅓ cup dry white wine and ⅓ cup strained mussel cooking liquid (see Mussels) to which you have added a sprinkle of chopped shallots. Drain the fish, put it on a hot platter, and surround it with mussel meats. Reduce the poaching liquor by ½, thicken it with 2 egg yolks and 1 tablespoon Fish Velouté Sauce, and finish with 5 tablespoons butter and a little chopped parsley. Pour the sauce over the sole and the mussels, and glaze.*

SOLE MARGUERY (*Sole Marguery*). Season a whole sole or flounder with salt and pepper. Poach it in a buttered pan in ½ dry white wine and ½ Fish Fumet. Drain the sole, put it on a hot platter, and surround it with cooked shrimp and mussels. Reduce the poaching liquid by ½, thicken it with Fish Velouté Sauce, finish it with butter, pour it over the sole and its garnish, and glaze.*

SOLE À LA NANTUA (*Sole à la Nantua*). Season a whole sole or flounder with salt and pepper. Poach it in a buttered pan in Fish Fumet and a little Mushroom Essence. Drain the sole, put it on a hot platter, and surround it with cooked jumbo shrimp or crayfish tails. Coat the sole with Nantua Sauce and decorate it with a row of black truffle slices.

SOLE À L'ARLÉSIENNE (*Sole à l'Arlésienne*). Season a whole sole or flounder with salt and pepper. Poach it in a buttered dish in Fish Fumet. Drain the fish and put it on a hot platter. Reduce the poaching liquid by ½. In another pan, cook together ½ onion, chopped and lightly sautéed in butter; 2 medium tomatoes, peeled, seeded, and chopped; a pinch of minced garlic; and 1 teaspoon chopped parsley. Simmer, covered, for a few minutes, and add the reduced poaching liquid. Also add squash cut in olive shapes and simmered in butter. Cover the sole with this garnish, and at each end of the dish place a heap of fried onion rings.

POACHING FILETS

Filets of sole and flounder must be stripped of any membrane adhering to them to prevent them from curling while being cooked. They may be poached flat or folded over, and sometimes they are rolled.

This meat, devoid of skin and membrane, is very, very delicate. In order to avoid softening the flesh and drawing out its flavor, it is usually poached in a minimum amount of liquid, usually about ½ cup of liquid for 4 filets. Part of the fish stands above the level of the liquid and is therefore steamed. To equalize cooking, regularly baste the tops of the filets, cover them snugly with waxed paper or parchment cut to fit the pan, and *cover the pan tightly.* It is not necessary, nor is it advisable, to turn the filets while cooking them.

Be sure the liquid does not boil, or the fish will cook too quickly and fall apart. The liquid should just show a few bubbles around the edge of the pan.

FILET OF SOLE WITH MUSHROOMS (*Filets de Soles aux Champignons*). In a covered pan, simmer ¾ cup small mushrooms in butter with ⅓ cup of water. Season the filets with salt and pepper, fold them, and poach them, covered, in the mushroom cooking liquid and 2 tablespoons butter. Drain the filets, arrange them on a hot platter in the form of an oval, and fill the center of the oval with the mushrooms. Reduce the poaching liquid by ⅔, thicken with 2 tablespoons Fish Velouté Sauce, and finish the sauce with 2 table-spoons butter. Pour the sauce over the fish and mushrooms.

FILETS OF SOLE HUNGARIAN (*Filets de Soles à la Hongroise*). Lightly sauté in butter 1 tablespoon chopped onion seasoned with a pinch of paprika. To the pan add 2 small tomatoes, peeled, seeded, and chopped; ⅓ cup Fish Fumet, and ¼ cup of dry white wine. Cover and cook for a few minutes. Season the filets with salt and pepper, fold them, and put them into a buttered pan. Pour over them the onion and tomato mixture, and poach them, covered. Drain the filets and arrange them on a dish in the form of a circle. Reduce the poaching liquid until it is syrupy. Then thin it with a few tablespoons of light cream and a sprinkle of fresh lemon juice. Pour this sauce over the filets.

FILETS OF SOLE LADY EGMONT (*Filets de Soles Lady Egmont*). In a covered pan, simmer ½ cup minced mushrooms in butter and ½ teaspoon of lemon juice. Season the filets with salt and pepper, and fold them. Poach them, covered, in ⅓ cup Fish Fumet and the liquid exuded by the mush-rooms. Drain the filets and put them on a hot platter. Reduce the poaching liquid by ½, finish the sauce with 2 tablespoons butter and 2 tablespoons heavy cream, and stir into this sauce the warm minced mushrooms and 2 tablespoons warm cooked asparagus tips. Pour this sauce over the filets, and glaze.*

FILETS OF SOLE WITH OYSTERS (*Filets de Soles aux Huîtres*). Poach 12 oysters in their own liquor. Season the filets with salt and pepper, and fold them. Poach them, covered, in the strained oyster liquor with 2 table-spoons butter. Drain the filets, arrange them on a hot platter in the form of an oval, and fill the center of the oval with the oyster meats. Reduce the poaching liquor by ½ and combine with Normandy Sauce. Pour this sauce over the sole and the oysters.

FILETS OF SOLE POLIGNAC (*Filets de Soles Polignac*). Season the filets with salt and pepper, and fold them. Poach them, covered, in ½ cup dry white wine, a few tablespoons of Mushroom Essence, and 2 tablespoons butter. Drain the filets and arrange them on a hot platter in the form of an oval. Reduce the poaching liquor by ½, thicken it with 2 tablespoons Fish Velouté Sauce, and swirl in* 2 tablespoons butter. Also add to the sauce 6 tablespoons cooked minced mushrooms and 1 tablespoon julienne* or truffle. Pour this sauce over the filets and glaze.*

FILETS OF SOLE VENETIAN (*Filets de Soles à la Vénitienne*). Season the filets with salt and pepper, and fold them. Poach them, covered, in ½ cup Fish Fumet. Drain and arrange them on a hot dish in the form of a circle. Between the filets, place heart-shaped pieces of bread sautéed in butter. Reduce the poaching liquid by ½, combine it with Venetian Sauce, and pour over the filets.

FILETS OF SOLE VÉRONIQUE (*Filets de Soles Véronique*). Season and fold the filets. Poach them, covered, in ¼ cup of Fish Fumet. Drain the filets and arrange them on an ovenproof platter in the form of an oval. Reduce the poaching liquid until it is syrupy and swirl in* 3 tablespoons butter. Pour this sauce over the filets and glaze* them. Serve the dish with a pyramid of cold, skinned, muscatel grapes placed in the oval.

Some traditional recipes for filets of sole do not incorporate the poaching liquid into the sauce. I only mention this here so you will not think I have become weary and have decided to leave things out.

FILETS OF SOLE WITH SHRIMP (*Filets de Soles aux Crevettes*). Season the filets with salt and pepper, and fold them. Poach them, covered, in Fish *Fumet*. Drain them and arrange them on a hot platter in the form of an oval. In the center of the oval put hot cooked shrimp. Coat the fish and shrimp with Shrimp Sauce.

FILETS OF SOLE CHAUCHAT (*Filets de Soles Chauchat*). Season the filets with salt and pepper, and fold them. Poach them, covered, in ¼ cup lemon juice and 2 tablespoons butter. Drain the filets, and arrange them in the form of an oval on a platter on a thin layer of Mornay Sauce. Surround the filets with potatoes cut in cork shapes and lightly sautéed in butter. Cover the filets and the potatoes with Mornay sauce and glaze* them.

FILETS OF SOLE OLGA (*Filets de Soles Olga*). Take 1 potato for each filet and bake it in the oven until the skin is crisp and golden. Cut a slice from the skin and scoop out the flesh, leaving only the crisp baked potato shell. In the bottom of each shell, put 1 tablespoon chopped cooked shrimp combined with White Wine Sauce. Season the filets with salt and pepper, and fold them. Poach them, covered, in Fish Fumet. Drain them and place them on top of the shrimp in the potato shells. Fill the shells with Mornay Sauce, sprinkle with grated Parmesan cheese, and glaze* them.

FILETS OF SOLE WILHELMINE (*Filets de Soles Wilhelmine*). Prepare baked potato shells as in Filets of Sole Olga (above). Into each shell put 1 tablespoon chopped cucumber with cream, 1 filet poached in Fish Fumet, and 1 raw oyster. Fill the shell with Mornay Sauce and glaze* in the oven.

✳ *BRAISED FISH*
(*Poissons Braisés*)

Braised fish are cooked partly in a flavorful liquid, partly in steam. The braising liquid is then made into a sauce.

Lean, whole fish weighing 3 to 4 pounds or more are braised, stuffed or unstuffed. Salmon steaks are also traditional candidates for braising. Braising, like poaching, is an excellent way to cook frozen fish because all of the thawed juices are saved.

The braising liquid is half wine, half Fish Fumet to which aromatic herbs and vegetables are added.

To braise a fish, scale it carefully. If you choose, remove the head and tail. Also, if you choose, stuff the fish with Forcemeat for Fish, and close the cavity with skewers and string or simply sew it up with string. In a shallow casserole or fireproof pan with a cover, put a bed of aromatic vegetables (a *Mirepoix*) as listed in the recipe. Season the fish, wrap it in cheesecloth lightly so it can be easily handled, place it on its side on top of the vegetables, and pour over it enough of the recommended braising liquid to cover it by about ⅓. Sprinkle melted butter over the fish, and if it is very lean, drape it with strips of blanched bacon. Also cover the fish with a piece of waxed or parchment paper trimmed to fit the pan, and in which you have cut a little hole to allow the steam to escape.

Bring the liquid to a boil, partially cover the pan, leaving a 1- or 2-inch opening, and simmer the fish on top of the stove or in a 375° oven. (We partially uncover the pan so that the liquid can reduce somewhat during the brief time it takes to cook a fish.) Baste the fish regularly throughout cooking to prevent its upper surface from drying. Cooking time should be about 8 to 10 minutes per pound, but test for doneness early.

When the fish is cooked, lift it from the liquid, drain it, and gently turn it out of the cheesecloth onto a hot serving platter. Remove its skin and keep it warm. Skim the fat from the surface of the braising liquid and boil it down over a hot fire until it is reduced to ½ or ⅓ its original volume. Finish the sauce as directed in the recipe. (As a rule, braising liquid made with white wine is thickened with white sauce, cream, or egg yolks; braising sauce made with red wine is thickened with *Beurre Manié*.) Strain the finished sauce over the fish, and garnish as suggested in the particular recipe.

BARBEL MARINER STYLE (*Barbeau à la Mode des Mariniers*). Use a catfish to make this dish. Lightly sauté in butter 2 onions, chopped, and 2 shallots, chopped. Put them in the bottom of a braising pan with ½ cup chopped walnuts and 1 cup chopped mushrooms. Skin a 2-pound catfish and make 2 or 3 diagonal cuts along either side. Place it on the bed of vegetables, and to the pan add enough red wine to cover the fish by ½. Sprinkle the top of the fish with ½ cup melted butter and drape it with blanched bacon strips. Cover the fish with waxed or parchment paper cut to fit the size of the pan. Bring the liquid to a boil, cover the pan leaving a 1- or 2-inch opening, and place it in a 375° oven. Braise it, basting frequently, for 15 minutes. Uncover the pan, remove the bacon strips, and sprinkle the fish with melted butter and fine, dry breadcrumbs. Continue cooking, uncovered, until the crumbs are browned and the fish is done. Put the fish on a hot platter, thicken the braising liquid with *Beurre Manié*. Pour the sauce over the fish and sprinkle with chopped parsley.

BRILL À LA CANCALAISE (*Barbue à la Cancalaise*). You may use gray sole or another flounder to make this dish. Make a cut from gill to tail along the middle of the fish on the dark side, and partially detach the filets. Season the fish with salt and pepper, and put 2 tablespoons butter into the cut. Put the fish in a buttered braising pan and add enough white wine to cover the fish by ½. Sprinkle with melted butter and braise. Drain the brill and put it on a platter dark side up. Remove the dark skin. Turn the fish over, wipe the dish clean, and keep warm. Boil down and strain the braising liquid and use it to make Normandy Sauce. Finish the sauce with a little Crayfish or Shrimp Butter. Surround the fish with poached oysters, heat it briefly in the oven, and pour the sauce over the fish and oysters.

ROYAL BRAISED SALMON (*Saumon Braisé Royale*). Braise a whole salmon in sauterne wine until it is almost cooked. Drain it, put it on an oven-proof platter, and carefully skin it from a point just behind the gills to a point 1 inch from the tail. Brush it lightly with its braising liquid and return it to the oven to glaze.* Serve the salmon surrounded by cooked shrimp, fish Quenelles, mushrooms, potato balls cooked *à l'Anglaise,* and truffle slices. Separately serve Normandy Sauce in a hot sauceboat.

✳ BAKED FISH
(Poissons au Four)

Fish are baked with careful basting in a moderately hot to hot oven. They are also gratinéed, a special kind of baking in which the fish is cooked in a sauce.

The best fish for baking are whole, fat, handsome fish weighing 3 pounds or more. They should be whole and large and fat to better retain their moistness in the face of the oven's dry heat. They should be handsome because they are served whole. Lean fish can be baked with special precautions, precautions that are wise to take when cooking fat fish as well. We can bard* the fish with sheets of pork fat or strips of blanched bacon, especially around the tail, where the meat is at its smallest dimension. We can moisten the hot air of the oven by adding liquid to the baking pan. We can fill the fish with a very moist stuffing. And whatever else we do, we baste, baste, baste. Consequently we can bake bass, bluefish, red snapper, grouper, pompano, mullet, whiting, whitefish, salmon, and cod.

To bake a whole fish, scale it carefully and trim the fins (or cover them with foil to prevent them from charring). Stuff it, if you choose, with a Forcemeat appropriate to the fish (a creamy shrimp stuffing in a mild-flavored fish can perform at the table as a sauce). Sew up the cavity or close it with skewers and string. Place the fish on a rack in a preheated baking pan (so that the cooking may begin all the sooner), or on top of a *Mirepoix* of vegetables spread in the bottom of the pan. Brush the fish thickly with melted butter (or dot it with pieces of butter), drape it with pork fat or blanched bacon if it is very lean, and place it in a 350° to 400° oven. The smaller the fish, the hotter the oven. Bake the fish, basting frequently with butter, for about 8 to 10 minutes per pound, but test early for doneness. If the fish seems too dry, add a little wine or water to the baking pan.

Carefully remove the fish to its serving dish, laying it on its side or standing it upright—on its belly. You may replace the eyes with stuffed olives. Make the sauce with the pan juices if the recipe requires, and serve with the recommended sauce and garnishes.

For gratinéed fish you can use small whole fish, steaks, or filets. The fish is baked in a sauce or liquid that is calculated to thicken to the proper consistency and form a glaze at the precise moment the fish is done. All this is very difficult to judge, so you must rely on the recipe. Examples to follow are *Sole au Gratin* and *Sole-sur-le-Plat,* which is a short form of the gratin called a glazing.*

STRIPED BASS À LA LIVORNAISE (*Bar à la Livornaise*). Butter an ovenproof serving dish large enough to hold 3 or 4 small striped bass. In the bottom of the dish place a bed of Tomato Fondue mixed with chopped onion and a pinch of minced garlic. Place the bass on this bed, sprinkle with breadcrumbs and olive oil, and bake in a 400° oven for about 10 minutes. Serve the fish sprinkled with chopped parsley.

RED MULLET WITH SHALLOTS (*Rouget à l'Échalote*). You may use American gray mullet or striped mullet to make this dish. Butter an ovenproof serving dish. In the bottom of the dish place a bed of chopped shallots thoroughly cooked in white wine. Make a series of shallow cuts, every 2 inches, along the back of a mullet. Place the mullet on the bed of shallots, sprinkle with a few tablespoons of dry white wine, and dot liberally with butter. Bake the fish in a 350° oven, basting frequently. When cooked, sprinkle with lemon juice and chopped parsley, and serve in the dish.

SHAD AU PLAT (*Alose au Plat*). Mix 1 tablespoon chopped parsley, 1 teaspoon chopped shallot, and a little salt and pepper in 3 tablespoons butter. Spread this flavored butter inside a 1½-pound shad. Place the shad on a buttered ovenproof serving dish, sprinkle with ½ cup dry white wine, dot with butter, and bake in a 375° oven, basting frequently. If the liquid in the dish dries up, add a little water or wine. Serve the shad in the dish, sprinkled with chopped parsley.

STUFFED SHAD À LA MÉNAGÈRE (*Alose Farcie à la Ménagère*). Stuff the shad with breadcrumbs, lightly sautéed onions, butter, chopped parsley, and chopped chervil, seasoned with salt and pepper. Bake in the same manner as Shad au Plat (above).

SHAD CLAUDINE (*Alose Claudine*). Butter an ovenproof serving dish. In the bottom of the dish place a bed of chopped shallots thoroughly cooked in white wine, sliced raw mushrooms, and chopped parsley. Cut the shad into steaks, place them on the bed of vegetables, season with salt and pepper, sprinkle with a few tablespoons of dry white wine, and dot liberally with butter. Bake in a 375° oven, basting frequently. When the shad is almost cooked, pour heavy cream over the dish and glaze* it.

ROAST COD (*Cabillaud Rôti*). Cut the cod in large pieces and marinate them for one hour in a little oil and lemon juice. Drain the pieces, place them on a rack in a baking pan, sprinkle them with melted butter, and bake in a 350° oven, basting frequently with butter. Arrange the fish on a hot platter. Add a little dry white wine to the pan juices and reduce the mixture by ½. Thicken with *Beurre Manié,* and serve the sauce with the fish.

COD À L'INDIENNE (*Cabillaud à l'Indienne*). Butter an ovenproof serving dish. In the bottom of the dish place a bed of lightly sautéed chopped onions; peeled, seeded, and chopped tomato; chopped parsley; and a pinch of minced garlic. Cut the cod into thick steaks, season with salt and pepper, and place on the bed of vegetables. Sprinkle with ½ cup dry white wine, and dot the fish with butter. Bake in a 375° oven, basting frequently, for about 10 minutes. Begin basting with heavy cream, frequently, until the cod is done. Put the cod on a hot serving platter. Boil down the pan juices and mix with Curry Sauce. Serve the cod with Rice à l'Indienne.

SOLE ON THE DISH (*Sole sur le Plat*). Partially detach the filets on the dark side of a sole or flounder but leave the skin on. Season inside the cut̃ with salt and pepper, and tuck 2 tablespoons butter beneath the loosened filets. Place the sole in a well-buttered ovenproof serving dish, sprinkle with ½ cup concentrated Fish Fumet and a squeeze of lemon juice, dot the fish with butter, and bake it in a 375° oven. Baste very often. By the time the fish is cooked, the cooking liquid will have become syrupy, giving the sole the translucent and glossy coat that is characteristic of this dish.

This dish may be also achieved by cooking with wine to which a little Meat Glaze is added. Thus, you can use champagne to make *sole sur la plat au champagne,* Saint-Émilion to make *sole sur la plat Saint-Émilion,* etc.

SOLE BERCY (*Sole Bercy*). Partially detach the filets on the dark side of a sole or flounder but leave the skin on. Salt and pepper inside the cut and put 2 tablespoons butter beneath the loosened filets. Place the sole on a bed of lightly sautéed onions in a well-buttered ovenproof serving dish. Surround the fish with mushroom slices sautéed in butter. Sprinkle with ½ cup of dry red Burgundy wine, dot the fish with butter, and bake in a 375° oven, basting frequently. When the sole is almost cooked, remove from the oven and drain off the cooking juices. Reduce these juices a little, thicken with *Beurre Manié,* and swirl in* 2 tablespoons butter. Pour this sauce over the fish, and glaze* it in the oven.

✳ GRILLED AND BROILED FISH
(*Poissons Grillés*)

Broiling and grilling require great alertness on your part, because even 30 seconds overcooking in this fiercely hot environment can dry out and spoil a fish. The fish is assaulted at once by hot iron, superheated air, and rays of radiant heat. But the delicious products of the broiler and grill—the crispness and creaminess and delicate smoke flavors—are powerful incentives for acquiring skill in this method.

Fish are grilled or broiled whole or cut into steaks or filets. The meat must be at least ½ inch thick so that it may brown before it is cooked through, and it should not be more than 2 inches thick so that the interior may be cooked before the surface burns. Observe the rule for broiling and grilling; that is, place thinner fish closer to the flame. Thick fish may be seared close to the flame, and then moved farther away to complete their cooking. All fish are protected with bastings of fat. Lean fish and thin filets are protected with coatings of flour or breadcrumbs as well.

GRILLED FISH

To grill whole, sliced, or fileted fish, roll it in butter or olive oil. If the fish is whole, cut 1 or 2 diagonal slashes on both sides to prevent the fish from curling and to open pathways for the heat into the interior. If it is a lean fish, dredge it first in flour, slapping it smartly to remove the excess, and roll in butter or oil. This will produce a protective crust.

Oil the grill and heat it until it is very, very hot. If it is not hot enough, the fish will stick to it and will be destroyed when you attempt to turn it over. The hot grill will also leave handsome brand marks that are characteristic of grilled fish. (A Japanese hibachi grill is excellent for this purpose.)

Baste the fish regularly with fat, and turn it when it is deliciously brown on the first side. (Halfway through the cooking of this first side, you may shift the fish so the brown brand marks are crisscrossed.)

Use a spatula and fork to turn the fish over without piercing it. If there is a clear space on the grill, place it there, for there the iron is likely to be hotter. How long you cook the second side depends upon the thickness, density, and moistness of the particular fish. Test for doneness by probing with a fork or poultry skewer. The fish is cooked when its flesh flakes and the interior flesh is opaque.

BROILED FISH

To broil whole, sliced, or fileted fish, prepare it for cooking exactly as grilled fish. Oil the broiler pan and heat it until it is very, very hot to prevent the fish from sticking. Place the fish in the pan and broil, basting often with butter. Delicate filets usually need not be turned, as the hot pan cooks their bottom side; they are usually done when the top is a beautiful golden brown, in about 8 minutes. Whole fish and fish steaks are almost done when the top is nicely browned. Baste with butter, turn them over, and cook for a few minutes on the second side. They are done when the flesh flakes and is opaque in the interior.

Send grilled or broiled fish to the table on a very hot platter, garnished with sprigs of parsley and slices of lemon. The fish is usually served with Maître d'Hôtel Butter.

GRILLED SMELT (*Éperlans Grillés*). Clean the smelt, make a cut along their backs, and remove their backbones. Season with salt and pepper, dredge in flour, and sprinkle them copiously with melted butter. Grill the smelt very quickly, close to the flame, basting with butter and turning once. Serve the smelt in a row on a long, hot platter, and garnish with slices of lemon and fried parsley. Separately serve Maître d'Hôtel Butter. (The smelt may be split open (butterflied) so that their flesh may absorb more of the delicious smoke and are thereby cooked even more quickly.)

GRILLED WHOLE SHAD (*Alose Grillée*). Make diagonal cuts along each side of the shad. Season it with salt and pepper, and marinate it for one hour in oil and lemon juice, to which you have added a little parsley, bay leaf, and thyme. Grill the shad, basting with butter. Put it on a hot platter and garnish with lemon slices and fried parsley. Separately serve Maître d'Hôtel Butter.

SKEWERED SALMON (*Brochettes de Saumon*). Cut salmon in 1½-inch cubes, and impale these cubes on skewers alternating with half-sautéed mushrooms. Season with salt and pepper, roll in melted butter, and then roll in fine, dry white breadcrumbs. Press the breadcrumbs into the salmon so that they may adhere closely. Grill the salmon, basting with butter. Lay the skewers diagonally on a long, hot platter and garnish with parsley and lemon slices. Separately serve Maître d'Hôtel Butter.

RED MULLET À LA BORDELAISE (*Rouget à la Bordelaise*). Make shallow cuts along the back of the mullet. Season with salt and pepper, brush it with olive oil, and broil it in the broiler, turning once. Put it on a hot platter, garnish with lemon slices and parsley, and separately serve Bordelaise Sauce made with white wine.

The American gray mullet or striped mullet may be used for the above recipe.

PLAICE À LA NIÇOISE (*Carrelet à la Niçoise*). Make a few cuts along the back of the fish. Season with salt and pepper, brush it with olive oil, and broil it in the broiler. Put the fish, white side up, onto a serving platter on a bed of seeded, peeled, and chopped tomatoes that you have cooked lightly in butter and flavored with minced garlic and chopped tarragon. Lay a criss-cross grid of anchovy filets on top of the fish, and scatter over it 1 tablespoon capers. Surround the fish with green or black olives, and sprinkle with chopped basil.

Flounder, fluke, or chicken halibut may be used in the above recipe.

FILETS OF BRILL À LA TYROLIENNE (*Filets de Barbue à la Tyrolienne*). Season the filets with salt and paprika, brush them with olive oil, and broil them. Serve the filets on a bed of Tomato Fondue and cover them with fried onion rings.

Filets of flounder, halibut, or other fine-grained white fish may be used in the above recipe.

❋ SAUTÉED FISH
(*Poissons Sautés* or *à la Meunière*)

À la meunière means "in the manner of the miller's wife," and it comes to us from the days when people, not companies, milled flour. The fish is always dredged in flour and sautéed quickly in very hot butter. The flour gives it its characteristic golden brown color, without which the fish is improperly cooked. The miller's wife would be outraged.

All small whole fish up to about 2 pounds, and steaks of all larger fish, can be sautéed or cooked *à la meunière*. The procedure seems simple enough, but it has its pitfalls. The most terrible of these yawns before you if the butter is·not hot enough. The surface of the fish will not be sealed and it will leak its juices into the pan. The juices, evaporating into the kitchen air, will cool the fat even more. The fish will stick to the pan. It will not brown, but turn dirty gray and horrid-looking. The flour will taste pasty. The butter will penetrate the flesh of the fish and make it greasy throughout. Believe me, the fat must be hot, hot as you dare make it without smoking and burning it.

To cook fish *à la meunière,* use a heavy steel or cast-iron skillet or sauté pan large enough to hold all the fish with ample space between them. If you are sautéing a large fish of 2 pounds, you should have an oval fish sauté pan. (Unless you are very serious about this, I recommend you limit whole fish to this 2-pound size. Larger fish require pans so large the home range burner will only heat a portion of them, and pans large enough to span 2 burners would very likely be too large for sautéable fish.)

Cover the bottom of the pan with ⅛ inch Clarified Butter, and heat it until it begins to turn brown. Season whole fish with salt and freshly ground pepper, and roll and rub them in flour. (To help the flour to adhere, you may dip the fish first in milk or flat beer.) Slap the fish sharply over the sink to dislodge excess flour that would burn in the pan. If the fish are whole, slash them diagonally every 2 inches on each side so they will not curl and the heat can penetrate. Immediately after dredging, place the fish in the pan. The fish will cool the butter, so turn the fire up full so that the butter may be more quickly restored to its proper temperature.

Turn the fish when it is golden brown and cook the second side. Small fish and steaks will take about 12 minutes from start to finish, but be sure to check for doneness early. The fish is done when it flakes easily and the flesh is opaque in the middle. Larger fish of 2 pounds will not cook in the time it takes the surface to brown, so you must compromise and lower the heat after the first side is seared in hot butter. Fifteen minutes from the time cooking begins, turn the fish over and turn up the heat to brown the second side. Then again reduce the heat and cook for 10 to 15 minutes or until the fish is done.

Just before the fish is finished cooking, heat enough clarified butter in another pan to sauce the fish. Cook the butter slowly until it turns light brown and exudes a nutty odor. Remove the cooked fish to a hot platter, garnish with parsley and lemon slices, and pour the sizzling brown butter over the fish *à la meunière*.

GOLDEN SOLE (*Sole Dorée*). Pepper the fish lightly, dip it in flour, pat it smartly to remove the excess, sauté it in Clarified Butter until the fish is golden brown, salt it with very fine salt, and serve with a row of peeled lemon slices placed on top of it. This very simple method, which, however, requires careful cooking, is used for all small fish and for filets and steaks of larger fish.

SOLE À LA MEUNIÈRE (*Sole à la Meunière*). This is identical to the above dish except that the sautéed fish is sprinkled with lemon juice and chopped parsley at the last moment, and sizzling hot Brown Butter is poured over the fish. The fish is served while the lemon juice is still frothing in the hot butter.

BASS À LA PROVENÇALE (*Bar à la Provençale*). Make a few shallow cuts along the back of a small striped bass. Season with salt and pepper, dredge with flour, and sauté the fish in olive oil. Put the fish on an ovenproof serving dish, cover with Provençale Sauce, sprinkle with breadcrumbs and olive oil, and glaze* it in the oven. Serve the fish sprinkled with chopped parsley.

SAUTÉED HERRINGS À LA LYONNAISE (*Harengs Sautés à la Lyon-naise*). Make a few shallow cuts along the sides of the fish. Season with salt and pepper, dredge with flour, and sauté the fish in Clarified Butter. When the first side is cooked, turn the herring and add to the pan ½ onion, thinly sliced and partially sautéed in butter. Put the herring on a hot serving platter and strew the onion slices over it. Wipe out the sauté pan and brown some fresh clarified butter in it. Add a little vinegar to the butter, warm it, and pour the brown butter and vinegar over the fish.

SMELT À L'ANGLAISE (*Éperlans à l'Anglaise*). Clean the smelt, make a cut along their backs, and remove their backbones. Dip in beaten egg, roll in fine, dry white breadcrumbs, and sauté the smelt in Clarified Butter. Put the smelt on a hot platter, and pour melted Maître d'Hôtel Butter over them.

CUTLETS OF SALMON WITH MUSHROOMS À LA CRÈME (*Côtelettes de Saumon aux Champignons à la Crème*). Divide salmon steaks from top to bottom to form cutlet-shaped pieces. Season with salt and pepper, dredge them in flour, and sauté in Clarified Butter. When the first side is cooked, turn the cutlets and add 3 or 4 small mushrooms for each cutlet. Place the cooked cutlets on a hot round platter, arranging them in a circle on top of heart-shaped pieces of bread sautéed in butter. Place the mushrooms on top of the cutlets. Add a few tablespoons of Madeira wine, heavy cream, and butter to the juices in the pan, and thicken with a few tablespoons of Fish Velouté Sauce. Cook for a few minutes until the sauce is at the right consistency, strain it, and pour it over the fish.

FILETS OF BRILL À LA DUXELLES (*Filets de Barbue à la Duxelles*). Season filets of brill, gray sole, or another flounder with salt and pepper. Dredge them in flour and sauté them in Clarified Butter. Arrange them on a hot platter on a bed of *Duxelles* mixed with Tomato Sauce. Garnish the filets with slices of peeled lemon and chopped parsley. Clean the pan, add fresh clarified butter, and brown it (or do this in a separate pan while the fish is cooking). Pour the sizzling brown butter over the fish.

✳ DEEP-FRIED FISH
(*Poissons Frits*)

Fish are fried deeply immersed in hot oil. There must be enough oil so that its heat is not seriously reduced when the fish are plunged into it. The fish are coated in some manner to create a barrier between the oil and the fish.

Only small fish or small pieces and filets can be successfully deep-fried. As in sautéing, the fish must be cooked in the center by the time the surface is golden brown. Deep-frying is a much faster process, however, taking only 1 or 2 minutes. Also, as in sautéing, the fat must never be allowed to cool to the point where it will penetrate the fish. It should be kept between 360° and 380°, the higher temperature being used for the smaller fish or pieces. Use olive oil or a fresh vegetable oil.

There are four kinds of protective coatings for deep-fried fish. Small whole fish with their skins on may be simply (1) dipped in milk or flat beer and dredged with flour. Small pieces and small filets are more usually (2) dipped in flour, then in egg beaten with a little milk and oil, and then rolled in fine, dry white breadcrumbs (*à l'Anglaise*). The raw egg congeals instantly in the hot fat, sealing the fish in a crisp and tender but impenetrable crust. (The fat must be kept at the proper temperature, however, or this crust will become soggy and tough.) The fish may also be (3) dipped in Batter or (4) enclosed in pastry dough as a kind of *Rissole*.

To deep-fry fish, season and coat it in one of the ways listed. Use tongs or a heated frying basket to immerse it in the very hot oil, taking care that the temperature of the oil does not fall below 360°. If it does, begin with the oil at a higher temperature, or fry fewer pieces of fish at a time. The fish is cooked in 1 or 2 minutes, or when it is a handsome golden brown. (If in doubt, test a cooked piece.) Lift out the fish, draining it, and serve it on a napkin. (If several batches of fish must be fried, withdraw them from the oil a few seconds early. When all the fish are thus cooked, run the batches through the oil again for a few seconds.) Deep-fried fish is always served with a garnish of Fried Parsley.

WHITING COLBERT (*Merlan Colbert*). Make a cut along the back of the fish and remove the backbone. Season with pepper, dredge with flour, dip in egg beaten with a little milk and oil, roll in fine, dry white breadcrumbs, and deep-fry. Arrange the fish on a long dish, and season with very fine salt. Into the cut along the backbone of each fish, put a little Maître d'Hôtel Butter.

Many other small fish may be prepared in the same way.

WHITING À L'ESPAGNOLE (*Merlan à l'Espagnole*). Prepare as for Whiting Colbert (above), but serve on a bed of garlic-flavored Tomato Fondue and garnish with deep-fried onion rings.

SKEWERED FRIED SMELT (*Éperlans Frits en Brichettes*). Pepper the smelt, dip them in milk, and dredge them in flour. Impale them on a skewer, running the skewer through the eyes, and deep-fry them. Drain the fish, sprinkle with very fine salt, and serve them on their skewers garnished with lemon slices and Fried Parsley.

SALMON ATTEREAUX (*Attereaux de Saumon*). Marinate 1-inch cubes of salmon for 1 hour in lemon juice and a little olive oil to which you have added salt, pepper, and a little chopped parsley. Sauté the salmon very briefly in butter to stiffen the flesh. Impale the salmon cubes on skewers, coat them with Villeroi Sauce, and allow them to cool until the sauce is set. Dip in beaten egg, roll in breadcrumbs, and deep-fry. Serve on the skewers with lemon and Fried Parsley.

FILETS OF SOLE ORLY (*Filets de Sole Orly*). Marinate filets of sole or flounder for 1 hour in lemon juice and a little olive oil to which you have added salt, pepper, chopped shallots, parsley, bay leaf, and a little thyme. Drain the filets, dry them, dip in Batter and deep-fry them. Arrange them in a circle on a hot round dish garnished with Fried Parsley. Separately serve Tomato Sauce or Tartar Sauce.

❋ *SOME OTHER PREPARATIONS OF FISH*

FISH IN PAPER CASES
(*Poissons en Papillotes*)

This is a very pleasant way to cook and serve fish, and so easy to do you need not wait for a special occasion to enjoy fish this way. There is more to this method than just a pleasing presentation. The paper cases seal in the good juices and flavors and keep the fish hot to the last bite. All filets of fish and small whole fish (with heads and tails removed) can be prepared in this way.

Prepare the paper cases by cutting parchment paper (or heavy 8½ by 11" bond typing paper) in the shape of flattened hearts. Butter the hearts on one side. Lightly sauté or broil the fish or filet until it is golden brown and barely cooked. Spread ½ of the buttered paper heart shapes with a thick warm sauce for fish—Velouté, Béchamel, Mornay, Normandy, White Wine, or Duxelles Sauce, which is particularly suited to this dish. Place the fish on the sauce and fold the other half of the heart over it, forming a case. Roll the edge of the case to seal tightly. Place the cases on a baking sheet and bake them in a 400° oven for 5 minutes, or until the paper begins to brown and puff up. Remove to individual serving plates, cut a semicircle ¾ way around the top of the case, fold back, and serve with the delicious steam rising from the warm brown heart.

SALPICON OF FISH
(*Salpicon de Poisson*)

Skin and bone cooked fish (preferably boiled or poached), dice it, and bind the dice together with a thick hot sauce for fish such as Béchamel, Normandy, Fish Velouté, Mornay, or White Wine Sauce. You may also mix into this *salpicon* diced cooked shellfish, mushrooms, and tiny *Quenelles*.

CROQUETTES OF FISH
(*Croquettes de Poisson*)

Skin and bone cooked fish (preferably boiled or poached), and flake it. To 2 cups flaked fish, add ¾ cup cooked and diced mushrooms, 3 table-spoons diced truffles (if you have them), and ¼ cup Madeira (if you choose). Cover and heat gently in the oven. To 2 cups very thick Velouté Sauce or Béchamel Sauce, add 3 beaten egg yolks. Combine the sauce and fish. Heat, stirring, until the mixture is thoroughly blended and leaves the sides of the pan. Chill the croquette mixture in a flat pan, buttering it to prevent a skin from forming. When chilled, take egg-sized pieces of the mix-ture, flour them, dip in egg beaten with olive oil, and roll in fine, dry white breadcrumbs. Press them in the shape of corks, balls, cubes, cones, patties, or whatever shape you choose. Deep-fry until golden, drain them, and season with fine salt. Use as a garnish or serve alone, heaped on a napkin-covered dish and garnished with parsley, or put in a nest of Straw Potatoes.

BARQUETTES and TARTLETS OF FISH
(*Barquettes et Tartelettes de Poisson*)

Prepare a *Salpicon* of fish, mushrooms, and truffles in the proportions given for Croquettes of Fish (above). Bind the salpicon together with a thick, hot sauce for fish such as Béchamel, Fish Velouté, Normandy, Mornay, or White Wine Sauce. Fill round Tartlet shells or boat-shaped *Barquettes* with the salpicon. Heat and serve as a garnish or appetizer.

BEIGNETS OF FISH
(*Beignets de Poisson*)

Prepare a *Salpicon* of fish as in the recipe for *Barquettes* and Tartlets of Fish (above), and chill it thoroughly. On a floured board, shape the mixture into small balls. Dip the balls in a light batter and deep-fry them. Season with fine salt, heap them in a mound on a napkin-covered plate, and garnish with parsley. Separately serve Tomato Sauce or Périgueux Sauce.

BRANDADE OF SALT COD
(*Brandade de Morue*)

The French, who dearly love fresh fish, also dearly love salt cod. Here is an unusual way of eating it that is favored in Languedoc.

Wash the loose salt from 2 pounds of salt cod, cut it in pieces, and soak for 24 hours in several changes of cold water. Poach the pieces in water for 8 minutes, drain them, and flake them, removing every vestige of skin and bones. Dry the flaked fish briefly in a warm oven. Put 1 cup olive oil in a heavy 4-quart saucepan and heat until it smokes. Add the cod and 1 clove of garlic, crushed, and pound and mash the cod with a heavy wooden spoon until it becomes a smooth paste. Reduce the flame to its lowest point and begin adding, little by little, 2 cups of warm olive oil, stirring constantly to thoroughly blend the cod paste and oil. As the mixture thickens, alternately add, little by little, about 1 cup of warm heavy cream. The consistency of the *brandade* is correct when it has the consistency of mashed potatoes. Season with salt, if necessary, and white pepper.

Put the brandade in a hot, deep bowl, heaped up in the middle to form a dome. Sauté triangles of bread in olive oil and place them all around the edge of the bowl in a sawtooth pattern, angled outward.

Brandade of salt cod is also used as a filling for *Vol-au-Vent* pastry cases, providing an unusual and surprising fish course. The dish is called *vol-au-vent de morue*.

PAUPIETTES OF SOLE

Paupiettes are small filets of sole, spread with a thin layer of fish Forcemeat, and rolled up like a scroll. They are usually poached very gently, and are then served in some imaginative way befitting their cylindrical shape. Use only the finest, firmest American flatfish for this dish to assure that the fish will not fall apart during cooking. Gray sole, winter flounder, rex sole, and California sand dab are recommended.

PAUPIETTES OF SOLE MONT-BRY (*Paupiettes de Soles Mont-Bry*). Spread the filets thinly with fish Forcemeat, roll into *paupiettes,* and poach gently in Fish Fumet. Meanwhile, remove a slice from the top of a tomato for each paupiette, scoop out the inside of the tomato, brush with olive oil, and bake until cooked. Half-fill the tomato case with saffron-seasoned Risotto. Arrange the tomato cases on a round dish in the form of a crown. Drain the paupiettes and slip one into each tomato. Reduce the poaching liquor by ⅔, and finish with heavy cream, chopped chervil, and chopped tarragon. Pour the sauce over the paupiettes.

QUENELLES OF PIKE
(*Quenelles de Brochet*)

Quenelles of pike, extensively used as a garnish for elaborate fish dishes, are also the principal ingredient in a number of traditional dishes. They can be made in several ways, but this preparation, made with Mousseline Forcemeat, is the lightest and finest.

Finely grind 1 pound of skinless, boneless raw pike. Put the meat in a mortar, add 1 teaspoon salt, ½ teaspoon white pepper, and a pinch of nutmeg, and pound to a paste. Gradually add to this paste the white of 2 eggs, beating them in with a wooden spoon. Put the mixture through a food mill or rub it through a sieve, place it in a cold bowl set in crushed ice, and gradually beat into it about 2 cups of heavy cream until the mixture is well blended, smooth, and light. (Or, you may put the sieved mixture in a bowl, cover with a little heavy cream to prevent it from drying, and chill it in the refrigerator. When chilled, gradually beat in about 2 cups cold heavy cream.)

To form the quenelles, use 2 metal spoons kept hot in hot water. Scoop up a spoonful of the forcemeat with one hot, moist spoon and shape the mixture in the form of an egg with the second hot, moist spoon. Slip the shaped forcemeat into the second spoon and slide it into a well-buttered saucepan. Fill the saucepan with the quenelles, allowing about an inch between them. They will swell during cooking.

To cook the quenelles, pour into the pan boiling salted water or stock to cover the quenelles, bring to the simmer, and simmer for 10 or 15 minutes until the quenelles rise to the top of the liquid. Remove and drain them, dry them carefully, and proceed as directed in any recipe requiring pike quenelles, or as in one of the recipes given below.

QUENELLES OF PIKE IN CREAM (*Quenelles de Brochet à la Crème*). Arrange cooked Quenelles of Pike (above) on slices of Fried Bread and cover them with hot Cream Sauce.

QUENELLES OF PIKE À LA FLORENTINE (*Quenelles de Brochet à la Florentine*). Place cooked Quenelles of Pike (above) on an ovenproof serving platter on a bed of Spinach in Butter. Pour Mornay Sauce over the *quenelles*, sprinkle with grated Parmesan cheese and melted butter, and glaze* quickly in the oven or broiler.

QUENELLES OF SALMON (*Quenelles de Saumon*). Prepare exactly as Quenelles of Pike (above), but use raw salmon. Small salmon *quenelles* are used as a garnish; large ones as a small entree.

FISH STEWS
(*Matelotes*)

Matelotes are fish stews made with fresh-water fish and red or white wine. In some regions, these stews are called *meurettes,* and in others, *pauchouses.*

MATELOTE À LA BOURGUIGNONNE (*Matelote à la Bourguignonne*). Butter a deep skillet and cover the bottom with 1 onion, finely sliced; 1 carrot, finely sliced; 2 cloves of garlic, crushed; 3 sprigs of bruised parsley; ½ bay leaf, crumbled; a pinch of thyme; salt; and pepper. On this bed of vegetables, place 2 pounds of a variety of fresh-water fish cut in pieces. (Bass, perch, pike, lake trout, whitefish, carp, catfish, and an eel for its gelatinous qualities are ideal for this stew.) Add 2 cups dry red wine and bring to a boil. Warm 3 tablespoons brandy, pour it over the fish, and light it. When the flames die down, cover and simmer for 6 or 8 minutes until the fish are done. Remove the fish, drain them, and keep warm. Reduce the liquid in the skillet by ⅓ or ½, press it through a sieve to extract all the juices from the vegetables, thicken it with *Beurre Manié,* and finish by swirling in* 8 tablespoons butter cut in small pieces. Pour the sauce over the fish and serve in a deep dish or bowl garnished with squares of sautéed bread rubbed with garlic.

MATELOTE À LA MARINIÈRE (*Matelote à la Marinière*). Prepare as for *Matelote à la Bourguignonne* (above), but omit the carrot from the aromatic vegetables, use dry white wine instead of red, and thicken the sauce with Fish Velouté Sauce. Add to the sauce separately cooked mushrooms and small Glazed Onions, and garnish the stew with fresh-water crayfish (or shrimp) and heart-shaped pieces of bread sautéed in butter.

PAUCHOUSE (*Pauchouse*). Proceed as for *Matelote à la Bourguignonne* (above), but cook small Glazed Onions and mushrooms along with the fish, and add to the stew boiled breast of pork cut in large dice and sautéed in butter until crisp and golden.

MATELOTE À LA NORMANDE (*Matelote à la Normande*). This *matelote,* which is an exception to the rule, is prepared with salt-water fish. Prepare as for Matelote à la Bourguignonne (above), but omit the carrot from the

aromatic vegetables, use cider as the liquid instead of wine, and burned calvados instead of burned brandy. Thicken the liquid with a thick Fish Velouté
Sauce, and finish the sauce with about ½ cup heavy cream to bring it to the
desired consistency. Finish the stew by adding poached mussels, oysters, crayfish (or shrimp), and mushrooms, and garnish with heart-shaped pieces of
bread sautéed in butter.

✳ SHELLFISH

When the colonists came to America, they found the shores teeming with
shellfish. The cockles and winkles of England had given them a taste for these
boneless fish, and they set out to indulge that taste to their hearts' content.
Great red lobsters, big as turkeys, made American tables groan with their
weight. Chowder was invented to cook the large, tough, flavorful clams. And
no sooner were cities built than oysters were hawked in their streets.

This craving for shellfish reached a peak during the famous "oyster craze"
of the nineteenth century, when oysters-on-the-half-shell were devoured everywhere in America. Light, fast wagons rushed the oysters at a gallop to Pitts-
burgh, and from there by riverboat to Cincinnati. The Abraham Lincoln family, in their log cabin in southern Illinois, feasted on oysters raw, poached,
stewed, baked, and fried. If fresh oysters are not available everywhere today,
it is only because our food distribution system is in a sad decline.

America's favorite shellfish today are shrimp, oysters, lobsters, crabs,
clams, and scallops. Locally, the spiny lobster (*langouste*) and conch of
Florida, the abalone of California, and the fresh-water crayfish of Louisiana
are in high esteem. (Crayfish are also commercially harvested in Wisconsin
and Minnesota.)

The French taste for shellfish differs. Clams and oysters are mostly eaten
raw, and shrimp are served mainly as hors d'oeuvres or as garnishes for larger
dishes. In France, raw oysters, lobsters, *langoustes, langoustines,* scallops,
mussels, and fresh-water crayfish are the *fruits de mer* in most demand.

Nevertheless, there is no great difficulty in applying traditional French
recipes to American shellfish. American crabs can be cooked like crayfish or
small tender clams like mussels. I have taken the liberty of making some of
these applications in the following recipes.

SHRIMP
(*Crevettes*)

In France shrimp are sold live, like lobster, and killed just before cooking or plunged alive into boiling water or oil. Nevertheless, traditional French cooking is not too concerned with shrimp, using them primarily as garnishes or hors d'oeuvres, and employing the larger prawns as major ingredients. (The Japanese are fanatically devoted to fresh shrimp. Having discovered a way to keep them alive in dry sawdust for 4 days, they distribute them about their country like so many bags of beans.) A few live shrimp are available in Gulf ports here, and if you can get them you will find them inestimably sweet-fleshed.

Only the tails of shrimp are eaten. Fresh shrimp tails, called "green" shrimp, are absolutely the best, but they are becoming harder and harder to find. Many shrimp, like tuna, are frozen right aboard the boat that catches them. Shrimp that have been frozen and thawed are frequently available. This "store thawing" or "slacking" of fish or any other food is an absolutely indefensible practice. Any frozen food you buy should be taken home frozen hard as a rock.

Shrimp also come cooked, canned, and frozen with or without the shell. In the supermarket you will mostly find shrimp frozen and shelled, with pink stripes on the meat. These shrimp have already been partly cooked and need little further cooking.

Tiny shrimp—the California gray and the Alaska pink—weigh in at more than 125 tails to the pound. The larger shrimp tails, from the Gulf and south Atlantic coast, range from 8 to 70 per pound. Of these, what are called large shrimp average 20 per pound; jumbo shrimp may weigh in as heavy as 8 per pound. Shrimp are also imported, small ones from Iceland and Holland (up to 300 tails per pound!), and large ones from all over the world.

Virtually all the large American shrimp are one of three varieties—the white shrimp of Louisiana and South Carolina, brown shrimp of Texas and Mexican waters, and the pink or brown-spotted shrimp of Florida. The actual color of the raw shrimp is deceiving, but if you have mature, unshelled shrimp you can determine the variety by feeling alongside the ridge at the top of the next-to-last tail segment. If there is a groove alongside the ridge large enough to admit your fingernail, you have a brown shrimp. If the groove is there but too narrow to admit your fingernail, and there is a small brown spot on the side of the third tail segment, it is a pink (or brown-spotted) shrimp. If there is no groove, it is a white shrimp.

I tell you all this only so you can pick and choose among the shrimp to find the taste you like best. White shrimp are usually sweeter. Pink shrimp usually have more of the tangy iodine taste of the sea. Medium shrimp have a more decided taste than large shrimp. Tiny shrimp are the sweetest. Frozen shrimp have less taste than fresh shrimp. And live shrimp taste best of all.

To buy fresh shrimp, choose those that have shiny shells. Pinch them; the flesh should be firm and springy. Smell them; they should have the fresh smell of the sea.

COOKING SHRIMP

Like other fish, shrimp are very delicate and should be cooked only briefly. If overcooked, they become tough, dry, and tasteless. Properly cooked, shrimp are firm and juicy. They should actually crunch in your mouth. If the flesh is soft when properly cooked, the shrimp was probably waterlogged. One pound of fresh shrimp tails with the shell on will give you about ½ pound of shrimp meat.

The shells of shrimp are flavorful, and if the dish you are preparing allows a choice, leave them on during cooking. (The shrimp meat will also look smoother, rounder, and pinker.) The shells will turn red, and if you have no further use for them, pound them in a mortar with a little shrimp meat to color and flavor Shrimp Butter.

You may devein the shrimp or not, as you choose. (Some people point out that the vein is nutritionally rich with plankton.) To devein before cooking, loosen the shell halfway along the back and use a skewer to probe and fish the vein out. To devein after cooking, peel the shrimp, make a cut with a sharp knife along the ridge of the back, and scrape the vein out.

To "butterfly" shrimp, shell them (leaving the fan-shaped terminal portion of the shell on) and slit them down the back almost all the way through. Flatten lightly, taking care not to break the shrimp in two. They will spread out more when cooked. You may butterfly shrimp in the shell by first snipping the shell up the back with a sharp kitchen shears.

To boil shrimp: Leave the shells on the shrimp and plunge them into rapidly boiling water that has been well-salted with 2 tablespoons of salt per quart. (This heavy salting helps equalize the osmotic pressure between the shrimp's juices and the water, thereby reducing the tendency of the water to penetrate the flesh and dilute the flavor of the shrimp.) Return the water to the simmer, and simmer for 4 to 6 minutes. Test for doneness by squeezing the shrimp. It is cooked when it feels firm all the way through. Or break off a piece to see if the flesh in the center is opaque. Or taste it.

To add flavor to large shrimp or frozen shrimp, boil them in a Court Bouillon with Vinegar.

To poach shrimp: Poach the shrimp if you are going to use the liquid in which it cooks to make a sauce. Follow the directions for poaching fish, using white wine and other ingredients to provide the basis for a sauce. This is an excellent way to conserve and enhance the flavor of frozen shrimp. You may shell the shrimp before cooking, so that they may more readily absorb the surrounding flavors. But cook the shells along with the shrimp, removing them when the pan juices are reduced and strained to make the sauce. Shrimp may be served with white sauces for fish, and glazed.*

To bake shrimp: "Butterfly" the shrimp in their shells. Marinate the shrimp for 2 hours in ½ olive oil and ½ white wine, with seasonings; or in olive oil and a few tablespoons of vinegar or lemon juice, with seasonings. Bake quickly in a 400° oven, basting frequently with oil or butter.

To broil shrimp: "Butterfly" the shrimp in their shells. Marinate them as for baking (above). Broil with the cut side up, basting frequently, and taking great joy in the way the shell blackens and chars. Serve these juicy, flavorful, "pink and black" shrimp sizzling in their charred shells.

To sauté shrimp: Toss the shrimp, in their shells, in very hot Clarified Butter until the shells are red and the meat cooked through. Or shell the shrimp, dredge them in flour, and cook until golden brown as for Sole à la Meunière.

To deep-fry shrimp: Shell the shrimp, "butterfly" them, dry, dredge in flour, and dip them in a light Batter. Deep-fry in 360° oil for about 2 minutes, until golden brown.

SHRIMP ON SKEWERS (*Brochettes de Crevettes*). Poach the shrimp until they are almost cooked. Peel them, impale them on skewers, alternating with cooked mushroom caps, season the whole with salt and pepper, and sprinkle with melted butter. Broil for a few minutes, turning the skewers. Serve on the skewers on a bed of cooked rice.

SHRIMP IN SHELLS (*Crevettes en Coquilles*). Poach, shell, and devein the shrimp. Border scallop shells or shell-shaped dishes with Duchess Potatoes piped through a pastry bag. In the bottom of each shell put 2 tablespoons White Wine Sauce into which you have mixed a little chopped truffle. Put a number of shrimp meats in each shell, cover with more white wine sauce with truffles, and glaze* briefly in a hot oven.

SHRIMP WITH CURRY SAUCE (*Crevette à l'Indienne*). Mix 1 pound cooked and shelled shrimp meats with 1½ cups Curry Sauce. Serve on a bed of boiled rice.

SHRIMP PILAF (*Pilaf de Crevettes*). Add cooked and peeled shrimp meats to Rice Pilaf. Serve with Shrimp Sauce.

THE LOBSTER AND THE LANGOUSTE
(*Le Homard et la Langouste*)

At Hyannisport on Cape Cod I presided over many a clambake that required neither pot nor pan. A pit was dug, and hot stones were rolled into it and covered with an iron plate. On top of this we heaped wet rockweed, clams, more rockweed, corn in the husk, more rockweed, whole chickens, more rockweed, lobsters, more rockweed, and a heavy tarpaulin tied down over all. It was not the kind of cooking I was taught at Restaurant Laperouse in Nantes. But, steamed in their own sweet juices, these have to be the most pure and honest-tasting lobsters of all, and I highly recommend this colonial American style of cooking. But be sure the rocks are hot enough. I have heard of occasions when the famished guests have torn off the covering tarpaulin only to free a horde of sweaty, cranky lobsters that stalked off in all directions.

The lobster and the langouste are related, but they differ importantly in that the langouste has no claws. It is also called crawfish, rock lobster, and spiny lobster, and the tail of the langouste is found in most supermarkets, imported frozen from South Africa. The langouste is also sold live where it is caught, along the southern Atlantic, Gulf, and Pacific coasts.

France is well supplied with langouste, and what is perhaps French cooking's most famous lobster dish, *homard à l'américaine,* very likely began as a Provençal recipe for langouste. Both langouste and lobster are cooked in the same manner.

The lobster is one of America's most important contributions to gastronomy. This is so well recognized that the beast has escaped the freezing that is the fate of so many other seafoods. You can still buy lobsters alive.

Lobsters, like oysters, are a pet subject for writers. You can find articles on lobsters most anywhere, so I will discuss only those points which I think are most important to the buying and cooking of them.

Although lobsters are caught as far south as North Carolina, about 85 percent of our live lobsters come from northern waters, half from Maine and half from Nova Scotia. The supply has leveled out, and no matter how many more traps are put into the water, just about the same amount of coastal

lobsters are caught every year. State laws prohibit the taking of undersize lobsters (Maine laws prohibit the taking of oversize lobsters as well), and most
coastal lobsters are from 1 to 4 pounds in weight. Big lobsters, 50 years old
and weighing 30 pounds, are now being taken far at sea at the edge of the
continental shelf.

The taste of a particular lobster depends on many things. As to size, I
think a 2- to 4-pound lobster tastes best. Chicken lobsters, weighing little more
than 1 pound, have not had time to develop their flavor (although they may
be 6 years old). No one eats soft-shelled lobsters (except some Maine lobster-
men who say the flesh is more tender, sweet, and juicy when the lobster is
absorbing sea water after having thrown off its old shell). I have not tasted
the very large deep sea lobsters. Those who fish them claim they taste every
bit as good as the coastal variety, and one company engaged in this growing
fishery insists that it will give us "lobster every Sunday," with a fresh 10-pound
lobster steaming on the dinner table in place of the proverbial chicken.

You know, of course, that fresh lobsters must be alive when you buy them.
And you know they're alive if they *move*. But lobsters can live as long as two
weeks out of water, and frequently you will find them being offered when their
two weeks are almost up. These feeble, torpid, half-dead lobsters are not the
best ones to buy. In Maine, where they know their lobsters, they like them best
when their tails crack like a whip. Pick up any live lobster you buy and
straighten out its tail. If the lobster doesn't get mad at you and snap its tail
back, look for another one. Also, a lobster, like an artichoke, should feel heavy
for its size.

Male lobsters are better for boiling because their flesh is firmer. They are
also liked for show, because their shells turn a more brilliant red. Female lobsters, however, contain the coral, or roe, which is a great delicacy to be eaten
alone or mixed into a sauce. You can take your choice if you remember that
the tail of the male lobster is narrower than the female's, and the two uppermost fins in the tail are stiff and hard.

One more thing. If you have lobster at a restaurant, and the flesh sticks
to the shell when you eat it, the lobster was dead before it was cooked. Good
luck.

COOKING LOBSTER

I hesitate to tell Americans how to cook lobster, particularly those Americans in Maine. A classic French method is to plunge the live lobster head first
into a boiling Court Bouillon made with wine. But the jiffy Maine method of
half-boiling, half-steaming lobster in a pot has to reveal the very most a lobster

can offer. The method duplicates the clambake without the stone-rolling labor. Bring 2 to 3 inches of salted water to a rolling boil, drop the lobster in on its back, and clamp on the lid. Boil for 18 minutes and serve with a bib and plenty of melted butter.

For the benefit of you who are not overly familiar with lobsters, here are some things you should know.

To kill a lobster: Hold the lobster flat, place the point of a knife on the top of its shell directly between the eyes, and stab it to death. Or, place the point of the knife in the center of the back in the interstice at which it joins the tail, and stab it to death. Piercing the lobster in either place kills it almost instantly. You can also kill the lobster by plunging it into boiling water. It is well agreed that the lobster's sense of pain is much less acute than our own, but the S.P.C.A., concerned nevertheless, has developed a method of killing by boiling which is absolutely painless to the lobster. Place the lobster in cold salted water and light the fire. As the water warms the lobster shows no discomfort whatsoever. At 154° it keels over. At 176° it is dead. It is believed the heat slowly penetrates and anesthetizes the lobster's nervous system.

To clean a lobster: Lay the killed lobster on its back. Beginning at the mouth, make a deep cut the length of the body and the tail. Open the lobster and remove the sack (the stomach) lying just back of the head, and the intestinal vein, which runs from the stomach through the body and tail. The spongy material (the lungs) lying alongside the body is also discarded. The gray stuff (the tomalley or liver) is delicious and turns green when cooked. The black stuff (the coral, or roe) in female lobsters is especially delicious and turns red when cooked.

To cut up a lobster: Clean the lobster, reserving the tomalley and the coral if any. Remove and crack the large claws. Cut off the tail and cut across it to divide it in two. Cut the body in two, crossways, and then cut the front half in two, lengthwise. This will give you 7 pieces of approximately equal size.

To boil lobster: Plunge the lobster head first into a boiling Court Bouillon made with vinegar. A 2-pound lobster will need about 15 to 20 minutes of boiling. Remove and drain the lobster, clean it, split it open lengthwise, and serve in the shell surrounded by curly parsley and with a sauceboat of melted butter. This dish is called *homard au court bouillon*. Served with mealy boiled or steamed potatoes, the dish becomes *homard à la hollandaise*.

If the lobster is to be served cold in some manner, boil it for 10 minutes only and allow the lobster to cool in the liquid.

To poach lobster: Clean the lobster and cut it in pieces. Poach it in the shell, following the directions for poaching fish.

To bake lobster: Clean the lobster on its back, taking care not to spill any of its juices. Place the lobster on its back in a baking pan, spread with 4 or 5 tablespoons butter, and bake in a 350° oven for 30 to 40 minutes, basting regularly. Season with salt and pepper after cooking.

(Instead of plain butter, I particularly like to baste plain baked or broiled lobster with a basting made as follows: Mash the raw tomalley and roe of the lobster with a little cognac, and blend it with soft creamed butter, chopped tarragon leaves, and a little pepper.)

To broil lobster: Clean the lobster and split it down the middle from end to end. Place on the broiling pan, cut side up, and spread each half with 3 tablespoons butter (or use the flavored basting suggested for baked lobster, above). Broil far from the flame, basting frequently with butter, for about 15 minutes, or until the firmness and opacity of the tail meat tell you the lobster is done. (The cooking should be so adjusted that the top of the lobster browns when the cooking ends, so move the lobster closer to or farther from the flame as required.) Salt and pepper the lobster, and serve.

To sauté lobster: Clean the lobster and cut it in pieces without removing the shell. Toss the pieces in very hot Clarified Butter until the shells are red and the meat cooked through.

LOBSTER AMERICAN (*Homard à l'Américaine*). Clean and cut up a 2-pound lobster, reserving the tomalley and coral. Sauté the pieces in a skillet in very hot olive oil and a little butter for 5 to 10 minutes or until the flesh stiffens and the shells turn red. Put a little of the hot oil into a saucepan, add 2 shallots, chopped, and 1 clove of garlic crushed, and cook them for a few minutes. Then add the lobster pieces, ½ cup dry white wine, ½ cup Fish Fumet, and 1 tablespoon Meat Glaze if you have it. Bring to the simmer, pour over ¼ cup heated brandy, and ignite it. Then add 3 tomatoes, peeled, seeded, pressed, and chopped (or ½ cup Tomato Purée), 1 teaspoon chopped parsley, and a pinch of cayenne. Cover the saucepan and cook for 20 minutes, or until the lobster is done. Remove the lobster pieces, shell them, dry them, and put them in a hot serving bowl. Boil down the cooking liquid to ¾ cup. Crush the tomalley (and coral if you have it) and cream it with 1 tablespoon butter and 1 teaspoon flour. Stir this into the sauce to thicken it. Add 1 teaspoon chopped parsley and ½ teaspoon chopped tarragon, heat the sauce without allowing it to boil, and finish it off the fire by swirling in* 2 tablespoons butter. Strain the sauce and pour it over the hot lobster meat. Sprinkle with chopped parsley and tarragon, and serve with broiled rice.

LOBSTER À LA FRANÇAISE (*Homard à la Française*). Clean a 2-pound lobster, split it in half, and remove and crack the claws. Thinly slice 1 carrot and 1 onion and parboil for 5 minutes. Place half the vegetables in a well-buttered pan, place the lobster halves on top of the vegetables, sprinkle with 1 teaspoon chopped shallots and 1 tablespoon chopped parsley, and cover with the rest of the vegetables. Arrange the tender-meated claws on top (so they will cook more slowly), add ¼ cup white wine and ¼ cup Fish Fumet, cover the lobster with waxed or parchment paper to fit the pan, and poach the lobster for 20 minutes, or until done (see Poached Fish). Remove, drain, shell the lobster, replace the meat in the half shells without chopping it, and keep warm. Reduce the poaching liquid by ⅔, blend in ½ cup Cream Sauce, and finish the sauce by swirling in* 1 tablespoon butter. Taste the sauce, add salt and pepper if necessary, then add 1 tablespoon cognac and ½ teaspoon chopped chives. Taste again, pour the unstrained sauce over the lobster, and serve.

LOBSTER À LA NAGE (*Homard à la Nage*). Make a special Court Bouillon as follows: Thinly slice 3 medium carrots, 4 onions, and 4 inner stalks of celery. Add 1 crumbled bay leaf and 2 sprigs or a good pinch of thyme. Simmer all together in butter until the vegetables are soft but not brown. Add 2 cups dry white wine, and boil down by ⅔. Add 3 cups Fish Fumet, and simmer for a few minutes more. Boil the lobster in this liquid, and serve it whole on a deep platter with the court bouillon and its vegetables poured over it. Separately serve Hollandaise Sauce or melted butter.

LOBSTER IN CREAM (*Homard à la Crème*). Clean and cut up a 2-pound lobster. Sauté the pieces in Clarified Butter until the flesh has stiffened and the shell is red. Add 2 tablespoons brandy, 2 cups heavy cream, a little salt, and a pinch of cayenne. Swirl the pan to blend these liquids, cover, and simmer for 20 minutes or until the lobster is done. Remove, drain, shell, and dry the lobster meat, and put it in a hot deep dish. Reduce the cooking liquid by ½, and swirl in* 3 tablespoons butter and a small squeeze of lemon. Strain the sauce and pour it over the lobster.

LOBSTER THERMIDOR (*Homard Thermidor*). Clean and split a 2-pound lobster. Cover the bottom of a baking pan with oil and place the lobster halves in it, flesh side up, and liberally spread with butter. Bake in a 350° oven for 30 minutes, basting frequently, or until the lobster halves are done. While the lobster is baking, cook in a saucepan 1 tablespoon butter, 1 teaspoon chopped shallot, and ¼ cup dry white wine until the liquid is almost cooked away. Add 1 cup Mornay Sauce, 1 teaspoon chopped parsley, and ½ teaspoon dry English mustard. Cook and stir until the sauce is smooth. Taste the sauce and add salt and more mustard if desired. Remove the lobster meat from the shells, dice it, and wash and dry the half shells. Place them in an ovenproof serving dish, put a layer of sauce in the bottom of them, and place the diced lobster meat, mixed with a little of the sauce, on top. Finish the remaining sauce with 1 tablespoon whipped cream and spoon it over the lobster meat. Sprinkle with grated Parmesan cheese and glaze* in the broiler.

LOBSTER ON THE SPIT (*Homard à la Broche*). Plunge a 3- to 4-pound lobster in boiling water to kill it and stiffen its flesh. Fix it to a spit on an outdoor broiler, with a very hot charcoal fire at one side so that you may place a dripping pan beneath the spitted lobster. Melt a good half pound of butter and season it with freshly ground pepper, powdered thyme, and powdered or well-pounded bay leaf. Liberally baste the lobster with this flavored butter, and expose it to a very hot fire. Put a few tablespoons of dry white wine into the dripping pan to keep the drippings from burning. Cook the lobster, basting frequently with butter, for about 45 minutes or until the lobster is done. Separately serve the pan drippings. (Choose a male lobster for this treatment; the shell will turn redder. And be sure you have color film for your camera, because you will want to record for posterity this truly magnificent sight.)

CRABS
(*Crabes*)

"Crabs are cooked in salt water and dressed in the shell, seasoned and mixed with mayonnaise sauce, decorated with hard yolk and white of eggs and chopped parsley." This is the *only* recipe for crab in the French *Répertoire-de-la-Cuisine,* the 7,000-recipe handbook of classic French cooking that every French chef has tucked away in the kitchen somewhere. This is not because crabs do not exist in French waters; crabs are found everywhere. But they are not as plentiful as American crabs. Also, most crabs are so perishable they cannot be shipped live. They are usually cooked and canned or frozen first. And no French chef wants another's hand in his work. "Too many cooks spoil the broth." I am unable, therefore, to give you any bona fide classic French recipes for crab. And the truth of the matter is, you don't need them.

Much of America's best cooking is performed right on the beach, and in coastal cities where fresh-caught crab is landed live. Just thinking of it makes me hungry. But before I rush off to the kitchen, let us take a walk around our coasts to see what crabs we can find.

Beginning in Eastport, Maine, you will find scuttling along rocky and sandy bottoms New England's best known crab, the *rock crab*. This yellowish crab, measuring 4 inches across, and the larger brick-red *Jonah crab* are both called rock crab in New England. You may get some live ones if you can strike up a conversation with someone in Maine, or if you stay alert in Boston.

In southern Maine you will begin to meet up with the aggressive *green crab*. This 3-inch bundle of energy and good eating is a familiar sight to me, as it is found in French waters. In keeping with its pugnacious character, the French call this little crab *crabe enragé*.

Along about Cape Cod and all the way down to the Florida Keys, you will find the *calico crab,* named for its white shell, which is sprinkled with purple and red. The meat in this little 3-inch crab is so good it's worth going at with tweezers.

Also at Cape Cod and all the way down to Florida and the Gulf, you will begin to find the major crab of the East Coast, the *blue crab*. Measuring 6 inches across the back and 3 inches fore and aft, and weighing up to 1 pound with large, meaty claws, this is the crab that made Maryland cookery famous, and makes Maryland a good place to be from May to October. (Fish for this crab yourself, with a fish head on a string, and a net to land the crab with. The crab will greedily hold onto the bait as you lift him to the surface of the water, where you can quickly nab him.)

Most crab and soft-shell crab served in Eastern restaurants is the *blue crab*. Soft-shell crab, of course, is any crab that has just molted its hard shell. They are hard to catch, so crab fishermen keep hard-shell crabs that are beginning to molt (peelers) until they throw off their shells. They are cleaned and eaten whole, tasty soft shell and all.

From North Carolina all the way around Florida and the Gulf states to Texas, the southern *stone crab* is landed. Usually called *Florida stone crab* in the East, its large lobsterlike claws are cooked, shipped to New York, and sold at prices you hate to pay. It is difficult to judge the varying deliciousnesses of American crabs, but this may be the very best of all.

Leaping across to California we come to *Dungeness crab* country. This is the red-brown crab whose juices have stained the neckties of millions of tourists at San Francisco's Fisherman's Wharf. It is caught all the way up to the Aleutian Islands, and if you ask around and meet the boats, you can get some live ones. They're big, averaging 7 inches across and weighing from 1¼ to 2½ pounds. If you have a fisherman friend you may end up eating a 12-inch Dungeness.

This is *red crab* country, too, a crab equaling the Dungeness in size, and a crab that crab fanciers claim tastes even better than the Dungeness. Another fine Pacific Coast crab is the *rock crab* (no relation to the New England rock crab). It is smaller than the Dungeness but provides just as much meat with its larger, meatier claws. Both these crabs are hard to catch in quantity and are therefore less well known.

From Alaska comes the *king crab*. This crab is never available alive, fortunately perhaps, because it measures up to *nine feet* from claw to claw, and it just might eat *you*. The monster is finicky, and the herring bait it is caught with must be very fresh. It will not take any food more than 18 hours old. This must contribute mightily to the sweetness of its meat, all of which is contained in the long, gangly legs and claws. You can find this crab in most any supermarket, often cooked and frozen in the shell, looking for all the world like a large pink bone with a beautiful white marrow inside.

Hawaii has its crabs too. Best known are the *Samoan crab* and the *Kona crab*. I have never tasted these, but they are reputed to be as good-tasting as any crab you will ever eat.

Finally, there is another kind of crab, so small it almost escaped my notice. This crab is usually caught by oyster shuckers, because it lives in the mantle of the oyster. It is pale pink, slow-moving, measures only 1 inch across, and it has one amazing virtue. This little crab, the *oyster crab,* is permanently soft-shelled and needs no cleaning. Just sauté it lightly and eat it, one bite per crab. The Pacific Coast *pea crab*, which moves in with the horse clam, can be treated in exactly the same manner.

COOKING CRABS

To taste crabs *au naturel,* boil or steam live crabs like lobsters in well-salted water for about 10 minutes until the shells turn red. Break off the pointed tail and pull the shells apart. Scrape the whitish gills from the sides and remove the spongy parts from the middle. Crack the claws, dig the meat from claws and body, and eat hot with melted butter, or cold with a cold sauce for fish.

Soft-shell crabs are usually cooked by a dry heat method—sautéed, broiled, or deep-fried—and are killed and cleaned just before cooking. To kill the crab, use a sharp knife to cut off the face at a point just behind the eyes. Lift the points of the soft shell, and clean as indicated for hard-shell crabs (above). Cook the crab whole, in its shell. Soft-shell crabs are available from May through September.

Fresh-cooked crab meat is commonly available in the United States. It can be eaten cold in a seafood cocktail, or used in many excellent American recipes. Of the meat taken from the blue crab, the white lump meat of the two body muscles is best. White flake meat from the body and brownish meat from the claws (which contains shreds of fiber that must be removed) are less choice. Cooked meat from both the body and claws of the Dungeness crab is pinkish in color and is usually packed together.

DEVILED CRAB (*Crabe à la Diable*). Over gentle heat, heat 2 cups of crab meat with 2 tablespoons butter. Add 1 cup Mornay Sauce, 2 teaspoons English mustard mixed with water to form a thin paste, ¼ teaspoon salt, and a little pepper. Mix the crab meat and sauce, and pack it into individual baking dishes or a single ovenproof serving dish. Mix a few tablespoons whipped cream into ½ cup Mornay sauce, spread this over the crab meat, sprinkle with grated Parmesan cheese, and glaze* under the broiler.

CRAB MORNAY (*Crabe Mornay*). Over gentle heat, heat 2 cups crab meat with 2 tablespoons butter. Add 1½ cups Mornay Sauce, 1 teaspoon lemon juice, ¼ teaspoon salt, and a little pepper. Mix the crab meat and sauce, and pack it into individual baking dishes or a single ovenproof serving dish. Sprinkle with ½ cup grated Cheddar cheese and 1 cup soft breadcrumbs that you have tossed in 4 tablespoons melted butter. Put into a moderate oven until the cheese is melted and the breadcrumbs are browned.

SOFT-SHELL CRABS WITH BROWN BUTTER (*Crabes Mous Meunière*). Kill and clean the crabs. Dip them in milk and in flour, and sauté them briskly in ¼ inch of very hot Clarified Butter, turning to brown each side. In a separate pan slowly cook butter until it is brown and exudes a nutty odor. Put the crabs on a serving platter, sprinkle with salt, pepper, and lemon juice, and pour the sizzling brown butter over them.

DEEP-FRIED SOFT-SHELL CRABS (*Crabes Mous Frits*). Kill and clean the crabs. Sprinkle with salt and pepper, dip in flour, then in egg beaten with a little milk, and finally roll them in fine, dry white breadcrumbs. Fry in deep 370° fat for a few minutes or until golden brown. Drain and serve with lemon and Tartar Sauce.

OYSTERS
(*Huîtres*)

The oyster is best enjoyed raw, as a pure taste. Have it very cold in its shell, immersed in its clear, icy liquor. Put it into your mouth and chew slowly, bringing the meat to mouth temperature and releasing its flavors for you to savor. Swallow, and note the aftertaste. Follow with a cold sip of Chablis or Pouilly-Fuissé, these wines having an exceptional affinity for the flavor of oyster. Then a bite of brown bread with butter, to clear your taste buds for the next oyster. Pay the fullest attention as you do all this, and you will be rewarded as follows:

A bite of oyster is a clean, fresh bite of the sea. It is as if the sea had set, like a lump of flavorful aspic, in the pearly mold of the oyster's shell. The taste is protean, elemental. It includes the 8 salts of the sea, its metals and minerals in proportion to their concentration in the sea water in which the oyster lives its life, and glycogen, the sweet animal starch that the oyster manufactures as its own food reserve.

Thus, the oyster not only brings us the flavor of the sea, but the subtly *different* flavors of the sea at different places. We taste the copperiness of North Carolina's bays, the saltiness of Long Island's Great South Bay, the sweetness from Virginia's sweet-water rivers. If we pay attention, we detect these things in our mouths, just after we inhale the sea air surrounding the oyster as it approaches our lips, just before the masticated oyster washes down our throats like an iodine-rich tide.

For those who have learned to taste, eating oysters on the half shell is an exciting adventure. The oysters are sometimes flavored with a little fine-ground fresh pepper and a drop or two of lemon juice, but never the first one. The first one is always tasted for itself alone. Try this with your next half-dozen oysters: Eat the first oyster plain, tasting attentively. Sprinkle two drops of lemon juice on the second, give a half-turn of the pepper mill to the third, sprinkle both lemon and pepper on the fourth, taking care to have a sip of cold white wine and a bite of brown bread between each oyster. Eat the fifth oyster unadorned and review your conclusions. The sixth oyster is a free one; eat it in any of the four ways you like best. If you are eating in a relaxed situation, lift the shell and drink the liquor of each oyster after you swallow it.

Oyster eating goes back a very long time. The Chinese, the Greeks, and other ancient peoples all had their feasts of oysters. The Romans imported them from the British Isles. A Roman writer in 50 B.C. commented, "Poor Britons, there is some good in them after all. They produce an oyster."

The famous oysters of Europe are English Whitstables and Coldchesters, the native Dutch oyster, the large Portuguese oyster, and the French Belons, Marennes Blanches, and Marennes Vertes. These last are green with the chlorophyll they absorb from plants in the shallow waters where they fatten, and they have a taste reminiscent of hazelnuts.

There are two native American oysters, the Eastern oyster and the Olympia oyster. The Pacific oyster, which now makes up 15 percent of the United States supply, is not a native.

The American Eastern oyster is world famous, and the Blue Points of Long Island have held the gastronomic world in thrall. The Eastern oyster, which makes up 85 percent of the United States supply, is grown, mostly on cultivated beds, from Cape Cod to the Gulf states. Like many of our natural foods, it suffers from ecological and other disturbances, and many famous beds have been virtually destroyed by predators, the proverbial strange maladies, and silting, and many have been taken out of production due to pollution. (All oyster production is controlled by the Shellfish Sanitation Program; the waters above the beds are regularly tested, each seller has a certification number, and the producing area of every shipment of oysters is recorded.)

If you wished to collect the tastes of Eastern oysters like stamps, you would try to fill your taste album with Rhode Island Narraganset Bays, Silver Leafs, and Nayatt Points; Long Island Peconic Bays, Gardiners Bays and Gardiners Islands, Oyster Bays, and Fire Island Salts; Maryland Choptanks; Delaware Bays; Virginia Chincoteaques, Lynnhavens, Rappahanocks, and Robbins Islands; North Carolinas; and a host of Gulf oysters, Crystal Rivers, Apalachicolas, etc. Some of these famous beds are all but lost. Even so, as an oyster taste collector, you would have your work cut out for you.

I do not mention the Blue Point, because that famous oyster does not really exist anymore. A storm in the 1930's opened a new sea channel into Blue Point Bay, changing its character over a period of time so that it is no longer suitable for raising oysters. Oysters called Blue Points on menus all across the United States are usually one of the Long Island oysters.

The farther north you grow an oyster, the longer it takes to grow to marketable size—5 years in the north, against 2 to 3 years in the south. This is because northerly oysters hibernate. They spawn in the summer (the months without an *r*), then feed rapidly up until December. At this time they are at their peak of fatness, rich, plump, and creamy colored, and it is at this time that they close their shells against the cold water and hibernate until spring. Taken from the water in winter, the northern oyster is the firmest oyster you can get, containing over 20 percent solid, flavorful ingredients. Southern oysters stay awake and grow faster. They do not build up food reserves to the degree their northern cousin does, and their solid ingredients amount to about 10 percent.

On the West Coast the native Olympia oyster is in very short supply. It is a tiny oyster, about the size of your thumbnail, averaging about 2,000 meats to the gallon. Nurtured in Washington's Puget Sound, it is expensive to harvest, and shucked gallon prices have reached $68 in New York City. It's a coppery-tasting little mouthful, and you should be sure to look for it on the half shell if you visit the West Coast.

The Pacific oyster is grown from seed imported each year from Japan.

These oysters are very large. They are never eaten raw, but simmered in water for 5 minutes, even when sliced and used in a cold oyster cocktail. (For half-shell eating, Californians, like New Yorkers, eat the ubiquitous "Blue Point.")

COOKING OYSTERS

After all this talk about oysters on the half shell, I must reveal that only 15 percent of oysters are eaten this way in America. The rest are grilled, broiled, fried, stewed, or eaten in cocktails calculated to obliterate their taste. Oysters for these purposes are usually bought shucked, either frozen or fresh. Whatever the ultimate destiny of an oyster, here is how to open a fresh one. You realize, of course, that the oyster must be alive and its shell tightly closed.

To open an oyster: Scrub the shell under running water. Line the palm of your hand with several thicknesses of towel, grasp the oyster with the deep side down, and force the point of an oyster knife in at the hinge, forcing and twisting until the oyster relaxes. Slip the knife in under the flat top shell and cut the top muscle. Lift off the flat top shell, taking care not to spill the liquor in the deep bottom shell. Then slip the knife between oyster and bottom shell and cut the bottom muscle to free the oyster. Spread the "lips" of the oyster evenly to fill the shell and serve. (Americans often flip the oyster over so that its prettier side is uppermost, but the juices are often spilled during this operation.) I do not recommend "billing" the oyster, that is, chopping the thin edge with a hammer and inserting the knife in the resulting hole. Pieces of shell always seem to get into the oyster liquor.

Although raw oyster eating is great sport in France, a number of recipes have been developed for cooking oysters, especially in Normandy, where the oysters are firmer and whiter than the green Marennes.

When oysters are broiled, grilled, or fried, they are usually poached briefly to remove their viscous coating. Oyster cooking is a very delicate process, and they are considered cooked when their edges begin to ruffle and curl. Overcooking makes an oyster tough and tasteless.

OYSTERS AU GRATIN (*Huîtres au Gratin*). Open and free the oysters. Place them in their deep shells, and place the shells in an ovenproof serving dish on a bed of rock salt. Sprinkle with lemon juice, breadcrumbs sautéed in butter, and melted butter. Cook in the broiler or in a hot oven for 2 to 3 minutes, or until the edges of the oysters curl.

OYSTERS IN CREAM (*Huîtres Gratiné à la Crème*). Prepare as for Oysters au Gratin (above), but put 1 tablespoon heavy cream into the shell, place the oyster in the cream, sprinkle with grated Parmesan cheese and melted butter, and broil.

OYSTERS À LA BOURGUIGNONNE (*Huîtres à la Bourguignonne*). Open and free the oysters, place them in their deep shells, and place the shells in an ovenproof serving dish on a bed of rock salt. Put them into a 400° oven for 2 minutes. Remove and spread each oyster with a mixture consisting of 1 cup soft butter, 1 teaspoon finely chopped shallots, 1 garlic clove, minced, 1 teaspoon chopped chives, 1 teaspoon chopped parsley, 1 teaspoon chopped tarragon, salt, and pepper. Sprinkle with fine, dry white breadcrumbs and put into the broiler for 2 or 3 minutes, or until the crumbs are browned.

FRIED OYSTERS COLBERT (*Huîtres Frites Colbert*). Poach the oysters in their liquor for 2 minutes. Drain, dip in egg and fine, dry white breadcrumbs, and deep-fry in 360° oil. Drain and serve on a napkin-covered platter, with lemon and fried parsley. Separately serve Maître d'Hôtel Butter.

OYSTERS À LA VLADIMIR (*Huîtres à la Vladimir*). Poach the oysters in their liquor for 2 minutes. Return to their deep shells, into which you have put a spoonful of Supreme Sauce. Coat with supreme sauce, sprinkle with breadcrumbs tossed in butter and grated Parmesan cheese, and glaze* quickly under the broiler.

OYSTERS À LA FLORENTINE (*Huîtres à la Florentine*). Poach the oysters in their liquor for 2 minutes. Drain and return to their deep shells, into which you have put a bed of spinach that has been chopped, cooked in butter, and drained. Spoon Mornay Sauce over each oyster and glaze* quickly under the broiler.

OYSTERS À LA FAVORITE (*Huîtres à la Favorite*). Poach the oysters in their liquor for 2 minutes. Return them to their deep shells with 1 tablespoon Béchamel Sauce, and place these in an ovenproof serving dish on a bed of rock salt. Put a truffle slice on top of each oyster, and cover with 1 tablespoon béchamel sauce, grated Parmesan cheese, and melted butter. Glaze* quickly under the broiler.

OYSTERS ON SKEWERS (*Brochettes d'Huîtres*). Poach the oysters in their liquor for 2 minutes. Impale the oysters on skewers, alternating them with poached mushroom caps. Brush with melted butter seasoned with lemon juice and pepper, and roll in fine, dry white breadcrumbs. Broil for 2 or 3 minutes, or until the breadcrumbs are browned, and serve garnished with parsley and lemon slices. Separately serve Maître d'Hôtel Butter.

OYSTERS ON SKEWERS VILLEROI (*Brochettes d'Huîtres Villeroi*). Poach the oysters in their liquor for 2 minutes. Dip in Villeroy Sauce and allow them to cool. Then dip them in beaten egg and fine white breadcrumbs, skewer them, and deep fry in 360° oil. Drain and serve skewered on a napkin-covered platter, garnished with fried parsley and lemon slices.

MUSSELS
(*Moules*)

The French would give their eyeteeth to get at the vast beds of edible mussels that surround our shores. In fact, the same blue mussel that forms large and largely ignored shoals from Canada to Cape Hatteras is farmed in France like the oyster. This mussel, named for its handsome blue-black shell, is about 2½ inches long. The shell is a pearly violet color inside. The mussel meats are rich tan to orangish, and they are frequently served attached to their beautiful opened shells.

The Pacific Coast has its mussels too, with delicious orange-colored meat. From May to October, however, they may ingest a microscopic, phosphorescent, planktonic animal that is poisonous, and they should not be eaten during this time.

Mussels are available in northern New England markets mostly from January to May, and in the New York market all year round. They are sold in their shells.

COOKING MUSSELS

To prepare mussels for cooking, scrub them under running water with a very stiff brush, strip away the threads with which the animal fastens itself to rocks, and rinse in several changes of water. It is not usual to eat mussels raw. They are therefore frequently opened by steaming in a very little water or white wine, which is all the cooking the mussel needs. The sea water and liquids escaping from the mussels become the basis of their sauce.

MUSSELS À LA MARINIÈRE (*Moules à la Marinière*). Scrub the shells of 2 or 3 dozen mussels. Put them in a saucepan with 2 shallots, finely chopped, 2 tablespoons butter, 1 cup dry white wine, and a *Bouquet Garni* consisting of 1 sprig parsley, ½ bay leaf, and a sprig or pinch of thyme, tied in cheesecloth. Cover and cook briskly for 5 minutes, or until the mussels are opened. Remove the mussels, detaching one shell from each, and put them in a dish on their half shells. Reduce the poaching liquid by ½, remove the bouquet garni, and thicken the sauce with *Beurre Manié*. Taste and season the sauce with salt and pepper, and swirl in* 2 tablespoons butter. Pour this sauce over the mussels and sprinkle with chopped parsley.

MUSSELS À LA HONGROISE (*Moules à la Hongroise*). Cook the mussels as for Mussels à la Marinière (above), but add to the saucepan 1 teaspoon paprika. Strain the cooking liquid, add to it ½ cup chopped onions, which you have simmered in butter until very soft, ¼ cup Béchamel Sauce, and a few tablespoons of heavy cream and cook until the sauce is thick. Swirl in* 2 tablespoons butter and pour over the mussels.

MUSSELS IN CREAM (*Moules à la Crème*). Cook the mussels as for Mussels à la Marinière (above). Strain the cooking liquid and add 1½ cups Béchamel Sauce and a few tablespoons of heavy cream. Cook the sauce until it is quite thick, and stir in a few more tablespoons of cream. Strain the sauce again, bring it to the boil, swirl in* 4 tablespoons butter, and pour it over the mussels.

MUSSELS À LA PROVENÇALE (*Moules à la Provençale*). Scrub the shells of 2 or 3 dozen mussels. In a saucepan, cook 1 onion, chopped, and 1 clove garlic in 2 tablespoons butter until soft and golden. Add 3 large tomatoes, peeled, seeded, and chopped, and the mussels. Cover and cook briskly, shaking the pan, for 5 minutes or until the mussels are opened. Season with salt and freshly ground pepper and serve the dish as it is.

MUSSELS À LA POULETTE (*Moules à la Poulette*). Cook the mussels as for Mussels à la Marinière (above). Strain the cooking liquid, add to it 1½ cups Poulette Sauce and cook for a few minutes. Add a squeeze of fresh lemon and swirl in* 2 tablespoons butter. Pour the sauce over the mussels and sprinkle them with chopped parsley.

CLAMS
(Palourdes)

Clams are not very important in French cookery. The classic cuisine doesn't recognize them at all, and if you find a clam dish on the menu of a French restaurant in America it will most likely be an adaptation of a recipe for mussels or another mollusk. In France, clams are cultivated mostly for eating on the half shell. In Brittany large clams are sometimes stuffed.

In America, clams are enjoyed in many ways, and there is a clam to suit each method of presentation. I will take up each one of the commonly available and the famous but hard-to-find clams in turn.

The clambake clam is the *soft-shell,* also called *long-neck* or *steamer clam.* Traditionally the clam of New England, it has been introduced to Pacific waters and is the largest selling clam in California. Soft-shell clams average 3 inches in length. Their shell is open on both ends, with a protruding siphon or neck that is tough and not eaten. For a clam whose shell will not close, the soft-shell clam is very hardy out of water and it is sold live in the market. These clams are usually steamed in their shells (in a little water and rockweed if available), and the flavorful juice that runs from them is collected and served as broth. They are sometimes opened and the meat deep-fried.

The *hard-shell clam* is more common south of Cape Cod. Also called *quahog* or *littleneck clam,* it is entirely enclosed in a tough shell. The clam itself, tender when young, becomes very tough as it grows to 4 or 5 inches. The youngest of these clams are eaten raw; "littlenecks" are the smallest and "cherrystones" a little larger. Medium-size clams, up to 3 inches, are sometimes steamed. Beyond this size the hard-shell clam becomes very tough as well as very flavorful, and it is chopped and served in stuffed clam dishes or used in making clam chowder.

Razor clams of the East Coast are wonderfully sweet to eat, but their shells—shaped like the handle of an old-fashioned straight razor—will not close. Consequently, they expire very soon after being taken from the water and you cannot buy them in the shell. The West Coast *jackknife clam,* which is similarly but more protectively shelled, is available live. Razor clams are often fried.

The *surf clam* is the largest clam of the East Coast, measuring about 6½ inches across. Only the two muscles are eaten. These little 1-inch cylinders resemble scallop muscles, and are perhaps the best meat any of the clams have to offer.

The *butter clam,* about 3 inches in diameter, is the favorite clam of the Puget Sound area and is sold alive in Seattle and in other Western markets that demand it. It can be cooked in any way.

The *pismo clam* is famous for its flavor, and Californians have hunted it so aggressively that, even though rigorously protected, there are few to be found.

The *geoduck* is a huge clam weighing up to 13 pounds and it is plentiful in Puget Sound. An average geoduck weighing 3 pounds will yield almost half its weight in meat. The meat is sweet, and efforts are now being made to bring this clam to market. (One must always be on the alert for new tastes.)

COOKING CLAMS

Littlenecks, cherrystones, and butter clams are eaten raw like oysters, with a little pepper and lemon juice if you prefer. They are served very cold on the half shell, in a limpid pool of their own sweet liquor.

To open clams: These animals have very powerful muscles, and you must outwit them by employing the element of surprise. Scrub the shells in advance of opening them, and put them aside for 10 minutes to rest. Then, to avoid alarming the clam, place it very gently in the palm of your left hand, with the hinge resting against the heel of your hand. Gently place the sharp edge of a knife along the crack between the shells and curl the fingers of your left hand around the back of the blade. Then *squeeze* the knife into the crack. Do not press the knife with your right hand; it could slip and give you a bad cut. Once the knife is in, scrape it on the bottom of the upper shell to cut the muscle. The clam will then be opened, and you can cut the bottom muscle. If the clam does not open with a few squeezes of the knife, set it aside until an illusion of security causes it to relax again. Do not spill the liquor inside.

Soft-shell clams are easily penetrated and cut free with the point of a knife. Remove the necks of these long-necked clams.

BAKED CLAMS HYANNISPORT (*Palourdes au Four Hyannisport*). I am breaking my own rule here to give you a recipe that is not in the French repertoire. Use tender, small littleneck or cherrystone clams. Simmer 1 teaspoon chopped shallots in 1 tablespoon dry white wine until the wine is almost evaporated. Add 2 cloves garlic, chopped, 1 teaspoon chopped parsley, ¼ teaspoon black pepper, 1 tablespoon fresh breadcrumbs, 1 tablespoon grated Swiss cheese, and ¼ cup room-temperature butter. Mix with a spatula to form a paste, and season with salt to taste. Open 24 small cherrystone clams and save their liquor for another purpose. Place half shells on a bed of coarse salt in an ovenproof dish. Place a clam in each half shell, and spread with the prepared mixture. Bake in a 400° oven for about 10 minutes, or until the clams are cooked.

CLAMS AU GRATIN (*Palourdes au Gratin*). Prepare as for Scallops au Gratin, using tender littleneck or cherrystone clams. Do not slice them.

CLAMS IN CREAM (*Palourdes Gratinés à la Crème*). Prepare as for Oysters in Cream.

FRIED CLAMS COLBERT (*Palourdes Frites Colbert*). Prepare as for Fried Oysters Colbert, but do not poach the clams before frying.

GRILLED DEVILED CLAMS (*Palourdes Grillée à la Diable*). Open littleneck or cherrystone clams and save their liquor for another purpose. Dip them in melted butter that you have seasoned with salt, pepper, and lemon juice. Impale the clams on skewers, and roll them in fine breadcrumbs seasoned with a little cayenne. Grill gently, place the skewers of cooked clams on a long dish, and surround with peeled slices of lemon and parsley. Separately serve Devil Sauce.

CLAMS À LA BORDELAISE (*Palourdes à la Bordelaise*). Prepare a *Mirepoix* by finely chopping 1 carrot, 1 onion, and 1 sprig of parsley, and cooking them for 15 minutes in 3 tablespoons butter with ½ crumbled bay leaf and a pinch of thyme. Set the mirepoix aside. Scrub the shells of 2 or 3 dozen clams. Put them in a saucepan with 2 shallots, finely chopped, 2 tablespoons butter, 1 cup dry white wine, and a *Bouquet Garni* consisting of 1 sprig parsley, ½ bay leaf, and a sprig or pinch of thyme, tied in cheesecloth. Cover and simmer for 5 minutes, or until the clams are opened. Remove the meats from the shells and keep warm. Reduce the poaching liquid by ½, strain it very carefully, and put it in a clean saucepan. Add the prepared mirepoix, ¾ cup thick Velouté Sauce, 2 tablespoons Tomato Purée, and ½ cup heavy cream. Boil this sauce for 5 minutes, adding a little more cream if it becomes too thick. Season with salt, pepper, and lemon juice to taste, bring to the boiling point, remove fro mthe fire, and swirl in* 3 tablespoons butter. Pour this sauce over the clams, and sprinkle with chopped parsley.

CURRIED CLAMS (*Palourdes au Curry*). Scrub the shells of 2 or 3 dozen clams. Put them in a saucepan with 2 shallots, finely chopped, 2 tablespoons butter, 1 cup dry white wine, 1 teaspoon curry powder, 1 sprig parsley, ½ bay leaf, and a sprig or pinch of thyme. Cover and simmer for 5 minutes, or until the clams are opened. Reduce the poaching liquid by ½, strain it carefully, and put it in a clean saucepan. Add ½ cup chopped onion, which you have seasoned with curry powder and simmered very slowly in butter, ¼ cup thick Béchamel Sauce, and 4 tablespoons cream. Boil this sauce for 5 minutes, or until it is quite thick. Swirl in* 3 tablespoons butter and pour the sauce over the clam meats on a bed of Rice à l'Indienne.

SCALLOPS
(*Coquilles Saint-Jacques*)

Scallops are the swimming mollusks that clack their shells when taken from the water. Because of clacking and gaping, they lose their water quickly and are difficult to keep alive. Consequently, all we ever find in the market are the small, tender cylinders of meat that are their muscles. Each scallop has but one. It is the sweetest of all shellfish meats. And fresh scallop meats smell sweet.

The sweetest of the sweet scallop meats are those of the tiny Long Island bay scallops. The meats range in color from creamy white to light tan, orangish or pinkish. They measure about ½ inch in diameter and ½ inch high. The larger meats are those of the deep sea scallop, measuring perhaps 2 inches across. These are sweet but not so sweet as the little ones. Some unscrupulous dealers have been caught stamping out ray and skate wings with a cooky cutter, and selling them as deep sea scallops. This is a fine tribute to the flavor of the skate, but another good reason why you should know as much as possible about the foods you buy. You can tell the difference by examining the fine grain of the meat closely. The grain of the scallop muscle runs vertically, that of the skate's wings, horizontally.

In France scallops are called *coquilles Saint-Jacques,* the shell being worn as the badge of a pilgrim during the Crusades. The whole scallop is sold live, not just the muscle, and the scallop is often served with its orange roe in its own shell. French recipes for scallops can be prepared using the muscle meat only, and you can buy natural scallop shells to serve them in, or shells of porcelain.

COOKING SCALLOPS

Scallop meats lose their flavor quickly, so they should be very fresh. The meat must be firm and smell sweet and clean. The fact that they may be eaten raw like oysters indicates how little cooking they need. As with other small, tender foods, cook them in high heat so that the heat penetrates quickly and the cooking is over and done with before they dry and lose their delicate flavor.

SCALLOPS À LA MEUNIÈRE (*Coquilles Saint-Jacques à la Meunière*). Wash and dry the scallop meats. Dip in milk, dredge in flour, and quickly sauté them in very hot Clarified Butter for a few minutes, or until they are golden. In a separate pan, slowly cook clarified butter until it is brown and exudes a nutty odor. Put the scallops on a serving platter, sprinkle with salt, pepper, and lemon juice, and pour the sizzling brown butter over them. Sprinkle with chopped parsley and garnish with lemon.

SCALLOPS AU GRATIN (*Coquilles Saint-Jacques au Gratin*). Poach the scallops for 3 or 4 minutes in Court Bouillon made with white wine. Slice them thickly (if they are large sea scallops) and season with salt and pepper. Put the scallop slices, along with slices of mushroom sautéed in butter, into scallop shells containing 1 tablespoon of Duxelles Sauce. Cover the scallops and mushrooms with more of the sauce, sprinkle with white breadcrumbs and butter, and glaze* under the broiler. Sprinkle with chopped parsley and garnish with lemon.

SCALLOPS NANTAISE (*Coquilles Saint-Jacques Nantaise*). Prepare as for Scallops au Gratin (above), but instead of the mushroom slices use poached mussels and oysters.

SCALLOPS OSTENDAISE (*Coquilles Saint-Jacques Ostendaise*). Prepare as for Scallops au Gratin (above), but instead of the Duxelles Sauce and mushroom slices, use Nantua Sauce, poached shrimp and oysters, and truffle slices.

SCALLOPS À LA PARISIENNE (*Coquilles Saint-Jacques à la Parisienne*). Prepare as for Scallops au Gratin (above), but decorate the rims of the scallop shells with Duchess Potatoes piped through a pastry bag and brushed with egg. Also, in place of the Duxelles Sauce, use White Wine Sauce to which you have added a little chopped truffle.

FRIED SCALLOPS COLBERT (*Coquilles Saint-Jacques Frites Colbert*). Season the scallops with salt and pepper. Dredge in flour, dip in beaten egg, and roll in breadcrumbs. Fry in ¼ inch very hot Clarified Butter for a few minutes until golden. Drain and serve sprinkled with chopped parsley. Separately serve Colbert Butter.

SCALLOPS ON A SKEWER (*Coquilles Saint-Jacques en Brochette*). Wash and dry the scallop meats, and season them with salt and white pepper. Marinate for 2 hours in 1½ cups dry vermouth and ½ cup chopped fennel leaves. Impale the scallop meats on skewers, alternating with whole cherry tomatoes, and brush with olive oil. Grill or broil gently until the scallop meats are a light golden color.

9   *Birds for the Table*

*Adam and Eve sold themselves for an
apple. What would they have done for
a truffled turkey?*

—BRILLAT-SAVARIN

Many birds are good to eat, and the British Museum assures us that no bird—
of which there are 8600 species—is poisonous. Consequently many birds are
eaten whose names we hardly know. The Eskimos love little auks and cook
them by fermentation in the body of a fat seal. Figpeckers and larks are other
little birds that are eaten. In olden times little game birds were used as a stuffing for big game birds. The best game birds are wild ducks and geese, grouses,
partridges, peafowls, pheasants, plovers, ptarmigans, quails, snipes, and wood-
cocks. Many of these are now raised in captivity and you can buy them by
mail order. Although game birds are important in the French cuisine, they are
so tedious to buy I will speak no more of them here. Besides, they are frozen.

The edible birds readily available to us number five—the chicken, turkey,
duck, goose, and the newly arrived Rock Cornish hen. These domesticated
birds are bred to be meatier than their wild cousins, but their meat has less
flavor. In recent years poultry has become even less flavorful due to modern
poultry farming methods, which use special feeds to hurry sedentary flocks to a
marketable size. Chickens, for example, do not have the pronounced taste they

used to have because they are denied the bugs and worms, the running about, and the extra weeks of life it takes to grow tasty. Yet they come to us beautifully clean, tender, fat, fresh, and wholesome, and at such reasonable cost that King Henry IV's and President Hoover's promise of a chicken in every pot have been realized in our time. As for the flavor of these birds, we will rely upon good French cooking to enhance that.

Along with other items of the American food supply, poultry has become increasingly standardized. All of our commercial ducks are Pekin ducks; most of our geese are gray Toulouse geese. This leaves us wondering what delightful flavors we are missing. As French cooks, we must be on the scent of the elusive variety. Somewhere a farmer feeds a plump Nantes duck. Somewhere there honks a fat Emden goose. Whether we forage farms or poultry markets, running these rare birds to earth is one of the joys and triumphs of real French cooking.

In addition to being standardized, the American poultry supply has become increasingly frozen. Only the common chicken can be readily bought fresh, along with some fresh-killed turkey during the holiday season. Where is the sign reading, "Fresh Ducks"? You will look for it in vain. A famous chef, once said, "Frozen food is dead food." But then, better frozen ducks than no Duck with Peaches. Better frozen geese than no Braised Goose à l'Allemande.

On the plain of Bresse in southern Burgundy they rear a chicken that has been famous for flavor for hundreds of years. The Bresse poultrymen delight in their slow-maturing Bresse chickens. They pamper them in life, slaughter them lovingly, wash them in milk, powder their little carcasses white as snow, and sell them at outrageous prices that amply repay the care bestowed upon them. Is there a market for such a chicken in America? Are you willing, at least now and then, to pay extra to defray the cost of raising a chicken of superior flavor and marketing it fresh? Lately more and more brand name fresh chickens are coming to market. You owe it to yourself to taste them and see if they are worthwhile.

✳ CHICKEN IN THE POT

Which came first, the chicken or the egg? I can confidently answer this question, at least as far as the United States is concerned. The egg came first.

Up to 20 years ago, the supply of chicken meat in America was largely a by-product of commercial egg production. (The storied little red hen was a Rhode Island Red, a variety famous for egg-laying.) Chickens reached the market only after they had passed their egg-laying prime. They were prime old hens, a bit tough, but rich with the good chicken flavor it takes time to develop. They made great fricassees, great stews, great soups. Chicken with dumplings! Perhaps you can remember how good these used to taste.

Of course younger, tenderer chickens were on the market too. These were often males, or poor egg layers that had been culled out of the flock. But they were in limited supply, and because of the law of supply and demand these birds were more costly than the common little red hen.

Today all this has changed. A new industry has grown up, having nothing to do with egg production, that breeds and rears chickens for their meat only. Go to the store today and you'll find that the tough old stewing hen (if you can find her at all) often costs twice as much per pound as the young, plump, tender broiler barely two months old.

Commercial production of chickens for meat is dominated by the fact that the younger the chicken the more efficiently it converts feed to meat. Spectacular growth per pound of feed occurs up to 6 weeks of age; after this, the rate of growth declines. In as much as feed accounts for about 60 percent of the cost of producing a salable chicken, you can understand why chickens are being marketed younger and smaller. Six pounds of high-energy feed will produce a 2½ - to 3-pound chicken in 8 weeks or less. This is the broiler-fryer—the chicken you find most of in the stores, and at the lowest price.

This wonderfully tender little bird has one big drawback. It lacks flavor. It is like veal that has not had the time to develop into beef. As French cooks, we will have to exercise all our cunning to enhance and emphasize the wee flavors present in this little bird that has grown too quickly.

The roasting chicken you will find at the store is the same broiler-fryer reared to weigh 3½ to 4 pounds or more. It has been fed more, and therefore it will cost you more per pound. Being a few weeks older, it will have more flavor than the younger birds, but it too has undergone forced growth on special antibiotic feeds, and it will not have the rich flavor of the barnyard chicken of old.

The capon is a castrated male, grown to be tender, fat, and meaty. It will be 15 or more weeks old and will weigh 5 to 8 pounds. These specially treated birds cost more than ordinary roasters. Unfortunately, they come to you mostly frozen.

Finally we have the stewing chickens, egg-laying chickens past their prime and sold for meat. These are called fowls, and they are hard to find. They may weigh as little as 3 to 3½ pounds; the best laying hens are in this weight range. They may be 1 year old or more, tough and dry but rich in flavor. They are scarce because few people bother making chicken soups anymore, and the egg producers' exhausted laying flocks are bought up by the soupmakers. (They know where the flavor is!) Although these old chickens have paid for their feed in eggs, they are often high-priced, obeying the laws of supply and demand and rewarding the extraordinary entrepreneurship that brings them to the consumer market.

BUYING THE CHICKEN

Let us buy one of these chickens. We have already discussed the effect of age on flavor and tenderness. Beyond this, a broad-breasted, meaty, firm-fleshed, loose-skinned, fresh-smelling chicken is best.

All meat-type chickens are bred for broad-breastedness. Meatiness of the legs and breast (no sharp breastbone sticking out) is a reliable guide; you can see you're getting your money's worth of meat. Poke and pinch the chicken. The flesh should be firm and springy; the skin loose, not taut. Smell the chicken; there should be absolutely no odor. If the chicken is bagged in plastic beware of loose juices in the bag that may indicate the chicken has been frozen and thawed.

In some parts of America, a yellow-skinned chicken is preferred. Yellow-skinnedness, however, tells you nothing about the chicken's quality or flavor. In the past a yellow skin indicated the chicken was fed on corn, and corn-fed chickens did taste better. Today's computerized feeds may or may not contain significant amounts of corn. The preference for yellow-skinned chickens is easily satisfied by adding powdered marigold to the chicken feed. Egg-laying fowls that reach the market are usually white-skinned.

STUFFING THE CHICKEN

A chicken will accept about ½ cup of stuffing per pound of weight. First, salt and pepper the cavity. Stuff lightly; the stuffing swells with cooking. If you do not stuff the chicken, put inside some flavoring in addition to salt and pepper. An onion or piece of celery provides inner moisture for roast chicken. A little ball of butter provides inner butter basting for braised chicken. A handful of herbs will add flavor to a chicken that is poached. Skewer the cavity and secure it with soft string; better yet, sew it up. It is difficult to brown a chicken in a pan with skewers sticking out every which way. A trussing needle or a curved upholsterer's needle, found in any dime store, will do the job nicely. Rub the chicken all over with a cut half of lemon to clean and freshen it. Leave the tail of the chicken—the "Parson's Nose"—sticking out. It makes a handy trough for pouring out the juices of an unstuffed chicken.

TRUSSING THE CHICKEN

A chicken that is cooked whole must be trussed to prevent the heat from splaying out the legs and wings and unduly drying them during cooking. Use a piece of soft twine about 18 inches long. With the breast of the chicken facing upward and the legs pointing away from you, lay the center of the string across the lower ends of the legs. Cross the string beneath, draw it tight so that the legs are tucked under the end of the breastbone, and bring the halves of the crossed string underneath along the creases naturally separating the thighs from the body. Flip the chicken over and turn the legs toward you. The string is now in position to secure the wings to the body. Loop the string around the wings, draw it very tight (thereby pulling the legs snugly to the body), and tie it. This takes only one knot, and the string does not mark the breast.

CUTTING UP THE CHICKEN

Never buy cut-up chicken! Juices and flavor are quickly lost from cut surfaces. It is child's play to cut up a chicken yourself, fresh, just before cooking. If you want only the legs and thighs and breasts, use the rest of the chicken to make the Giblet Stock and sauce you need to bring these parts to the peak of flavor.

Begin with the legs; a chef's knife is best. Make a cut deep into the natural crease between the thigh and the body. Bend the entire leg and thigh outward, disjointing it from the hip. Flip the chicken over onto its breast and, holding the leg, cut the other half of the circle around the thigh. Cut high up on the body of the chicken so you get all the thigh meat. Separate leg from thigh with one cut, feeling for the joint between the two. Remove the other leg and thigh. Cut around the base of the wings and twist them off. Chop off the wing tips for the stockpot.

Now, take the breasts. Holding the knife horizontally, cut from the cavity toward the neck between the two sets of rib bones that angle toward the rear of the chicken on either side. Cut right on through to release the breast. Then whack the breast in two. (Detailed directions for boning the breast are given later in this chapter.)

BONING THE CHICKEN

Sometimes you will want to bone the entire chicken. This is a little complicated to put wholly into words, so here are some salient pointers. Use a thin, sharp knife and sharpen it often as you work. Begin by slitting the skin the entire length of the backbone. Little by little, begin scraping down from the backbone along the ribs, keeping the knife at a flat angle but *always* with the knife edge to the bone. As you progress, carefully lay back the skin and the meat. With patience you will be able to remove the entire backbone and breastbone in this manner.

To bone legs, thighs, and wings, remember that meat muscles are tenaciously attached to the bone at the joints. For the thighs, work from the inside out. Push back the skin and cut around the firm attachment of meat to the joint end of the bone. Then scrape outward, keeping the knife at a flat angle but always with the edge to the bone to avoid cutting the meat or the skin. Turn the meat inside out as you proceed, or push it ahead of you. When you reach the leg end of the thighbone, again cut around to release the meat. Then twist the thighbone free.

To bone the leg, work from the end of the leg inward. Cut skin and flesh free of the bone at the bottom of the leg. Scrape upward toward the thigh, turning the skin and flesh inside out as you go. When you reach the thigh end of the bone, cut around it to release the meat and pull the bone free. The first joint of the wings may be boned as you boned the thighs.

COOKING THE CHICKEN

Chicken cookery is protein cookery. The meat, however, is finer-grained and more delicate than beef. Also, the fat in young birds tends to be clumped outside the muscles, rather than inside, where it could be expected to provide inner basting, juiciness, and flavor. The meat of all chickens varies from the delicate, white, fat-free breast to the heavier, dark, juicier legs and thighs. As a result, when cooking chicken, we take steps to equalize the effects of cooking upon the various parts.

SOMETHING TO WATCH FOR

A final caution. After you have cooked and eaten your chicken, observe the bones. They should be white. If they are brown, the young chicken you bought as fresh-killed was in reality frozen and thawed. Freezing crushes the blood cells of bone marrow and can be seen as a deep red color on the uncooked bone which changes to dark brown during cooking.

✳ BOILED (POACHED) CHICKEN

Boiled chicken doesn't sound very appetizing, and perhaps this is why chicken is rarely prepared this way in America. Actually, in good cooking, the chicken is never boiled. It is poached in a flavorful liquid at a simmer well below the boiling point. The liquid, which is white stock with perhaps a half bottle or bottle of white wine added, can be given additional flavor by aromatic vegetables and herbs.

The object of poaching is to make tender the flesh of mature birds so that we can enjoy the more fully developed, richer flavor these birds possess. We take special pains to see that the flavor of the chicken does not escape into the stock in which it cooks. The dish is a failure if the chicken has no pronounced flavor of its own, if it is tough or dry, or if it is overcooked so that the flesh falls from the bones. The meat should be firm, moist, and flavorful.

Poached chicken is always cooked whole to retain its flavor and juices, it is trussed as for roasting, and it may be stuffed. It is served hot or cold, whole or cut up, with a variety of traditional sauces and garnishes. Poaching the whole chicken is also the best way to obtain juicy, full-flavored chicken meat for dishes requiring precooked chicken.

Chickens for poaching must have the hardness of flesh to withstand the attack of hot water. Roasters and capons of 4 to 5 pounds and more are the usual choice. Old stewing chickens can also be poached; they require longer cooking, however.

The stock in which chickens are poached should have a pronounced chicken taste, and the amount used should only just cover the chicken to concentrate wayward flavors. Also, we begin cooking the chicken in boiling stock to scald the skin and help seal in the flavor. You may cook with it a vegetable garnish, according to the recipe.

POACHED CHICKEN
(*Poularde Pochée*)

Chicken, a 4- to 5-pound roaster or capon

White Chicken Stock, 1 to 2 quarts, enough to just cover the chicken

Dry white wine, up to half the quantity of stock used (optional)

A stock pot or oval casserole of a size to fit the chicken snugly

Wash the chicken quickly inside and out in running water, and dry it. You may stuff it with your favorite stuffing, or put a peeled onion, leek, carrot, or some herbs inside for flavor. Sew up the vent and truss the chicken as for roasting. If it is white-skinned, and you want to retain this dazzling whiteness, rub the chicken all over with a cut half of lemon.

Place the chicken in a close-fitting pot and pour over it boiling White Chicken Stock or stock and dry white wine to cover. This stiffens the skin and prevents it from splitting, which might happen if you plunge the chicken into boiling liquid. Return the stock quickly to the simmering point, adjust the flame, cover, and let simmer for 50 minutes. Skim occasionally. Do not allow the stock to boil!

To test for doneness, use a wooden spoon or a skimmer to lift the chicken half out of the stock, being careful not to break the skin. Probe the thigh deeply with a poultry skewer and observe the juices that run from the hole. They should be clear. The thigh should feel soft (not rubbery) and should yield to the poke of your finger. If the thigh resists poking, or the juices run rosy, return the chicken to the pot. Mature birds are very variable, and cooking may take another half hour or so.

If the chicken is to be served hot, drain it in a colander and put it on a heated platter for saucing and garnishing according to the recipe. (If it is to be served cold, or if only precooked chicken meat is required, the chicken is cooled and stored in the stock to prevent drying. In this case, turn off the heat while the juices still run slightly pink, as the chicken will continue to cook in the stock until the stock has cooled.)

19 VARIATIONS ON HOT POACHED CHICKEN

There are many dishes in the French cuisine that employ hot poached chicken. Most of them are sauced with one of the variations of basic Velouté Sauce, which is made in advance. Traditionally, toward the end of the chicken's cooking period, some of its cooking liquid is added to the velouté and slowly simmered with it. The actual sauces used—Allemande, Supreme, etc.—are based on this velouté-and-stock mixture, and are usually but the work of a moment.

In those cases where no thickening sauce is used, the stock in which the chicken has cooked is reduced and thickened with arrowroot or cornstarch to make a Starch-Thickened White Stock. The vegetable garnish may or may not be cooked in the stock with the chicken, according to the individual recipe.

POACHED CHICKEN À L'ALLEMANDE (*Poularde Pochée à l'Allemande*). Poach the chicken. Coat it with Allemande Sauce to which you have added some of the chicken's cooking liquid, reduced by ½ or more.

POACHED CHICKEN WITH CUCUMBERS (*Poularde Pochée aux Concombres*). Poach the chicken. Serve it surrounded with chunks of Cucumbers in Butter. Pour over Allemande Sauce, which you have refreshed with a squeeze of lemon.

POACHED CHICKEN WITH MUSHROOMS IN WHITE SAUCE (*Poularde Pochée aux Champignons à Blanc*). Poach the chicken. Coat it with Allemande Sauce flavored with Mushroom Essence. Serve the chicken surrounded with poached and very white mushroom caps.

POACHED CHICKEN WITH RICE (*Poularde Pochée au Riz*). Poach the chicken. Coat it with Allemande Sauce to which you have added some of the chicken's greatly reduced cooking liquid. Serve with rice cooked in the chicken's broth and shaped in small molds.

POACHED CHICKEN WITH SPRING VEGETABLES (*Poularde Pochée à la Renaissance*). Poach the chicken. Coat it with Supreme Sauce flavored with Mushroom Essence. Serve it on a platter surrounded by separate mounds of spring vegetables—tiny carrots, little peas, asparagus, mushrooms, etc.—that have been boiled, braised, glazed, sautéed, or fried.

POACHED CHICKEN À L'IVOIRE (*Poularde Pochée à l'Ivoire*). Poach a very white-skinned chicken. Coat it with Supreme Sauce. Serve it surrounded with poached white mushroom caps and chicken Quenelles. (Or you can garnish this dish with buttered noodles and Mushrooms in Cream.)

POACHED CHICKEN AU VERT-PRÉ (*Poularde Pochée au Vert-Pré*). Poach the chicken. Coat it with Supreme Sauce to which you have added 2 tablespoons Printanier Butter per cup of sauce. Surround with a garnish of buttered peas, green beans, and asparagus tips.

POACHED CHICKEN WITH OYSTERS (*Poularde Pochée aux Huîtres*). Poach the chicken. Surround it with oysters poached in their own liquor and drained. Quickly boil down the oyster liquor and use it to flavor a Supreme Sauce. Pour the sauce over all.

POACHED CHICKEN À LA NANTUA (*Poularde Pochée à la Nantua*). Stuff the chicken with a mixture of ½ shrimp Purée and ½ very thick Velouté Sauce. Poach it, and serve it with Supreme Sauce that you have finished with 2 tablespoons Shrimp Butter per cup of sauce. (You may use a purée of crayfish, clams, oysters or other shellfish to stuff the chicken.)

POACHED CHICKEN DIVA (*Poularde Pochée Diva*). Stuff the chicken with a Rice Stuffing. Coat it with Supreme Sauce to which you have added ½ teaspoon paprika per cup of sauce. Serve with a separate garnish of *cèpes* in cream (see Mushrooms) or Mushrooms in Cream.

POACHED CHICKEN IN HALF MOURNING (*Poularde Pochée en Demi-Deuil*). Slip 6 or 8 thin slices of raw truffle beneath the breast skin of the chicken. Lard* the breasts and poach the chicken. Coat it with Supreme Sauce to which you have added some of the chicken's cooking liquid, reduced by ½ or more, and some thin slices of truffle. Serve remaining sauce in a sauceboat.

POACHED CHICKEN À L'AURORE (*Poularde Pochée à l'Aurore*). Poach the chicken. Coat it with Aurora Sauce and surround it with chicken Quenelles and oval slices of tongue. The chicken may be stuffed with a stuffing flavored with Tomato Purée.

POACHED CHICKEN À LA CHIVRY (*Poularde Pochée à la Chivry*). Poach the chicken. Coat it with Chivry Sauce to which you have added 2 tablespoons Printanier Butter per cup of sauce. Serve the chicken surrounded by artichoke bottoms garnished with tiny fresh peas or asparagus tips. (Or you may serve the chicken with a separate *Macédoine* of mixed, boiled vegetables—carrots and turnip balls or dice, diced green beans, diced asparagus tips, and peas—mixed with butter or thick fresh cream.)

POACHED CHICKEN À L'ANGLAISE (*Poularde Pochée à l'Anglaise*). Poach the chicken along with a ¾ pound piece of well-blanched salt pork or slab bacon. Fifteen minutes after cooking begins, add some carrots and turnips cut into olive shapes, slices of the white part of leeks, and a heart of celery. Garnish the dish with the vegetables and the salt pork or bacon, sliced. Send it to the table with a sauceboat of Parsley Sauce and a sauceboat of the cooking liquid for the vegetables.

POACHED CHICKEN À L'ÉCOSSAISE (*Poularde Pochée à l'Écossaise*). Stuff the chicken with a mixture of ½ pearl barley cooked in stock and ½ sausage meat; 1 onion, chopped and cooked in butter; and 2 tablespoons cream. Poach the chicken and coat it with Écossaise Sauce to which you have added some of the chicken's greatly reduced cooking liquor and a *Brunoise* of carrots, onions, celery, and leeks. Separately serve string beans with cream.

POACHED CHICKEN EDWARD VII (*Poularde Pochée Edouard VII*). Escoffier created this dish on the occasion of the coronation of Edward VII of England. Stuff the chicken with a Rice Stuffing. Poach it and coat it with Curry Sauce to which you have added 2 tablespoons diced red peppers per cup of sauce. Separately serve cucumbers in cream.

POACHED CHICKEN WITH COARSE SALT (*Poularde Pochée au Gros Sel*). Poach the chicken. Fifteen minutes after cooking begins, add carrots cut in olive shapes and small white onions. Serve the chicken surrounded with small heaps of carrots and onions. Separately serve a sauceboat of the chicken's cooking liquid, reduced and slightly thickened with arrowroot. Also serve a little bowl of coarse sea salt.

POACHED CHICKEN À LA MÉNAGÈRE (*Poularde Pochée à la Ménagère*). Poach the chicken in a rich White Stock made gelatinous by veal and chicken bones. Pour the stock into a saucepan, add to it equal quantities of sliced carrots, onions, and potatoes, and cook slowly until the liquid is reduced enough to coat a spoon. Serve the chicken in an oval cocotte with the vegetables and the sauce.

POACHED CHICKEN WITH TARRAGON (*Poularde Pochée à l'Estragon*). Poach the chicken with 6 sprigs fresh tarragon (or 2 teaspoons dried tarragon) added to the stock. Place the chicken on a dish and decorate the chicken with blanched tarragon leaves. Reduce the cooking stock, strain it, and add arrowroot to make a Starch-Thickened White Stock to which a few chopped tarragon leaves are added. Pour a little of this sauce into the bottom of the dish around the chicken, and serve the rest in a sauceboat. Very simple, and very good.

✳ THE BRAISING AND STEWING OF CHICKENS

Chicken takes well to these forms of moist heat cookery. Large fryers, roasters, and capons can all be used. Because of the tenderness and delicacy of their flesh, they take much less time to braise or stew than beef, veal, or pork. We will take care to conserve and present at the table any flavors necessarily lost from the meat during cooking.

Chickens to be braised are braised whole—first browned and then simmered slowly in a thickened stock or sauce. Chickens to be stewed are cut up. They may or may not be browned, according to the recipe. Generally they are cooked in a thickened stock that becomes their sauce. Two special kinds of stews are chicken fricassees and chicken blanquettes. We will treat each in turn.

BRAISED CHICKEN

Braised whole chickens are a rarity in America. The same birds you would use for braising are perfect for roasting, too, and roasting seems so much easier. But a roasting chicken will taste quite different if it is braised. Also braising will produce a sauce impossible to get by roasting. As French cooks, we are duty bound to search out this sauce and this taste.

To braise a chicken, it is first browned in hot fat and then simmered in rich stock with aromatic vegetables and herbs in a covered pot. Less stock is used than in braising other meats because tender young chickens cook quickly and there is less time for the stock to cook down. The chicken is basted frequently to keep the flesh moist. The stock, which reduces to about ½ its original quantity, becomes the base of the sauce. The cooking takes place partly in rich gelatinous liquid, partly in steam.

The object of braising chicken is to obtain tender, juicy, flavorful meat with a good, rich sauce. The chicken should look different from roasted chicken—moist, glossy, beautifully glazed. The dish is a failure if the meat is not more tender and succulent than that of roasted chicken, and if the sauce is not full-flavored and velvety to feel on the tongue, free of the fat and palpable flouriness encountered in hastily made pan gravies. Enough! Let us begin.

BRAISED CHICKEN
(*Poularde Braisé*)

Chicken, a 3- to 4-pound roaster, capon, or large fryer
Clarified Butter, 4 tablespoons
Carrots, 2 medium, thickly sliced
Onions, 2 medium, thickly sliced
White Stock, 3 to 4 cups
Dry white wine, 1 cup
Bouquet Garni—3 sprigs parsley, 1 celery rib, ½ bay leaf, and a sprig or pinch of thyme, tied in a cheesecloth bag

Cornstarch or arrowroot, 2 to 4 teaspoons
Sherry, Madeira, or port wine, 2 to 4 teaspoons
Salt and pepper
A heavy casserole with tight-fitting lid, preferably oval to fit the chicken snugly

Clean the chicken quickly inside and out under running water, and dry it. Stuff it if you wish, or place fresh herbs or parsley inside, sew up the vent, and truss it. Brown the chicken lightly in clarified butter, rolling it over and over. The chicken should sizzle until golden. You may now lard* or bard* the breast if you choose.

(Braised poultry is best cooked in a casserole that just fits the bird so that a minimum amount of braising liquid is used. An oval-shaped casserole is ideal, and a 3½-pound chicken fits snugly into a 2½-quart oval casserole. You may brown the chicken right in the casserole, but be sure to butter the chicken and the sides of the casserole first. If the raw, unbuttered skin hits a hot, unbuttered surface it will stick and tear. It is perhaps best to brown the chicken in a skillet, or even in the oven, handling it carefully with wooden spoons to keep the skin intact.)

Add more butter to the casserole if necessary, lower the heat slightly, and cook the carrots and onions until they just begin to brown. (Vegetables brown at lower temperatures than meat, and unclarified butter can be used.)

Now, the braising liquid. Pour into the casserole containing the browned vegetables 1 cup of White Veal or Chicken Stock and reduce this over a medium flame, stirring to scrape up the brown bits in the bottom of the casserole. When the stock begins to become thick and syrupy, add 1 cup more. When this in turn has thickened, add the white wine. Return the chicken to the casserole and add more stock until the chicken is ⅓ covered. The stock, which reducing has made more gelatinous, will now cling to the chicken with every basting and more effectively contain its juices and goodness. (If the chicken and vegetables have been browned in a skillet, reduce the stock in the same skillet, stirring to scrape up the flavorful brown bits. Then pour into the casserole.) Heat the casserole on the flame until the braising liquor has returned to a simmer. Add the bouquet garni.

You may finish the cooking tightly covered in a 325° oven or on the burner. Oven cooking is best because of its all-around heat, but if your casserole is thick and heavy the top of the stove will do fine. In either case adjust the heat carefully to maintain a perfect simmer and baste, baste, baste. Also cover the bird with a piece of buttered paper or aluminum foil the size and shape of the casserole, with a hole in the center to vent off the steam. (This encloses the bird even more snugly in a cocoon of rich, flavorful steam. Also, particularly for top-of-the-stove cooking, this prevents the steam that condenses on the inside of the relatively cool cover from dropping back as liquid onto the chicken, and washing away the gelatinous liquid you so carefully basted on.) In either case, also, the casserole may be uncovered in the oven for the last 15 minutes and the chicken basted every few minutes with the sauce to form a beautifully transparent glaze.

Today's tender chicken, cooked in this manner, should take only 15 minutes per pound. Check for doneness early, in about 45 minutes. *You must not overbraise chicken or any white meat;* it loses its perfection rapidly, becoming dry and stringy. The chicken is done when it exudes clear or yellowish juice when the thigh is probed deeply with a poultry skewer. (The juice should bubble somewhat freely from the hole: if not, the chicken has begun to dry out.) The thigh will also *feel* tender, and the legs will move freely when wiggled.

When the chicken is cooked absolutely perfectly, remove it carefully, taking care not to break the skin or disturb the glaze and place it atop a piece of toasted bread on a warm serving dish, keep warm, and finish the sauce. Tip the casserole and skim most of the fat from the surface. Discard the bouquet garni. Thicken the sauce by adding to the liquid 2 teaspoons arrowroot or cornstarch mixed with 2 teaspoons sherry, Madeira, or port. (Or you may thicken the sauce by adding an already thickened white stock.) Heat, skimming away any additional fat rising to the surface. If the sauce needs more thickening, add a little more starch in wine. The sauce should coat a spoon nicely. Season it to taste with salt and pepper and strain through a fine strainer or several layers of washed cheesecloth. That's it!

The chicken is brought to the table glistening with sauce and surrounded by a ring of watercress. More sauce is passed in a sauceboat. Separately serve buttered noodles and fresh peas, or olive-shaped Glazed Carrots and Glazed Turnips, mushrooms cooked in Brown Stock, small white Glazed Onions, or Green Beans in Cream.

4 TRADITIONAL VARIATIONS ON BRAISED CHICKEN

Braised chicken is always seared in hot fat before cooking to seal in the juices and stiffen the flesh. According to the intensity of this searing, braised chicken may be served white (*à blanc*) or brown (*à brun*). When braised white, the chicken is lightly seared without browning and the sauce is finished with a white sauce or cream. When braised brown, the chicken first receives a good browning and the sauce is finished with wine or a brown sauce or thickened brown stock.

A vegetable garnish may be cooked along with the chicken and served with the chicken or separately. Braised chicken is sometimes brought to the table in the casserole in which the chicken and vegetables were cooked. This method of serving is called *en cocotte*.

BRAISED CHICKEN WITH CARROTS VICHY (*Poularde Braisée Vichy*). Stuff the chicken with a Rice Stuffing. Brown it lightly and braise it. Reduce the braising liquid to 1 cup. Off the fire, stir in 1 cup Supreme Sauce, blend well, and pour over the chicken. Serve the chicken surrounded with small Tartlet shells filled with Carrots à la Vichy.

BRAISED CHICKEN WASHINGTON (*Poularde Braisée Washington*). Stuff the chicken with 3 to 4 cups of corn fresh-cut from the cob, to which you have added 1 onion, chopped, and ½ cup sausage meat, both simmered in butter. Braise the chicken, and glaze* it in the oven. Serve with a *Timbale* of Corn in Cream.

BRAISED CHICKEN À LA PAYSANNE (*Poularde Braisée à la Paysanne*). Braise the chicken with 2 medium carrots, 1 medium onion, and 1 rib of celery, all finely minced. Serve the chicken *en cocotte*.

BRAISED CHICKEN À LA BERGÈRE (*Poularde Braisée à la Bergère*). Brown 1 cup diced and blanched salt pork or bacon with ½ pound small whole mushrooms in 2 tablespoons butter. Remove the pork and mushrooms. Stuff the chicken with 1 medium onion and ¼ pound mushrooms, both chopped and simmered in butter, and mixed with 6 tablespoons butter and 1 teaspoon chopped parsley. Brown the chicken, return the pork and mushrooms to the pan. Add ½ cup dry white wine, reduce for 2 or 3 minutes while scraping the solidified juices from the pan, and add 4 tablespoons Starch-Thickened White Stock. Braise the chicken. When it is cooked, place it on a round dish and keep warm. Thicken the juices in the pan with *Beurre Manié* or arrowroot. Pour the sauce and the vegetables around the chicken, and surround it with fried Shoestring Potatoes.

CHICKEN STEWS

French stews, or ragouts, are made with meat cut into uniform pieces. There are two kinds of ragouts—brown and white. In brown ragouts (*à brun*) the meat is seared in hot fat to seal its surface before it is put to simmer in stock. The stock is often thickened before cooking, and the meat is simmered in this sauce. In white ragouts (*à blanc*) the meat is first blanched* and then put into the cold stock. The meat actually poaches in liquid stock that is thickened at the end of cooking.

Most French chicken stews are cooked *à brun*. The preliminary searing may be very light, the chicken remaining light golden in color. Or it may be heavy enough to turn the chicken a rich golden brown. (In America, chickens prepared in this manner are called white and brown fricassees.) The stock may be thickened before, during, or after cooking. In any case it is finished and served as the sauce. Also, the stock may include various liquids—White Veal or Chicken Stock, Poultry Glaze (see Meat Glaze), gravy, wine, cream, Mushroom Essence—in combinations according to the recipe.

Some chicken stews are very elegant, the sauce being carefully strained and finished apart from the chicken, and the vegetables cooked separately. More often the chicken and its garnishing vegetables are cooked together and served in the casserole.

There are many classic chicken stews to choose from. Here are a few that illustrate the method and the great variety the method makes possible. The most famous of all is the ancient *coq au vin*.

CHICKEN WITH WINE
(*Coq au Vin*)

Chicken, a 3-pound fryer, cut up	Onions, 12 small white
Butter, 5 tablespoons	Mushroom caps, 12 medium
Shallots, 2 finely chopped	Sugar, a pinch
Cognac or brandy, 2 tablespoons	*Beurre Manié*—2 tablespoons flour
Salt and pepper	and 2 tablespoons butter
Red Burgundy wine, 3 cups	A heavy casserole or skillet with
Bouquet Garni—4 sprigs parsley, 1	tight-fitting lid, just large enough
bay leaf, a pinch of thyme	to hold the chicken
Salt pork or bacon, ¼ pound, cut in	
½-inch dice	

Wash the chicken quickly, inside and out, under running water, and dry it. Cut the chicken into legs, thighs, breasts, and wings. Thoroughly dry the pieces and brown lightly in 4 tablespoons butter in a heavy skillet or casserole. The butter should not be overly hot and the chicken should sear only until it is a light golden color. Part of this searing may take place with the cover on, to stiffen the meat without browning. This should take about 10 minutes. Then sprinkle with shallots, cook for 1 minute more, and drain the butter from the pan.

Sprinkle heated cognac or brandy over the chicken in the pan and light it. When the flame burns down, lightly salt and pepper the chicken. Add red Burgundy wine and the *bouquet garni*. Cover and simmer for about 30 minutes, until the chicken's juices run clear when the thigh is pricked deeply with a poultry skewer. Do not allow the liquid to boil.

While the chicken is cooking, parboil bacon or salt pork for 5 minutes. Drain and dry the dice. Brown and cook them together with white onions and mushroom caps in 1 tablespoon butter to which you have added a pinch of sugar to aid in the browning.

When the chicken is done, place it on a hot serving platter, garnish it with the onions, mushrooms, and bacon or pork, and keep it warm. Skim the fat from the cooking liquid. Prepare a *beurre manié* by kneading together flour and butter, and drop little pea-sized balls of this into the gentle boiling liquid, stirring briskly with a wire whisk until the sauce is formed and thick enough to coat a spoon. Strain the sauce over the chicken and decorate the platter with heart-shaped slices of toasted white bread. Serve with the same red Burgundy wine you used to stew the chicken.

5 RAGOUTS OF CHICKEN
FROM THE FRENCH CUISINE

CHICKEN À LA BOURGUIGNONNE (*Poularde à la Bourguignonne*). You can prepare this as in the recipe for Chicken with Wine (above), except that after flaming and seasoning the chicken remove it from the pan. Add just 2 cups red Burgundy wine to the pan and boil it down to ½ its volume. Then add 2 cups Brown Sauce or rich Starch-Thickened Brown Stock. Return the chicken to the pan and proceed as for chicken with wine. The sauce should become thick enough during cooking not to need final thickening with *Beurre Manié*.

CHICKEN À LA BASQUAISE (*Poularde à la Basquaise*). Brown the chicken in 2 tablespoons butter and 2 tablespoons olive oil in a heavy skillet or casserole. Season the chicken with salt and pepper. To the pan add: 1 medium onion, sliced; 4 tomatoes, peeled, seeded, and chopped; 2 green peppers, seeded and sliced; 6 mushrooms, sliced; ½ cup diced Virginia ham; 1 garlic clove, minced. Simmer all together for 4 minutes. Then add ½ cup dry white wine and ½ cup Brown Sauce brought to the boiling point. Cover and simmer for 30 minutes or until the chicken is done. Serve in the casserole with a red and green sprinkling of 1 tablespoon diced pimentos and 1 tablespoon chopped parsley.

CHICKEN WITH LEMON (*Coq au Limon*). Brown the chicken in 4 tablespoons butter in a heavy skillet or casserole. Remove the chicken. To the pan add 1 tablespoon flour and mix it with the butter to form a White Roux. Cook for 3 minutes, then add 1 cup White Stock, 3 tablespoons rich Brown Sauce, and a *Bouquet Garni* consisting of 3 sprigs parsley, ½ bay leaf, crushed, and a sprig or pinch of thyme all tied in cheesecloth. Also add 1 large fresh lemon cut into dice. Return the chicken to the pan and cook for 30 minutes or until chicken is done. Remove the bouquet garni and pour the sauce over the chicken. Decorate the dish with slices of 1 fresh lemon.

CHICKEN FRANÇAISE (*Poularde Française*). Lightly brown ½ pound of ham cut into small dice in 8 tablespoons butter in a heavy skillet or casserole. Push the ham to one side, dredge the chicken pieces in flour, and brown them in the pan. To the pan add: 5 white onions, quartered; 1 cup chopped mushrooms; 1 clove of garlic, crushed; 1 tablespoon chopped parsley; 1 teaspoon salt and ¼ teaspoon pepper; and a good pinch of thyme. Cover and heat the vegetables thoroughly over low heat. Then add 2 tablespoons brandy and 1 cup dry red wine, bring to the simmer, cover, and cook for 45 minutes or until chicken is done. Remove the chicken to a hot platter and pour the sauce and vegetables over it.

CHICKEN CURRY (*Currie de Poulet*). Dice ½ pound of lean raw ham (or cured ham that is first parboiled for 3 minutes) and lightly brown it in 3 tablespoons butter in a heavy skillet or casserole. Push the ham aside, and lightly brown chicken pieces in the butter. Salt and pepper the chicken, cover the casserole, and simmer for 10 minutes to stiffen the meat. Sprinkle into the pan 1 tablespoon flour, stir it to form a White Roux with the butter, and cook for 2 minutes. Then add 1 cup White Stock; 2 teaspoons curry powder; one apple, cored and diced; and a *Bouquet Garni*—3 sprigs parsley, 1 rib celery, ½ bay leaf, crushed, and a sprig or pinch of thyme tied in cheesecloth. Cover and simmer for 30 minutes, or until the chicken is done. Remove the chicken, keep it warm, reduce the sauce slightly, and discard the bouquet garni. Pour the sauce with the diced ham over the chicken. Serve with Rice à l'Indienne.

CHICKEN FRICASSEES AND BLANQUETTES

French ragouts, both white and brown, have also been adapted to chicken cookery in two kinds of dishes that are similar to ragouts but not identical—fricassees and *blanquettes*. Like ragouts, both fricassees and blanquettes are simmered in stock with seasonings, and the reduced stock is made into a sauce. They differ from ragouts in that the sauce is always finished with egg yolks and cream.

Now, what are the differences between fricassees and blanquettes? The key difference between the two is that in fricassees the chicken parts are first seared in butter to seal them; in blanquettes they are not. Also, fricasseed chicken is sprinkled with flour after searing, thereby thickening the liquid in which the meat simmers; blanquettes are actually poached in unthickened liquid. Finally, the vegetable garnish in pure fricassees is cooked along with the chicken; in blanquettes these vegetables are always prepared separately.

As a result we can expect the meat of fricassees to retain more of its flavor than the meat of blanquettes, which is both unseared and cooked in liquid stock (containing the powerful solvent of water). On the other hand we can expect the sauce of blanquettes to be more flavorful and succulent, which it is. Fricassees, which combine meat and vegetable garnish in the pan, are more of a family dish. Blanquettes are more studied—elegant and formal.

The object of fricassees and blanquettes is to present juicy, tender chicken pieces in a rich, creamy sauce. The sauce must help intensify the flavor of the chicken and it should be very white. If the sauce is gray, which is the certain result when egg-yolk and cream-enriched sauces contact aluminum, the dish is a failure. These dishes must be prepared in enameled cast iron, tinned copper, or stainless steel pans.

OLD-FASHIONED CHICKEN FRICASSEE
(*Fricassee de Poulet à l'Ancienne*)

Chicken, a 3- to 4-pound fryer, or roaster, cut up
Butter, 4 tablespoons
Carrot, 1 medium, thinly sliced
Onion, 1 medium, thinly silced
Celery, 1 rib, thinly sliced
Salt and white pepper
Flour, 3 tablespoons
White Stock or dry white wine or both, 3 to 4 cups
Bouquet Garni—2 sprigs parsley, ½ bay leaf, crumbled, and a sprig or a pinch of thyme

White onions, 16 small
Mushroom caps, 16 medium
Egg yolks, 2
Heavy cream, ½ cup
Lemon juice, 1 tablespoon
Nutmeg, a pinch
Parsley or chives, chopped, 1 tablespoon
A heavy enameled cast iron, tinned copper, or stainless steel skillet or casserole to fit the chicken and vegetables

Wash the chicken, inside and out, under running water, and dry it. Cut the chicken into legs, thighs, breasts, and wings. Melt 4 tablespoons butter in a heavy casserole or skillet. (Do not use aluminum; it will darken the egg-enriched sauce.) Lightly sear the chicken pieces in the sizzling butter without browning them.

Remove the chicken and put into the pan the carrot, onion, and celery rib. Lower the flame and sear the vegetables lightly without browning them. Add a little more butter if necessary.

Return the chicken to the pan, season with a little salt and white pepper, and sprinkle with flour. Cook slowly over a low flame for about 5 minutes, turning the chicken pieces in the butter to prevent them or the flour from browning. (The flour cooks with the butter to form a White Roux.) Then add enough boiling white stock or dry white wine and white stock combined to just cover the chicken. Turn up the flame and bring quickly to the simmer, stirring and shaking the pan to mix the butter and flour roux with the stock.

This will thicken the stock and begin to form a sauce that will develop in flavor as it cooks with the chicken in the pan. Add the bouquet garni. Cover the pan and simmer slowly for about 30 minutes or until the thighs are tender to touch and the juices run clear when pierced deeply with a skewer.

Meanwhile, gently boil small white onions in a little white stock or water to cover. Ten minutes before the chicken is cooked, add these with their cooking stock to the pan. At the same time, add mushroom caps (with the stalks cut off flush with the base of the caps), which you have kept white in a little lemon water.

When the chicken is cooked, remove and keep warm. Skim the sauce of fat, increase the flame, reduce the sauce until it coats a spoon, remove the pan from the heat, and remove the bouquet garni. In a glass bowl, blend egg yolks with heavy cream. Begin beating in 1 cup of the hot sauce, first by spoonfuls and then by ¼ cupfuls. Slowly pour the egg-enriched mixture back into the sauce remaining in the pan, stirring and blending with a wooden spatula, taking care not to crush the onions or mushrooms. Return the pan to the fire and continue stirring until the sauce almost boils. Do not allow it to boil.

Add a little salt and white pepper if necessary, and a squeeze of fresh lemon juice and nutmeg to taste. Return the chicken to the pan, and turn it in the sauce until it is nice and hot. Transfer chicken, vegetables, and sauce to a hot serving dish and sprinkle with chopped parsley or chives.

4 VARIATIONS ON CHICKEN FRICASSEE

In a few words, a chicken fricassee is a dish of chicken parts, seared in butter, cooked in a thickening stock that is reduced to a sauce and enriched with egg yolks and cream, and served in the sauce with the garnishing vegetables. Once you grasp the basic method, many variations are possible that do not compromise the flavor of this excellent dish. For example, if your stock is concentrated and flavorful, you may dispense with the flavoring vegetables—carrot, onion, and celery. If your stock is thickened, or you are cooking in a sauce, you may dispense with the flour thickening. Also, you may cook the garnishing vegetables entirely by themselves, providing you add a little of their cooking water to the stock in the pan before it is reduced. Finally, you may sear the chicken pieces in butter for a longer time until they are golden brown. This makes the skin a little dryer and crisper, and adds more of a fried chicken flavor.

Other variations may be made in the sauce by adding various flavoring elements—tarragon, for example—to the sauce during cooking. The sauce, however, must be finished with egg yolks and cream if your dish is to be a true fricassee. If the yolks are omitted, or if both yolks and cream are omitted and the sauce thickened in another manner, the dish is a chicken *stew*.

You may also vary fricassees by your choice of the garnishing vegetables. There are many possibilities. Remember, however, that the flavor of these vegetables or the liquid in which they were cooked must be incorporated into the sauce, thereby subtly unifying the fricassee. Here are some traditional variations from the French repertoire:

CHICKEN FRICASSEE DIJON (*Fricassée de Poulet Dijon*). Brown the chicken pieces in 2 tablespoons butter in a heavy nonaluminum skillet or casserole, and season with salt and white pepper. Sprinkle 1 tablespoon flour into the pan and stir it well to mix with the butter and form a White Roux. Then add 1 cup hot white wine, 3 sprigs parsley, ½ bay leaf, crushed, and a pinch of tarragon and of thyme. Cover and simmer for 30 minutes, or until the chicken is done. Remove chicken and keep warm. In a bowl, lightly beat 2 egg yolks and ½ cup heavy cream. Skim the fat from the liquid in the pan and slowly add some of the liquid to the egg and cream mixture, stirring constantly. Return the mixture to the pan and add 1 or more teaspoons prepared Dijon Mustard to taste, and a pinch of cayenne. Bring the sauce to the simmer, stirring constantly, and simmer for 1 minute. Do not boil or the egg yolks will separate out. Taste the sauce, correct the seasoning with salt and white pepper, and strain it over the chicken.

CHICKEN FRICASSEE VALLE D'AUGE (*Fricassée de Poulet Valle d'Auge*). Lightly sear the chicken pieces without browning in 2 tablespoons butter in a heavy nonaluminum skillet or casserole. Season the chicken with salt and white pepper, add 1 small onion, chopped, and simmer for 2 minutes. Then add 2 tablespoons calvados or apple brandy (apple jack) and ½ cup boiling apple cider. Cover and simmer gently for 30 minutes or until the chicken is done. While the chicken is cooking, cook 8 small white onions, 12 baby carrots, and 12 small mushrooms in a little White Stock or water. Also while the chicken is cooking, lightly beat 2 egg yolks with 1 cup heavy cream in a mixing bowl. When the chicken is done, remove to a hot platter and keep warm. Skim the fat from the liquid in the pan and slowly add the liquid to the egg and cream mixture, stirring constantly. Return the mixture to the pan, bring the sauce to the simmer, stirring constantly, and simmer for 1 minute without boiling. Drain the onions, carrots, and mushrooms and arrange them on top of the chicken. Season the sauce to taste with salt and white pepper, and strain it over the chicken and vegetables.

CHICKEN FRICASSEE À LA MINUTE (*Fricassée de Poulet à la Minute*). Lightly sear the chicken pieces without browning in 2 tablespoons butter in a heavy nonaluminum skillet or casserole. Season the chicken with salt, white pepper, and a little nutmeg. Sprinkle 1 tablespoon flour into the pan and stir it well to mix with the butter and form a White Roux. Then add 1 cup boiling White Stock, 3 sprigs parsley, ½ bay leaf, crushed, and a pinch of thyme. Cover and simmer gently for 30 minutes or until the chicken is done. Halfway through cooking add 12 small white onions, partially cooked, and 12 small mushrooms. In a mixing bowl, lightly beat 2 egg yolks with 1 cup heavy cream. When the chicken is done, remove it to a hot platter and keep it warm. Skim the fat from the liquid in the pan and slowly add some of the liquid to the egg and cream mixture, stirring constantly. Return the mixture to the pan, bring the sauce to the simmer stirring constantly, and simmer for 1 minute without boiling. Take care not to crush the onions or mushrooms. Remove the sauce from the fire, season with salt, white pepper, and fresh lemon juice to taste, and pour sauce and vegetables over the chicken.

CHICKEN FRICASSEE À LA BERRICHONNE (*Fricassée de Poulet à la Berrichonne*). Brown 4 medium carrots, cut in the shape and size of large olives, in 4 tablespoons butter in a heavy nonaluminum skillet or casserole. Remove the carrots and brown the chicken pieces. Season the chicken with salt and white pepper. Sprinkle 1 tablespoon flour into the pan and stir it well to mix with the butter and form a White Roux. Return the carrots to the pan, and add 1 cup boiling White Stock and a *Bouquet Garni* consisting of 3 sprigs parsley, 1 rib celery, ½ bay leaf, crushed, and a pinch of thyme, all tied in cheesecloth. Cover and simmer gently for 30 minutes or until the chicken is done. In a mixing bowl, lightly beat 2 egg yolks with 1 cup heavy cream. When the chicken is done, remove it to a hot platter and keep warm. Remove the bouquet garni. Skim the fat from the liquid in the pan and add some of the liquid to the egg and cream mixture, stirring constantly. Return the mixture to the pan, bring the sauce to a simmer, stirring constantly, and simmer for 1 minute without boiling. Take care not to crush the carrots. Taste the sauce, correct the seasoning with salt and white pepper, and pour sauce and carrots over the chicken.

CHICKEN BLANQUETTE

Although a chicken blanquette can make use of the same garnishing vegetables as a chicken fricassee, the vegetables are always served separately, never in the sauce. This makes the blanquette ideal for a buffet service. The meat and skin of the chicken, which are not stiffened by searing, will be more tender than the fricassee, and the sauce richer and more elegant. Also, the chicken may be skinned and boned before serving in the sauce. Note that the chicken is actually cooked by poaching, thereby surrendering much of its flavor to the liquid in which it cooks. Never allow the water to boil, or the chicken will be toughened. (For some reason that escapes me, the chicken in blanquettes is not called *poularde* or *poulet,* but *volaille.*

BLANQUETTE OF CHICKEN
(*Blanquette de Volaille*)

Chicken, a 3- to 4-pound fryer or roaster, cut up
White Stock or stock and dry white wine, 3 to 4 cups
Salt, ½ teaspoon
White pepper, a pinch
Carrot, 1 medium, thickly sliced
Onion, 1 medium, thickly sliced
Celery, 1 rib, thickly sliced
Bouquet Garni consisting of 3 sprigs parsley, ½ bay leaf, crumbled, and a sprig or pinch of thyme, all tied in cheesecloth

Butter, 2 tablespoons
Flour, 3 tablespoons
White Chicken Stock, 1 cup
Mushrooms, chopped, ½ cup
Egg yolks, 2
Heavy cream, ½ cup
Lemon juice, 1 to 2 tablespoons
Nutmeg, a pinch
Parsley, chopped, 1 tablespoon
A heavy nonaluminum skillet or casserole, with cover, to fit the chicken pieces

Wash the chicken, inside and out, under running water. Cut the chicken into legs, thighs, breasts, and wings. Place the chicken pieces in a heavy casserole, cover with cold water, bring almost to the boil, and poach gently for 1 minute, thereby drawing out the scum. Rinse the chicken, clean the casserole, return the chicken pieces to it, and begin again.

Cover the chicken with White Stock or a mixture of stock and dry white wine. Add salt and white pepper. Bring to the simmering point, skim, and add carrot, onion, celery rib, and the bouquet garni. Cover and poach slowly. In about 40 minutes probe a thigh deeply with a poultry skewer. When the juices run colorless, the chicken is done. Do not overcook, or the chicken will become dry.

Meanwhile, prepare a White Roux by cooking butter and flour together for a few minutes. Cook very gently and do not allow the roux to color. Remove from the fire and pour into the roux 1 cup boiling white chicken stock, beating with a wire whisk to mix thoroughly and form a thick Velouté Sauce. Add chopped mushrooms and cook very slowly for 30 minutes, skimming the sauce and stirring frequently.

When the chicken is done, remove and keep warm. Skim the fat from the poaching liquid, then boil it quickly to reduce it by ½. Off the fire, strain the reduced liquid into the velouté sauce and beat it smooth with a wire whisk.

In a glass mixing bowl blend egg yolks with cream. Begin beating in 1 cup of the hot sauce, first by spoonfuls and then by ¼ cupfuls. Slowly pour the egg-enriched mixture back into the sauce in the pan, beating it smooth with a wire whisk. Bring the sauce almost to the simmer but do not let it boil. Add salt and white pepper if necessary, and fresh lemon juice and nutmeg to taste. The chicken pieces may be then warmed in the sauce. Or the meat may be removed in large pieces from the bones, the breasts cut in two, and warmed in the sauce. Serve the chicken sprinkled with chopped parsley.

VARIATIONS ON CHICKEN BLANQUETTE

The sauce is everything (*c'est tout!*) in chicken blanquettes, and variation is achieved by a subtle flavoring of it. You may add, during cooking, various herbs such as chervil or tarragon. You may vary the amount of wine used in the poaching stock. Also, you may finish the sauce with a little Madeira, sherry, port, or butter stirred in just before serving.

Traditionally, a chicken blanquette is served with small white boiled onions and mushroom caps cooked in water to which a squeeze of lemon is added to keep them very white. Fresh buttered noodles are also a traditional accompaniment. You may also serve rice or small boiled or steamed potatoes. If you want to add color to your garnish, you may serve Glazed Carrots and peas, or green beans, or asparagus tips. They will make your sauce look even whiter.

✳ *POËLÉED CHICKEN*

Poëléing, as a cooking term, is practically unknown in America. The method, however, is employed under other names such as pot roasting and casserole cooking. These names, which emphasize the cooking receptacle at the expense of the cooking method, lead to bad results. The ignorant, perceiving little more than a receptacle to fill, proceed to introduce their own improvements into the pot, debasing the method with nondescript recipes that fall somewhere in between poëléing and braising, and that can only lead to mediocre results. Invariably, you will find a delicious casserole dish to be a true poëlé. A poor one will be a debasement of the basic method.

Poëléings differ from braisings in that they cook in lots of butter with little or no liquid added. They cook mostly in the steam of their own juices. And they are cooked quickly. A true poëlé, according to Escoffier, is cooked quickly as a roast. The method is exceptionally suitable for tender meats like poultry.

A poëléd chicken is distinguished from a braised chicken by its rich, buttery flavor; its crisper skin (which is allowed to brown in the uncovered pot at the end of cooking); and its sauce, flavored mainly by the chicken's natural juices. The chicken is very lightly browned in hot butter. It is then placed on a bed of *uncooked* aromatic vegetables in a close-fitting pot, covered tightly, and cooked in a 400° oven with frequent butter basting. The result is halfway between roasting and braising, combining the juiciness of braised chicken with the flavor of roast chicken.

Cooking in this manner is known as cooking *en casserole*. Vegetables half cooked in butter may be added toward the end of cooking, and finished and served as a garnish with the chicken. In this case, of course, the pot must be large enough to admit the garnishing vegetables.

Poëléing chicken is similar to pot roasting beef in that little or no liquid is used. The difference lies in the heat and speed of cooking based upon the nature of the meat. Beef pot roasts are cooked slowly to make tough cuts tender, and the roast supplies its own basting fat as it cooks. Chicken poëlés are cooked quickly, in keeping with the tender meat of chicken, and generous amounts of butter are supplied for frequent basting. (The most tender roast of beef, the filet, is never pot-roasted but is sometimes poëléd.)

*Étuvées** are similar to poëlés in that the meat is cooked in butter in a close-fitting container with little or no liquid. The methods differ in that the meat in étuvées is cut into small, regular pieces and is partially cooked or very well browned before placing in the casserole. The cooking is completed very, very slowly with *no basting*. In this respect, étuvées are a kind of pot roasting for small pieces of meat. You might also describe them as being a waterless stewing.

POËLÉED CHICKEN (CHICKEN EN CASSEROLE)
(*Poularde Poëlée*)

Chicken, a 3- to 4-pound fryer or roaster

Clarified Butter, ½ cup

Carrots, 1 medium, diced

Onions, 1 medium, diced

Celery, 1 rib, diced

Bouquet Garni—3 sprigs parsley, ½ bay leaf, crushed, and a sprig or pinch of thyme

Salt and white pepper

White Stock, concentrated, 1 cup; or a mixture of concentrated stock and Madeira or port wine, 1 cup

A heavy casserole, preferably oval, to fit the chicken snugly

Wash the chicken quickly, inside and out, under running water, and dry it. Stuff the chicken if you like, or place inside a walnut-sized ball of butter and a handful of fresh tarragon or parsley. Sew up the vent, truss the chicken, rub it with melted butter, and place it in a close-fitting, preferably oval casserole in which the clarified butter is heating. Be sure the hot sides of the casserole are buttered to prevent the skin from sticking and tearing. (You may also sear the chicken in a heavy skillet, and transfer it to the casserole after.) As the casserole heats on the flame, roll the chicken over and over to baste it thoroughly and stiffen the skin. The butter should sizzle faintly, but do not allow the chicken to brown. It should be lightly golden.

Remove the chicken and in the bottom of the pan spread a layer of mixed, diced carrot, onion, and celery. Scatter in the ingredients of the bouquet garni. The uncooked vegetables and the chicken's own juices will provide all the moisture needed for cooking.

Salt and pepper the chicken, place it on this bed of vegetables breast up, and cover it with buttered paper or foil cut to fit the pan with a small hole in the center to vent the steam. Cover the pan tightly, heat it until the butter sizzles, and place it in a 375° oven. Baste the chicken regularly with butter from the casserole.

Test for doneness in 40 minutes. Prick the thigh deeply with a poultry skewer and observe the juices that run out. When they still have a slight tinge of pink, uncover the casserole, remove paper or foil, and allow the chicken to brown in the oven, basting frequently with butter from the pan.

When done, remove the chicken and keep it warm. Add to the juices and vegetables in the pan 1 cup concentrated white stock (which you have reduced from at least 2 cups); or reduced stock and wine. Cook gently over a moderate flame for 10 minutes until the liquid absorbs the flavors held in the butter and the vegetables. Then strain out the vegetables, skim the butter from the sauce, and reduce the sauce to the desired consistency, which should just coat a spoon. Place the chicken atop a piece of toasted bread on a platter, surround it with watercress or parsley, and send it to the table with a sauceboat containing the essence of its juices. Serve with it vegetables cooked in a variety of ways—sautéed, glazed, braised, or baked.

8 VARIATIONS ON POËLÉED CHICKEN

POËLÉED CHICKEN À LA BONNE FEMME (*Poularde en Casserole à la Bonne Femme*). Poëlé the chicken as for Poëléed Chicken, except add to the casserole, halfway through cooking, small white onions and small new potatoes (or mature potatoes cut into olive shapes) that have been browned in butter, and squares of blanched lean bacon. Mix juices and butter in the pan with 4 tablespoons Starch-Thickened Brown Veal Stock. Serve the chicken and vegetables in the casserole, *en cocotte*.

POËLÉED CHICKEN À LA BELLE MEUNIÈRE (*Poularde à la Belle Meunière*). Stuff the chicken with ¼ pound chicken livers, sliced, and ¼ pound mushrooms, quartered, both lightly cooked in butter. Under the breast skin slip 6 thin slices of black truffle. In place of the vegetables in Poëléed Chicken, add to the pan ¼ pound salt pork or bacon cut in squares and blanched, and ¼ pound mushrooms tossed lightly in butter. Poëlé the chicken.

POËLÉED CHICKEN À LA LOUISIANE (*Poularde à la Louisiane*). Stuff the chicken with Corn in Cream to which you have added 2 tablespoons diced green pepper. Poëlé it, and place it on an oval platter. On the sides of the platter, alternate *Timbales* of rice and fried bananas. At either end, place a *Croustade* filled with Corn in Cream. Serve the sauce separately.

POËLÉED CHICKEN WITH PEAS (*Poularde Clamart*). Poëlé the chicken. Halfway through cooking add to the casserole 2 cups half-cooked Peas à la Française. Finish the cooking and serve directly as is, *en cocotte*. Do not tinker with the cooking juices.

POËLÉED CHICKEN À LA LANGUEDOCIENNE (*Poularde à la Languedocienne*). Poëlé the chicken. To the juices in the pan add 1 cup dry white wine and 1 clove of garlic, crushed and simmer for 10 minutes. Skim the fat from the sauce and thicken it with 4 tablespoons Starch-Thickened Brown Veal Stock or Brown Sauce. Place the chicken on a round platter, pour the sauce over it, and sprinkle with chopped parsley. Around the chicken place Stuffed Tomatoes à la Languedocienne and rounds of eggplant sautéed in oil.

POËLÉED CHICKEN À LA NIÇOISE (*Poularde à la Niçoise*). Poëlé the chicken. To the juices in the pan add 1 cup dry white wine, 1 clove of garlic, crushed, and 1 tablespoon Tomato Purée. Simmer for 10 minutes, skim the fat from the sauce, and thicken it with 4 tablespoons Starch-Thickened Brown Veal Stock or Brown Sauce. Place the chicken on a round platter, pour the sauce over it, and sprinkle with chopped tarragon. Surround the chicken with 8 small new potatoes and 8 quartered artichokes, both simmered in butter; 8 braised zucchinis; and black olives.

POËLÉED CHICKEN À LA POLONAISE (*Poularde à la Polonaise*). Stuff the chicken with 2 cups chicken liver Forcemeat mixed with 1 cup fresh breadcrumbs soaked in milk and squeezed dry, and 1 teaspoon chopped parsley. Poëlé the chicken. Put it on a platter, squeeze over it the juice of ¼ lemon, and pour over ½ cup Brown Butter in which you have browned ¼ cup dry white breadcrumbs.

POËLÉED CHICKEN CHÂTELAINE (*Poularde Châtelaine*). Brown the chicken lightly and poëlé it. Skim the fat from the juices and thicken them with ½ cup Starch-Thickened White Stock. Place the chicken on a round platter and around it alternate artichoke bottoms simmered in butter and dressed with Soubise Sauce, and small mounds of glazed chestnuts (see Chestnuts). Pour a little of the sauce in the bottom of the platter, and serve the remainder separately.

❄ ROAST CHICKEN

Centuries ago in Europe, and even today in Texas, whole oxen were spitted and roasted over open fires. Cuts tough and tender, fat and lean, all were cooked together. When you roast a whole chicken—legs and thighs, breasts and wings—you must do the same. Roasting these different parts all at once is our first problem.

A second problem lies in the nature of roasting itself. Roasts were born on spits over open fires, and their characteristic savor is best obtained in this way. We try to duplicate this environment when we use our enclosed ovens for roasting. The oven must be hot and dry—hot enough to keep the meat from stewing inside, dry enough to absorb any cooking steam.

Whether we are roasting a chicken in the oven or on a spit out-of-doors, there are several things we do to protect the dryer, more delicate breast meat from the hot, dry heat needed to properly roast the legs and thighs. We truss it snugly, partially protecting the breast and thighs. We baste it often with fat. We roast the chicken partly on its sides, as the fiercest heat is reflected from the top of the oven. Also, we can bard* the chicken by tying thin sheets of fat around the breast and wings. And sometimes we lard* the breast with strips of fat so that it receives an internal basting.

OVEN-ROASTED CHICKEN
(*Poulet Rôti au Four*)

Chicken, a roaster or capon, 4 or more pounds	White Stock or dry white wine, 1 cup
Lemon, ½	A low-sided baking pan of a size
Salt and pepper	just a little larger than the chicken,
Clarified Butter, sweet, 8 tablespoons	and a rack to fit it

Wash the chicken quickly, inside and out, under running water and dry it. Freshen it inside and out by rubbing with a cut half of lemon. Salt and pepper the inside, and stuff it if you wish. Or put inside a little ball of butter with a handful of tarragon or parsley or thyme, or a medium onion for juice and flavor. Sew up the vent and truss the chicken. Dry it carefully.

Rub the chicken all over with unsalted (sweet) butter that you have clarified.* Unsalted butter is less likely to draw moisture to the surface of the chicken; clarified butter is less likely to burn in the roasting pan. Now, if you choose, you may lard* or bard* the breast. Place the chicken on its side on a rack in the roasting pan.

(A good roasting pan is shallow, to prevent steam from collecting around the sides of the chicken. Also it should fit the chicken nicely—too big a pan will become overly hot and burn the fat and drippings. The chicken must be placed on a rack above the drippings, else it would fry.)

You have a choice of heats. You can roast the chicken at a constant brisk heat from start to finish—375° for roasters up to 5 pounds, 350° for roasters and capons over 5 pounds. Or you may vary the heat, cooking at 425° for the first 30 minutes of roasting, and then reducing the heat to 350° for chickens up to 5 pounds, 325° for chickens over 5 pounds. The second method acts to seal the skin of the chicken early, but I do not consider it necessary for well-basted chickens. It is more important to keep the heat as high as possible throughout cooking, thereby preventing the chicken from stewing inside. With either method, the cooking time is the same—about 20 minutes per pound for unstuffed chickens up to 5 pounds, 15 minutes per pound for larger birds. For stuffed chickens, add 5 minutes per pound.

Place the roasting pan with the chicken on its side in a preheated 375° oven. Baste regularly all over every 5 minutes, at first with melted clarified butter and then with fat from the pan. Baste with fat only. Avoid scooping up any nonfat juices that would evaporate on the surface of the chicken, thereby cooling it and causing it to steam. Also, baste quickly to prevent the oven temperature from falling. Ambient temperatures can ruin a roast.

After 20 minutes turn the chicken onto its other side, taking care not to break the skin of the legs or breast. Continue roasting, continue basting. Be sure the fat or other drippings falling into the roasting pan do not smoke or burn. If they do, you will have to pour in ¼ cup of water to cool the pan.

After 20 more minutes turn the chicken breast up. Continue roasting and basting until the chicken is done, adding a little water to the pan if the valuable drippings begin to burn. If the unbarded breast begins to brown too much too soon, protect with a piece of foil or cloth soaked in fat.

About 10 to 15 minutes before the chicken is done, you will hear a great furor of spluttering in the oven as the almost-cooked chicken begins to give up its juices as a prelude to drying out. At this time, remove the bard (if there is one) from the breast and keep basting until the chicken is done.

The chicken is done when the legs relax and move easily, when the thigh meat feels tender, when the thigh exudes a clear juice when pierced deeply with a poultry skewer, and when (in the case of an unstuffed chicken) the juices that pour from the vent when the chicken is lifted are perfectly clear and free of rosiness. These gelatinous juices should be poured into the pan; they are invaluable in making the sauce.

Tilt the pan and skim off most of the fat. Add white stock or white wine and reduce on the burner, scraping up the drippings stuck to the pan. Add salt and pepper to taste, and finish with 1 tablespoon butter swirled in.* This simple sauce, which should just coat a spoon, is traditional for roast chicken. There is barely a cupful to be spooned over individual servings.

If more sauce is required, you can add some Starch-Thickened White Stock to the pan. Also, a thickly sliced carrot and onion may be added during roasting to give the sauce additional flavor. Take care the vegetables do not burn.

The character of oven-roasted chicken is that of chicken roasted over an open fire. The garnishing vegetables should enhance this character, and should be mostly cooked in dry heat—oven-roasted or sautéed potatoes, Glazed Carrots, Glazed Onions, broiled mushrooms or tomatoes, peas or green beans tossed in butter. Crisp, golden fried potatoes are a memorable garnish.

VARIATIONS ON ROAST CHICKEN

Roast chicken, simply served, is the practice in French gastronomy, and the number of traditional garnishes is not great. Traditionally, the chicken is served as a separate course, accompanied only by its sauce and a fresh salad of watercress or Boston lettuce.

ROAST CHICKEN À L'ANGLAISE (*Poulet Rôti à l'Anglaise*). Stuff the chicken with a Sage and Onion Stuffing. Roast it. Bring it to the table surrounded with slices of sautéed bacon or grilled sausages, and serve with Bread Sauce.

ROAST CHICKEN À LA SICILIENNE (*Poulet Rôti à la Sicilienne*). Stuff the chicken with 3 cups of cooked and buttered lasagna that you have seasoned with salt and white pepper and bound together with 1 cup of pistachio nut Purée. Roast the chicken, and 15 minutes before it is done sprinkle with fine, dry white breadcrumbs. Serve with a sauceboat of reduced pan juices.

✳ BROILED CHICKEN
(*Poulet Grillé*)

Chickens are broiled whole by splitting them open down the back and flattening them slightly. Chickens are also broiled after being cut up. Whether you are cooking the chicken in a broiler or on a grill, it is best to half bake the chicken first, then complete the cooking by broiling. In as much as the meat is delicate and the parts rather thick, you must use moderate heat. Also, the surface of the meat must be protected by breadcrumbs and frequent basting.

Chicken, a 2- to 2½-pound broiler	Breadcrumbs, 1 cup
Salt and pepper	A low-sided baking pan
Butter, ¼ cup	

Wash the chicken quickly, inside and out, under running water, and dry it. If broiling the chicken whole, cut it down the length of the back and remove the backbone. Flatten the chicken with a mallet, disjointing the bones, and remove as many bones as can conveniently be got at. Thrust a long skewer through the wings to hold them flat. Or, you may cut the chicken into legs and thighs, breasts and wings.

Roll the chicken in melted butter and bake it in a 325° oven for 20 minutes, basting with butter several times. Remove the chicken from the oven and sprinkle it with salt and pepper, melted butter, and fine, dry white breadcrumbs. Press the crumbs into the meat to make them adhere closely. Sprinkle again with melted butter and broil in the broiler or on the grill for 10 to 15 minutes, or until the chicken is done. Serve the chicken with a highly seasoned sauce, such as Mustard or Béarnaise or Devil Sauce.

DEVILED CHICKEN (*Poulet Grillé Diable*). Roll the chicken (whole and split, in quarters, or pieces) in melted butter and bake it in a 325° oven for 20 minutes, basting frequently with butter. Remove the chicken and coat it with ½ cup prepared Dijon Mustard to which you have added a pinch of cayenne pepper (the mustard will become mild during cooking). Sprinkle with fine, dry white breadcrumbs, pressing the crumbs into the mustard to form a thick, compact coating. Sprinkle with butter and broil in the broiler or on the grill for 10 to 15 minutes, or until the chicken is done. Serve the chicken on a round platter encircled with gherkins and half slices of lemon. Separately serve a sauceboat of Devil Sauce.

❉ *THE CHICKEN SAUTÉES*

We come now to a delightful method of cooking chicken that is quick, easy, delicious, and provides endless variety for the table. The chicken cooks happily, practically unattended, while you are preparing the vegetables. Then you make the sauce right in the pan the chicken was cooked in. If you have some of the basics on hand, such as Brown Sauce or *Velouté* you can quickly achieve many of the grand dishes of the French cuisine. If not, you will still achieve delightful variety making sauces housewife style, *à la ménagère,* using different wines and broths.

Remember that a sauté is food in small pieces cooked quickly in just enough fat to keep it from sticking. Very little fat and *no liquid.* The food must cook in its own juices, and must be cooked briskly enough so that it does not stew. Your chicken sauté should be slightly crispy outside, juicy inside. I will try to teach you every trick I know to make it come out this way.

CHICKEN SAUTÉ
(*Poulet Sauté*)

Chicken, a 3-pound fryer, cut up
Clarified Butter, 3 tablespoons, or
  butter and oil
Salt and pepper
White Stock or dry white wine, or a
  combination of both, 1 cup

Brown Sauce or Starch-Thickened
  Brown Veal Stock, 4 tablespoons
A heavy skillet or sauté pan just
  large enough to hold the chicken
  pieces

Wash the chicken quickly, inside and out, under running water, and dry it. Cut the chicken into legs and thighs, breasts and wings. In order that the chicken will lie flat in the pan, bone the breast, leaving the long bone attached to prevent the meat from shriveling. Also, chop off the end of the leg bone. (Make a circling cut around the skin, push the skin back, and cut again to loosen the flesh from the bone. Push skin and flesh back and give the bone a whack with a chef's knife.) Dry the chicken pieces thoroughly.

Heat the clarified butter or butter and oil in a heavy skillet or sauté pan. The butter should be hot but not too hot. Chicken parts are too thick and too delicate a meat to sauté at the extreme heat used for other thin-sliced meats. The butter is hot enough after it begins to sizzle.

Put the pieces of chicken into the pan skin side down. This is the side that will be up when you serve the chicken, and it is best to cook these with full attention so their color will be very appetizing. Leave plenty of room between the pieces. If they don't all fit, brown them 4 at a time. Crowding the pieces uses up too much heat, and they will steam instead of brown. Turn the pieces when they are beautifully golden (they will color a little more as they cook), and cook on the other side. Adjust the heat to prevent scorching, but be sure the chicken continues to fry. Use your ears. You should *hear* the chicken sizzling.

When the pieces are well colored, in about 10 minutes, remove them from the pan. Be sure the fat in the pan has not burned; if it has, pour it off and replace it.

Heat the pan so that it is less hot than when you were browning, salt and pepper the legs and thighs, put them in the pan and roll them in the butter, partially cover the pan, and cook for 8 minutes. Only then, salt and pepper the breasts and wings, which take less time to cook, and roll them in the butter as you put them in the pan. Now, all the pieces will be cooked at the same time.

You will notice that we partially covered the pan. This is not usual in sautés. Normally the pan is never covered. But the pieces of chicken are too thick to sauté in the usual manner. Leave about an inch of space between the cover and the pan to vent the steam. And be sure the pan stays hot enough so you can hear the chicken frying. This will keep the skin of the chicken crisp.

During cooking, turn the pieces 2 or 3 times so they cook evenly and keep their protective coating of butter. Ten or 15 minutes after adding the breasts (a total of 20 to 25 minutes after browning) the chicken should be done. For the crispiest chicken, uncover the pan and increase the heat slightly during the last 5 minutes of cooking. Test for doneness by poking the thigh with your finger (it should feel soft) and pricking it deeply with a poultry skewer (the juices should run clear). The breasts will stiffen slightly when they are cooked. Remove the chicken and keep it warm, uncovered in a turned-off oven.

And now, the sauce. Pour off the fat and add to the pan the white stock or white wine or a mixture of both. Boil this down quickly by ½, deglazing the pan by scraping up and dissolving any brown bits. Thicken with Brown Sauce or Starch-Thickened Brown Veal Stock. Serve the sauce according to the individual recipe.

SAUCE MAKING À LA MÉNAGÈRE

If you do not have a thickening sauce on hand, you can make your sauce *à la ménagère*. Remove the chicken from the pan, roughly skim off the fat, and sprinkle 1 tablespoon flour into the pan. Heat slowly, stirring, for 2 or 3 minutes as the flour and butter cook to form a Blond Roux. Then add 1 cup of flavorful liquid—White Stock, white wine, clear soup, vegetable cooking water, etc., or a combination of these—stir to dissolve the roux and brown bits in the pan, and reduce to ½ cup. Then add 1 cup more of liquid—stock, wine, etc.—and cook, stirring, for 10 minutes. Strain the sauce and serve it over the chicken. This sauce will not be as brilliant or clear as sauces thickened with Brown Sauce or Starch-Thickened Stock.

19 VARIATIONS ON CHICKEN SAUTÉ

CHICKEN SAUTÉ WITH BUTTER (*Poulet Sauté au Beurre*). This is performed so quickly the dish is sometimes called chicken *à la minute*. Sauté the chicken in butter and place it in a serving dish. Squeeze lemon juice on the chicken, pour over it the butter from the pan, and sprinkle it with chopped parsley. *Fini.*

CHICKEN SAUTÉ À LA MEUNIÈRE (*Poulet Sauté à la Meunière*). Proceed as for Chicken Sauté with Butter (above), but add ½ cup Brown Sauce or concentrated Starch-Thickened Brown Veal Stock.

CHICKEN SAUTÉ WITH BASIL (*Poulet Sauté au Basilic*). Sauté the chicken. To the juices in the pan add 1 tablespoon basil and 1 cup dry white wine. Reduce by ½, stirring to incorporate the juices solidified in the pan. Off the heat, swirl in* 2 tablespoons butter and pour over chicken.

CHICKEN SAUTÉ MARSEILLAISE (*Poulet Sauté Marseillaise*). This sauté is sauced with a vegetable garnish cooked along with the chicken. Sauté the chicken in olive oil. Halfway through cooking, add 2 medium tomatoes, peeled, seeded, and quartered; 2 medium green peppers, finely chopped; and 2 garlic cloves, crushed—all half cooked by sautéing in oil. Remove the chicken when cooked and drain off the oil from the pan. Add ½ cup dry white wine, a squeeze of lemon juice, and cook until the wine is almost boiled away. Cover the chicken with this garnish and sprinkle with chopped parsley.

CHICKEN SAUTÉ PROVENÇALE (*Poulet Sauté Provençale*). Sauté the chicken in olive oil. Halfway through cooking add 2 garlic cloves, crushed. Remove the cooked chicken. Sprinkle 2 teaspoons of flour into the pan, cook 1 minute, and add ½ cup dry white wine. Add 2 medium tomatoes, peeled, seeded, and chopped; about 16 black olives, pitted and blanched; 8 small mushrooms, sautéed in oil; 2 tablespoons of finely chopped onions; and a pinch of basil. Simmer together for 5 minutes, and pour over the chicken.

Then dress the chicken with 8 flat anchovy filets and sprinkle with chopped parsley.

CHICKEN SAUTÉ NIÇOISE (*Poulet Sauté Niçoise*). Sauté the chicken in olive oil. To the juices in the pan add 1 crushed garlic clove and ½ cup dry white wine. Reduce by ½ and add ⅔ cup Tomato Sauce. Serve the chicken with small new potatoes, artichokes cut in quarters, and small zucchini—all simmered in olive oil or butter—and 16 pitted black olives. Pour the sauce over the chicken and sprinkle with chopped parsley or tarragon.

CHICKEN SAUTÉ WITH WINE (*Poulet Sauté au Vin*). Sauté the chicken in butter. To the juices in the pan add ½ cup wine and reduce by ½. Add ⅔ cup Starch-Thickened Brown Veal or Chicken Stock, simmer for a few minutes and finish the sauce by swirling 2 tablespoons butter around in the pan. Pour the sauce over the chicken. This sauté assumes the name of whatever wine it is made with. Thus, just by changing the wine, you have *poulet sauté au champagne, au Chablis, au Riesling, au porto, au Madeira,* etc. If the wine you use is particularly strong-flavored, add just ¼ cup and then more to taste.

CHICKEN SAUTÉ BORDELAISE (*Poulet Sauté Bordelaise*). Sauté the chicken in butter and finish the sauce as for Chicken Sauté with Wine (above). Place the chicken on a serving dish and surround it with quartered artichoke bottoms, blanched and finished in butter; sliced potatoes sautéed in butter; slices of onion deep-fried, and a few sprigs of Fried Parsley.

CHICKEN SAUTÉ WITH HERBS (*Poulet Sauté aux Fines Herbes*). Sauté the chicken in butter. To the juices in the pan add ⅔ cup dry white wine. Reduce the wine by ½ and add ⅔ cup Brown Sauce. Simmer for 2 minutes. Remove from the fire and finish the sauce with 3 tablespoons butter and 1 teaspoon each of chopped parsley, chervil, and tarragon. Pour the sauce over the chicken.

CHICKEN SAUTÉ WITH MUSHROOMS (*Poulet Sauté aux Champignons*). Sauté the chicken in butter. Fifteen minutes before the chicken is done, add ½ pound sliced mushrooms, simmered in butter. Remove chicken and mushrooms and add ¼ cup Madeira wine to the pan, along with the juice exuded from the mushrooms when they were stewed. Reduce by ½, and add ½ cup Brown Sauce. Swirl 2 tablespoons butter in the pan and pour over the chicken, which you have garnished with the mushrooms.

CHICKEN SAUTÉ WITH POTATOES (*Poulet Sauté Parmentier*). Sauté the chicken in butter. Halfway through cooking, add 4 potatoes cut in large dice or 16 potato balls lightly browned in butter until ¾ cooked. Remove chicken and potatoes, and to the juices in the pan add ½ cup wine. Reduce by ½ and add ¾ cup Starch-Thickened Veal Stock, simmer for a few minutes, and finish the sauce by swirling 2 tablespoons butter around in the pan. Arrange the potatoes in little heaps around the chicken, pour the sauce over the chicken, and sprinkle with chopped parsley.

CHICKEN SAUTÉ PARISIENNE (*Poulet Sauté Parisienne*). Prepare as for Chicken Sauté with Potatoes (above), but do not include the potatoes. Instead, spread a thick layer of Duchess Potatoes in a serving dish, brush the potatoes with egg, and brown them in the oven. Place the sautéed chicken on this bed of potatoes, garnish it with buttered asparagus tips, and pour the sauce over the chicken.

CHICKEN SAUTÉ CHASSEUR (*Poulet Sauté Chasseur*). Sauté the chicken in half butter, half olive oil. Fifteen minutes before the chicken is cooked, add ¼ pound sliced mushrooms simmered in butter and olive oil. Remove chicken and mushrooms and add to the pan ½ cup white wine, the juice exuded by the mushrooms when they were simmered, and 1 shallot, chopped. Reduce by ½ and add ½ cup Brown Sauce and ¼ cup Tomato Sauce. Simmer for 2 minutes. Off the fire, swirl in 1 tablespoon brandy, pour the sauce over the chicken, and sprinkle with chopped parsley.

CHICKEN SAUTÉ DUROC (*Poulet Sauté Duroc*). Prepare Chicken Sauté Chasseur (above). Garnish the chicken with small peeled tomatoes simmered in butter, and small new potatoes sautéed in butter.

CHICKEN SAUTÉ LYONNAISE (*Poulet Sauté Lyonnaise*). Sauté the chicken in butter. Halfway through cooking, add 3 medium-large onions, chopped and lightly browned in butter. Remove the chicken. Add ½ cup Starch-Thickened White Veal Stock, reduce by ½, and pour sauce and onions over chicken. Sprinkle with chopped parsley.

CHICKEN SAUTÉ WITH CARROTS (*Poulet Sauté Vichy*). Sauté the chicken in butter. Halfway through cooking, add ½ pound of half-cooked Carrots à la Vichy. Place the chicken and carrots on a serving dish. Add ¼ cup concentrated White Veal Stock to the pan, swirl it around, and pour over the chicken and carrots.

CHICKEN SAUTÉ ANNETTE (*Poulet Sauté Annette*). Sauté the chicken in butter. To the pan add 1 shallot, chopped, and ½ cup dry white wine. Reduce by ½ and add ½ cup Brown Sauce or Starch-Thickened Brown Veal Stock. Simmer for 2 minutes, remove from the fire, and add 1 teaspoon each of parsley, chervil, and tarragon. Add a squeeze of fresh lemon and 1 table-spoon butter and swirl it around in the pan. Serve the chicken on a bed of Annette Potatoes and pour over the sauce.

CHICKEN SAUTÉ À LA BOURGUIGNONNE (*Poulet Sauté à la Bour-guignonne*). Sauté the chicken in butter. Three-fourths way through cooking, add ½ cup diced, blanched, and lightly fried bacon; 12 small onions, glazed; and 12 small mushrooms simmered in butter. Remove chicken, bacon, onions, mushrooms and add to the pan 1 garlic clove, crushed, and 1 cup dry red wine. Reduce by ½ and add 1 cup Brown Sauce. Simmer for 1 minute and strain over the chicken surrounded by its garnish.

CHICKEN SAUTÉ CYNTHIA (*Poulet Sauté Cynthia*). Sauté the chicken in butter. To the saucepan add ¾ cup dry champagne and reduce it by ½. Add 1 tablespoon chicken Meat Glaze and simmer for 1 minute. Remove the pan from the fire and finish the sauce with 4 tablespoons butter, 2 tablespoons fresh lemon juice, and 1 tablespoon dry curaçao. Surround the chicken with peeled and seeded grapes and peeled orange sections. Pour the sauce over the chicken.

❋ THE BREASTS OF CHICKENS
(*Les Suprêmes des Volailles*)

The raw breast meat of chicken is one of the most delicate meats we have to deal with in cooking. It is very tender, very fine-grained, very lean, and rela-tively dry. It is also very delicately flavored. Meat like this is best cooked quickly to develop its flavor before it becomes too dry. Chicken breast meat is amazingly juicy and flavorful when sautéed, broiled, fried, or poëléed—that is, when it is cooked to suit its character. Nevertheless you will find many recipes for chicken breasts that are fricassees or poachings. Both of these methods, to my mind, rob the meat of its delicate flavor.

The French repertory for chicken breasts is very large. We will begin our mastery of this subject by learning the proper nomenclature.

In French cooking, the piece of boneless and skinless meat removed raw from each side of the breastbone is called a *suprême*. Each *suprême* has two parts—the upper, larger portion, which is called the *filet*, and the lower, smaller, but thicker portion (a sort of flap running lengthwise beneath the *filet*), which is called the *filet mignon*. The *filet mignon* of large chickens is sometimes removed, shaped into a little arc or ring, cooked separately, and used to garnish the filet. If the chicken is small, the filet mignon remains part of the filet. The meat is slightly flattened between two pieces of plastic or waxed paper with a smooth mallet or side of a chef's knife. A *suprême de volaille,* then, is one-half the breast meat of a chicken—raw, skinned, boned, and slightly flattened.

BONING THE BREASTS

To·bone the breast, cut along the ridge of the breastbone for its entire length. Peel back the skin and scrape the edge of your knife down the breastbone. When you reach the wing, cut around it and disjoint it by twisting the point of your knife in the socket between the bones. Continue scraping down along the ribs until the meat separates entirely from the breastbone. Turn the meat bottom up, slip the point of your knife under the end of the white tendon running the length of the meat, take hold of the end of this tendon, and, with the cutting edge of the knife held upward against it, scrape and pull it out. Trim off the ragged edges of the meat, flatten it, and you have a suprême. Wrap it immediately in plastic or foil, as the air will dry it quickly.

Now if, during the boning of the suprême, you leave the first joint of the wing (including its bone) attached to it, the suprême becomes a *côtelette* (the French word for cutlet or chop, which the meat now resembles). The skin is removed from the joint of the wing, and the côtelette flattened in the usual manner. On French menus the côtelette is sometimes called *l'aileron,* or wing.

COOKING SUPRÊMES AND CÔTELETTES

Suprêmes and côtelettes are cooked in exactly the same manner. Cooked *à brun,* they are usually sautéed in very hot Clarified Butter, but they are also broiled or even deep-fried. Cooked *à blanc,* they are seared in foaming butter, put into a very hot oven in a covered pan, and poëléed. They are sometimes rolled in breadcrumbs before cooking, and sometimes stuffed. Usually they are dressed with a sauce made from the juices remaining in the pan.

You will find some recipes that call for the poaching of suprêmes in stock, and some that direct you to add liquid to the pan after preliminary browning. This is a very dangerous practice. The delicate flesh of suprêmes is almost certain to become toughened by any liquid hot enough to cook them in reasonable time, or the flesh will be leached of its flavor by any liquid cool enough to avoid this toughening. It is safer to keep the heat hot and dry, and finish the cooking in 6 to 8 minutes. If poached suprêmes are necessary, as in some cold dishes, poach the chickens whole and remove the breasts and bone them. (Properly speaking, poached and boned breast meat of chicken is known as *blanc de poulet*.)

Following are recipes for sautéed, broiled, deep-fried, and poëléed suprêmes. Whatever you do, serve the suprêmes almost immediately after they are cooked, taking only 2 or 3 minutes to make the sauce. They are so delicate they will shrink, dry, and toughen on exposure to air alone. Five minutes' delay can turn triumph into tragedy.

SAUTÉED BREAST OF CHICKEN
(Suprême de Volaille Sauté)

This basic recipe for 4 suprêmes employs the butter in which the meat is cooked as a Brown Butter sauce (*beurre noisette*). Nothing could be simpler, or faster.

Heat 6 to 8 tablespoons Clarified Butter in a skillet or sauté pan that will contain 4 suprêmes without crowding. Heat until the butter just begins to brown. At the last moment, thoroughly dry and lightly salt and pepper 4 suprêmes, dredge them in flour, and slap them sharply over the sink to dislodge any loose flour that might burn in the pan.

Cook the suprêmes quickly, adjusting the heat to keep the butter from turning brown. After 3 minutes, turn the suprêmes. The cooked side should be crisp and golden. Cook for 3 minutes more. Test for doneness.

It is simple to tell when suprêmes are done. Tap them with your fingers while they are still underdone and they will feel soft. Note this softness and keep tapping frequently as they cook. Very rapidly they will lose their softness and become springy, resilient. As soon as they do, they are cooked. Put them on a hot serving platter and keep them warm.

Now make the sauce, quickly! Add more clarified butter to the butter remaining in the pan so there are 6 to 8 tablespoonfuls. Turn up the heat, swirling the butter in the pan, until it browns evenly. Keep swirling or the butter will burn. In 2 or 3 minutes, when it is light brown and smells nutty, remove from the fire. Add 1 tablespoon finely chopped parsley and a good squeeze of lemon. Taste, and add more lemon or salt and pepper if necessary, and pour the sauce over the chicken quickly. Run!

Serve the suprêmes with crisp golden potatoes or diced eggplant fried in butter, little Peas à la Française, asparagus tips in cream, braised lettuce, mushrooms simmered in butter, creamy vegetable purées, or other delicate vegetable garnishes that are crisply fried or softly braised in butter. Or try one of the traditional garnishes suggested below.

Chicken in Champagne Sauce with Truffles

Duck à l'Orange

Stuffed Green Peppers

Paupiettes of Veal with Rice Timbales

BREAST OF CHICKEN SAUTÉ WITH BROWN BUTTER

When served with brown butter, breast of chicken sauté is varied by flavorings complementary to brown butter, by flavored coatings on the meat, or by various garnishes.

BREAST OF CHICKEN SAUTÉ DORIA (*Suprême de Volaille Doria*). Sauté 4 suprêmes in butter. Garnish with pieces of peeled and seeded cucumber, cut in the shape of garlic cloves and simmered in butter. Pour Brown Butter over the chicken.

BREAST OF CHICKEN SAUTÉ JARDINIÈRE (*Suprême de Volaille Jardinière*). Sauté the suprêmes in butter. Garnish *à la jardinière*—with glazed carrots and turnips cut in olive shapes; peas, green beans, and kidney beans all finished in butter; and knobs of cauliflower brushed with butter. Arrange the vegetables in little heaps all around the chicken. Pour Brown Butter over the chicken.

BREAST OF CHICKEN SAUTÉ WITH PARMESAN (*Suprême de Volaille au Parmesan*). Proceed as for Sautéed Breast of Chicken, but dip the suprêmes in beaten egg after dredging with flour, and roll them in freshly grated Parmesan cheese. Press the cheese into the meat, and let stand for 10 minutes before cooking. When cooked, place the suprêmes on top of Polenta croutons sautéed in butter, and pour Brown Butter over all.

BREAST OF CHICKEN SAUTÉ GABRIELLE (*Suprême de Volaille Gabrielle*). Proceed as for Sautéed Breast of Chicken, but first coat the suprêmes with a thin layer of finely chopped *Mirepoix* cooked in butter, and coat with egg and buttered breadcrumbs. Serve garnished with crisp shredded lettuce dressed with thick, cool cream. Pour Brown Butter over the chicken.

BREAST OF CHICKEN SAUTÉ WITH VARIOUS SAUCES

By adding flavor and thickness to the butter remaining in the pan, very quick pan sauces are made. The flavoring element is frequently wine; thickening and flavoring are supplied by a ready-made sauce or a starch-thickened stock. The traditional recipes specify the liquids to be used, and the garnishes. Generally, suprêmes are luxuriously garnished.

The first recipe below permits you to change subtly the character of the dish by your choice of wine, which is the major flavoring element. It also illustrates the problem of adding any liquid, such as mushroom liquor, that is not already thickened. It must be incorporated quickly. The suprêmes are cooked and waiting! You have 2 or 3 minutes, no more!

BREAST OF CHICKEN WITH WINE (*Suprême de Volaille au Vin*). Sauté 4 suprêmes in butter. Remove the chicken and turn the fire up full. Avert your eyes and add ½ cup hot wine (any dry white wine, or a dry Bordeaux red, sherry, Madeira, or port). Boil furiously for 1 minute, while scraping the bottom of the pan with a wooden spoon to loosen and dissolve the solidified pan juices. Then thicken with ½ cup hot, rich, Starch-Thickened White Veal or Chicken Stock. Stir briefly to blend the flavors, and pour over the suprêmes.

BREAST OF CHICKEN WITH MUSHROOMS (*Suprême de Volaille aux Champignons*). Sauté the suprêmes in butter. Surround them with minced mushrooms lightly simmered in butter and pour over Mushroom Sauce.

BREAST OF CHICKEN WITH ARTICHOKE HEARTS (*Suprême de Volaille aux Fonds d'Artichauts*). Sauté the suprêmes in butter. Place them on top of a garnish of sliced artichoke bottoms, simmered in butter and sprinkled with *Fines Herbes*. Serve separately a rich Starch-Thickened White Chicken Stock.

BREAST OF CHICKEN ARLESIENNE (*Suprême de Volaille Arlesienne*). Sauté the suprêmes in butter. On a round serving platter, place a ring of eggplant slices that you have deep-fried in oil. Place the chicken on top of the eggplant. Garnish the dish with rings of Deep-Fried Onions and tomatoes sautéed in oil. In a sauceboat, serve a Demi-Glace Sauce that you have flavored to taste with a little cooked Tomato Purée.

BREAST OF CHICKEN MARYLAND (*Suprême de Volaille Maryland*). Season the suprêmes, roll them in butter, coat them with fine, dry white breadcrumbs, and sauté in butter. Put a slice of grilled or fried bacon on top of each suprême, and surround with small fried cakes of cornmeal and fried slices of banana. Separately serve Horseradish Sauce mixed with heavy cream.

BREAST OF CHICKEN GISMONDA (*Suprême de Volaille Gismonda*). Proceed as for Sautéed Breast of Chicken, but after dredging in flour, dip 4 suprêmes in 1 egg beaten with 1 tablespoon water, and roll in ¼ cup freshly grated Parmesan cheese mixed with ¾ cup dry white breadcrumbs. Sauté the chicken, remove from the pan and keep warm. To the pan add ¼ pound mushrooms, sliced and simmered in butter. Turn up the heat and cook the mushrooms for 1 minute. Add 2 tablespoons Brown Sauce and cook for 1 minute more. Place the chicken on a bed of hot, cooked, coarsely chopped spinach, pour sauce and mushrooms over the meat, and sprinkle with chopped parsley.

BREAST OF CHICKEN FLORIO (*Suprême de Volaille Florio*). Cook 1 cup Béchamel Sauce with ½ cup milk and ½ cup White Chicken Stock until thickened. Off heat blend in ½ cup Hollandaise Sauce and ¼ cup dry white wine. Sauté 4 suprêmes in butter with a sprinkle of marjoram. In a buttered casserole, put a bed of hot buttered noodles. Spread over them ½ pound chopped mushrooms simmered in butter, and put the chicken on top. Pour the sauce over all, sprinkle on plenty of fresh-grated Parmesan cheese, and brown quickly under the broiler.

BROILED BREAST OF CHICKEN
(*Suprême de Volaille Grillé*)

Protected by a thick coating of breadcrumbs and basted with butter, suprêmes can be quickly brought to perfection under the broiler or on the grill. Although the heat is intense, the cooking is so quick the meat is finished before its juices can escape.

BREAST OF CHICKEN ST. GERMAIN (*Suprême de Volaille St. Germain*). Dry and salt and pepper the suprêmes. Dip them in Clarified Butter and roll them in dry white breadcrumbs. Place them under the broiler and sprinkle copiously with clarified butter. Broil at medium heat for 4 minutes, or until golden brown. Turn them over, sprinkle again with butter, and continue broiling until they are springy to the touch. Serve with Béarnaise Sauce and a *Timbale* filled with a purée of *Foie Gras* blended with heavy cream.

DEEP-FRIED BREAST OF CHICKEN
(*Suprême de Volaille Frit*)

In order to meet the requirement of quick cooking, suprêmes that are stuffed, rolled, or marinated are fried in deep, hot fat. In this highly efficient cooking medium the center of the suprême is perfectly cooked by the time the surface, protected by a layer of crumbs, has turned golden brown. The fat is heated to about 375°. Cooking time is 6 to 8 minutes. Any sauce to be served is, of course, made separately.

BREAST OF CHICKEN ORLY (*Suprême de Volaille Orly*). Marinate the suprêmes for one hour in a Marinade of ½ cup oil and ¼ cup lemon juice, with a few parsley sprigs and a little finely sliced onion. Turn them several times. Dry them thoroughly, season with salt and pepper, dip them into a coating *à l'Anglaise,* and fry them. Drain the suprêmes and serve them on a napkin surrounded by crisp Fried Parsley. Send to the table with a sauce-boat of Tomato Sauce.

BREAST OF CHICKEN KIEV (*Suprême de Volaille Kiev*). Flatten suprêmes or côtelettes a little more than usual. On the meat place a piece of chilled butter the size of a finger, sprinkle it with chopped parsley, and roll it up. Press the meat to seal the butter inside (or skewer with a toothpick). Salt and pepper the suprême, dredge it with flour, pat it to remove the excess, dip it in a mixture of 1 beaten egg to 2 tablespoons milk and 1 tablespoon oil, and roll it in fine, dry white breadcrumbs. Allow to set for a few minutes, dip and roll in breadcrumbs again, and refrigerate for 1 hour. Fry in deep hot fat, at about 375°, for 6 to 8 minutes until golden brown, and serve immediately.

POËLÉED BREAST OF CHICKEN
(*Suprême de Volaille Poëlé*)

Suprêmes are cooked *à blanc* by poëléing* in butter in a covered casserole. The cooked meat should be very light in color, and it is dressed with a white sauce of some kind. Poëléing gives the meat a soft, creamy, braised quality appropriate to the rich white sauces with which it is served. These dishes are very elegant, very *haute cuisine.*

Clarified Butter, 4 tablespoons	Parchment or waxed paper
Chicken, 4 boned half breasts (suprêmes)	An ovenproof casserole or skillet with tight-fitting cover, to fit the 4 suprêmes
Lemon, ½	
Salt and pepper	

Heat the butter in a skillet with an ovenproof handle and tight-fitting cover, or in a casserole. Dry the suprêmes thoroughly, rub them with lemon to keep them white, and when the butter foams up, roll them briefly in the butter to sear their surface. Salt and pepper the suprêmes and cover them with buttered parchment paper or waxed paper cut to fit the pan. Cover the pan and put it into a hot, 425° oven.

The suprêmes will cook quickly. Poke them with your fingers after 6 minutes. As soon as they lose their softness and become springy to the touch, they are done. The juices in the pan may or may not be used in the sauce, according to the individual recipe. As in sautéing, the suprêmes must be served within 2 or 3 minutes of the time they are cooked.

POÊLÉED BREAST OF CHICKEN ÉCOSSAISE (*Suprême de Volaille Écossaise*). Poêlé the suprêmes. Cover them with Écossaise Sauce and surround them with little mounds of green beans finished in butter.

POÊLÉED BREAST OF CHICKEN WITH MUSHROOMS IN WHITE SAUCE (*Suprême de Volaille aux Champignons à Blanc*). Poêlé the suprêmes, adding to the pan after preliminary searing 2 tablespoons greatly reduced Mushroom Essence. On a round serving platter, arrange the chicken and some perfectly white mushroom caps, simmered separately in lemon juice and butter, in the form of a crown. Combine ½ cup Allemande Sauce with the pan juices, and coat the chicken lightly. Serve the remaining sauce in a sauceboat.

POÊLÉED BREAST OF CHICKEN WITH TONGUE (*Suprême de Volaille Écarlate*). Make 6 to 8 little incisions on the top of each suprême, and insert part way into these little discs of red, salted tongue about the size of a nickel. Poêlé the suprêmes. Place them atop flat Quenelles of chicken Mousseline Forcemeat shaped to fit the suprêmes, and sprinkle with chopped very red tongue. Coat with Supreme Sauce. You should be able to see the red of the tongue through the sauce.

POÊLÉED BREAST OF CHICKEN WITH OYSTERS (*Suprême de Volaille aux Huîtres*). This dish achieves interest with contrasting temperatures. Poêlé the suprêmes. Place them in a circle on an icy cold platter with a cold bed of bread in the center. On top of the bread place a dozen icy cold oysters on the half shell. The chicken should be very, very hot and the shellfish very, very cold. Serve with a sauceboat of Supreme Sauce.

BREASTS OF CHICKEN IN OTHER WAYS

During your cooking life you will come across many recipes in which chicken breasts are neither sautéed, nor broiled, nor poêléed, nor fried. Analyze these recipes carefully. Discover their purpose. Very often you will find they are simple stews indulging someone's fancy for outlandish ingredients, and for which, if they have any merit at all, chicken parts would be more appropriate. For example, if the recipe calls for baking the breasts in kumquat juice and vinegar in an open pan in a moderate oven for an hour or two, take care! You will not be tasting breast of chicken and you will not be cooking French.

On the other hand, there are traditional ways of cooking suprêmes that call for a combination of cooking methods. These are valid recipes, in that very compromise you make in cooking hot and dry you get something in while in return.

EASTS OF CHICKEN IN PAPER CASES (*Suprême de Volaille en* *pillotes*). Cut parchment paper into heart shapes for cooking *en papillote*,* and butter or oil the paper. On each piece of parchment paper, place a slice of ham trimmed to the size of the suprêmes. Cover the ham with one table-spoon reduced Italian Sauce. Put on top a browned suprême. Top the suprême with another one tablespoon Italian sauce and another slice of ham. Fold the paper around these contents, pleating the edges to seal it. Place the *papillotes* in a baking pan and put into a hot, 425° oven. About 8 minutes should complete the cooking of the suprêmes and the heating of the ham. The *papillotes* will puff out handsomely. Serve the chicken *en papillote*, cutting a small slit in the top of the paper to allow the delicious steam to escape and tantalize the nose.

❋ TURKEY
(*Dindonneau / Dinde*)

In 1794 the French father of gastronomy, Brillat-Savarin, visited Hartford, Connecticut. And within five leagues of there, in crisp October, on the farm of a Mr. Bulow, he shot, on the wing, a Connecticut wild turkey, which, upon being served up in company with partridge wings *en papillote* and gray squirrel stewed in Madeira to a select group of American friends, was pronounced, "Very good! Exceedingly good!" and "Oh, my dear sir, what a glorious bit."

"The turkey," said Brillat-Savarin, "is assuredly one of the finest gifts made by the New World to the Old."

The turkey made its appearance in France at the end of the seventeenth century, and it quickly found a place in classic cookery. Many of the classic recipes for pullets or roasting chickens have been assigned to it. The turkey of these recipes, however, is smaller than the turkey we are used to, weighing about 5 or 6 pounds.

Attempts have been made in America to make turkey more suitable for everyday cooking. One such attempt, to breed a smaller turkey, resulted in the Beltsville White. But the awesome efficiency of commercial feeds has confounded this attempt. In just 10 years the mature weight of the Beltsville White tom skyrocketed from 21 to 30 pounds, larger than the Broad Breasted Bronze it was meant to supplant. As a result, a 10-pound turkey today is much younger than it was just a few years ago. The meat is more tender but less flavorful. In general, the larger the turkey, the more turkey flavor.

Eighty to 90 percent of turkeys are sold frozen. Make every effort to get a fresh-killed turkey. Turkey meat is drier than the rich dark meat of duck or goose, and the juices lost in thawing are irreplaceable. When turkey is roasted by dry heat, as is frequently the case, even more juices are lost.

Turkey is cooked exactly like chicken. It is the same class of bird, containing both white and dark meat. The only allowance we must make is for the turkey's larger size, which requires longer cooking at somewhat lower temperatures. Very young turkeys, weighing 4 to 6 pounds, can be cooked using the methods and recipes given for chicken fryers—grilled, sautéed, stewed, and fricasseed. Larger turkeys can be treated as roasting chickens and capons—poached, braised, poëléed, and roasted. Like chicken, turkey must be cooked to the well-done stage, and all precautions given for keeping chicken meat moist are scrupulously followed.

To prepare turkey for cooking, wash it quickly inside and out under running water, and dry it thoroughly. Cut off the last joint of the wings, and use them with the giblets for the stock pot. Season the cavity with salt and pepper, stuff it if you choose, and truss the bird as you would a chicken. Cook the turkey following any of the recipes given for chicken, changing cooking times and temperatures to conform with those given in the following recipes. These recipes are traditional or considered especially appropriate for turkey.

ROAST TURKEY
(Dindonneau Rôti)

Clean the turkey, season the cavity with salt and pepper, stuff it if you wish, and truss it. Rub it all over with soft unsalted butter and place it on its side on a rack in a low roasting pan. Roast the turkey in a preheated 425° oven for 15 minutes. Turn the turkey onto its other side, and roast for 15 minutes more. Turn the turkey breast up, and reduce oven heat to 325°. Bard* the breast with a sheet of pork fat. If you do not have a bard, cover the breast with 2 or 3 layers of cheesecloth dipped in melted butter. Baste the entire turkey frequently with butter—the oftener you baste, the juicier the turkey will be. Allow about 20 minutes per pound for unstuffed turkeys up to 10 pounds, 15 minutes per pound for turkeys up to 15 pounds, and 10 to 12 minutes per pound for larger turkeys. Add 3 to 5 minutes per pound for stuffed turkeys. The turkey is done when the thigh and leg become soft to the touch. When pricked deeply with a skewer, a clear juice should emerge. About 1 hour before cooking is completed, add sliced carrots and onions to the baking pan to give their savor to the drippings. During the last 20 minutes, uncover the breast so it will brown.

ROAST TURKEY À L'ANGLAISE (*Dindonneau Rôti à l'Anglaise*). Prepare the following sage and onion stuffing. Sauté 4 cups chopped onion in 6 tablespoons butter until soft. Soak 1 pound of soft breadcrumbs in milk, press them out, and toss to loosen them. Lightly mix the crumbs with the onions and season with 2 teaspoons salt, pepper, 1½ tablespoons sage, and ¼ teaspoon nutmeg. Finally, mix in ½ pound finely chopped fat of veal, beef, or pork. This will provide 8 to 10 cups of stuffing; allow about ¾ cup per pound of turkey. Stuff the turkey with this mixture, roast it, and serve it with grilled sausage and pan gravy.

ROAST TURKEY WITH CHESTNUT STUFFING (*Dindonneau Rôti Farci aux Marrons*). Prepare the following chestnut and sausage stuffing. Cut slots in the flat sides of 2 pounds of chestnuts, boil them for 10 minutes, and peel and skin them while they are still hot. Simmer the peeled chestnuts in White Stock or turkey Giblet Stock until they are almost cooked, about 30 minutes. In a large bowl, put 2 pounds of finely ground pork sausage, or a mixture of ¾ pound veal, ¾ pound pork, and ½ pound pork fat, all finely ground. Sauté ½ cup finely minced onions in butter for 3 minutes, add ½ cup Madeira wine, and reduce the wine by ½. Add the onions and wine to the pork mixture, along with 1 teaspoon chives, ½ teaspoon powdered thyme, ¼ teaspoon pepper, 1 clove of garlic, finely minced, and 1½ cups soft breadcrumbs soaked in milk, squeezed dry, and tossed to loosen. If you used fresh meat instead of sausage meat, add 1 teaspoon salt. Beat this mixture with a wooden spoon until thoroughly blended. Finally, mix the chestnuts into the stuffing. This makes 8 to 10 cups of stuffing. Stuff the turkey, roast it, and serve with pan gravy.

BRAISED TURKEY
(*Dindonneau Braisé*)

Turkey, like chicken, is juiciest and most flavorful when it is braised. To braise turkey, follow the recommendations given for braising chicken, with the following allowances for the turkey's larger size.

It is difficult to brown a large turkey on the stove. Brown it in a 425° oven, allowing 15 minutes on each side. You will need additional braising liquid, partly because the bird is larger, partly because it will cook longer and the liquid will evaporate more. Use the braising liquid given for braised chicken, doubling or tripling the amount of liquid and doubling the amount of flavoring vegetables. Finally, you will need a large braising pan. You might use a covered roaster. Braise turkey in a 325° oven for about 20 minutes per pound. To glaze* the turkey, uncover it for the last 15 minutes and baste it with its braising liquid.

BRAISED TURKEY À LA BOURGEOISE (*Dindonneau Braisé à la Bourgeoise*). Braise the turkey. About 1 hour before cooking is completed, add to the braising liquid half-cooked Glazed Carrots cut in olive shapes; half-cooked small Glazed Onions; and diced, blanched, and browned salt pork or bacon. Glaze* the turkey and serve it surrounded with the carrots, onions, and salt pork. Separately serve the braising liquid, skimmed, reduced, strained, and thickened as a sauce.

BRAISED TURKEY À LA BOURGUIGNONNE (*Dindonneau Braisé à la Bourguignonne*). Braise the turkey, using dry red wine in the braising liquid in place of white wine. About 1 hour before cooking is completed, add to the braising pan whole or quartered mushrooms lightly sautéed in butter; half-cooked small Glazed Onions; and diced, blanched, and browned salt pork. Glaze* the turkey and serve it on a platter with the mushrooms, onions, and salt pork arranged around it. Skim, reduce, strain, and thicken the braising liquid, and pass it in a hot sauceboat.

BRAISED TURKEY NIVERNAISE (*Dindonneau Braisé Nivernaise*). Braise the turkey and glaze* it. Serve it surrounded with heaps of small Glazed Onions; Glazed Carrots and Turnips cut in olive shapes; Braised Lettuce; boiled potatoes. Separately serve the braising liquid, finished as a sauce.

BRAISED TURKEY À LA BOUQUETIÈRE (*Dindonneau Braisé à la Bouquetière*). Stud* the breast of the turkey with strips of pork fat. Braise the turkey and glaze* it. Serve it surrounded with heaps of Glazed Carrot and Turnip balls; boiled cauliflowerets, peas, and diced green beans, all tossed in butter; and potatoes cut in olive shapes and sautéed in butter. Separately serve the braising liquid, finished as a sauce.

✳ DUCK
(*Caneton / Canard*)

The Tour d'Argent, established in 1852, is the oldest restaurant in Paris. A specialty of this house is pressed Rouen duck, one of the best-known dishes of France. The Rouen duck is a cross between domesticated duck and wild duck captured in the Seine estuary. It is killed by smothering so that none of its blood is lost. It is then two-thirds roasted and the breast meat is sliced thin. The carcass is put into a duck press to squeeze out all its blood. The blood is used to thicken a sauce made with duck stock, cognac, and Madeira. The handsome, ruddy meat, bathed in this sauce, is juicy, mildly gamy, a joy to eat. This dish, which receives its final preparation at the table, is called a *salmis*. Depending on how and where it is made, it appears on the menu as *canard* or *caneton à la presse, au sang, à la rouennaise,* or *à la Duclair.* (If you order this duck at the Tour d'Argent, you will be assigned a duck number. The restaurant has been numbering its ducks since the 1890's. For example, on May 16, 1948, Princess Elizabeth ate Duck No. 185,397.)

It is not possible to make a proper salmis with our domesticated duck, not only because it is bled, but because it is very fat. This makes our duck more difficult to cook, because we must relieve it of its excess fat without over-cooking its fine flesh. But we shall manage, and the result is well worth while.

Our duck is the White Pekin duck, found frozen in almost every super-market. A gourmet of a sea captain brought it here from China in 1873 and it has flourished in the fresh-water inlets of Long Island, New York, where it is raised mostly today. It is also raised in Massachusetts, Virginia, and the Middle West. Ninety percent of ducks are sold frozen. If you live close to duck farms, you may be able to get fresh duck from April to November. If not, be assured that duck freezes more successfully than chicken, and every frozen duck I have seen has been beautifully plucked, drawn, and cleaned.

Almost all these ducks are properly labeled duckling, for they are quite young. They weigh about 5 or 6 pounds. Nevertheless, a duckling of this size will serve no more than 4 people because there is much less meat on it than on a comparably sized chicken. Also, duck is more difficult to carve. These problems are all solvable, and I will suggest solutions as we review the basic methods of cooking the White Pekin duck.

ROAST DUCK
(Caneton Rôti)

Roast duck is at its juiciest and best when cooked to the medium-rare stage. Unfortunately, when the breast is cooked just right the legs are still underdone. Of course you can serve only the breasts and wings, reserving the legs and thighs for additional cooking on another day. But if the scheme is to enjoy an entire roast duck, what is one to do? Also, how can one rid this duck of excess fat in the little time it takes to roast it properly? Here are some French solutions.

Take a 5- to 6-pound duckling. Wash in running water inside and out, dry it, and cut off the first two joints of the wings. (Use these wing joints along with the duck giblets to make a duck Giblet Stock as the foundation for your sauce.) Remove any loose fat from the cavity and season the inside with ½ teaspoon salt and a little pepper. You may also rub the cavity with ½ teaspoon sage and put in a few slices of onion. Or put in a few slices of apple and stalks or leaves of celery. Or stuff the duck with your choice of dressing. Close the cavity and truss the duck (see Chicken). Now, using a skewer or a sharp-pointed knife, prick the skin of the duck all around the back and the base of the thighs and breasts. This will allow the fat to run out. Dry the duck; do not rub it with fat.

Place the duck on its back on a rack in a shallow roasting pan. Put it into a 450° oven and allow it to brown for 15 to 20 minutes. Lower the heat to 350°, turn the duck on its side, and roast for about 20 minutes more. During this period you may remove some of the accumulating fat from the pan and add 1 onion, sliced, and 1 carrot, sliced, as a flavoring for a pan sauce. Do not baste the duck, and be sure the oven is hot enough so that you can *hear* the duck roasting.

Now turn the duck on its other side and roast for 20 minutes more. Then turn the duck on its back to finish browning the breast and complete the cooking. This will require about 15 minutes more, allowing about 12 minutes per pound for the total cooking time. If you like a crispy-skinned duck, you may now baste the duck during the last 15 minutes with liquid—stock, wine, lightly salted water, orange juice, or 1 part honey to 2 parts water.

Test the duck for doneness. The breast should now be cooked medium rare and it should feel soft. But the legs and thighs are still firm! Thrust a skewer deeply into the leg or thigh and a rosy red juice runs out. The legs and thighs need more cooking. Here is how it is done.

Remove the duck from the oven and cut off the legs and thighs whole. Make a few cuts in the underside of each leg and thigh, and put them in a moderate broiler to cook for 6 or 8 minutes. Their cooking will be completed and the last of their excess fat expelled while you are preparing the duck and its sauce.

While the legs and thighs are broiling, make the sauce with the drippings in the roasting pan according to the recipe you are using. Then you can prepare the duck for easy serving in one of two ways.

First, you can remove each of the breasts in one piece. Slice them thinly on a carving board, put the slices with the wings on a hot serving platter, and keep warm. When the legs and thighs are done, they are divided and added to the platter. The sauce is poured over, the platter appropriately garnished, and the precarved duck is ready to serve.

A second way to serve duck is to remove the breasts, slice them thinly, and return the reassembled slices to their original place on the carcass of the duck. The broiled legs and thighs are put back in their place, and your little subterfuge is masked with a few spoonfuls of sauce.

ROAST DUCK WITH PEACHES (*Canard Rôti aux Pêches*). Roast the duck. While the duck is roasting, brown 1 teaspoon chopped shallots in a saucepan with 1 teaspoon butter. Add the juice from a 1-quart can of preserved peach halves, and ¼ cup peach liqueur or Triple Sec. Reduce over a high flame until the liquid is ½ the original quantity. Add 1 cup Brown Sauce and ¼ cup currant jelly, bring to a boil, stir to blend all ingredients, and remove from heat. Place peach halves in a buttered baking dish, sprinkle with confectioners' sugar, and bake them in the oven until they are appetizingly browned. Place the roast duck on a hot platter, garnish it with the peaches, and pour some of the sauce over it. Pass the remaining sauce in a hot sauceboat.

ROAST DUCK WITH ORANGE SAUCE (*Caneton Rôti à l'Orange*). Roast the duck. While it is roasting, caramelize* 2 tablespoons sugar in 2 tablespoons red wine vinegar until result is a rich brown color. Add 2 cups brown duck Giblet Stock or 2 cups Brown Sauce, stirring to blend. Now, if you used the duck giblet stock, thicken it with 2 tablespoons arrowroot dissolved in a little Madeira or port wine. Finally, add to the sauce the rind of 2 oranges, carefully removed with a vegetable peeler so that none of the pith clings to it, cut in fine julienne,* parboiled for 5 minutes, drained, and dried. When the duck is roasted, remove the fat from the roasting pan and deglaze* the pan with ½ cup Madeira or port wine. Reduce quickly to 2 tablespoons and add this to the orange sauce. Finally, flavor to taste with spoonfuls of Grand Marnier or orange liqueur, and lemon juice. Serve the duck garnished with orange segments from which all the membrane has been removed, and pour some of the sauce over the duck. Duck with orange sauce is also made with braised and poêléed duck. For the sauce recipes, see Bigarade Sauce.

POÊLÉED DUCK
(*Caneton Poêlé*)

Poêléing or roasting *en casserole* is an excellent method of cooking duck. The legs and thighs can be cooked to the medium rare stage without the breast becoming too dry, the fat is melted out of the body, and the duck's own juices are collected for its sauce.

To poêlé the duck, clean it, truss it, and prick the skin all along the back and at the base of the breasts and thighs, as for roasting. Brown it slowly in a few tablespoons of butter in a snug-fitting oval casserole, being careful to grease the sides of the casserole to prevent the skin from sticking and tearing. Roll the duck over and over to sear it on all sides and release its fat.

When the duck is browned, pour the fat from the casserole, turn the duck breast up, and lightly salt it. Add a *Bouquet Garni* consisting of 3 sprigs parsley, ½ bay leaf, and a sprig or pinch of thyme, tied in cheesecloth. Cover the duck with a piece of buttered paper or foil, cut to fit the casserole, with a small hole punched in it to vent the steam. Cover tightly and place in a 350° oven. Remember, poêléing is quick cooking. After browning, only about 60 minutes is required to bring a 5½-pound duck to the desired medium-rare stage.

Ten minutes before the cooking is completed, you may uncover the casserole and brown the duck to the appetizing color you desire. You may also baste the duck with stock or wine to give it a crispier skin. When the duck is done, remove it from the casserole and keep it warm. Remove the bouquet garni, skim the fat from the casserole, and use the remaining liquor (the duck's own juices) to make the sauce according to the recipe.

POÊLÉED DUCK IN MADEIRA (*Caneton Poêlé au Madère*). Poêlé the duck. Skim the fat and deglaze* the casserole with ½ cup Madeira wine. Reduce by ½ and add 1 cup starch-thickened brown duck Giblet Stock or Brown Veal Stock. Strain the sauce and swirl in 2 tablespoons butter. Pour some of this sauce over the duck, and pass the remainder in a hot sauceboat. By using port or sherry wine in place of Madeira, this dish becomes *caneton au porto* or *caneton au xérès*.

POÊLÉED DUCK IN CHAMPAGNE (*Caneton Poêlé au Champagne*). Poêlé the duck. Skim the fat and deglaze* the casserole with 1 cup dry champagne. Reduce by ½ and add ½ cup Starch-Thickened White Veal Stock. Strain the sauce, swirl in 2 tablespoons butter, pour some of this sauce over the duck, and pass the rest in a hot sauceboat.

POÊLÉED DUCK WITH MINT (*Caneton Poêlé à la Menthe*). Rub the cavity of the duck with 2 tablespoons soft butter to which you have added ½ teaspoon chopped fresh mint. Poêlé the duck. Skim the fat and deglaze* the casserole with ½ cup White Veal Stock. Thicken the stock with 2 to 3 teaspoons arrowroot dissolved in a little veal stock. Flavor with lemon juice to taste, and strain. Just before serving, add ½ teaspoon finely chopped fresh mint and pour over the duck.

POËLÉED DUCK À LA BONNE FEMME (*Caneton Poëlé à la Bonne Femme*). Poëlé the duck, adding to the casserole after it is half cooked and skimmed of fat: ½ pound lean bacon slices cut in squares and blanched, 2 cups small onions parboiled and tossed in butter, and 2 cups potatoes cut in olive shapes and lightly browned in butter. When the duck and vegetables have completed cooking, arrange them on a hot platter. Skim the fat and deglaze* the casserole with 1 cup White Veal or Chicken Stock. Thicken the stock with 2 to 3 teaspoons arrowroot dissolved in a little cold stock, and strain. Pour some of the sauce over the duck, and sprinkle with chopped parsley.

POËLÉED DUCK WITH TURNIPS (*Caneton Poëlé aux Navets*). Poëlé the duck, adding to the casserole after it is half cooked and skimmed of fat: 4 cups turnips cut in olive shapes and parboiled for 10 minutes. When the duck and turnips are cooked, arrange them on a hot platter. Skim the fat and deglaze* the casserole with 1 cup White Veal or Chicken Stock. Thicken the stock with 2 to 3 teaspoons arrowroot dissolved in a little cold stock, and strain. Pour some of the sauce over the duck, and sprinkle with chopped parsley.

BRAISED DUCK
(*Caneton Braisé*)

If for reasons of variety or taste you would like your duck well done, braise it. Duck roasted to the well-done stage is just too dry and tough to eat. A properly braised duck can be eaten with a spoon.

To braise the duck, clean it, truss it, and prick the skin all along the back and at the base of the breasts and thighs, as for roasting or poëléing. Brown it well in a few tablespoons of butter in a snug-fitting oval casserole, rolling the duck over and over to brown all sides and release its fat. Take care to grease the sides of the casserole to prevent the duck's skin from sticking and tearing.

Remove the browned duck, pour all but 2 tablespoons of fat from the casserole, and in the remaining fat brown a *Mirepoix* consisting of 1 carrot, chopped, and 1 onion, chopped. Deglaze* the casserole with 1 cup dry white wine and reduce almost completely until the wine is syrupy. Place the duck breast up in the casserole on the bed of vegetables, and add the braising liquid. For example, you may use 2 cups of Brown Veal or Chicken Stock or duck Giblet Stock, which have been slightly thickened by reduction or with arrowroot. Or you may use 1 cup of Brown Sauce thinned with 1 cup of Brown Stock. The liquid should come about halfway up the sides of the duck.

Now, add a *Bouquet Garni* consisting of 3 sprigs parsley, ½ bay leaf, and a sprig or pinch of thyme, all tied in cheesecloth. Bring the braising liquid to a boil and cover the duck with a piece of buttered paper or foil, cut to fit the casserole, with a small hole punched in it to vent the steam. Cover tightly and place in a 325° oven. (For details of what occurs during the braising process, see Braised Chicken.)

Cook the duck for about 1½ hours, reducing the heat to 300° if the liquid seems to be bubbling too merrily. At the end of this period the legs and thighs should feel soft, not stiff. Probe the thickest part of the thigh with a skewer; a clear yellow juice should run out.

Remove the duck to a hot platter. You may now glaze* the duck by spooning some of its braising liquid (not the fat on top) over it and returning it to the oven. Repeat this operation several times to build up a glossy, transparent coating. In the meantime, remove the bouquet garni from the braising liquid, skim off all the fat, and finish the sauce according to the recipe you are using.

Just as in the braising of beef and chicken, you may cook garnishing vegetables in the casserole along with the duck.

BRAISED DUCK WITH GREEN PEAS (*Caneton Braisé aux Petits Pois*). In an oval casserole chosen to fit the duck snugly, brown in butter 1 cup diced, blanched salt pork or bacon and 1 cup small white onions. Remove the pork and onions and brown the duck in the casserole. Remove the duck and deglaze* the casserole with ½ cup Brown Stock. Return the duck to the casserole and add 1 cup Demi-Glace Sauce; a *Bouquet Garni* consisting of 3 sprigs parsley, ½ bay leaf, and a sprig or pinch of thyme, all tied in cheesecloth; the pork and onions; and 3 cups fresh green peas. Braise the duck and vegetables. Remove the duck to a hot platter, and discard the bouquet garni. Skim the fat from the casserole, and reduce the sauce until it just covers the peas, pork, and onions. Cover the duck with the sauce and garnish.

BRAISED DUCK WITH OLIVES (*Caneton Braisé aux Olives*). Brown the duck in butter in a snug-fitting oval casserole. Remove the duck, pour out the fat, and deglaze* the casserole with 1 cup dry white wine. Reduce the wine almost completely, add 1 cup Brown Stock and 1 cup Brown Sauce, return the duck to the casserole and braise it. Remove the duck to a hot deep platter. Skim the fat from the casserole, strain the sauce, and bring it to the boil. Glaze* the duck, by spooning some of its sauce over it and putting it in a hot oven. Repeat this operation several times until a transparent glaze is built up. To the hot sauce, add 2 cups pitted and blanched green olives. Serve the glazed duck on its platter in a sea of green olives and sauce.

BRAISED DUCK WITH MIXED VEGETABLES (*Caneton Braisé Macédoine*). Braise the duck in 1 cup white wine and 1 cup slightly thickened Brown Veal Stock, brown Chicken Stock, or brown duck Giblet Stock. Glaze* the duck and serve it surrounded with mounds of carrots and turnips cut in olive shapes, sliced green beans, green peas, and kidney beans—all boiled and tossed in butter. Separately serve the sauce in a hot sauceboat.

✳ GOOSE
(*Oie*)

These birds are becoming harder and harder to find at the supermarket, even at Christmastime. This is unfortunate, for the dark, rich, fine-grained meat of goose is exceptionally flavorful both hot and cold.

There are many varieties of geese, but America seems to have settled upon two—the gray Toulouse goose and the white Embden. The goose has escaped the tinkering of geneticists and has remained much the same for decades. Its ability to forage for itself, which made the goose the most populous fowl of poorer realms, is of little advantage today. Today's supermarket goose eats the foods made *de rigueur* by mass production.

Old goose is tough, but the goose you buy at the store will most likely be less than 6 months old, weighing up to 10 pounds, and quite tender. It will be frozen, and can be frozen more successfully than chicken, for example. Like other meats it is best thawed slowly in the refrigerator, and a 10-pound goose will defrost in about 2 days.

The complaint I hear most about goose is that it is too fat. But this is no problem. Proper cooking will drain the fat from the goose, and the fat thus collected is a great prize for your larder. Goose fat is matched only by clarified butter as a superior fat for cooking.

To release the fat from a goose, we need only treat it as we do the fat White Pekin duck. Prick the skin of the goose with a sharp-pointed knife or skewer all around the back and the base of the thighs and breasts to allow the fat to run out during cooking. In fact, we cook goose exactly as we do duck.

To prepare goose for cooking, wash it quickly under running water and dry it thoroughly. Pull out the mass of fat in the cavity and reserve it for rendering (see Fats and Oils). Cut off the wings at the elbows, and simmer these with the neck, gizzard, and heart, onion, carrot, parsley, bay leaf, and thyme, to make a Giblet Stock for the sauce.

ROAST GOOSE
(*Oie Rôtie*)

Goose is roasted like duck. Allow a total cooking time of about 12 minutes per pound for an unstuffed goose, about 15 minutes per pound for a stuffed one. The goose is browned for 20 minutes at 450°, the oven heat is reduced to 350°, and the cooking is completed. As for duck, the goose can be basted with a liquid toward the end of cooking to make its skin very brown and crisp. Roast goose, like roast duck, is best cooked only to the medium or medium-rare stage. The leg muscle should feel soft to the touch, and when the thigh muscle is pricked deeply with a skewer the juices should run faintly pink.

If you stuff the goose with fruit, such as apples or prunes, sew up the cavity and truss it as you would a chicken. If you stuff the goose with a bread-based stuffing, such as sage and onion, you may want to first rid the goose of some of its fat so this will not saturate the stuffing. To do this, prick the skin of the goose as described and heat it in a 375° oven for 15 minutes. Allow the goose to cool, and repeat the process 1 or 2 more times. This will expel much of the fat. Cool the goose, stuff it, and truss it. It is now ready for roasting.

ROAST GOOSE À L'ANGLAISE (*Oie Rôtie à l'Anglaise*). Stuff the goose with traditional Sage and Onion Stuffing. Roast the goose. Serve it and its stuffing with sugared applesauce. Separately serve pan gravy, Bread Sauce, or Parsley Sauce.

ROAST GOOSE WITH POTATOES (*Oie Rôtie aux Pommes de Terre*). Roast the goose. When it is half roasted, drain most of the fat from the baking pan with a bulb baster. Add to the pan the desired amount of half-boiled potatoes, turning them in the pan to coat them with fat. About 15 minutes before the goose is done, add to the pan the desired amount of quartered hard-cooked eggs and brush them with goose fat. Place the goose on a platter, drain fat from the potatoes and eggs, arrange them around the goose, and garnish the platter with watercress. Deglaze* the pan with goose Giblet or Chicken Stock, and thicken with *Beurre Manié* to make pan gravy.

BRAISED GOOSE
(*Oie Braisée*)

Goose is braised like duck, making allowances for the larger size of the goose. It is an excellent method of cooking goose, relieving it of all excess fat.

Clean and dry the goose, stuff it if you wish, truss it, and prick the skin as described above. Brown it in a 450° oven for about 20 minutes. Prepare sufficient braising liquid with white wine and stock according to the proportions given for Braised Duck. Braise the goose in a 325° oven, allowing about 20 minutes per pound. The goose is cooked when the point of a knife can be thrust into the leg without meeting any resistance. The juices, of course, should run clear. To glaze* the goose, uncover it for the final 15 minutes and baste with the braising liquid.

BRAISED GOOSE À L'ALLEMANDE (*Oie Braisée à l'Allemande*). Stuff the goose with peeled, quartered green apples that you have half cooked in butter. Braise the goose. Serve it on a platter surrounded by small whole green apples, peeled, cored, and stewed gently in butter. Garnish the apples with red currant jelly. Separately serve the braising liquid, finished as a sauce.

BRAISED GOOSE WITH HORSERADISH (*Oie Braisée au Raifort*). Braise the goose. Serve it on a platter surrounded with fresh-cooked noodles tossed with butter. Skim, strain, and reduce the braising liquid and sprinkle it over the noodles. Separately serve Albert Sauce.

BRAISED GOOSE À LA BOURGUIGNONNE (*Oie Braisée à la Bourguignonne*). Braise the goose as for Braised Turkey à la Bourguignonne.

✺ 10   *Meat*

> *"Our lodges are red with meat."*
> AMERICAN INDIAN SAYING

When the colonists arrived in America, they joined the ranks of Laplanders, Tartars, and Eskimos as the world's heaviest consumers of meat. Visiting Europeans went home exclaiming with wonder, "Why, they eat meat three times a day!" Much of this early American meat was game, ranging from deer meat to buffalo tongues and beaver tails. Today this exotic diet has been replaced by butcher's meat, and we eat about 30 percent of the world's supply. But before you start thinking you are too well fed, I must point out that the Argentinians, Uruguayans, Australians, and New Zealanders all eat more meat per person than we do.

Although a small amount of rabbit and goat meat is raised, butcher's meat in America consists almost entirely of beef, veal, pork, and lamb. For cooking purposes, these meats are divided into two classifications. Beef and lamb are red meats, full of juice; beef may be eaten rare, and lamb may be eaten rare or medium rare. Veal and pork are dry white meats, and they must be eaten well done. Aside from these, all other meats eaten in America are game.

(It is interesting to contemplate the domestication of other animals for addition to our meat supply. An attempt has been made to introduce herds of caribou in Maine. The squandered American bison, if its ill temper can be curbed, might be returned to the American table. These huge beasts grow to weigh more than a ton. Today there are 30,000 of them in the West. They were so wantonly slaughtered that these 30,000 are descendants of bison from New York's Bronx Zoo.)

Meat, like poultry, is now scientifically raised on special feeds that speed the animals to market. As a result, the meat we eat is from animals considerably younger than were marketed just a few years ago. This meat is more tender, finer-grained, and generally less flavorful than the meat of older animals. It requires less cooking than the meat you bought in 1960, and more than ever it requires a good searing and browning to preserve and develop its flavor.

Now, I want to warn you of a continuing threat hanging over us all. Some of the people who distribute our meat, desirous of making their own lives easier, are pressing a plan that will put an end to America's supply of fresh meat. The plan is to centrally cut the meat in retail-size cuts, package it, freeze it, and then get you to buy it. The plan is called "centralized meat packaging." This means a side of beef can go down an assembly line and be cut up, not by butchers, but by anyone who can be taught to slice a chop here or saw a bone there. The retail-sized cuts are then frozen and distributed with no fear of immediate or apparent spoilage. This scheme will be presented to you with a "massive consumer re-education program" to convince you that this is a convenient, superior way to buy your meat. It is not.

When meat is frozen, ice crystals form inside it. These crystals physically crush the meat's tissues and wring their juices from them. When the meat is thawed, even carefully, much of its juices leak out. Poke the meat and you will find it soft and mushy. Some methods of freezing are better than others, because smaller-sized ice crystals are formed. But the meat is damaged nevertheless, and this meat can never be as juicy and flavorful as when it was fresh.

You should also be fully aware that frozen meat, like fresh meat, will spoil. On its way to becoming totally inedible, it progressively loses its flavor. Fresh meat announces when it has lost its bloom; frozen meat is inscrutable. You never know what you have until the meat is taken home and thawed.

Clean, fresh meat does not spoil readily, and the fresh meat you buy at the supermarket or butcher shop is most likely about 10 days old, which is the time it takes to route the meat through the channels of distribution. The meat, which should be in large pieces and protected by its own fat, is always refrigerated, of course. During this period the meat develops flavor and tenderness by a process known as aging; that is, the meat is improved by this leisurely trip to market. The rib and loin of beef and lamb are sometimes deliberately aged for up to 6 weeks, and you will pay a premium price for this special treatment.

Fresh meat will continue to age in your refrigerator, although small pieces, stripped of their protective fat, should be used within 5 days. Keep the meat loosely wrapped so that there is air circulation over its surface.

Although we speak of cooking beef, pork, veal, and lamb, in practice most of our fresh meat cookery is concerned with beef. We are now eating 110 pounds of beef per person a year, compared to 65 pounds of pork (a large proportion of which is cured as ham, bacon, or sausage), and just 3 or 4 pounds of veal and 3 or 4 pounds of lamb. There are reasons for this imbalance, and we will examine some of them in the pages ahead.

❋ BEEF
(Boeuf)

The people of every beef-raising country think their beef is best. The English are great cattle breeders, and the cattle of all large beef-raising nations share an English ancestry. The French are very fussy about their beef, and the famous Charolais, Limousin, Normandy, and other oxen are painstakingly graded even to the degree of plow pulling they may have done during their long lives. The Indians raise more cattle than anyone else (with a cattle population more than double that of the United States), and although they do not eat beef, Indian Brahman cattle are breeding stock for new varieties all over the world. The Japanese, perhaps, are the most prideful of all. They quench the thirsts of their famous Matsuzaka beef with great draughts of beer to make them hungrier; they burn incense in their comfortable stalls to keep the mosquitoes away; and every day they massage the great beasts to distribute their fat more evenly.

Just a few years ago, American cattle roamed the range in the great Western tradition. They grazed on range grasses, some of them were grain-fattened in feed lots, and in 3 years' time they arrived on our tables as beef. Today these same animals, penned up and fed computerized diets, are frequently ready for market in less than 1½ years. Their meat is finer-grained and more tender than that of range beef. It also contains more interior fat, which makes the meat juicy and flavorful. But it does not have the full flavor of the older, tougher, range-exercised animals. Their lean, flavorful meat is less and less available in the United States, and that which is still produced goes to the meat processors.

In the early 1960's this new American beef was shipped to Europe in hopes of creating a new market. But Europeans didn't like it. They found it "too mushy" for their taste. They preferred their own tough, stringier beef produced by grass-fed range cattle. They also prefer their cattle big.

American beef has become increasingly lighter and the cuts smaller, reflecting the commercial practice of slaughtering the animal before it can eat too much of its expensive antibiotic feed. Average weight ranges from 1100 to 1400 pounds. The younger and smaller the beef, the more it is like old veal, and old veal is not fit to eat. Some parts of the country resist these small cuts and are eating more flavorful beef as a reward for their resistance.

Although we might lament the absence of older, more flavorful beef for making stocks and *pot-au-feu,* a thick American steak, tender as butter, is a great consolation. Some of this beef is so tender, particularly after aging, that cuts of rump or round can be broiled like steaks, and chuck roasted like sirloin. One way to tell if a normally tough cut of beef is this tender is to press your finger deeply into the beef and *feel* how soft it is.

The finest beef is Prime grade beef, sold directly to expensive restaurants. Almost all beef sold in supermarkets and butcher shops is now Choice grade beef. As I have said, America produces very little beef of leaner, lower grades than these. Much of the lower grade beef used in canned meat and sausage products is imported.

When the government inspector stamps "Choice" on a piece of meat, that is not the end of your problem. Some Choice is better than other Choice, and you must pick and choose among the pieces offered. Some sellers consistently offer a better quality of Choice than others, and there are few people in life who can do more for your table than a good, conscientious butcher. Find one and stay with him. And, just to keep him interested, look closely at the meat you buy.

Fine beef is a bright red cherry color, not pinkish (too young), not brown (drying out), not dark red (too old or too lean). It has a bluish color where freshly cut, but this will turn brilliant red after a few minutes' exposure to the air. Also, large cuts of well-aged meat may have a crusty, blackish surface where the lean is exposed to the air; this is normal.

The flesh is fine-grained, particularly when the cut is taken from the rib or loin. Less tender cuts are coarser in grain but not overly so. Teach your eye by observing the grain closely in all the beef you buy. Fine beef is soft-looking, satiny in appearance, and smooth to the touch.

There are small drifts and flecks of fat intermixed with the lean. This fat, called marbling, is evidence of additional microscopic grains of fat spread throughout the lean. This fat melt and bastes the inside of the meat as you cook it, keeping it juicy, providing a "juiciness" of its own and contributing importantly to the flavor of the meat.

Larger chunks of fat, surrounding and in between the large muscles, are firm to the touch and creamy white in color. It is neither translucent nor greasy, but rather opaque and dry, crumbly, and brittle in texture.

When you poke the meat lightly, it feels firm and resilient to your touch, and the impression left by your finger quickly fills in again. The bones are red and porous where cut.

Finally, good fresh beef smells fresh and clean with no "heavy" odor.

THE CUTS OF BEEF

For cooking purposes we can organize the beef carcass into four categories. The first category is the tenderest, and is roasted, poëléed, sautéed, grilled, or broiled. The second category is tougher, and it is braised, pot-roasted, or stewed. The third category is exceedingly tough and is stewed or used for soup. The fourth category includes the variety meats, which are prepared in many different ways.

THE FIRST CATEGORY OF BEEF

Proceeding from front to back, this category consists of the rib section, the loin section, and the sirloin section. Large cuts from this section are almost always roasted or poëléed, and the steaks are sautéed, grilled, or broiled.

THE RIB SECTION supplies us with the magnificent rib roast standing on its rack of bones. The roast contains a large muscle called the eye of the rib. When this muscle is stripped out of the rib roast, it becomes a Delmonico or rib eye roast. *Cut into steaks,* these roasts become rib steaks, boneless rib steaks, and Delmonico or rib eye steaks.

THE LOIN AND SIRLOIN SECTIONS provide a huge roast that includes the entire side of beef beginning at the end of the ribs and continuing to the rump. This roast is rarely seen whole, and is more likely to be seen divided into its loin and sirloin sections. *Cut into steaks,* from front to back, this roast gives us the club steak, the T-bone steak, the porterhouse steak, and the sirloin steaks—pin bone sirloin, flat bone sirloin, and wedge bone sirloin.

If you remove the tenderloin, which is the tender inside muscle running almost the entire length of the loin and sirloin sections, the roast is then known as a shell of beef, a top loin roast, or top sirloin roast. *Cut into steaks,* it provides top loin steaks (also called New York strip or Kansas City steaks) and top sirloin steaks.

The tenderloin itself provides a roast, and it, too, can be cut into steaks. In America, the roast is known as a tenderloin roast, and the steaks as tenderloin or filet mignon steaks. (The French, who because of the way they cut their beef have many more tenderloins on hand than Americans do, divide the tenderloin into five different kinds of steaks, as we shall see.)

THE SECOND CATEGORY OF BEEF

This category of beef spreads out from the tender central section to include the rump, the round (rear leg), the chuck (shoulder and arm), the brisket and plate (breast), and the flank (belly).

THE RUMP gives us the rump roast, bone-in or boned and rolled, which is pot-roasted or braised. It also gives us the rump steak, which is the portion of the rump nearest the sirloin. It is rather tough.

THE ROUND gives us the top and bottom round roasts, the eye of round roast, and the sirloin tip roast, all of which are lean, tough, dry, and flavorful. They should be pot-roasted or braised. From this section we also get the round steak (which can be divided into top round—the most tender; bottom round; and eye of round steaks) and the sirloin tip steak, all of which are tough, and the cube steak, which is pounded into tenderness.

THE CHUCK gives us the chuck roasts, both blade and arm roast cuts, which are very flavorful for pot roasts and braising. The blade cuts are more tender than the arm cuts. (Note the shape of the blade bone. The tenderest of the blade cuts are nearest the rib and contain the straight, flat blade bone. As you proceed toward the neck, which is tougher, this bone becomes shorter and a ridge forms on it giving it the shape of a "7". The shorter and more pronounced this "7," the tougher the meat will be.) Blade or chuck steaks are sometimes cut from the chuck, but they are gristly and not dependable for broiling. Steaks cut from the arm are tougher still. Two ways to distinguish arm steaks from round steaks is that the round arm steak bone is near the uncut end of the steak, and close to this bone is a distinctive round muscle of darker-colored lean meat that contains noticeable amounts of connective tissue.

THE BRISKET provides a boneless piece that is frequently made into corned beef. Fresh brisket is excellent for boiling. The lean and fat are in layers, the lean being relatively thick.

THE PLATE gives us juicy plate beef, containing alternating layers of fat, lean, and bone, which makes it excellent for boiling and making *pot-au-feu*. The plate may also be rolled and tied for pot-roasting or braising, or cut into little rounds called skirt steaks. This section also gives us the short ribs, which are the ends of the ribs taken from the rib roast. They contain a good layer of flavorful lean and are excellent braised.

THE FLANK produces the flank steak (a coarse-fibered cut that is scored with a knife in crisscross fashion). This piece is often sold as London broil, which is made tender by cooking rare and carving thin.

THE THIRD CATEGORY OF BEEF

This consists of the bony extremities—the neck, the ends of the legs (shank or shin), and the tail—which are stewed or used for soup.

THE FOURTH CATEGORY OF BEEF

The fourth and final category of beef includes all the variety meats— liver, kidney, brains, sweetbreads, heart, tongue, and tripe. These range from being very lean and tough to very fat and tender.

COOKING BEEF

Beef is the great laboratory of protein cookery because every conceivable variety of meat is found on the carcass. There are fat ribs and lean rounds, tender sirloins and tough flanks, full-flavored chuck and delicately flavored filet. Other meats are more consistent than beef. Veal is lean; lamb is tender; pork is fat. But beef is a bit of everything, and once you understand how it is cooked you can apply the basic methods to any meat, fish, or fowl that falls into your hands.

What happens when meat is cooked has already been discussed in Chapter 3. If you are at all in doubt as to what goes on inside a sirloin roast you are roasting or a piece of rump simmering in a *pot-au-feu*, you can turn back to this section and refresh your memory now.

Very briefly, beef is mature red meat, containing cuts both tough and tender. The proteins of beef, like those of other meats, begin to coagulate at 140°. At this temperature beef is *fully cooked* to the rare stage. Tender cuts of beef contain less flavor than the tough cuts, and they should be cooked rare or medium rare because cooking beyond this point will usually toughen them, dry them, and destroy their flavor. Tough cuts of beef must be cooked slowly with moist heat until well done to soften their connective tissues. They survive this longer cooking because they are more flavorful, and because the flavor they lose is recaptured in their sauce or broth.

✳ BOILED BEEF
(Boeuf Bouilli)

The French treatment of hot boiled beef is limited almost entirely to one centuries-old dish, the *Pot-au-Feu*. There are many recipes for leftover boiled beef, but common sense suggests that by putting a larger-than-necessary piece of meat into the pot-au-feu you will enjoy your triumvirate of hot beef, bouillon, and vegetables and get the leftover boiled beef you need, too. You will find the recipe for pot-au-feu in Chapter 6. If you do not choose to serve the bouillon from the pot-au-feu, here is a variation for hot boiled beef:

BEEF WITH COARSE SALT (*Boeuf au Gros Sel*). Poach the beef with garnishing vegetables. Serve the hot vegetables and the hot beef with coarse salt, Cornichons (pickled gherkins), and Dijon Mustard, and/or Horseradish Sauce.

Boiled beef is almost always taken from the less tender parts of the animal. There is one exception in which the most unlikely cut of all, the filet of beef, is poached.

FILET OF BEEF ON A STRING (*Filet de Boeuf Ficelle à la Vilette*). (A *ficelle* is a piece of string; La Vilette is the largest slaughter house in Paris.) Brown a piece of filet or other tender cut of boneless meat. Tie it well with butcher's twine, leaving a long trailing piece of string to lift the meat with. Plunge the meat into boiling rich Brown Stock and simmer it for about 15 minutes per pound. Lift it regularly with its piece of string to test for doneness. The meat is retrieved from the pot while it is still very rare (squashy in the center), before it has time to dry and toughen. Serve with a garnish of boiled vegetables.

There are many recipes for leftover boiled beef, and I will list some of these presently.

✳ BRAISED BEEF

Braised beef is the greatest triumph of French cooking. The sheer flavor that saturates this meat astounds the taste. Its succulence is unequaled in all of cooking. Its tenderness and texture are inexplicable. It is at once firm without resistance, juicy without moistness. It is like carving, chewing, and swallowing a rich brown sauce. It bathes the throat in a savory glory. It is a mystery. And it takes some careful cooking.

I am going to give you two recipes for basic braised beef—a full dress one and a shorter one. Both produce excellent results. Both let you taste the true taste of braised beef. Both will provoke cries for "More!" so you must plan on more meat per serving than you would ordinarily allow. We will begin with the grand recipe.

BRAISED BEEF IN THE GRAND MANNER
(*Boeuf Braisé à la Grande Manière*)

Beef, a 5-pound roast from the rump, round, or chuck
Larding fat (optional)
Salt, 2 teaspoons
Pepper, ½ teaspoon
Thyme, 2 teaspoons
Red wine, dry, 3 cups
Brandy, ¼ cup (optional)
Olive oil, 4 tablespoons
Bay leaf, 1
Garlic, 1 clove, peeled
Parsley, 3 sprigs
Carrot, 1 medium

Onion, 1 medium
Celery, 1 rib
Beef fat or oil, 2 to 4 tablespoons
Barding fat (optional)
Brown Stock, 3 to 4 cups
Brown Sauce, 1 to 1½ cups; or ⅔ cup Starch-Thickened Brown Stock to ⅓ cup Tomato Purée
A heavy skillet for browning the meat
A heavy braising pan that just fits the meat

The procedure can be divided into 7 steps—marinating, larding (may be omitted), browning, the first cooking, the second cooking, glazing, and the making of the sauce.

Beef for braising is cut in smaller pieces than beef roasts. The sauce must percolate through the beef, so it must not be overly large—6 to 8 pounds at most. The classic French cut for braising is a piece from the rump, called the *pièce de boeuf*.

The meat should be a compact, chunky roast cut in one piece. These roasts are usually referred to as pot roasts: rump, chuck, sirloin tip, eye of round, top round, and bottom round. (A rolled and tied roast will do, but let us be purists in this recipe; by knowing what is best, we can compromise intelligently when we must.)

Examine the roast carefully. American beef usually has enough fat marbling to eliminate the need for larding. But the rump, round, and sirloin tip are exceptionally lean parts of beef. Larding will improve them, making them juicier, more flavorful, and more tender. Now is a good time to reread the detailed instructions for larding* in Chapter 3. And do not neglect to marinate the lardoons in brandy and spices.

Whether you lard or not, the next step is to marinate the meat. Rub the roast all over with salt, freshly ground pepper, and thyme. Work these well into the surface of the meat. Place the meat in a dish or bowl just large enough to hold it, and pour over it dry red wine, brandy if you prefer, and olive oil. Add to this marinade crumbled bay leaf, garlic, and parsley.

Roll the meat over and over in this marinade, thoroughly impregnating its surface with the wine and oil. Then add to the marinade carrot, onion, and celery, all sliced. Push these vegetables down into the liquid, soaking them thoroughly. Then heap half of them on top of the roast to keep the top moist and to transfer their flavor to the meat.

Leave the meat to marinate for 6 to 8 hours at room temperature, or from 18 to 24 hours in the refrigerator. (These are minimums; you can marinate the meat in the refrigerator for up to 4 days.) Frequently turn the meat over in the marinade, soaking all surfaces as you do so, and heap part of the marinade-soaked vegetables on top of it. About ½ hour before cooking, remove the meat and the vegetables and allow them to drain, reserving the liquid.

Dry the meat thoroughly so it will not steam, and brown the meat so that it will not give up its juices too soon. Heat beef fat or oil to the smoking point in the braising pan (or better yet, in a separate skillet to make browning easier and more effective). Brown it on all sides and ends, turning to obtain a good brown crust. Use wooden spoons or a skimmer to turn the meat; do not poke holes in it.

Remove the meat and tie it from side to side and fore and aft with butcher's twine. There should be a binding of string every 1½ inches. If the meat is very lean with little covering fat of its own (and particularly if you have not larded it), you can bard* the meat with thin sheets of fresh pork or beef fat tied securely in place.

Next brown the vegetables used in the marinade, first removing the parsley. Add more fat to the pan if needed, and stir the vegetables to brown them on all sides—their total surface is quite extensive and will impart a good brown color and flavor to the sauce.

When the vegetables are well browned, pour over them the liquid marinade. Cook briskly for a few minutes, scraping up and dissolving the solidified juices in the pan with a wooden spatula. Then restore the parsley from the marinade to the pan, and place the meat on top of this bed of aromatic vegetables. (If you performed the browning in a separate skillet, deglaze* the skillet and pour liquid and vegetables into the braising pan.) Cover the pan and cook briskly, reducing the wine from the marinade until it has a syrupy consistency.

After the wine is reduced, add hot Brown Stock to the pan. Ideally, the liquid should come just barely to the surface of the roast. (If the braising pan is too large, too much liquid is needed and it will require additional reduction to make the sauce when cooking is finished.) Bring the liquid to a boil. Cover the roast with a piece of buttered paper or foil cut to fit the size of the pan. Cut a small hole in this paper to vent steam. Cover the pan tightly and put it into a 325° oven.

You are now performing the first cooking of the meat. After it has been in the oven for 15 minutes, check to see that the liquid is simmering gently; if it is beginning to boil, reduce the heat to 300°. The first cooking will take about 3 hours. Check from time to time to see that the liquid is not boiling, which toughens the meat. As the heat penetrates the roast, inner pressures build up. You will see the roast straining against its binding of strings, particularly at the narrow ends, which bulge from the pressure. Poke the meat and it seems to reverberate inside—the center is still jellylike. (As an experiment, pierce the meat with a poultry skewer. The juices spurt from the hole, driven by pressure built up inside by the heat.)

In about 3 hours the roast will have stiffened. It will no longer reverberate when you poke it. Probe it with a skewer. Juices will run out. If they are red, leave the meat to cook a little longer. When the center of the roast becomes hot enough (about 140°) the last of the liquid protein will coagulate, the juices will lose their red color and run clear, the meat will be just well done, and the first cooking will be completed.

Remove the pan from the oven, and remove the meat from the pan. Poke the meat. You will find it is quite stiff, almost hard. The meat is now at its toughest, much tougher than it would have been if you had removed it while the center was still rare. The muscle fibers have toughened, and the connective tissue has not yet softened. But we shall reduce this meat to melting tenderness during the second cooking.

You will notice that the liquid in the pan has reduced somewhat during cooking. Put the pan on a burner and reduce it still more, to about ½ of its original volume. Then strain the liquid, discard the vegetables and seasonings, clean the pan, and return the strained liquid to it.

We will now make the sauce. Add to the strained liquid, which should be about 1 or 1½ cups, an equal volume of Brown Sauce. If you do not have brown sauce on hand, use a tomato-flavored Starch-Thickened Brown Stock. (To ⅔ cup of starch-thickened brown stock add ⅓ cup Tomato Purée or 2 medium tomatoes, chopped.) Put the meat back into the pan, roll it in the sauce, bring the sauce to a boil, replace the buttered paper or foil, cover the pan, and put it back into a 325° oven for the second cooking.

During the second cooking the meat softens, relaxes, and pours forth its juices into the sauce. The sauce, in turn, penetrates the relaxed and porous meat, enriching it with its own juices, which have been themselves enriched, and creating a succulence in the meat no other method of cooking can equal. The meat is literally saturated with sauce, impregnated inside and out.

There is a danger to be faced during this second cooking. The meat is no longer covered or mostly covered by liquid. Half of it or more stands high and must not be allowed to get dry. You must baste frequently during the second cooking. And you must turn the roast regularly, to allow its upper half to receive its communion with the sauce. Do not shirk your duty at this point. The end is in sight, and the reward is magnificent.

Two hours should suffice to complete the second cooking. Toward the end of this period poke the meat with your fingers. Notice how it has softened. You have some freedom here. If dinner is held up, just reduce the oven heat; the meat will even gain by the delay. The meat is done when you can push a knife into it without meeting *any* resistance. The meat will be solid and firm for cutting. But the point of a knife will enter it as if it were soft butter.

Now, the final touches. Remove the meat from the pan, remove its bard if it has one, and remove the trussing strings. Place it on a hot serving platter, brush over it some of its sauce, and put it in a warm oven to glaze.* The gelatinous sauce will set quickly. Paint it with sauce again. Repeat this procedure 8 times if you wish, building up layer after layer of transparent glaze through which guests can peer at the meat. It is one of the most magnificent views French cookery has to offer.

In the meantime, finish the sauce. Skim off the fat, strain the sauce through a sieve lined with two layers of rinsed and wrung-out cheesecloth, allow it to rest for a few minutes, and skim again. Taste and add salt if necessary. Everything else is already there. The sauce should roll softly over the bowl of a wooden spoon. If it is too thin, reduce it. If too thick, thin it with a little brown stock. Serve the sauce in a hot sauceboat.

And eat the braised beef.

BRAISED BEEF, HOME STYLE
(*Boeuf Braisé Chez Vous*)

The preceding recipe is not overly tedious, yet to some degree it is a labor of love. By all means make it for company if you enjoy wild acclaim. For everyday cooking you can still enjoy the good taste of braised beef by making a few adroit short cuts in the grand recipe. The result may not be so elegant to see, but I must confess this recipe produces braised beef that tastes every bit as good as you will get from the fussier recipe. And it is the taste that counts most. If you compare the two recipes, you will find that no essential ingredient or important procedure has been unaccounted for.

Beef, a 5-pound roast, standing or rolled, preferably from the chuck, with some fat inside it
Salt, 2 teaspoons
Pepper, ½ teaspoon
Thyme, 2 teaspoons
Red wine, dry, 3 cups
Olive oil, 4 tablespoons
Bay leaf, 1
Garlic, 1 clove, peeled
Parsley, 3 sprigs
Carrot, 1 medium, sliced
Onion, 1 medium, sliced
Celery, 1 rib, sliced
Beef fat or oil, 2 to 4 tablespoons
Brown Stock, 3 to 4 cups
Arrowroot or cornstarch, 3 to 4 teaspoons
Vegetables—of your choice, to cook and serve with the meat (see below)
A heavy braising pan that just fits the meat and vegetables
A heavy skillet for browning the meat

Choose the roast from a flavorful portion of the animal that is not overly lean. The shoulder or chuck is well interspersed with fat. Thus the roast comes to you naturally larded.* Rub it with salt, pepper, and thyme.

Marinate if you have time in red wine, olive oil, crumbled bay leaf, garlic, parsley, carrot, onion, and celery. Two hours marinating at room temperature will accomplish much. If you do not have time to marinate, proceed to the next step.

Thoroughly dry the roast, brown it in beef fat or oil, and tie it if necessary. Brown the vegetables listed above, whether or not you used them to marinate. Deglaze* the pan with the marinating liquor, or 3 cups of dry red wine if you did not marinate. Put roast, vegetables, and seasonings into the braising pan. Cover and boil down until the liquid is syrupy. Add brown stock, bring to a boil, cover the meat with buttered paper or foil into which you have cut a little hole, cover the pan tightly, and place it in a 325° oven. Look inside after 15 minutes to make sure the liquid is just simmering, not boiling.

Cooking time is the same as in the grand recipe, about 5 hours all told. This time, however, you are going to combine the first and second cookings. No lugging roasts in and out of pans for you. You will remove the roast from the pan only when it is ready to eat.

After about 3 hours of cooking, remove the pan from the oven and place it on a burner. Mix arrowroot or cornstarch in a few tablespoons of water. Little by little, stir this mixture into the liquid in the pan over a moderate fire. When the sauce sufficiently thickens, spoon some of it over the roast.

Now place in the pan with the roast whatever vegetables you choose to eat. Carrots, small onions, small potatoes or potato balls, and peas are typical selections. Bring the sauce to a boil, re-cover the roast with its paper or foil, cover the pan, and return it to a 325° oven. Baste frequently with the sauce until the roast is done, in about 2 hours. It is cooked when the point of a knife thrust into it meets no resistance whatsoever.

Remove the roast and the garnishing vegetables to a hot platter. Roughly skim the sauce of fat and strain it—the fat is not completely removed in this kind of dish, as it adds richness and flavor. Pour the sauce over the roast and the vegetables, and sprinkle with a little chopped parsley. That is all, except to say that a calf's or pig's foot braised along with the roast will do wonders for the sauce. Serve its meat with the roast.

8 VARIATIONS ON BRAISED BEEF

Boeuf à la Mode is the most renowned braised dish in French cooking. Wherever in the world you order *boeuf à la mode,* you should get it as described in the following recipe, complete with the meat from the calf's feet. Other braised beef dishes on the menu can be usually recognized by the title *pièce de boeuf,* braised beef often receiving this name whether or not it is made from the true *pièce de boeuf* (rump).

Roasts from the first category of beef are also braised—moderately sized pieces from the rib, sirloin, and even whole filet. To my mind, however, it seems foolish to braise these roasts in home cookery in as much as these pieces are eminently roastable, can be enjoyed rare, and are not as good for braising as the tougher, more flavorful, and less expensive cuts.

BEEF À LA MODE (*Boeuf à la Mode*). This masterpiece of home cooking was appropriated, named, and elevated to *haute cuisine* by an eighteenth-century Paris restaurant, Le Boeuf à la Mode. Lard* the beef, rub it with salt, pepper, and nutmeg, and marinate* it. Braise it along with one or more blanched calf's feet. When ¾ cooked, skim the fat from the braising liquid, strain, and return the liquid to the pan. Remove the calf's feet, cut their meat into small square pieces, and return these pieces to the pan. Also put into the pan carrots cut in olive shapes and small onions, both vegetables half cooked and glazed* in butter. When the meat is done, put it on a hot platter, glaze it until it gleams, and surround it with the vegetables and the calf meat.

Skim fat from the braising liquor, reduce to thicken if necessary, and serve separately in a sauceboat.

BRAISED BEEF À LA BOURGEOISE (*Pièce de Boeuf à la Bourgeoise*). Proceed as for Beef à la Mode (above), but use white wine instead of red wine when making the marinade.

BRAISED BEEF À LA LORRAINE (*Pièce de Boeuf à la Lorraine*). Lard* (if necessary), marinate,* braise, and glaze* the beef. Serve with balls of Braised Cabbage, separately braised in red wine, and Potatoes Fondantes. Separately serve the reduced braising liquor and grated horseradish or Horseradish Sauce.

BRAISED BEEF À LA NOAILLES (*Pièce de Boeuf à la Noailles*). Lard* (if necessary), marinate,* and braise the beef in its marinade mixed with Starch-Thickened Brown Veal Stock. When ½ cooked, add 8 medium onions, minced and lightly sautéed in butter, and ¼ cup raw rice. When the meat is done, remove, trim, and slice it. Rub the vegetables remaining in the pan through a fine sieve. Place a spoonful of this between the beef slices, and reassemble the roast in its original shape. Pour the rest of the sauce over the beef, sprinkle with buttered breadcrumbs and melted butter, and brown it in the oven.

BRAISED BEEF À LA LYONNAISE (*Pièce de Boeuf à la Lyonnaise*). Lard* (if necessary) marinate,* braise, and glaze* the beef. Serve it with braised Stuffed Onions and Potatoes Fondantes. Separately serve Lyonnaise Sauce in a hot sauceboat.

BRAISED BEEF À LA BOURGUIGNONNE (*Pièce de Boeuf à la Bourguignonne*). Lard* (if necessary), marinate* in a red wine marinade, and braise the beef in its marinade mixed with ¼ part Brown Sauce and ¾ part Starch-Thickened Brown Veal Stock. When ⅔ cooked, skim and strain the braising liquor and return it to the pan with quartered mushrooms, small onions, and diced blanched bacon, all half cooked in butter. When the meat is done, glaze* it, place it on a hot platter, and surround it with the vegetables. Roughly skim the sauce of fat, thicken it by reduction if necessary, and pour over the meat and the vegetables.

BRAISED BEEF À L'ALSACIENNE (*Pièce de Boeuf à l'Alsacienne*). Lard* (if necessary), marinate,* braise, and glaze* the beef. Surround it with poached pork sausage slices, boiled potatoes, and braised sauerkraut. Separately serve the reduced braising liquor in a hot sauceboat.

BRAISED BEEF À LA FLAMANDE (*Pièce de Boeuf à la Flamande*). Lard* (if necessary), marinate,* braise, and glaze* the beef. Surround it with balls of Braised Cabbage, dice of bacon and slices of Italian sausage cooked with the cabbage; carrots and turnips cut into olive shapes and simmered in butter; and boiled potatoes. Separately serve the reduced braising liquor in a hot sauceboat.

✳ *BEEF STEWS*

A beef stew is beef braised in small pieces. The braising time is usually shorter than for large cuts of meat, because the small pieces cook more quickly. Nevertheless, the meat undergoes the same braising treatment—toughening as it cooks to the well-done stage, then relaxing and softening as its connective tissue breaks down and the sauce penetrates the meat.

Beef stews are very variable, and there is a long series of options you have in the cooking of these stews. The exercise or nonexercise of these options changes the character of a stew as fully as a variation of its ingredients. The important options are: whether or not the meat is marinated; whether or not each piece is larded; whether or not the meat is browned; whether it is cooked in a thickened sauce or in liquid; whether a lot of liquid is added to the pot, or just a little; whether or not the sauce is skimmed, strained, seasoned, and returned to the pot part way through cooking (as in a classic, full-dress braising); whether or not the meat is served with garnishing vegetables; and whether or not these vegetables are cooked in the same pot with the meat. About all that is common to all beef stews is that they are covered and cooked slowly in a flavorful liquid with aromatic vegetables.

The beef stews of France masquerade under different names. These names come to us from the provinces, or from the distant past, or from abroad. In as much as many well-known stews have not been admitted to *haute cuisine,* terminology is somewhat vague. If you have a good recipe for beef stews, you may not much care whether it is a ragout, a *daube,* an *estouffade,* a goulash, or *carbonades.* Yet it is good to be as precise as possible in these matters, so you may at all times know what you are about. Classification of stews is also an excellent aid to remembering recipes.

Consequently I will list for you what I consider to be most characteristic for each of the different stews, and give you one or two recipes for each. You will always be able to find recipes that do not fit the pattern, but as I said, this whole business of stew making is terminologically vague.

RAGOUTS

Ragoût is the French name for stew. Ragouts are brown or white. For brown ragouts (*à brun*) the meat is browned; for white ragouts (*à blanc*) it is not. When I think of a ragout, however, I conceive it mostly as beef pieces that have been marinated, sometimes larded, browned, cooked in a thickening sauce made with brown stock, red wine, and the marinating liquid, and served in a not too thick sauce with vegetables that may or may not have cooked along with the meat.

Beef à la bourguignonne is the best-known of French ragouts. Of all typically French dishes, it is probably the one most often cooked in American homes. There is danger in too easy familiarity, however, and slipshod cooking of this fine stew threatens to discredit it. If you find your beef à la bourguignonne is not getting the acclaim the dish deserves, follow this recipe carefully. Omit nothing. The pork rind in this dish is every bit as important as the beef, adding a special succulence to the sauce. And be sure the beef is taken from the tougher, more flavorful cuts; expensive meat will spoil the stew. The cooking of this dish is similar to beef braised in the grand manner.

BEEF À LA BOURGUIGNONNE
(*Boeuf à la Bourguignonne*)

Beef, 4 pounds lean rump, chuck, or round, cut in 2-inch cubes
Salt, 1 teaspoon
Pepper, ¼ teaspoon
Red Burgundy wine, 3 cups
Carrot, 1, thinly sliced
Onion, 1, thinly sliced
Parsley, 3 sprigs
Bay leaf, 1, crumbled
Thyme, a pinch
Garlic, 3 cloves, crushed
Bacon, fresh pork fat or salt pork with rind, ½ pound
Lard, 1 tablespoon

Sugar, ½ teaspoon
Flour, 3 tablespoons
Tomato Purée, 3 tablespoons
Brown Stock, 3 to 4 cups
Small white onions, 24
Clarified Butter, 4 tablespoons
Mushrooms, 1 pound, halved or quartered
Parsley, 3 tablespoons chopped
A heavy skillet or frying pan in which to brown the meat
A heavy casserole with tight-fitting lid

Season the meat with salt and pepper. Marinate it for 4 hours in wine, to which you have added carrot, onion, parsley, bay leaf, thyme, and garlic.

Cut the rind from bacon, fresh pork fat, or salt pork, and save the rind. Cut the fat into Lardoons, little sticks of fat ¼ inch thick and 1½ inches long. If you are using bacon or salt pork, simmer the lardoons in water for 5 minutes to remove their cured or salt taste, drain and dry them. Lightly sauté the lardoons in lard. Remove from the pan.

Drain the meat, reserving the marinade. Thoroughly dry each piece of beef and brown it on all sides in the very hot lard. Do not crowd the pieces; they must not steam. Remove the meat, lower the heat slightly, and in the pan brown the sliced carrot and sliced onion from the marinade, sprinkling them with sugar to help them brown and to add a good brown color to the stew.

Next, pour off the fat from the pan. Return to it the beef and lardoons, and sprinkle with flour, stirring to coat the beef and brown the flour without burning. (Or place the pan in a hot 450° oven, stirring once or twice until the flour is browned, in about 10 minutes.)

Place the pork rind in the bottom of a heavy casserole, and add the beef, lardoons, and browned vegetables. Deglaze* the skillet with the marinade, and pour this into the casserole along with the parsley, bay leaf, and garlic cloves it contains. Add tomato purée and brown stock to just cover the meat. Bring the liquid to a boil, cover the casserole tightly, and place it in a 325° oven. Cooking time is about 4 hours. The meat is done when a knife pierces it with no resistance whatsoever. Turn the meat a few times in the sauce. Do not overcook or the meat will become dry and stringy.

About 1 hour before the meat is done, separately brown white onions in clarified butter and simmer them in brown stock or red wine until just tender. Also sauté in butter halved or quartered mushrooms (depending upon the mushrooms' size) and keep warm.

When the meat is done, remove the beef and the lardoons. Strain the sauce into a saucepan, and discard the pork rind. Clean the casserole and return the beef and lardoons to it, and place the onions and mushrooms on top of the meat. Skim the sauce of fat. The sauce should just coat a spoon. If it is too thin, thicken by reducing it or stir in a little *Beurre Manié*. Pour the sauce over the meat and vegetables, and serve the stew in the casserole accompanied by potatoes or noodles.

BEEF STEW WITH VEGETABLES (*Ragoût de Boeuf aux Légumes Diverses*). Prepare the stew as in Beef à la Bourguignonne (above). Separately prepare such vegetables as carrots cut in olive shapes and braised in butter; small white onions sautéed in butter and finished in stock; boiled potatoes; braised hearts of celery; turnips cut in olive shapes, parboiled and glazed in butter. Also, you may cook along with the beef 3 tomatoes, peeled, seeded, and chopped. For a less rich stew, omit the lardoons.

BEEF STEW WITH RED WINE (*Ragoût de Boeuf au Vin Rouge*). Cut 4 pounds lean beef into 2-inch cubes. Dredge the beef in flour and brown it in a skillet. Remove the beef to a heavy casserole, and lightly brown ¾ cup each of chopped carrots, onions, and leeks; 2 tablespoons chopped chives; and 2 cloves garlic, crushed. Pour 3 tablespoons flaming brandy over the meat in the casserole. Add the chopped vegetables, sprinkle with 1 teaspoon salt. Also add 12 peppercorns, crushed, ¼ teaspoon marjoram, and a *Bouquet Garni*. Cover the meat with dry red Burgundy wine, tightly cover the casserole, and put into a 325° oven for 3 to 4 hours. When the meat is cooked, transfer it to a hot serving dish. Strain the sauce through a sieve, pressing through some of the vegetables, skim it, and pour it over the meat.

BEEF STEW BORDELAISE (*Ragoût de Boeuf Bordelaise*). Cut 4 pounds lean beef into 2-inch cubes. Marinate for 2 hours in 2 cups dry red Bordeaux wine to which you have added 1 teaspoon salt, 12 peppercorns, crushed, 2 cloves garlic, crushed. Cut ½ pound of bacon into Lardoons, parboil for 5 minutes, and brown in a skillet in 1 tablespoon lard. Remove the bacon, turn up the heat, and brown the beef in very hot fat. Put beef and bacon into a heavy casserole. Pour off the fat from the skillet, deglaze* the pan with the marinade, and pour the hot marinade over the beef. Add Brown Stock to cover the meat and a *Bouquet Garni* tied in cheesecloth. Bring the liquid to a boil, cover the casserole tightly, and put into a 325° oven for 3 to 4 hours, or until the meat is done. Halfway through cooking add carrot and turnip balls, small white onions, and mushroom caps. When meat and vegetables are done, discard the bouquet garni, skim the sauce, add 2 cups cooked green peas, and sprinkle parsley over the whole. Serve in the casserole.

BEEF STEW WITH ASSORTED GARNISHES (*Ragoût de Boeuf aux Garnitures Diverses*). Cut 4 pounds lean beef in 2-inch squares. Brown the pieces in hot fat. Remove the meat from the pan and brown 1 carrot, sliced, and 1 onion, sliced, sprinkled with ½ teaspoon sugar. Deglaze* the pan with Brown Stock. Place the beef in a casserole, add brown stock to cover, a *Bouquet Garni,* and 2 cloves garlic, crushed. Cook in a 325° oven for about 2 hours. Remove the beef, reserving the sauce. Clean the casserole and return the beef to it. On top of the beef place the garnishes—carrots or turnips in olive shapes, hearts of celery, halved or quartered mushrooms, chestnuts, Chipolata Sausages. Strain the sauce into a saucepan, skim off the fat, reduce the sauce by ½, and pour it over the beef and vegetables. Bring the sauce to a boil, cover the casserole, and return it to a 325° oven. The vegetables are steamed as the meat finishes cooking. Cook for 1 hour, or until beef and vegetables are done. Serve in the casserole.

DAUBES

The term *daube* is taken from the verb *dauber,* "to stew." A daube may consist of a single large piece of beef (braised beef) as well as the small pieces of beef (beef stews) we are considering here. When I think of a daube, I conceive it mostly as pieces of beef that have been marinated and stewed *à blanc* with flavoring vegetables and some kind of fat meat (pork, ham, or blanched bacon) and liquid in a pot tightly sealed with flour and water paste. The cooking is very, very slow (much slower than the meat actually requires) and it is uninterrupted. The vegetables cooked with the daube disintegrate into its sauce; garnishing vegetables must be cooked separately. (In olden times, daubes were cooked in sealed earthenware pots buried in hot cinders.)

DAUBE OF BEEF À LA BÉARNAISE
(*Daube de Boeuf à la Béarnaise*)

Beef, 4 pounds lean rump, chuck, or round, cut in 2-inch cubes	Lard, 4 tablespoons
	Ham, 4 to 6 slices ¼ inch thick, preferably Bayonne ham
Lardoons, seasoned, 1 for each piece of meat (see below)	Flour, 1 cup
Salt, 1 teaspoon	*Bouquet Garni*—consisting of 3 sprigs parsley, 1 celery rib, 1 bay leaf, a sprig or pinch of thyme, all tied in cheesecloth
Pepper, ¼ teaspoon	
Red wine, dry, 3 cups	
Brandy, 3 tablespoons (optional)	
Carrots, 7 medium	Garlic, 2 cloves, crushed
Onions, 7 medium	Brown Stock, 1 to 2 cups
Parsley, 3 sprigs	Flour and water paste
Bay leaf, 1	A heavy casserole with a tight-fitting lid
Thyme, a pinch	

Lard* each beef cube with a lardoon that you have sprinkled with brandy and rolled in chopped garlic, parsley, and thyme. Season the meat with salt and pepper. Marinate the meat for 2 to 4 hours in dry red wine and brandy (optional) to which you have added 1 thinly sliced carrot, 1 thinly sliced onion, parsley, bay leaf, and thyme.

Slice 6 carrots and 6 onions in rounds, and lightly sauté them in lard. Line a heavy casserole with slices of Bayonne ham (or salted and smoked ham that you have parboiled for 10 minutes to rid it of salt and smoke flavors). Roll the meat in flour and place it in the casserole in layers, alternating it with layers of the mixed onions and carrots. In the center of this, thrust the bouquet garni.

Heat the wine marinade with its vegetables, add to it the garlic and 1 cup brown stock. Simmer for 30 minutes and strain this liquid over the meat. If the meat is not fully covered, add a little more brown stock to cover it.

Bring the liquid to a boil on a burner. Cover the casserole and seal the cover with a thick paste of flour and water, leaving a small hole to vent interior pressures. Place in a slow 275° oven and cook for 5 to 6 hours. Then break the seal, remove the bouquet garni, skim fat from the surface of the sauce, and serve the stew in the casserole with separately prepared vegetables, rice, or noodles.

(The Béarnais serve this daube with *broyo,* corn meal cooked in vegetable bouillon, cooled, sliced, and drenched with hot sauce from the stew. To make broyo, follow the recipe for Polenta, using vegetable stock as the liquid and omitting the Parmesan cheese.)

DAUBE OF BEEF À LA PROVENÇALE (*Daube de Boeuf à la Provençale*). Proceed as for Daube of Beef à la Béarnaise (above), but use white wine in place of red wine for the marinade, and add 3 tablespoons olive oil. Also, in addition to the sliced carrots and onions, layer the meat in the casserole with fresh bacon rinds and blanched bacon cut in fine dice; chopped mushrooms; peeled, seeded, and chopped tomatoes; crushed garlic cloves; and pitted black olives. To the *Bouquet Garni* add a slice of bitter orange peel. Pour into the casserole the cooked and strained marinade and enough Brown Veal Stock to barely cover the meat. Bring the liquid to the boil, seal the casserole lid with a paste of flour and water with a small hole to vent the steam, and cook in a 275° oven for 5 to 6 hours. Serve with noodles tossed in olive oil, fresh grated Parmesan cheese, and a little sauce from the stew. (This serving of pasta with stew is called a *macaronade.*)

ESTOUFFADES

The term *estouffade* is taken from the verb *étouffer,* "to smother." I know of no consistent difference between estouffades and daubes.

(Do not confuse this term with *étouffée* or *étuvée,* which describes cooking in a tightly closed pot with little or no liquid, that is, pot roasting. Also do not confuse with the identical term *estouffade,* which is the classic word for brown stock.)

CARBONADES

The term *carbonades* refers to the method of cutting the beef, in thin strips or squares. (Originally the word described thin strips of beef grilled over the coals.) Today *carbonades de boeuf* are browned, layered in a casserole with onions, and cooked in beer and brown stock. The cooking is slow and usually uninterrupted, the pot being sealed with a paste of flour and water.

CARBONADES OF BEEF À LA FLAMANDE
(Carbonades de Boeuf à la Flamande)

Beef, 4 pounds lean rump, chuck, or round, cut in 1½-inch squares ½ inch thick
Flour, 1 cup
Lard, 4 tablespoons
Salt, 1 teaspoon
Pepper, ¼ teaspoon
Onions, 2 pounds, thickly sliced
Garlic, 6 cloves, crushed
Brown Stock, 2 cups
Red wine vinegar, 2 tablespoons
Brown sugar, 2 tablespoons
Parsley, 4 tablespoons chopped
Bay leaf, 1
Thyme, 1 teaspoon
Beer, 2 12-ounce bottles light imported beer
Flour and water paste
A skillet to brown the beef and onions
A deep, heavy casserole with tight-fitting cover

Dredge the pieces of beef in flour, slapping them smartly to remove excess, and brown them in a sauté pan or skillet in very hot lard. When well browned, remove from the pan and season with salt and pepper.

Put onions and garlic into the pan. Add more lard if necessary and sauté until the onions are lightly golden. Place beef and onions in alternate layers in a deep casserole.

Pour the fat from the pan, deglaze* it with brown stock and pour this over the beef and onions along with the vinegar, brown sugar, parsley, bay leaf, and thyme. Then add light Belgian or other imported beer and stir lightly to blend the liquids. Heat until the liquid comes to a boil, and seal the lid of the casserole with a thick paste of flour and water, leaving a small hole to vent interior pressures. Place the casserole in a 325° oven for 2½ to 3 hours. Serve with the same brand of beer you used for braising, along with potatoes or rice.

GOULASHES

Goulash is the Hungarian name for stew. This name has been appropriated by the French cuisine to apply to stews containing typically Hungarian ingredients, notably paprika. Tomatoes and onions are usually present also.

Goulashes are usually cooked with a very little liquid that is naturally thickened by vegetables added at the beginning of cooking. Other vegetables are added part way through cooking. Goulashes are therefore rather thick, often without the separation of solid and liquid ingredients you find in a French ragout. Goulashes are often served on beds of noodles.

HUNGARIAN GOULASH
(*Gulyas de Boeuf à la Hongroise*)

Beef, 4 pounds lean rump, chuck, or round, cut in 2-inch cubes

Lard, ¼ pound

Onions, ¾ pounds (about 4 medium), sliced

Salt, 1 teaspoon

Paprika, 2 tablespoons

Tomatoes, 1½ pounds (about 6 medium), peeled, seeded, and chopped

Water, 2 cups

Potatoes, 4 medium, cut in quarters

A heavy skillet or sauté pan to brown the beef and onions, and to stew in

Brown the beef in a heavy skillet in the hot lard. When the beef is well browned, add and brown the onions. Sprinkle the beef and onions with salt and paprika, and add tomatoes and 1 cup water. Cover and simmer for 1½ hours.

Add 1 cup hot water and the potatoes, cover, and simmer for one hour more, or until meat and potatoes are cooked. Serve in a deep dish, accompanied by or on a bed of noodles. Also, a happy thing to do is to garnish the edges of the dish with a little border of separately cooked fresh green peas.

This goulash may also be made by adding 2 tablespoons flour to the browned meat and onions and stirring to form a brown Roux. In place of water use 1 cup Brown Stock. In place of tomatoes use 1 cup Tomato Purée. Also add a *Bouquet Garni*. Separately cook the potatoes.

✳ ROAST BEEF

The important roasts of beef are the rib roast, the loin roast, the sirloin roast, the rib eye roast, and the tenderloin roast. Other pieces of meat called roasts should be pot roasted.

All these roasts are eminently tender and need cooking only to develop their flavor. If cooked beyond the rare stage they begin to toughen. Consequently, we cook them only until they reach an internal temperature of 120° to 130°. The roast is then allowed to stand in a warm place for about 20 minutes. The roast will continue to cook in its own heat (inner temperature of a large roast can increase by as much as 20°). After this peak is reached the inner juices will settle back into the meat fibers from whence they came. The roast can then be more easily carved, and less juice will escape from it.

ROAST RIB OF BEEF
(*Côtes de Boeuf Rôti*)

The bigger the roast, the better it cooks. However, you will probably not often need as large a rib roast as you can get—a full 7-rib roast will weigh from 25 to 30 pounds. Figure on about 3½ pounds per rib. The first ribs are the best (counting from the back of the animal forward).

Beef, an 8-pound (about 2 ribs) standing rib roast with backbone and short ribs removed, long ribs left in	Salt, 2 teaspoons
	Brown Stock or Brown Veal Stock, 1 cup
Melted fat, 2 tablespoons	A low-sided baking pan to just fit the roast

This roast comes with a natural barding of its own fat, and a natural rack of rib bones upon which it stands in the oven. Brush the bare faces of the roast with melted fat, place it in a low-sided roasting pan just large enough to hold it, and put it to brown in a 450° oven for 20 to 30 minutes. When it is well browned on the ends, salt it all over and reduce oven heat to 350°.

Be certain you can always *hear* the roast cooking. If it ceases to sizzle, turn up the heat a little. Also, be careful the drippings in the pan do not burn. If they begin to smoke, carefully add a very little water to the pan (about ⅛ cup) to cool it. Continue to baste the faces of the roast with its melting fat. Cooking time is about 2 hours, or 15 minutes per pound.

To test for doneness, thump the face of the meat with your fingers. If the meat still trembles, jellylike, inside, it needs a little more cooking. Do not rely on the faulty practice of cutting between the ribs to look at the meat near the bone. This meat, protected by the bone, will continue to be rare long after the center is well done and ruined. This roast, like all roasts, should be served rare. If you use a meat thermometer, remove the roast when it reaches 130° and allow it to rest in a warm place for 20 minutes. The meat will continue cooking in its own heat.

Pour off the fat, deglaze* the pan with brown stock or brown veal stock, and cook down a little. This juice, which contains a good proportion of the meat's own juices, is traditionally sent to the table in a sauceboat. It is not thickened with starch, but may be made a little thicker and enriched by swirling in* a few tablespoons of butter. The meat is consequently served, not with a sauce, but with juice (*au jus*).

ROAST LOIN OF BEEF
(*Aloyau de Boeuf Rôti*)

This is the grandest roast of all. It consists of all the American steaks in one monumental piece. A roast of these proportions is rarely encountered, but an 8-inch-thick slice will give you a well-dimensioned roast from whatever part you take it. The filet portion of this roast, which is the most tender part, should retain a good portion of its covering fat to protect it during cooking, otherwise it will become dry before the rest of the roast is done. Cook this roast exactly as a rib roast, being certain to place it on a rack above the surface of the roasting pan.

ROAST SIRLOIN OF BEEF
(*Contre-Filet de Boeuf Rôti*)

This cut of beef is also called a shell of beef in America. It is the upper, larger portion of all the steaks (with the tenderloin and tail removed). The entire roast weighs about 12 pounds, boned.

Beef, a 6-pound sirloin roast, boned	Brown Stock or Brown Veal Stock,
Barding* fat	1 cup
Melted fat, 2 tablespoons	A rack and a low-sided roasting pan
Salt, 1½ teaspoons	to just fit the roast

Like the rib roast, this roast comes with a natural barding of its own fat on top. The underside should also be barded* and the roast tied in both its dimensions with butcher's twine. The roast is placed on a rack so it will not fry in its own fat. Dry the raw faces of the roast, rub them with melted fat, and put the roast in a 450° oven to brown. When it is well browned on both ends, salt it all over and reduce the oven heat to 400°. This roast, being thinner from top to bottom than the rib roast, is cooked at a higher heat.

Observe the same precautions as for the rib roast. Thump the meat to test for doneness; it should be springy when adequately cooked. A meat thermometer will register 120° to 125° for a rare roast, and this roast is essentially ruined when cooked much beyond the rare stage. Allow the roast to rest in a warm place for 20 minutes after cooking. Pour off the fat, deglaze* the pan with brown stock or brown veal stock, reduce it, and serve this unthickened juice separately with the roast. You may enrich this juice by swirling in* a few tablespoons of butter.

ROAST RIB EYE OF BEEF

This roast is the boned central portion of the rib roast. It is sometimes called a Delmonico roast. It is of about the same thickness across as the sirloin roast, and it should be barded* and cooked exactly the same as the sirloin roast.

ROAST TENDERLOIN (FILET) OF BEEF
(*Filet de Boeuf Rôti*)

Many elegant roasts are produced from this costly cut, the tenderest of all the beef pieces. We will consider these roasts separately.

ROAST BEEF COOKED IN SALT. An excellent method of cooking beef roasts is in a casing of salt. Moisten coarse salt with water and pack it all around the roast in a layer about ½ inch thick. This will harden like cement in the heat, protecting the meat and containing its juices. To test for doneness, a meat thermometer is best. Remove the roast when its center reaches 120°. Allow the roast to rest for 20 minutes, then crack the salt casing with a hammer.

7 GARNISHES FOR ROAST BEEF

These garnishes may be used with any roast—rib, loin, sirloin, and tenderloin.

ROAST BEEF WITH BRUSSELS SPROUTS (*Boeuf Rôti à la Bruxelloise*). Roast the beef. Garnish the roast with Brussels sprouts and olive-shaped potatoes or potato balls sautéed in butter. In a hot sauceboat, separately serve the skimmed pan juices, or rich hot Brown Stock, or a thin Demi-Glace Sauce.

ROAST BEEF À LA DAUPHINE (*Boeuf Rôti à la Dauphine*). Roast the beef. Serve the roast with Dauphine Potatoes. Separately serve the skimmed pan juices or rich hot Brown Stock.

ROAST BEEF À LA DUCHESSE (*Boeuf Rôti à la Duchesse*). Roast the beef. Serve the roast with a surrounding garnish of Duchess Potatoes. Separately serve the skimmed pan juices or rich hot Brown Stock.

ROAST BEEF À LA PARISIENNE (*Boeuf Rôti à la Parisienne*). Roast the beef. Serve the roast with Braised Lettuce and Parisian Potatoes. Separately serve the pan juices reduced with a little white wine and Brown Veal Stock.

ROAST BEEF À LA JARDINIÈRE (*Boeuf Rôti à la Jardinière*). Roast the beef. Serve it surrounded by little heaps of peas, green beans, and kidney beans, all cooked in butter; olive-shaped Glazed Turnips and Glazed Carrots; and boiled cauliflowerets kept very white. Separately serve the skimmed pan juices or rich hot Brown Stock.

ROAST BEEF MACÉDOINE (*Boeuf Rôti Macédoine*). Roast the beef. Serve the roast with a *Macédoine* of vegetables. These vegetables are the same as those for *à la Jardinière* (above), mixed together and tossed in butter. Separately serve the skimmed pan juices or rich hot Brown Stock.

ROAST BEEF NIVERNAISE (*Boeuf Rôti Nivernaise*). Roast the beef. Serve it surrounded with carrots cut in olive shapes and glazed* in butter and sugar. (Small Glazed Onions may also be served.) Separately serve the skimmed pan juices or rich hot Brown Stock.

✳ POT-ROASTED BEEF

Pot roasting has been so thoroughly confused with braising that I fear the matter will never be clarified, and many a poor woman will go through life without ever having really pot-roasted a piece of beef. I will try to dispel the fog.

A "pot roast" is a piece of meat taken from the less tender parts of the animal. It can be poached in liquid, braised, or pot-roasted. When it is braised, it is cooked very slowly in a flavorful liquid that covers or partially covers the meat. This liquid reduces naturally to form a sauce during cooking. The meat is cooked partly in liquid, partly in steam.

On the other hand, when the meat is pot-roasted, it is cooked in very little or no added liquid at all. The moisture in pot-roasted beef is supplied by the meat itself and the vegetables that are cooked along with it (which is why the method is called pot *roasting*). A pot roast cooks in the steam of its own juices. The result in flavor and texture differs considerably from braised beef.

Pot roasting, then, is a form of poëléing, the method being adapted to tough cuts of meat. In true poëléing, the tender meat is lightly browned and cooked quickly at high heat. In pot roasting, the tougher meat is given a good brown searing to retain its juices better. And it is cooked very, very slowly with frequent basting so that it can become tender without drying out.

Pot roasts can be marinated in wine before cooking to both flavor and tenderize them. But first you should try the following basic recipe, which gives you the true basic taste of pot roast pure and simple.

BEEF POT ROAST
(*Boeuf à l'Étuvée*)

Beef, a 3- to 4-pound pot roast from the rump, chuck, or round
Lard, 4 tablespoons
Clarified Butter, ½ cup
Carrots, 2, sliced
Onions, 2, sliced
Celery, 2 ribs, sliced
Garlic, 2 cloves, peeled
Salt, 1 teaspoon
Pepper, ¼ teaspoon
Brown Stock, 2 cups

Parsley, 3 sprigs
Bay leaf, 1, crumbled
Thyme, a pinch
Arrowroot or cornstarch, 2 teaspoons; or *Beurre Manié,* 2 tablespoons
Parsley, chopped, 1 tablespoon
A skillet or sauté pan to brown the meat in
A heavy casserole with a tight-fitting cover

The meat may be one boneless piece, or boned and rolled, or the bone may be left in as in a blade chuck pot roast. Brown the meat thoroughly in lard in a heavy skillet or sauté pan, taking 10 to 15 minutes to give it a good brown crust. Remove it from the pan, pour off the fat, and add clarified butter. Heat to sizzling, and lightly brown the carrots, onions, celery, and garlic. Place these browned vegetables in the bottom of a heavy casserole.

Season the meat with salt and pepper. If necessary, tie the meat with butcher's twine so it will hold its shape (a flat blade chuck pot roast needs no tying). Place the meat in the casserole on the bed of vegetables.

Deglaze* the skillet with ¼ cup brown stock, using a wooden spoon to scrape up thickened juices in the bottom of the pan. Continue simmering for a few minutes until most of the brown stock has evaporated. What remains in the pan is a flavored butter. Pour this over the meat.

Heat the casserole until the vegetables sizzle. Heap some of these vegetables on top of the meat, and add parsley, bay leaf, and thyme. Then cover the meat with a piece of buttered parchment paper or aluminum foil cut to fit the pan, with a small hole cut in it at one end to vent the steam. Turn down the heat as far as you can and cook very, very slowly, basting the meat with additional butter from time to time, or with rendered fat and butter from the pan. Or you may cook the pot roast in a 300° oven, basting frequently.

The thick browning you gave the meat will help it to retain most of its juices, but some of these and the juices of the vegetables will be transformed into a gentle, flavorful steam. In this benign, flavorful, steamy atmosphere the connective tissue of the meat will soften and change to gelatin. The gelatin will be released to enrich the sauce forming in the bottom of the pan.

Cook the pot roast, basting frequently with butter and fat, for 3 to 4

FRENCH COOKING FOR THE AMERICAN TABLE

hours. The meat will react as it does when braised—it will stiffen and toughen as it becomes well done all the way through, and then it will relax and soften as the connective tissue dissolves in the gentle, humid heat. The meat is done when it feels thoroughly soft to your touch, or when you can pierce it with a knife without meeting any resistance. It will have retained much of its juices, with which meat is generously supplied. Take care not to overcook, or the meat will eventually become dry and stringy.

When perfectly cooked, remove the meat from the pan and keep it warm. Place the pan on the flame and add to it 1½ cups brown stock. Cook, stirring with a wooden spoon, to scrape up any solidified juices and to thoroughly absorb the flavors held by the butter and the vegetables. Simmer for 6 to 8 minutes to thoroughly complete this absorption, then strain the sauce into a saucepan through a sieve, pressing through some of the vegetable purée. Allow the sauce to rest for 1 or 2 minutes, and skim the fat from the surface. Season to taste with salt and pepper, and thicken if necessary with 2 teaspoons cornstarch or arrowroot mixed in a few tablespoons of brown stock or red wine, or with about 2 tablespoons *beurre manié*.

Just before serving, butter the surface of the pot roast, sprinkle it with 1 tablespoon chopped parsley. Separately serve the sauce and whatever vegetables you have prepared as garnish.

POT ROAST OF BEEF À LA MATIGNON (*Boeuf Étuvée à la Matignon*). This method of pot roasting comes to us from old cookery. Prepare 2 cups of *Matignon*—a mixture of minced carrots, onions, celery, and ham, with thyme and bay leaf, lightly browned in butter and moistened with Madeira wine. Lightly brown the pot roast, tie it, and butter it thickly. Spread some of the matignon on a large piece of buttered parchment paper or a piece of foil. Place the meat on this bed, and heap the rest of the matignon over the top and sides of the meat. Wrap it tightly in the paper to hold the matignon in close contact with all surfaces of the meat, and cook as in the recipe above. When making the sauce, be sure to simmer the matignon in Brown Stock to extract all its flavors.

✳ THE BEEFSTEAKS

French steaks differ from American steaks in that they are usually boned. Actually, they are cut from the long muscles or roasts that have been previously stripped out of the carcass and trimmed. The French butcher has little use for a saw, and a T-bone is seldom seen in France.

As a result French steaks are almost always smaller, because they are cut from meat that forms only a portion of an American steak. A porterhouse steak, for example, is cut across three different muscles of beef—the loin (French *contre-filet*), the tenderloin (French *filet*), and a portion of the flank (the tail of the porterhouse), a poor, tough piece of meat that never finds its way into a French *bifteck*.

As in America, the French grill, broil, and pan-broil their steaks. They also sauté steaks in butter. Sautéed steaks are usually cut thinner and are flattened a little before cooking.

Whether steaks are cut in the French or American manner, they still obey the laws of cooking. If you do not choose to make the effort to get French cut steaks, the cooking directions are nevertheless applicable to the steak you have. Take note, however, of the differences in flavor, texture, and tenderness among the different portions of porterhouse, T-Bone, and sirloin steaks. Having to cook these unlike portions under identical circumstances, you will never be able to get the whole steak *exactly* right. The loss, however, to millions of American steak eaters, has proved to be only marginal.

In addition to being boned, frequently sautéed, and generally smaller, French steak service differs from the American mostly in its garnishes. These are varied and numerous. Five perfect *tournedos,* arranged in a coronet, inspire elegancies of garnishing that have won permanent places in *haute cuisine*. These same elegant and delicious garnishes would look perfectly laughable alongside a monster sirloin.

French steak service differs also in its liberal use of sauces and flavored butters. But enough of differences. The meat is at hand, carved—in whatever fashion—from the tender first category of prime or choice beef. Let us cook this meat.

GRILLED AND BROILED BEEFSTEAK
(Entrecôte Grillé)

A steak—rib, club, T-bone, porter-house, sirloin, or tenderloin steak (filet mignon), cut at least 1½ inches thick	Clarified Butter Pepper Salt

This is tender meat. We will cook it only to maximize its flavor without toughening it or drying it out. This calls for high, dry, and relentless heat. You must pour it on.

To get a head start on cooking, let the steak stand out of the refrigerator for an hour to bring it to room temperature. If you have a large steak rimmed

Roast Sirloin of Beef

Roast Filet of Beef au Poivre Vert, with Braised Lettuce, Stuffed Onions

Roast Loin of Pork

with fat, trim some of this away, leaving a rind of about ½ inch thickness. Slash this rind of fat every 1 or 2 inches, cutting the membrane between fat and lean to prevent it from shrinking and thereby curling the meat. Pepper the steak with freshly ground pepper and rub it all over with clarified butter. Do not salt the steak. Salt will draw moisture to the surface and interfere with the cooking.

Adjust the broiling pan or grill to suit the thickness of the steak. A 1½-inch steak should lie about 3 inches from the flame. Steaks thicker than this are first seared to brown their surface, and then moved farther from the flame to prevent the surfaces from charring before they are cooked inside. Steaks thinner than 1½ inches are cooked nearer to the flame, so that the heat may brown their surfaces and develop full flavor in the flavor compounds before the juicy redness of the center is forever lost. All steaks should be cooked only until they are rare.

Heat the broiler or stoke the grill until it is very, very hot. You must surprise the steak with the suddenness and ferocity of your fiery attack. Grease the broiling pan or grill with oil or the fat you trimmed from the steak. Then, dry the steak thoroughly and commit it to the fire. If grill or pan is as hot as it should be, an explosive hiss is heard and a cloud of steam will billow forth as the hot metal vaporizes the moisture on the steak's surface. And if the grill or pan is as hot as it should be, the steak will not stick.

I cannot predict when the steak will be cooked, or tell you how long to cook it on each side. Five minutes, 7 minutes, maybe more—it all depends on the steak and the heat. You, standing on the spot, can tell much better than I. The clues are different for broiling and grilling. Let us take grilling first.

THE GRILLED STEAK

The grilled steak is receiving intense heat from underneath. The hot metal of the grill has branded it with carbon stripes and continues to conduct heat into the meat. Convected heat from the coals is working on the meat between the bars of grill metal, instantly drying the moisture that tries to sweat out. Radiant heat at the same time is probing deep into the meat, exciting its molecules, coagulating its protein. A veritable wall of heat—conducted, convected, and radiated—rises upward through the meat. Now, watch the surface.

In 5 minutes, maybe more, little beads of red juice appear on the surface of the meat. Energized by the heat pressure building inside the meat, they flee from the heat in defiance of gravity. These beads are your signal that

Side 1 is done. When they appear on a steak you are grilling, turn the steak over and begin cooking Side 2. Use tongs to turn the steak; a fork will spill its juices.

Ssssssss! An explosive hiss and a cloud of steam as the water in these flavorful beads vaporizes in the heat, depositing on the meat their precious burden of flavor compounds. Now, you have tricked the meat juices. The heat again fully assaults them and they reverse their direction, fleeing the heat, striving to reach the cooling upper surface of the steak. Do not let them reach the surface!

You must anticipate. You must remove the steak from the grill just before these liquid rubies can emerge, because at this point the meat is still rare or medium rare. When they do reach the surface, the steak will be well on its way to the medium stage and will have lost its characteristic juiciness and flavor.

You can tell when the beads are about to emerge by prodding the steak with your fingers. Begin poking after you turn it. Note and remember the response, a kind of soft acquiescence felt beneath the surface. Continue poking until you feel the steak respond with a defiant resiliency. Then it is cooked enough. (Practice this until you get the "feel" of steak that is cooked rare. Until you become expert, watch like a hawk for the beads of juice and whisk the steak off the grill the instant they appear.) Season the steak and serve it.

One other caution. Do not cut alongside the bone to see how the meat is doing. The bone is a cooling influence and meat alongside the bone will remain rare while the rest of the steak is being overcooked.

THE BROILED STEAK

When the broiled steak hits the broiling pan, it is partly seared on the bottom by contact with the ridged hot metal. At the same time it is attacked from above by the heat of the flame and heat radiating from the hot top of the broiler. As the flame heats the top of the steak, it also passes heat to that part of the pan exposed around the sides of the steak, keeping it hot (but not as hot as it became during preheating). Cooked from both sides at once (although more effectively from above), the broiled steak will be done a few minutes before the grilled steak.

As the heat from the flame takes effect, the surface of the steak will become dotted with puddles of melting fat. These perform a self-basting operation, protecting the browned surface of the meat from drying out and becoming too crusty.

When cooked on the grill, beads of red juice appearing on the surface of the steak tell you it's time to turn it. In the broiler these beads are lost in melted fat or dried by the heat as they reach the surface. You cannot, therefore, rely on this signal. Instead turn the steak (with tongs) when the surface looks appetizingly brown, or in about 5 minutes.

The underside of the steak will be grayish, due to the unavoidable entrapment of steam between the meat and the grooves in the broiling pan. Poke it with your fingers and establish in your mind its "feel." Continue cooking the steak and as it browns continue poking the steak. As soon as it loses its softness and feels resilient, it is done rare. If you cook the steak longer, juices will begin to run out at the bottom. Salt the steak and serve it.

9 VARIATIONS ON GRILLED OR BROILED BEEFSTEAK

The French insist that a great affinity exists between beefsteak and butter, and even when butter is not important to the method of cooking they manage to put the two tastes together by the simple expedient of buttering the steak. All of these garnishes and dressings are excellent on all American steaks. The French word *entrecôte* refers to all American steaks minus their tenderloin portion if they have one.

STEAK À LA BERCY (*Entrecôte à la Bercy*). Just before serving, butter the steak with Bercy Butter, or serve the melted butter separately.

STEAK MARCHAND DE VIN or WINE MERCHANT'S STEAK (*Entrecôte Marchand de Vin*). Just before serving, butter the steak with Marchand de Vin Butter, or serve the melted butter separately.

STEAK MAÎTRE D'HÔTEL (*Entrecôte Maître d'Hôtel*). Just before serving, butter the steak with Maître d'Hôtel Butter, or serve the melted butter separately.

STEAK AU VERT-PRÉ (*Entrecôte au Vert-Pré*). Surround the steak with little mounds of Straw Potatoes alternated with bunches of watercress. Just before serving, butter the steak with Maître d'Hôtel Butter.

STEAK À LA MIRABEAU (*Entrecôte à la Mirabeau*). When the steak is ½ cooked on the second side, remove it and garnish it with a latticework made with thin strips of anchovy filets. In the diamond shapes formed by the latticework, place slices of green olive. Return the steak to the broiler and finish the cooking. Butter the steak with Anchovy Butter and surround it with Château Potatoes.

STEAK À LA BÉARNAISE (*Entrecôte à la Béarnaise*). Surround the steak with Château Potatoes alternated with bunches of watercress. Separately serve Béarnaise Sauce.

STEAK À LA BORDELAISE (*Entrecôte à la Bordelaise*). When the steak is almost finished cooking, spread its upper surface with a mixture of ½ cup bone Marrow, poached, drained, and diced; and 2 tablespoons finely chopped shallots. Finish the cooking and sprinkle the steak with chopped parsley. Separately serve Bordelaise Sauce.

STEAK À LA TYROLESE (*Entrecôte à la Tyrolienne*). Decorate the steak with large onion rings sautéed in butter, and surround it with Tomato Fondue to which you have added Pepper Sauce. Sprinkle with chopped parsley.

STEAK WITH ROQUEFORT (*Entrecôte au Roquefort*). Cream 4 tablespoons Roquefort cheese and 2 tablespoons finely chopped parsley, chives, or chervil in ¼ cup soft butter. Season to taste with salt, pepper, and lemon juice. Spread this over the steak.

SAUTÉED BEEFSTEAK

A steak—boned rib steak, club, T-bone, porterhouse, sirloin, or tenderloin steak (filet mignon), cut about 1 inch thick or less	Clarified Butter, 2 tablespoons Salt and pepper

If the steak has a rind of fat, trim it so that only ½ inch of the fat remains. Slash this rind of fat every 1 or 2 inches to prevent it from shrinking and thereby curling the meat. Flatten the steak slightly so it will contact the pan over its whole surface.

Heat the clarified butter in a sauté pan or heavy skillet until it is very hot but not yet browning. Thoroughly dry the steak, pepper it if you choose, and place it in the pan (dropping the part farthest away from you into the pan last to avoid splashing hot fat on yourself). Sear the steak thoroughly for 1 or 2 minutes, then turn the heat down slightly to avoid drying the steak too much. Let the butter be your guide; do not allow it to burn.

Continue sautéing at brisk heat until beads of moisture appear on the surface of the meat. As in broiling, the juices are fleeing the source of heat and bubbling to the cooler surface. Using tongs, immediately turn the steak over (remembering to drop the farthest part into the pan last to avoid burning yourself). Turn the heat up full for 1 or 2 minutes, and then reduce it slightly again.

Now you must begin tapping the steak, as cooking is very swift, faster than grilling because the total surface of the pan is efficiently applying high heat directly to the steak. At first the steak feels soft beneath its surface. Continue tapping until the softness passes out of the steak and it becomes resilient. Immediately remove the steak from the pan. If the beads of red juice appear on the surface of the steak, it is most likely almost cooked to the medium stage. You must anticipate the appearance of these beads to sauté steak as it should be sautéed, rare. Salt and pepper the steak after cooking.

7 VARIATIONS ON SAUTÉED BEEFSTEAK

STEAK À LA BOURGUIGNONNE (*Entrecôte à la Bourguignonne*). Surround the steak with mushrooms sautéed in butter, glazed small onions, and diced salt pork that you have blanched and browned. Deglaze* the pan with ½ cup dry red wine, add ½ cup Demi-Glace Sauce, reduce slightly and strain over the steak. (Do not skim off the butter.)

STEAK À LA NIÇOISE (*Entrecôte à la Niçoise*). This steak may be sautéed in olive oil in place of clarified butter. Surround it with Tomato Fondue à la Niçoise, small potatoes or potato balls sautéed in butter, and string beans tossed in butter. Deglaze* the pan with ½ cup dry white wine, add ½ cup Starch-Thickened Brown Veal Stock to which you have added 1 tablespoon Tomato Purée, reduce slightly, and strain over the steak.

STEAK WITH MUSHROOMS (*Entrecôte aux Champignons*). When the steak is ¾ cooked, add 12 mushroom caps to the pan and complete their cooking with the steak. Surround the steak with the mushrooms. Deglaze* the pan with ½ cup dry white wine, add ½ cup Demi-Glace Sauce, reduce slightly, remove from the heat, strain, and swirl in one tablespoon butter. Pour over the steak.

STEAK À LA BONNE FEMME (*Entrecôte à la Bonne Femme*). When the steak is ½ cooked, add to the pan boiled, half-cooked potatoes cut in olive shapes; half-cooked small Glazed Onions, and ½ cup diced and parboiled salt pork or bacon. Complete the cooking of the meat and vegetables together. Surround the steak with the vegetables. To the butter in the pan, add a few tablespoons of Brown Veal Stock or water and pour this over the steak. Sprinkle with chopped parsley.

STEAK À LA LYONNAISE (*Entrecôte à la Lyonnaise*). When the steak is ¾ cooked, add 2 tablespoons minced onion lightly sautéed in butter. To the butter remaining in the pan, add 1 tablespoon vinegar, 2 tablespoons white wine, and ½ cup Demi-Glace Sauce. Reduce this sauce a little, and pour over the steak. Sprinkle with chopped parsley.

PEPPER STEAK (*Entrecôte au Poivre*). This is a famous French steak dish usually made with individual portion-sized steaks, sautéed. (It can also be made with a single large steak, cut thick and broiled.) For 4 individual portion club or strip steaks (or 1 huge sirloin or porterhouse), coarsely crack 2 tablespoons peppercorns. Dry the steaks and rub them all over with Clarified Butter. Press the cracked pepper into the steaks on both sides, working it into the meat with the heel of your hand, and let the steaks stand ½ hour. Sauté the steaks and remove to a hot platter. Pour off the fat, deglaze* the pan with ½ cup Brown Sauce, pour this over the steak, and sprinkle with chopped parsley.

FLAMING PEPPER STEAK (*Entrecôte au Poivre Flambé*). Pepper steak is sometimes flamed. Proceed as above, but heat ¼ cup cognac and pour it flaming over the steaks. You may also finish cooking the steaks at the table in a chafing dish, adding the sauce and the hot cognac, igniting it, and spooning the flaming result over the meat.

PAN-BROILED BEEFSTEAK

The pan broiling of steaks belongs more to American than French cookery, which relies more on sautéing. Carried to the extreme, pan broiling produces the so-called "black and blue" steaks—charred black on the outside, raw and blue in the center. (Raw beef is indeed blue; it turns red after brief exposure to the air.)

To pan-broil, you must have a heavy skillet, preferably of cast iron, which is least likely to cause sticking. Heat the skillet until it is very, very hot, so hot that beads of water will bounce off its surface. If you rubbed beef fat into this pan it would instantly burn; instead rub the steak with a little rendered beef fat or oil. Trim the steak of excess fat and make cuts through the fat and the membrane between fat and meat to prevent the steak from curling. Do not salt.

If you have a range hood fan, turn it on. Put the steak into the pan. Ignore the smoke and the noise; a necessary crust is forming on the bottom of the steak.

If the steak is one inch thick, red pearls of moisture will appear on its surface in 2 or 3 minutes. Lift the steak with tongs, hold it in the air for one minute while the pan gathers in the heat from the flame, and then put the steak down on its other side. Smoke and steam will puff from the pan as the second crust forms. Begin poking the steak with your fingers. As soon as it stiffens to the touch, in about 2 minutes, it is done rare and should be served.

If the steak is 1½ to 2 inches thick, lower the heat after it has cooked on the first side for 2 minutes. When pearls of moisture appear on the uncooked surface, turn the fire up full, lift the steak with tongs, hold it for one minute until the pan heats up, and then put the steak down on its uncooked side. Cook at high heat for 2 minutes, reduce the heat, and continue cooking until the steak stiffens to your touch.

The residue in the pan is burned and is of no use. Salt and pepper the steak and top it with butter, or one of the compound butters or sauces appropriate for broiled steak.

STEAKS FROM TOUGH CUTS OF BEEF

Occasionally one gets a tender steak cut from the second category of choice beef—such as the rump steak next to the sirloin or the chuck steak next to the ribs—and these can be sautéed or broiled like first category beef. It is wiser, however, to give these steaks special treatment to keep them tender. These steaks must all be served rare, as the slightest bit of overcooking will make them tough as nails.

FLANK STEAK or LONDON BROIL. This is a stringy piece of meat about 1 foot long, 6 inches wide, and 1 inch thick. Score the meat on both sides to prevent it from curling during cooking. Marinate* it for at least 2 hours at room temperature, for up to 48 hours in the refrigerator, with the following marinade: ¼ cup Vinaigrette, 1 tablespoon lemon juice, 2 tablespoons soy sauce, 2 garlic cloves, finely chopped, 3 tablespoons finely chopped shallots or scallions, and a few drops of Tabasco. When ready to cook, drain and dry the meat and rub it all over with oil or Clarified Butter. Broil or grill it quickly, close to the flame, using high heat for about 3 minutes per side. Remove to a hot platter, pour over 4 tablespoons Brown Butter and chopped parsley. Slice the steak thinly, slanting your slices across the grain.

STEAK À LA NORMANDE (*Entrecôte à la Normande*). Prepare a marinade with 2 cups sweet cider, ½ cup calvados or apple brandy (applejack), 4 tablespoons lemon juice, 1 lemon rind cut in strips, 3 cloves, and a pinch of nutmeg and of cinnamon. Marinate the meat for 8 hours at room temperature or for up to 48 hours in the refrigerator. Strain the marinade and reduce it by ½. Dry the steak and sauté it. To the reduced marinade add 1 cup thick cream, blend in, and simmer while the steak cooks. Season the steak with salt and pepper and pour the sauce over it.

✳ THE HAMBURGER

Minced or ground beef taken from the most flavorful parts of the animal, shaped into small cakes, and grilled or sautéed are also called *bifteck* by the French. These are not served on a bun, but if you should choose to eat them that way, there is nothing to prevent you.

Hamburgers made from very rare meat are sterile tasting. They need some fat for flavor and richness, but not so much that they will shrink too much in cooking. Ten to 15 percent fat is about right. The only way you can certainly control this is to grind or mince the beef yourself. These hamburgers will taste quite different from the store-ground kind.

HAMBURGER STEAK
(*Bifteck à la Hambourgeoise*)

Beef, 1 pound ground or minced, containing 10 to 15 percent fat	Water, 2 tablespoons
Onions, ½ cup minced	Egg, 1
Salt, 1 teaspoon	Clarified Butter, 2 tablespoons
Pepper, a pinch	Flour, ½ cup
Nutmeg, a pinch	A heavy skillet or sauté pan

If you grind the beef yourself and it is very lean, add to 1 pound of beef ¼ cup finely chopped beef kidney fat or beef marrow. Also add minced onions, slightly sautéed in butter; salt, pepper, and nutmeg; water; and lightly beaten egg. Mix gently but thoroughly and shape into 4 cakes, taking care to handle the meat delicately and not to pack it too tightly.

Heat clarified butter in a heavy skillet or sauté pan until it is very hot. At the last moment, dredge the hamburgers in flour, slapping them smartly to remove excess flour that might burn in the pan. Sauté the hamburgers briskly, burning them when beads of moisture appear on their surfaces. Sauté on the other side, tapping them with your fingers, until they become just firm and springy. Remove to a warm serving platter. They should be slightly rare in the center. Serve the hamburgers coated with a sauce made in the pan—such as Madeira, Bordelaise, or Pepper Sauce.

✳ FILET OF BEEF

A filet of beef is the tenderloin portion of all the American steaks in one piece. Trimmed of fat, it is a teardrop-shaped piece of lean meat about 20 inches long, 4 inches thick at its thickest part, and weighing about 5 to 7 pounds. The whole filet or part of it is used as a roast, and it may be roasted, poëléed, or braised. The filet may also be sliced into steaks, to be grilled, broiled, or sautéed. Either way, this is elegant meat and the most expensive part of beef. There are only 2 of these filets on a thousand-pound steer.

In America, as in France, the roast is known as a filet of beef roast. Descriptively, it can be divided into 3 major sections. Beginning at the large end of the filet at the rear of the animal, approximately the first third of its length is taken from the sirloin section, that is, it is the tenderloin portion of all the sirloin steaks. This is the head of the filet (*la tête de filet*). It is the coarsest part, and it is frequently removed from American filet of beef roasts.

Approximately the next third of the filet is taken from the porterhouse section. This is very choice meat, about 4 inches in diameter throughout its length. It is called the heart of the filet (*le coeur du filet*).

The third and final section of the filet is taken from the T-bone section of American beef. This is the tail of the filet (*la queue de filet*), and it becomes progressively smaller in diameter until it ends against the club steak in the vicinity of the ribs.

Steaks sliced from the filet are known as filet mignon in America. In French cooking, these steaks receive 5 different names according to the part of the filet they are taken from. We will examine these steaks more closely after we are done with the roast.

THE FILET OF BEEF COOKED WHOLE

The whole filet, or its thickest part, is roasted, poëléed, or braised. In preparation for these operations you must trim the filet of excess fat and membrane. Very carefully skin the membrane from the top or smooth side of the filet (the ridged side is the underside). Try not to overly loosen the 2 strips of meat laying along either side of the main muscle, or remove them if you choose. Trim excess fat from the underside of the filet, leaving enough to provide a natural bard.

Filet of prime grade is usually well marbled, and is sometimes cooked without the addition of fat. Choice grade filet is less well marbled. In as much as this is very lean meat, you must lard* or stud* or bard* it with fat to prevent it from drying out. (Lard the meat *before* tying and browning it. Stud or bard the meat *after* tying and browning it.)

So that the meat will hold its shape when cooking, tie the filet with butcher's twine at one-inch intervals along its length. (If the tapering tail is included in the cut, fold 2 inches of the tail back upon the main body of the meat to form a cylindrical roast about 4 inches in diameter throughout.)

MEAT   389

Next, thoroughly dry the roast with paper towels and brown it. Filet meat is so tender, and a filet roast so small in diameter, it is best to perform this operation in very hot fat in a skillet. This browns the roast quickly and effectively without overly precooking the meat. Now stud* or bard* the meat if you choose, and proceed to roast, poêlé, or braise it.

ROAST FILET OF BEEF
(Filet de Boeuf Rôti)

Trim, lard* (if necessary), tie, season with pepper, and brown the roast in hot beef fat rendered from the trimmings, or in oil. Stud* or bard* the meat if you choose. Do not salt.

This meat must be cooked quickly to the very rare or rare stage. Beyond this point it will begin to toughen and dry out. Therefore, roast the meat in a hot oven at 450° throughout. If the roast is not barded, baste it with fat. Cooking time is about 10 minutes per pound for very rare, 12 minutes per pound for rare. In any event cooking should not last much longer than 45 minutes. Test for doneness by pressing the roast with your fingers. When it loses its softness and becomes resilient to your touch, it is done. A meat thermometer will read about 120°.

Five minutes before you expect the roast to be done, remove the roast from the oven and quickly cut off the ties. Spread it with a few tablespoons of Meat Glaze and return it to the oven to glaze.* Allow the finished roast to rest for 5 or 10 minutes before serving. Here are some of the traditional ways to serve *filet de boeuf rôti*.

FILET OF BEEF CLAMART *(Filet de Boeuf Clamart)*. Roast the filet. Surround it with boiled artichoke bottoms heaped with Peas à la Française finished in butter, and potato balls lightly sautéed in butter. Separately serve the roast's juices, slightly thickened.

FILET OF BEEF DU BARRY *(Filet de Boeuf Du Barry)*. Roast the filet. Surround it with cauliflowerets that you have coated with Mornay Sauce, sprinkled with grated cheese, and browned in the oven. Separately serve the roast's juices, slightly thickened.

FILET OF BEEF BRILLAT-SAVARIN *(Filet de Boeuf Brillat-Savarin)*. Roast the filet. Garnish the roast with asparagus tips and Duchess Potatoes, deep-fried and hollowed out to form little nests that are filled with a *Salpicon* of truffles and *foie gras* in a thick Demi-Glace Sauce. Separately serve the demi-glace sauce.

FILET OF BEEF BOUQUETIÈRE *(Filet de Boeuf Bouquetière)*. Roast the filet. Surround it with mounds of carrot and turnip balls, diced string beans, peas, and flowerets of cauliflower, all boiled and finished in butter; and potatoes cut in olive shapes and sautéed. Separately serve the skimmed and strained pan juices, slightly thickened; or Starch-Thickened Brown Veal Stock.

FILET OF BEEF À LA NIÇOISE (*Filet de Boeuf à la Niçoise*). Roast the filet. Surround the roast with small potatoes sautéed in butter, small to-matoes sautéed in butter with garlic, and green beans finished in butter. Separately serve the roast's skimmed and strained juices; or Starch-Thickened Brown Veal Stock to which you have added 2 tablespoons Tomato Purée per cup.

FILET OF BEEF RICHELIEU (*Filet de Boeuf Richelieu*). Roast the filet. Surround it with mounds of small stuffed tomatoes and stuffed mushrooms, small potatoes or potato balls sautéed in butter, and braised halves of lettuce, all artfully alternated with an eye to their color. Separately served the skimmed and strained juices, slightly thickened; or Starch-Thickened Brown Veal Stock.

FILET OF BEEF ST. GERMAIN (*Filet de Boeuf St. Germain*). Roast the filet. At the ends of the roast place a mound of Glazed Carrots cut in olive shapes. On each side of the carrots place mounds of small potatoes or potato balls sautéed in butter. Along each side of the filet place a row of small *Timbales* filled with Purée of Peas. Separately serve the skimmed and strained juices, slightly thickened; or Starch-Thickened Brown Veal Stock.

FILET OF BEEF WITH GREEN PEPPERCORNS (*Filet de Boeuf au Poivre Vert*). Roast the filet. Serve garnished with Braised Lettuce and Stuffed Onions. Pour over the roast Demi-Glace Sauce or Starch-Thickened Brown Veal Stock in which you have simmered green peppercorns. (Green peppercorns can be found in cans in specialty food shops. They are imported from Madagascar or India.)

POËLÉED FILET OF BEEF
(*Filet de Boeuf Poêlé*)

Beef, a filet roast weighing up to 4 pounds
Clarified Butter, 3 tablespoons
Salt and pepper
Carrots, 2 medium, chopped
Onion, 1 medium, chopped
Bouquet Garni—3 sprigs parsley, 1 bay leaf, crumbled, a pinch of thyme, 1 celery rib

Brown Stock or Brown Veal Stock, 3 cups
Cornstarch or arrowroot, 1 tablespoon
Wine, dry port or white wine, ¼ cup
Butter, 3 tablespoons
A heavy skillet for browning
A heavy casserole, preferably oval, to just fit the roast
A hot sauceboat

Poëléing, you will remember, is cooking in a tightly covered casserole at good heat with little or no added liquid. It is a cross between roasting and braising, and is suitable only for tender meats. Aromatics are cooked with the meat to give it flavor and to provide a base from which to make a sauce.

Trim, lard* (if necessary), and brown the roast in a heavy skillet in hot beef fat or clarified butter. Salt and pepper the meat, tie it with butcher's twine, and stud* or bard* the meat if you choose.

In the skillet in which the meat was browned, lightly brown the carrots and onion. Place the vegetables in the bottom of a heavy casserole that just fits the meat. Put the meat in the casserole, heaping some of the vegetables over it, and add the bouquet garni. Heat the casserole on a burner until the fat sizzles. If the meat is unbarded, cover it with a sheet or overlapping sheets of fresh pork or beef fat. Heat the casserole on a burner until the vegetables start to cook. Cover the pan tightly and place it in a hot 400° oven.

The meat must be cooked quickly to the rare or the very rare stage. Cooking time is about the same as for roasting, about 10 minutes per pound. Baste the roast once during the cooking, turning the roast and heaping the vegetables over it. Work quickly to prevent the oven from cooling.

While the roast is cooking, deglaze* the skillet in which you browned the meat and vegetables with brown stock or brown veal stock, and reserve this liquid for the sauce.

Test for doneness by pressing the roast with your fingers. When it loses its softness and becomes resilient to your touch, it is done. (If you use a meat thermometer, the roast is cooked when the temperature reaches 120°.) Remove the roast to a heated platter and make the sauce.

Roughly skim the fat from the casserole and reduce the pan juices over a brisk flame for 3 or 4 minutes. Strain the juices into a saucepan, skim again, and thicken with cornstarch or arrowroot mixed into dry port wine or dry white wine, adding this mixture little by little until the sauce just coats a spoon. Season to taste with salt and pepper and simmer the sauce for a few minutes more.

Coat the meat with 3 or 4 tablespoons of this sauce, and put it to glaze* in the cooling oven. Just before serving remove the sauce from the heat and stir in 3 tablespoons cold butter to further enrich and thicken it. Serve *filet de boeuf poëlé* in one of the following traditional ways:

FILET OF BEEF RENAISSANCE (*Filet de Boeuf Renaissance*). Poëlé and glaze* the filet. Surround it with carrots and turnips cut into grooved balls and glazed; little bundles of asparagus tips; peas; green beans; cauliflower knobs; small potatoes or potato balls sautéed in butter. Serve separately the poëlé liquor, skimmed, strained, and thickened with arrowroot.

FILET OF BEEF LORETTE (*Filet de Boeuf Lorette*). Poëlé and glaze* the filet. At the ends of the roast place heaps of Lorette Potatoes. Along the sides place mounds of asparagus tips finished in butter. Separately serve Demi-Glace Sauce blended with 4 tablespoons Tomato Purée per cup.

FILET OF BEEF À LA FRANÇAISE (*Filet de Boeuf à la Française*). Poëlé and glaze* the filet. Surround the roast with littles nests made with Duchess Potatoes dipped in egg and dry white breadcrumbs, deep-fried and hollowed out, and filled with a mixed vegetable dice. Also arrange among the nests Braised Lettuce quarters, cauliflower flowerets, asparagus tips tied in bunches, and all topped with Hollandaise Sauce. It is a sight to behold. Separately serve a thin Demi-Glace Sauce or Starch-Thickened Brown Veal Stock, using arrowroot as the starch.

FILET OF BEEF À L'ANDALUSIAN (*Filet de Boeuf à l'Andalusian*). Poëlé and glaze* the filet. Surround it with grilled green pepper halves stuffed with Rice à la Grecque; and one-inch-thick slices of eggplant fried in oil, partially scooped out, and filled with chopped tomatoes sautéed in oil. Arrange these alternately around the roast and place a Chipolata Sausage between each. Separately serve the skimmed and strained pan juices, slightly thickened.

FILET OF BEEF CHÂTELAINE (*Filet de Boeuf Châtelaine*). Poëlé and glaze* the filet. Surround it with artichoke bottoms heaped with thick Soubise Sauce, chestnuts cooked in the pan juices, and potato balls lightly sautéed in butter. Separately serve the skimmed, strained, and reduced pan juices added to Madeira Sauce.

FILET OF BEEF MONTMORENCY (*Filet de Boeuf Montmorency*). Poëlé and glaze* the filet. Separately serve the skimmed, strained, and reduced pan juices added to Madeira Sauce. To each cup of this sauce, add 2 tablespoons red current jelly, 1 tablespoon horseradish, and 18 lightly poached and drained cherries.

BRAISED FILET OF BEEF
(*Filet de Boeuf Braisé*)

This tenderest of all beef cuts is often braised in French cooking. This is not so unusual when you consider that the filet is not as full-flavored as the more exercised parts of beef. Marinating and braising allow the chef to bolster this mild flavor.

Actually, the treatment accorded to the filet (and other tender roasts) is not true braising at all. The meat is cooked only to the rare stage and removed long before the braising liquor can fully penetrate the meat. However, to "braise" the filet, you can follow in general the directions already given for braised beef with the following important exceptions:

1. Reduce the marinating time to 2 to 4 hours at room temperature. It is not necessary to tenderize this beef; you are marinating only to add flavor.

2. Omit the brandy (it is too decided in taste) and use a light wine in the marinade—a Rhine wine, a delicate Bordeaux, or Madeira.

3. Brown the filet only lightly to avoid precooking it too deeply.

4. Be sure to lard* or stud* with fat, or bard* the filet.

5. Only half cover the filet with braising liquor. It will not have time to cook down.

6. Baste the filet every 10 minutes, quickly, to avoid cooling the oven and the pan.

7. Severely reduce the braising time, to about 15 minutes per pound. Unlike other braised meats, the filet and other tender first category roasts are braised rare. Test for doneness by poking the filet with your fingers; it is done when it ceases to feel soft. (At 120° on the meat thermometer the filet is very rare; at 125° rare.)

8. When the filet is cooked, skim the fat from the pan, reduce the sauce quickly to ⅓ of its volume, and flavor it with a little of the same wine the filet was marinated in.

Braised filet is very *haute cuisine*, elaborately garnished and often expensively stuffed. Here are two typical recipes:

FILET OF BEEF À LA MATIGNON (*Filet de Boeuf à la Matignon*). Brown the filet and stud* it with strips of very red salt beef tongue alternating with strips of truffle. Completely cover the roast with a layer of *Matignon*, wrap it in a Bard of fresh pork or beef fat, and tie it. Braise the filet in Madeira wine, and glaze* it. Surround the roast with artichoke bottoms filled with matignon sprinkled with buttered crumbs, and browned in the oven; and Braised Lettuce. Skim, strain, and reduce the braising liquor. Pour a little of this in the bottom of the platter, and send the rest to the table in a hot sauceboat.

FILET OF BEEF À LA PÉRIGOURDINE (*Filet de Boeuf à la Périgourdine*). With a larding needle or a long thin knife, make a hole through the center of the filet from end to end. Working from each end, thrust pieces of truffle into this hole until they meet in the center. Braise the filet in Madeira wine and Brown Veal Stock. Serve the roast surrounded with slices of *foie gras* lightly sautéed in butter, alternating with small Tartlets containing a *Salpicon* of truffles. Skim, strain, and reduce the braising liquor and pour it over the roast.

THE STEAKS OF THE FILET

Imagine, if you will, the teardrop-shaped filet with its head at your left and its tapering tail at your right. The names of the steaks taken from the filet for French cooking are, from left to right, *bifteck, chateaubriand, filet steak, tournedos,* and *filet mignon.*

The cooking of all these pieces—whether grilled, broiled, or sautéed—is similar to the cooking of other beefsteaks. However, this meat, being dryer and more delicate than the meat of strip, club, or rib steaks, should be cooked even more quickly if possible. This requires that grilled or broiled steaks from the filet be exposed to even greater heat than ordinary steaks, while being protected by more frequent basting with Clarified Butter.

Sautéed steaks from the filet should be cooked quickly, too, and basted with butter as they cook. As an added precaution, before cooking rub these steaks with plenty of Clarified Butter and be sure they are warmed to room temperature before you set them to cook. Finally, panbroiling, which can be very drying, is not recommended for steaks of the filet.

With these little adjustments, and other refinements to be given for each cut, you may follow the directions given in the previous section for cooking ordinary beefsteaks. Tests for doneness are the same.

As to garnishes, you have a great deal of freedom. Steaks from the filet may be served with any garnish appropriate to ordinary beefsteaks (*entre-côtes*). They may also receive any garnish belonging to the whole filet of beef, providing the garnish is so arranged as to suit the size and shape of the steak. It is clear, for example, that the Rossini garnish for tournedos—which consists of arranging the 2-inch-diameter tournedos in the form of a crown and topping each with a 2-inch-diameter round of *foie gras* and a slice of truffle—would be rather gross if applied to a large chateaubriand or rib steak. Also, tradition has something to say in the matter. I will therefore apportion garnishes to cuts of steak with which they are associated by their nature or tradition. You may substitute according to your own good judgment.

BIFTECK

Biftecks are the tenderloin portion of American sirloin steaks, the least tender part of the filet lying close to the rump. (In France, the name bifteck is also sometimes given to strip or shell steaks and hamburgers.) They may measure up to 4 inches across, are cut about 1 inch thick, and weigh 5 or 6 ounces. They are grilled, broiled, or sautéed. (This cut is sometimes sold in America as New York butt tenderloin steak.)

Before cooking, trim and slightly flatten the bifteck. Brush it with Clarified Butter, pepper it only, and cook it with brisk heat. Serve it with any garnish appropriate to ordinary beefsteaks, with garnishes listed under whole filet of beef, with garnishes listed under other steaks from the filet, or with the following:

STEAK WITH MUSHROOMS (*Bifteck aux Champignons*). Sauté the steak. Halfway through cooking add to the pan sliced mushrooms that you have ¾ cooked in a little stock. Remove the cooked steak to a hot platter. Deglaze* the pan with the mushroom cooking liquor, boiled down, and finish the sauce with a little dry white wine and Demi-Glace Sauce. Swirl in* a little cold butter and pour sauce and mushrooms over the steak.

STEAK SOUBISE (*Bifteck Soubise*). Grill the steak. Serve it with Soubise Sauce.

STEAK À LA PERSANE (*Bifteck à la Persane*). Broil the steak. Serve it with green peppers stuffed with rice; grilled tomato halves; and fried slices of bananas. Separately serve Chateaubriand Sauce.

STEAK WITH TARRAGON (*Bifteck à l'Estragon*). Grill the steak. Dress the top of the steak with parboiled fresh tarragon. Separately serve Starch-Thickened Brown Veal Stock flavored with chopped fresh tarragon.

STEAK À LA PORTUGAISE (*Bifteck à la Portugaise*). Sauté the steak. Surround it with Château Potatoes and small tomatoes stuffed with Duxelles. Deglaze* the pan with a little white wine, thicken this liquid with a little Demi-Glace Sauce flavored with Tomato Purée, and pour the sauce over the steak.

CHATEAUBRIAND

Chateaubriands are the most formidable steaks of the filet, consisting of the large tenderloin portion of American porterhouse steaks. They are cut 2 inches thick and weigh up to 1¾ pounds. On menus they usually appear as "Chateaubriand for two persons." (It is said that François Chateaubriand, whose name this steak bears, was thus honored for his method of cooking it, that is, grilling it between two other steaks so that it could be enjoyed evenly rare throughout. Actually, the method was invented by Chateaubriand's chef, Montmireil. Chateaubriand, therefore, stole the credit.)

A chateaubriand is usually grilled. Being a thick steak, it is first placed close to the fire to seal its surface. It is then removed farther from the fire, or the flame is reduced, to finish the cooking.

This steak is traditionally served with Château Potatoes and sauced with Maître d'Hôtel Butter, Chateaubriand Sauce, or Colbert Sauce. It is also served with garnishes appropriate to ordinary beefsteaks, with garnishes listed under the whole filet, with garnishes listed for other steaks of the filet, or with the following:

CHATEAUBRIAND PARMENTIER (*Chateaubriand Parmentier*). Grill or broil the steak. Serve it with potatoes cut into large dice or small balls, lightly cooked in butter, and sprinkled with chopped parsley.

CHATEAUBRIAND À LA PROVENÇALE (*Chateaubriand à la Provençale*). Grill or broil the steak. Serve it with stuffed Tomatoes à la Provençale, and mushroom caps stuffed with garlic-flavored *Duxelles*.

CHATEAUBRIAND VALENCAY (*Chateaubriand Valencay*). Grill or broil the steak. Serve it with ham-and-noodle Croquettes. Separately serve Chateaubriand Sauce.

CHATEAUBRIAND À LA SARDE (*Chateaubriand à la Sarde*). Grill or broil the steak. Serve it with tomatoes and 3-inch cucumber sections, both vegetables braised, partially hollowed out, stuffed with *Duxelles,* sprinkled with buttered crumbs and butter, and browned in the oven. Also serve Croquettes of rice and egg yolk, flavored with saffron, dipped in batter, and deep-fried.

FILET STEAK

Filet steaks, like chateaubriands, are taken from the American porterhouse. They are cut about 1 inch thick and weigh about 6 ounces. They are similar to the *bifteck* in size, but they are finer. Grill, broil, or sauté them. Serve them with any garnish listed for ordinary beefsteaks, the whole filet, other steaks from the filet, or the following:

FILET MIGNON MASSENA (*Côte de Filet Massena*). Broil, grill, or sauté the steak. Remove it to a hot platter and decorate the top with slices of poached and drained beef bone Marrow. Surround the steak with small artichoke bottoms simmered in butter and topped with thick Béarnaise Sauce.

FILET MIGNON RACHEL (*Filet de Boeuf Rachel*). Grill or broil the steak. Surround it with artichoke bottoms simmered in butter, topped with slices of poached and drained bone Marrow, and put under the broiler flame for 1 minute. Separately serve Bordelaise Sauce.

FILET MIGNON FORESTIÈRE (*Côte de Filet Forestière*). Sauté the steak. Serve it surrounded with heaps of noodles alternated with heaps of potatoes cut in large dice and sautéed in butter.

FILET MIGNON BRABANCONNE (*Côte de Filet Brabanconne*). Grill, broil, or sauté the steak. Serve it with Potatoes Fondantes or Tartlet shells filled with Brussels sprouts that you have parboiled and simmered in butter, covered with Mornay Sauce, and browned under the broiler.

TOURNEDOS

Tournedos are taken from the tenderloin portion of the larger of the American T-bone steaks. They are trimmed to be perfectly round—about 2 inches in diameter and 1½ inches thick, weighing 3 to 4 ounces. Usually 2 are made up from a single slice of filet, and 2 or 3 are served per person. They are usually cooked with a Bard of fat tied around their circumference. Tournedos are sometimes called *medaillons* of beef.

These elegant pieces are most often sautéed in Clarified Butter, after having been rubbed with butter and peppered lightly (they are salted after cooking). They are often placed on sliced of bread cut in rounds the same size as the tournedos and sautéed in butter until they are crisp and golden. The bread helps raise the tournedos up above their surrounding garnish. Tournedos are served with any garnish appropriate to ordinary beefsteaks, whole filet of beef, other steaks from the filet, and especially the following:

TOURNEDOS MARIE-LOUISE (*Tournedos Marie-Louise*). Sauté the tournedos. Arrange them in the form of a crown atop round slices of bread sautéed in butter. On top of each tournedos place an artichoke bottom, simmered in butter and filled with a mound of Mushroom Purée mixed with thick Soubise Sauce.

TOURNEDOS ROSSINI (*Tournedos Rossini*). Sauté the tournedos. Arrange them in the form of a crown atop round slices of bread sautéed in butter. On top of each tournedos place a round slice of *foie gras*, seasoned, dredged in flour, and sautéed in butter. On top of each slice of *foie gras* place a slice of truffle. Separately serve Starch-Thickened Brown Veal Stock flavored with Madeira wine.

TOURNEDOS BEAUHARNAIS (*Tournedos Beauharnais*). Sauté the tournedos. Arrange them in the form of a crown atop round slices of bread sautéed in butter. On top of each tournedos place an artichoke bottom filled with Béarnaise Sauce and sprinkled with finely chopped tarragon. Fill the center of the crown with small potato balls sautéed in butter. Pour Madeira Sauce around the tournedos.

TOURNEDOS ALGERIAN (*Tournedos Algérienne*). Sauté the tournedos. Arrange them in the form of a crown. Top each tournedos with a round cake of sweet potato Croquette. Surround the crown of tournedos with small peeled and seeded tomatoes simmered in olive oil.

TOURNEDOS MARÉCHALE (*Tournedos Maréchale*). Sauté the tournedos. Arrange them in the form of a crown atop round slices of bread sautéed in butter. On top of each tournedos place a slice of glazed* truffle. Surround the crown of tournedos with mounds of asparagus tips in butter.

TOURNEDOS HENRY IV (*Tournedos Henri IV*). Grill the tournedos. Arrange them in the form of a crown atop round slices of bread sautéed in butter. Using a pastry bag, pipe a ring of Béarnaise Sauce around the top of each tournedos. In the center of this ring, place an artichoke bottom filled with tiny potatoes balls lightly sautéed in butter.

TOURNEDOS CHORON (*Tournedos Choron*). Sauté the tournedos. Arrange them in the form of a crown atop round slices of bread sautéed in butter. Using a pastry bag, pipe a ring of Choron Sauce around the top of each tournedos. In the center of this ring, place an artichoke bottom filled with peas in butter. Surround the crown of tournedos with potatoes cut in olive shapes and lightly sautéed in butter.

TOURNEDOS LESDIGUIÈRES (*Tournedos Lesdiguières*). Grill the tournedos. Arrange them in the form of a crown atop large onions that you have poached until they are almost cooked, hollowed out to form a natural receptacle, filled ⅔ with spinach in cream and the remaining ⅓ with Mornay Sauce, and browned in a hot oven.

TOURNEDOS CINDERELLA (*Tournedos Cinderella*). Sauté the tournedos. Arrange them in the form of a crown atop butter-braised artichoke bottoms that you have topped with a Soubise Purée containing chopped truffles, and browned in the oven.

TOURNEDOS BALTIMORE (*Tournedos Baltimore*). Sauté the tournedos. Arrange them in the form of a crown atop small Tartlet shells filled with Corn in Cream. Place on top of each tournedos a thick slice of tomato and a slice of green pepper, both sautéed in butter. Separately serve Chateaubriand Sauce.

TOURNEDOS ST. MANDE (*Tournedos St. Mande*). Sauté the tournedos. Arrange them in the form of a crown atop mounds of Potatoes Macaire molded like tarts. Fill the center of the crown of tournedos with Peas in Butter.

TOURNEDOS À LA MÉNAGÈRE (*Tournedos à la Ménagère*). Sauté the tournedos. Place them on a bed of vegetables in a deep platter or cocotte, the vegetables having been prepared in advance as follows: In a heavy casserole or cocotte, put 1 cup each of finely diced new carrots, small onions, and peas. Mix into the vegetables ½ cup Printanier Butter in small pieces. Season the vegetables, add ¼ cup water, cover the cocotte, and simmer the vegetables until they are just tender.

FILET MIGNON

Filet mignons are taken from the tenderloin portion of the smaller of the American T-bone steaks, at the tail end of the teardrop-shaped filet. Although the French sometimes call these "little filets" (*petits filets de boeuf*), they are sometimes larger in diameter than tournedos because not more than one is obtained per slice. They are usually trimmed round, barded with fat around their circumference, cooked like tournedos (although they are more often grilled), and they may be served with any of the garnishes already given for steak or whole filet, as well as the following:

FILET MIGNON BÉARNAISE (*Filet Mignon Béarnaise*). Grill or broil the steaks. Arrange them in the form of a crown atop round slices of bread sautéed in butter. Brush the steaks with Meat Glaze and surround them with a ring of Béarnaise Sauce. In the center of the crown of steaks, place a mound of Château Potatoes.

FILET MIGNON MONTGOMERY (*Filet Mignon Montgomery*). Grill or broil the steaks. Place them on top of a spinach cake cooked in a Tartlet mold. With a pastry bag, decorate the tops of the steaks with rosettes of thick Soubise Sauce, and place a round of truffle on the rosette.

FILET MIGNON ARLÉSIENNE (*Filet Mignon Arlésienne*). Sauté the steaks in butter and oil and remove them to a hot platter. Place slices of deep-fried onion on the steaks, and surround them with alternating slices of egg-plant and tomatoes, sautéed.

FILET MIGNON ROUMANILLE (*Filet Mignon Roumanille*). Grill or broil the steaks. Arrange them in the form of a crown atop grilled or broiled to-mato halves, coat the steaks with Mornay Sauce and glaze* them in the oven. In the center of the crown of steaks place a mound of deep-fried eggplant slices. On top of each steak place a poached stuffed olive with an anchovy filet wrapped around its base.

✳ *LEFTOVER BEEF*

There are many French dishes using leftover beef, both hot and cold. Cold beef dishes are no problem. When the beef is reheated, however, you run the risk of drying it out and getting a "leftover" taste.

The best beef for reheating is boiled beef, followed by leftover braised beef. When properly cooked to begin with, these meats retain a good amount of moisture. They may be lightly sautéed or slowly simmered in sauce without drying out too much.

Roast beef is too dry for further cooking, and it is best eaten cold. It may be warmed by slicing it very thinly and pouring boiling hot sauce over the thin slices. Obviously, the rarer the beef, the juicier it will be.

POOR MAN'S BOILED BEEF (*Boeuf Bouilli au Pauvre Homme*). This dish is reputed to have been prized by King Louis XV of France. Arrange thin slices of cold boiled beef on a baking dish. Sprinkle with salt, pepper, chopped scallions and parsley, a little garlic, and a few tablespoons of stock fat. Pour over 1 cup Brown Stock and sprinkle with breadcrumbs. Heat the dish in a 325° oven for 15 minutes.

COLD BOILED BEEF À LA PARISIENNE (*Boeuf Bouilli Froid à la Pari-sienne*). Place thin slices of cold boiled beef in a row on a long dish. Sur-round the beef with alternating heaps of boiled potato slices, tomato slices, green beans, quartered hard-cooked eggs, and watercress. Scatter thin-sliced onion over the meat and sprinkle it with Vinaigrette Sauce. Decorate with chopped parsley, chervil, and tarragon.

DEVILED BOILED BEEF (*Boeuf Bouilli à la Diable*). Thickly slice cold boiled beef. Spread it with Dijon Mustard, sprinkle with butter and dry white breadcrumbs, pressing the crumbs into the mustard. Lightly broil or grill the slices and serve with Devil Sauce.

BOILED BEEF À LA HONGROISE (*Boeuf Bouilli à la Hongroise*). Cut 1 pound cold beef in ¾-inch dice and lightly brown it in a skillet. Add ½ cup chopped onions and cook until they are transparent. Season with salt, pepper, and 2 teaspoons paprika. Just before serving stir in 1 cup Cream Sauce.

BOILED BEEF À L'INDIENNE (*Boeuf Bouilli à l'Indienne*). Prepare as for à la Hongroise (above), but in place of the paprika add 2 teaspons curry powder. Serve with Rice à l'Indienne.

BOILED BEEF À LA PROVENÇALE (*Boeuf Bouilli à la Provençale*). Prepare as for à la Hongroise (above), but in place of the cream sauce use 1 cup garlic-flavored Tomato Fondue. Sprinkle with chopped parsley.

BOILED BEEF À LA LYONNAISE (*Boeuf Bouilli Sauté à la Lyonnaise*). Lightly sauté 1 pound of sliced cold boiled beef in butter. To the pan add 1 cup sliced and sautéed onions. Add salt and pepper, and cook onions and beef together for a few minutes. Place beef and onions on a hot platter and sprinkle with chopped parsley. Deglaze* the pan with 2 tablespoons vinegar and pour over the beef and onions.

CHOPPED BOILED BEEF AU GRATIN (*Coquilles de Boeuf au Gratin*). Chop and season leftover boiled beef. Put the chopped beef into a scallop shell. Using a pastry bag, lay down a decorative border of Duchess Potatoes around the rim of the shell. Sprinkle with breadcrumbs, grated cheese, and melted butter, and lightly brown in the oven.

THIN SLICED BOILED BEEF IN SAUCE (*Émincés de Boeuf*). Thinly slice leftover beef and arrange it on a serving dish. Cover the beef with a boiling sauce—Burgundy or Madeira, Piquant or Pepper, Robert, Devil, Bordelaise, Chasseur, or Duxelles Sauce.

MIROTON OF BEEF (*Miroton de Boeuf*). Place in the bottom of a baking dish a bed of lightly sautéed onions and Lyonnaise Sauce. Place thin overlapping slices of cold boiled beef on this bed of sauce and onions, pour over hot Lyonnaise Sauce and a few tablespoons of hot melted butter. Brown lightly in the oven, sprinkle with chopped parsley, and serve.

FRICADELLES OF BEEF (*Fricadelles de Boeuf*). Mince 1 pound of leftover beef and mix it with 1⅓ cups Potato Purée, ½ cup chopped onion, 2 eggs, salt, pepper, and a pinch of nutmeg. Shape into 4 cakes, dredge them with flour, brown them in butter, and bake them in a 350° oven for 20 to 30 minutes. Serve with a spicy sauce—Robert, Pepper, Piquant, or Devil.

BEEF HASH (*Hachis de Boeuf*). Finely dice leftover boiled beef, mix it with Demi-Glace Sauce, bring to the simmer, cover, and place in a 300° oven for 30 minutes. Add more sauce during cooking if mixture becomes too dry. Serve the hash in a deep dish with or without a border of Duchess Potatoes. Hachis de Boeuf may also be made with Curry Sauce (*à l'Indienne*), with Hungarian Sauce (*à la Hongroise*), with Italian Sauce (*à l'Italienne*), and with Lyonnaise Sauce (*à la Lyonnaise*).

✳ VEAL
(*Veau*)

Veal is the meat of calves 12 weeks old or less. The best veal is from dairy herd calves. In France and Italy these calves are raised exclusively on milk and finished on milk and eggs. The flesh is very white, with not a tinge of pink, and very delicate in flavor. What little fat is found on this veal is very white and smooth and exudes a faint, fresh odor of milk. With meat like this to work with, it is not surprising that veal is very important in French cookery.

Unfortunately it is almost impossible to find real veal in America. Your best hope is to locate a good Italian butcher who, by determined effort, has managed to find people who will raise veal according to his specifications. The veal one usually finds ranges from pale pink to a grayish, deeper pink, and finally to red. Pale pink veal is acceptable; never buy the red.

The reasons we do not have good veal are complicated. Yes, the cost of milk is high, but the calf consumes this milk only for a short 12 weeks at most. Another reason is the cost of butchering; a calf takes almost as much slicing and sawing as a steer and produces much less meat. As a result, calves are quickly put on a grain or grass diet and their growth forced for 12 or even 14 weeks to make butchering them worth while. Both their diet and their age contribute redness to their meat. People taste this red meat veal and conclude that veal is not very good, certainly not worth paying a premium for. Thus, a vicious circle has developed and an excellent meat is absent from our tables. We each eat only 3 to 4 pounds of veal a year.

If every woman in America went to the supermarket tomorrow and asked, "Do you have any *whiter* veal?" a good stride would be taken in the right direction. Wanting this, I suggest you examine the veal carefully every time you go to the store. Frequently you will find both light and dark veal blatantly displayed together. Fix the range of color in your mind, and the first time you see whitish, light pink veal, cancel your previous shopping plan and buy it. This will be from a younger, smaller animal, and although not entirely milk fed, the meat will be delicate and good. Prepare it according to one of the classic French recipes that follow, and you can confidently expect your family to do the dinner dishes as your reward.

The best grades of veal, like beef, are Prime and Choice, but the grade does not tell you how old the animal is. You must learn to read the meat itself.

THE CUTS OF VEAL

Veal is cut much like beef. From front to rear, there are arm roasts, shoulder roasts, rib roasts, loin roasts, sirloin roasts, rump roasts, and roasts cut from the leg. Also, there are rib and loin chops, corresponding to beef-steaks. Because of its smaller size, veal offers some cuts nonexistent in beef. Taken from the rib section is a crown roast, which is the rib turned inside out and placed so the bones stand upright like a crown. The lower (shank) half of the leg often becomes a roast. The whole breast of a side of veal is removed in one piece, corresponding to the brisket and plate of beef. Finally, the renowned scallops of veal (*escalopes de veau*) are thin, boneless, flattened slices of meat, cut across the grain and taken from the round, loin, or rib. (I have seen thin pounded pieces of veal meat called scallops that are not scallops at all, but slices of meat taken lengthwise from the leg. These curl when cooking, so it is best to cut your own.)

COOKING VEAL

Veal cookery is protein cookery, but it differs considerably from the cooking of beef. Although young, veal contains much of its protein in the form of connective tissue. Also, it contains hardly any fat. Consequently, although a careful roasting is possible (it should be larded*), veal is best cooked by moist heat to soften its surfeit of tough connective tissue and prevent it from drying out. An exception is veal scallops, which are tenderized by crosscutting and pounding.

Putting the cuts of veal and recommended cooking methods together, we have sautéed veal scallops; sautéed or braised veal chops; roasted or braised loin and rib roasts; braised rump, round, and shoulder roasts; braised veal knuckle; braised breast; veal stews made from cubes of neck, shoulder, and breast (especially fricassees and *blanquettes*); and pan stews (paradoxically called veal sautés).

✳ BRAISED VEAL

Because of the high proportion of connective tissue contained in calf's meat, large pieces of veal are best braised. The braising of veal and other white meats differs from the braising of beef. You will recall that a complete, long-form braising of beef requires two stages of cooking. Veal is braised in one stage, similar to the short-form braising of beef. And *most important, you must take care that veal or any other white meat is not overcooked during the braising.* Unlike beef, which at the end of its braising period readily absorbs the rich sauce surrounding it, veal will become tough, dry, and tasteless. The procedure for braising veal is as follows:

(1) Lard* the veal if you choose, carefully dry it with paper towels, and brown it lightly to stiffen its surface. To do this, you may turn it in hot Clarified Butter in a skillet or casserole. Or you may spread it with butter and brown it in a hot 425° oven for about 30 minutes, or until it is golden brown.

(2) Tie the meat with butcher's twine if necessary, and season it with salt and pepper. Place it in a casserole on a bed of raw or lightly browned aromatic vegetables consisting of 1 carrot, sliced, and 1 onion, sliced. (If you brown the meat in the oven, these vegetables may be added at the beginning.) The casserole should be large enough to hold the meat without the cover touching it.

(3) To the casserole add 1 cup Brown Veal Stock; 2 or 3 sawed veal bones; and a *Bouquet Garni* consisting of 1 stalk celery, 3 sprigs parsley, ½ bay leaf, and a sprig or pinch of thyme, all tied in cheesecloth. Reduce this stock, either in the hot oven or over a brisk fire, until it has almost disappeared. Then add another 1 cup of stock and reduce it, basting the meat frequently, until it is almost a glaze. (The purpose of this is to create a gelatinous braising liquid that will cling to the meat during cooking and more effectively prevent it from drying out.)

(4) Now, add more brown veal stock to just about half cover the meat. Cover it with a piece of buttered paper cut to fit the size of a pan, and with a small hole cut in it to vent the steam. Cover the pan tightly and put it in a 375° oven.

(5) Cook the meat, basting regularly, until it is done. From the time the cover is replaced, the meat will require about 30 minutes' cooking per pound. But you must test for doneness early. Unlike beef, veal and other white meats will dry out very quickly if they are overcooked. Test for doneness by pricking the meat deeply with a poultry skewer. It is done when the juices that bubble from the hole are absolutely colorless.

(6) When the meat is just cooked, uncover it and allow it to glaze* in the hot oven for 10 minutes, basting very frequently with the braising liquid to prevent it from drying and to give it a handsome, translucent coating.

(7) Remove the meat to a hot platter, and use the braising liquid to prepare a sauce as indicated in the recipe you are following.

All of the following recipes for large braised pieces of veal are more or less interchangeable, and the garnishes for one cut of meat may be used for any other.

BRAISED RIB OF VEAL À LA CLAMART (*Carré de Veau Braisé à la Clamart*). Have the backbone removed to make carving easier. Braise the veal and glaze* it. Serve it garnished with artichoke hearts filled with peas with butter, and potato balls sautéed in butter until golden. Separately serve the braising liquid, skimmed, reduced, strained, and slightly thickened with Demi-Glace if this is necessary.

BRAISED RIB OF VEAL À LA JARDINIÈRE (*Carré de Veau Braisé à la Jardinière*). Have the backbone removed to make carving easier. Braise the veal and glaze* it. Put it on a hot platter, and surround it with heaps of Glazed Carrots cut in olive shapes, Glazed Turnips cut in olive shapes, peas, green beans cut in ½-inch slices, and kidney beans mixed in butter. You may also serve cauliflowerets dressed with butter or Hollandaise Sauce. Separately serve the braising liquid, skimmed, reduced, and strained.

BRAISED LOIN OF VEAL À LA RENAISSANCE (*Longe de Veau Braisée à la Renaissance*). Braise the loin and glaze* it. Put it on a hot platter. At the ends place a heap of boiled cauliflowerets. Along the sides, place Braised Carrots and Braised Turnips cut in olive shapes, green beans cut in ½-inch slices, peas, asparagus tips in butter, and small potato balls cooked in butter. Separately serve the braising liquid, skimmed of fat, reduced, and strained.

BRAISED LOIN OF VEAL PAPRIKA (*Longe de Veau Braisée Paprika*). Lard* the meat. In addition to the salt and pepper, season it well with paprika. Braise it on a bed of chopped onions only (omitting the carrots), and glaze* it. Garnish with nests of Duchess Potatoes filled with cooked cauliflowerets coated with Mornay Sauce into which you have mixed a little chopped onion simmered in butter and seasoned with paprika. Skim and reduce the braising liquor. Season it with paprika, add heavy cream equal to the amount of braising liquid, and press through a sieve. If necessary, thicken with a little Béchamel or Velouté Sauce. Serve the sauce separately in a hot sauceboat.

BRAISED SHOULDER OF VEAL À LA BOULANGÈRE (*Épaule de Veau Braisée à la Boulangère*). Have the shoulder boned, rolled, and tied. At home, untie it and season the inside with salt and pepper. Retie the shoulder and braise it. Thirty minutes before cooking is completed, remove the meat and keep it warm. Skim the braising liquid and quickly reduce it by ½. Strain it and return it to the clean braising pan with the meat. Add small white onions that you have very lightly sautéed in butter. Cover and resume cooking until the veal and onions are done. Serve the onions with the veal. Separately serve the braising liquid, skimmed of fat and strained.

BRAISED SHOULDER OF VEAL À LA BOURGEOISE (*Épaule de Veau Braisée à la Bourgeoise*). Prepare as for Braised Shoulder of Veal à la Boulangère (above), but add to the braising pan small Glazed Onions, Glazed Carrots cut in olive shapes, Braised Celery, and fresh peas.

BRAISED STUFFED SHOULDER OF VEAL (*Épaule de Veau Braisée et Farcie*). Have the shoulder boned, rolled, and tied. At home, untie it, pound the inside surface with a mallet, and season it with salt and pepper. Spread the surface with a thick layer of Sausage Meat or Forcemeat mixed with chopped herbs such as parsley, chives, thyme. Roll up the shoulder, tie it, braise it, and glaze* it. Separately serve the braising liquid, skimmed of fat and strained.

BRAISED RUMP OF VEAL À LA BRIARDE (*Noix de Veau Braisée à la Briarde*). Lard* and braise the rump of veal. Serve it garnished with braised lettuce stuffed with Sausage Meat or Forcemeat and carrots cut in olive shapes and mixed in cream. Separately serve the braising liquid, skimmed, reduced, and strained.

BRAISED RUMP OF VEAL NIVERNAISE (*Noix de Veau Braisée Nivernaise*). Lard* and braise the rump of veal. Serve it garnished with Glazed Carrots cut in olive shapes, and small Glazed Onions. Separately serve the braising liquid, skimmed, reduced, and strained.

BRAISED STUFFED BREAST OF VEAL (*Poitrine de Veau Braisée et Farcie*). Endeavor to get a large breast of veal, weighing about 6 pounds. You will most likely have to bone the meat yourself. With a sharp knife, outline the bones on the underside where they are close to the surface. Slip the knife beneath them, and bend them back until they come loose, scraping the knife against the bone as you work. Now, scrape along the breastbone, keeping the edge of the knife against the bone. Continue cutting and scraping along the length of the meat until the breastbone is free. Trim away excess fat but do not remove the long flap of meat that runs lengthwise.

The meat is now triangular in shape, with a thick base at the bottom.

Placing one hand on the side of the meat, begin slicing a deep pocket into the thick base. Follow the progress and position of the knife with your hand, to make sure it does not pierce the surface of the meat. When the pocket is made, stuff it with Sausage Meat or Forcemeat and sew it up. Braise the breast. Remove it to a hot platter and keep warm. Skim, reduce, and strain the braising liquid. If it is not thick enough, thicken it with a little cornstarch in water. Also, you may enrich the sauce with a little cream. Slice the stuffed breast at an angle to assure large slices. Ladle a little of the sauce over it, and send the rest to the table in a hot sauceboat.

BRAISED BREAST OF VEAL WITH SPINACH (*Poitrine de Veau Braisée aux Épinards*). Bone the breast or not, as you choose. Braise and glaze* it. Garnish with simmered Spinach in Butter. Skim the braising liquid, reduce it, and strain it. Sprinkle a little over the breast, and serve the rest in a hot sauceboat.

BRAISED BREAST OF VEAL WITH MUSHROOMS (*Poitrine de Veau Braisée aux Champignons*). Proceed as for Braised Breast of Veal with Spinach (above), but garnish with whole mushrooms stewed in butter.

BRAISED BREAST OF VEAL À LA PROVENÇALE (*Poitrine de Veau Braisée à la Provençale*). Bone the breast or not, as you choose. Brown lightly in olive oil. Place on a bed of finely chopped and sautéed onion; peeled, seeded, and chopped tomato; a few cloves of garlic, crushed; and a *Bouquet Garni*. Half cover the breast with braising liquid made with ½ white wine, ½ Brown Veal Stock. Braise the breast. Separately serve the braising liquid, skimmed of fat, reduced, and strained.

BRAISED VEAL CHOPS (*Côtes de Veau Braisées*). All veal chops can be braised, but it is perhaps best to braise only the shoulder chops or steaks cut from the round, reserving the more tender chops for poëléing or sautéing. Have the chops cut at least 1 inch thick. Brown them lightly in butter, and braise them in a liquid consisting of ½ white wine, which you have boiled down until it is almost entirely reduced, and ½ Brown Veal Stock. Arrange the cooked chops on a hot platter. Skim, reduce, and strain the braising liquid, and pour it over the chops.

BRAISED PAUPIETTES OF VEAL (*Paupiettes de Veau Braisées*). Prepare meat as for Veal Cutlets (*escalopes*), and pound to a ¼-inch thickness. Spread the escalopes with Pork Forcemeat mixed with *Duxelles,* chopped parsley, and beaten egg. Roll them up, bard* them with blanched salt pork or bacon, and tie them with soft string. Put them in a braising pan on a bed of chopped carrots and onions, lightly sautéed in butter. Season with salt and pepper, cover, and cook on a low flame for 15 minutes. Add 1 cup dry white wine, and boil down until the wine is almost entirely reduced. Add Starch-Thickened Brown Veal Stock to cover the *paupiettes* by ½, and a *Bouquet Garni* consisting of 3 sprigs parsley, ½ bay leaf, and a sprig or pinch of thyme, all tied in cheesecloth. Cover the pan, bring to the boil, and braise in a 325° oven, basting frequently, for about 45 minutes or until the veal is done. Remove the bards from the paupiettes, and reduce the braising liquid by ½. Strain this sauce and use some of it to glaze* the paupiettes. Serve the remaining sauce separately.

✳ SAUTÉED VEAL

Rib chops, loin chops, and the boneless, flattened pieces of meat called cutlets or *escalopes,* are all sautéed. Sometimes, also, the breast of veal is sautéed after having been cut up as for a stew.

VEAL CHOPS

Veal contains a large proportion of connective tissue, and, unless tenderized in some manner, it must therefore be sautéed slowly to give this tissue time to become tender. Consequently, veal chops for sautéing should be cut about one inch thick to prevent them from drying out during the relatively long sautéing period. Veal chops are sometimes broiled or grilled slowly with care, but this form of heat is too hot and dry to suit them.

To sauté veal chops, season the chops with salt and pepper and dredge them in flour, slapping the chops smartly so that there is no excess flour to burn in the pan. Put the chops in very hot Clarified Butter and reduce the heat so that they sauté slowly, 10 to 15 minutes per side. Turn the chops when beads of moisture appear on the uncooked side. When beads of moisture again appear on the cooked side, continue cooking for a few minutes longer and press the chop with your finger to be sure it is firm in the center and well done. The chops should be golden brown in color.

When the chops are cooked, remove them to a hot serving platter. Pour off excess butter from the pan, and deglaze* the pan with whatever liquid (wine or stock or mushroom essence) is called for in the recipe. These pan juices are then thickened with Demi-Glace Sauce, Starch-Thickened Stock, *Beurre Manié,* or cornstarch, according to the recipe.

VEAL CHOPS BOURGUIGNONNE (*Côtes de Veau Bourguignonne*). Sauté the chops in Clarified Butter. When they are half cooked, add to the pan small Glazed Onions, mushrooms, and squares of parboiled lean bacon. When the chops are cooked, remove them to a hot platter. Deglaze* the pan with dry red wine, reduce a little, and thicken with *Beurre Manié*. Finish the sauce with a little Demi-Glace Sauce and cook for a few minutes to blend the flavors. Off the fire, swirl in a little butter and pour the sauce, with the vegetables and bacon it contains, over the chops.

VEAL CHOPS CHASSEUR (*Côtes de Veau Chasseur*). Sauté the chops in Clarified Butter, remove them to a hot platter, and keep warm. To the pan add 1 tablespoon chopped shallots and 1 cup sliced mushrooms. Cook over a lively flame until the vegetables are browned. Add ¾ cup dry white wine and reduce almost entirely. Add 1 cup Starch-Thickened Brown Stock and 1 tablespoon Tomato Sauce. Cook and stir for a few minutes to blend the sauce. Off the fire, add 1 teaspoon chopped chervil and 1 teaspoon chopped tarragon. Swirl in 1 tablespoon butter and pour the sauce, shallots, and mushrooms over the chops.

VEAL CHOPS À LA CRÈME (*Côtes de Veau à la Crème*). Sauté the chops in Clarified Butter, remove them to a hot platter, and keep warm. Deglaze* the pan with ½ cup dry white wine or Madeira wine. Cook down by ½ and add a few tablespoons of thick cream. Cook down again, until the sauce thickens (or thicken it with a little Velouté Sauce). Strain the sauce and pour it over the chops.

VEAL CHOPS WITH MUSHROOMS À LA CRÈME (*Côtes de Veau aux Champignons à la Crème*). Prepare as for Veal Chops à la Crème (above), but add mushroom caps to the pan when the veal is half cooked. Remove the cooked veal and mushrooms to a hot platter, prepare the sauce, and pour it over the chops and mushrooms.

VEAL CHOPS À LA PORTUGAISE (*Côtes de Veau à la Portugaise*). Sauté the chops in olive oil, and remove to a hot platter. Deglaze* the pan with ½ cup dry white wine. Add 6 or 8 tablespoons Tomato Fondue and a little minced garlic. Reduce until the sauce thickens, add 1 teaspoon chopped parsley, and pour over the chops.

VEAL CHOPS À LA LYONNAISE (*Côtes de Veau à la Lyonnaise*). Sauté the chops in Clarified Butter. When they are almost cooked, add to the pan ⅓ cup chopped onion, which you have simmered in butter. Remove the cooked chops to a hot platter. To the pan add 2 tablespoons vinegar, 2 table-spoons Demi-Glace Sauce, and 1 tablespoon chopped parsley. Heat and pour the sauce and onions over the chops.

VEAL CUTLETS

Veal cutlets, or *escalopes,* are boneless pieces of meat taken from the loin, tenderloin, or round and cleared of all visible connective tissue. They should be cut across the grain from a single muscle with no separations, and are trimmed in round or oval shapes. They are cut somewhat thinner than veal chops, and are tenderized by pounding. They weigh 3 or 4 ounces, and after pounding they should be about ½ inch thick.

Escalopes de veau are sautéed in one of two ways. They may be simply dredged in flour and sautéed in Clarified Butter. Or, they are beaten until very thin, dipped in flour, egg, and breadcrumbs (*à l'Anglaise*), and then sautéed. In either case, because they have been somewhat tenderized and are thinner than veal chops, they are sautéed more quickly over a brisk flame. They require no more than 6 or 7 minutes to cook.

VEAL CUTLETS WITH GREEN VEGETABLES (*Escalopes de Veau aux Légumes Verts*). Sauté the cutlets briskly in Clarified Butter and remove to a hot platter. Garnish the cutlets with green beans, or asparagus tips, or peas, or lima beans, boiled and dressed with butter. Surround the cutlets with a thick Starch-Thickened Brown Veal Stock and pour the butter from the pan over them.

VEAL CUTLETS À L'ANGLAISE (*Escalopes de Veau à l'Anglaise*). Flatten the cutlets, dip them in flour, egg, and fine dry white breadcrumbs, and sauté them briskly in Clarified Butter. Arrange them in the form of a crown on a hot serving dish, and sprinkle with Brown Butter.

VEAL CUTLETS À LA VIENNOISE (*Escalopes de Veau à la Viennoise*). Flatten the cutlets, dip them in flour, egg, and fine, dry white breadcrumbs, and sauté them briskly in Clarified Butter. Arrange the cutlets on a round dish in the form of a crown, on top of a thin layer of Anchovy Butter. Place a slice of peeled lemon on top of each cutlet. Place an olive wrapped in a filet of anchovy on top of each slice of lemon. Surround the cutlets with little mounds of chopped egg white, chopped egg yolk, capers, and chopped parsley.

VEAL SAUTÉS

Veal sautés are not sautés at all, but rather a kind of pan stew. I place them here because this is what they are called, and if you came upon them unaware in the section on veal stews you might think I was badly in need of rest.

These "sautés" are made with the same cuts used in making stews, that is, shoulder, neck, and breast, boned or unboned, and cut into pieces about 1 inch thick and 2 inches square. The meat is blanched before cooking to expel its scum. Cover the pieces with cold water, bring to a simmer, and simmer for 5 minutes. Wash the pieces under running water, and proceed with the recipe.

VEAL SAUTÉ WITH RED WINE (*Sauté de Veau au Vin Rouge*). Blanch 2 pounds of veal stewing meat. Sauté lightly for 10 minutes in butter with 1 onion, coarsely chopped. Season with salt and pepper. Add 3 cups dry red wine, 1 cup White Stock, 1 clove of garlic, crushed, and a *Bouquet Garni*. Cover and simmer until the veal is tender, about 1½ hours. Remove the veal and place it in a clean saucepan with 16 small Glazed Onions and 16 mushrooms sautéed in butter. Skim the cooking liquid, reduce it by ½, thicken it with *Beurre Manié,* strain it, and pour it over the veal and vegetables. Cover and simmer the veal for about 15 minutes.

VEAL SAUTÉ WITH EGGPLANT (*Sauté de Veau aux Aubergines*). Blanch 2 pounds of veal stewing meat. Sauté lightly in olive oil for 10 minutes, and season with salt and pepper. Add 2 cups dry white wine, 2 cups Brown Veal Stock, 4 tablespoons Tomato Purée, and 1 clove of garlic, crushed. Cover and simmer for 1½ hours, or until the veal is done. Remove the veal to a hot deep serving dish and keep warm. Skim the liquid in the pan and reduce it by ½. Thicken it, if necessary, with a little cornstarch diluted in water or white wine. Add to the veal 2 to 3 cups of eggplant cut in large dice and sautéed in oil. Strain the sauce and pour it over the veal and eggplant.

VEAL SAUTÉ À L'INDIENNE (*Sauté de Veau à l'Indienne*). Blanch 2 pounds of veal stewing meat. Sauté lightly in butter for 5 minutes. Add ¼ cup chopped onion and cook for 5 minutes more. Season with salt and pepper. Add 1 teaspoon curry powder and 1 tablespoon flour and cook, stirring, for a few minutes until the flour and butter form a Blond Roux. Add 4 cups White Veal Stock and a *Bouquet Garni,* cover, and simmer for 1½ hours or until the veal is done. Remove the veal to a hot deep serving dish. Skim the liquid in the pan and reduce it by ½. Thicken it, if necessary, with a little cornstarch diluted in water or white stock. Strain the sauce and pour it over the veal.

✳ *VEAL STEWS*

Stews of veal are noted for their delicate flavor, which is attributable to the delicacy of calf's meat, and the succulence of their sauce, attributable to the gelatinous quality of calf's meat and bones. Stewing veal is taken from the neck, shoulder, and breast. It may be boned or unboned. The meat is cut into 2-inch-square pieces about one inch in thickness. The pieces are first blanched by putting them in cold water, bringing the water to a simmer, and simmering for 5 minutes. They are then rinsed clean under running water.

Veal stews, or ragouts, are of two kinds, brown and white. For brown ragouts, the meat is seared in hot fat to seal and stiffen its surface. For white ragouts, the meat is put to simmer in the stewing liquid without this pre-liminary searing. Brown and white stews are adapted to become special kinds of stews, called fricassees and *blanquettes*. Like brown stews, the meat of fricassees is seared before simmering in liquid. Like white stews, blanquettes are put into the stewing liquid without searing. Fricassees and blanquettes differ from ordinary stews in that they receive a final thickening and enrich-ment with egg yolks and cream. Following are examples of these four kinds of veal stews.

VEAL STEW PRINTANIER (*Ragoût de Veau Printanier*). Blanch 2 pounds of veal stewing meat. Sauté lightly in butter for 10 minutes, and season with salt and pepper. Add 3 cups Brown Stock, ⅔ cup Demi-Glace Sauce, and a *Bouquet Garni,* and simmer for 1 hour. Remove the veal and put it in a clean saucepan. Add about 1 cup of new carrots cut in olive shapes, 1 cup of new turnips cut in olive shapes, and 1 cup of small new potatoes or potato balls. Skim and strain the sauce, pour it over the veal and vegetables, and cook for about ½ hour more or until the meat is done. Transfer the stew to a deep serving dish, and sprinkle over it ½ cup cooked peas and ½ cup cooked green beans cut in ½-inch sections.

VEAL STEW À L'ANGLAISE (*Ragoût de Veau à l'Anglaise*). Blanch 2 pounds of veal stewing meat. Slice 2 pounds of potatoes (about 8 cups) and chop 4 medium onions (about 3 cups). Put a layer of meat in the bottom of a casserole, season it with salt and white pepper, and add a layer of sliced potatoes and chopped onions. Put on top a *Bouquet Garni,* and continue to add the remaining ingredients in layers, seasoning each layer of meat. Add 2½ cups of water, cover tightly, and put in a 300° oven for about 1½ hours, or until the veal is done. Remove the bouquet garni. The sauce of this stew is thickened naturally by the starch of the potatoes.

OLD-FASHIONED VEAL FRICASSEE (*Fricassée de Veau à l'Ancienne*). Veal fricassee is prepared almost exactly like fricassee of chicken, except, of course, the cooking time for veal is longer than for chicken. Blanch 2 pounds of veal stewing meat. Dry the pieces thoroughly, and sauté them in butter in a heavy casserole or skillet until the meat is lightly seared. (Do not use aluminum; it will darken the egg-enriched sauce.) Remove the veal. In the same pan, sauté lightly without browning 1 medium carrot, 1 medium onion, and 1 celery rib, all sliced. Return the veal to the pan, season with salt and white pepper, and sprinkle with 3 tablespoons flour. Cook slowly over a low flame for 5 minutes, turning the pieces and adding a little butter if necessary so that the butter and flour will form a White Roux. Then add enough White Veal Stock to barely cover the veal, about 3 or 4 cups. Turn up the flame and bring to a simmer, shaking the pan to mix the flour and butter roux with the stock to thicken it slightly. Add a *Bouquet Garni,* cover tightly, and simmer slowly on the fire (or place in a 300° oven) for 1½ hours, or until the veal is done.

Ten minutes before cooking is completed, add 16 poached small white onions and the water or white stock in which they were simmered. Also add 16 mushroom caps, wiped clean and kept white in a little lemon water. When the veal is cooked, remove it and keep warm. Remove the bouquet garni. Skim the sauce, reduce it quickly until it just coats a spoon, and remove from the fire. Beat 2 egg yolks with ½ cup heavy cream, blend in a little of the hot sauce, and return this mixture to the pan, stirring and blending with a wooden spoon and taking care not to crush the onions or mushrooms. Return to the fire and stir until the sauce almost reaches the boiling point. (Do not allow it to boil!) Finish the seasoning with salt and white pepper, a squeeze of fresh lemon juice, and nutmeg to taste. Return the veal to the pan, turning it in the sauce until it is hot. Serve the stew in a hot deep serving dish sprinkled with chopped parsley or chives.

OLD-FASHIONED BLANQUETTE OF VEAL (*Blanquette de Veau à l'Ancienne*). *Blanquette* of veal is prepared almost exactly like blanquette of chicken. Blanch 2 pounds of veal stewing meat. Put the meat into a non-aluminum casserole and season with salt and white pepper. Add 1 medium carrot, 1 medium onion, and 1 celery rib, all sliced. Also add a *Bouquet Garni*. Then add enough White Veal Stock to cover the veal, about 3 or 4 cups. Cover tightly and simmer on a low flame (or put into a 300° oven) for 1½ to 2 hours, or until the veal is done.

Meanwhile, prepare a thick Velouté Sauce with 3 tablespoons butter, 3 tablespoons flour, 1 cup white veal stock, and a little chopped mushrooms. Simmer, slowly stirring and skimming, for 30 minutes. When the veal is done, remove it and keep warm. Skim the fat from the poaching liquid, then boil it quickly to reduce it by ½. Off the fire, strain the reduced liquid into the velouté and beat it smooth with a wire whisk. Beat 2 egg yolks with ½ cup heavy cream, blend in a little of the hot sauce, combine this mixture and the remaining sauce, and beat with a wire whisk until smooth. Place the sauce in a clean saucepan and heat almost to the boiling point. (Do not allow it to boil!) Finish seasoning the sauce with salt and white pepper, a squeeze of fresh lemon, and nutmeg to taste.

Put the veal into the sauce, and add 16 poached small white onions and 16 cooked small white mushroom caps. Heat the veal and vegetables thoroughly, and serve in a hot deep serving dish sprinkled with 1 tablespoon chopped parsley. Fresh buttered noodles are a traditional accompaniment for this dish.

✳ PORK
(Porc)

Not long after the colonists arrived in America, the pigs they had brought with them were running wild in the forest, multiplying prodigiously, and growing fat and delicious on acorns and other nuts they foraged for. They were hunted like game, and the country-cured hams of Virginia and Kentucky soon took their place alongside the hams of York and Westphalia and Prague and Bayonne as Great Hams of the World.

American pork has recently been redesigned. The new meat-type hog has less back fat and a higher proportion of lean. The animal is slaughtered between 7 and 12 months of age.

The meat of this young pork is light to grayish pink, firm, fine-textured, and moderately marbled with fat (avoid pork with soft, watery lean). The fat is white and firm, although naturally softer than the fat of other butcher's meats. The bones are red, soft, and spongy at their cut ends. Beyond one year of age pork meat is less desirable. The lean becomes rosier, darker in color; the grain becomes coarser; and the meat is more heavily marbled with fat. The bones lose their redness and sponginess.

Unlike beef, veal, and lamb, pork is not graded by the government, partly because there is less variation in the quality of pork and a greater uniformity of the age at which it is slaughtered.

In earlier times pork meat was mostly cured so that it would keep without refrigeration. Pork meat responds so wonderfully to salting and curing with smoke and sugar that most of the animal is still treated in this way because it is thought to taste better. Consequently, pork is not shipped about like carcasses of beef but is divided up at the packing house and the sections consigned to their ultimate destiny.

THE CUTS OF PORK

The major cuts of pork are the picnic (arm), the Boston butt (shoulder), the loin (which comprises the whole of the back—ribs, loin, and sirloin), the bacon or belly (including the spareribs), and the ham (rear leg).

The fatter portions are usually cured—picnic hams from the arms, salt pork and bacon from the belly, pig's feet and hocks from the lower arms and legs, jowls from the cheeks, and hams from the legs.

The leaner portions are usually eaten fresh—Boston butt from the shoulder, spareribs from the breast, and the whole loin of pork extending from the shoulder to the leg. As a roast, the loin can be divided (front to rear) into the blade loin roast, the center loin roast, and the sirloin roast. To recognize these roasts, look for the rib and blade bones in the blade loin roast, and the hipbone in the sirloin roast. The center loin roast, which contains the tenderloin and only the backbone, is preferred.

Lean fresh hams are usually cut in two and are called butt half (which is meatier) and shank half (which contains a greater proportion of bone). If, instead of being called butt half or shank half, the ham pieces are called butt *portion* and hank *portion,* this indicates that the choice center of the ham has been removed from the leg.

These roasts are also cut into fresh chops, giving you (from front to rear), blade steaks and chops, rib chops, loin chops, and sirloin chops. A top loin chop is a loin chop with its tenderloin removed. (The stripped-out tenderloin is sometimes available as a tenderloin roast. The whole tenderloin or rib eye roast becomes Canadian bacon when cured.) Center cut slices of ham are called ham steaks.

COOKING PORK

For years we have been told to cook pork to an interior temperature of 185° in order to assure the destruction of a certain parasite (trichinae) that may be lurking in the flesh. This amount of cooking, and perhaps the tendency of American women to cook even beyond this temperature to gain a good margin of safety, has given pork the reputation of being an exceedingly dry meat. Recently this temperature has been revised downward to 170° (the parasite is actually destroyed at 137°, according to the United States Government). Cooked to 170°, pork will surprise you with its juiciness. It will still be well done, and should be cooked until well done to properly develop its flavor.

All cuts of pork are tender, largely because of the good distribution of fat throughout the meat, and may therefore be cooked by dry heat. Large pieces are roasted, and pork chops are sautéed and broiled or grilled. However, because pork must be cooked to the well-done stage, care must be taken in broiling and grilling to prevent the meat from becoming too dry. Because of this necessity of cooking until well done, pork lends itself well to braising. Fresh pork is sometimes boiled. (Cured hams, of course, are frequently boiled.) It is rarely cut up and made into a stew. The lean meat of pork changes in color from pink to grayish-white when cooked.

✳ ROAST PORK

Pork is an excellent meat for roasting and other dry heat cooking methods. Although it must be well done, it is liberally endowed with interior fat that protects it from the high heat. And it is this high heat that activates the meat's flavor extractives, releasing their good flavor in an aromatic flood that will make your table a joy to sit at.

In as much as all cuts of pork are tender, you may cook them all in the same way. Consequently, the following comments apply to both boned and unboned picnic, arm, Boston butt, blade loin, center loin, sirloin, and fresh ham roasts.

The flavor of pork can be enhanced by preseasoning. At least 2 or 3 hours before cooking, sprinkle the meat with salt, pepper, and a little powdered thyme and powdered bay leaf. Rub these seasonings into the meat and fat. You may also rub it with a little mashed garlic.

Just before cooking, dry the roast thoroughly. Place it, with its fattest side up, on a rack in a small baking pan or shallow casserole that can be brought to the table. (A few tablespoons of butter may be added to the pan to use as basting before the pork drippings begin to flow.) Brown the roast in a preheated 450° oven for 30 minutes, or until the fat begins to brown and crisp and become translucent. Reduce the heat to 350° and continue cooking until the meat is well done, basting occasionally. Allow 20 to 25 minutes per pound for slender roasts like pork loin, and 30 to 35 minutes per pound for rolled roasts or fresh ham.

The meat is cooked when an absolutely clear juice is released when the roast is pricked to its very center with a poultry skewer. However, I suggest that you use a meat thermometer when cooking pork. Make sure the tip of the thermometer is centered in the roast away from any bones. You may then remove the roast when the thermometer reads 160° in the expectation that the heat will "coast" upward to at least 170° as the roast rests before carving. The center of the roast must reach 170°.

While the roast is resting, make gravy from the drippings by pouring off the excess fat from the pan and thickening the remaining juices slightly with *Beurre Manié*. However, since a well-cooked pork roast will not yield much juice, it is usually necessary to extend the juice by adding a Starch-Thickened Brown Veal Stock. The juice may also be mixed into one of the spicy sauces suitable for pork, which are made separately. These include Robert, Piquant, Pepper, and Devil Sauces.

ROAST LOIN OF PORK À LA BONNE FEMME (*Longe de Porc à la Bonne Femme*). Several hours in advance, rub the roast with salt, powdered bay leaf, and powdered thyme. Roast the pork in a shallow oval-shaped casserole to which you have added a few tablespoons of butter. When the pork is half cooked, surround it with potatoes cut in olive shapes and small onions, both lightly sautéed in butter. Bury in this garnish a *Bouquet Garni*. Complete the cooking, basting frequently. Remove the bouquet garni and serve the pork in the casserole, sprinkled with chopped parsley.

ROAST LOIN OF PORK À LA PROVENÇALE (*Longe de Porc à la Provençale*). Twelve hours in advance, rub the roast with salt, powdered bay leaf, and powdered thyme. Cut a number of small slits in the roast, and insert into these whole sage leaves. Cover the meat with crushed garlic and sprinkle with a few tablespoons of olive oil. Just before cooking, remove the garlic and put it in the roasting pan. Roast the pork and serve with the skimmed pan juices poured over it.

ROAST SHOULDER OF PORK À LA SOISSONNAISE (*Palette de Porc à la Soissonnaise*). Several hours in advance, season the roast with salt, powdered bay leaf, and powdered thyme. Roast the shoulder in a shallow oval-shaped casserole that can be brought to the table. When it is ¾ cooked, fill the casserole with cooked and drained white beans or kidney beans. Complete the cooking. The beans will grow plump on the flavorful drippings falling from the pork. Serve in the casserole.

ROAST SHOULDER OF PORK WITH BRUSSELS SPROUTS (*Palette de Porc aux Choux de Bruxelles*). Several hours in advance, rub the roast with salt. Roast the shoulder in a shallow casserole that can be brought to the table. When it is ¾ cooked, surround the pork with Brussels sprouts that you have half cooked in water. The Brussels sprouts complete their cooking in the deliciously rich drippings of the roast. Serve in the casserole. (The Brussels sprouts may be replaced with green cabbage to obtain *palette de porc au chou vert,* and with red cabbage to obtain *palette de porc au chou rouge.*)

ROAST FRESH HAM OF PORK À LA BOULANGÈRE (*Jambon de Porc Frais à la Boulangère*). Several hours in advance, rub the ham with salt, powdered bay leaf, and powdered thyme. Roast the pork in a shallow oval-shaped casserole. About 45 minutes before cooking is completed, surround the ham with ½-inch-thick slices of potatoes and onions, both lightly browned in butter. Baste with the drippings and complete the cooking of the ham and vegetables together.

ROAST FRESH HAM OF PORK ST. CLOUD (*Jambon de Porc Frais Saint Cloud*). Remove the skin, shave the fat to a ½-inch thickness, and score it lightly in a crisscross pattern. Several hours before cooking, rub the ham with salt and pepper. Cut a number of small slits in the ham and into these insert slivers of garlic. Put 2 tablespoons butter and 1 cup dry white wine into a shallow oval-shaped casserole. Roast the pork, basting frequently with the mixture of butter, wine, and drippings. About ½ hour before the pork is done, remove it from the oven and pour off ¾ of the drippings from the casserole. Spread the roast with a layer of applesauce, and surround it with thin slices of apple sprinkled with brown sugar. Return to the oven and continue the cooking, basting the apple slices until they are tender. Then add ½ cup heavy cream to the casserole and cook for 5 minutes more. Serve in the casserole.

❋ POT-ROASTED PORK

Pork is pot-roasted like beef, and the method is explained under pot roasts of beef, which I suggest that you reread at this time. Any of the cuts for roasting may be pot-roasted, although they are usually first boned. Pot-roasted meat, like braised meat, makes its own sauce as it cooks.

At least several hours in advance of cooking, rub the roast with salt, pepper, a little powdered thyme and powdered bay leaf, and a little mashed garlic if you prefer. You may also marinate the pork by rolling it (after you have rubbed it with the dry seasonings) in ¼ cup olive oil mixed with ¼ cup lemon juice.

Just before cooking, dry the roast thoroughly, and brown it in very hot oil. Put it in a close-fitting casserole with 1 raw carrot, sliced, 1 raw onion, sliced, and a *Bouquet Garni*. Heat the casserole on the fire, and cover the pork with a piece of buttered paper or foil cut to fit the casserole, and with a small hole cut in it to vent the steam. Cover tightly, and put into a 325° oven. Cook until done, basting frequently, and take care the pork does not become overcooked. Allow about 40 minutes per pound.

When the pork is cooked, remove it to a hot platter. To the casserole add ½ cup dry white wine or Brown Stock, and cook gently for about 5 minutes to absorb the flavor of the fat into the liquid. Pour off the fat, leaving a few tablespoons, and reduce the liquid by ⅓. Strain the sauce, rubbing the aromatic vegetables through the sieve along with the sauce. Send it to the table separately in a hot sauceboat.

POËLÉED LOIN OF PORK À LA CHIPOLATA (*Longe de Porc Poëlée à la Chipolata*). Preseason or marinate the pork, brown it, and pot-roast it. Place it on a hot serving dish and surround it with Chipolata Sausages, braised Chestnuts, poached mushrooms, and small Glazed Onions. You may also add Braised Carrots to this garnish. Prepare the pan juices as described above, and pour over the pork and its garnish.

✳ BRAISED PORK

Roast pork is so delicious that braising is not often called for. Pork is braised like veal, and the method is fully explained under the heading of braised veal. I suggest you follow these directions exactly, noting especially that the meat must not be overcooked.

There are, however, two notable braised pork dishes based on the exceptional affinity that exists between the flavors of cabbage and sauerkraut, on the one hand, and pork and pork fat on the other hand. The pork is braised in cabbage or sauerkraut that has already been half braised in broth and wine.

BRAISED SHOULDER OF PORK WITH RED CABBAGE (*Palette de Porc Braisé au Chou Rouge*). Prepare braised Red Cabbage à la Flamande, and cook it for 3 hours. Several hours in advance, rub the pork with salt and pepper. Brown it in hot fat in a skillet, and put it into the casserole with the cabbage, cover tightly, and cook in a 325° oven until the pork is done, allowing about 40 minutes per pound. Uncover the pork for the last 10 minutes to glaze* it. Remove the pork to a hot serving platter, surround it with the well-drained braised cabbage, and keep warm. Skim the fat from the braising liquid, reduce a little, and pour it over the cabbage.

BRAISED SHOULDER OF PORK WITH SAUERKRAUT (*Palette de Porc Braisée avec Choucroute*). Follow exactly the directions for Braised Shoulder of Pork with Red Cabbage (above), substituting sauerkraut prepared according to the recipe for Red Cabbage à la Flamande.

✳ PORK CHOPS

Pork chops are sautéed, grilled, broiled, and braised. The best chops are the loin chops, followed by the rib chops. Pork chops, like all pork, must be cooked until well done. If they are overcooked, even when braised, they will become tough, dry, and tasteless. To test for doneness, press the chops; they should feel firm and not squashy. Also probe them with a poultry skewer; the emerging juice must be absolutely clear.

SAUTÉED PORK CHOPS

Chops for sautéing should be cut about ¾ inch thick. Trim the chops, leaving no more than ¼ inch of fat, and slash through the fat just into the meat to prevent the chops from curling. Season them with salt and pepper. Dredge the chops in flour, slapping them sharply to remove any excess. (This retards the escape of juices from the relatively dry meat.) Sear both sides in hot pork fat or hot Clarified Butter, reduce the heat, and sauté for about 12 minutes per side, or until the chops are done. (The sautéing must be gentle to assure that the chops will cook through before they become too brown.) Remove the chops to a hot serving platter. Pour off excess fat from the pan, deglaze* with ½ cup Brown Stock or dry red wine, and reduce the sauce by ½. Strain and pour over the chops.

PORK CHOPS À LA FLAMANDE (*Côtes de Porc à la Flamande*). Trim and season the chops, and sauté them on both sides until they are half cooked. Place them in an ovenproof serving dish on a bed of apple slices. Bake the chops and apples in a 325° oven until cooked, basting frequently with butter. Serve the chops in the baking dish.

PORK CHOPS À LA BAYONNAISE (*Côtes de Porc à la Bayonnaise*). Rub the chops with salt, pepper, powdered thyme, and powdered bay leaf. Make 4 or 5 incisions in each chop, and insert slivers of garlic. Sprinkle with oil and vinegar and let the chops stand for at least one hour. Drain and dry the chops, and sauté them until they are ½ cooked. Arrange them on an oven-proof serving dish and surround them with half-sautéed potato balls or new potatoes and *cèpes* or mushrooms sautéed in oil. Complete the cooking in a 350° oven and sprinkle with chopped parsley.

GRILLED AND BROILED PORK CHOPS

Cut the chops about ¾ inch thick, trim the fat to leave ¼ inch, and slash through it just into the lean to prevent the chops from curling. Brush the chops with melted butter and sprinkle them with fine, dry white bread-crumbs. Sear the chops close to the flame, then grill them gently away from the flame, basting frequently, until they are cooked.

PORK CHOPS À LA CHARCUTIÈRE (*Côtes de Porc à la Charcutière*). Grill or broil the chops. Arrange them on a round dish in a ring. Into the center of the ring put a heap of Mashed Potatoes. Separately serve Charcutière Sauce (that is, Robert Sauce to which you have added a few tablespoons of gherkins minced or cut in julienne*).

BRAISED PORK CHOPS

Chops for braising should be cut about 1 inch thick. They are braised like veal chops. First, trim the chops to leave no more than ¼ inch of fat. Brown them lightly in butter, or in the fat rendered from their own trimmings. Season with salt and pepper, add ¼ cup dry white wine for each chop, and boil until the wine is almost entirely evaporated. Add Brown Veal Stock or Brown Stock to cover the chops by ½. Bring to the boil, cover, and simmer on the stove or in a 350° oven for about 1 hour, or until done. Do not over-braise pork chops or any other white meat, or it will become tough, dry, and tasteless. Arrange the chops on a hot platter. Skim, reduce, and strain the braising liquid, and pour it over the chops.

PORK CHOPS À L'ALSACIENNE (*Côtes de Porc à l'Alsacienne*). Braise the chops. Arrange them in a ring on a round dish, and fill the center of the ring with sauerkraut and poached Strasbourg or Frankfurt sausages. Surround the chops with boiled potatoes. Skim, reduce, and strain the braising liquid, and pour it over the chops.

✳ LAMB
(*Agneau*)

Poor lamb! First, American panthers feasted off the stock brought over by the colonists, and by the time the land was made safe for lamb, Americans had lost their taste for it. Next, the sheepmen and the cattlemen fought over the grazing lands in the West, and the sheepmen lost. Finally, Americans, adopting English methods of cooking mutton, overcooked lamb until it was well done. Leg of lamb, pierced with a few slivers of garlic and cooked until just medium rare, is one of nature's most delightful gifts. Yet we each eat no more than 3 or 4 pounds of lamb a year. Mutton, which is highly prized in many countries, is almost not eaten at all, averaging 1/5 pound per person in a year.

Classified according to age, there are four kinds of lamb. The younger lamb is more available early in the year. The youngest is milk-fed lamb (*agneau de lait*). Like milk-fed veal its flesh is white and delicate in flavor, and it is difficult to find. Spring or Pascal lamb is mostly available at Easter time. In the United States lamb is considered to be spring lamb up to 6 months of age. Ordinary lamb is from 6 to 14 months old. Mutton is older. The best grades of lamb are Prime and Choice.

The younger the lamb, the more delicately flavored it is. In America this delicate flavor is much preferred to the strong, "muttony" taste of mutton or old lamb. You can judge the age of lamb by the color of its flesh and its size. A leg of spring lamb may weigh from 3 to 6 pounds. A leg of ordinary lamb weighs up to 10 pounds. The younger the lamb, the lighter the color of its lean meat. You will be happy with lamb that has pinkish-red, fine-grained meat that looks very smooth when cut. The fat, which is white or pinkish in color, is firm and brittle. Cut surfaces of the bones are soft, red and porous. As lamb becomes older the flesh is darker red in color and heavier layers of fat are evident. Mutton, prized in France, England, and many other countries, is darker red in color and fatter than beef.

THE CUTS OF LAMB

Lamb cuts are similar to veal cuts, only smaller. From front to rear, there are shoulder roasts, rib roasts, loin roasts, and sirloin roasts. The leg of lamb is cooked whole or divided into the lower shank half and the upper sirloin half (called the rump roast when taken from veal). The best chops are rib chops, loin chops, and sirloin chops. The rib section also provides the elegant crown roast of lamb. The breast of lamb is removed whole, and it may be boned and stuffed. Finally, lamb *noisettes* are delicate round pieces of bone-less meat taken from the rib or loin and weighing about 3 ounces. They are similar to the *escalopes* of veal.

COOKING LAMB

Lamb, except for the shanks and neck, is all tender meat. It may there-fore be cooked by any method. Also, full-fledged lamb is a mature, red meat, and like beef it can be served rare. Rare lamb is so good that perhaps the best way to cook a leg of lamb is to roast it, but it may also be cooked well done by pot-roasting or braising. Lamb chops are perhaps best grilled or broiled, although they may also be sautéed and braised. Lamb *noisettes* are best sautéed. Lamb also is famous as the ingredient for "brown" and "white" stews—*navarins,* Irish Stews, *blanquettes,* and fricassees.

If you do not care for the decided muttony flavor of older lamb, you should give it a long braising with the cover of the braising pan slightly askew. This expels the acid odors that are the source of your displeasure, giving the meat a more delicate flavor.

Finally, lamb differs from other meats in that its fat has a very high melting point. If cooled slightly, the fat congeals to a pasty consistency and becomes muttony in character. Consequently, when you serve lamb be sure to bring it to the table very hot.

✳ ROAST LAMB

Mature lamb is roasted like beef, and you can reread my remarks on roast beef for details. (Also see Chapter 3 for the various tests for doneness.) In general, the roast of lamb is first browned in a hot 450° oven for 20 minutes, and its cooking is completed at 350°. For medium rare, a large 6- to 7-pound bone-in roast of lamb will take about 12 minutes per pound all told; a smaller roast takes about 15 minutes per pound. A boneless roast, weighing about 4 pounds, will require from 22 to 25 minutes per pound to cook medium rare. These times are only approximate, however. Press the roast with your fingers, and when it loses its softness and becomes springy, probe it deeply with a poultry skewer. If the juices run red, cook a little longer. The lamb is medium rare when the juices turn a rose color. A meat thermometer should read 140° (the interior temperature will continue to climb after the roast is removed from the oven).

ROAST LEG OF LAMB
(*Gigot d'Agneau Rôti*)

Lamb, a 6- to 7-pound whole leg of lamb
Garlic, 1 or 2 cloves
Salt and pepper
Carrot, 1, chopped
Onion, 1, chopped

Fat, 6 tablespoons
Watercress, a handful
Starch-Thickened Brown Stock or Starch-Thickened Brown Veal Stock, 1 cup

You may partially bone the leg to aid in carving. From the rump end, remove the large pelvic bone and the smaller tail bone above it by scraping along the bones with a sharp knife and wresting them free. At the shank end, loosen the flesh from the knob of bone and press it back, loosening it from the bone with your knife, until 2 or 3 inches of bone are exposed. Break the exposed bone by rapping it sharply with the back of a chef's knife. Remove the broken piece, and sew the loose meat together.

Pare away most of the surface fat, leaving a thin layer for self-basting. Do not peel away the membrane; it helps preserve the shape of the meat.

Lamb and garlic have a nice affinity. Make 6 or 8 thin cuts into the flesh, and insert into them thin slivers of garlic. (This may be done several days in advance of cooking.)

Season the lamb with salt and pepper. Strew the bottom of a baking pan with chopped carrot, chopped onion, the bones and the meat trimmings of the leg, and sprinkle with melted fat. Dry the leg of lamb, rub it all over with melted fat, and place it on a rack in the baking pan. Brown the roast in a 450° oven for about 20 minutes, and reduce the heat to 350°. Cook for about 1¼ hours all told, basting frequently. Begin testing for doneness by pressing the roast with your fingers. When it loses its softness and becomes springy, probe it deeply with a poultry skewer. If the juices run red, cook a little longer. The lamb is medium rare when the juices turn a rose color. A meat thermometer should read 140°.

Place the leg on a serving platter and garnish it with watercress. Pour off the fat from the baking pan, and deglaze* the pan with starch-thickened lamb stock prepared from the bones and trimmings, or Starch-Thickened Brown Stock, or Starch-Thickened Brown Veal Stock. Strain the sauce, pressing the juice from the vegetables, skim away the last of the fat, and serve in a hot sauceboat. Or, serve the lamb with traditional Mint Sauce.

PARSLIED LEG OF LAMB (*Gigot d'Agneau Persillé*). To 2 cups fine fresh white breadcrumbs, add ¼ cup melted butter, ¼ cup finely chopped parsley, 2 garlic cloves, finely minced (optional), ½ teaspoon salt, a little pepper, and a squeeze of lemon juice. Roast the lamb until it is almost cooked. Remove from the oven and coat it with the breadcrumb and parsley mixture, pressing this firmly to the surface of the meat. Return the lamb to the oven and complete the cooking. The roast will take on a magnificently golden color. Serve garnished with parsley or watercress and slices of lemon. Separately serve sauce made from the pan juices thickened with Starch-Thickened Brown Veal Stock.

ROAST LEG OF LAMB À LA BOULANGÈRE (*Gigot d'Agneau Rôti à la Boulangère*). Brown the roast in an ovenproof serving dish and remove it. To the dish, add onions and potatoes cut in ½-inch-thick slices and lightly sautéed in butter. Season the vegetables and sprinkle them liberally with melted butter. Pour 1 to 2 cups of Brown Veal Stock into the dish to almost cover the vegetables. Place the lamb on this bed of vegetables and complete the cooking together. Serve the lamb and its garnish in the baking dish.

ROAST LEG OF LAMB À LA RENAISSANCE (*Gigot d'Agneau Rôti à la Renaissance*). Roast the lamb. Surround it with carrots and turnips cut into grooved balls and glazed,* little bundles of asparagus tips, peas, green beans, cauliflower knobs, small potatoes or potato balls sautéed in butter. Separately serve the pan juices thickened with Starch-Thickened Brown Veal Stock.

ROAST LEG OF LAMB À LA DAUPHINE (*Gigot d'Agneau Rôti à la Dauphine*). Roast the lamb. Garnish with Dauphine Potatoes. Separately serve the pan juices thickened with Starch-Thickened Brown Veal Stock.

ROAST LEG OF LAMB À LA BRUXELLOISE (*Gigot d'Agneau Rôti à la Bruxelloise*). Roast the lamb. Garnish with Brussels sprouts finished in butter, and potatoes cut in olive shapes and sautéed in butter. Separately serve the pan juices thickened with Starch-Thickened Brown Veal Stock.

ROAST SHOULDER OF LAMB À LA PARISIENNE (*Épaule d'Agneau Rôtie à la Parisienne*). Roast the lamb. Garnish with Braised Lettuce and Parisian Potatoes. Separately serve the pan juices thinned with white wine and thickened with Starch-Thickened Brown Veal Stock.

ROAST SHOULDER OF LAMB À LA JARDINIÈRE (*Épaule d'Agneau Rôtie à la Jardinière*). Roast the lamb. Serve it surrounded by little heaps of peas, green beans, and kidney beans, all cooked in butter; olive shaped and Glazed Turnips and Carrots; and boiled cauliflower knobs kept very white. Separately serve the pan juices thickened with Starch-Thickened Brown Veal Stock.

ROAST LOIN OF LAMB À LA CLAMART (*Carré d'Agneau Rôti à la Clamart*). Roast the lamb. Surround it with boiled artichoke bottoms heaped with Peas à la Française finished in butter, and potato balls lightly sautéed in butter. Separately serve the pan juices thickened with Starch-Thickened Brown Veal Stock.

ROAST LOIN OF LAMB À LA BOUQUETIÈRE (*Carré d'Agneau Rôti à la Bouquetière*). Roast the lamb. Surround it with mounds of carrot and turnip balls, diced string beans, peas, and flowerets of cauliflower, all boiled and finished in butter; and potatoes cut in olive shapes and sautéed. Separately serve the pan juices thickened with Starch-Thickened Brown Veal Stock.

ROAST LOIN OF LAMB MARIE-LOUISE (*Carré d'Agneau Rôti Marie-Louise*). Roast the lamb. Garnish with Noisette Potatoes sautéed in butter, and boiled artichoke bottoms filled with Mushroom Purée and topped with Soubise Sauce. Separately serve the pan juices thickened with Starch-Thickened Brown Veal Stock.

✳ POT-ROASTED LAMB

Lamb is pot-roasted like beef, and you can follow the basic recipe for Pot-Roasted Beef with two exceptions. First, lamb is naturally tender and can be cooked in half the time, about 30 minutes per pound. Second, the liquid for deglazing* the browning pan and for making the sauce should be lamb or Veal Stock, instead of the brown stock that might disguise the flavor of the lamb. The usual cuts for braising are semiboned leg and boned shoulder.

LEG OF LAMB À LA BORDELAISE (*Gigot d'Agneau à la Bordelaise*). Brown the lamb and put it into a casserole. Pot-roast the leg until it is half cooked. To the casserole add small potato balls and mushroom caps, both lightly sautéed in butter, and finish cooking the lamb and vegetables together. Uncover the casserole and sprinkle with Brown Butter in which you have tossed dry white breadcrumbs, chopped parsley, chopped shallots, and minced garlic. Separately serve the pan juices thickened with Starch-Thickened Brown Veal Stock.

LOIN OF LAMB À LA NIÇOISE (*Carré d'Agneau à la Niçoise*). Brown the lamb and put it into a casserole. To the casserole add peeled and seeded tomatoes cut in large pieces, zucchini cut in large dice, and small potatoes or potato balls, all lightly sautéed in olive oil. Season with salt and pepper, cover, and cook in a 300° oven. Serve in the cocotte, sprinkled with chopped parsley.

LOIN OF LAMB À LA BONNE FEMME (*Carré d'Agneau à la Bonne Femme*). Brown the lamb in Clarified Butter and put it into a casserole. To the casserole, add small onions, small potato balls, and strips of bacon, all lightly sautéed in butter. Season with salt and pepper, sprinkle with melted butter, cover, and cook all together in a slow 300° oven. Serve in the casserole.

LOIN OF LAMB WITH NOODLES (*Carré d'Agneau aux Nouilles*). Brown the lamb, put it into a casserole, cover, and cook until it is almost done. Remove the lamb, and partially fill the casserole with a bed of freshly cooked noodles tossed in butter. Return the lamb to the casserole, cover, and finish the cooking. Just before serving, sprinkle the lamb and noodles with Starch-Thickened Brown Veal Stock. Sprinkle with chopped parsley and serve in the casserole.

✳ BRAISED LAMB

Lamb is braised like beef. We do not braise lamb to tenderize it; the meat is naturally tender. We apply the braising method so that we can bring lamb to the well-done stage without drying it, allowing additional time for a salutary interchange to take place between the meat and the sauce. About 45 minutes per pound will suffice.

In general the leg and shoulder of lamb are braised. The leg should be partially boned, as for roasting. The shoulder of mature lamb is usually boned; the shoulder of very young lamb is not. The bones are saved and cooked along with the meat to extract their goodness.

Lamb need not be marinated, unless you wish to give it a game taste. Other than this, it may be braised just like beef, and you may follow the basic recipe for Braised Beef with any large cut of lamb. Very briefly, here is the procedure:

(1) Carefully dry the lamb and brown it. To do this, turn it in a skillet in very hot Clarified Butter, or rub it with clarified butter and put it into a hot 450° oven for 30 minutes, or until it is browned. Along with the lamb brown any lamb bones that have been removed from the meat.

(2) Tie the meat if necessary, and season with salt and pepper. Put it in a casserole on a bed of sliced carrots and sliced onions, browned in butter in a skillet or browned along with the lamb in the oven. Tuck the browned bones around the meat. Also add a *Bouquet Garni* consisting of 1 stalk celery, 3 sprigs parsley, 1 bay leaf, 1 clove of garlic, crushed, and a sprig or pinch of thyme, all tied in cheesecloth.

(3) Deglaze* the baking pan or skillet in which the lamb and vegetables were browned with white or red wine, with lamb or Veal Stock, or with a combination of wine and stock. Add 1 cup of this liquid to the casserole, and cook briskly over a hot flame until it is almost entirely reduced. Add 1 more cup of this liquid, and reduce again until it is thick and syrupy.

(4) Add more stock or stock and wine to the casserole to almost cover the meat. Bring the liquid to a boil and place on top of the meat a piece of buttered paper or foil cut to fit the size of the pan, with a small hole cut in it to vent the steam. Cover the pan tightly and put it in a 325° oven.

(5) Cook the lamb, basting regularly, until it is done. This will require about 45 minutes per pound for a leg or an unboned shoulder, or about 55 minutes per pound for a boned or boned and stuffed shoulder. If your guests are delayed, reduce the heat to 300° and you can braise the lamb for an hour more or even longer.

(6) When the lamb is cooked, uncover the casserole, turn up the oven heat to 375°, and allow the meat to glaze* in the oven for about 10 minutes, spooning its sauce over it to give it a handsome coating.

(7) Remove the meat to a hot platter, and use the braising liquid to prepare a sauce as indicated in the recipe you are following.

BRAISED LEG OF LAMB À LA SOUBISE (*Gigot d'Agneau Braisé à la Soubise*). Brown and braise the lamb until it is ⅔ cooked. Remove it from the braising pan, clean the pan, strain the braising liquid, and return it to the pan with 2 pounds of sliced onions and ½ pound of Carolina Rice. Return the meat to the pan, cover, and complete the cooking. Remove the meat to an ovenproof serving platter and glaze* it in the oven. Put the onions, rice, and braising liquid through a sieve, and finish this Soubise Sauce with 2 tablespoons butter and serve separately in a hot sauceboat.

BRAISED LEG OF LAMB WITH A SPOON (*Gigot d'Agneau Braisé à la Cuiller*). Lamb is a mature meat, and unlike the white meats it may be braised for a very long time without becoming dry or tough. In fact, if kept moist, it will become tender enough to scoop out with a spoon, hence the name of this recipe. Braise the lamb in the usual manner, except cook it for 5 hours, basting often, and replacing the braising liquid if it is too reduced in cooking.

BRAISED SHOULDER OF LAMB À LA BOURGEOISE (*Épaule d'Agneau Braisée à la Bourgeoise*). Brown and braise the lamb until it is half cooked. Remove it from the braising pan and clean the pan. Strain the braising liquid and return it to the pan with carrots cut in olive shapes and half cooked in butter, small Glazed Onions, and pork belly cut in dice, parboiled for a few minutes, and browned. Cover and complete the cooking together.

BRAISED SHOULDER OF LAMB EN BALLON (*Épaule d'Agneau Braisée en Ballon*). Bone the shoulder and season the inside. Roll and shape it to form a round ball, tying it with string vertically from top to bottom until it has the appearance of a slightly flattened pumpkin. Brown, braise, untie, and glaze* the *ballon* of lamb, and serve it on a round dish. Reduce, strain, and thicken the braising liquid, and pour it over the ballon.

STUFFED SHOULDER OF LAMB EN DAUBE À LA BOURGUI-GNONNE (*Épaule d'Agneau en Daube à la Bourguignonne*). Bone the shoulder and stuff it with 1 pound of pork Forcemeat to which you have added 1 onion, chopped and simmered in butter, ¼ cup *Duxelles,* and 1 teaspoon chopped parsley. Roll the shoulder into the shape of a ball, tie it, brown it, and braise it in a braising liquid made with red wine until it is ½ cooked. Remove the lamb, untie it, and place it in a shallow casserole. To the casserole, add mushrooms tossed in butter, small Glazed Onions, and pork belly cut in large dice, parboiled for a few minutes, and browned. Strain and add the braising liquid. Heat the casserole on the stove until the liquid is simmering. Add a few tablespoons of blazing brandy, let it burn out, and cover the casserole. Seal the cover with a paste of flour and water, leaving a small hole for some of the steam to escape. Put the casserole in the oven to finish cooking the lamb. Serve in the casserole.

❊ LAMB STEWS

Lamb stewing meat is taken from the breast, short ribs, shoulder, and neck. Cut the meat in 1½- to 2-inch cubes. Leave the bones in the meat for the flavor and gelatin they add to the sauce. They can be easily slipped out of the flesh just before serving.

"White" lamb stews include *blanquettes,* fricassees, and Irish stew. "Brown" stews of lamb or mutton are called *navarins.*

LAMB STEW À L'ANGLAISE, or **IRISH STEW** (*Ragoût d'Agneau à l'Anglaise, ou Ragoût Irlandais*). Prepare exactly as for Veal Stew à l'Anglaise.

OLD-FASHIONED BLANQUETTE OF LAMB (*Blanquette d'Agneau à l'Ancienne*). Prepare exactly as for Old-Fashioned Blanquette of Veal, using young spring lamb.

OLD-FASHIONED FRICASSEE OF LAMB (*Fricassee d'Agneau à l'Ancienne*). Prepare exactly as for Old-Fashioned Fricassee of Veal, using young spring lamb.

CURRY OF LAMB (*Curry d'Agneau*). Cut 2 pounds of lamb stewing meat into 1-inch cubes. Sauté briskly in very hot Clarified Butter with 1 onion, chopped. When the meat is browned, sprinkle with 3 tablespoons flour, 1 to 2 tablespoons curry powder, and 2 teaspoons salt. Cook for a few minutes, stirring, to form a Roux with the flour and the fat in the pan. Add 3 cups water or stock and bring to a simmer, stirring to dissolve the roux into the liquid. Then add a *Bouquet Garni* consisting of 3 sprigs of parsley, 1 bay leaf, and 1 sprig or pinch of thyme, all tied in cheesecloth. Bring the liquid to a simmer, cover, and cook in a 325° oven for 1½ hours, or until the lamb is done. Discard the bouquet garni and remove the lamb to a serving dish. Reduce the sauce if necessary to thicken it, flavor it with a squeeze of fresh lemon, correct the seasoning, and pour it over the lamb. Separately serve Rice à l'Indienne.

LAMB STEW PRINTANIER (*Navarin Printanier*). Cut 2 pounds of lamb stewing meat in 1½-inch cubes. Sauté briskly, a few pieces at a time, in very hot Clarified Butter until brown. Place the lamb in a casserole, sprinkle with 1 teaspoon sugar, and cook over a brisk flame for a few minutes until the sugar begins to melt and brown (the sugar gives a good brown color to the sauce). Pour off the fat and sprinkle the meat with 1 teaspoon salt, a little pepper, and 3 tablespoons flour. Cook for a few minutes, stirring, to form a Roux with the flour and the fat remaining on the meat and in the pan. Add 3 cups water or stock and bring to a simmer, stirring to dissolve the roux into the liquid. Then add 1 large tomato, chopped (or ¼ cup Tomato Purée); 1 clove garlic, crushed; 3 sprigs parsley; 1 bay leaf; and 1 sprig or pinch of thyme. Return the liquid to a simmer, cover, and cook in a 325° oven for 45 minutes. Transfer the pieces of lamb to a clean casserole, and strain the sauce over them. To the casserole, add: 1 cup carrots and 1 cup turnips cut in olive shapes; 1 cup small onions; and 1 cup potato balls or small new potatoes. Also add ½ cup fresh peas and ½ cup green beans cut in 1-inch lengths. Bring the sauce to the simmering point, cover the casserole, and return it to the oven, basting occasionally, for 45 minutes or until the lamb and vegetables are done.

PILAF OF LAMB (*Pilaf d'Agneau*). Cut 2 pounds of lamb stewing meat into 1½-inch cubes, and prepare as for Lamb Stew Printanier (above), up until the point when the Roux is dissolved in the 3 cups of liquid. Then add 4 large tomatoes, peeled, seeded, and chopped (or 1 cup Tomato Purée); 1 clove garlic, crushed; ½ teaspoon ginger (or 2 good pinches saffron); 3 sprigs parsley; 1 bay leaf; and 1 sprig or pinch thyme. Return the liquid to a simmer, cover, and cook in a 325° oven for one hour. Transfer the pieces of lamb to a clean casserole, and strain the sauce over them. To the casserole, add: ½ cup peeled and diced sweet peppers and 2 cups parboiled converted rice. Bring the sauce to the simmering point, cover the casserole, and return it to the oven for ½ hour or until the lamb and rice are cooked.

✳ *LAMB CHOPS*

Lamb chops to be grilled or broiled are cut 1½ to 2½ inches thick. Trim the fat, leaving a thin layer, and slash through this barely into the meat in 3 or 4 places to prevent the chops from curling. Season them with salt and pepper, brush with melted Clarified Butter, and dip them in fine, dry white breadcrumbs. Grill or broil them 3 to 4 inches away from the flame for 4 or 5 minutes per side. Tests for doneness are similar to the tests for Grilled and Broiled Beefsteak. Serve rare or medium rare.

LAMB CHOPS À L'ANGLAISE (*Côtelettes d'Agneau à l'Anglaise*). Grill or broil the chops. Arrange them on a dish in the form of a crown, and garnish with strips of grilled bacon, boiled potatoes, and watercress.

LAMB CHOPS DU BARRY (*Côtelettes d'Agneau Du Barry*). Grill or broil the chops. Arrange them on an ovenproof dish with flowerets of cauliflower coated with Mornay Sauce and sprinkled with Parmesan cheese. Brown in the broiler and serve.

BARMAN LAMB CHOPS (*Côtelettes d'Agneau Barman*). Grill or broil the chops. Arrange them on a round dish in the form of a crown, and garnish with broiled tomatoes, large broiled mushroom caps, and watercress. On top of each chop put a slice of grilled or broiled bacon.

LAMB CHOPS NAVARRAISE (*Côtelettes d'Agneau Navarraise*). Mix together ¼ cup chopped cooked ham, ½ cup chopped sautéed mushrooms, and 1 teaspoon chopped red peppers. Bind the mixture together with a very thick Béchamel Sauce flavored with truffle Essence. Grill or broil the chops on one side, and place them on a baking pan, cooked side up. Heap the ham and vegetable mixture on each of the lamb chops in the form of a dome. Sprinkle with melted butter and grated Parmesan cheese, and finish cooking in a 400° oven. Serve the chops on top of tomato halves sautéed in oil and placed in a ring, and surround with a ribbon of Tomato Sauce.

Lamb chops for sautéing are cut about 1 inch thick. Trim away the excess fat, leaving a thin rind, and slash through this barely into the meat in 3 or 4 places to prevent them from curling. Lamb chops are usually treated *à l'Anglaise,* that is, seasoned with salt and pepper, dipped in flour, then in egg beaten with a little oil, and finally in fine, dry white breadcrumbs. Sauté them quickly in hot Clarified Butter for 3 or 4 minutes per side. Tests for doneness are similar to the tests for Sautéed Beefsteak. They are best rare or medium rare.

LAMB CHOPS MARÉCHALE (*Côtelettes d' Agneau Maréchale*). Dip the chops in egg and breadcrumbs and sauté them in Clarified Butter. Arrange them on a dish in the form of a crown, and put a slice of truffle on each chop. Garnish the center of the dish with a heap of buttered asparagus tips.

LAMB CHOPS MONTROUGE (*Côtelettes d'Agneau Montrouge*). Dip the chops in egg and breadcrumbs and sauté them in Clarified Butter. Arrange them on a dish in the form of a crown, and garnish the center of the dish with a thick Mushroom Purée. Surround the dish with a ribbon of Demi-Glace Sauce finished with butter.

LAMB CHOPS À LA PARISIENNE (*Côtelettes d'Agneau à la Parisienne*). Dip the chops in egg and breadcrumbs mixed with finely chopped truffles, and sauté them in Clarified Butter. Arrange them on a dish in the form of a crown, and garnish the center of the dish with mushrooms cooked in cream. Surround the dish with a border of asparagus tips in butter.

LAMB CHOPS À LA MINUTE (*Côtelettes d'Agneau à la Minute*). Pound the chops to flatten them, season with salt and pepper, and sauté in Clarified Butter over a very hot flame. Sprinkle the chops with chopped parsley and lemon juice, and pour over them sizzling hot butter from the pan.

✳ VARIETY MEATS
(*Abats*)

Aside from steaks and roasts, food animals supply us with a wealth of odds and ends that can be summed up as variety meats. Heads, feet, tails, tongues, brains, and other items enter into this supply, which, depending upon the particular item and the animal from which it is obtained, fills bowls in the humblest cottage or graces plates in the most exalted restaurants.

Cooking these meats is a delightful final examination of what you have learned about cooking. The variety of methods used is as extraordinary as the variety of tastes that result. From the quick 4-minute sautéing of calf's liver, to the 12-hour simmering of tripe *à la mode de Caen,* from the *haute cuisine* elegance of sweetbreads to the simple joys found in a bowl of oxtail soup, the variety meats will keep you on your toes both cooking and tasting.

Leaving aside the outrageous (a Roman is said to have served a dish made with the tongues of 10,000 tiny birds who had been taught to say a few words) and the outdated (we rarely see a stuffed calf's head served up anymore), here are some of the most commonly eaten and available variety meats.

✳ SWEETBREADS
(Ris de Veau)

Sweetbreads are the thymus gland taken from the throat of the calf. This gland disappears as the animal grows to become beef. Very white, very tender, and delicately flavorful, sweetbreads are the most elegant and expensive of all the fresh variety meats, and they have been happily consumed by kings, little princesses, financiers, judges, and fashionable doctors for centuries.

A whole sweetbread is actually a matched pair, weighing about one pound. Each one of the pair is made up of two parts—an elongated portion called the throat sweetbread and a firmer, more compact, rounded portion called the heart sweetbread. The heart sweetbread is preferred because the throat sweetbread contains some connective tissue. Both are equally flavorful.

One of the curious things about sweetbreads is that they retain their tenderness even when cooked again and again. Given this opportunity, it has become commonplace to cook sweetbreads three times over. The first cooking or blanching stiffens them. The second cooking flavors them. And the third cooking transforms them into the dish we want them to be.

Sweetbreads are very perishable, and they should receive their first cooking or blanching as soon as you get them home. Before blanching, soak sweetbreads in several changes of water or in running water for 3 or 4 hours, or until all traces of blood in them have been dissolved away. Pick off as much as you can of the membrane covering their surface, taking care not to tear or pull away the flesh. Place the sweetbreads in 1 quart of cold water, add 1 tablespoon of lemon juice or vinegar and 1 teaspoon salt, and bring to the simmer. Simmer gently for 10 minutes, drain, and plunge the sweetbreads into several changes of cold water to cool them swiftly. Arrange them in a single layer on a plate or platter, cover with another plate, put a weight on top, and put the whole into the refrigerator for several hours. This flattens the sweetbreads evenly and squeezes excess water out of them. This process also stiffens the sweetbreads for any cutting or slicing you may want to do.

If you are going to braise the sweetbreads, they need no further preparation. However, if you are going to sauté or broil them, you can give them additional flavor by poaching them in a flavorful liquid.

Make a Court Bouillon by gently boiling 1 sliced carrot, 1 sliced onion, 3 sprigs parsley, 1 tablespoon vinegar, and ½ teaspoon salt in 1 quart water for 20 minutes. Add the sweetbreads and a few peppercorns and simmer very gently for 15 minutes. Drain and dry the sweetbreads, and they are ready for sautéing or broiling. (If you braise the sweetbreads, this poaching in a flavorful liquid is included in the braising process.)

SAUTÉED SWEETBREADS
(*Ris de Veau Sautés*)

Having soaked, blanched, and poached the sweetbreads as described above, they can be again chilled in the refrigerator to make them firm preparatory to further cooking. They are sautéed as follows.

Carefully split the sweetbreads in two lengthwise. Dry the pieces and coat them *à l'Anglaise,* that is, dip them in flour, then into a mixture of one egg beaten with 2 tablespoons milk, 1 teaspoon salad oil, and ½ teaspoon salt, and then roll them in fine, dry white breadcrumbs. Sauté the sweetbreads in Clarified Butter for 4 or 5 minutes per side.

When sweetbreads are of a good size, they may be more conveniently prepared for sautéing or broiling by slicing them to form ½-inch-thick slices or *escalopes.* Sweetbread escalopes or cutlets are the form in which you are most likely to encounter sweetbreads in the restaurants. According to the recipe you are using, these may be coated *à l'Anglaise,* they may receive another flavorful coating, or they may be simply dredged in flour and sautéed for 2 or 3 minutes on each side.

SAUTÉED SWEETBREAD CUTLETS À LA MARÉCHALE (*Escalopes de Ris de Veau Sautés à la Maréchale*). Poach, chill, and slice the sweetbreads. Coat the cutlets *à l'Anglaise* and sauté them in Clarified Butter. Arrange them in a circle on a dish, alternating the sweetbread cutlets with slices of truffle. Garnish the center of the circle with a mound of asparagus tips tossed in butter, and sprinkle the sweetbread and truffle slices with brown butter from the pan, or separately prepared Brown Butter.

SAUTÉED SWEETBREAD CUTLETS GRAND DUKE (*Escalopes des Ris de Veau Sautés Grand Duc*). Prepare as above, but do not coat the cutlets or dip them in flour. Sauté very gently in butter so they will cook without browning. Before adding the asparagus garnish in the center, coat the sweetbread and truffle slices with Mornay Sauce and glaze* in the oven.

SAUTÉED SWEETBREAD CUTLETS ROSSINI (*Escalopes de Ris de Veau Sautés Rossini*). Poach, chill, and slice the sweetbreads. Season the cutlets with salt and pepper, dredge in flour, and sauté them in Clarified Butter. Arrange them in the form of a crown on top of cutlet-shaped pieces of sautéed bread. On top of each cutlet, place a slice of *foie gras,* seasoned, dredged in flour, and sautéed in butter, and a slice of truffle. Deglaze* the pan with Madeira wine, reduce, finish the sauce with a few tablespoons of Demi-Glace Sauce, and pour over the sweetbreads and their garnish.

SAUTÉED SWEETBREAD CUTLETS FLORENTINE (*Escalopes de Ris de Veau Sautés Florentine*). Poach, chill, and slice the sweetbreads. Season the cutlets with salt and pepper, dredge in flour, and sauté in Clarified Butter. Transfer them to a heatproof platter, on top of a bed of spinach finished in butter. Cover with Mornay Sauce, sprinkle with Parmesan cheese and melted butter, and brown.

SAUTÉED SWEETBREAD CUTLETS À L'ALLEMANDE (*Escalopes de Ris de Veau à l'Allemande*). Poach, chill, and slice the sweetbreads. Season the cutlets with salt and pepper, dredge in flour, and sauté in Clarified Butter. Place them on slices of Fried Bread cut in the shape of the cutlets, and pour Allemande Sauce over each.

SAUTÉED SWEETBREAD CUTLETS À L'ITALIENNE (*Escalopes de Ris de Veau Sautés à l'Italienne*). Poach, chill, and slice the sweetbreads. Season the cutlets with salt and pepper, dredge in flour, and sauté in olive oil. Arrange them on a dish, and cover with Italian Sauce.

BROILED SWEETBREADS
(*Ris de Veau Grillés*)

Sweetbreads for broiling are prepared as for sautéed sweetbreads—first blanched, then poached in a flavorful liquid, and then chilled to make them firm. They may be grilled whole, but it is more usual to halve them lengthwise or to cut each into 3 or 4 cutlets. They are then seasoned with salt and pepper, dipped in Clarified Butter, and broiled under a moderate flame for 6 to 8 minutes, basted frequently with butter. Serve them with vegetables tossed in butter, sautéed or grilled mushrooms or tomatoes, Maître d'Hôtel Butter or Bercy Butter, or according to one of the following recipes.

BROILED SWEETBREADS JOCELYNE (*Ris de Veau Grillés Jocelyne*). Make potato cases by slicing potatoes 1½-inch thick and shaping the slices a little larger than the sweetbread slices. About ¼ inch inside the edge of these slices, make a circular cut 1 inch deep all around the rim. Deep-fry the potato slices until they are golden brown, and scoop out the pulp in the center to form the case. Fill the potato case with Soubise Sauce flavored with a little curry. Poach, chill, slice, and broil the sweetbreads. Arrange the potato cases on a dish, place a broiled sweetbread on top of each, and place a grilled tomato half and a grilled green pepper half on top of each sweetbread.

BROILED SWEETBREADS ST. GERMAIN (*Ris de Veau Grillés Saint-Germain*). Poach, chill, halve, and broil the sweetbreads. Arrange them on a dish surrounded by alternate mounds of sautéed potato balls and Glazed Carrots cut in olive shapes. Separately serve a Purée of Peas, and pass a sauceboat of Béarnaise Sauce.

BRAISED SWEETBREADS
(*Ris de Veau Braisés*)

Sweetbreads to be braised need only to be soaked and blanched before their cooking begins. They are a delicate white meat and are braised like chicken.

Salt and pepper the blanched sweetbreads. Put them in a casserole with 1 sliced carrot, 1 sliced onion, and 2 tablespoons blanched salt pork or bacon, all browned in butter. Add 3 sprigs parsley, ½ bay leaf, and 1 sprig or pinch of thyme. Add ½ cup dry white wine and boil down until it is syrupy. Then add enough reduced veal or chicken stock or Starch-Thickened Veal or Chicken Stock to cover the sweetbreads by about ½. Cover tightly and cook in a 325° oven for about 45 minutes to 1 hour, basting frequently with the braising liquid. Sweetbreads are done when they tend to break apart and when their edges crumble. The sweetbreads can be browned and glazed by removing the cover halfway through cooking, but they must be basted often.

When the sweetbreads are cooked, remove them to a hot platter. Skim the fat from the braising liquid, reduce it to the desired consistency, strain it, and pour it over the sweetbreads. Serve with vegetables braised or tossed in butter, such as carrots, peas, green beans, corn, mushrooms, celery, or lettuce, or with various purées of vegetables served separately, or in one of the following ways.

BRAISED SWEETBREADS CLAMART (*Ris de Veau Braisés Clamart*). Braise blanched sweetbreads in white wine and Starch-Thickened Brown Veal Stock. Arrange them on a dish with potato balls sautéed in butter and artichoke bottoms filled with green peas tossed in butter. Skim and reduce the braising liquid, and strain it. Pour some of this sauce over the sweetbreads, and pass the rest in a hot sauceboat.

BRAISED SWEETBREADS À LA JARDINIÈRE (*Ris de Veau Braisés à la Jardinière*). Braise the blanched sweetbreads in white wine and Starch-Thickened Brown Veal Stock. Arrange them on a dish, and surround them with alternating heaps of Glazed Carrots cut in olive shapes; Glazed Turnips cut in olive shapes; green beans, kidney beans, cauliflowerets, and peas, all tossed in butter. Skim and reduce the braising liquid, strain it, and pour some of it over the sweetbreads. Separately pass the remaining sauce in a hot sauceboat.

BRAISED SWEETBREADS À LA PÉRIGOURDINE (*Ris de Veau Braisés à la Périgourdine*). Braise the sweetbreads in white wine and Starch-Thickened Brown Veal Stock. Arrange them on a platter with thin slices or dice of truffles. Skim and reduce the braising liquid to the desired consistency, strain it, and off the fire stir in a few tablespoons of Madeira wine to taste. Pour some of this sauce over the sweetbreads, and pass the rest in a hot sauceboat.

BRAISED SWEETBREADS À LA PRINCESSE (*Ris de Veau Braisés à la Princesse*). Braise the sweetbreads in white wine and Starch-Thickened White Veal or White Chicken Stock. Arrange them on a platter with Asparagus Tips in Cream and thin slices or dice of truffles. Skim and strain the braising liquid and use it to make Allemande Sauce. Pour some of this sauce over the sweetbreads, and pass the remainder in a hot sauceboat.

BRAISED SWEETBREADS TALLEYRAND (*Ris de Veau Braisés Talleyrand*). Stud* the sweetbreads with slivers of truffle. Braise them in white wine and Starch-Thickened White Veal Stock. Skim and strain the braising liquid, thicken it with about ½ cup thick Chicken Velouté Sauce, and return to the boil. Remove from the fire and add to 1½ cups of this sauce 4 to 6 tablespoons heavy cream and ¼ cup Madeira wine. Swirl in* 2 tablespoons butter, and add 1 tablespoon each of finely chopped truffle, pickled tongue, and cooked *Mirepoix*. Pour some of this sauce (Talleyrand Sauce) over the sweetbreads, and pass the rest in a hot sauceboat.

BRAISED SWEETBREADS À LA CRÈME (*Ris de Veau Braisés à la Crème*). Braise the sweetbreads in white wine and Starch-Thickened White Veal Stock, and keep them warm. Meanwhile, prepare 1½ cups thick Béchamel Sauce. Off the fire, blend into this sauce 1 egg yolk beaten in ½ cup heavy cream. Season to taste with salt. Add ¾ cup diced cooked white chicken meat and ¾ cup sliced poached mushrooms. Heat to just below the boiling point, remove from the fire, and stir in 2 or 3 tablespoons Madeira wine to taste. Finally, cut the sweetbreads in large dice and carefully swirl them into the sauce, taking pains not to break them. Serve the creamed sweetbreads in Tartlet shells or on toast.

SWEETBREAD CUTLETS AU GRATIN (*Escalopes de Ris de Veau au Gratin*). Braise the sweetbreads in White Wine and Starch-Thickened Brown Veal Stock. Slice them in cutlets, and arrange them on an ovenproof dish surrounded by poached, sliced mushrooms. Cover the whole with Duxelles Sauce, sprinkle with fine, dry white breadcrumbs, and brown in the oven. Just before serving, sprinkle with lemon juice and chopped parsley.

✸ *BRAINS*
(*Cervelles*)

Brains are very similar to sweetbreads in their texture and cooking. They are sautéed, broiled, and braised like sweetbreads, and many of the recipes for these two meats are completely interchangeable. If anything, brains will stand more cooking than sweetbreads, prolonged cooking serving to set them more firmly. The brains of beef, calf, lamb, and pork are all eaten, but those of calf and lamb are preferred.

To prepare brains for cooking, soak them for 3 or 4 hours in cold water, carefully peel away the membrane covering them, and trim away any white connective tissue. Cover them with 1 quart boiling water and add 2 tablespoons lemon juice or vinegar and 1 teaspoon salt. Return to the simmer and simmer for 15 minutes. Do not plunge the blanched brains into cold water; instead, allow them to cool in the blanching liquid. Drain the brains, arrange them in a single layer on a platter, place a weight on top to flatten them, and put them in the refrigerator. The brains are now ready for further cooking. This should all be done as soon as you get home from the store.

If you are going to braise the brains, you may proceed with the recipe. However, if you are going to sauté or broil the brains, you should first poach them in a flavorful liquid. Use the Court Bouillon suggested for sweetbreads, adding an extra 1 tablespoon of vinegar. Gently poach calf, lamb, and pork brains for 15 minutes; poach beef brains for 30 minutes. Allow them to cool in the liquid, drain them, and put them in the refrigerator to chill and stiffen for subsequent slicing. They are now ready for broiling or sautéing.

Poached brains can be sliced and sautéed following the recipes for Sweetbread Cutlets. Thus you can prepare sautéed brains à la Maréchale, Grand Duke, Rossini, Florentine, à l'Allemande, and à l'Italienne. Or you can prepare them in one of the following ways.

CALF'S BRAINS IN BROWN BUTTER (*Cervelles de Veau au Beurre Noisette*). Dredge slices of poached brains in flour, season them with salt and pepper, and sauté them in Clarified Butter. Separately prepare Brown Butter, add to it a little chopped parsley, and pour it over the brains. Put in a few teaspoons of vinegar or lemon juice in the hot pan in which you browned the butter, and sprinkle it over the brains.

CALF'S BRAINS À LA BOURGUIGNONNE (*Cervelles de Veau à la Bourguignonne*). Dredge slices of poached brains in flour, season them with salt and pepper, and sauté them in Clarified Butter. Arrange the brains on slices of sautéed bread and garnish the platter with small Glazed Onions and sautéed mushrooms. Cover the brains with Bourguignonne Sauce.

✳ *LIVER*
(*Foie*)

Liver is a grainless, soft meat, high in protein, that becomes tough as shoe leather if overcooked. Although the livers of the different animals react similarly to heat, their cooking differs, depending upon their flavors. These range from very delicate to strong. In the order of their delicacy, I would arrange the commonly available livers as follows:

Calf's liver is the most delicate, delicious, and expensive. It is the first choice for good cooking, and is best cooked sautéed or broiled to the rare or medium-rare stage.

Chicken liver is equally delicate in taste, but its small size and exceptionally soft texture relegate it to combination dishes or use as a garnish.

Baby beef liver is more decided in taste, depending upon how "baby" the beef is. It is cooked like calf's liver or beef liver.

Pork liver, after being soaked in milk for 2 hours, is equal in delicacy to baby beef liver. Pork liver, of course, must be cooked well done. (It is a first choice for pâtés.)

Beef liver is the strongest-tasting and usually requires careful cooking and saucing to mitigate its strong flavor. It is best braised.

Lamb liver, like beef liver, is strong-tasting, and should be presented with a piquant sauce no matter how it is cooked.

Liver is usually cooked in one of three ways. It is sliced thinly and quickly sautéed. It is sliced more thickly and broiled. Or it is left whole and braised. Because liver is a very lean meat, it is frequently larded with fat when braised.

Except for pork liver, which is soaked in milk for two hours, liver requires little preparation. You may wipe the liver with a damp cloth; do not put it in water. When sliced for sautéing or broiling, the elastic membrane should be peeled from the rims of the slices to prevent curling during cooking. This membrane is left on when liver is braised whole to hold the meat in shape; it will become tender and unnoticeable during the braising process.

SAUTÉED CALF'S LIVER (*Foie de Veau Sauté*). Cut the liver in thin slices ¼ to ⅜ inch thick, and peel away the membrane on the edges. Season with salt and pepper, dredge lightly in flour (slapping the slices over the sink to remove excess flour), and sauté briskly in Clarified Butter. Cook for 2 or 3 minutes on the first side, and for 1 or 2 minutes on the second side, or until the liver is just pink inside (when pricked with a skewer, a pale pink juice will run out). Arrange on a dish, and sprinkle with butter from the pan or, if the butter is burned, separately prepared Brown Butter.

SAUTÉED CALF'S LIVER À L'ANGLAISE (*Foie de Veau Sauté à l'Anglaise*). Slice and sauté the liver (as above) in Clarified Butter. Arrange the slices on a platter alternating them with slices of sautéed or grilled bacon. Sprinkle with Brown Butter. Separately serve boiled or steamed potatoes.

SAUTÉED CALF'S LIVER À LA LYONNAISE (*Foie de Veau Sauté à la Lyonnaise*). Slice the liver and sauté as for Sautéed Calf's Liver (above). In a second skillet, sauté thin slices of onion in butter. Arrange the slices of liver on a platter and put a slice of sautéed onion on top of each. To the butter in the onion pan, add 2 tablespoons Meat Glaze or Starch-Thickened Veal Stock, blend for a few minutes, and pour over the liver and onions. In the same pan, reduce 2 tablespoons wine vinegar by half. Sprinkle the vinegar and chopped parsley over the liver and onions.

SAUTÉED CALF'S LIVER À LA BORDELAISE (*Foie de Veau Sauté à la Bordelaise*). Slice the liver and sauté as for Sautéed Calf's Liver (above). Arrange the slices on a platter alternating them with slices of ham sautéed in butter. Pour Bordelaise Sauce over the liver and ham.

SAUTÉED CALF'S LIVER À L'ITALIENNE (*Foie de Veau Sauté à l'Italienne*). Slice the liver and sauté as for Sautéed Calf's Liver (above). Arrange the slices on a platter and pour Tomato Sauce over them.

SAUTÉED CALF'S LIVER À LA PROVENÇALE (*Foie de Veau Sauté à la Provençale*). Slice the liver and sauté as for Sautéed Calf's Liver (above). Arrange the slices in a circle on a dish, and pour Tomato Fondue into the center of this circle. Garnish the dish with black olives and a good sprinkle of chopped tarragon.

SAUTÉED CALF'S LIVER À LA BOURGUIGNONNE (*Foie de Veau Sauté à la Bourguignonne*). Slice the liver and sauté as for Sautéed Calf's Liver (above). Arrange the slices on a platter and garnish with tiny Glazed Onions and sautéed mushrooms, whole or quartered. To the butter in the pan, providing it is not burned, add ½ cup dry red wine and ½ cup Demi-Glace Sauce. Reduce by ½, strain, and pour over the liver and its garnish. (Or, instead of making this pan sauce, use separately prepared Burgundy Sauce.)

BROILED CALF'S LIVER (*Foie de Veau Grillé*). Cut the liver in ½-inch-thick slices, and peel away the membrane on the edges. Season with salt and pepper, dredge lightly with flour (slapping the slices over the sink to remove excess flour), and brush them with melted butter. Broil the slices about 5 inches from the flame, for 3 or 4 minutes on each side. The liver is done when it just becomes firm to the touch (when pricked with a skewer, a pale pink juice will run out). Serve with Maître d'Hôtel Butter or Bercy Butter, or with Piquant, Bordelaise, Italian, Devil, or another spicy sauce.

BROILED CALF'S LIVER À L'ESPAGNOLE (*Foie de Veau Grillé à l'Espagnole*). Slice and broil the liver as for Broiled Calf's Liver (above). For each piece of liver prepare a Grilled Tomato half. Arrange the slices of liver on an oval platter and place a grilled half tomato on top of each. Garnish one end of the platter with Deep-Fried Onions and the other end with Fried Parsley.

BROILED CALF'S LIVER EN BROCHETTE (*Brochettes de Foie de Veau Grillés*). Cut the liver in ⅔-inch-thick slices and cut these into 1½-inch squares. Cut equal amounts of blanched salt pork or lean bacon in the same size. Sauté the pork and the liver in butter for 1 or 2 minutes to set the surface. Put the pork and liver into a bowl with parboiled mushroom caps, and toss with thick Duxelles Sauce until the pieces are well coated. Impale the liver, pork, and mushroom caps alternately on skewers, dip in fine, dry white breadcrumbs, and sprinkle with melted butter. Broil under a moderate flame for 8 minutes, basting with butter and turning the skewers to assure that the pork is well cooked. Serve with Duxelles Sauce or any of the butters or sauces recommended for Broiled Calf's Liver (above).

BRAISED CALF'S LIVER (*Foie de Veau Braisé*). Lard* or stud* a whole calf's liver with ¼-inch square strips of blanched salt pork that you have sprinkled with pepper, nutmeg, and chopped parsley, and marinated in brandy for 2 hours. Brown the liver in a skillet with 3 tablespoons Clarified Butter, reserving the skillet and the butter. In a casserole just large enough to hold the liver, brown 2 carrots, chopped, and 2 onions, chopped, in butter. Place the liver on this bed of vegetables, and add 1 rib celery, 3 sprigs parsley, ½ bay leaf, and 1 sprig or pinch of thyme. To the skillet in which the liver was browned, add 2 tablespoons flour, blending and cooking it with the butter for 3 or 4 minutes to form a roux. Add 1½ cups dry red wine and 1½ cups Brown Stock and cook until the sauce thickens. Pour this sauce over the liver, adding more brown stock if necessary to cover it. Bring the liquid to a simmering point on the stove. Cover the liver with a piece of foil cut to fit the pan, with a small hole cut in it to vent the steam. Cover tightly and braise in a 350° oven for 2½ to 3 hours, turning and basting the liver as the sauce cooks down. Remove the liver to a hot serving platter. Skim fat from the braising liquid and reduce it to ½ of its original quantity. Strain the sauce, sprinkle some of it over the liver, and serve the remainder in a hot sauceboat.

❊ KIDNEYS
(Rognons)

Beef kidneys are tough and strong-flavored, and pork kidneys have a peculiarly sweetish taste that is not much appreciated. This is not to say that these meats cannot be made palatable, but in fine cooking the choice of kidneys is usually limited to veal and lamb.

Lamb kidneys are small, weighing about 2 ounces, measuring a finger's length, and shaped like a kidney bean. You may wipe them with a damp cloth; do not soak them or put them under running water. Trim off any fat remaining on the kidney, cutting away the firm button of fat on the concave side. Carefully peel away the membrane surrounding the kidney, and it is ready to cook.

Veal kidneys are larger, weighing up to ½ pound, and their exterior shape suggests a cluster of balls. They may or may not be surrounded with a layer of beef kidney fat, or suet. If you plan to poêlé the kidneys, this layer of fat should be trimmed to a thickness of about ½ inch, thereby providing an excellent natural Bard. If you are going to sauté or broil the kidneys, remove the fat and carefully peel away the membrane in which the kidney is encased. If the kidneys come to you already free of fat, prepare them like lamb kidneys.

Lamb and veal kidneys are naturally tender, but they will become quite tough and dry if they are not cooked properly. They will not stand long cooking. Cook them briskly in dry heat. Either sauté them in very hot butter, or broil them under a hot flame, or poêlé them in a hot oven. They are best cooked medium-rare.

SAUTÉED KIDNEYS (*Rognons Sautés*). Peel membrane from the kidneys, cut away any remaining fat, and slice them ¼-inch thick. Season with salt and pepper and dredge lightly in flour, slapping the pieces sharply over the sink to dislodge any excess flour. Sauté the kidneys briskly in very hot Clarified Butter for about 2 minutes per side. Drain the kidneys on several thicknesses of paper towel to rid them of some of the juices they contain. While the kidneys are draining, make a sauce according to the recipe you are using in the pan in which the kidneys were cooked. Warm the drained kidneys in this sauce, without allowing the sauce to boil.

SAUTÉED KIDNEYS WITH MUSHROOMS (*Rognons Sautés aux Champignons*). Slice and sauté the kidneys and drain them. Add one cup sliced mushrooms to the pan, sauté them, and set them aside. Add ½ cup Madeira wine to the pan and reduce almost entirely. Add ⅔ cup Demi-Glace Sauce or Starch-Thickened Brown Veal Stock and cook for a few minutes more. Return the kidneys and mushrooms to the pan to warm them. Finally swirl in* 2 tablespoons butter and serve in a serving bowl.

SAUTÉED KIDNEYS WITH WINE (*Rognons Sautés au Vin*). Slice and sauté the kidneys and drain them. Add 1 cup wine to the pan and reduce it almost entirely. Add ⅔ cup Demi-Glace Sauce or ⅔ cup Starch-Thickened Brown Veal Stock and cook for a few minutes more. Return the kidneys to the pan, warm them, and swirl in* 2 tablespoons butter. Serve the kidneys and their sauce in a serving bowl. You may use Madeira or sherry wine, champagne, and almost any dry red or white wine in this recipe, to create *rognons sautés au Madère, au Xérès, au Champagne,* and so on.

SAUTÉED KIDNEYS À LA BORDELAISE (*Rognons Sautés à la Bordelaise*). Slice and sauté the kidneys and drain them. Deglaze* the pan with ⅔ cup Bordelaise Sauce and add to it: ⅓ cup poached diced marrow, ⅔ cup sliced *cèpes* or mushrooms lightly sautéed in oil and butter; and ½ teaspoon finely chopped parsley. Warm the drained kidneys in this sauce and serve in a serving bowl.

SAUTÉED KIDNEYS À L'INDIENNE (*Rognons Sautés à l'Indienne*). Slice and sauté the kidneys and drain them. Dice one onion and sauté it in butter until soft. To the onion add ⅔ cup Velouté Sauce and ½ teaspoon curry powder. Cook for 4 or 5 minutes to blend the flavors, and rub the sauce through a fine sieve. Warm the kidneys in the sauce, without allowing the sauce to boil. Serve them in a serving bowl accompanied by Rice à l'Indienne.

SAUTÉED KIDNEYS CHASSEUR (*Rognons Sautés Chasseau*). Slice and sauté the kidneys and drain them. Deglaze* the pan with ½ cup dry white wine and reduce the wine almost entirely. Add ⅔ cup Chasseur Sauce, cook for a few minutes to blend the flavors. Warm the kidneys in the sauce, without allowing the sauce to boil, and serve them in a serving bowl.

SAUTÉED KIDNEYS BERCY (*Rognons Sautés Bercy*). Slice and sauté the kidneys and drain them. To the pan add one tablespoon minced shallot and cook for 1 minute. Add ⅔ cup dry white wine and reduce by ½. Finally, add 2 tablespoons Meat Glaze and a squeeze of lemon juice, and cook for a few minutes to blend the flavors. Return the kidneys to this sauce, and swirl in* 5 tablespoons butter without allowing the sauce to boil. Serve the kidneys in a serving bowl with their sauce, and sprinkle with chopped parsley.

BROILED KIDNEYS (*Rognons Grillés*). Peel membrane from the kidneys and cut them in two lengthwise, without completely severing the two parts. Trim away any fat, and impale the butterflied kidneys on small skewers to prevent them from closing up in the heat. Season the kidneys with salt and pepper, brush them with melted butter, and broil them, basting frequently. Broil veal kidneys about 5 inches away from the flame for about 6 to 8 minutes per side. Broil lamb kidneys, which are smaller, closer to the flame for about 5 minutes per side. Serve with Maître d'Hôtel Butter.

BROILED KIDNEYS AU VERT PRÉ (*Rognons Grillés au Vert Pré*). Broil the kidneys (as above). Garnish the platter with mounds of Shoestring Potatoes and bouquets of parsley.

BROCHETTES OF KIDNEYS (*Brochettes de Rognons*). Cut the kidneys in 1½-inch round or square pieces about ⅓ inch thick. Season with salt and pepper and sauté in Clarified Butter for 1 or 2 minutes to just set the surface. Impale the pieces of liver on skewers, alternating with similarly sized pieces of blanched salt pork or bacon and slices or whole caps of parboiled mushrooms. Roll in fine white dry breadcrumbs, sprinkle with melted butter, and broil under a moderate flame for 8 minutes, basting with butter and turning the skewers to assure that the pork is well cooked. Serve with Maître d'Hôtel Butter or Bercy Butter.

✳ HEART
(Coeur)

Only veal hearts are of enough culinary interest to merit cooking for themselves alone, and they are very good indeed. They may be sliced, sautéed, and served with a sauce and garnish made in the pan. Or they may be cooked whole—braised, roasted, or poëléed.

When cooking whole veal heart, cut it open part way lengthwise, wash away the blood that collects in the center, remove the arteries, and tie the heart tightly with soft butcher's twine. The heart may be stuffed. When sautéing veal heart, slice it crossways, cut out the cross sections of artery, wash out the clots of blood, and dry the slices thoroughly.

Veal hearts weigh from ¾ to 1½ pounds, the largest being most suitable for braising.

SAUTÉED VEAL HEART À L'ANGLAISE (*Coeur de Veau Sauté à l'Anglaise*). Slice the heart crossways into thin slices ¼ to ⅜ inch thick. Remove arteries, wash away the blood that collects in the center, drain and dry the slices carefully. Season with salt and pepper, dredge in flour, and sauté in very hot Clarified Butter or good beef fat. Cook for only 2 or 3 minutes per side; the slices should be pink inside. Serve with fried or grilled bacon and boiled or steamed potatoes.

SAUTÉED VEAL HEART À LA BORDELAISE (*Coeur de Veau Sauté à la Bordelaise*). Sauté the slices of heart and finish as for Sautéed Kidneys à la Bordelaise.

VEAL HEART EN CASSEROLE À LA BONNE FEMME (*Coeur de Veau en Casserole à la Bonne Femme*). Clean, tie, and season the heart with salt and pepper. Brown it in Clarified Butter in a casserole a little larger than the heart. Add to the casserole small parboiled potatoes or potato balls, tiny Glazed Onions, and squares of bacon lightly sautéed in butter. Cover and cook the heart in a 375° oven, basting frequently with butter, for 30 minutes or until its juices run pink when probed with a skewer. Baste with 4 tablespoons Starch-Thickened Veal Stock and leave it to glaze* for a few minutes in the oven. Serve the heart and vegetables in the casserole.

ROAST VEAL HEART (*Coeur de Veau Rôti*). Clean the heart, dry it, and tie it. Season with salt and pepper, sprinkle with ¼ cup olive oil and a little lemon juice, and turn it in this marinade for about 1 hour. Bard* the heart with pork fat, put it on a rack in a baking pan, and roast in a 375° oven for one hour or until the juices run pink when probed with a skewer. Serve with the juices of the pan, thickened with Starch-Thickened Veal Stock.

BRAISED VEAL HEART (*Coeur de Veau Braisé*). Clean the heart, dry it, and tie it. Braise the heart, following the procedure given for Braised Calf's Liver, but cook in a 300° oven for about 4 hours.

❋ *BEEF TONGUE*
(*Langue de Boeuf*)

Beef tongue is lean, firm, fine-flavored meat. A whole tongue weighs 3 to 4 pounds, containing a high proportion of usable meat that is every bit as good cold as hot. Veal, pork, and lamb tongues are also eaten, but they are not so flavorful. Beef tongue is available at most supermarkets fresh and salted.

Salt tongue, pickled with brine, seasonings, and saltpeter, is handsomely colored and is known in France as scarlet tongue (*langue de boeuf à l'écarlate*). It is frequently used as a decorative garnish.

Before cooking, salt tongue is scrubbed with a brush and soaked in water for 4 to 8 hours to relieve it of its salt. It is then poached or braised.

Fresh tongue is a more perishable meat than it appears to be, and you should either cook it immediately or preserve it by salting. Scrub the tongue as soon as you get it home and soak it in water for 2 hours. If you are not going to cook the tongue the same day, dry it carefully, put it in a nonmetallic or ceramic dish, surround it with a layer of coarse salt, cover, and refrigerate. Wash off the salt before cooking. Fresh tongue is usually braised.

POACHED TONGUE (*Langue de Boeuf Pochée*). Simmer the tongue for about 3 hours in water with 2 large carrots, sliced, 2 large onions, sliced, 1 rib celery, sliced, a handful of parsley, 2 bay leaves, and 2 sprigs or big pinches of thyme. (If the tongue was not salted, add 1 teaspoon per quart of water.) Tongue will require about 3 hours to cook, and is done when it can be easily pierced with a fork. Remove the cooked tongue, skin it, and trim it, removing any loose bones at the base. Carve it by slicing across the grain. Tongue lends itself to wine sauces such as Madeira, piquant sauces such as Pepper, Piquant, Vinaigrette, Robert, Lyonnaise, Devil, and Tomato Sauces. If the tongue is to be served cold, allow it to cool in the poaching liquid.

BRAISED TONGUE (*Langue de Boeuf Braisée*). Braise the tongue exactly as you would rump roast of beef (see Braised Beef). Part way through the cooking, when you are straining the sauce, skim and trim the tongue, removing any loose bones at its base. When the tongue is cooked, glaze* it in the oven and serve with a sauce made from the braising liquid. You may use any of the garnishes recommended for braised beef to create such dishes as *langue de boeuf braisée à la bourguignonne, à la jardinière, à la lorraine, à la Noailles, à la lyonnaise, à l'alsacienne, à la bourgeoise,* and *à la flamande.*

Leftover braised or poached tongue is very good as it is. It can also be treated as follows:

BEEF TONGUE AU GRATIN (*Langue de Boeuf au Gratin*). Arrange slices of cold tongue in a ring on a buttered ovenproof dish, alternating them with slices of boiled ham. Place a braised mushroom cap on top of each slice of tongue, and cover the whole with Duxelles Sauce. Sprinkle fine, dry white breadcrumbs and melted butter over the dish, and brown in the broiler or a hot oven.

DEVILED BEEF TONGUE (*Langue de Boeuf à la Diable*). Cut cold tongue in ½-inch-thick slices. Spread the slices with Dijon Mustard, dip them in melted butter, roll them in fine, dry white breadcrumbs, and sprinkle with butter. Broil the slices on both sides until they are well browned and serve with Devil Sauce.

Finally, whole poached tongue makes a resplendent dish when prepared and served in the following manner.

BEEF TONGUE IN ASPIC (*Langue de Boeuf en Gelée*). Skin, debone, and trim a poached, salted beef tongue, wrap it tightly in plastic wrap, and chill it in the refrigerator. Place the tongue on a long platter and coat it with several layers of meat Aspic that you have colored with red food coloring. Surround the tongue with diced aspic jelly and garnish the ends of the platter with parsley or watercress.

✳ *TRIPE*
(*Gras-double*)

Tripe is taken from the four stomachs of beef animals. All four stomachs are eaten, but in America the only tripe usually available is the handsome honeycomb tripe (French, *bonnet*) of the second stomach. This is a pouchlike affair, very tough and rubbery when you buy it, with its outer surface covered with polygonal structures resembling a honeycomb.

Although the tripe you get at the store should already be parboiled, it will require about 4 hours more cooking to make it tender enough to eat. If you plan to sauté the tripe, this cooking must be done in advance. Simmer the tripe whole in lightly salted water to which you have added 1 tablespoon flour to aid in keeping the tripe white. The cooked tripe is then cut up in sizes appropriate for additional cooking.

The taste of tripe cannot be likened to anything else, and its unique flavor remains dominant in the dishes that have been devised for it. It is usually stewed or sautéed.

SAUTÉED TRIPE À LA LYONNAISE (*Gras-double à la Lyonnaise*). Cut one pound of precooked tripe in small strips or squares and sauté in Clarified Butter. To the pan, add ½ cup chopped onion sautéed in butter and continue cooking until the tripe is golden brown. Transfer the tripe to a hot serving platter, and pour over it the pan butter and onions. Add 2 tablespoons vinegar to the pan, cook for 1 minute, and sprinkle the tripe with this vinegar and 1 tablespoon chopped parsley.

SAUTÉED TRIPE À LA POLONAISE (*Gras-double à la Polonaise*). Cut 1 pound of precooked tripe in small strips or squares and sauté in Clarified Butter until golden brown. Transfer the tripe to a hot serving platter and sprinkle with chopped egg yolk, chopped parsley, lemon juice, and vinegar. Brown ½ cup fine, dry white breadcrumbs in the butter remaining in the pan, adding more butter if needed, and pour over the tripe.

TRIPE À LA FERMIÈRE (*Gras-double à la Fermière*). Sauté ¼ cup diced onion and ¼ cup diced carrot in 2 tablespoons butter until they have softened. Add 2 tablespoons flour and cook, stirring, for 2 or 3 minutes to form a Roux. Add 3 cups White Veal Stock and cook, stirring for a few minutes until the stock thickens. Add 1 pound precooked tripe cut in small strips and seasoned with salt and pepper, cover the pan and simmer for 1 hour. For the last 10 minutes of cooking, add 1 cup sliced mushrooms sautéed in butter.

TRIPE EN BLANQUETTE (*Gras-double en Blanquette*). In an enameled or other nonaluminum saucepan, sauté 2 tablespoons diced onion in 2 tablespoons butter until soft. Add 1 tablespoon flour and cook, stirring, for 2 or 3 minutes to form a Roux. Add 3 cups White Veal Stock and cook, stirring, for a few minutes until the stock slightly thickens. Add 1 pound precooked tripe cut in small strips and seasoned with salt and pepper. Simmer the tripe, uncovered, for 1 hour. Just before serving, thicken the sauce with 2 or 3 beaten egg yolks and add 1 tablespoon chopped parsley and a good squeeze of lemon. Swirl in* 2 tablespoons butter and serve on a hot platter.

✖ 11   *Vegetables in a Blue Light*

It is barely dawn when M. Touzeau, chef of the Restaurant Laperouse, and I enter the ancient market place at Nantes. The air is dewy and cool. Bare electric bulbs, paling in the growing blue light of morning, throw their glare onto the slick cobbles of the street. Around my ears echo the clop of horses, the rumble of iron-rimmed wheels, the clatter of crates and boxes, the greetings and gibes of men. The fragrance of croissants and coffee wafts through the thin smell of rain. I am thirteen years old in my first year of apprenticeship. I am carrying two large *paniers*. M. Touzeau and I have come to buy the day's vegetables.

Spilling out of wagons and baskets, heaped high on rickety stalls, the vegetables of France glow softly in the blue light. Here is the celery, creamy and crisp. Here are plump purple artichokes, bouquets of red radishes, sheaves of parsley, eggplants black as obsidian, shiny as cellophane. M. Touzeau strolls through this dewy profusion, poking, hefting, sniffing.

Plunk! Into my right-hand basket go six green cabbages, heavy as cannonballs. Thump, thump! Into my left-hand basket go big white potatoes, smelling of earth. Poke, heft, sniff, plunk! Here come bunches of bright orange carrots, alabaster cauliflowers wrapped in their own fresh leaves, golden onions, copper shallots, fat leeks, green beans so crisp they crackle in my mouth. And purple turnips, great handsome things, but oh, so heavy. . . .

A few blocks from my home in San Francisco is the famous Safeway Supermarket where Premier Khrushchev was shown the bounty of America. I frequently go there to shop for my vegetables. In place of the paniers of Restaurant Laperouse I push a stainless steel cart. In place of the bare bulbs of Nantes, fluorescent tubes glow brightly. The store opens at nine and the dawn is long past. But I still see the vegetables in a blue light.

I sense M. Touzeau standing at my elbow. Poke! Heft! Sniff! "Ah, there is a cauliflower worthy of the pot. Take this, and this! But not that, not that! Pinch those beans! Smell that celery!" But it is hard to do. The plastic wrappings keep getting in the way. And though it is perhaps of little importance, I cannot smell the earth these foods grew in.

The mechanization of vegetable growing and mass distribution are not designed to provide the wide variety of fresh, flavorful vegetables real French cooking demands. You must therefore take care to skim the cream from this vast mass supply. This search for the best is great sport.

Let us begin at the store, in the produce department run by a man who takes pride in his vegetables. Before your eyes are laid out the roots, bulbs, tubers, seeds, stems, flowers, leaves, and "fruits" that make up our vegetable supply. Most of these are packaged for self-service, by the supplier or the produce man himself. These vegetables are handsome—bright-colored, fresh-looking, very clean. You would be amazed to know the expense and care required to bring you these vegetables in such prime condition. Unfortunately, much of what you see is a sham.

As French cooks, we are interested mostly in the flavor of our vegetables. To be of good flavor, a vegetable must be fresh. If it is fresh it will look fresh. But you must be on your guard. All fresh-looking vegetables are not necessarily fresh. And all fresh vegetables are not necessarily good-flavored. Let us look at freshness first.

Take the little peas in their pods, for example. Bedecked with beads of moisture, they look so succulent, fresh, and green. But taste one. It is almost invariably starchy. There is almost no way, through the channels of mass national distribution, that these peas can be gotten to you without losing an important amount of their fresh sweetness.

Not all vegetables are as perishable as peas and corn. Other vegetables, carefully handled, can reach your supermarket in good condition. A bundle of California asparagus, quick-cooled in the field to prevent its withering in its own heat, washed in soft water, packed upright in a tray of damp moss, shipped in a refrigerated and humidified freight car, and expeditiously handled by the supermarket, can arrive at a New York table crisp, fresh, and sweet. Although it is six or eight days old, it will have lost less of its fresh flavor than asparagus picked that morning and displayed in the withering sun on a quaint roadside stand.

Unless you have your own vegetable garden, you will have to cook in the French manner the vegetables of our mechanized farms. You can make certain, however, that they are as fresh as it is possible for them to be. No slipups along the line. (I will tell you exactly what to look for in each vegetable so you can be as certain of its freshness.) Also, keep your eyes open for locally grown vegetables—asparagus, peas, corn, beans, and all perishable in-season vegetables that have been both recently picked *and* respectfully handled.

It is more difficult to judge the freshness of the hardy vegetables, such as potatoes, carrots, and onions. Properly stored, they resist showing their age. Although they can remain fresh-looking for months, their flavor suffers nevertheless. With these vegetables, use common sense. The packages will usually tell you what state the vegetables come from. If it's a northern state you know the vegetable was harvested last autumn. Just count the months. If the package doesn't tell you where the vegetable comes from (the store brand packages in some chain stores do not), you are being deprived of an important source of buying information.

Getting your hands on fresh vegetables is only part of the great search. The freshest, most handsome vegetables may be tasteless or downright poor in flavor. There are many reasons for this. Bad weather, forced growth, sprays and fertilizers, overmaturity, all can affect vegetable flavor. Most of these, however, are responsible for only isolated or temporary setbacks in flavor. The one big reason for poor flavor in today's vegetables will raise the hackles on your neck!

Many vegetables do not taste as good as they used to because the original variety is not around anymore. Good-tasting varieties have been discontinued in favor of new varieties that have "high commercial quality." These new varieties grow faster. They yield more per acre. They resist blight and insects. They look fresher, longer, so they may travel for days or store for months. They have tougher skins to resist rough handling. They are even bred to ripen simultaneously, so that machines can pick them all with a single pass. And there are other reasons. The new tomato, for example, was designed to be a tough-skinned, brittle-stemmed, simultaneously maturing fruit on a *two-foot-tall bush*. In short, the tomato is designed to fit the requirements of a tomato-picking machine! Do you wonder why you haven't tasted any good tomatoes lately?

Of all natural foods, the vegetables are most susceptible to overnight varietal change. A fruit tree is good for forty years. Most vegetables are annuals. A new variety can dominate commercial production in just one season. And flavor is not a very important determinant of what that variety will be.

One reason why flavor is minimized is that it is difficult to measure. Yields per acre, skin thickness, color, size, profitability, all can be measured quantitatively. Flavor is elusive, variable, subjective. Yet flavor is what vegetable eating is all about. The plight of flavor is especially serious in that the threat to it is so insidious. Little by little we forget the tastes that were and we become inured to the tastes that are.

You cannot blame the growers for this. They do not set out to grow poor-tasting vegetables. You perhaps cannot even blame the U. S. Department of Agriculture, which is responsible for many of these new wonder seeds. Flavor has taken a backseat mainly because there is no great body of vegetable lovers informed or outraged or organized enough to demand better-tasting vegetables.

But enough of this grim stuff. All is not yet lost. Although asparagus production is standardized on the Washington varieties, they are not bad-tasting. Although there are many poor-tasting carrots, there are other varieties still being commercially grown. And tomatoes we can always grow ourselves in pots.

And there is something you can do. Find out all you can about the variety and origin of vegetables for sale at your store. Then buy two kinds at once and cook them and taste them together—the differences in flavor will often surprise you. The plastic package vegetables come in will tell you where they're from. I will try to tell you how to identify common varieties. In return for just a little effort, you and your family can enjoy better-tasting vegetables from now on.

Vegetables offer a variety of good tastes in a variety of beautiful colors. French cooks make the most of these tastes and colors, and frequently take pains to reshape and present a vegetable in especially appealing ways. Carrots are cut into little olive shapes. Potatoes are shaped with a ball cutter. Lavish care upon any vegetable and it will reward you by tasting better.

The French cooking of vegetables is in many ways similar to the nutritional cooking so widespread in America. In general, unless the vegetable is braised, the cooking is quick and the vegetables are never the least bit overcooked. The same techniques that preserve natural flavors also preserve vitamins and minerals. But nutritionists insist that vegetables be cooked in their skins, or left whole, or cooked in very little water. French cooking admits no such restrictions. Vegetables are cooked to achieve a desired taste, not the retention of Vitamin C. Yet France hasn't had a case of scurvy in years.

Vegetables are similar to one another in that they are made up of cellulose-walled cells that are bound together by protopectin. The cells contain more or less water, starch, sugar, vitamins, minerals, and flavor compounds. When heated the cellulose softens and raw flavors are changed to cooked flavors. Beyond this, vegetables vary so much it is best to give the particulars of cooking them vegetable by vegetable. But first, here are some general rules based on the physics and chemistry of cookery. They read amazingly like common sense.

To serve vegetables at their very best: blanch and cool them in advance of cooking, finish their cooking at the very last minute, and serve immediately and simply with butter, salt, and pepper. Never reheat vegetables unless they have been braised.

To make a vegetable taste milder: blanch it before cooking; cook it in lots of water, uncovered; pare it and cut it in small pieces before cooking in water.

To retain more of a vegetable's natural flavor: cook it quickly, covered, in very little water; boil it quickly in its skin; steam it; or cook it in dry heat.

To retain more of a vegetable's freshness of flavor: cook it quickly, until just tender, and serve immediately. Do not allow it to stand in its own heat, or both flavor and texture will rapidly deteriorate.

To retain the color of green vegetables: blanch them in plenty of boiling salted water and cool them quickly before cooking in another way; or boil them quickly, uncovered, in plenty of water that is completely free of acid. Do not use bicarbonate of soda.

To retain the color of white vegetables: cook them quickly in boiling salted water to which you have added lemon juice, milk, or flour (see *Blanc*).

To retain the color of red vegetables: cook them in water acidulated with vinegar, lemon juice, or tart apple slices.

To keep cooked vegetables firmer: cook them in water acidulated with vinegar or lemon juice.

To remove water from a vegetable so it will cook firmer and absorb butter or flavorful braising liquids: blanch it whole or in pieces; or sprinkle cut pieces with salt and allow to stand for 30 to 60 minutes; or put the vegetable in a pot, cover it, and bake in the oven for 10 minutes to "sweat" out the water.

To reheat braised vegetables: heat very slowly in a covered dish.

To remove astringency and bitterness from certain vegetables: sprinkle cut pieces with salt, place a weight on top, and allow to stand for 30 to 60 minutes.

To more effectively brown a vegetable: sprinkle it with a little sugar when browning.

To serve leftover vegetables: marinate them in Vinaigrette Sauce and serve cold. Do not reheat them.

To "crisp" wilted vegetables (which I hope you will never have to do): soak them in unsalted water.

✳ *ARTICHOKES*
(*Artichauts*)

The artichoke is two vegetables in one. One of these vegetables is the whole artichoke, including its edible leaf bases. The other vegetable is the white base, bottom, or heart of the artichoke as it is variously called, which may be cooked and eaten alone or with a filling.

The artichoke has a taste all its own, like a plump, creamy nut flavored with a breath of fresh vegetable green. The ancient Romans, who were not beyond drinking ground-up pearls in their wine, paid more for the taste of artichokes than any other vegetable in the garden.

Artichokes are delicious hot or cold, and children find them more fun to eat than any other vegetable around. Using your fingers, you pluck a leaf at a time, dip the meaty, creamy base of the leaf into a sauce or melted butter, put it in your mouth, bite down, and squiggle off the soft, meaty pulp between your teeth. When all the leaves are disposed of, and discarded on your plate like a fan of playing cards, you then attack the nutty white artichoke heart with your fork. Whole boiled artichokes are always served alone, coming to the table in solitary splendor on special plates that are so divided as to provide spaces for the artichoke, its sauce, and the discarded leaves.

All of our artichokes are grown just south of San Francisco, on a narrow strip of land within sight of the sea. They are most plentiful from October through May, with peak supplies in April. The one variety available is the Globe, or French, artichoke, which measures up to 4½ inches across. In France and Italy, many varieties of artichoke are grown and eaten.

Buying artichokes: When handling artichokes, avoid the sharp spine at the tips of the leaves. Look for bright green artichokes with leaves that are firm, fleshy, closely packed, and clinging to form a compact globe that feels heavy for its size. Avoid open artichokes with loose, spreading leaves, or with hard-tipped leaves spreading at the tip end, or with very purple centers. Brown spots on the outer leaves may indicate old age or bruising. Pry the leaves apart and peer down at their inner sides. If they are fresh and green down to the base of the leaf, and the brown spots do not penetrate the artichoke, they are merely bruised and therefore acceptable.

Preparing artichokes: With a sharp knife, cut about 1 inch off the top of the artichoke. Remove the bottom row or two of coarse outer leaves by bending them backward (they will snap if the artichoke is fresh). If the stem is long enough, break it off so you may thereby pull away any stringy fibers extending into the base. Trim the stem even with the base of the artichoke and trim away the stubs of the missing leaves. With scissors, snip about ½ inch off the tips of all the remaining leaves, giving the artichoke the appearance of an elegant green rosette with a golden center. Brush all cut surfaces with lemon juice to prevent the flesh from darkening.

Next, spread the trimmed outside leaves to expose the center of the artichoke. Reach in, twist out, and throw away the cone of small leaves in the center. With a teaspoon reach down into the center and carefully scoop out the fuzzy ring or "choke." Scrape it all out, leaving the cuplike bottom of the artichoke white and clean, and brush its surface with lemon juice. (You may also remove the choke after cooking and before serving, if there is time.)

Finally, freshen up the artichokes with an hour's dip in cold, salted water to which you have added 1 or 2 tablespoons of lemon juice.

Cooking artichokes: Whole artichokes pose a problem in that they are both a green and white vegetable. The white bottoms of artichokes are of such a composition that they will turn gray unless their cooking water is acidulated, and acidulated water will turn the green leaves olive drab. One solution is to tie a slice of peeled lemon to the base of the artichoke, leaving the choke in to protect the upper side of the base. Then boil, uncovered, in plenty of water. In as much as the relatively long cooking that artichokes require will somewhat discolor the leaves anyway, you may want to go ahead and acidulate the water with a few tablespoons of lemon juice or vinegar. In addition to boiling, whole artichokes are braised. The bottoms alone can be cooked in many ways.

BOILED ARTICHOKES (*Artichauts Bouillis*). Trim and clean the artichokes (see preparations above) and shake them dry. Plunge them into a large quantity of boiling salted water, and return quickly to the boil. The artichokes will float, so weigh them down with a plate that will fit inside the pot, or drape them with washed cheesecloth. Boil, uncovered, for 25 to 45 minutes. Test for doneness by pulling at a leaf; it should come loose easily. Also, the bottom should be tender when pierced with a fork. Drain the artichokes upside down, and squeeze gently to press out the water. If the choke is not removed, remove it now. Serve hot with melted butter or Hollandaise Sauce. If the artichokes are to be served cold, immediately plunge them into cold water to cool them, drain, and store covered in the refrigerator. Serve cold artichokes with Mayonnaise or Vinaigrette Sauce.

BRAISED ARTICHOKE QUARTERS (*Quartiers d'Artichauts Braisés*). Prepare 6 artichokes in the usual manner, but cut ⅓ to ½ off the top. Quarter the artichoke from top to bottom, scrape out the choke, and brush the cut surfaces with lemon juice. Blanch the artichokes for 5 minutes in boiling salted water to which you have added 1 to 2 tablespoons lemon juice or vinegar per quart. Drain and dry the artichokes.

Put ½ cup diced carrots and ½ cup diced onions in a casserole with butter or olive oil and simmer for a few minutes without allowing the onions to brown. Add the artichoke quarters, 1 teaspoon chopped garlic, and season with salt and pepper. Cover the casserole and cook over low heat for 10 minutes to expel moisture from the artichokes. Add ½ cup dry white wine and boil until the liquid is almost entirely reduced. Add 1 cup Brown Stock or enough to cover the artichoke quarters by ½. Place in the midst of the artichokes a *Bouquet Garni* consisting of 3 sprigs parsley, ½ bay leaf, and a sprig or pinch of thyme, all tied in cheesecloth. Cover the artichokes with a piece of heavy oiled paper, cut to fit the casserole and with a small hole cut in it to vent the steam. Cover the casserole and braise in a 325° oven, basting frequently, for one hour, or until the artichokes are tender and the liquid is greatly reduced. Transfer the artichokes to a serving platter, boil down the braising liquid to a few tablespoons, and sprinkle over the artichokes.

BRAISED ARTICHOKES À L'ITALIENNE (*Artichauts Braisés à l'Italienne*). Prepare as for Braised Artichoke Quarters (above). To the reduced braising liquid add Italian Sauce and pour over the artichokes.

ARTICHOKES CLAMART (*Artichauts Clamart*). Prepare 4 artichokes as for Braised Artichoke Quarters (above), but blanch them for 15 minutes. Put them in a casserole with 4 tablespoons butter, cover, and cook over low heat for 10 minutes. Mix 2 cups fresh peas with 2 cups shredded lettuce and add to the casserole. Sprinkle with a little salt and one teaspoon sugar, and add ¼ cup water. Bring to the boil, cover tightly, and braise in a 325° oven for 40 minutes or until the artichokes are tender. Serve in the casserole, dotted with butter.

ARTICHOKES CRÉCY (*Artichauts Crécy*). Prepare as for Artichokes Clamart (above), but use 3 cups carrots in place of the lettuce and peas.

STUFFED BRAISED ARTICHOKES À LA BARIGOULE (*Artichauts Braisés Farcis à la Barigoule*). Blanch 6 whole artichokes for 10 minutes, drain them, remove their chokes, and season them with salt and pepper. Fill them with *Duxelles* that you have mixed with ¼ cup chopped pork fat or blanched bacon or ham, and 1 teaspoon chopped parsley per cup of duxelles. Bard* each artichoke with fresh pork fat or blanched salt pork or bacon, tying the bard in place with soft string. Place the artichokes in a casserole that just fits them, on a bed of 1 carrot, sliced, and 1 onion, sliced. Add ½ cup dry white wine and bring to the boil. Cover the casserole and braise in a 325° oven for about 1¼ hours, or until the artichokes are tender when pierced with a fork. Remove the bards and place the artichokes on a serving dish. Skim the fat from the juices in the casserole, thicken the juices with Demi-Glace Sauce, Brown Sauce, Starch-Thickened Brown Stock, or *Beurre Manié,* and reduce to about ½ cup. Pour the sauce over the artichokes.

STUFFED BRAISED ARTICHOKES À LA MÉNAGÈRE (*Artichauts Braisés Farcis à la Ménagère*). Prepare as for Stuffed Braised Artichokes à la Barigoule (above), but stuff the artichokes with chopped boiled beef mixed with chopped pork fat or blanched bacon, and parsley.

STUFFED BRAISED ARTICHOKES À LA LYONNAISE (*Artichauts Braisés Farces à la Lyonnaise*). Prepare as for Stuffed Braised Artichokes à la Barigoule (above), but stuff the artichokes with Pork Forcemeat (sausage meat) mixed with sautéed chopped onion and parsley.

ARTICHOKE HEARTS
(*Fonds d'Artichauts*)

The bottom, base, or heart of the artichoke is the darling of French chefs. The delicate, nutty flavor and cuplike shape of this morsel invite all kinds of delightful fillings, and there are enough artichoke hearts "*à la*" this and "*à la*" that to keep you busy for weeks. Unfortunately, artichokes are much more expensive in America than in Europe, and using only the heart of an artichoke cannot be an everyday proposition. Nevertheless, you should know how to prepare them for special occasions, and you can buy them more economically canned.

Prepare artichoke hearts for cooking as you would whole artichokes, but break off the leaves until you are above the level of the heart, and then cut off the top of the artichoke. Have plenty of lemon juice on hand and brush cut parts with the juice as you proceed, as the attractiveness of the heart depends upon its whiteness (it can turn a horrible gray color). Trim away the leaf ends, but leave the chokes in place. As you trim each heart, put it into cold water to which you have added 2 tablespoons lemon juice per quart.

Boil the artichoke hearts in a nonaluminum pan, uncovered, in a *Blanc* consisting of 2 tablespoons flour, 2 tablespoons lemon juice, and 1½ teaspoons salt per quart of water. They will be cooked in about 30 minutes. Drain and remove the chokes. If you are not going to use the hearts immediately, let them cool in their cooking water. Remove the chokes and store the hearts in the refrigerator submerged in the cooking water.

For a cold garnish, drain the hearts and carefully pat them dry. Fill them with cold shrimp, crab, lobster; caviar; cold fish and shellfish purées; cold vegetables in aspic jelly; or cold *Salpicons*.

For a hot garnish, drain the hearts, pat them dry, and brush them liberally with melted butter. To reheat, put them cut side down in a buttered casserole, heat the casserole gently, cover it tightly, and put it into a 325° oven for 15 minutes. Remove the artichoke hearts and fill them with any of the hot *Salpicons* in Chapter 4, with any Purée, or in one of the following ways.

Fonds d'Artichauts Saint-Germain. Fill the hearts with Purée of Peas.

Fonds d'Artichauts Vichy. Fill the hearts with Carrots à la Vichy.

Fonds d'Artichauts Compoint. Fill the hearts with green Asparagus Purée.

Fonds d'Artichauts Princesse. Fill the hearts with asparagus tips and diced truffles.

Fonds d'Artichauts Choron. Fill the hearts with a thick Choron Sauce.

Fonds d'Artichauts Béarnaise. Fill the hearts with a thick Béarnaise Sauce.

Fonds d'Artichauts Lucullus. Fill the hearts with chopped truffles in Madeira Sauce.

When artichoke hearts are filled and glazed* in the oven, they are said to be stuffed. Following are a few suggestions for stuffed artichoke hearts.

Fonds d'Artichauts Farcis à la Florentine. Fill the hearts with spinach simmered in butter, top with Mornay Sauce, sprinkle with grated Parmesan cheese and melted butter, and brown.

Fonds d'Artichauts Farcis Soubise. Fill the hearts with thick Soubise Sauce, sprinkle with grated Parmesan cheese and melted butter, and brown.

Fonds d'Artichauts Farcis à la Duxelles. Fill the hearts with a thick *Duxelles* for garnishing vegetables, sprinkle with grated Parmesan cheese and melted butter, and brown.

Artichoke hearts are also blanched, stewed gently in butter, and served sprinkled with chopped parsley and chervil (*fonds d'artichauts fines herbes*). or covered with Allemande Sauce (*fonds d'artichauts à l'allemande*), or finished in cream that is allowed to boil down until it is almost entirely reduced (*fonds d'artichauts à la crème*), or made into a purée.

PURÉE OF ARTICHOKES (*Purée d'Artichauts*). Boil the artichoke hearts in a *Blanc* (see above) for 15 minutes, and finish their cooking by stewing them gently, covered in butter. Put the hearts and their cooking butter through a food mill, or rub them through a sieve. Add mashed potatoes or Potato Purée to equal ½ the volume of the artichoke, heat, bring to the desired consistency with butter and cream, and season to taste with salt and white pepper.

✳ *ASPARAGUS*
(*Asperge*)

Of all our vegetables the asparagus is held most in thrall by the ancient rhythm of the seasons. The first green shoots begin to dot the beds in California in mid-February. In March, California asparagus can be found in every supermarket. In April comes the green deluge as New Jersey and Washington begin to harvest their first green spears. In May, California's beds are almost exhausted, and Washington, New Jersey, Illinois, and other states struggle to fill the gap. But in June the supply has fallen to less than half that of April. And in July it is all over. There is no more fresh asparagus, not even if you are a movie star, not even if you are a king.

At least this is the way things have stood until very recently. There are strange things happening in the mountains of Mexico, and you may come across a bundle of asparagus at an unlikely time of year. In California, too, wizards are at work, coaxing a few green spears untimely from their beds in October and November. Nevertheless, fresh asparagus is still our most seasonal vegetable, and your enjoyment of it is regulated by the earth's passage around the sun.

The French enjoy asparagus hugely and have many green, white, and purple varieties to choose from (see Chapter 1). In America we have settled on the Washingtons—Mary, Martha, and Waltham. All are blight-resistant, dark green asparagus, although Mary and Martha tend to have purple tips. These varieties are used for canning, too, and most canned "White" asparagus is actually green asparagus that has been blanched white by growing underground.

The Washingtons, although lacking in variety, are good-tasting asparagus. They grow straight and true and can be machine-harvested to arrive at your table faster and fresher. Like many vegetables, asparagus loses sugar rapidly after harvesting, particularly during the first 24 hours. This loss is minimized by chilling the asparagus to the near-freezing point immediately after cutting.

Nothing contributes more to the pleasure of the table than a fat bundle of fresh green asparagus dripping with butter and flecked with salt. But because of its strict seasonality, we must frequently resort to frozen. Frozen asparagus, however, is but a promise of the real thing to come. I can easily distinguish between cooked asparagus that is fresh or frozen by taste, smell, sight and feel. The fresh asparagus has the essential green vegetable taste. It is crunchier, clean-flavored, more intact, and juicier with its own fresh juices. It smells like a green field. And what is more, you can peel it. Yet asparagus freezes better than many other vegetables, and frozen asparagus is welcome in winter.

Canned asparagus is something unto itself. Its odd flavor is only distantly related to fresh or frozen asparagus. A taste for it can be acquired, and before the days of freezing great quantities were served up at the grand resorts of Deauville and Monte Carlo and Newport. You may want to try the famous Argenteuil asparagus of France, which is imported in glass jars.

Buying asparagus: Look for asparagus that is firm, smooth, round, and freshly green for most of its length, with compact, tightly closed green or purplish tips. Early-season asparagus is pencil thin and vividly green for almost its entire length. The fibrous white base is tough and inedible, but it helps seal in and preserve the flavor and freshness of the stalk. As the season progresses the stalks become thicker—very large asparagus attaining one inch of thickness or more. The color is not quite so vivid a green, and the base is dense and woody, but this is asparagus in its prime—lusty, plump, mature in flavor, proud of its very asparagusness. To equalize cooking, all stalks should be of about the same thickness.

Avoid asparagus with open, spread tips, flattened stalks, or stalks that have thin, fibrous ribs running lengthwise up and down. This asparagus has begun to dry out because it is old or badly cared for (asparagus at the store should be displayed in bundles standing upright in a pan of water). Avoid asparagus with flattened or angular stalks, which are likely to be tough and woody. Avoid wilted asparagus. And avoid asparagus with too much white in the stalks, which has to be discarded.

Preparing asparagus: When you get your fresh asparagus home, wash it in water, taking care to remove any sand that may be lodged in the tips. If you cannot use it the same day, treat it like a florist treats a flower. Stand the stalks on end in one inch of water, invert a plastic bag over the tops, and store in the refrigerator.

To prepare thin, early-season asparagus, cut off the white bases to equalize length of spears and tie in bundles; these tender shoots need no peeling and are too thin to peel anyway.

To prepare mature asparagus, use a swivel-bladed vegetable peeler. Place a stalk on the counter with the tip away from you, holding the base in your left hand. Peel downward, stroking from below the tender tip toward the base, leaving the ends of the peelings attached to the base, and revolving the spear with your left hand as you peel all around the stalk. Then "wipe" the peelings downward with your hand and snap off the base where it breaks naturally. Wash the asparagus to remove loose peelings, trim the bottoms to equalize length, and tie the spears in serving-size bundles at top and bottom with soft butcher's twine. The peeled stalks are now a beautiful fresh pale green and white color, and they will now cook quicker, crisper, and more tender.

Cooking asparagus: Asparagus is cooked as simply as possible. One method is to stand it upright in a covered pot half filled with boiling water so the bottoms boil while the tips steam, which is a method I highly recommend for broccoli. This is not at all necessary for peeled asparagus, which when boiled in water cooks evenly and quickly. It is superior in tenderness, crispness, flavor, and color—the color of freshly boiled peeled asparagus being one of the most beautiful in nature.

HOT BOILED ASPARAGUS (*Asperges Bouillies Chaudes*). Peel, trim, and wash the asparagus, and tie at top and bottom with soft cotton twine in serving-size bundles of 6 to 10 stalks, reserving a few average-size stalks to test for doneness. Place the bundles in a large volume of rapidly boiling salted water, add the loose stalks, return quickly to the boil, and boil gently, uncovered for 10 to 18 minutes. Test for doneness by lifting the loose stalks with a fork. They are done when their ends bend downward, but are overcooked when their ends droop vertically. Taste for tenderness and crispness. The bundled stalks will take perhaps a minute longer to cook. As a final test, press a knife into the butt ends of the stalks; it should enter easily. Remove the bundles by lifting them by the strings, place them on a napkin, cut the strings and drain them well. Serve hot or warm asparagus with melted butter, Hollandaise, Mousseline, Maltaise, or Butter Sauce.

COLD BOILED ASPARAGUS (*Asperges Bouillies Froides*). Prepare as for Hot Boiled Asparagus (above). Plunge the cooked asparagus briefly in cold water, or cool it under a gently running cold tap. Drain and serve with Mayonnaise, Vinaigrette, or Chantilly Sauce.

ASPARAGUS À LA FLAMANDE (*Asperges à la Flamande*). Prepare Hot Boiled Asparagus (above). Separately serve halves of hot hard-cooked eggs and hot melted butter. Each diner crushes an egg, seasons it with salt and pepper, and mashes it with butter as a sauce.

ASPARAGUS À LA POLONAISE (*Asperges à la Polonaise*). Prepare Hot Boiled Asparagus (above), and arrange in overlapping tiers on a serving dish so the tips in each layer are displayed. Sprinkle the tips with chopped hard-cooked egg yolk mixed with ½ as much chopped parsley. Just before serving, pour over the tips sizzling hot Brown Butter in which you have browned ½ as many tablespoons of fine, dry white breadcrumbs as you have tablespoons of butter.

ASPARAGUS AU GRATIN (*Asperges au Gratin*). Prepare Hot Boiled Asparagus (above), and arrange in overlapping tiers on an ovenproof serving dish so the tips in each layer are displayed. As you lay down each layer, dot the tips with Mornay Sauce. Cover the exposed top layer of stalks with buttered paper or foil, and pour Mornay sauce over all the tips to cover them completely. Sprinkle the sauce with grated Parmesan cheese and melted butter, brown in the oven, remove the paper, and serve.

ASPARAGUS À L'ITALIENNE (*Asperges à l'Italienne*). Prepare as for Asparagus au Gratin (above), but omit the Mornay sauce and sprinkle the platter and the tips of the asparagus with grated Parmesan cheese. Then sprinkle with Brown Butter and brown in the oven.

ASPARAGUS TIPS IN BUTTER (*Pointes d'Asperges au Beurre*). Prepare the asparagus as for Hot Boiled Asparagus (above). Peel, trim, and wash the asparagus. Line up the heads of the stalks and cut them across 2 inches down the stalk to form 2-inch-long asparagus tips. Tie the tips in bundles and cut the rest of the stalks in ¼-inch dice. Drop the dice in boiling salted water, boil for 5 minutes, and add the asparagus tips. Boil for a few minutes more, until the tips are tender. Remove and drain the asparagus, keeping the tips warm in a towel. Toss the dice in a buttered saucepan to dry them, season with salt and pepper, and dress generously with butter off the fire. Spread the dice in the bottom of a serving dish and place the asparagus tips on top. Or put the dice in the bottom of Tartlet or Barquette shells and garnish with the tips.

ASPARAGUS TIPS IN CREAM (*Pointes d'Asperges à la Crème*). Prepare as for Asparagus Tips in Butter (above), but cover the dried and seasoned asparagus dice with boiling cream, and boil down quickly until it is almost entirely reduced. Add a few more tablespoons of heavy cream, shake the pan to mix the sauce, remove from the fire, and finish with a little butter. Serve as for asparagus tips in butter.

ASPARAGUS PURÉE (*Purée d'Asperges*). Boil the green part of asparagus until tender. Drain, squeeze out excess water, chop, and dry in a buttered saucepan over a brisk fire. Put the asparagus through a food mill or rub it through a sieve. Season to taste with salt and pepper, reheat, blending in one tablespoon butter per cup of asparagus, and bring to the desired consistency by stirring in heavy cream.

✳ *BEETS*
(*Betteraves*)

Beets are an essential ingredient of three favorite American dishes—the New England boiled dinner, "red flannel" hash, and sweet-sour Harvard beets. Nevertheless, consumption of fresh table beets has continuously fallen across the United States and they are now considered a minor fresh vegetable, although the consumption of canned beets has increased.

Beets are boiled or baked. I think Americans would eat more fresh beets if they began baking them, which is the preferred method in France. In fact, baked beets was a favorite dish of the colonial Americans. They cooked them slowly in the brick oven tunneled into the side of the early American fireplace, slipped off their skins, and served them whole with salt, pepper, melted butter, and a touch of apple vinegar to cross swords with their natural sweetness.

Boiled or baked beets are served hot as a vegetable dish, or they may be served cold as a pickled dish or in a salad. Their bright color makes them a most useful garnishing vegetable, and the French use fancy truffle cutters to stamp out little stars, diamonds, and other shapes from thin beet slices.

Buying beets: Look for young small- to medium-size beets under 3 inches in diameter. In as much as beets are usually cooked whole, they should be of the same size. Choose firm, deep red, smooth-skinned beets with slender tap roots at the bottom. Avoid soft, cracked, or shriveled beets. If the beets have no tops, avoid those showing numerous leaf scars at the stem end. If the tops are on, do not be discouraged if they are somewhat wilted as this will not affect the taste of the beet if it has met the qualifications I have given. On the other hand, if the tops are fresh and crisp, you can cook and eat them like any other green.

Preparing beets: Remove the tops, leaving a full 1 inch of stem. Do not cut the tap root at the bottom. Wash the beets in running water, scrubbing them with a brush and taking care not to break the skin or the root. Dry carefully and store like potatoes in a cool, airy place.

Cooking beets: Beets require a few special cooking accommodations. Although they are baked or boiled like potatoes, they are more watery than potatoes and their color bleeds easily. For this reason they are best cooked whole, in their skins, with 1 inch of stem left on. Also, when boiling beets like other red-pigmented vegetables, add 2 teaspoons of vinegar or lemon juice to each quart of water to help prevent them from turning purple and to retain their fresh red color.

Because of variations in age, some beets may require twice as long to cook as others of the same size. Also, when beets are baked they must be slowly baked in a moderate 325° oven (the odor of burned beet is not good), and they will require longer cooking than baked potatoes. Nevertheless, baking is the best way to cook beets whether they are served as a hot or cold dish, and I recommend that you bake some to discover their true flavor.

BAKED BEETS (*Betteraves au Four*). Scrub and trim the tops from young beets, leaving 1 inch of stem. Bake them in a pan in a 325° oven until tender all the way through. Test for doneness by squeezing them in a cooking mitt, or by probing them with a skewer. Remove from the oven, slip off the skins, slice the beets or leave small ones whole, and serve hot with butter, salt, and pepper.

BOILED BEETS (*Betteraves Bouillies*). Scrub and trim the tops from young beets, leaving 1 inch of stem. Plunge them into boiling water to which you have added 1 teaspoon salt and 2 teaspoons vinegar or lemon juice per quart. Test for doneness by squeezing them in a cooking mitt. Avoid probing with a skewer until you are fairly certain they are done. Plunge into cold water to loosen and slip off the skins and serve whole. Or slice large boiled beets and sauté the slices very lightly in butter for a few minutes. Serve with butter, salt, and pepper.

BEETS À LA POITEVINE (*Betteraves à la Poitevine*). Combine sliced baked or boiled beets in a skillet with Lyonnaise Sauce, chopped parsley, and wine vinegar to taste. Heat gently for a few minutes, tossing the beets in the sauce.

BEETS IN CREAM (*Betteraves à la Crème*). Peel and slice raw beets and cook very slowly in butter in a covered pan until they are soft. Remove the slices and keep warm. To the pan juices, add 1 to 2 cups medium cream and quickly reduce by ½. Season to taste with salt and pepper, finish the sauce by swirling in 2 to 4 tablespoons butter, and pour over the beet slices.

BEET SALAD (*Salade de Betteraves*). To 2 cups of thin slices or julienne* of baked beets, add ½ cup diced baked onion or the chopped white and green of scallions. Toss lightly with ½ cup Vinaigrette Sauce or Mustard Cream Sauce and 1 tablespoon chopped parsley or tarragon.

BEET PURÉE (*Purée de Betteraves*). Put baked beets through a food mill or press through a sieve, and cook gently in a pan to evaporate excess moisture. For a hot purée, to 1 cup of this beet hash add ½ cup thick Brown Sauce or Starch-Thickened Brown Stock or thick Béchamel Sauce, return to the simmer, season to taste with salt and pepper, and finish by stirring in 1 teaspoon butter. For a cold purée, cool the beet hash and mix with ½ cup thick Mayonnaise.

✳ *BROCCOLI*
(*Brocoli*)

The French, who love cauliflower, pay little attention to broccoli. This is curious because the two vegetables belong to the same species and variety and are frequently practically identical. In fact, white broccoli that forms a solid head is essentially a late, long-season cauliflower. This white broccoli is often sold as cauliflower or cauliflower-broccoli.

Green or sprouting broccoli is a branching form of cauliflower. It has a single large central head with several smaller heads surrounding it. Large and small heads are usually bundled and sold fresh with a good portion of their stalks and leaves, all of which is edible. Frozen broccoli usually consists of the smaller heads and stalks only. Most green broccoli grown in the United States is the Italian Calabrese variety.

Fresh broccoli is available throughout the year, with greatest supplies from October to May. California grows 90 percent of our broccoli, with the remainder coming from Oregon, Arizona, Texas, New York, and New Jersey.

Buying broccoli: Look for firm plump, tender stalks and firm, compact heads. The color of various strains may vary from light to dark green and blue-green, but it should look fresh. When broccoli is overmature, the heads become loose and dry and show traces of tiny yellow or purple flowers that indicate that the head, which is actually a giant bud, is beginning to bloom. Broccoli is very perishable, so examine it closely.

Preparing broccoli: Trim tough ends of stalks and discard large, coarse leaves. Soak a whole head of broccoli in cold salted water for 1 hour to expel any insects. Or cut the head into stems and flowerets and soak for ½ hour. Drain, dry, and store covered in the refrigerator, or blanch the broccoli at this time.

Blanching broccoli: If the broccoli is to be boiled it need not be blanched. Otherwise, blanch it first. To blanch a whole head of broccoli, peel the stalks and make a lengthwise slit through each of them. Plunge the whole head into a large amount of boiling salted water, boil for about 6 minutes, then plunge into cold water to stop the cooking. To blanch broccoli in pieces, first peel the stalks. Cut the head into flowerets with stems about 3 inches long, cut the larger stalks into 3-inch pieces, and make a lengthwise slit through each of them. Plunge the stalks into a large amount of boiling salted water and boil for about 4 minutes. Add the flowerets, which are very delicate, and cook at a gentle boil for 4 minutes more. Then plunge the broccoli in cold water to stop the cooking, and drain it. You may store blanched broccoli, covered, in the refrigerator.

Cooking broccoli: Broccoli may be cooked like cauliflower. Both are members of the cabbage family and ordinarily are cooked quickly, uncovered, in plenty of water to prevent strong flavors from developing (see Cabbage). This treatment will also help preserve the green color of broccoli.

BOILED BROCCOLI (*Brocoli Bouilli*). Prepare and cook the broccoli as described for blanching broccoli, above, but cook for 10 to 15 minutes all told, until the stalks are tender when pierced with the point of a knife. Drain well and serve hot with melted butter, Hollandaise Sauce, Mousseline Sauce, Maltaise Sauce, Cream Sauce, sour cream, or grated cheese. Or serve the broccoli cold with Vinaigrette Sauce, Ravigote Sauce, or Mayonnaise.

STEAMED BROCCOLI (*Brocoli à la Vapeur*). I am partial to this method of cooking broccoli, which has the advantage of preserving the delicate texture and flavor of the buds. Do not cut up the broccoli. Merely trim away the tough ends of the stalks and peel stalks and stems while still attached to the buds. Slit stalks and stems to hasten the cooking. Finally, blanch the broccoli uncovered in a large quantity of boiling salted water for 2 minutes only, tie it in a bunch with soft twine, and stand it on end in boiling salted water in a tall pot with a cover. The tender buds should be above the water. Cover the pot and boil gently until the broccoli is cooked.

BROCCOLI WITH CREAM (*Brocoli à la Crème*). Cook as for Cauliflower with Cream.

BROCCOLI À LA POLONAISE (*Brocoli à la Polonaise*). This is broccoli dressed with chopped egg yolk, parsley, and breadcrumbs. Cook as for Cauliflower Polonaise.

BROCCOLI À LA MILANAISE (*Brocoli à la Milanaise*). This is broccoli dressed with Parmesan cheese. Cook as for Cauliflower Milanaise.

BROCCOLI AU GRATIN (*Brocoli au Gratin*). This is broccoli finished in Mornay Sauce. Cook as for Cauliflower au Gratin.

BROCCOLI PURÉE (*Purée de Brocoli*). Cook as for Cauliflower Purée.

✳ BRUSSELS SPROUTS
(*Choux de Bruxelles*)

We all should eat more Brussels sprouts. A mound of freshly boiled, barely cooked sprouts, their golden centers still crunchy to the teeth, their bright green leaves wreathed with steam, sprinkled with sea salt and pepper and hot yellow butter, will give you warm mouthfuls of delicate cabbage flavor subtly seasoned with nuts, and will supply you with conclusive proof that great cooking is simplicity itself.

These morsels of the cabbage family are prized in Europe. In America we eat only about ⅓ pound per person a year. The only explanation I can conceive for this is that most people who have tried them have overcooked them. And if the heart of a Brussels sprout isn't still crunchy, it has been overcooked.

Frozen Brussels sprouts, of course, are available all year. Fresh sprouts are in season from September through March, with peak supplies in November. California grows most of them, within a mile of the sea, in the same area where artichokes are grown. Most of the rest of our supply comes from Long Island, New York.

Buying Brussels sprouts: Brussels sprouts are sold in pint-size containers. Buy the smallest sprouts you can find. They should be hard, compact, round, and very green. Puffy, soft sprouts are tasteless. Wilted, yellow-leaved sprouts are old and stale.

Preparing Brussels sprouts: Remove bruised or battered outside leaves and trim a thin slice from the base of the sprout. With a pointed knife, pierce a cross in the center of the base to speed cooking. Wash and soak the sprouts for 10 minutes in cold salted water with a little vinegar added. Drain, dry, and store covered in the refrigerator, or blanch the sprouts at this time.

Blanching Brussels sprouts: No matter how you cook the sprouts, they should first be blanched. You may blanch and refrigerate them for up to 24 hours, or blanch them just before cooking. To blanch, plunge the sprouts, a few at a time, into rapidly boiling salted water, keeping the water at the boil. When all the sprouts are in the pot, cook uncovered at a gentle boil for 5 to 8 minutes. The sprouts should be softened, but their centers should be still firm. Remove from the water, plunge into cold water to stop the cooking, and drain.

Cooking Brussels sprouts: Brussels sprouts are boiled, stewed in butter, and sautéed. They may also be steamed and deep-fried. As I have said, they should be cooked as briefly as possible. They are a full-fledged member of the cabbage family and if overcooked will become strong-tasting and unpleasant (see Cabbage). All precautions listed for cabbage are equally applicable to Brussels sprouts.

Also, Brussels sprouts are a green vegetable and you must take care to preserve their fresh green color. When you blanch Brussels sprouts as a first step in cooking, this requirement is met. Steaming is an exception that sacrifices some color for an intensification of flavor.

BOILED BRUSSELS SPROUTS (*Choux de Bruxelles Bouillis*). Proceed as for blanching (above), but cook the sprouts at a gentle boil for a total of about 10 minutes, or until the sprouts are tender with crunchy centers. Test for doneness by cutting a sprout in two. Drain the sprouts, dry them slightly in an open pan over moderate heat, season with salt, pepper, and melted butter.

BRUSSELS SPROUTS WITH BROWN BUTTER (*Choux de Bruxelles au Beurre Noisette*). Boil the sprouts, drain and dry them, and arrange them on a platter. Just before serving, sprinkle with lemon juice and Brown Butter.

BRUSSELS SPROUTS STEWED IN BUTTER (*Choux de Bruxelles Étuvés au Beurre*). Cooking *à l'étuvée* is a slow stewing in butter without added liquid. As the sprouts cook, they will absorb the butter. Boil the sprouts until they are about half cooked, drain and dry them, and put them in a pan with about 4 tablespoons butter per quart of sprouts. Season with salt and pepper, cover with a piece of buttered paper or foil, tightly cover the pan, and cook slowly in the oven or over a low fire for about 10 minutes or until they are tender.

BRUSSELS SPROUTS À LA LIMOUSINE (*Choux de Bruxelles à la Limousine*). Prepare the sprouts as for Brussels Sprouts Stewed in Butter (above). When they are cooked, toss them lightly with Braised Chestnuts.

BRUSSELS SPROUTS IN CREAM (*Choux de Bruxelles à la Crème*). Cook as for Brussels Sprouts Stewed in Butter (above), but after stewing in butter for 5 minutes, roughly chop the sprouts in the pan and cover them with hot heavy cream. Simmer until done, add a little more butter, and serve.

BRUSSELS SPROUTS HOUSEWIFE STYLE (*Choux de Bruxelles Ménagère*). Sauté ½ cup diced salt pork or bacon in butter until golden, adding 1 tablespoon minced onion for the last minute of cooking. Add 1 quart boiled and drained Brussels sprouts and toss together for a few minutes. Season with salt and pepper, and serve with a sprinkling of chopped parsley.

BRUSSELS SPROUTS AU GRATIN (*Choux de Bruxelles au Gratin*). This is Brussels sprouts finished in Mornay Sauce. Cook as for Cauliflower au Gratin.

BRUSSELS SPROUTS MILANAISE (*Choux de Bruxelles Milanaise*). This is Brussels sprouts dressed with Parmesan cheese. Cook as for Cauliflower Milanaise.

BRUSSELS SPROUTS POLONAISE (*Choux de Bruxelles Polonaise*). This is Brussels sprouts dressed with chopped egg yolk, parsley, and breadcrumbs. Cook as for Cauliflower Polonaise.

STEAMED BRUSSELS SPROUTS (*Choux de Bruxelles à la Vapeur*). Prepare the Brussels sprouts but do not blanch them. Place on a rack in a tightly covered pan and steam over boiling water for 15 minutes or until done. Season with salt and pepper and serve with hot melted butter.

SAUTÉED BRUSSELS SPROUTS (*Choux de Bruxelles Sautés*). Boil the sprouts until almost done, drain them well, and toss them in hot butter until lightly browned. Season with salt and pepper and sprinkle with chopped parsley.

DEEP-FRIED BRUSSELS SPROUTS (*Choux de Bruxelles Frits*). Boil the sprouts until ½ cooked, drain them well, and stew them in butter until they are almost cooked. Dip them in frying Batter and deep-fry them in 375° fat until they are golden brown. Drain, season with salt and pepper, sprinkle with fried parsley, and serve on a napkin. Separately serve Tomato Sauce.

PURÉED BRUSSELS SPROUTS (*Purée de Choux de Bruxelles*). Boil the sprouts until they are almost cooked, drain and dry them, and finish their cooking by stewing in butter. Put them through a food mill and blend into them ¼ cup mashed potato for each cup of sprouts. Heat the purée, season with salt and pepper, and finish by stirring in a little butter.

✳ THE CABBAGES
(Les Choux)

Cabbage is the head of a great vegetable family. Not only is cabbage itself represented among the green, white, and red vegetables, but cabbage's close cousins make up an impressive roster of vegetables eaten for their stalks, leaves, buds, and roots. These include cauliflower, broccoli, Brussels sprouts, kale, kohlrabi, and collard. Rutabaga, or "Swede" (French: *navet de Suède*), is an ancient cross between the cabbage and the turnip.

The relationship of these vegetables is important in cookery. All have a similarity of taste based on a sulfurous compound they contain. Also, all of these vegetables require knowledgeable cooking if this compound is not to decompose and become strong-tasting. It is this decomposition that has given these vegetables a bad name. Although we still eat 8 pounds of cabbage and 1½ pounds of sauerkraut per person each year, this is ⅓ the amount Americans ate 50 years ago. And we eat only 1 pound of cauliflower, 1 pound of broccoli, and ⅓ pound of Brussels sprouts. Clearly something must be done to support these worthy vegetables.

Consequently, in this section I will tell you all the tricks for cooking delicious cabbage dishes, with the understanding that the chemistry of these methods applies to cauliflower, broccoli, and Brussels sprouts as well.

Buying cabbage: There are five kinds of cabbages regularly sold in the United States, and you will find one or more of them in good supply at any time of year. They are grown in many states, mostly in Florida, Texas, California, New York, and New Jersey. These cabbages differ in seasonality, cooking times, cooking precautions, and flavor.

Danish Cabbage, also called *Hollander cabbage,* is winter cabbage and is usually stored. It is a veritable cannon ball of a vegetable, growing large and heavy and weighing up to 6 pounds. The heads are usually round, very smooth and solid, the smooth, almost rubbery leaves clinging tightly to the head and overlapping greatly at the crown. Even at the base, where other cabbages are soft between the leaf ribs, the leaves of Danish cabbage are firm and tightly compacted. In as much as some of the outside green leaves are likely to have been trimmed away after storage, exposing the white inner leaves, Danish cabbage is sometimes called "white" cabbage. Buy those that appear as I have described, avoiding any that feel light or have discolored veins in the leaves. Also avoid heads when the leaves have snapped off at the base; these are likely to be strong-tasting and coarse in texture.

Domestic cabbage is "green" or summer cabbage and is sold fresh. It is not as large or hard or heavy as the Danish winter cabbage, weighing up to 3 pounds. The heads are less heavy for their size, the leaves less compacted and rubbery, more crumpled, greener, and crisper, and they overlap less at the crown. If you press the leaves at the base of the head, you will find it to be noticeably softer. This cabbage does not keep well, so you must be on the alert when buying it. Although it is a softer cabbage than Danish, it should be reasonably firm. Very early domestic cabbage may have been harvested before maturity and is very perishable. Avoid cabbages that are puffy and soft and those with yellowed leaves.

Pointed cabbage is a small, green spring cabbage that is smaller than domestic. The heads are pointed or sometimes conical. It should be reasonably firm, fresh-looking, and be free of yellowing leaves or discolored veins.

Savoy cabbage is a relatively loose, greenish-yellow, crinkle-leaved cabbage. It is the favorite green cabbage of France. It is the mildest of the cabbages, with a fine, delicate flavor, and can be cooked in the shortest time.

Red cabbage is hard- to medium-headed, shaped like domestic or Danish cabbage, with dark red to purple leaves. Avoid cabbages with leaves that are darkened and puffy.

Preparing cabbage: All cabbages are prepared by removing battered outside leaves. Depending upon the dish you are creating, the cabbage is left whole, or cut into wedges, or separated into leaves, or shredded. However it is cut, the cabbage should be soaked in cold salted water for 20 to 30 minutes. If it is to be cooked in any other manner than by boiling, it must then be blanched.

Blanching cabbage: Cabbage that is to be steamed, braised, or stuffed and baked and old white cabbage that is boiled must first be blanched. Plunge the cabbage into rapidly boiling salted water, boil for the required time, then plunge it into cool water to stop the cooking, and drain it well. Savoy cabbage and young green cabbage are blanched for 2 minutes when shredded, 4 minutes when cut in quarters, 8 minutes when left whole. Older white cabbage and red cabbage are blanched for 3 minutes when shredded. 5 minutes when cut in quarters, 10 minutes when left whole. Add 2 tablespoons vinegar or lemon juice to each quart of water in which red cabbage is blanched.

Cooking cabbage: The cooking of cabbage is an education in itself, teaching a great deal about the adjustment of flavor and the retention of color in vegetable cookery. The most important law learned in cooking cabbage is that overcooking is death on vegetables. Yet, in some dishes, we cook cabbage for 4 or 5 hours! Bear with me a moment, and I shall explain.

Cabbage and all members of the cabbage family contain a sulfurous compound that breaks down when subjected to heat and gives forth a disagreeable odor and flavor. Our first concern in cooking cabbage is to disarm this sulfurous compound. Here are two ways we can do so when boiling cabbage.

First, we can shred the cabbage or cut it in thin slices. Put the cabbage pieces into a small amount of rapidly boiling salted water. Return the water to the boil as quickly as possible and boil the cabbage for one minute uncovered. Then tightly cover the pot and continue cooking at a full boil until tender. Here is what happens when you cook cabbage by this method:

As the cabbage hits the water and the heat begins to penetrate it, the sulfurous compound it contains begins to decompose. This decomposition is hastened by an enzyme in the cabbage. While the water is returning to the boil and during the first minute of boiling uncovered, decomposition proceeds and some mildly sulfurous odors are given off into the air. Having allowed these odors to escape from the pan, we clap the cover on tightly and boil as quickly as possible. Does the enzyme continue to urge the sulfurous compound to produce more disagreeable odors and flavors? No, because the enzyme is destroyed by the heat, which penetrates the small pieces of cabbage swiftly. Before the sulfurous compound can decompose further on its own, the cooking is finished. Cabbage cooked in this manner is fresh-tasting, with a robust cabbage flavor (which has been trapped under the cover) but none of the disagreeable taste associated with cabbage that is overcooked.

A second method of cooking cabbage produces a more mild-flavored result. This method also allows you to cook large wedges of cabbage or other cabbage family vegetables that you may want to cook whole. To implement this method, plunge the vegetable into a large amount of rapidly boiling salted water, and boil, uncovered, until it is cooked. Here is what happens:

Again the enzyme that hastens the decomposition of the sulfurous compound is activated. This time the heat penetrates more slowly, and the enzyme remains active longer. However, the larger amount of water returns to the boil more quickly or even immediately and cooking is speeded somewhat. Plant acids that contribute to the enzyme reaction are diluted in the water and their effects are greatly neutralized. The uncovered pot allows the volatile odors that are produced to escape freely. Cooking will take a little longer, but by removing the cabbage as soon as it is tender very little disagreeable odor or flavor will be produced, and these will be adequately dispersed. This cabbage will taste milder than that cooked in water just to cover it, and some will prefer it this way. For the mildest taste of all, slice the cabbage thinly and cook it by this method. This, of course, will produce the mildest flavor in any vegetable you cook.

No matter how you cook cabbage—whether you intend to braise its leaves or bake it whole and stuffed—it should first receive a preliminary blanching to rid it of disagreeable flavors. When you blanch cabbage, you are doing nothing more than partially cooking it in lots of boiling salted water, as in the second method discussed above. It is then plunged into cold water to stop the cooking before you proceed to the next step.

Obviously, when you braise cabbage, you must cook it further. Will more disagreeable odors and flavors develop? Yes. But when braising you will persist in cooking—3, 4, maybe even 5 hours. During this time a great transformation will take place, as the sulfurous compound is completely decomposed and its unpleasantness cooked entirely away. What results is an entirely new taste, reminiscent of cabbage but greatly mellowed and modified by the prolonged cooking and the mingled flavors of other ingredients cooked in the braising pan.

A final problem in cooking cabbage has to do with the retention of color. Color is bound to be lost when cabbage is baked, braised, or steamed, so these remarks apply only to boiled cabbage.

Cabbage comes in 3 colors—green, white, and red. Again the cooking of cabbage is very educational, in as much as the methods for retaining these colors in cabbage can be applied to all vegetables. And again, the greatest troublemaker is overcooking. Overcooked green cabbage becomes a grayish olive drab; white cabbage turns yellow or dirty gray; red cabbage becomes purplish-gray and eventually green when overcooked. For both flavor and color, cook cabbage as quickly and briefly as possible.

Green cabbage, like all green vegetables, will retain a better color if it is quickly cooked uncovered in a large volume of boiling salted water. Never add acid ingredients to the water if you want a fresh green color.

White cabbage will stay whiter if you cook it in a *Blanc,* adding 2 tablespoons flour, mixed to a paste in a little water, and 1 tablespoon vinegar or lemon juice to each quart of salted cooking water. However, the acid will firm the vegetable tissues slightly, making it necessary for you to cook the cabbage longer. To avoid this, cook the cabbage in a nonacid blanc, adding 2 tablespoons flour mixed in ¼ cup milk to each quart of water.

Red cabbage, which takes longer to cook, definitely needs acid to protect its color. This is especially important in that most municipal water supplies are slightly alkaline, and alkalinity is very destructive of red vegetable pigments. Add 2 tablespoons lemon juice or vinegar to each quart of boiling salted water. Or add a whole tart apple, peeled and sliced. The apple will supply the necessary acid to the water as the cooking progresses.

As I have said, the principles of cabbage cookery given here are applied to all the vegetables of the cabbage family—cauliflower, broccoli, Brussels sprouts, kale, kohlrabi, and collard. And if I have seemed to belabor the cookery of cabbage, it is only in defense of this worthy family. From the rough, coarse leaves that made the first cabbage soup to the aristocratic white cauliflower of modern *haute cuisine,* this ancient family has served mankind well for many thousands of years.

BOILED CABBAGE, FIRST METHOD (*Chou à l'Anglaise*). Shred the cabbage by quartering it, cutting it in thin slices, and removing tough pieces. Soak the shredded cabbage in cold salted water for 20 minutes, and drain it well. Put it into a skillet (not iron) filled with about 2 inches of boiling salted water. Return quickly to the boil and boil for 1 minute, cover, and continue boiling until tender. Savoy cabbage will take about 3 minutes' boiling all told. Test for doneness by tasting a piece. Young green cabbage will take about 4 minutes, older white cabbage will take about 8 minutes, and red cabbage will take 10 to 15 minutes. Add 2 tablespoons vinegar or lemon juice to each quart of water in which red cabbage is cooked. Drain the cooked cabbage well, place it between two plates, hold over the sink, and squeeze hard to extract all the water you can from the cabbage. Serve with salt, pepper, and hot melted butter.

Shredded cabbage may also be cooked by the following method. It will require a little less time to cook than the method just described, the taste of the cabbage will be milder, and its color will be fresher.

BOILED CABBAGE, SECOND METHOD (*Chou à l'Anglaise*). Cut the cabbage in wedges and remove the core, or shred the cabbage as described above. Soak the prepared cabbage in cold salted water for 20 minutes, and drain it well. Plunge it into a large volume of rapidly boiling salted water, return swiftly to the boil, and boil, uncovered, until tender. Wedges of Savoy cabbage will take about 6 minutes, wedges of young green cabbage will take about 8 minutes, wedges of older winter cabbage will take about 15 minutes, and wedges of red cabbage will take about 20 minutes. Shredded cabbage will take about ½ the time given. Add 2 tablespoons vinegar or lemon juice to each quart of water in which red cabbage is cooked. Sandwich the cooked cabbage wedges between two plates and squeeze tightly to press out the moisture. Trim the pressed cabbage into rectangular or diamond shapes, and serve with salt, pepper, and hot melted butter.

STEAMED CABBAGE (*Chou Vert à la Vapeur*). Shred the cabbage or cut it in wedges. Blanch it, plunge it into cold water to cool it, and drain it well. Pull wedges of cabbage apart and remove the core and the thickest midribs from the leaves. Pick over the cabbage, pulling wedges apart and removing the core and thickest midribs from the leaves. Heap the cabbage in the tray of a steamer, cover, and steam until tender. Blanched green cabbage will take 4 to 5 minutes, blanched white cabbage will take about 8 minutes. Red cabbage will take 15 minutes or more. Press the cabbage between two plates to squeeze out excess moisture, and serve with salt, pepper, and butter.

BRAISED CABBAGE (*Chou Vert Braisé*). Cut the cabbage in quarters, blanch it, plunge into cold water to cool, and drain it. Pull the wedges apart and remove the thickest midribs from the leaves. Line a casserole with fresh pork fat, blanched salt pork, or blanched bacon and place the cabbage leaves in the casserole, sprinkling them with salt, pepper, and nutmeg. Add 1 carrot, cut in quarters, 1 onion, cut in half, and a *Bouquet Garni* consisting of 3 sprigs parsley, ½ bay leaf, and a sprig or pinch of thyme all tied in cheesecloth. Add Beef Consommé or Veal Stock to cover the cabbage, and cover the whole with strips of pork fat. Bring to the boil, cover tightly, and cook in a 325° oven for 4 hours.

WHOLE STUFFED CABBAGE (*Chou Vert Farci*). Take a head of young green or Savoy cabbage, blanch it for 10 minutes, cool it in cold water, and drain it. Place the head on a cloth, carefully spread out the leaves, and cut out the core of the cabbage to within 1 inch of the bottom. Stuff the center of the cabbage with a ball of highly seasoned Pork Forcemeat (pork sausage) or another meat mixture, and close a few leaves around it. Continue to close the leaves of the cabbage, sprinkling them with salt and pepper and sandwiching layers of forcemeat between them. Re-form the cabbage in its original shape and wrap it with Bards of fresh pork fat or blanched salt pork. Then wrap the cloth up around it and tie tightly. Put the cabbage into a casserole with 1 carrot, sliced, and 1 onion, sliced, and a *Bouquet Garni* consisting of

3 sprigs parsley, ½ bay leaf, and a sprig or pinch of thyme. Add Beef Consommé or Veal Stock to cover the cabbage, bring to the boil, cover, and cook in a 325° oven for 4 hours. Drain the cabbage, remove it from the cloth, and place it on a serving dish. Reduce the braising liquid by ½, thickening it if necessary with Demi-Glace Sauce or Starch-Thickened Brown Stock, season to taste, and pour this sauce into the dish around the cabbage.

STUFFED CABBAGE ROLLS (*Petits Choux Farcis*). Take a head of young green or Savoy cabbage, blanch it for 10 minutes, cool it in cold water, and drain it. Carefully remove the outer leaves, and cut the heavy midribs from them. Allow enough leaves to provide for the number of cabbage rolls required, using more than 1 leaf section to form each roll if necessary. Chop the remaining cabbage finely and mix with an equal amount of highly seasoned Pork Forcemeat (pork sausage) or another meat mixture. Place a leaf or several overlapping leaves on a piece of cheesecloth, place a ball of stuffing in the center, fold the leaves over the stuffing, and twist the cheesecloth to form a regularly shaped ball, taking care not to split the leaves. Continue in this manner until all the rolls are formed. Place the rolls in a skillet lined with sheets of pork fat, and proceed as for Braised Cabbage above. Cabbage rolls are used to garnish braised and boiled meats.

RED CABBAGE À LA FLAMANDE (*Chou Rouge à la Flamande*). Slice red cabbage in wedges, remove core and coarse leaf ribs, and cut into fine julienne.* Put the cabbage into a heavily buttered casserole, and sprinkle with salt, pepper, nutmeg, and vinegar. Cover tightly and cook in a 325° oven for 2 hours. Now add to the casserole 3 tart apples, peeled and quartered, and sprinkle in 1 tablespoon brown sugar. Return to the oven and cook, covered, for about 1 hour more.

RED CABBAGE À LA VALENCIENNE (*Chou Rouge à la Valencienne*). Prepare as for Red Cabbage à la Flamande (above), but cook Chipolata Sausages along with the cabbage.

RED CABBAGE À LA WESTPHALIENNE (*Chou Rouge à la Westphalienne*). Prepare as for Red Cabbage à la Flamande (above), but add 1 cup chopped onion and ½ cup dry red wine at the beginning of cooking.

RED CABBAGE À LA LIMOUSINE (*Chou Rouge à la Limousine*). Prepare as for Red Cabbage à la Flamande (above), but add 1 cup chopped raw chestnuts, ½ cup Beef Consommé or Veal Stock, and ½ cup melted pork fat or pork drippings at the beginning of cooking.

MARINATED RED CABBAGE (*Chou Rouge Mariné*). Slice red cabbage in wedges, remove core and coarse leaf ribs, and cut into fine, regular julienne.* Put it into a bowl, sprinkle with 1½ teaspoons salt for every quart of cabbage, and allow it to stand for 2 days, tossing it from time to time. Drain the cabbage, return it to the bowl, and add 1 bay leaf, 1 clove garlic, mashed, and 6 peppercorns. Cover the cabbage with red wine vinegar that you have boiled and cooled, and allow it to stand for 1 or 2 days more. Serve as an hors d'oeuvre or as a garnish for cold meat.

✳ CARROTS
(*Carottes*)

Carrots are indispensable in the French kitchen. Along with onions they form the fundamental ingredients of the *Mirepoix,* the vegetable flavor base that underlies the entire superstructure of French cooking. Thus we should know what we are about when choosing our carrots.

Once upon a time you could tell how fresh carrots were by a glance at their green tops. No more. Today almost all carrots are topped before shipping, and they come to us in plastic bags. This is just as well, because the green tops continue to feed on the carrots and sap their goodness as long as they are attached. There are other ways to judge the freshness of carrots, as well as other carrot characteristics to look for.

The flavor of carrots varies widely as to variety, where grown, and the different parts of the carrot itself. The skin is bitter. The core is less sweet, and the core of old carrots is downright coarse and soapy-tasting. What we want in carrots is the characteristic fresh carrot taste, a reasonable sweetness, and lack of bitterness. A bite of the skinned raw carrot will tell you this. You will want to compare carrots from different parts of the country (look for the state on the plastic bag) to discover which taste you like best. Also, watch for local carrots in season. Taste them regularly, religiously. You will soon discover that carrots are not at all the same.

At one time the Chantenay and the Nantes varieties of carrots made up 70 percent of our supply. These were excellent carrots, containing no more than 35 percent core. (The Chantenay is about 5½ inches long and 2 inches in diameter, cylindrical, blunt-ended and smooth-skinned, with a light reddish-orange color; the Nantes is about 6 inches long and 1½ inches in diameter, cylindrical, blunt-ended, and smooth-skinned, with a bright orange color and an occasionally purplish tinge at the shoulders.) Today these varieties are seldom seen (the Nantes does not ship well), and many of the new varieties may contain 50 percent core or more.

California produces most of our carrots, which is good because they are first quality, followed by Texas, Michigan, Wisconsin, and Washington. According to season, you are most likely to find California carrots in late fall, California and Texas carrots in winter, Arizona carrots in the spring, California carrots again in early summer, New Jersey and Illinois carrots in late summer, and in early fall a rash of carrots from Massachusetts, Connecticut, New York, Michigan, Wisconsin, Minnesota, Texas, Colorado, Washington, and Oregon. I mention all these sources only so that you may look for and choose your carrots carefully and remember where the best-tasting come from.

Buying carrots: Almost all carrots come topped, in 1-pound see-through plastic bags that may be tinted to accentuate the carrots' orange color. Slender, immature carrots are always shipped fresh. Mature, full-sized carrots may be shipped fresh or come from storage. If you see a stub of green stalk at the top of the carrots in the bag, the carrots are fresh from the field. If the stalks have been trimmed flush with the top of the carrots, they are from storage— the tops having been removed completely to prevent spoilage. This test holds true because it costs more to trim carrots completely, and this trimming is unnecessary if the carrots are shipped fresh. If you have a choice, avoid the storage carrots, which are to some degree coarser, less sweet, more bitter, and less delicate in flavor than the shipped-fresh kind.

Aside from this, look for carrots that are bright-colored, well shaped, smooth, clean, free of rootlets, with firm flesh. Avoid carrots that are soft or flabby (bend the ends) or show green sunburned areas at the top.

Preparing carrots: Peel carrots with a vegetable peeler (the skin is flavorful but bitter). Young carrots are cooked whole. Mature carrots are cut into rounds, dice, balls, sticks, clove shapes, and small carrot shapes. When cutting in rounds, hold the knife at an angle when cutting the small end, gradually straightening the knife as you proceed, cutting up the carrot to equalize the diameter of the slices. When cutting mature storage carrots, cut off all four sides and discard the square center containing the core. Then cut the sides into sticks, dice, or garlic clove shapes.

Blanching carrots: Mature carrots that have been long in storage may require blanching to ameliorate their heavy flavor. Peel them, and plunge them whole or in pieces into boiling salted water. Blanch whole carrots for 5 minutes; blanch pieces for one minute. Plunge them into cold water, drain, and dry.

Cooking carrots: Carrots are always cooked in moist heat, although they may be lightly sautéed at the end of their cooking. The basic method for preparing carrots is braising, because their flavor is persistent and long, slow braising with butter makes them mellow and richer-tasting. Boiling draws out much of the carrot's flavor, and is best reserved for old carrots. For a very pure carrot taste, steam them.

BOILED CARROTS (*Carottes Bouillies*). Put carrots into boiling salted water and boil until tender. Cook small, young carrots whole or cut in 1½-inch lengths. Cook mature carrots quartered lengthwise and cut in 1½-inch lengths, or cut in olive or garlic clove shapes, or cut in sticks, dice, balls, or rounds. Discard the cores of old storage carrots. Boiling time for whole young carrots and cut-up mature carrots is 10 to 20 minutes. Drain and dry the carrots and toss them in a pan with hot butter (*carottes au beurre*), or serve melted butter separately (*carottes à l'anglaise*).

STEAMED CARROTS (*Carottes à la Vapeur*). Cut carrots in one of the ways described for Boiled Carrots (above). Put into the steaming tray and steam for 20 to 30 minutes, until the carrots are tender. Serve with melted butter.

BRAISED CARROTS (*Carottes Braisées*). Cut 1 pound carrots into 1½-inch lengths, olive shapes, garlic clove shapes, or thick rounds—all of about equal thickness. You should have 4 cups of carrot pieces. Put them in a saucepan, add 1 cup of water (to barely cover the carrots), ¼ teaspoon salt, 2 teaspoons sugar, and 1 tablespoon butter. Bring to the boil, cover, and boil gently for 30 minutes until the liquid has almost entirely reduced and the carrots are tender. Uncover and toss the carrots until their cooking liquid has disappeared.

CARROTS IN CREAM (*Carottes à la Crème*). Prepare Braised Carrots (above). Barely cover them with boiling heavy cream and simmer, uncovered, until the cream has reduced by ⅔. Off the fire, stir in 2 tablespoons butter. Serve sprinkled with chopped parsley.

GLAZED CARROTS (*Carottes Glacées*). Prepare 1 pound carrots as for Braised Carrots (above). Put them in a saucepan with 1 cup of water or Brown Stock, ¼ teaspoon salt, 1 tablespoon and 1 teaspoon sugar, and 4 tablespoons butter. Bring to the boil, cover, and boil gently for 30 minutes or until the liquid is reduced to a syrup and the carrots are tender. Uncover and toss the carrots in the syrup and butter until they are glazed and shiny.

CARROTS À LA VICHY (*Carottes à la Vichy*). Slice 1 pound carrots in thin rounds. Cook as for Glazed Carrots (above), using 1 cup water, and serve sprinkled with chopped parsley. (It is traditional to use Vichy water if you have it.)

GLAZED CARROTS WITH ONIONS (*Carottes à la Nivernaise*). These two vegetables were made for each other, and appear frequently together as a garnish for braised meats and poultry. Just before serving, mix Glazed Carrots and Glazed Onions and arrange them on the platter around the meat.

CARROTS AUX FINES HERBES (*Carottes aux Fines Herbes*). Prepare as for Glazed Carrots (above), and serve sprinkled with chopped parsley, chervil, and chives.

CARROT PURÉE (*Purée de Carottes*). To 2 cups chopped carrots (about ½ pound) add ¼ teaspoon salt, 2 teaspoons sugar, 1 tablespoon butter, ¼ cup raw rice, and 2 cups water. Bring to the boil, cover, and boil gently for 30 minutes until the rice and carrots are cooked and the liquid has almost entirely disappeared. Put the rice and carrots through a food mill or rub them through a sieve. Heat the purée in a saucepan to dry it a little, and bring it to the desired consistency by stirring in 1 tablespoon butter and a few tablespoons heavy cream.

CARROT MOLD (*Pain de Carottes*). Prepare Carrot Purée (above). After drying the purée, remove it from the fire, cool it a little, and blend in 3 whole eggs, beaten. Butter a cylindrical (charlotte) mold and decorate its bottom and sides with strips or rounds of cooked carrot. Pour the purée-and-egg mixture into the mold, place the mold in a pot of hot water so that the water is at the same level as the mixture, and cook in a 325° oven for 30 to 40 minutes, or until the mixture has set. Allow this pudding to cool a little, and unmold it on a serving dish. Serve with Cream Sauce or Mousseline Sauce.

❋ CAULIFLOWER
(*Chou-Fleur*)

There are few dishes more elegant than a whole head of snowy white cauliflower, surrounded with a rosette of its own green leaves, brought steaming to the table, sprinkled with egg yolk and parsley, and drenched at the last moment with sizzling brown butter and breadcrumbs. It will look for all the world like a plump, savory pudding and you can slice it like a cake.

Unhappily, this is a sight not often seen. We eat only about one pound of cauliflower per person a year. As with other members of the cabbage family, this lack of popularity is most likely the result of overcooking.

California produces the most of this vegetable, and California cauliflower is in the market all year round, with the greatest supplies from November through May. New York is the second largest producer, and Long Island cauliflower is mostly available in September, October, and November. Arizona and Texas also send us cauliflower during winter months. Varietal names for cauliflower are seldom used, but the heads are usually identified by the name of the state in which they are grown. Sizes begin at about 1 pound, with the white heads about 4 inches in diameter. The largest cauliflower, Veitch Autumn Giant, is more than 8 inches in diameter. It is harvested in autumn in the East, a truly magnificent vegetable.

Buying cauliflower: Look for firm, solid, white to creamy-white heads surrounded by fresh green leaves. If the flowers in the head have begun to bloom, the head will take on a granular appearance resembling cooked rice. This condition, described as "riciness," indicates that the vegetable has passed its prime. Also avoid cauliflower that is beginning to brown (too old), is grayish-brown and soft (has been frozen), or is spotted, smudgy, or speckled (insect injury, mold, and decay). Yellowed leaves that break easily from the stem are another sign of overmaturity.

Preparing cauliflower: The fresh green leaves as well as the white head of cauliflower are edible and delicious, and you may leave them on if you choose. To prepare a whole head of cauliflower, make crosswise cuts in the base of the stem with a pointed knife. Soak the head for one hour in cold salted water with a little vinegar or lemon juice. Or cut individual cauliflowerets from the stem, and soak for ½ hour. Drain, dry, and store covered in the refrigerator, or blanch the cauliflower at this time.

Blanching cauliflower: If the cauliflower is to be boiled, it may be cooked without blanching. For all other methods of cooking, the cauliflower should be blanched first. Plunge the vegetable into a large quantity of rapidly boiling salted water and return swiftly to the boil. Boil heads gently, uncovered, for 6 to 8 minutes. Boil cauliflowerets gently, uncovered, for 2 minutes. Plunge into cold water to cool as quickly as possible, drain, and dry.

Cooking cauliflower: To prevent the development of strong flavors, cook cauliflower as rapidly as possible, taking care, however, not to damage the delicate head as it softens. Do not overcook; the cauliflower should be firm and just fork-tender. Cauliflower is a full-fledged member of the cabbage family, and all cooking precautions listed for this family must be observed (see Cabbage).

Cauliflower is cooked whole or in pieces. However, when cooked in pieces, the cauliflowerets are frequently reassembled in a dome shape before serving to resemble somewhat the original head. It is nice to look at, and a thoughtful touch. To mold cooked cauliflowerets, place them head side down in a warm bowl, beginning in the middle of the bowl with the longest-stemmed cauliflower and surrounding it with the others so that all stems point toward the center. Cover the bowl with a serving dish, invert it, and gently shape the mound of cauliflowerets to form a head.

BOILED CAULIFLOWER (*Chou-fleur Bouilli*). Prepare and begin cooking the cauliflower as described for blanching cauliflower, but add 2 tablespoons flour mixed in ¼ cup milk to each quart of cooking water to keep the cauliflower white. Cook the whole heads for 15 to 25 minutes all told, including blanching time if the vegetable is blanched. Cook cauliflowerets for 8 to 12 minutes all told. The cauliflower is cooked when it is just barely fork-tender. Drain thoroughly, and serve with hot melted butter, Cream Sauce, Hollandaise Sauce, or Mousseline Sauce. Or plunge the cauliflower into cold water to stop the cooking, and serve cold with Vinaigrette Sauce, Mayonnaise, or another cold sauce.

STEAMED CAULIFLOWER (*Chou-fleur à la Vapeur*). Blanch the cauliflower. To steam a whole head, place it in boiling salted water to cover it by ⅓, cover the pot, and steam for about 30 minutes, or until it is fork-tender. To steam cauliflowerets, place in a steaming tray and steam for 10 to 15 minutes. Drain and serve with melted butter or with sauces listed for Boiled Cauliflower (above).

CAULIFLOWER WITH CREAM (*Chou-fleur à la Crème*). Boil cauliflowerets, drain, and arrange them in the shape of a cauliflower head. Season with salt and white pepper, cover with Cream Sauce, and decorate with sprigs of fresh parsley.

CAULIFLOWER À LA POLONAISE (*Chou-fleur à la Polonaise*). Boil whole cauliflower or cauliflowerets, drain, arrange on a serving dish, season with salt and white pepper, and sprinkle with mixed hard-cooked egg yolks and chopped parsley. At the last moment, pour over the cauliflower Brown Butter in which you have browned one teaspoon fine, dry white breadcrumbs per tablespoon of butter.

CAULIFLOWER À LA MILANAISE (*Chou-fleur à la Milanaise*). Boil whole cauliflower or cauliflowerets until just barely tender, drain, arrange on an ovenproof serving dish, and season with salt and white pepper. Sprinkle the cauliflower with melted butter and grated Parmesan cheese, and put it in a hot 450° oven to brown. Just before serving, sprinkle with Brown Butter.

CAULIFLOWER AU GRATIN (*Chou-fleur au Gratin*). Boil whole cauliflower or cauliflowerets and drain well. If you are using cauliflowerets, mold them in a bowl (see above). Place the cauliflower on an ovenproof platter coated with Mornay Sauce. Season the cauliflower with salt and white pepper and cover it completely with more of the sauce. Sprinkle with grated Parmesan, browned breadcrumbs, and melted butter, and place in a hot 450° oven until the cheese has melted and the sauce has browned.

SAUTÉED CAULIFLOWER (*Chou-fleur Sauté*). Boil cauliflowerets until they are almost cooked, and drain them very well. Prepare 3 tablespoons Brown Butter in a sauté pan, add the drained cauliflower, and sauté briskly, taking care not to crush the tender flowerets. Arrange on a dish, season with salt and white pepper, sprinkle with a little butter from the pan and finely chopped parsley.

CAULIFLOWER FRITTERS (*Chou-fleur en Fritots*). Boil cauliflowerets until they are ¾ cooked, and drain them. Sprinkle with oil, lemon juice, salt, and white pepper and allow them to stand in this marinade for 30 minutes, turning them occasionally. Dip in a Batter for deep-frying vegetables and deep-fry in 380° fat for 1 or 2 minutes, until golden-brown. Drain and serve on a napkin with Fried Parsley and Tomato Sauce.

CAULIFLOWER SALAD (*Salade de Chou-fleur*). Season chilled, boiled cauliflower with oil, lemon juice, salt, and white pepper. Sprinkle with parsley or chopped chervil.

CAULIFLOWER PURÉE (*Purée de Chou-fleur,* or *Purée Du Barry*). Boil the cauliflower, drain it well, and put it through a food mill or rub it through a sieve. Heat it in a saucepan to dry it a little, and add ¼ cup mashed potatoes for every cup of cauliflower. Season with salt and white pepper, and add enough heavy cream to bring the purée to the desired consistency. Finish the purée off the fire by stirring in 1 or 2 tablespoons butter.

✳ CELERY
(Céleri)

The ancient Greeks and modern medicine have both used celery as a sedative, so if you find yourself nodding off on a celery diet, do not be oversurprised.

Celery, which has become a work horse of the kitchen, contains a highly volatile oil that gives it its characteristic flavor. In the wild state it has a ferocious taste, which, I suppose, suggested its use as a medicine. Then along about the seventeenth century the French got to sniffing and tasting it and they began using it to flavor soups, stews, and sauces. Before long they were eating it all by itself. Today it is eaten fresh, as in America, but it is even more widely eaten cooked.

Almost all celery is sold fresh, and we eat about 7 pounds apiece each year. There are both green and yellow varieties. For most of our celery-eating history the yellow variety has been dominant. It is called Golden Self Blanching, and French farmers have been perfecting it for generations. But in recent years we have discovered that green varieties need not be bitter or stringy, and the overwhelming proportion of celery grown and eaten in the United States is now green. The two major green varieties are Utah and Pascal. Although more Utah celery is grown, green celery is usually called "Pascal" celery in the supermarket.

California grows most of our celery, and it is available all year but most plentiful in June and July, November and December. Florida grows about half as much as California, and you can expect to find Florida celery in the market from December through June.

As to nomenclature, in the following discussion a rib of celery is one of the individual stems attached to the head at the base.

Buying celery: Choose fresh-looking, solid, rigid heads of medium length with individual ribs thick and brittle enough to break with a snap. Feel inside the ribs for a smooth surface; if it is puffy or irregular the celery is pithy and may have been frozen. If the celery is wrapped, press the center of a rib to test for pithiness. Yellow celery should be creamy or light golden. Green celery should be light green or medium green. The ribs of both should look glossy, and the leaflets remaining at the top should be mostly green. Do not buy soft celery, or celery with flabby branches at the top. Also avoid celery that is discolored on the inside of the outer ribs near the base, or on the inner ribs.

Preparing celery: Celery is not soaked. Pull off excessive coarse or damaged outside ribs. Trim the root end of the head and cut off the top just below the first fork in the individual ribs, which gives you about 8 inches of stalk. The tops and leaves are stronger-tasting and are used for flavoring stocks. Depending upon how you are going to eat the celery, either pull the ribs from the head and wash them clean under running water, or leave the head whole, spread the ribs without snapping them, and manipulate the head under forcefully running water to clean the ribs where they attach at the base of the head. Finally, use a sharp knife to cut and strip away the strings from the outside ribs. Store, covered, in the refrigerator, or blanch the celery at this time.

Blanching celery: Plunge the whole head of celery in boiling salted water and boil for 15 minutes. If the head is large, first cut it in two lengthwise. Refresh the celery by plunging it into cold water. The ribs are now flexible and easy to spread, so you may wash them again under forcefully running water to flush out any dirt remaining at the root end. Drain the celery thoroughly, squeeze it tightly in a towel to remove as much excess water as possible, and tie in at least two places with soft white twine. The celery is now ready for cooking.

Cooking celery: Celery is always braised, cooked in a flavorful stock or stock and wine to give it a rich, mellow flavor. Long, slow cooking promotes the interchange of flavors between the celery and the braising liquid, which becomes, of course, the sauce. The celery may be braised up to 24 hours in advance of serving and reheated gently, covered, in its sauce.

BRAISED CELERY (*Céleri Braisé*). Line a casserole with fresh pork fat, or with salt pork or bacon that you have blanched by simmering in water for 10 minutes. Place in the bottom a bed of sliced carrots and onions, place blanched and tied heads of celery on this bed of vegetables, season with salt and pepper, cover the casserole and put it into a 350° oven for 10 minutes to reduce excess moisture. Then add a *Bouquet Garni* consisting of 3 sprigs parsley, 1 bay leaf, and a sprig or pinch of thyme, all tied in cheesecloth. Pour in enough White Stock or Brown Stock to barely cover the celery, combining with this stock ½ cup or 1 cup dry white wine if you wish. Finally, cover the whole with more fresh pork fat or blanched bacon and a piece of buttered paper or foil cut to fit the casserole, with a small hole cut in it to vent the steam. Cover the casserole tightly and braise in a 350° oven for 1½ hours.

Remove and drain the celery, cut the strings, cut the heads in single-service portions lengthwise, bend them in two if they are long, and place in a serving dish. Skim the fat from the braising liquid, strain it into a saucepan, and quickly reduce it to the amount of sauce you need. Thicken the liquid

486   FRENCH COOKING FOR THE AMERICAN TABLE

with arrowroot or cornstarch mixed in a little stock or Madeira wine, or thicken it with *Beurre Manié*. Off the fire, beat in a few tablespoons butter and pour the sauce over the celery. Sprinkle with chopped parsley.

CELERY IN CREAM (*Céleri à la Crème*). Braise the celery as for Braised Celery (above). Drain thoroughly, cut lengthwise into single-service portions, folding them in two if the ribs are long. Or cut the celery crosswise in 1½-inch pieces for serving by the spoonful. Season the celery with salt and white pepper and keep it warm in a well-buttered skillet.

Skim the fat from the braising liquid, and reduce it quickly to about ½ the quantity of sauce required. Thicken the liquid with Béchamel Sauce or by adding it to a Blond Roux, using enough sauce or roux to make it quite thick. Now add enough fresh heavy cream to give it the consistency of a sauce, and season to taste with salt and pepper. Bring the sauce to a boil and pour it over the celery in the pan. Shake the pan to coat the celery pieces, or roll the single-service portions in the sauce.

CELERY WITH BÉCHAMEL SAUCE (*Céleri a la Béchamel*). Braise the celery, cut it in the desired portions as for Celery in Cream (above), season with salt and white pepper, and cook gently in butter for 15 minutes. Add Béchamel Sauce to the pan and simmer for 10 minutes more.

CELERY IN BUTTER (*Céleri au Beurre*). Place blanched and tied celery heads or ribs in a saucepan with several tablespoons of butter. Season with salt and pepper, add a few tablespoons of White Stock or Brown Stock or stock and wine, cover, and simmer slowly for 1 hour.

CELERY WITH PARMESAN (*Céleri au Parmesan*). Braise the celery and drain it well. Arrange it in an ovenproof dish, season with salt and pepper, and pour over it Demi-Glace Sauce or Starch-Thickened Brown Stock. Sprinkle with grated Parmesan cheese and brown in a hot oven.

CELERY MORNAY (*Céleri Mornay*). Proceed as for Celery with Parmesan (above), but use Mornay Sauce.

CELERY À LA MILANAISE (*Céleri à la Milanaise*). Proceed as for Celery with Parmesan (above), omitting the sauce and sprinkling the celery with grated Parmesan cheese and melted butter. Just before serving, sprinkle with Brown Butter.

CELERY AU JUS (*Céleri au Jus*). Braise the celery, drain it well, arrange it on a platter, and season with salt and pepper. Dress it with Starch-Thickened Brown Veal Stock to which you have added 2 tablespoons butter per cup.

CELERY PURÉE (*Purée de Céleri*). Slice blanched celery crosswise in 1½-inch pieces, and stew it slowly in butter and a little White Stock in a covered saucepan for 1 hour. Drain it well, and put it through a food mill or rub it through a sieve or purée in the blender. Skim the fat from the cooking liquid and add it to the celery. Thicken the mixture to the desired consistency with mashed potatoes or Potato Purée, heat, stirring, and season to taste with salt and white pepper. Finish the purée by stirring in a little butter.

✳ CORN
(*Maïs*)

Fresh sweet corn on the cob is one of the most American of dishes, and one of the first great vegetable delicacies I discovered at the American table. Strangely enough, corn on the cob is not often eaten in Europe. They do not know the joys of a platterful of steaming corn, the golden ears molten with butter and flecked with salt and aromatic pepper, the plump kernels ripe to bursting with hot, sweet cream.

To be good, fresh corn must be fresh. There is much truth in the American saying that the cooking water must be boiling before the corn is picked. In the first 2 hours after it is picked, sweet corn can lose as much as 10 percent of its sugar if it is not promptly cooled to near freezing. Corn picked at dawn and left to stand at summer temperatures on a quaint farm stand can lose up to 50 percent of its sugar in one day. However, corn that is immediately cooled, preferably in an ice water bath, and shipped at the freezing point, will retain about 80 percent of its sugar for as long as 4 days. This corn is quite satisfactory, so you do not have to despair if a cornfield is not accessible to you. Nevertheless, to get the freshest corn, you must get to the supermarket or your local farm stand early in the morning. Look for corn kept on ice.

Florida grows most of our sweet corn, followed by California, New York, Michigan, New Jersey, Ohio, Pennsylvania, and Massachusetts. Florida sends us fresh corn throughout the year, but mainly in April, May, and June. California corn is available mostly from June through October. Almost every state grows sweet corn, so watch for the corn-harvesting season in your area.

Buying sweet corn: Since corn must be fresh, and since even your vegetable man may not know the history of a batch of corn, you must choose it carefully. To begin with, look at the cut end of the ear; it should not be discolored or dried looking. Next, look at the husks. They should be fresh, green, and succulent looking. If corn is old, or if it is packed without cooling, the husks will begin to dry, wilt, and yellow. Now, strip the husk part way down the ear. The kernels should be plump and yellow, and they should fill the cob to the tip of the silk end. Small, soft, white kernels at the tip indicate that the corn is not fully grown, and therefore not as sweet as it should be. The kernels should be just large enough to fill the ear without leaving any space between the rows. If the kernels are large, pressed tightly against one another, the corn is overmature. If the kernels are dark yellow, with depressions on their surface, the corn is old and drying out.

If the corn has passed your examination up to this point, press one of the kernels with your thumbnail. It should offer slight resistance to pressure, and then it should pop. Observe the contents closely. If it is thin or watery or just cloudy in appearance, the corn is too young. If the inside of the kernel is mealy and doughlike, the corn is old and stale. If the corn is in prime condition, the kernels will contain a thick, white, sweet cream. As a final test, taste it.

Preparing sweet corn: Put corn into the refrigerator as soon as you get it home. Before cooking, trim the stem end. Peel back the husk, pull it off, and remove all the strings of silk at the tip. Or leave the husk on the ear, removing the silk only. Corn is neither soaked nor blanched.

Cooking sweet corn: Corn is boiled, steamed, and sometimes roasted. There are no special precautions other than the standard one of avoiding overcooking. Some say that corn should not be boiled in salted water, as it toughens the kernels. I do not believe this.

BOILED CORN ON THE COB (*Maïs Frais au Naturel Bouilli*). Cook the corn with or without its husk. Plunge into rapidly boiling salted water, cover, and return the water quickly to the boil, and boil from 3 to 8 minutes. Drain the corn. If the husk is still in place, fold it back and trim it. Serve immediately with butter, salt, and pepper.

STEAMED CORN ON THE COB (*Maïs Frais au Naturel à la Vapeur*). Remove husk and silk but leave the stems on the ears. Stand each ear on its stem in a few inches of boiling water so that all, or almost all, of the kernels are above the water level. Cover and steam for 10 to 15 minutes. Serve immediately with butter, salt, and pepper. (Steamed corn, which is tastier than boiled corn, can also be steamed in the husk, although this requires 5 to 10 minutes more cooking.)

ROASTED CORN ON THE COB (*Maïs Frais au Naturel au Four*). Remove silk from the corn, brush the kernels with melted butter, and reshape the husk around the ear. Put the ears on a baking sheet, leaving room between them, and bake at 400° for 10 to 15 minutes, or until the kernels are swollen and tender. Serve with salt, pepper, and butter.

CORN IN BUTTER (*Maïs au Beurre*). Boil the corn. Strip the kernels from the cob with a sharp knife, put them into a saucepan, sprinkle them with a little salt and sugar, and heat for a few moments to dry them. Add a generous amount of fresh butter to the pan and toss lightly.

CORN IN CREAM (*Maïs à la Crème*). Boil the corn, strip the kernels from the cob, put them into a saucepan, and heat for a few moments to dry them. Add heavy cream to barely cover the kernels and simmer for 4 or 5 minutes until the cream is reduced by ½. Season to taste with salt and a little sugar.

CORN PURÉE (*Purée de Maïs*). Boil the corn. With a sharp knife, cut the ears lengthwise along the middle of each row of kernels. Using the back of the knife, press out the pulp into a saucepan. Add a little butter, season to taste with salt and pepper, and heat gently. At the last moment, blend in a few tablespoons of heavy cream.

✳ CUCUMBERS
(*Concombres*)

Aside from those that are pickled, cucumbers are mostly eaten fresh and raw in the United States, and we eat about 3 pounds per person each year. The French eat their cucumbers cooked as well, and there are a number of ways the cucumber can be prepared to bring new vegetable variety to your table.

Cucumbers are available all year, but they are most plentiful from May through August. Florida sends us most of our supply, followed by California, the two Carolinas, Virginia, and New York.

Buying cucumbers: This vegetable is quite perishable and becomes coarse when old or overgrown. Look for firm, regularly shaped fruits about 6 or 7 inches long, with round ends and bright green skin. Green to white tips at the end of fresh cucumbers change to yellow as the cucumber becomes too old. Avoid soft, withered cucumbers (tough, bitter flesh), or those that are large, puffy, and dull-skinned (tough flesh, hard seeds, overmature), or those that have sunken areas (decay). Usually the skins of cucumbers are waxed to help preserve freshness.

Preparing cucumbers: Cucumbers are rather difficult to keep at home in as much as they require a moist 50° environment. Kept in the refrigerator for a few days, they are likely to develop dark watery spots that encourage mold. It is better to buy cucumbers only as you need them.

For eating cucumbers fresh, peel and slice them or cut them into sticks or lozenge shapes. If you are unfortunate enough to have bought overmature cucumbers, cut them in half lengthwise and scoop out their seeds before you slice them. Sprinkle the pieces with salt and let them stand for 30 minutes or longer to draw off some of their moisture and a bitterness they sometimes contain.

When cooking cucumbers, you must first draw off some of their water so they will not disintegrate during the cooking. For cut cucumber, sprinkle with salt and allow the pieces to stand for 30 minutes or longer. Whole, unpeeled cucumbers should be blanched.

Blanching cucumbers: Plunge whole, unpeeled cucumbers in boiling salted water, boil gently for 10 minutes, cool them in cold water, and dry them.

Cooking cucumbers: Cucumbers may be cooked like summer squash (see Squashes and Pumpkins in this chapter) or in one of the following ways.

STEAMED CUCUMBERS (*Concombres à la Vapeur*). Peel the cucumbers, cut them in half, scoop out their seedy centers, and cut the meat in slices, sticks, or lozenge shapes. Sprinkle with salt and allow to stand for 30 to 60 minutes. Steam them in a vegetable steaming tray for 10 to 15 minutes, or until the pieces are soft and translucent. Serve with salt, pepper, and butter.

CUCUMBERS IN BUTTER (*Concombres au Beurre*). Prepare the cucumbers as for Steamed Cucumbers (above). Put them in a skillet or sauté pan with 2 tablespoons butter and 2 tablespoons water per cup of cucumber. Season with salt and white pepper, cover, and simmer very slowly for about 45 minutes, rolling the cucumbers in the butter, until they are tender but not mushy.

STUFFED CUCUMBERS (*Concombres Farcis*). Cucumbers make excellent and decorative *Timbales* that are eminently edible. Blanch whole, unpeeled cucumbers for 5 minutes, cool them, and cut them crosswise to form thick 2-inch slices. Cut thin, lengthwise strips from the skin to give the slices a green-and-white striped effect. Stand the slices on end and hollow out the seeds and center pulp to within ½ inch of the bottom. This forms the cucumber case.

Fill the cucumbers with a savory stuffing, such as one of those suggested for Summer Squash, or with one of the Forcemeats (see Chapter 4). Stand the filled cases in a well-buttered pan just large enough to hold them, placing them on top of a bed of sliced carrots and onions. Add enough Brown or White Stock (appropriate to the stuffing) to cover the cucumbers by ½, and a *Bouquet Garni.* Bring the stock to the boil, and cover the cucumbers with a piece of foil cut to fit the pan, with a small hole cut in it to vent the steam. Cover the pan and cook in a 325° oven for 45 minutes. Remove the cucumbers and keep them warm. Reduce the stock quickly, thicken it with cornstarch, Starch-Thickened Stock, or *Beurre Manié,* and pour the sauce over the stuffed cucumbers.

For additional recipes for cucumbers, see and follow the recipes for Summer Squash to prepare *concombres glacés, à la crème, sautés, au gratin, à la milanaise, à la provençale, frits,* and *purée de concombres.*

✳ *EGGPLANT*
(*Aubergine*)

This handsome vegetable is very popular in many parts of the world, and some of the world's most famous dishes are based on its delicate flesh—such as Italian eggplant *parmigiana,* Greek *moussaka,* and Turkish *imam baaldi.* This Turkish dish, the name of which translates as "the priest who fainted," is eggplant stuffed with onions, tomatoes, and raisins, simmered in seasoned oil for hours, allowed to absorb all the oil, and served cold. It is rather like a fruit preserved in syrup, and is named for a priest who fainted with pure pleasure upon tasting it.

Eggplant is one of the most versatile of vegetables. It may be cooked in a great many ways, and it has a great affinity for tomatoes, onions, garlic, and cheese. We eat about ½ pound of fresh eggplant apiece each year. It is not a minor vegetable, but there is room for improvement.

There are many varieties of eggplant. In America we eat mostly the large purple varieties. Almost all comes from Florida and New Jersey. It is harvested in Florida all year round, and in New Jersey in the summertime. It is most plentiful in August and September.

Buying eggplant: The best purple eggplants are firm, smooth, heavy for their size, and uniformly black-purple. The color should be clear and glossy and extend over the entire surface. Different varieties of eggplant may be pear-, oval-, globe-, or somewhat triangular-shaped. Choose smaller eggplants; the largest tend to be coarser in the center and less flavorful. Avoid eggplants that are flabby, soft, wrinkled, or mottled with dark brown spots, which are evidence of decay.

Preparing eggplant: Eggplant is relatively perishable, and will keep only for about 10 days after harvesting. Store it in the refrigerator, keeping it moist. When you are ready to cook, wash the eggplant under running water and trim away the green stalk. Depending upon the recipe, you will cut the unpeeled eggplant in two lengthwise, or peel it (using a vegetable peeler) and slice it or cut it in sticks. Whatever course you take, sprinkle the cut flesh of the eggplant with salt and allow it to stand for 30 minutes to draw out excess water and puckery juices. Drain the flesh, squeeze lightly to remove more water, dry in paper towels, and proceed with the cooking. Eggplant is neither soaked nor blanched.

Cooking eggplant: Eggplant is a very watery vegetable with a spongy flesh. This allows it to be cooked in a variety of ways. Because it is watery, it may be baked in the oven contained in its own skin. Because it is spongy it can be successfully sautéed, deep-fried, or broiled after some of its excess water has been squeezed out. When stewed it cooks down very quickly, readily absorbs the liquid surrounding it, and eventually disintegrates like a tomato.

SAUTÉED EGGPLANT (*Aubergine Sautée*). Peel the eggplant, cut in ½-inch-thick slices, sprinkle with salt, and allow to stand for 30 minutes with a weight on top. Drain away the extracted juices, and press the slices dry with a paper towel. Dip the slices in milk, shake away the excess, and dredge them in flour. Sauté briskly in ¼ inch very hot oil for 2 or 3 minutes per side, until golden brown and soft all the way through. Drain on paper towels, season with salt, and serve immediately sprinkled with Brown Butter and chopped parsley.

BROILED EGGPLANT (*Aubergine Grillée*). Peel the eggplant, cut in ½-inch-thick slices, sprinkle with salt, and allow to stand for 30 minutes with a weight on top. Drain away the extracted juices, and press the slices dry with a paper towel. Brush them with oil or Clarified Butter and broil in the broiler for 3 to 4 minutes per side, until golden brown and soft all the way through. Season with salt and serve with Maître d'Hôtel Butter.

FRIED EGGPLANT (*Aubergine Frite*). Peel the eggplant, cut in ½-inch-thick slices lengthwise, sprinkle with salt, and allow to stand for 30 minutes with a weight on top. Drain away the extracted juices, and press the slices dry with a paper towel. Cut the slices in sticks, ½ inch square and 2 inches long. Dredge them in flour, tossing them with the flour in a paper bag. Slap the sticks to remove excess flour and deep-fry in 390° hot oil for about 2 minutes, until they are golden brown. Drain on paper towels and sprinkle with salt. Serve immediately or the eggplant will soften. (Fried eggplant can also be cut in ⅓-inch-thick round slices and coated *à l'Anglaise*.)

EGGPLANT AU GRATIN (*Aubergine au Gratin*). Cut the eggplant in two lengthwise. With a knife (preferably a curved grapefruit knife), make a deep cut ¼ to ½ inch inside the skin, all around the circumference of each eggplant half, taking care not to break the skin. Within the boundaries of this cut, make deep crisscross incisions to within ½ inch of the bottom of the eggplant. Sprinkle with salt and let stand, cut side down, for 30 minutes. Squeeze gently to remove excess water and dry the cut surface with a towel. Sauté gently in oil, cut side down, for 10 minutes or until the pulp is softened and can be scooped out. Remove most of the pulp, leaving a thin layer next to the skin. Chop the pulp, add to it about ½ its volume of dry *Duxelles,* and season with salt and pepper. Pack this mixture back into the skins, sprinkle with melted butter and dry breadcrumbs, and brown in the oven or under the broiler. Place the stuffed eggplant halves in a serving dish, and surround them with Demi-Glace Sauce or Starch-Thickened Brown Stock.

EGGPLANT À LA LANGUEDOCIENNE (*Aubergine à la Languedocienne*). Prepare as for Eggplant au Gratin (above), but in place of the *duxelles* use lightly sautéed, chopped Pork Forcemeat and 1 small clove garlic, minced. Omit the sauce.

EGGPLANT À LA REINE (*Aubergine à la Reine*). Prepare as for Eggplant au Gratin (above), but in place of the *duxelles* use a *Salpicon* of chicken in Velouté Sauce, equal in quantity to the pulp. Omit the sauce.

EGGPLANT À LA PROVENÇALE (*Aubergine à la Provençale*). Prepare as for Eggplant au Gratin (above), but in place of the *duxelles* use chopped tomatoes simmered in olive oil with a little garlic. Serve the eggplant halves surrounded with Tomato Sauce.

EGGPLANT À LA NÎMOISE (*Aubergine à la Nîmoise*). Prepare as for Eggplant à la Provençale (above), but add chopped pimentos and chopped parsley to the stuffing. Omit the sauce.

❊ GREEN AND WAX BEANS
(*Haricots Verts et Haricots Mange-Tout*)

The green or snap bean has always fared less well than the pea in American cooking pots. Perhaps this is because the pea is so small and helpless looking, while the green bean looks more robust. But do not be fooled by appearances. Green beans are one of the greatest vegetable delicacies when they are properly cooked, and in France *haricots verts* are treated with fully as much deference as the famed *petits pois*.

What is more, fresh green beans are almost everywhere available, whereas the perishability of peas has made them an uncommon item among fresh vegetables. Green beans, cooled quickly after they are picked, and kept cool and dry, will arrive at the supermarket in excellent condition. They are at their best when simply cooked, boiled quickly until just tender, drained, and put into a sauté pan with butter for a minute or two to dry them and give them a glossy shine.

Although we eat about 9 pounds of green beans apiece each year, the consumption of fresh green beans has declined to only about 20 percent of the total. This is disturbing news for our palates. The delicate, nutty taste of fresh green beans is unique among vegetables. Florida sends us the most fresh beans, and they are in the market from November through May. During the remaining months other states make up the supply, mainly North Carolina, New York, Virginia, California, New Jersey, South Carolina, and Michigan. Peak months for green beans are June and July.

There are many varieties of snap beans, both green and yellow (wax), growing on bushes or poles, and with pods that are round, oval or relatively flat in cross-section. All are good eating as long as they are very fresh and very young. Both green and yellow (wax) fresh snap beans can be cooked in the same manner.

Buying snap beans: The younger the beans, the better, so look for the skinniest you can find. (Green beans in France are marketed when they are less than ¼ inch in diameter.) The pods must be a fresh green color throughout (or bright yellow for wax beans), without mottling or russeting. Bush bean pods grow to about 6 inches in length; pole bean pods reach 8 inches. Pods should be firm and flexible, with no hint of wilt or wateriness, and they should break with a crisp snap when bent. Snap beans are virtually stringless today, so stringlessness is no longer a guide to maturity. Inside the pods, the smaller and more immature the beans the better they will be. Disregard the color of the immature beans; they vary greatly depending upon the variety. Avoid beans with thick, fibrous pods in which the bulge of the beans can be seen, indicating overmaturity.

Preparing snap beans: Wash beans under running water, and remove tips at the ends by breaking them off with your fingers and stripping away any stray strings that might be attached. Leave the beans whole, cut them in two lengthwise, or cut them on the diagonal into 1½-inch pieces (diagonal cutting makes the beans look better). Dry the beans thoroughly and store in the refrigerator until ready to cook, or blanch them.

Blanching snap beans: The blanching of green beans ordinarily takes place just before their cooking. Also, green beans, unlike many other vegetables, are blanched until they are almost fully cooked. To blanch, dry the beans well and plunge them, whole or in pieces, into a large amount of rapidly boiling salted water. Add beans a few at a time to prevent the water from coming off the boil. Boil the beans briskly, uncovered, for 8 to 12 minutes, testing from time to time by biting into one, until they are tender but still crunchy. Drain the beans well and proceed with the recipe. Or you may place the beans in a colander and cool them quickly under cold running water, drain them and store covered in the refrigerator.

Cooking snap beans: Green beans have this peculiarity: they are detectably fresher and finer-tasting if their blanching and cooking take place in one session, without allowing the beans to cool. The difference in taste is marginal, however, and you should blanch in advance if by doing so you can better control the time of their serving, because green beans must be served as soon as they are cooked. Perhaps more than any other vegetable, their just-cooked freshness is quickly lost, and a few minutes' delay between cooking and serving can make the difference between chortles of delight and a stony silence from your guests.

A second concern in cooking green beans is to preserve their delicate flavor. The best way to do this is to cook the beans whole. Flavor is lost from the ends of sliced green beans, and lost even more quickly when the beans are cut lengthwise (this lengthwise cut, called "Frenching," gives beans the slim appearance of French green beans; it is not done in France).

Finally, you must preserve the color of the cooked beans so that they are even more vividly green than when fresh. This is assured when they are properly blanched and cooked very quickly. Yellow (wax) beans present no color problem.

BOILED GREEN BEANS (*Haricots Verts Bouillis*). Proceed as for blanching snap beans (above), boiling them for 12 to 15 minutes, or until they are tender but still slightly crunchy to the teeth. Drain them well, put them into a saucepan, and shake them over the fire for 1 or 2 minutes to evaporate their surface moisture. Season with salt and pepper, add 6 tablespoons butter per pound of beans, and toss over a brisk fire to melt the butter and coat the beans. Serve immediately. This dish is also called *haricots verts à l'anglaise*.

GREEN BEANS IN BROWN BUTTER (*Haricots Verts au Beurre Noisette*). Boil the beans, drain and dry them thoroughly in a towel, season with salt and pepper, and put them into a sauté pan with hot Clarified Butter that has begun to brown (Brown Butter). Toss them in the butter for 1 or 2 minutes and serve sprinkled with very fresh, chopped parsley.

GREEN BEANS IN CREAM (*Haricots Verts à la Crème*). Boil the beans until they are ⅔ cooked. Drain them well, put them into a saucepan, and shake them over the fire for 1 or 2 minutes to evaporate their surface moisture. Season with salt and pepper, add a little butter, and toss for 1 minute more. Add heavy cream to barely cover the beans, bring to the boil, cover the pan leaving a 1-inch opening, and simmer for 4 or 5 minutes until the beans are tender and the cream is reduced by ½. Serve sprinkled with chopped fresh parsley.

GREEN BEANS AU GRATIN (*Haricots Verts au Gratin*). Prepare Green Beans in Cream (above). Sprinkle an ovenproof serving dish with grated Parmesan cheese, add the beans, sprinkle with more Parmesan and melted butter, and brown in the oven.

GREEN BEANS À LA NORMANDE (*Haricots Verts à la Normande*). Prepare Green Beans in Cream (above). Off the fire stir in 2 beaten egg yolks and heat gently, stirring, until the sauce thickens. If it is too thick, add a little more cream. Just before serving, stir in 1 tablespoon butter.

GREEN BEANS À LA TOURANGELLE (*Haricots Verts à la Tourangelle*). Prepare as for Green Beans in Cream (above), but in place of the cream add a thin Béchamel Sauce in which you have simmered a little garlic. Finish the cooking in the sauce and sprinkle the beans with chopped parsley.

SAUTÉED GREEN BEANS (*Haricots Verts Sautés*). Boil the beans, drain them, and dry thoroughly in a towel. Season with salt and pepper, and sauté briskly in a little Clarified Butter until they are slightly browned. Serve sprinkled with chopped parsley.

GREEN BEANS À LA PROVENÇALE (*Haricots Verts à la Provençale*). Proceed as for Sautéed Green Beans (above), using olive oil instead of butter. Just before serving add a little minced garlic to the pan and toss it with the beans for a few seconds. Serve sprinkled with chopped parsley.

GREEN BEANS À LA LYONNAISE (*Haricots Verts à la Lyonnaise*). Boil the beans, drain them, and dry them thoroughly in a towel. In a sauté pan, lightly brown in Clarified Butter ¾ to 1 cup thin sliced onions per 1 pound beans. Add the beans, season with salt and pepper, and sauté briskly until the beans are slightly browned. At the last moment, sprinkle the beans in the pan with vinegar, toss, and serve sprinkled with chopped parsley.

GREEN BEANS, HOUSEWIFE STYLE (*Haricots Verts à la Bonne Femme*). Boil the beans until they are ⅔ cooked, drain them, and dry thoroughly in a towel. In a saucepan, sauté ½ pound diced blanched salt pork or bacon until the fat is partially rendered and the dice are browned. Add the beans, season them with salt and pepper, and sprinkle with ¼ cup Starch-Thickened Brown Stock. Cover tightly and simmer for 5 to 8 minutes, or until the beans are tender. Turn the beans and pork into a serving dish, sprinkle with chopped parsley and top with fresh butter.

GREEN BEAN SALAD (*Salade de Haricots Verts*). Boil the beans, cool them quickly under running water, drain and dry them in a towel. Toss lightly in Vinaigrette Sauce.

GREEN BEAN PURÉE (*Purée de Haricots Verts* or *Purée Favorite*). Boil the beans, drain, and dry them in a towel, and stew them very slowly, covered, in butter for about 5 minutes. Put the beans through a food mill or rub them through a sieve, add to them half their volume of mashed potato or Potato Purée, season with salt and pepper, and reheat. Just before serving stir in a little butter.

✻ LETTUCE AND CHICORY
(*Laitue* and *Chicorée*)

Americans eat a large amount of lettuce, about 20 pounds per person each year. Practically all of this poundage is eaten raw in salads. Lettuce salads are discussed in Chapter 12. Here I will describe the various lettuces and members of the chicory family, and give recipes for their use as hot, cooked vegetables.

Californians eat more lettuce than anyone else. California produces by far the most lettuce and sends it around the country throughout the year. Arizona lettuce is available from November through May, and the New York and New Jersey lettuce crops are in season from June through November.

Many other states add to the supply to make lettuce evenly available in every month.

Five kinds of lettuce account for almost all of our supply—crisphead, butterhead, Bibb, romaine, and leaf lettuce. Three members of the chicory family—chicory or curly endive, escarole, and Belgian endive—are frequently assumed to be lettuces and are both cooked and used as salad greens. Watercress, also, is a common salad green.

The flavor of lettuce, at best, is very delicate. Usually there is an element of sweetness with an undertone of bitterness. There is also a hint of chlorophyll green (a flavor that tastes like grass smells). All too often, however, you will find lettuces that are absolutely tasteless.

Crisphead lettuce, commonly called *iceberg* or *head* lettuce, is large, solid, and hard, with brittle, greenish-white outer leaves and crisp white-to-yellow inner leaves that are tightly rumpled. In volume, this lettuce surpasses all the others put together by far, because it ships and keeps excellently. Most of the leaves of this lettuce are pale and coarse, and they do nothing for the appearance of a salad. In prime condition, it is quite juicy and tends to be sweet in flavor.

Butterhead lettuce, also called *Boston* lettuce, is smaller than crisphead, forming soft, smooth, loose-leaved rosettes of green and yellow. The leaves are soft and tender. The inner leaves feel buttery, giving this variety its name. It is a very handsome lettuce in salads and a preferred lettuce for cooking. It is delicately flavored and chewy in texture.

Bibb lettuce (sometimes called *limestone* lettuce) is named for Major John Bibb, who developed the variety about the time of the Civil War. It is a small, crisp, butterhead variety. Leaves are brittle, ribbed, and green, becoming greenish-white in the center. It has a delicate but distinctive flavor, and is very choice for salads and cooking.

Romaine lettuce, or *cos,* is a large, long, upright lettuce with stiff, coarse, dark green leaves that become greenish-white in the center of the head. Outer leaves tend to be leathery and tough, inner leaves more tender and crisp. It is more flavorful than any of the above lettuces, with a combination of sweet and slightly bitter flavors and a more pronounced taste of green.

Leaf lettuce is a large, spreading lettuce. It resembles butterhead in texture, but the soft, tender leaves do not form a rosette. Different varieties are flat- or curly-leaved. The leaves may be all green or green with brown or red tips. It is delicately flavored.

Chicory, or *curly endive,* forms a loose head with tightly curled dark green outer leaves and yellow heart leaves. The leaves have large ribs and a bitey texture. It has a bitter flavor.

Escarole resembles curly endive, although the leaves are broader, heavier, and tougher, and not quite so curly. Leaf color ranges from green outer leaves to a yellow-green center. It has a bitter flavor.

Belgian endive is small, tightly headed, and spindle-shaped with a pointed end and compact, blanched-white leaves. It is bitter.

Watercress is a little plant with long stems and small round green leaves that grows in running water. It has a distinctive, spicy, peppery flavor.

Buying lettuce: All lettuce should look fresh. Green colors should be bright, yellows rich, and white clean white or white-green. Look at the cut stem. If it has become rust-colored and dry, the lettuce has been around for a while. Crisphead lettuce, Bibb, and romaine should have brittle leaf ribs; other lettuces should have succulent leaves without evidence of wilting. Avoid lettuces with rust-colored stains in the leaves, or any other discoloration, or soft, slimy spots.

Preparing lettuce: Store lettuce in plastic bags in the refrigerator. If you wash it before storing, wash lightly and shake it well to dry it. For eating raw in salads, prepare lettuce according to the suggestions given in Chapter 12. For cooking the lettuce, trim away bruised outside leaves and cut a thin slice from the stem. Wash the lettuce by agitating it in a bowl of cold water, continuing until no more sand or soil is deposited in the bottom of the bowl. Shake the lettuce to dry it, and blanch it.

Blanching lettuce: Lettuce is very watery, and it must be blanched before further cooking to rid it of some of its water and empty its cells for a more flavorful filling. Plunge the trimmed, washed heads into a large quantity of boiling salted water and boil for about 5 minutes. (Escarole and chicory, which are tougher, should be boiled for 10 minutes.) Remove and plunge into cold water, or cool under running water. Drain the lettuce, squeeze it to remove excess water, and it is ready for cooking.

Cooking lettuce: Lettuce, chicory, and escarole are greatly reduced in volume during cooking. One pound of lettuce will produce about 4 quarts of lightly packed leaves. After blanching and squeezing, you will have no more than a scant 2 cups of material to work with. After blanching, lettuce is always braised in a flavorful liquid to give it flavor and succulence. And after braising the lettuce may still receive additional cooking in order to produce a classic dish.

BRAISED LETTUCE (*Laitues Braisées*). Blanch heads of Bibb or Boston lettuce, cool them and squeeze out the excess water. If the heads are small, leave them whole. If they are large, cut them in half, lengthwise, and fold each half from top to bottom with the large outer leaves on the outside. Season the folded lettuce with salt and pepper and put in a pan on a bed of blanched pork rind, blanched salt pork, or blanched bacon, covered with sliced onions and carrots. Add a *Bouquet Garni* consisting of 3 sprigs parsley, ½ bay leaf, and a sprig or pinch of thyme all tied in cheesecloth. Cover the pan and let it stand in a 325° oven for 10 minutes to draw moisture from the vegetables. Remove the pan from the oven and pour in enough White Stock or Brown Stock to just cover the lettuce. Bring the stock to the boiling point, cover the lettuce with a piece of buttered paper cut to fit the pan and with a small hole cut in it to vent the steam. Cover the pan and cook in a 325° oven for about 1½ hours. Drain the lettuce and put it on a serving platter. Skim and strain the braising liquid and reduce it until it coats a spoon, or reduce the liquid to the desired quantity and thicken with Starch-Thickened Stock. Off the fire swirl into it 1 or 2 tablespoons butter. Pour this sauce over the lettuce.

LETTUCE IN BROWN BUTTER (*Laitues au Beurre Noisette*). Braise the lettuce, drain it, arrange it on a dish, and sprinkle with a few tablespoons hot Brown Butter.

LETTUCE AU GRATIN (*Laitues au Gratin*). Braise the lettuce, drain it, and arrange it on a buttered ovenproof serving dish on a bed of Mornay Sauce. Cover with more Mornay sauce, sprinkle with grated Parmesan cheese and melted butter, and brown in the oven.

PURÉE OF LETTUCE (*Purée de Laitue*). Braise the lettuce, drain it, and put it through a food mill or rub it through a sieve. Heat the purée in a buttered pan for a few minutes to dry it, thicken it with ¼ to ½ its volume of mashed potatoes, and bring it to the desired consistency with heavy cream. Off the fire, beat in a little butter.

LETTUCE IN CREAM (*Laitues à la Crème*). Blanch and shape the lettuce as for Braised Lettuce (above). Put the folded lettuce in a casserole, season with salt and a pinch of sugar, cover, and heat in a 325° oven for 10 minutes. Remove the casserole from the oven and pour in enough Velouté Sauce made with White Stock to cover the lettuce. Bring to a boil and cover with a piece of buttered paper cut to fit the pan with a hole cut in it to vent the steam. Cover the casserole, and braise in a 325° oven for 1½ hours. Remove from the oven, put the casserole over a low flame, and add about ¼ as much hot heavy cream as you have sauce in the pan, swirling the pan to blend it. Off the fire swirl in* 1 or 2 tablespoons butter.

CHICORY AND ESCAROLE (*Chicorée* and *Escarole*). These vegetables may be cooked exactly like lettuce, except that after blanching the leaves are chopped. In as much as they are quite flavorful in themselves, they may also be cooked like Spinach.

BRAISED BELGIAN ENDIVE (*Endives Belges Braisées*). This vegetable is not blanched. Trim the stems from 8 to 12 endives, remove hard outer leaves, wash under running water, and dry them. Butter a fireproof enamel casserole and add the endives in 1 or 2 layers, sprinkling them with 1 tablespoon lemon juice, ½ teaspoon salt, and 4 tablespoons melted butter. Heat the casserole briefly on the flame, cover it, and put it into a 325° oven for 10 minutes to draw moisture from the endives. Return to the stove, add ½ cup water, bring to the boil, and cover the endives with buttered paper with a hole cut in it to vent the steam. Cover the casserole, return to the 325° oven, and braise for 1 hour. Remove the endives, drain them, and put them on a serving dish. Strain the pan juices and reduce quickly to ½ cup. Off the fire, swirl in* 1 tablespoon butter, and pour the sauce over the endives.

✳ MUSHROOMS
(*Champignons*)

Mushrooms as a flavoring, a vegetable garnish, and a stuffing are as essential as onions to French cooking.

In France there is always a delightful variety of wild mushrooms to herald the seasons of the year—morels, cèpes, chanterelles, and many others. These all have distinctive flavors and perfumes, and it is great sport to set your teeth for a certain mushroom taste and be able to enjoy it. Wild mushrooms are not commercially important in the United States, but they are imported from various countries in dried and canned form.

The French began domesticating the mushroom during the reign of that hearty eater King Louis XIV. The cultivated mushroom—*Agaricus campestris* —is derived from the common field mushroom. In France cultivated mushrooms are called *champignons de couche*. The little button mushrooms are called *champignons de Paris*. These mushrooms, especially a white version, are the only mushrooms cultivated in the United States. They are grown in the dark—in caves or special houses—in the vicinity of most major cities. Leading mushroom-producing states are Pennsylvania and New York. Fresh mushrooms are most plentiful from November through April.

Buying mushrooms: Mushrooms are very perishable and show their age readily. Very fresh mushrooms are mostly white or creamy white (although there is a brown version that is liked on the West Coast), and they are moist, firm, and velvety in appearance. The cap will be tightly closed, showing no gills. As the mushroom ages, the skin darkens and the cap unfolds to reveal the mushroom's gills. As aging progresses, the skin of the mushroom becomes dry and brownish and the gills become brown and eventually black. The mushroom loses moisture and withers. However, quite fresh mushrooms may have brown spots due to bruising or water, and these spots do not affect flavor. Opened or brown mushroom that have not deteriorated too much are still good eating, sautéed or used as a stuffing or flavoring ingredient. The size of mushrooms has no relation to flavor; mushrooms with diameters of 1 inch and 3 inches can both be the same age.

Preparing mushrooms: When you get mushrooms home, handle them as little as possible and store them, covered, in the refrigerator. Use them as soon as possible and clean them just before using. Cut a thin slice from the hardened end of the stem. If the mushrooms are quite clean, simply wipe them with a damp paper towel. If they are flecked with compost or soil, wash them individually under running water, wiping them with a wet towel. Drain the mushrooms and dry them with a towel. Washing will bruise the mushroom flesh and they will begin to darken. If you are not going to cook them immediately, and you wish to keep them white, brush them with lemon juice. Domesticated mushrooms need not be peeled.

Just before cooking, cut the mushrooms in the desired shape. Mushrooms with the stems on are sliced vertically, top to bottom, cut vertically in quarters, or left whole if they are small. The stem is a little tougher than the cap and you may want to remove it. Cut it flush with the base of the unopened cap. If the cap has begun to open, simply pull out the stem. Reserve the stems for flavoring.

If you have more mushrooms on hand than you can safely store fresh, cook them as for Steamed Mushrooms or one of the other methods listed below, and store them. On a future occasion you may reheat them, or add them to a dish for the last few minutes of cooking. Or you may use them to make *Duxelles.*

One pound of fresh mushrooms contains about 20 mushrooms of medium size. One pound of sliced mushrooms equals about 5 cups; 1 pound of diced mushrooms equals about 4 cups. Mushrooms will cook down considerably, to ½ or less the original quantity.

Dried imported mushrooms should be washed and then soaked in luckwarm water or wine for 30 minutes to 1 hour to full reconstitute them.

Drain them, squeeze them dry, and use the liquid as a flavoring ingredient. Since the taste of wild mushrooms may be unexpectedly strong, a good trick is to mix and cook them with the blander cultivated variety.

Cooking mushrooms: There are a few tricks to cooking mushrooms, which can be best described under the following recipes. If mushrooms must be kept white for blanquettes or garnishing, they are cooked in an acid steam. Browning, however, adds to their flavor. In general they are cooked quickly, but if overcooked they lose flavor and become tough.

POACHED MUSHROOMS (*Champignons à Blanc*). This method of cooking keeps the mushrooms quite white. To ¼ cup water in a saucepan, add 1 tablespoon lemon juice, 1 tablespoon butter, and a pinch of salt. Bring to the boil and add ½ to ¾ pound of mushrooms. Cover and shake the pan to coat the mushrooms with the liquid, and boil for 5 minutes, shaking the pan occasionally. The mushrooms will cook in the steam. Drain the mushrooms, reduce the cooking liquid by ¾, and store it as Mushroom Essence (see Chapter 4).

You may also steam mushrooms by rubbing them with lemon juice and simmering them for 10 minutes in a covered pan with 1 tablespoon butter, a pinch of salt, and 2 or 3 tablespoons White Stock or Madeira wine.

GRILLED MUSHROOMS (*Champignons Grillés*). Use medium to large mushroom caps, brush with oil or Clarified Butter, season with salt and pepper, and place cup side up in the broiling pan. Broil for 5 minutes under a moderate flame, turn the mushrooms over, baste with oil or butter, and broil for 5 minutes more. Serve with Maître d'Hôtel Butter.

SAUTÉED MUSHROOMS (*Champignons Sautés*). Dry the mushrooms carefully, slice them, season with salt and pepper, and sauté them briskly in very hot Clarified Butter for 3 to 5 minutes, or until they are golden brown. Leave plenty of room in the pan, shake the pan to cook evenly and keep the mushrooms dry, and keep the heat as high as possible without burning the butter. This will prevent mushroom juices from collecting in the pan, and will prevent the mushrooms from steaming. Also, this allows the mushrooms to cook and brown before they become too dry and leathery. They should sizzle while cooking. Serve covered with butter from the pan and sprinkled with chopped parsley.

MUSHROOMS IN CREAM (*Champignons à la Crème*). Sauté ½ pound mushrooms until they are lightly browned. Lower the heat, add 2 tablespoons finely minced shallots or onions, and cook for 1 minute more. Sprinkle with

2 teaspoons flour, and cook, stirring, for 2 minutes to form a White Roux. Add fresh cream to barely cover the mushrooms, partially cover the pan, and boil rapidly for 4 or 5 minutes until the cream has reduced and thickened. Stir in a few tablespoons heavy cream and season to taste with salt and pepper. At the last moment, you may add a squeeze of lemon juice or 2 tablespoons Madeira wine, and boil for 1 minute more. Serve in Barquette or Tartlet shells, *Croustades, Vol-au-Vents,* or other pastry cases.

MUSHROOMS À LA LYONNAISE (*Champignons à la Lyonnaise*). Sauté the mushrooms in Clarified Butter. For the last few minutes of cooking, add a few tablespoons minced onion. Serve sprinkled with lemon juice, chopped parsley, and Brown Butter from the pan.

MUSHROOMS IN MADEIRA (*Champignons au Madère*). Sauté the mushrooms in Clarified Butter. Remove them from the pan and deglaze* the pan with Madeira wine. Reduce the wine by ½, and thicken it with Brown Sauce or Starch-Thickened Brown Stock. Return the mushrooms to the pan and cook for 1 or 2 minutes more. Off the fire stir in a little butter.

MUSHROOMS À LA POULETTE (*Champignons à la Poulette*). Sauté the mushrooms in Clarified Butter. Off the fire, add Poulette Sauce and serve sprinkled with chopped parsley.

STUFFED MUSHROOMS (*Champignons Farcis*). Break the stems out of medium to large mushroom caps of the same size. Brush with oil or melted butter, season with salt and pepper, put them in an oiled baking pan, cup side up, and bake in a 400° oven for 5 minutes. Take the pan from the oven and stuff the mushrooms with small mounds of *Duxelles* into which you have mixed a little Brown Sauce or Tomato Sauce and fresh breadcrumbs. Top the stuffing with dry breadcrumbs, sprinkle with butter, and brown in a hot oven or in the broiler.

You may also stuff the mushrooms with various *Salpicons* (see Chapter 4), sprinkled with dry breadcrumbs and butter and browned as above.

DUXELLES (*Duxelles*). This flavorful mushroom hash receives constant use as a flavoring for sauces, an ingredient in stuffings, and as a filling for stuffed vegetables. Dry *Duxelles* will keep for about 2 weeks in the refrigerator. See the recipe for dry and other duxelles mixtures in Chapter 4.

MARINATED MUSHROOMS (*Champignons Marinés*). See Chapter 5.

MUSHROOM PURÉE (*Purée de Champignons*). Put 1 pound cleaned mushrooms through the food mill or blender, or rub through a sieve. Squeeze dry in a towel, put the mushrooms into a saucepan with a little butter, and heat, stirring, for a few minutes to dry the mixture. Add ⅔ cup very thick Béchamel Sauce and ¼ cup heavy cream, season with salt, white pepper, and nutmeg, and cook, stirring, for a few minutes until the ingredients are well blended and the sauce reduced to the proper consistency. Remove from the fire and beat in 3 tablespoons butter.

✳ THE ONION FAMILY
(La Famille Des Oignons)

No great subtlety in cooking is possible without a complete understanding of the flavors and cooking characteristics of all the various members of the onion family. These include chives, green onions or scallions, Bermuda, Spanish, and grano-granex onions, red Italian onions, white onions, yellow globe onions, leeks, shallots, and garlic. We have our work cut out for us.

Onions are plentiful throughout the year, although some varieties are seasonal. We eat 10 to 12 pounds a year. California grows most of our onions, followed by New York, Texas, Oregon, Michigan, Idaho, and Colorado.

In general, the warmer the climate the milder the onion, and the more perishable it is. Mediterranean onions and garlic are very mild, compared to those grown in more northerly latitudes.

Most of our onions are marketed dry, that is, with their green tops removed. Chives, scallions, and leeks are marketed fresh. We will begin with the dry onions.

DRY ONIONS

Dry onions make up the bulk of our onion supply. These are onions that have been cured by allowing their outer layers of skin and soft necks to dry thoroughly in moving air, thereby protecting them from decay and leaving them fresh and juicy inside. The length of time onions will keep depends upon how well they are cured and their variety.

The flavor of a given variety of onions may vary according to the stage of maturity at which they are picked and their age. In general, the younger and fresher the onion the milder its flavor. I have arranged the onions listed below in order of increasing pungency with the understanding that this order may not always hold true.

Bermuda onions are mild, sweet, and juicy. They are squat and flattened, and measure from 2 up to 3½ inches in diameter. Most are yellow (some white and red). These onions are excellent raw in salads and sandwiches, and they may be stuffed and baked. Bermuda onions are becoming harder to find, but you should look for them during the spring. They do not keep well.

Spanish or *Valencia* onions are also mild, sweet, and juicy. They are globe-shaped and large, measuring about 3 inches in diameter. They may be white-, yellow-, or tan-skinned. Like Bermuda onions, they are used raw in salads and sandwiches, or stuffed and baked. They are mostly available from August through April. They keep a little longer than Bermudas.

Grano-granex are sweet, mild onions that are largely replacing Bermudas. They are round- to top-shaped, and measure from 2 to 4 inches in diameter. They are used for the same purposes as Bermuda and Spanish onions (their seed was imported from Spain). They do not keep well.

Red Italian or *Creole* onions are stronger than any of the above, but still mild enough to be enjoyed raw. They are oval with slightly flattened ends, and measure 2 to 2½ inches in diameter. Most are purplish-red (although there are white varieties, too). Their handsome color and pungent flavor make them an excellent raw salad or sandwich onion when thin-sliced, and a raw garnish when chopped. Almost all are grown in Louisiana. They keep excellently.

White onions, also called *White Boilers* or *Pearl* onions, are too pungent to eat raw. The smallest pearl onions are pickled as cocktail onions. Larger white onions, measuring from ¾ inch in diameter up, are the classic boiling onion for use as a vegetable, in *blanquettes,* fricassees, and other stews. In general these onions are oval with pointed ends, with flaky white to silvery skins. They are very compact and hold their shape when cooked in stews. They are fairly good keepers.

Globe onions are pungent and oniony. These are our standard onion, the yellow variety making up 75 percent of our onion supply. They are variously shaped from oval, to round, to flattened, and measure 2 to 2¼ inches in diameter. Although most are yellow, you will also find white-, red-, and tan-skinned varieties on the market. These full-flavored onions are the flavoring onions, indispensable in the vegetable *Mirepoix* that provides a foundation flavor for so many French dishes. As a cooking onion, they are more general in purpose than any other onion, and may be baked, stuffed, braised, grilled, sautéed, and deep-fried. They are excellent keepers and always available, and the least expensive onion of all.

Shallots are pungent and flavorful, but somehow more subtle than the standard globe onion. There is less sweetness hidden in their flavor, replaced with a hint of garlic, and they are sometimes regarded as a bridge between onions and garlic. Shallots form a small, brown-skinned bulb containing individual cloves similar to those of garlic. The peeled cloves are creamy with a purplish tinge. Shallots are very important in French cooking, and the odor of shallots, butter, and white wine simmering together is characteristic of the French kitchen. They are minced and used as a raw garnish (sprinkled over fresh tomatoes, or steak, for example) or as a flavoring for shallot butter. They are frequently used whole as a cooked garnish in stews and braised dishes, and they are minced and used to flavor cooked sauces and panned sauces, frequently along with onions. In this role, shallots are superior to onions in that they emulsify better and aid in holding quickly made pan sauces together. Shallots are more available in America than ever before (French cooks used to have to order by mail) and can be found in many supermarkets. They keep well and are available all year long.

Garlic is the strongest, most pungent member of the onion family. The bulbs are about 1½ inches in diameter, and they divide into individual cloves. Raw garlic must be used with great restraint. Cooking ameliorates its flavor and long-cooked garlic may be eaten with impunity. Whole garlic is everywhere available throughout the year.

Buying dry onions: All dry onions should be bright and shiny-looking, clean and hard, symmetrically shaped, with small dry necks and crackling-dry, papery outer skins. One way to test onions is to listen to them. Vigorously shake a bag of onions; if they are firm and dry they will rattle. Avoid misshaped onions, those with green sunburned spots, with woody necks (that may extend through the onion), with wet or soft necks or skins (indicating that decay has set in), or with sprouts. These qualifications apply to all dry onions.

Preparing dry onions: Store onions in a cool, dry, airy place and peel them just before using. To peel, cut a thin slice from the stem end and peel back the skin to the root. If the first layer of flesh has shriveled somewhat, peel this back also. If you are going to cook the onion whole, cut a very thin slice from the root end, leaving enough of the base to hold the layers of flesh together. With a sharp pointed knife cut a deep cross in the root end to facilitate the cooking.

When cutting onions use a very sharp knife to avoid mashing cells and squeezing out the juice or splattering it in your eyes. To slice the onion, leave the root on and cut a thin slice from one side to steady the onion while slicing. Slice crosswise, from stem end to root end.

To dice the onion, leave the root on and cut the onion in two lengthwise, from stem to root. Place the onion cut side down and make vertical cuts almost to the root without cutting through the root. Hold the knife horizontal to the cutting board and make horizontal cuts almost to the root. Finally, slice the onion crosswise, stem to root, and the dice will fall free.

Peeling a great number of onions can be tedious. To speed this process, drop the onions in boiling water for 10 to 15 seconds. Cut a thin slice from the root and the stem end and slip off the skin.

Onions used to flavor brown stocks or sauces need not be peeled. Wash them clean and use them sliced or whole. Brown onion skins will help give a good brown color to the liquid. (To intensify color, you may also cut the onion in two and hold it over a flame to char it. Much of the charred color will be the result of the sugar in the onion caramelizing in the heat, an excellent source of rich brown color.)

Blanching dry onions: Strong or old onions, used as a vegetable, may be blanched to tame their flavor. Drop them, with their skins on, into boiling salted water and boil for up to 5 minutes. Drain, cool in cold water, cut thin slices from the ends, and slip off the skins.

Cooking dry onions: All onions contain a sulfurous compound that gives the onion family its oniony flavor and pungent, sometimes burning taste. This compound is very volatile, that is, it becomes gaseous when heated and evaporates rapidly. After this compound has been cooked away, all onions become mild. They also become sweet to the taste, which is evidence of the large amount of sugar they contain. The flavor of the sugar in onions can be further developed depending upon how they are cooked. Thus, there are two stages in onion cookery—an early stage when you are manipulating the characteristically pungent raw onion flavor, and a later stage (which you may or may not progress to) when you are manipulating the flavor of the sugar.

GREEN ONIONS

These members of the onion family are used fresh like any other green vegetable.

Chives are the mildest members of the onion family. Only the long, slim, tubular green leaves are eaten. They are too mild to be cooked without losing their flavor, although they may be warmed in a dish just before serving, or cooked briefly with eggs. Usually they are chopped and sprinkled raw over or in a dish. They are included as one of the classic *Fines Herbes*.

Scallions are sweet, mild onions with the most delicate flavor of any onion but chives. The plant is long, slender, and bulbless, with a white portion extending from 2 to 3 inches above the root and shading into light and darker green leaves. Scallions are produced from bulbless varieties, or from white onions that are harvested before the bulb has formed. They are eaten raw in sandwiches or sliced crosswise in salads or as a garnish. They may also be cooked very gently and served as a vegetable.

Leeks have a much lustier onion flavor than scallions, but they are milder than globe onions. They resemble scallions in shape, but their cylindrical stem is much heavier and thicker, measuring up to 1 inch in diameter or more. They are white for 2 to 3 inches above their root end, shading off into broad, flat, dark green leaves. Leeks are an important vegetable in French cuisine, and are considered by many to be indispensable to cooking. They are used as a flavoring, frequently along with onions, and in soups, and they are braised and served as a vegetable. Unfortunately, leeks are often difficult to find in American stores, and are inordinately expensive.

Buying green onions: Both scallions and leeks should have fresh green tops, with crisp stems that are white for 2 to 3 inches upward from the root. Bulbs and white stems should be young-looking and tender, without longitudinal fibers. Avoid scallions or leeks with wilted or yellowing tops, or with flabby, tough, fibrous stems. Chives, of course, are bought growing in pots and are always fresh.

Preparing green onions: Chives are left to grow in their pots, and are cut up just before using. Scallions and leeks should be kept moist in the refrigerator. To prepare scallions, simply wash them, remove coarse or wilted green leaves, trim the tops and remove coarse or wilted green leaves, and trim away the root. Slice them with a sharp knife, using the white part only or both white and green. Or tie them, whole, in bundles for cooking as a vegetable.

To prepare leeks, trim root and leaves as for green onions. Leeks, above all vegetables, gather quantities of soil among their leaves while growing and they must be carefully washed. Using a sharp-pointed knife, make an incision through the middle of the leek just above the root end. Cut upwards the entire length of the leek, slicing it lengthwise through the middle of the stem. If the leek is large, give it a quarter turn and make another lengthwise cut, dividing the stem of the leek in quarters that are firmly attached at the root end. Carefully separate the leaves and wash under forcefully running water, flushing out the soil hidden between the leaves. If necessary, soak the leeks in cold salted water, agitating them to flush out soil. (If you leave the leeks in water too long, their cut ends will begin to curl.) Tie the leeks in bundles for braising as a vegetable, use whole leeks for flavoring stocks, or slice them for soups.

510 FRENCH COOKING FOR THE AMERICAN TABLE

Blanching green onions: Only old, strong-flavored leeks may require blanching. Plunge them whole into boiling salted water, boil for up to 5 minutes, drain, and plunge into cold water to stop the cooking.

Cooking green onions: Scallions and leeks are boiled or braised like any other green vegetable.

SAUTÉED ONIONS (*Oignons Sautés*). Peel and slice or dice the onions. Put them in a skillet or sauté pan with a generous amount of hot Clarified Butter, and shake the pan to settle the onions. Cook over a moderate flame, shaking the pan and turning the onions with a spatula so they will cook evenly. The onions should sizzle while cooking. During the first 2 or 3 minutes the onions emit a strong raw onion odor and the dice or rings become translucent although their centers are still crisp. In the next 2 or 3 minutes the raw odor mellows and a sweetish aroma arises as the sugar content of the onion, formerly concealed by the volatile oils, makes itself known. The onion pieces also become soft all the way through and wilted in appearance, and they will begin to color. Shortly thereafter, as their water is cooked off, the onions brown swiftly and exude a sweet, caramel fragrance resulting from the caramelization of their sugars.

Thus you have your choice of cooked onion flavors and textures, ranging from onion pieces with (1) a still-pungent flavor and crisp, crunchy centers; (2) a delicate, sweet taste and juicy, tender centers; or with (3) a heavier brown-caramel-sweet flavor and firmer, chewier centers.

Sautéed onion rings are used as a vegetable garnish for sautéed foods, or in onion soup. Sautéed onion dice are used as a flavoring, and if sautéed until brown will give a good color to stocks and sauces.

BOILED ONIONS (*Oignons Bouillis*). Peel small white boiling onions. Cut a thin slice from the neck and a very thin slice from the root end so the onions will hold together. Pierce a cross into the root end to aid in cooking the centers. Drop the onions into boiling salted water. For a stronger flavor, use water just to cover and cook with the cover on. For a milder flavor, use plenty of water and cook with the cover off. Boil the onions for 20 to 25 minutes, until tender. Drain and dry in a pot over low heat. Serve with salt, pepper, and melted butter.

WHITE-GLAZED ONIONS (*Oignons Glacés à Blanc*). Peel small white boiling onions to make 2 cups. Put them in a saucepan with 1 cup boiling White Stock, 2 tablespoons butter, and 2 teaspoons sugar. Cover and simmer for 30 to 40 minutes, or until the onions are tender and the liquid has almost entirely cooked away. Uncover, turn up the heat, and continue cooking, shaking the pan, until the liquid has cooked away and the onions are well glazed.

BROWN-GLAZED ONIONS (*Oignons Glacés à Brun*). Peel small yellow or white onions to make 2 cups. Put them in a saucepan with 2 tablespoons butter and a good pinch of powdered sugar. Cover the pan and simmer the onions in the butter for 10 to 15 minutes, shaking the pan so they cook evenly, until they are lightly browned. Add ½ cup Brown Stock (which you have reduced from 1 cup), and sprinkle with 2 teaspoons sugar. Cover the pan and cook gently for 20 to 30 minutes, or until the onions are tender and the liquid is almost entirely reduced, and proceed as for White-Glazed Onions (above).

ONIONS IN CREAM (*Oignons à la Crème*). Prepare White-Glazed Onions (above), taking care to keep the onions very white. When the onions are barely tender and the liquid entirely reduced, add ½ cup thick Béchamel Sauce mixed with ¼ cup fresh cream. Simmer the onions in the sauce for 5 minutes. Season to taste with salt and white pepper, and serve sprinkled with chopped parsley.

BRAISED ONIONS (*Oignons Braisés*). Use Spanish, Bermuda, or grano-granex onions of medium size or larger. You may stuff them as for Stuffed Onions (below). Place them in a pan with enough Starch-Thickened Brown Stock to cover them by ⅓ or ½, bring to a boil, cover, and put them into a 350° oven. Braise the onions for 30 to 45 minutes, basting them frequently with their braising liquid, until they are just barely tender. Uncover and continue cooking, basting frequently, until the onions are brown. Remove the onions to a serving dish and quickly reduce the braising liquid. Off the fire, swirl in* a few tablespoons butter, season to taste with salt and pepper and a few tablespoons Madeira or sherry wine. Strain the sauce over the onions.

STUFFED ONIONS (*Oignons Farcis*). Use Spanish, Bermuda, or grano-granex onions of medium size or larger. Peel them, cut a very thin slice from the root end, and cut off ¼ of the onion at the stem ends. Blanch the onions in boiling salted water for 5 minutes, cool them in cold water, and drain them. Remove their centers, leaving 2 layers of onion as a case. Chop the centers finely, mix with ingredients suggested in recipes below, and stuff the onions with this mixture. Braise the stuffed onions as for Braised Onions (above). Just before serving, sprinkle the onions with dry white breadcrumbs and butter, and brown in a hot oven.

STUFFED ONIONS À LA PARISIENNE (*Oignons Farcis à la Parisienne*). Stuff the onions with a mixture of chopped onion, *Duxelles,* and chopped cooked ham. Braise the onions. Just before serving, sprinkle with grated Parmesan and butter and brown in the oven.

STUFFED ONIONS À L'ITALIENNE (*Oignons Farcis à l'Italienne*). Stuff the onions with a mixture of chopped onion, Risotto, and chopped cooked ham. Braise the onions. Just before serving, sprinkle with grated Parmesan cheese and butter and brown in the oven.

STUFFED ONIONS À LA CATALANE (*Oignons Farcis à la Catalane*). Stuff the onions with a mixture of chopped onion, Risotto, chopped pimentos simmered in oil, and chopped hard-cooked eggs. Braise the onions. Just before serving, sprinkle with dry white breadcrumbs and butter, and brown in the oven.

Onions may also be stuffed with mashed potatoes or spinach. They may also be filled with various soufflé mixtures based on cheese, spinach, tomatoes, and other vegetables (see Chapter 7).

BAKED ONIONS (*Oignons Rôtis au Four*). Use Spanish, Bermuda, or grano-granex onions of medium size. Trim the root ends slightly, but leave the necks and skins on. Place them in a buttered pan and bake slowly in a 325° oven for 1½ hours, or until soft and tender. Serve with salt, pepper, and butter.

DEEP-FRIED ONIONS (*Oignons Frits*). Peel and slice onions ¼ inch thick. Punch out the slices to form individual onion rings, dip the rings in milk, and drain them. Shake the rings in a bag with salt, pepper, and flour and deep-fry in 380° oil until the onions are browned. Drain, dry, and serve immediately with salt.

DEEP-FRIED ONIONS IN BATTER (*Oignons en Fritots*). Peel and slice the onions ¼ inch thick. Punch out the slices to form individual rings, dredge with flour, dip in a Batter for deep-frying vegetables, and deep-fry, a few at a time, in 380° oil until the batter is golden. Drain, dry, and serve immediately with salt.

ONION PURÉE (*Purée d'Oignons* or *Purée Soubise*). This is identical with Soubise Sauce (see Chapter 4).

BOILED LEEKS (*Poireaux Bouillis*). Trim, clean, and tie the leeks in bunches with soft string. Put into boiling salted water and boil for about 40 minutes, until the leeks are tender when pierced with a knife. Drain, dry, and serve with salt, pepper, and melted butter (*à l'Anglaise*), or with Hollandaise, Mousseline, or Cream Sauce.

BRAISED LEEKS (*Poireaux Braisés*). Clean and trim the leeks so they are about ½ white, ½ green. Place them in layers in an oval casserole, add enough water to cover them by ¼, sprinkle with a little salt and pepper, and add ½ tablespoon butter per leek. Bring to the boil, cover the casserole, and simmer for about 40 minutes or until the leeks are tender when pierced with a knife. Uncover the casserole and boil quickly if necessary to reduce the liquid to ¼ cup. Place the casserole, uncovered, in a 325° oven and cook the leeks, basting frequently with butter and their braising liquid, for 10 minutes more or until they have begun to turn golden. Turn the leeks in the remaining liquid and serve sprinkled with chopped parsley.

LEEKS IN CREAM (*Poireaux à la Crème*). Use the white part only of leeks. Put them in a saucepan with ½ tablespoon butter per leek, season with salt and white pepper, cover, and simmer very slowly for 20 minutes. Add to the pan enough light cream to barely cover the leeks, cover, and simmer for 30 minutes more or until the leeks are tender. Place the leeks in a serving dish. Add a few tablespoons heavy cream to the pan juices. Cook, stirring, for 1 minute, and correct the seasoning. Off the fire swirl in* 1 or 2 tablespoons butter and pour over the leeks.

LEEKS AU GRATIN (*Poireaux au Gratin*). Use the white part only of leeks. Blanch for 5 minutes in boiling salted water. Drain, dry the leeks in a sauté pan, season with salt and white pepper, add ½ tablespoon butter per leek, cover, and simmer slowly for about 45 minutes or until the leeks are tender. Place the leeks in an ovenproof serving dish, sprinkle them with grated Parmesan cheese and melted butter, and brown in the oven.

LEEKS MORNAY (*Poireaux Mornay*). Cook the leeks as for Leeks au Gratin (above). Place them in an ovenproof serving dish on a bed of Mornay Sauce, pour more of the sauce over them, sprinkle with grated Parmesan cheese and melted butter, and brown in the oven.

SCALLIONS or GREEN ONIONS (*Ciboules*). These may be prepared like leeks (above). However, they are much more delicate in flavor and texture, and require much less cooking.

✳ PEAS
(Pois)

Peas are one of the most perishable of vegetables. Their sugar begins to change to starch the moment they are picked, and only extraordinary care and expedition can get them to market with their sweetness relatively intact. As a result, almost all of the 6 pounds of peas we eat per person each year are canned or frozen, and fresh peas are now considered a minor vegetable. Nevertheless, I am duty bound to tell you how to choose and prepare any fresh local peas that may fall into your hands. They are well worth going out of your way to get.

Buying peas: Buy only peas in the pod. The pods should be a bright, light green, shiny, yet velvety to the touch. Break open a pod; it snaps crisply. The peas inside are well developed and almost fill the pod, or fill it without crowding. The raw pea is tender and tastes sweet, and tasting a pea is your best test of proper maturity and freshness. Avoid dark green pods that are flat and flabby (immature), or pods that are light-colored, speckled gray, distended, and filled to bursting with large peas (overmature), or pods that are yellowish or whitish (stale). You will obtain about 1 cup of shelled peas for every ¾ to 1 pound of peas in the pod.

When buying canned or frozen peas, which must often be the case, let taste and experience be your guide. Canned or frozen peas can be excellent when they are carefully processed at the peak of their freshness. In fact, canned peas are served in some of the finest Paris restaurants when fresh peas are inferior or out of season. Remember, different brands and styles of canned or frozen peas are not all the same. Some are excellent, some are poor. The most devastating way to test these foods is to buy and cook two different brands or varieties in different pots at the same time, and to taste-test the result. Next time you serve the vegetable, taste the winner along with another brand or variety. Continue in this manner until you have found the taste and texture you like best.

Preparing peas: Keep peas in their pods. Wrap them in plastic to keep them moist and store in the refrigerator, but use them as soon as possible. Shell the peas just before cooking. Peas are not soaked in water, but for some recipes they may be blanched.

Blanching peas: Drop peas in rapidly boiling salted water and boil, uncovered, for 5 to 10 minutes until the peas are tender but not quite fully cooked. Test by tasting a few. Immediately plunge the peas into cold water, and drain them as soon as they are cool.

Cooking peas: Peas are boiled, uncovered, in lots of boiling salted water, or they are blanched and stewed. The large amounts of water used in boiling or blanching cooks the peas quickly and helps retain their fresh green color.

The following recipes can be adapted to frozen and canned peas. Just remember, frozen peas are already blanched. Thaw them until they are loose, and cook them in very little water until they are cooked (for boiled peas), or until they are completely thawed and heated through (for peas that will receive further cooking). Canned peas are already cooked. Drain their liquid into a saucepan and boil it until it is almost entirely reduced. Add the peas, cover the pan, and toss them in the liquid to heat them through. Canned peas cannot be successfully cooked with fresh ingredients. Instead, cook the fresh ingredients separately and add the canned peas at the last moment.

BOILED PEAS, ENGLISH STYLE (*Petits Pois à l'Anglaise*). Drop the peas into a large amount of rapidly boiling salted water. Boil the peas for 5 minutes (for very young, small, tender peas) to 15 minutes (for large, mature peas), or until the peas are tender to the teeth but not mushy. Drain the peas, put them back into the saucepan, and toss over the fire to evaporate surface moisture. Serve with butter passed separately.

PEAS IN CREAM (*Petits Pois à la Crème*). Prepare Boiled Peas, English Style (above), leaving them slightly undercooked. Cover the drained and dried peas with boiling heavy cream, and simmer until the cream is reduced by ½. Season to taste with salt and a little powdered sugar. Just before serving, stir in 1 or 2 tablespoons fresh cream.

PEAS IN BUTTER (*Petits Pois au Beurre*). Prepare Boiled Peas, English Style (above). Season with a generous pinch of powdered sugar, shake the peas, and off the fire add 3 tablespoons butter cut in small pieces for every 2 cups peas.

PEAS WITH MINT (*Petits Pois à la Menthe*). Prepare Peas in Butter (above), but add a handful of fresh mint leaves to their cooking water. Place the peas in a serving dish and garnish them with mint leaves that you have parboiled for 1 or 2 minutes.

PEAS, FRENCH STYLE (*Petits Pois à la Française*). You may prepare this dish for cooking several hours in advance. Put into a saucepan 4 tablespoons melted butter and 2 cups fresh peas. Add 6 or 8 very small white onions (or the white tips of 6 or 8 scallions). Sprinkle with 2 teaspoons sugar and ½ teaspoon salt. Mix thoroughly. In the center of the peas place 2 sprigs of parsley and 2 sprigs of fresh chervil (or 2 pinches of dried chervil) tied in cheesecloth. Shake the pan to settle the ingredients, and cover them with 1 head of Boston lettuce, quartered. Cover and keep cool. When ready to cook, sprinkle with ¼ cup water. Cover the pan, bring the liquid to the boil, and simmer slowly for 25 to 30 minutes, or until the peas are tender but not mushy. Remove the parsley and chervil. Shred the lettuce, return it to the pan, and mix it thoroughly with the peas and onions. If too much liquid remains in the pan, reduce it to almost nothing by shaking the pan over a hot fire. Just before serving, mix in 1 tablespoon fresh butter off the fire.

PEAS À LA BONNE FEMME (*Petits Pois à la Bonne Femme*). Lightly brown in butter ½ cup diced and blanched salt pork or bacon, and 6 or 8 very small white onions. Remove the fat and onions, sprinkle in 1 tablespoon flour, and cook for a few moments to form a blond Roux. Add ¾ cup White Stock and cook, stirring, until the sauce thickens. Return the pork fat and the onions to the pan, add 2 cups fresh peas and 2 teaspoons sugar, and mix thoroughly. Tie 3 sprigs of parsley together with string and bury in the peas. Cover the pan, bring the liquid to the boil, and simmer slowly for 25 to 30 minutes, or until the peas are tender but not mushy. Remove the parsley. If the sauce is too thin, reduce it by shaking the pan over a hot fire.

PEAS À LA FLAMANDE (*Petits Pois à la Flamande*). Prepare 2 cups Carrots à la Vichy. When the carrots are half cooked, add 2 cups fresh peas and finish cooking together. Off the fire, add 4 tablespoons butter cut in small pieces.

PURÉE OF PEAS (*Purée de Pois Frais* or *Purée Clamart* or *Purée St. Germain*). Boil the peas in enough lightly salted water to cover them, adding a good pinch of sugar and a few lettuce leaves and parsley sprigs to the water. Drain the peas, put them through a food mill or rub them through a sieve. Reduce the cooking water almost entirely and add it to the purée. Finally, beat in 4 tablespoons butter for every 2 cups purée.

✳ SWEET PEPPERS
(*Piments Doux*)

Coming as it does from a fiery family, the sweet pepper surprises us with its diffident flavor. It has a mild, refreshing pungency when raw, and a mellow, pleasantly bitter quality when cooked. Because of their shape, the little things are stuffed with all kinds of foods, but their flavor and texture are also welcome in stews and salads.

Florida, Texas, and Mexico grow most of our fall-winter-spring peppers, California and New Jersey deluge the market in late summer, and there is a good supply on hand throughout the year.

Buying sweet peppers: Sweet peppers are bell- or barrel-shaped. Most are sold when green, but some varieties will turn a brilliant red or yellow if left to mature, without much change in taste. Look for peppers with a medium to dark green color or bright red or yellow color that are glassy-looking, with thick firm sides. They should feel heavy for their size. Avoid peppers with thin sides, or peppers that are flabby, or peppers with watery, sunken, blisterlike spots. Peppers that are pale in color, with soft seeds, are immature.

Preparing sweet peppers: Peppers have a relatively tough skin that is the very devil to remove. You must spear the pepper on a fork and hold it over a flame until the skin scorches, blisters, and blackens before you can peel it off. Or you can leave the skin on. In this case, cut the stem from the top and carefully remove all the seeds and the thick white ribs inside, and blanch the pepper before cooking.

Blanching sweet peppers: Plunge the emptied peppers into boiling salted water, boil for 10 minutes, plunge into cold water to stop the cooking, and drain.

Cooking sweet peppers: Sweet peppers present no special cooking problems. When braised, a preliminary blanching will preserve more of their green color.

GRILLED SWEET PEPPERS (*Piments Doux Grillés*). Empty the peppers and put them into the broiler under a moderate flame. Cook, turning the peppers, until their skins are scorched on all sides. Peel, cut into julienne,* and dress with Vinaigrette Sauce.

SWEET PEPPERS AU GRATIN (*Piments Doux au Gratin*). Empty and peel the peppers, cutting them in quarters if they are large. Stew gently, covered, in butter until they are soft. Put them in an ovenproof dish on a bed of Mornay Sauce to which you have added 1 tablespoon chopped and lightly sautéed onion. Arrange the peppers in the dish, cover them with Mornay Sauce, sprinkle with grated Parmesan cheese and melted butter, and brown in the oven.

SWEET PEPPER RAGOUT À L'ESPAGNOLE (*Ragoût de Piments Doux à l'Espagnole*). In a saucepan, simmer ½ onion, sliced, in olive oil for a few minutes, until wilted. Sprinkle in 1 tablespoon flour and cook, stirring, for 2 minutes more. Add 4 peppers, peeled, seeded, and cut in quarters, and season with salt and a pinch of red pepper. Add 1 clove garlic, crushed, 1 cup Brown Stock, and 2 tablespoons Tomato Purée. Stir to blend well and simmer, covered, for 30 minutes or until the peppers are tender. Serve sprinkled with chopped parsley.

STUFFED SWEET PEPPERS (*Piments Doux Farcis*). Peel and seed peppers. Or leave skins on, remove seeds, and blanch for 10 minutes. Fill them halfway with half-cooked Rice Pilaf. Pack the peppers in a saucepan, half cover them with Brown Stock, cover, and simmer slowly until the peppers are tender and the rice is fully cooked.

Peppers can be stuffed with a variety of well-seasoned Forcemeats (see Chapter 4). However, the stuffing should be light and should fill the pepper only partway to allow for expansion. Heavy, soggy fillings of any kind are unpleasant.

SWEET PEPPER PURÉE (*Purée de Piments Doux*). Remove the seeds from sweet red peppers and chop peppers coarsely. Put the peppers in a saucepan, and for each 1 cup chopped pepper add 5 tablespoons raw rice. Add enough Brown Stock to come ½ inch over the top of the peppers, cover, and simmer for about 30 minutes until the peppers are tender and the rice is cooked. Put the peppers and rice through a food mill, or rub them through a sieve, or purée in a blender. Cook over a low fire for a few minutes to dry the purée, and stir in 1 tablespoon butter per cup.

❋ *POTATOES*
(*Pommes de Terre*)

One October afternoon I ate a potato cooked by boy campers on an outing near Aberdeen, Idaho. The potato was from a mature crop of Russet Burbanks, fresh-dug that morning. The boys had flung a bushel of these into the ashes of a hickory fire that had warmed us through the chill afternoon.

My potato had baked for an hour and a half. It was fished out of the ashes on a spade, brushed with a towel, and presented to me hot as a coal. Fortunately I was wearing thick wool gloves.

Boy campers eat mostly with their hands, and I ate as they did, wrapping my gloved hands around my potato and using my teeth to tear open one end. The steam gushed forth, and I sat there warming my hands by squeezing the potato while inhaling the delicious steam as the potato dried in its own heat. Soon it was ready to eat.

Butter went into the open end, and salt. As the butter melted and ran down into the crushed insides, I bit into that potato as I would an apple. The skin crunched and crackled in my mouth to produce three intermingled flavors—the odd, dry taste of the wood ash that still crusted the skin; the elemental taste of carbon in the blackened flakes of the surface; and the dominant taste of the inner layers, rich, nutty, aromatic as the crust of fresh-baked bread. But this was not all! The mealy flesh of the potato, yellow-streaked with butter and alive with salt, became a kind of fluffy *sauce* for the main course of crusty skin. Never did a sauce more aptly fit a dish! I ate and ate. The sound of the skin crackled in my ears as I chewed, fluffy bits of white potato flecked my lips, the warm, salty butter ran down my chin. I suddenly realized that this was the best baked potato I had ever eaten, and that all the boys had fallen silent, watching me.

All baked potatoes should be cooked by boys in the ashes of a hickory fire near Aberdeen, Idaho, on a cold afternoon in October when the Russet Burbanks are being dug.

The potato is our most delicate vegetable. Its bland flavor is at the mercy of heat, rainfall, sunlight, minerals in the soil, fertilizers, pesticides, maturity, age, and storage conditions. Also the flavor of potatoes varies remarkably from variety to variety, and there are dozens of varieties to choose from, many of them all but impossible to identify. If, after running this gamut, you can secure a fine potato, you can still ruin it easily in cooking. Potato cookery allows no mistakes. In spite of all these pitfalls, potatoes account for one-third of all the vegetables we eat (an average of one medium potato per person per day), so it is important that we do our utmost to choose and cook them wisely.

When cooked, potatoes reveal themselves to be either waxy or mealy (floury). Waxiness in a cooked potato is seen as a glistening, pasty, translucent appearance of the cut surface. The French have some very waxy potatoes, such as the *Dutch yellow long,* which are chosen for potato salads and other recipes where the potatoes must hold together and remain firm when cooked. In America, waxy potatoes are rather casually divided into fryers, boilers, and general-purpose potatoes. Theoretically, fryers are the waxiest and are so called because they will hold together when boiled and subsequently sautéed in fat. Boilers are waxy potatoes that are firm enough so that their flesh will not slough off when boiled. General-purpose potatoes, which make up most of our supply, are supposed to be good for everything, which is tantamount to saying that they excel at nothing. Another class of potato, the immature, or "new," potato, red or white, is waxy irregardless of whether it might ultimately become mealy if allowed to mature.

At the opposite extreme is the mealy (floury) potato. It has a dryer, less soggy flesh, and close inspection will show the cooked flesh to be loose and granular, almost crystalline in consistency, reflecting light like crushed diamonds. Potatoes filling this description have a high specific gravity. I know a scientific gourmet who tests his potatoes by plunging them into a solution of one pound of salt dissolved in a gallon of water. He will eat only those that sink to the bottom.

This mealy potato is usually described as a baking potato. In general, if it is truly mealy, it is the best potato to use for baking, mashing, sautéing, deep-frying, steaming, and even boiling if it is boiled in its skin or boiled gently. This is true because, in general, the mealier the potato the better it will taste. And do not think for a moment that the differences in taste between types or varieties of potatoes are minor. They are, in fact, startling.

Mealiness in potatoes is very variable. Some varieties tend to be mealy, and remain relatively mealy wherever they are grown. Some varieties are basically waxy, but become mealy if grown in certain states. Although there is variation from year to year, some of America's mealiest potatoes are the Russet Burbank grown in Idaho and Washington, the White Rose grown in Idaho, the Irish Cobbler from Wisconsin, the Green Mountain from New York, and the Sebago from Washington. With the exception of Sebago, all these varieties originated in the nineteenth century, which is another way of saying that some of the best potatoes are not the new varieties that are now so widely grown.

Except for the Russet Burbank, identifying potatoes in your supermarket is next to impossible. The varieties are kept secret. Growers and packers have concluded you don't know or care about varieties, and they're probably right. Not knowing, however, makes it impossible to reward the best potato varieties with your patronage and discourages the growing of good-eating potatoes in favor of easy-to-grow ones.

The Idaho Russet Burbank is available most of the year and is easy to identify. The potato is long and russet-colored. The skin has a network of fine, raised lines. The bags are marked "Grown in Idaho," and the potato costs more. The Russet Burbank flourishes in Idaho's volcanic soils, and effective publicity has practically made it Idaho's own, although this variety from Washington State is equally mealy and good-tasting. Unfortunately, this potato's reputation as a baker has obscured its excellence for mashing, boiling, steaming, sautéing and French-frying. You should try it all of these ways.

Identifying other varieties is difficult even for experts. You can see whether the potato is a long or round variety, and whether it is red, white, or russet-skinned. The potato bag will tell you the origin and grade, almost invariably "U.S. No. 1." Beyond this even the produce manager may have no information. However, based on the volume of production in the major potato-producing states, chances are good you will be getting mealy potatoes if you buy: round whites from Wisconsin, upper New York State, or Colorado; reds from North Dakota; russets from Idaho or Washington.

The only way to be sure of potato quality is to cook and eat the potatoes. Buy bags of two different growers and states at the same time, cook some from each bag, and taste them at the same time. You'll often be amazed at the differences in taste, and how much you'll prefer one over the other. Then compare the winner with another potato grower's offering. Your family will soon be enjoying their potatoes more than ever before.

Buying potatoes: Look for hard, well-shaped potatoes with clean, intact skins. (New potatoes have thin skins that are normally somewhat tattered.) Avoid soft, shriveled, or sprouting potatoes. Also avoid potatoes with a green color caused by exposure to sunlight or artificial light in the store; these potatoes will be bitter-tasting. You will not be able to detect hollow heart, a dark-walled cavity in the center of a potato, but you can just cut it out. It is also difficult to detect freezing in the store, but if you find a dark ring in the flesh of the potato when you cut it across, the potato has been frozen and will have poor flavor. Store potatoes in a dry, cool place, in the dark to prevent greening.

Preparing potatoes: Potatoes are simply washed and cooked in their skins, or peeled and cut into various shapes. Peeled potatoes will darken upon exposure to the air, so they should be kept in cold salted water until they are cooked. Do not keep them in the water for too long, however, or some of their flavor will be lost.

Cooking potatoes: Potatoes are boiled, steamed, mashed, baked, stuffed, braised or scalloped, sautéed, grilled, and fried. I will discuss the problems posed by these cooking methods in the recipes to follow.

BOILED POTATOES (*Pommes de Terre à l'Anglaise*). Boil the potatoes whole and unpeeled, whole and peeled, or peeled and cut into pieces of the same size. Drop them in boiling salted water, putting the largest potatoes in first, and cook at a gentle boil. Large whole potatoes may take 45 minutes to cook; smaller pieces may cook in much less time. Potatoes are done when they are just soft in the center, which you can discover by probing with a thin skewer. Do not overcook, or they will become watery. Drain and dry the potatoes by returning them to the pot and shaking them gently over the flame. Serve immediately with salt, pepper, and butter. (Potatoes boiled in their skins are called *pommes de terre à l'anglaise en robe de chambre*.)

PARSLIED POTATOES (*Pommes de Terre Persillées*). Boil the potatoes, dry them, roll them in hot butter, season with salt and pepper, and serve sprinkled with chopped parsley.

STEAMED POTATOES (*Pommes de Terre à la Vapeur*). This is one of the simplest and finest ways to cook potatoes. Fine-flavored dry, floury baking potatoes can be used without the sloughing off of their flesh that sometimes happens when they are boiled. Also, steaming retains more of a fine potato's delicate flavor. They are less watery.

Peel the potatoes and cut them in the shape of small eggs. Put them in the tray of a vegetable steamer, cover, and steam for 30 to 40 minutes, or until soft and tender throughout. Salt lightly, and serve with salt, pepper, and melted butter. Steamed potatoes, like boiled potatoes, are also called potatoes à l'anglaise.

MASHED POTATOES OR POTATO PURÉE (*Purée de Pommes de Terre* or *Purée Parmentier*). Take 2¼ to 2½ pounds of potatoes, which will weigh about 2 pounds when peeled. Peel them, slice them thickly or quarter them, and boil them as for Boiled Potatoes (above). Drain and dry them, and put them through a potato ricer or press them vertically through a coarse sieve without rubbing them across the mesh. This "ricing" of the potatoes will greatly improve their texture. Put the potato (you should have about 4 cups) in a saucepan over a moderate fire and beat until the potato is smooth and begins to stick to the bottom of the pan. Beat in 4 to 6 tablespoons butter (1 to 1½ tablespoons per cup of purée). Next beat in about ½ cup boiling milk or cream, or enough to make the purée as soft or firm as you choose. Season to taste with salt and white pepper and serve immediately.

POTATOES AU GRATIN (*Pommes de Terre au Gratin*). Prepare Mashed Potatoes (above). Spread the potato in a buttered ovenproof serving dish, sprinkle with browned breadcrumbs, grated Parmesan cheese, and melted butter, and brown in the oven.

POTATO CROQUETTES (*Croquettes à Pommes*). Prepare Mashed Potatoes (above) up until the point when the potato pulp is drying in the pan. Season with 1 teaspoon salt, white pepper, and a little nutmeg. Beat in 3 tablespoons butter. Off the fire thoroughly blend in 2 eggs and 2 egg yolks, lightly beaten. Spread the mixture on a buttered pan to cool quickly, and brush its surface with melted butter to prevent drying. When the mixture has cooled, shape small quantities of the mixture to form cylindrical shapes the size of wine corks, pear shapes, balls, or small cakes. Coat the croquettes with egg and breadcrumbs *à l'Anglaise,** and deep-fry in 375° fat until golden.

DUCHESS POTATOES (*Pommes de Terre Duchesse*). Prepare Potato Croquette mixture (above). Allow the mixture to cool and shape on a floured board to form small loaves, patties, cakes or cork shapes and place these on a buttered baking sheet. Or use the mixture while still warm and pipe it through a pastry bag to form a decorative border or rosette shapes on a buttered serving platter. Brush the mixture with beaten egg and slowly brown in a 400° oven or quickly in the broiler, taking care that the top does not burn.

DAUPHINE POTATOES (*Pommes de Terre Dauphine*). Prepare Potato Croquette mixture (above). To this mixture, add ½ as much unsweetened Cream Puff Paste (see Chapter 14). Shape and deep-fry as for Potato Croquettes, with or without an *à l'Anglaise** coating.

LORETTE POTATOES (*Pommes de Terre Lorette*). Prepare Dauphine Potato mixture (above). Form the mixture into small crescent shapes and deep-fry in 375° fat until golden.

DUCHESS OF CHESTER POTATOES (*Pommes de Terre Duchesse de Chester*). Prepare a Potato Croquette mixture (above), blending in ¼ cup of grated Cheshire cheese per cup. Shape into small cakes, place on a buttered pan, brush with beaten egg, top with a thin slice of Cheshire cheese, and heat in the oven until the cheese bubbles.

PARMESAN POTATOES (*Pommes de Terre au Parmesan*). Prepare Potato Croquette mixture (above), blending in ¼ cup grated Parmesan cheese per cup of mixture. Shape into small cakes, place on a buttered pan, top with a slice of Swiss cheese, and heat in the oven until the cheese melts and bubbles.

BAKED POTATOES (*Pommes de Terre au Four*). Scrub baking potatoes clean and carefully dry them. Puncture the skin a few times with a skewer to vent inner pressures. If you want a lighter-colored skin, rub the potatoes with oil. Place the potatoes, with space between them, on a rack in a 425° oven. Bake for 1 hour or longer for a crusty, full-flavored skin. Test for doneness by squeezing a potato in the palm of your hand protected by a cooking pad or mitt, or test the centers by probing with a skewer. The potato is cooked when the center is soft. Cut a large cross in the center of the potato and squeeze to fluff the meat and release steam. The potato will dry in its own heat. Serve with butter and salt.

POTATOES BAKED IN ASHES (*Pommes de Terre sous le Cendre*). Boy Scouts take note. Clean the potatoes, puncture their skins with a skewer a

Boston Lettuce

Pommes Frites

Pears à l'Impératrice

few times to prevent explosions, and bake in ashes with live embers on top. They will take about 1½ hours. Do not wrap the potatoes in foil; it will make them soggy.

POTATOES MACAIRE (*Pommes de Terre Macaire*). Bake the potatoes. Remove their pulp, rice it and mash with salt, pepper, and 1 tablespoon butter per cup. Spread the potato mixture in a buttered skillet, and bake until brown in a 400° oven.

POTATOES BYRON (*Pommes de Terre Byron*). Prepare Potatoes Macaire* (above). Place the browned potato cake on a buttered ovenproof serving dish, sprinkle grated Cheshire cheese and cream, and glaze* in the oven or broiler.

STUFFED POTATOES (*Pommes de Terre Farcies*). Use long baking potatoes, either large or small, depending upon whether they are intended for use as a garnish, an hors d'oeuvre, or small entree. Bake the potatoes in their jackets.

You may open the potatoes in one of three ways. Cut them in two lengthwise. Cut an oval-shaped opening from their long side, reserving the cutout piece as a cover if necessary. Or remove a thick slice from one end through which to empty the potato, cutting a small slice from the other end so the potato will stand upright. However you open the potatoes, scoop out ⅔ to ¾ of their pulp.

(A very elegant way to serve stuffed potatoes is to bake them peeled. Shape the peeled potatoes handsomely, cut a slice from one end so they stand upright, brush them all over with butter, and bake until they are a rich, golden brown. Then cut a slice from the top of the potato and scoop out the cooked pulp.)

You may stuff the potatoes with their mashed pulp, seasoned and mixed with butter, cream, eggs, cheese, herbs, mushrooms, chopped cooked meats, ham, chicken, various vegetables, and sauces. After stuffing, the potatoes are reheated in the oven, frequently sprinkled with butter, crumbs, and cheese. For some other stuffings, including very elegant ones, see *Salpicons* and Forcemeats in Chapter 4. Or stuff the potatoes in one of the following ways:

STUFFED POTATOES À LA FLORENTINE (*Pommes de Terre Farcies à la Florentine*). Stuff the potatoes with Spinach in Butter, cover with Mornay Sauce, sprinkle with grated Parmesan cheese and butter, and brown in the oven.

STUFFED POTATOES À LA PRINCESSE (*Pommes de Terre Farcies à la Princesse*). Stuff the potatoes with Asparagus Tips in Cream, and garnish with chopped truffles.

STUFFED POTATOES À LA VICHY (*Pommes de Terre Farcies à la Vichy*). Stuff the potatoes with Carrots à la Vichy.

STUFFED POTATOES À LA DUXELLES (*Pommes de Terre Farcies à la Duxelles*). Stuff the potatoes with *Duxelles*.

STUFFED POTATOES À LA PROVENÇALE (*Pommes de Terre Farcies à la Provençale*). Stuff the potatoes with tuna fish marinated in Vinaigrette Sauce and chopped hard-cooked eggs, all mixed in Tomato Sauce.

STUFFED POTATOES À LA HONGROISE (*Pommes de Terre Farcies à la Hongroise*). Stuff the potatoes with their mashed pulp mixed with butter, sautéed onion, salt, pepper, and paprika.

POTATOES ANNA (*Pommes de Terre Anna*). This is a famous and delicious potato dish that is well worth your while to learn how to prepare. Peel 2½ to 3 pounds of long baking potatoes, shape them in uniform cylinders, and slice them in thin rounds no more than ⅛ inch thick. Prepare 1½ cups Clarified Butter, pour half of it into the bottom of a deep, heavy 8- or 10-inch skillet, and heat until the butter is quite hot. Dry the potato slices carefully, and place one slice in the center of the pan. Working quickly, overlap this slice with a ring of overlapping potatoes. Then overlap this ring of slices with another overlapping ring of slices laid down in the opposite direction. Thus you will have concentric rings of potato slices, one running clockwise and the next running counterclockwise, with each potato slice overlapping the adjoining slice, and each ring overlapping the adjoining ring. Continue in this manner until the bottom of the pan is filled and the edge of the outside ring is pressed firmly against the sides of the pan. Season this layer with salt and pepper and spoon 2 tablespoons of hot clarified butter over it. Shake the pan to settle the potatoes and to prevent them from sticking to the bottom of the pan, adjusting the flame so the butter does not burn.

Add more layers of potatoes in the same manner, seasoning each layer with salt and pepper and sprinkling with butter, until the potatoes are all used up. You should have about 5 layers. Sprinkle the remaining butter over the potatoes, shake the pan to assure that the bottom layer is not sticking, press the potatoes down firmly to settle them, cover tightly, and place in a 425° oven. Bake covered for 30 minutes, uncover, and bake for 15 minutes more, or until a brown crust has formed around the potatoes and a knife can be pressed into their center without meeting any resistance. Pour off the excess butter (reserving it for another use), loosen the potato cake if it has stuck to the pan, and unmold onto a serving platter.

POTATOES ANNETTE (*Pommes de Terre Annette*). Prepare as for Potatoes Anna (above), but cut the potatoes into thin julienne,* and pack the julienne tightly in the pan.

POTATOES À LA DAUPHINOISE (*Pommes de Terre à la Dauphinoise*). Peel 2½ pounds boiling potatoes and slice them in thin rounds no more than ⅛ inch thick. Rub a shallow fireproof serving dish with garlic and then with soft butter. Layer the potatoes into the dish, sprinkling them with 4 tablespoons melted butter, 1 cup grated Gruyère or Swiss cheese, 1 teaspoon salt, and a little white pepper. Thoroughly mix 1 beaten egg and a pinch of nutmeg with 2 cups of milk that you have brought to the boiling point and cooled. Pour this over the potatoes, heat until the milk is simmering, sprinkle with grated Gruyère cheese and melted butter, and bake at 350° for 40 minutes, or until the potatoes are thoroughly tender and plump with milk and the sauce is reduced and thickened.

POTATOES À LA SAVOYARDE (*Pommes de Terre à la Savoyarde*). Prepare Potatoes à la Dauphinoise (above), but use White Stock in place of the boiled milk.

POTATOES IN CREAM (*Pommes de Terre à la Crème*). Boil 2 pounds firm boiling potatoes. Peel the potatoes and slice into ¼- to ⅜-inch rounds. Put them in a saucepan, season with ½ teaspoon salt, a little white pepper, and a pinch of nutmeg, and add enough boiling milk or light cream to barely cover the potatoes. Cook over moderate heat, shaking the pan frequently, until the cream has reduced by ¾. Finish the dish by swirling in* a few tablespoons heavy cream, and off the fire swirl in 2 tablespoons butter.

MAÎTRE D'HÔTEL POTATOES (*Pommes de Terre Maître d'Hôtel*). Prepare as for Potatoes in Cream (above), but cook in milk to which you have added 4 tablespoons butter. Reduce the milk entirely, and serve the potatoes sprinkled with chopped parsley.

PARISIAN POTATO SALAD (*Salade de Pommes de Terre à la Parisienne*). For the French method of making potato salad, see Chapter 12.

POTATOES FONDANTES (*Pommes de Terre Fondantes*). Peel the potatoes and cut them in the shape of large garlic cloves. Put them in a skillet in a single layer in a generous amount of butter, cover, and cook very slowly until they are golden on one side. Turn them carefully, and continue cooking until the other side is golden and the potatoes are very soft and tender, adding fresh butter if the potatoes have absorbed the butter in the pan. Season with salt and arrange on a dish.

SAUTÉED POTATOES (*Pommes de Terre Sautées*). Peel the potatoes, cut them in the desired shape, dry them carefully, and sauté in Clarified Butter, tossing the potatoes or turning them with a spatula so they will brown evenly. Sauté small pieces or thin slices of potato over a brisk fire. Sauté large potato pieces over a moderate fire so they will cook through before they become too brown. Or, to speed the cooking, you may partially cook the potato pieces in boiling salted water, drain and dry carefully, and then sauté. Small new potatoes can be partially boiled in their jackets, peeled, dried, and sautéed.

CHÂTEAU POTATOES (*Pommes de Terre Château*). Cut the potatoes in the shape of large olives. Sauté the potatoes until golden, season with salt and pepper, and serve sprinkled with chopped parsley.

NOISETTE POTATOES (*Pommes de Terre Noisette*). Use a ball cutter to cut the potatoes in balls the size of hazelnuts. Sauté the potatoes until golden, and season with salt and pepper.

PARISIAN POTATOES (*Pommes de Terre Parisienne*). Use a ball cutter to cut potatoes in balls a little smaller than for Noisette Potatoes (above). Sauté until golden, season with salt and pepper, add a few tablespoons of Meat Glaze to the pan, roll the potatoes to coat them well, and serve sprinkled with chopped parsley.

PARMENTIER POTATOES (*Pommes de Terre Parmentier*). Cut the potatoes into ½-inch dice. Sauté until golden, season with salt and pepper, and serve sprinkled with chopped parsley.

POTATOES À L'ALLEMANDE (*Pommes de Terre à l'Allemande*). Cut the potatoes in thick round slices, sauté until golden, and season with salt and pepper.

POTATOES À LA LYONNAISE (*Pommes de Terre à la Lyonnaise*). Sauté potato slices until golden. Add to the potatoes ¼ their quantity of thin onion slices that you have sautéed until lightly browned. Toss the potatoes and onions together in the pan, season with salt and pepper, and serve sprinkled with chopped parsley.

FRENCH-FRIED POTATOES
(*Pommes Frites*)

We now come to the French dish all Americans like and eat above all others, the deep-fried or French-fried potato. This dish is not at all difficult to prepare, and you are assured of perfect results if you select the right potatoes and strictly observe the proper cooking procedures. However, this will avail you nothing if the fried potatoes are not served immediately. No one has yet devised a method that will keep the fried potato from perishing in its own heat and juices, and the first golden stick you eat from a plate will be better than any of the following ones. As a result, it is next to impossible to serve French-fried potatoes to guests. They are best served at a family dinner, when you can run back and forth to collect sizzling batches of freshly fried potatoes from the stove. This is a constant practice in French homes, and it is good exercise.

The best available fats for deep-frying are beef kidney fat, vegetable oil, or vegetable shortening that contains no emulsifiers (see Fats and Oils in Chapter 4). These fats can be heated to the high temperatures required. You will need a large quantity of fat in proportion to the amount of food to be fried in one batch; the more fat you use, the less its temperature will drop when the food is put into it, the less it will be absorbed by the food, and the more economical it will be.

You will need a heavy metal pan that will retain a lot of heat. To guard against the fat bubbling over, the pan should be large enough so that the fat fills it only halfway; that is, for 2 quarts of fat, use a 4- or 4½-quart pan. You will also need a deep-frying basket to fit the pan, and a deep-frying thermometer or a candy thermometer for taking the temperature of the fat. Finally, have a large pot cover handy to smother the flame if the fat should bubble over and catch fire.

The mealier (more floury) a potato, the better it is for deep-frying. Use only "baking" potatoes. They will give you a French-fry that is better-tasting, less oily, firmer and much crisper than "frying" or "boiling" potatoes. Remember, the mealiness of baking potatoes can vary from year to year, and from state to state, and you must continually test them for mealiness. The cut surface of the cooked potato should be granular and sparkling, not pasty, glistening, and translucent.

Best results are obtained if the ratio of fat to potatoes is high, that is about 8 to 1 or 6 to 1 by weight. Use about 2 cups of potato for 2 quarts of oil. Turn the burner up to full flame so the fat will return swiftly to 375°. Lift the frying basket with a cooking mitt, put the well-dried potatoes into it, and submerge it in the fat. If it bubbles up too much the potatoes are not sufficiently dried; lift the basket, then submerge it again. Fry the potatoes for 4 minutes, shaking the basket from time to time so the potatoes will remain loose and cook evenly. After 4 minutes lift the basket, drain the fat back into the pan, spread the potatoes on absorbent paper towels, and blot excess fat from their surface. They will still be white.

Check the fat to see that it is 375°, and continue to fry batches of potatoes in this manner until you have the amount required. You may hold these prefried potatoes for several hours, but they are best if they receive their final frying and are served immediately.

For the final frying, heat the fat to 390°. Fry the potatoes as before. They should require about 1½ minutes to turn golden brown and complete their cooking. Drain them, spread them on absorbent paper towels, and quickly blot off excess fat, but do not under any circumstances cover the potatoes with the toweling or they will soften. Serve immediately.

This will give you French-fried potatoes that are a uniformly light golden-brown color, with a crisp, tender crust and a dry, mealy interior like a fine baked potato. The potatoes will not be oily, and if you eat them immediately you will be eating the best French-fries you have ever tasted.

FRENCH-FRIED POTATOES (*Pommes Frites Pont-Neuf*). Use long baking potatoes. Shortly before cooking, peel and cut them lengthwise into ½-inch-thick slices, and again lengthwise into ½-inch-thick square sticks. You may keep the sticks in cold water briefly to preserve their white color, but it is best to wash them quickly under running water. Drain and dry the potatoes thoroughly, stick by stick, with an absorbent towel. (If you wish to deep-fry potatoes that are thicker than ½ inch, soak them in water for 10 minutes to extract some of the sugar from their surface layers, which would cause the potatoes to brown before they were fully cooked inside.)

If the potato pieces are large, they are fried in 2 stages, once to prefry them and once to finish them. Small, thin pieces are fried only once.

Put the frying basket in the deep-fry pan, add the oil, and heat it to 375°. Failure to preheat the frying basket will cause the temperature of the oil to fall unduly when the potatoes are put into the pan.

SHOESTRING POTATOES (*Pommes Frites en Julienne*). Cut the potatoes into long 1/5-inch-square sticks. Prefry for 2 minutes at 375°, and refry for 1 minute at 390°. Drain and serve immediately.

POTATO STICKS (*Pommes Frites en Allumettes*). Cut the potatoes in ⅛-inch-square sticks about 2 inches long. Deep-fry in 390° fat for 1 or 2 minutes, until golden brown. Drain and serve immediately.

STRAW POTATOES (*Pommes Frites Paille*). Cut the potatoes into very thin strips, resembling straw. Deep-fry in 390° fat for 1 minute, or until golden brown. Drain and serve immediately.

POTATO CHIPS (*Pommes Frites Chip*). Cut the potatoes in very thin slices. Deep-fry in 390° fat for 1 minute, or until golden brown. Drain and serve immediately.

COLLERETTE POTATOES (*Pommes Frites Collerette*). Cut the potatoes in cork shapes, and slice in thin rounds. Deep-fry these small potato chips in 390° fat for 1 minute, or until golden brown. Drain and serve immediately.

SOUFFLÉED POTATOES
(*Pommes Frites Souflées*)

This astounding dish was discovered by accident when a panicky chef, who had been forced to delay the serving of fried potatoes, plunged them at the last moment into very hot fat that had continued to heat on the fire. Eureka! They ballooned to form great golden shells! And something new to eat was born.

Peel long baking potatoes and trim them to form oval shapes about 2½ inches long. Slice the potatoes lengthwise in ⅛-inch-thick slices, discarding the outside slices. Soak the slices in ice water for 15 minutes. Dry carefully, place in a preheated frying basket (see French-Fried Potatoes, above), and cook for about 5 minutes in relatively cool 300° fat, turning them over once to equalize cooking. Drain the potatoes, spread them on paper towels, and blot them to remove excess fat. Cool the potatoes, uncovered, in the refrigerator for at least 5 minutes or several hours.

When you are ready to serve the potatoes, heat the fat above 400°, going as high as 425° if you can reach this temperature without the fat smoking. Put the potatoes, a few at a time, into the preheated frying basket and submerge them in the hot fat. They should puff up instantly. As soon as they are browned, remove and drain them on paper towels. Serve immediately.

 RICE
(*Riz*)

Rice is divided into long-, medium-, and short-grained types. Partly because of these dimensions, short-grained rice in general will be softer when cooked through than long-grained. The grains will be puffier, less distinct, and will tend to stick together. Consequently, short-grained rice is preferred for creamy desserts and puddings, and for thickening purée mixtures. Long-grained rice is preferred for use as a vegetable where it is desirable that the grains remain distinct and separate. Careful cooking, however, will enable you to use all these rices interchangeably.

Long-grained American rice, called "Carolina" rice by the French, is very likely the finest all-around long-grained rice in the world. American medium- and short-grained rices are excellent also. You may be interested to know how the United States Government has rated many of the world's rices when cooked. The best-looking and least sticky is Indian long-grained, the tenderest is Brazilian long-grained, and the best-tasting is American long-grained.

Brown rice, which is unmilled whole-grain rice, contains more of rice's natural vitamins. Converted rice, which has been partially cooked in a vacuum, also is more nutritious than polished white rice.

Buying rice: No problem here. American rice comes to you washed and free of loose starch, and needs no further washing. Long-grained rice is so popular you may have to hunt for the shorter grains, which will cook softer. Raw white rice is the least expensive and may be used for all purposes.

Cooking rice: The basic recipes that follow are for raw white rice. The standard formula is 2 cups of liquid for each cup of raw rice, which will provide 3 cups of cooked rice. If you like your rice softer, use a little more liquid; for firmer rice, use a little less. The minerals in some water supplies will discolor white rice; to avoid this, add 1 teaspoon of lemon juice per 2 cups of liquid.

Raw brown rice takes twice as long to cook as white rice, and will require ¼ more liquid.

Converted rice, although it is partially precooked, will also take longer to cook than raw white rice. Use the quantities of rice and liquid and the cooking time suggested on the package, but follow the cooking procedures given below for best results. Converted rice when cooked yields grains that are very separate and distinct yet tender. This is the perfect texture for rice as a vegetable and for use in some stuffings. For creamier rice, use raw white rice.

BOILED RICE (*Riz au Blanc*). Put 1 cup raw rice in an ovenproof saucepan with a little melted butter and toss lightly to coat the grains. Add 2 cups boiling water and one teaspoon salt, shake the pan to distribute the rice evenly, and return the water to a boil. Cover the pan tightly and put it into a 350° oven and cook for about 18 minutes. If necessary, you may cook the rice in a heavy saucepan over a low flame. In either case, do not disturb the rice while it is cooking.

When the rice is cooked and tender to the teeth, use a fork to part the rice gently to see if all the liquid in the bottom of the pan has been absorbed. If not, cook for a few minutes more. Transfer the rice to a serving dish, treating it very gently so as not to crush the grains. Dot with a few small pieces of warm butter, and toss very lightly with a fork (preferably a long, two-tined fork), to barely coat each grain. Season to taste with salt and white pepper.

RICE À L'INDIENNE or STEAMED RICE (*Riz à l'Indienne ou Riz à la Vapeur*). Little by little, add one cup raw rice to a large quantity of boiling salted water so that the water remains at the boil. Boil brisky, uncovered, for 15 minutes. Drain the rice in a sieve or colander and hold the sieve under the water tap to wash the rice thoroughly. Drain again and wrap in several thicknesses of damp, washed cheesecloth. When ready to serve, heat the rice in its cheesecloth, covered, in a 325° oven or in a vegetable steamer for 20 to 30 minutes, or until the rice is warmed through. Season to taste with salt and white pepper.

RICE PILAF (*Riz Pilaf* or *Pilau*). In an ovenproof pan, lightly cook 2 table-spoons finely minced onion in 2 tablespoons butter for 3 or 4 minutes, until the onion is soft and transparent. Add one cup raw rice, mix well, and cook for 2 or 3 minutes more, or until the rice loses its transparency and becomes opaque. Add 2 cups boiling stock—Beef or Chicken Consommé, White or Brown Stock, or White Chicken Stock, according to the flavor you desire. Season lightly with salt and white pepper, add a *Bouquet Garni* consisting of 3 sprigs parsley, ½ bay leaf, and a sprig or pinch of thyme, all tied in cheesecloth. Shake the pan to distribute the rice evenly, return the stock to a boil, cover the pan tightly, and finish cooking as for Boiled Rice (above).

RICE À LA TURQUE (*Riz à la Turque*). Prepare Rice Pilaf (above), adding ¼ teaspoon saffron to the cooking water to give the rice a rich golden color. Just before serving, toss the rice with ½ peeled, seeded, and chopped raw tomato.

RICE À LA CRÉOLE (*Rice à la Créole*). Prepare Rice Pilaf (above). Just before serving, toss the rice with ¼ cup each thinly sliced raw mushrooms, ¼ cup raw tomatoes, peeled, seeded, and chopped, and 1 tablespoon diced pimentos.

RICE À LA GRECQUE (*Riz à la Grecque*). In a covered saucepan, gently cook ¼ cup loose sausage meat, ¼ cup chopped onion, and one cup shredded lettuce in one tablespoon butter. Prepare Rice Pilaf (above). Just before serving, toss the rice with the onion-sausage-lettuce mixture, ¼ cup cooked peas, and ¼ cup diced pimento.

RISOTTO (*Risotto*). A true risotto is made in a special way, using Italian short-grained or another short-grained rice. The rice grains in the finished dish are distinct, but they adhere somewhat to form a light, fluffy, creamy mass that is characteristic of risotto. In practice, many dishes labeled risotto are made according to the method given for Rice Pilaf (above), the grains being distinct and separate. Although the textures of the two dishes differ, recipes for them are interchangeable.

To prepare basic risotto, in a saucepan sauté ½ cup minced onion in 2 tablespoons butter or olive oil until the onion is transparent. Add 1 cup raw rice and heat for a few minutes, tossing to coat every grain. Do not allow the rice to brown. Bring about 3 cups White Stock or Brown Stock to the boil. Add ½ cup boiling stock to the rice, stir, cover, and simmer for a few minutes until the liquid is absorbed. Add more stock, stir briskly with a wooden spoon, cover, and simmer again. Continue in this manner until the rice is just tender. Stir in 1 to 2 tablespoons butter and ¾ cup grated Parmesan cheese, and any other warmed ingredients called for in specific recipes. Cook for a few minutes more, until the rice reaches a fluffy and creamy but not sticky consistency. Season to taste with salt and pepper.

RISOTTO À LA PIÉMONTAISE (*Risotto à la Piémontaise*). Prepare as for Risotto (above), but add ¼ teaspoon saffron to the hot stock. Along with the butter and cheese, you may add thin slices of white Italian truffle and diced ham.

RISOTTO À LA MILANAISE (*Risotto à la Milanaise*). Prepare as for Risotto (above), but add ¼ teaspoon saffron to the hot stock. Along with the butter and cheese, add ¼ cup chopped raw mushrooms and ¼ cup raw tomatoes, peeled, seeded, and chopped.

RICE STUFFING (*Farce de Riz*). Rice that is partially cooked may be seasoned and mixed with many different foods and used to stuff poultry, fish, and vegetables. Prepare Rice Pilaf (above), cooking the rice until it is only ¾ cooked. Mix it with the desired ingredients, which may be cooked just-cooked meat, fish, ham, chicken livers, or partially cooked vegetables, raw tomatoes, mushrooms, *foie gras* truffles, or other ingredients (see *Salpicons*). Add a little cream or sauce to provide the moisture required to complete the cooking of the rice. Stuff loosely, as the rice will swell as it cooks.

❋ SPINACH AND OTHER GREENS
(Épinards et Herbes Potagères Diverses)

Spinach absorbs butter. When I was a young apprentice I read in Brillat-Savarin of a spinach lover who stewed his spinach in butter for days on end, allowing it to cool each night and adding fresh butter every morning, until it attained an incredible succulence and flavor. I resolved to repeat this experiment and rejoiced, day by day, as the spinach absorbed gob after gob of yellow butter just as the book said it would. Then, alas, I tasted it. It was acrid with the taste of metal. Thus I learned that, although spinach absorbs butter, it even more readily absorbs the flavor of iron or aluminum pans. Avoid them when cooking spinach.

Spinach is a very delicate vegetable when it is very fresh and cooked just before eating. When it is old, or cooked in advance, or overcooked, it can be vile. We must be doing something wrong, because we eat only 1/5 the fresh spinach that we ate 30 years ago, and we eat twice as much canned spinach as fresh!

Fresh spinach is in the market all year long. Texas and California are the largest producers, supplying most of our winter spinach. New Jersey, Maryland, Virginia, and Colorado send us spinach during spring, summer, and fall. July, August, and September are the least productive months.

Aside from spinach and the lettuces, a number of other plants are eaten as cooked greens. These include kale, turnip tops, collards, beat tops, Swiss chard (the leaves are eaten as greens; the white stems are peeled and cooked like celery), mustard greens, dandelion greens, chicory, endive, escarole, and the French favorite, sorrel. These all can be cooked like spinach, until just tender, although you may have to cook them for a longer time.

Buying spinach: Most of our fresh spinach comes washed and packed in plastic bags. Look for leaves that are fresh and crisp with a good green color. Whole plants should be stocky with large, tender leaves. Do not buy spinach with leaves that are wilted, turning yellow, showing evidence of sliminess, or have coarse, fibrous stems. Remove packaged spinach from its plastic bag as soon as you get it home, sprinkle it with water, and store it loosely, uncovered, so that the air circulates around it.

Preparing spinach: Spinach grows best in sandy soils, and even prewashed spinach requires additional washing to rid it of every speck of sand. Using a stainless steel knife, trim away the stems of plants and coarse ribs of leaves. Wash the spinach by agitating the leaves in a large bowl of water, changing the water until not a single grain of sand falls to the bottom of the bowl. Shake the leaves dry, and store in the refrigerator.

Blanching spinach: Very young tender spinach need not be blanched, but most spinach you buy will be mature enough or old enough to require a preliminary blanching before further cooking. Drop the spinach, a little at a time, into a large quantity of rapidly boiling salted water, keeping the water at the boil. Boil for 5 minutes. With a slotted spoon, remove the spinach and plunge it into a bowl of cold water to stop the cooking, leaving any sand that may have escaped you in the blanching pot. Place the spinach between two plates (the bottom of one plate fitting into the top of the other) and squeeze over the sink to remove all excess water. Store in the refrigerator, covered.

Cooking spinach: The simplest cooking of spinach is to boil it, drain it, and serve with butter, and very young tender spinach can be cooked in the water clinging to its leaves after washing. However, spinach is very versatile and its flavor combines wonderfully with meat, fish, poultry, eggs, and cheese. It has an important role as a filling, stuffing, and soufflé base, and many an elegant dish is served on a bed of chopped, buttered spinach.

Although spinach can be boiled in water in an aluminum pot without noticeable effect, remember to keep it away from direct contact with iron or aluminum pans. Do not even chop spinach with a carbon steel knife or it will take on a metallic flavor. Use stainless steel knives and tinned food mills.

Spinach is a watery vegetable and it cooks down alarmingly, with 1 pound of fresh leaves producing about 1 cup of cooked spinach.

BOILED SPINACH (*Épinards Bouillis*). Use fresh or blanched spinach. Boil it in boiling salted water for 5 to 10 minutes until the leaves are tender. Remove from the pot with a slotted spoon, drain, and press between two plates to squeeze out the water. Leave the spinach leaves whole or chop them, but do not use an iron knife. Put the spinach in an enameled or stainless steel saucepan with ½ tablespoon hot butter per cup of cooked spinach. Season with salt, pepper, and a little nutmeg. Cook uncovered over a brisk fire, stirring the spinach and shaking the pan, until the spinach has evenly dried. Serve with melted butter.

SPINACH IN BUTTER (*Épinards au Beurre*). Blanch and cool the spinach, squeeze it dry, chop it, season it, and dry it as for Boiled Spinach (above). When it is quite dry, add one tablespoon butter per cup of cooked spinach, cover, and stew very slowly for 10 to 15 minutes, stirring from time to time, until the spinach is cooked and the butter has been absorbed. Off the fire, toss the spinach with 1 tablespoon butter per cup, and serve.

SPINACH IN CREAM (*Épinards à la Crème*). Blanch and cool the spinach, squeeze it dry, chop it, season it, and dry it as for Boiled Spinach (above), but use 1 full tablespoon butter per cup of blanched spinach. When it is quite dry, sprinkle in 1 teaspoon flour per cup of spinach and cook, stirring, for a few minutes to form a Roux. Add ¼ cup heavy cream per cup of spinach, cover, and simmer slowly for 15 minutes, stirring from time to time, until the spinach is tender and the cream sauce is quite thick. Stir in a few tablespoons of cream if necessary to bring the sauce to the desired consistency. Off the fire, stir in ½ tablespoon butter per cup.

SPINACH AU GRATIN (*Épinards au Gratin*). Prepare Spinach in Butter (above), but stew the spinach in 3 tablespoons butter per cup. When the spinach is cooked, stir into it ¼ cup grated Parmesan cheese per cup. Place the spinach in a well-buttered ovenproof serving dish, sprinkled with more grated Parmesan and melted butter, and brown in the oven. This dish may also be prepared using Spinach in Cream (above).

SPINACH PURÉE (*Purée d'Épinards*). Use blanched spinach. Chop it finely or put it through a food mill. Put the spinach in a saucepan with 1 tablespoon butter per cup of spinach, and cook over moderate heat, stirring, for a few minutes or until the spinach has given up all its loose water. Season with salt, pepper, and a little nutmeg.

✳ *THE SQUASHES*
(*Les Courges et Courgettes*)

There are very many of these vegetables. For cooking purposes we can divide them into "summer" squash and "winter" squash, although these terms do not refer to their seasonal availability in the market.

SUMMER SQUASH

Summer squashes are those that are harvested and cooked while still immature. Both their skin and seeds are soft and edible, and they are juicier than winter squash. Five summer squashes make up most of our supply.

Zucchini or *Italian* squash is shaped like a cucumber with an enlarged end. It is usually 6 to 8 inches long. The skin is dark green with narrow, darker green stripes running lengthwise. The flesh is pale greenish-white in color, and fine-textured when young. It is available all year.

Cocozelle is another Italian-developed squash with the size and shape of zucchini. Its skin is smooth with wide, shallow ribs and dark green with pale greenish-yellow stripes that are more prominent than the stripes of zucchini. It is available all year.

Yellow Crookneck is pear-shaped with a long, curled-over neck. It is usually 8 to 10 inches long, with warty yellow skin (becoming darker as the squash grows older). The creamy yellow flesh tends to be granular. Available all year.

Yellow Straightneck looks like the crookneck with its neck straightened out. Its skin is smoother than the crookneck and pale yellow. Available all year.

Scallop, also called *Cymling, Patty Pan,* and *Dollar Squash,* is disc-shaped and smooth with well-defined ribs radiating from the center and forming a scalloped rim. It is usually 3 or 4 inches in diameter but is better when it is smaller. Skin color changes from pale green to white as the squash matures. The flesh is tinged with green. Other varieties have skins that are all yellow, or white with pale green stripes.

WINTER SQUASH

Winter squashes are those that are harvested when mature and ripe. Their skin and seeds are hard and inedible, and they are dryer than summer squash, containing only about 88.5 percent water in comparison to 95 percent for summer squash. Some are small and some are large, and the largest reported is said to have weighed 400 pounds.

Acorn squash has an over-all acorn shape, with deep, wide ridges running from top to bottom. Usual sizes are about 7 inches from end to end, and 5 inches in diameter. The skin is smooth, thin, and hard, with a dull, dark green color, changing to orange as the squash ages in storage. The flesh is deep yellow to orange, dry and sweet, but it becomes stringy as the squash matures or ages. It is available all year.

Butternut squash is cylindrical and about 10 inches long with a distinct bulbous end about half as thick as the squash is long. The skin is smooth, hard, and creamy light brown to yellow. The flesh is deep yellow, firm, dry, sweet, and fine-grained. Available all year.

Buttercup squash is shaped like a maharaja's turban, with a protuberance bulging from the center of the squash opposite the stem end (where the maharaja's head would normally go). It measures about 5 inches from top to bottom, and about 8 inches in diameter. The skin of the turban is smooth, hard, and dark green with gray spots and faint gray stripes. The bulge opposite the stem end is light gray, sometimes bluish. The flesh is orange, dry, fine-textured, and very sweet, with the flavor of sweet potato. Generally available from late summer through winter.

Hubbard squash is shaped like a light bulb, with a thick, curved neck at the stem end and a small, spindly neck at the bottom end. It is a large squash, about 15 inches long and 12 inches thick at the bulbous end. The skin is very hard, ridged, and warty, varying in color among different varieties of Hubbard from bronze-green to blue-gray to orange-red. The flesh is yellowish-orange and sweet. Available from late summer through February.

Delicious squash is similar in shape to Hubbard, but more top-shaped and somewhat smaller. Skin is hard, ridged, and warty, varying from bright red-orange with green splotches or creamy stripes to dark green with lighter green stripes. The flesh is orange and fine-grained. Available from late summer through March.

Banana squash is shaped like a large cucumber with somewhat rounded ends. It is a large squash, up to 2 feet long and 6 inches in diameter. Skin is medium hard, smooth with shallow wrinkles, varying in color from grayish olive to creamy pink. Flesh is yellowish-orange, sweet, dry, and fine-grained. It does not taste like bananas.

What we call *pumpkins* include both summer and winter squash varieties. True pumpkin flesh is less fine-grained and stronger in flavor than that of the squashes, and is usually reserved for pies. However, much of the canned "pumpkin" meat for pies is actually the richer meat of various squashes. Pumpkin may be blanched and cooked as winter squash.

Buying squashes: Summer squash should be fresh-looking and heavy for its size with a soft, tender skin. In general, the smaller summer squash is, the better it will be. Toughening of the skin, so it cannot be easily pierced with a fingernail, suggests that the seeds inside are becoming hard and inedible, and the flesh is becoming coarse and stringy.

The skin of winter squash is likewise a good indicator of quality. It should be hard, firm, and dry. Soft skin is an indication of immaturity and watery, flavorless flesh. Also avoid winter squash with soft spots or wet areas, which are indicative of decay.

Preparing squashes: Store summer squash in the refrigerator, keeping it moist until ready for use. Store winter squash in a dry, cool place at about 55°. Summer squash need not be peeled, and may be cooked whole, sliced, or otherwise cut into convenient pieces. Winter squash is peeled, its seeds are removed, and its stringy center is scraped off the firm flesh of the walls.

Cooking summer squash: Summer squash is very watery, and in order to make the vegetable palatable, some of this water must be removed during or before cooking. When it is boiled, excess water is drawn from the vegetable as it cooks, and the vegetable is dried in butter after cooking. When cooked in other ways, excess water is removed in advance by heating the vegetable in a covered pot in the oven for about 10 minutes; or by blanching in boiling salted water for 15 minutes; or by slicing the vegetable, salting the cut edges, and allowing it to stand for 30 to 60 minutes so that its excess water is drawn out. Beyond this, there are no special cooking problems other than that of taking pains to preserve the squash's delicate flavor.

Cooking winter squash: Winter squash is firmer and dryer than summer squash. It requires about twice as much time to cook to tenderness, but young, fresh winter squash is nevertheless delicately flavored and should not be blanched or overcooked. Because of its hard skin, winter squash is ideal for baking; because of its dry flesh, it should be well basted when baking.

GLAZED SUMMER SQUASH (*Courgettes Glacées*). Thickly slice 1 pound unpeeled summer squash, or peel the squash and cut it into large olive or garlic clove shapes. Put the squash in a saucepan with about 1 cup water (to cover the squash well), ¼ teaspoon salt, 2 teaspoons sugar, and 4 table-spoons butter. Bring to the boil, cover, and boil gently for 15 to 20 minutes or until the squash is tender. Uncover and toss the pieces until the water has entirely disappeared and they are coated with the butter and sugar.

SUMMER SQUASH IN CREAM (*Courgettes à la Crème*). Thickly slice 1 pound unpeeled summer squash, or peel the squash and cut it into large olive shapes. Blanch the pieces for 2 minutes and drain them well. Put them in a saucepan with 4 tablespoons butter, season with salt and white pepper, cover, and simmer very slowly until the squash pieces are almost tender. Sprinkle with 1 teaspoon flour, cook for a few minutes to form a Roux, barely cover the squash with boiling light cream, and simmer, uncovered, until the cream has reduced by ⅔ and the sauce has thickened. Off the fire stir in 2 tablespoons butter.

SAUTÉED SUMMER SQUASH (*Courgettes Sautées*). Peel the squash and slice it ⅓ inch thick or cut it in ½-inch dice. Sprinkle it with salt and allow it to stand for 30 to 60 minutes to expel excess water. Dry the pieces in a towel, dredge them in flour, and sauté in very hot olive oil, Clarified Butter, or a mixture of butter and oil for 6 to 8 minutes, until the squash is tender and lightly browned. Season with salt, pepper, and lemon juice if desired, and serve sprinkled with chopped parsley.

SUMMER SQUASH AU GRATIN (*Courgettes au Gratin*). Prepare Sautéed Summer Squash (above). Put it in a buttered, ovenproof serving dish on a bed of Mornay Sauce. Cover the squash with more of the sauce, sprinkle with grated Parmesan cheese and melted butter, and brown in the oven.

SUMMER SQUASH À LA MILANAISE (*Courgettes à la Milanaise*). Prepare Sautéed Summer Squash (above). Layer it in a buttered ovenproof serving dish, sprinkling it liberally with grated Parmesan or Swiss and Parmesan cheeses, and with melted butter or olive oil.

SUMMER SQUASH À LA PROVENÇALE (*Courgettes à la Provençale*). Sauté the squash as for Sautéed Summer Squash (above). Place the slices in an oiled baking dish on a bed of rice boiled in White Stock, sautéed tomato slices, sautéed onion slices, chopped parsley, and a little minced garlic. Add another layer of squash, and another layer of rice and vegetables, until the dish is filled. Sprinkle the top with grated Parmesan cheese and melted butter and brown in the oven.

DEEP-FRIED SUMMER SQUASH (*Courgettes Frites*). Peel the squash and cut it crosswise or lengthwise into ½-inch-thick slices. Salt the slices and let stand for 30 to 60 minutes to draw out excess water and dry them. Leave crosswise slices as they are. Cut lengthwise slices into ½-inch-square sticks about 2 inches long. Dredge in flour in a paper bag, shake off excess flour and deep-fry in 385° hot oil for about 2 minutes, until the slices or sticks are golden brown. Drain on paper towels, sprinkle with salt, and serve immediately. (Fried squash can also be cut in ⅓-inch-thick round slices and coated *à l'Anglaise*.)

STUFFED SUMMER SQUASH (*Courgettes Farcies*). Use zucchini, cocozelle, or yellow straightneck squash. Blanch the unpeeled squash for 10 minutes. Cut them in half, lengthwise, and make a deep cut ¼ inch inside the skin, all around the circumference of each squash half. Within the boundaries of this cut, make deep crisscross incisions to within ¼ inch of the bottom of the squash, taking care not to break the skin. Sprinkle with salt and let stand, cut side down, for 30 to 60 minutes. Squeeze gently to remove excess water and dry the cut surface with a towel. Sauté gently in butter and olive oil, cut side down, for about 5 minutes or until the pulp is softened and can be scooped out. Remove most of the pulp, leaving a thin wall next to the skin. Squeeze the pulp to remove excess water, chop it, and add to it an equal volume of dry *Duxelles* (or prepare one of the alternate stuffings listed below). Season with salt and pepper, pack the mixture back into the skins, sprinkle with melted butter and fine dry breadcrumbs, and brown in the oven or under the broiler.

Summer squash may also be stuffed as for Eggpant, that is, *à la langue-*

docienne, à la reine, à la provençale, and *à la nîmoise.* They may also be stuffed as for Onions, *à la parisienne, à l'italienne,* and *à la catalane.* For other possible stuffings see *Salpicons* in Chapter 4.

When following these recipes you will, of course, incorporate some of the pulp of the squash into the stuffing mixture.

PURÉE OF SUMMER SQUASH (*Purée de Courgettes*). Peel the squash, slice it, and boil it with an equal quantity of potato slices. When tender, drain the squash and potatoes and put them through a food mill or a sieve. Put the purée in a saucepan, beat in 1 tablespoon butter per cup, and cook for a few minutes to dry the mixture. Bring the purée to the desired consistency with heavy cream, and season with salt and white pepper.

Winter squash is not common in France, and few recipes exist for it beyond those established for pumpkin. Pumpkin, in general, is coarse-fleshed and stronger in flavor, and should be blanched before cooking. To preserve the delicate flavor of young winter squash, it should be baked. If you wish to cook it partially by boiling, boil it whole in its heavy skin.

GLAZED WINTER SQUASH (*Courge Glacée*). Pare the squash, cut it in pieces, and scrape out seeds and stringy fibers from the center. Boil in salted water to cover for about 15 minutes, or until the squash is almost tender. *Or,* scrub the squash and cook it whole in plenty of boiling water for about 30 minutes, or until a skewer will pass through it with a light resistance. Drain, pare, cut in half, remove the seeds and stringy fibers, and cut in pieces.

For 2 cups squash, put into a skillet 4 tablespoons each of butter, brown sugar, and water, and a pinch of cinnamon or nutmeg. Bring to the boil, add the squash, and toss it in the liquid. Cover the pan and simmer gently for 5 minutes or until the squash is tender. Uncover, and cook for 5 minutes longer until the liquid is reduced and the squash is well glazed.

BAKED WINTER SQUASH (*Courge au Four*). Scrub the squash but do not peel it. Cut small squash in half, cut large squash in bowl-like segments, and remove the seeds and stringy fibers from their centers. Cut a thin slice from the skin side of the squash so that the halves or "bowls" will stand without rocking. Brush the cut sides with melted butter, place cut side down in a baking dish, and bake in a 350° oven for about 20 minutes. Turn the squash cut side up, brush generously with melted butter, sprinkle with brown sugar, salt, pepper, and a pinch of cinnamon or nutmeg, and dot with more butter. Bake, basting frequently with the buttery syrup they contain, for 20 to 25 minutes more, or until the squash are tender. Serve the squash in their skins.

BAKED STUFFED WINTER SQUASH (*Courge Farcie au Four*). Prepare the squash as for Baked Winter Squash (above). Brush with butter and bake cut side down for 30 minutes. Season the squash with salt and pepper, and fill it with a savory stuffing such as sautéed chopped mushrooms and onion, shredded cheese and chopped parsley, heaping the mixture in a dome. Sprinkle with grated cheese, dry breadcrumbs, and melted butter, and bake for 15 to 20 minutes more. Or you may stuff the squash with one of the fillings suggested for Summer Squash.

PURÉE OF WINTER SQUASH (*Purée de Courge*). Bake the squash whole in a 375° oven until a skewer will pass into it easily. Cut the squash in half, scoop out seeds and stringy meat in the center, and scoop out the pulp. To each cup of pulp, add 1 tablespoon butter, 1 tablespoon brown sugar, ¼ teaspoon salt, and a pinch of cinnamon or ginger. Mix the pulp and seasonings well, and beat in enough hot heavy cream to bring the purée to the desired consistency.

❋ SWEET POTATOES AND YAMS
(*Patates*)

Sweet potatoes are sweet, starchy tuberous roots. What we call yams are a variety of sweet potato (real yams are something else again). Neither sweet potatoes nor our yams are potatoes, but members of the morning-glory family. Enough of this.

The major culinary difference between sweet potatoes and what we call yams is that the cooked yam has a softer flesh and the cooked sweet potato has a firmer, mealier flesh. Also, yams tend to be sweeter and have copper or pinkish tan skin and deep yellow to orange-red flesh, while sweet potatoes have more yellowish skin and lighter yellow flesh, although there are exceptions.

We used to eat large quantities of sweet potatoes in this country, but the yearly amount has declined to about 4 pounds per person fresh, and about 1½ pounds canned. They are available the year round, with greatest supplies from September through March. Louisiana grows most of our sweet potatoes, followed by New Jersey, California, and North Carolina.

Buying sweet potatoes and yams: Look for thick, chunky, medium-size tubers that taper at the ends. They should be smooth (although sometimes veined), clean, well shaped, and bright-looking. Misshapen potatoes or those with growth cracks are wasteful. Avoid the slightest amount of decay; it spreads rapidly and gives a bad flavor even to sound portions of the potato. Decay appears, frequently at the ends of the potato, as soft, wet areas; or as shriveled, depressed, discolored areas; or as greenish-black circular spots.

Finally, when you buy sweet potatoes be certain that you are buying all the same variety so that they will cook the same and produce the same flavor, color, and texture of flesh.

Preparing sweet potatoes and yams: These vegetables bruise easily and should be carefully handled. Store them in a cool place, but not where the temperature is likely to fall below 50°. Sweet potatoes chilled below this temperature form a dark, bitter layer under the skin which quickly turns to rot. Sweet potatoes are prepared for cooking like ordinary potatoes.

Cooking sweet potatoes and yams: These vegetables can be boiled, baked, mashed, sautéed, fried, and puréed just like potatoes, and you may follow many of the recipes for potatoes given in this chapter. Also, sweet potatoes may be cooked like Potato Croquettes, Potatoes in Cream, Braised Carrots, Glazed Carrots, Carrots à la Vichy, and Carrots aux Fines Herbes. Or, for an exceptional treat, prepare the following.

SWEET POTATOES À LA LAVIGERIE (*Patates à la Lavigerie*). Bake the potatoes in a 400° oven for 30 minutes to 1 hour, until crushably soft. Remove a slice from the side or end, scoop out the pulp, mash it with butter, and mix it with some braised Chestnuts (see Chapter 4), which you have passed through a food mill or rubbed through a sieve. Season to taste with salt and pepper, stuff the potatoes with this mixture, brush with melted butter, and return to the oven to heat through.

❋ TOMATOES
(*Tomates*)

The best tomatoes are those of a flavorful variety that are allowed to ripen on the vine. Unfortunately these two criteria are seldom met, and tomatoes do not taste like they used to.

I have already commented, in the introduction to this chapter, on the abandonment of the old-time tomato varieties in favor of new varieties that more adequately meet the vicissitudes of mass marketing and farming. So many specific requirements have been built into these new tomatoes that flavor, which is what tomato eating is all about, has been relegated to what is "acceptable." Much more demanding are the requirements for tough skins, machine-harvestable plants, brittle stems, hard flesh, and by all means a good rich red color. Color is all important to the canners who accept only fruits that are rich red and vine-ripe. This brings us to the second problem.

Tomatoes for fresh market are never allowed to ripen fully before shipment. Those that are shipped long distances, or will be otherwise delayed, are picked when they are what is called "mature green." These tomatoes are hard and green all over, with perhaps a spot of white at the bottom. Jelly has begun to form in their seed cavities, and the seeds are hard enough to slip aside if you try to cut them with a knife (if the seeds can be cut, the tomato will never ripen). Mature green tomatoes will turn red while they are passing through the marketing pipeline. In fact, they will turn a beautiful red because redness has been bred into them. But they will never have the good flavor of vine-ripened tomatoes.

Some tomatoes are allowed to remain on the vine until they began to grow pink or red. These are picked anywhere from the time that they show a faint pink blush at the bottom up until the time when they are 90 percent red. In general, the closer you are to the tomato fields, the riper the tomatoes are likely to be when they are picked. And the riper and redder the tomatoes when picked, the better they will taste.

Greenhouse tomatoes are grown mainly in the East and Middle West to supply local markets during winter. Special varieties have been developed for the greenhouse, many of them designed for forced growth. Most greenhouse tomatoes are vine-ripened until they are more than 50 percent red (some of these varieties ripen pink). Many greenhouse tomatoes are prepackaged in see-through boxes. You can also identify greenhouse tomatoes by the presence of a circle of leaves (sepals) and a clipped-short stem at the top of the plant. The stem keeps the tomatoes moister and fresher for a longer period of time. Fully colored (red or pink) tomatoes with fresh sepals indicate that the tomatoes are fresh and vine-ripened. Taste-test these tomatoes and make a note of the grower's name.

Most tomatoes, 5 out of every 6, are processed before they are sold, appearing in the market as catsup, sauces, purées, juices, and whole canned tomatoes. If you are planning to chop and cook the tomatoes, as a vegetable or as a flavoring for sauces, canned tomatoes will often be better-flavored than fresh tomatoes, in as much as they are picked when vine-ripe. When using canned tomatoes you may also try the imported varieties from Italy, where machine-harvestable varieties are not yet necessary.

The best chance you have of buying good-tasting tomatoes is to buy those that are harvested close by and picked by hand so that machine-harvestable varieties are not a requirement. Thus, watch for tomatoes grown in your state when they come into season.

The best way of all to get good tomatoes is, of course, to grow your own. It is rather hard to believe, but government figures show that the per capita consumption of home-grown tomatoes in America is 16 pounds a year! Compare this with 10 pounds bought fresh, and you will take heart in the knowledge that there are still a lot of good-eating tomatoes to be found.

To summarize, grow tomatoes in pots if you have to, and buy local tomatoes in season. During the months when fresh local tomatoes are unavailable, use canned tomatoes if possible, and carefully taste-test every fresh tomato purchase. Inquire at the store as to the state of origin, and compare with competing fresh tomatoes. Most autumn, winter, and early spring tomatoes come from California, Florida, Mexico, and Texas, and you should choose selectively among them to search out a grower who is taking pains to allow his tomatoes to ripen somewhat on the vine.

Buying tomatoes: In addition to what I have already said, look for tomatoes that are heavy, plump, red, and firm. When buying local tomatoes, do not be repelled by small deformities in shape, healed growth cracks, minor scars, or other minor irregularities. Locally grown and harvested tomatoes rarely have the artificial perfection of machine-harvested varieties, but they will make up for their imperfections with their flavor. Tomatoes exhibiting some green will usually ripen fully in a day or two. Avoid any tomatoes that feel light and look puffy, and avoid mushy, overripe tomatoes.

Preparing tomatoes: Ripe tomatoes are highly perishable, and you must use them in a day or two. If they are partly green, do not put them on the window sill in the sunlight to ripen. This looks very charming, but the tomatoes will become too hot. Also, do not put tomatoes in the refrigerator, as it is much too cold for them. Keep them at room temperature.

Tomatoes for flavoring sauces need not be skinned, as their skins will be removed when the sauce is strained. Also, tomatoes that are baked whole may be baked in their skins. Tomatoes for all other uses (especially the new thick-skinned tomatoes) must be skinned. There are three ways to do this.

Tomatoes that are to be cooked are skinned by dipping them in boiling water for 10 or 15 seconds, and then peeling away the loosened skin. Or, you may impale the tomato on a fork and revolve it over a flame to loosen the skin for peeling. If the tomatoes are to be served raw, do not use either of these methods, as they will make the surface of the tomato mushy. Instead, scrape the skin all over with the blade of a knife. This will loosen the skin enough so that it can be peeled away.

Tomatoes are very watery, and for most uses they should be relieved of some of this water as well as their seeds. Cut the tomato in half crosswise, reach into the seed cavities with your finger, and remove all the locular jelly and seeds. To remove even more moisture, salt the tomato and allow it to stand with its cut side down. These half-tomatoes may be reconstituted to form whole, solid, seedless, small tomatoes by twisting them in a towel. Tomato slices or quarters for salads can be relieved of their seeds and salted to remove moisture in the same way as tomato halves.

Cooking tomatoes: Aside from their wateriness, tomatoes pose no cooking problems and may be cooked for long or short periods depending upon their use.

GRILLED TOMATOES (*Tomates Grillées*). Peel the tomatoes. Cut large tomatoes in half. Cut a slice from the stem end of smaller tomatoes. Scoop out seeds, squeeze gently to expel jelly and water, and season with salt and pepper. Brush the tomato thoroughly, inside and out, with melted butter or oil, and grill or broil gently for 10 to 15 minutes, or until the tomatoes are soft.

SAUTÉED TOMATOES (*Tomates Sautées*). Peel, seed, and drain the tomatoes. Cut them in thick slices, sprinkle with salt and pepper, dredge in flour, and sauté in olive oil or Clarified Butter for 8 minutes, until each side is lightly browned.

SAUTÉED TOMATOES À LA PROVENÇALE (*Tomates Sautées à la Provençale*). Peel, halve, seed, and drain the tomatoes, and season with salt and pepper. Sauté them in olive oil, cut side down, for about 6 minutes, until they are half cooked. Place them in an oiled ovenproof serving dish, cut side up, and sprinkle with 1 cup fresh white breadcrumbs mixed with 1 tablespoon parsley and ½ garlic clove, minced. Sprinkle the tomatoes with oil from the pan, and put them in a 350° oven for about 5 minutes more, until they are tender and the crumbs are browned.

SAUTÉED TOMATOES À LA LYONNAISE (*Tomates Sautées à la Lyonnaise*). Peel, halve, seed, and drain the tomatoes, and season with salt and pepper. Sauté them in Clarified Butter, cut side down, for about 5 minutes, until they are half cooked. Turn the tomatoes over and cook for 5 minutes more, or until they are tender. Serve the tomatoes on a bed of chopped onion sautéed in butter. Pour over the tomatoes the tomato cooking butter, to which you have added a few tablespoons of sautéed minced onion.

DEEP-FRIED TOMATOES (*Tomates Frites*). Peel, seed, and drain the to-matoes, and cut them in thick slices. Season with salt and pepper, dredge in flour, and dip in a Batter for deep-frying. Fry them in 380° oil for 2 or 3 minutes, or until they are browned. Drain and serve immediately with Fried Parsley.

TOMATO FONDUE (*Fondue de Tomates*). Peel, seed, squeeze, drain, and chop the tomatoes. Season with salt and pepper and simmer very slowly in butter, in a covered pan, until the tomatoes are soft and relatively dry. If necessary, uncover the pan to dry the tomatoes to the consistency of a moist hash.

TOMATO FONDUE À LA NIÇOISE (*Fondue de Tomates à la Niçoise*). Simmer 2 tablespoons chopped onion in a little olive oil. Prepare 2 cups chopped tomatoes as for Tomato Fondue (above), add them to the pan with ½ cup diced pimentos, salt, paprika, ½ teaspoon minced garlic, and one teaspoon chopped tarragon. Cover and simmer until the tomatoes are relatively dry.

TOMATO FONDUE À LA GRECQUE (*Fondue de Tomates à la Grecque*). Prepare as for Tomato Fondue à la Niçoise (above), but omit the chopped tarragon.

STUFFED TOMATOES (*Tomates Farcies*). Do not peel the tomatoes. Cut large tomatoes in half crosswise; cut a slice from the stem end of medium tomatoes. Scoop out the seeds, squeeze out the jelly, and season the tomatoes with salt and pepper. You may begin their cooking in one of two ways. Arrange them on an oiled baking dish, cut side up, sprinkle with olive oil or melted butter, bake in a 450° oven for 10 minutes, remove them, and drain them again. Or, sauté the tomatoes in olive oil or Clarified Butter, cut side down, for 5 minutes. Stuff the partially cooked tomatoes with the filling called for in one of the following recipes, and bake them in a 350° oven for 10 minutes, or until the tomatoes and their stuffing are done.

STUFFED TOMATOES AU GRATIN (*Tomates Farcies au Gratin*). Prepare and half cook the tomatoes as for Stuffed Tomatoes (above). Fill them with *Duxelles,* sprinkle with dry breadcrumbs and olive oil, and brown in the oven. Serve the tomatoes surrounded with a border of Demi-Glace Sauce flavored with Tomato Purée.

STUFFED TOMATOES À LA PROVENÇALE (*Tomates Farcies à la Provençale*). To 2 cups peeled, seeded, drained, and chopped tomato, add 2 tablespoons chopped onion sautéed in oil, 1 teaspoon parsley, 1 garlic clove, crushed, and 1 tablespoon olive oil. Cover and stew gently for 10 minutes, and add ¼ cup fresh breadcrumbs that you have soaked in White Stock and tossed to loosen, 2 tablespoons anchovy paste, and a few tablespoons Starch-Thickened Brown Stock, and toss all these ingredients to mix them. Prepare and cook tomatoes as for Stuffed Tomatoes (above), leaving them in the oven for 10 minutes or until they are almost cooked. Stuff the tomatoes with the prepared filling heaped in a dome, sprinkle them with dry breadcrumbs, grated Parmesan cheese, and olive oil, and brown in the oven.

STUFFED TOMATOES À LA PORTUGAISE (*Tomates Farcies à la Portugaise*). Prepare and ¾ cook the tomatoes as for Stuffed Tomatoes (above). Stuff them with Rice Pilaf to which you have added ¼ cup chopped tomato per cup. Serve sprinkled with chopped parsley.

STUFFED TOMATOES À LA NIÇOISE (*Tomates Farcies à la Niçoise*). Prepare and partially cook the tomatoes in oil as for Stuffed Tomatoes (above). Fill them with a mixture of Rice Pilaf, fresh breadcrumbs, chopped eggplant sautéed in olive oil, chopped parsley, and a little chopped garlic, all seasoned with salt and pepper. Sprinkle with dry breadcrumbs and oil, and brown in the oven.

STUFFED TOMATOES À LA REINE (*Tomates Farcies à la Reine*). Prepare and partially cook the tomatoes in butter as for Stuffed Tomatoes (above). Fill them with a *Salpicon* of white meat of chicken, mushrooms, and truffles in Velouté Sauce. Sprinkle with dry breadcrumbs and melted butter, and brown in the oven.

STUFFED TOMATOES À LA LANGUEDOCIENNE (*Tomates Farcies à la Languedocienne*). Prepare and partially cook the tomatoes in oil as for Stuffed Tomatoes (above). Fill them with a mixture of Pork Sausage sautéed in oil, chopped onion sautéed in oil, chopped hard-cooked egg yolks, chopped parsley, and a little minced garlic. Sprinkle with dry breadcrumbs and oil, and brown in the oven.

TOMATO PURÉE (*Purée de Tomates*). See Chapter 4.

✳ *TURNIPS AND RUTABAGAS*
(*Navets et Navets de Suéde*)

The turnip and the rutabaga are similar vegetables, the rutabaga being a cross between the cabbage and the turnip. Most turnips are white-fleshed and most rutabagas are yellow-fleshed, although the reverse sometimes holds true. The turnip is juicier, more tender, and more delicate in flavor than the rutabaga, which is dryer, denser, and incidentally more nutritious. Both are cool-weather vegetables, although the turnip is successfully grown in the South. These vegetables are most plentiful from September through March, with fresh young turnips appearing in fall and early winter.

Buying turnips: Turnips may measure from 1½ to 6 inches in diameter, and the smaller turnips are frequently sold with their edible green tops attached. Most are globe-shaped and white with a purple crown; some are flattened. Small fresh turnips are the most delicate in flavor. Look for small- to medium-sized turnips that are heavy, smooth, and hard. Tops should be fresh, green, and sprightly-looking. Avoid turnips that are soft or shriveled or show many leaf scars around their crown, or are very large and light for their size, or have more than just a few fibrous roots at their base, or have limp, yellowed leaf tops.

Buying rutabagas: Rutabagas are larger than turnips, measuring up to 8 inches in diameter. They may be globe-shaped or elongated, with cream- or yellow-colored sides and purple crowns. They are shipped fresh or from storage. All storage rutabagas and some fresh rutabagas are coated with wax, which helps prevent them from drying. Choose smooth, firm rutabagas that are heavy for their size, with very few leaf scars at their crown and very few fibrous roots at their base.

Preparing turnips and rutabagas: These vegetables are always peeled. Small young turnips may be left whole; larger vegetables are cut in various shapes. Frequently, turnips are cut in the shape of baby carrots or large garlic cloves. After shaping the vegetable, old turnips and rutabagas should be blanched before further cooking to lessen their strong flavor.

Blanching turnips and rutabagas: Plunge the cut and shaped vegetable into boiling salted water and boil for 5 minutes. Drain, then proceed with the cooking.

Cooking turnips and rutabagas: Both turnips and rutabagas, like dried beans, are noted for their ability to glut themselves with butter and other fats during cooking. Consequently, they are frequently cooked with fatty meats (Duck with Turnips, for example). They will absorb the fat and become incredibly rich in flavor. Turnips also perform as a flavoring for stocks and soups, although they are used with discretion. As a vegetable in themselves, turnips and rutabagas are cooked like carrots.

BOILED TURNIPS (*Navets Bouillis*). Cook as for Boiled Carrots. Boil small young turnips whole for 20 to 30 minutes, until tender. Blanch old turnips and rutabagas, drain them, and boil again in new salted water.

BRAISED TURNIPS (*Navets Braisés*). Cook as for Braised Carrots.

TURNIPS IN CREAM (*Navets à la Crème*). Cook as for Carrots in Cream.

GLAZED TURNIPS (*Navets Glacés*). Cook as for Glazed Carrots.

TURNIPS IN BUTTER (*Navets au Beurre*). Peel and shape the turnips and parboil them in boiling salted water until they are half cooked. Drain, dry, and put them in a saucepan with a generous amount of butter. Stew very slowly until the turnips are tender and have absorbed the butter.

TURNIPS AUX FINES HERBES (*Navets aux Fines Herbes*). Peel and shape the turnips. Parboil them in boiling salted water until they are almost cooked. Drain, dry, season with salt and pepper, and sauté in butter with a pinch of powdered sugar to help them brown. Serve sprinkled with chopped parsley.

STUFFED TURNIPS (*Navets Farcis*). Peel medium-sized turnips of equal size. With a round cutter or a sharp-pointed knife, make a deep circular incision around the stems, taking care not to cut all the way through the turnips. Parboil the turnips for about 20 minutes, until they are just tender all the way through. Drain them and remove the cut centers. Put the centers through a food mill or rub them through a sieve. To this purée add an equal amount of mashed potatoes or Potato Purée, dry in a saucepan over a low fire, stir in a few tablespoons butter, and season with salt and white pepper. Stuff the turnip cases with this mixture, place them in a buttered baking dish, and sprinkle them copiously with melted butter. Put them in a 325° oven and finish the cooking, basting frequently with butter.

As alternatives to the filling above, you may stuff the turnips with well-seasoned meat hashes; with Spinach in Cream; with cooked rice and diced turnip in butter sprinkled with Parmesan cheese and browned; or with mashed turnip and *Duxelles*.

TURNIP PURÉE (*Purée de Navets* or *Purée Freneuse*). Slice the turnips and braise them. Put them through a food mill or rub them through a sieve. Combine this purée with ½ its quantity of mashed potatoes or Potato Purée, dry in a pan over a low fire, stir in a few tablespoons butter, and season with salt and white pepper.

✿ 12   *Salads and Their Dressings*

It is spring, and the earth is a great brown fruit. The April sky has moistened it with fresh rains and now the sun peers at it warmly. Inside this moist warm brown fruit countless trillions of tiny seeds know their time has come. They soak up the warmth and the moisture. They swell. Their brown husks split and send forth tender white shoots that clamber to the surface to make their tiny claim for light and warmth and air. And we salad eaters, fork in hand, are waiting.

There are two kinds of salads: plain (*salade simple*) and combination (*salade composée*). Plain salads consist of a single green, or a mixture of greens, or a single cooked, cold vegetable. The plain green salad is served as a salad course. The plain cooked vegetables salad is usually served as an hors d'oeuvre.

A combination salad may be almost any combination of foods. Two or more items of meat, fish, shellfish, vegetables, cheese, beans, rice, and hard-cooked eggs are usually dressed in advance and heaped in a dome on a bed of greens. The top and sides of this dome are decoratively garnished with such ingredients as radishes, celery, parsley, mushrooms, beets, gherkins, anchovy filets, hard-cooked eggs, tomatoes, and truffles. These salads can be very elegant. They are brought to the table in a crystal bowl so that everyone may gasp in admiration before the ingredients are all tossed together. This salad is served as an hors d'oeuvre or as a main dish.

But enough of analysis. Let us make salads. I will begin with the simplest salads and their dressings and finish with a few of the more complicated ones. Fruit salads, which are in the domain of sweet dishes, do not appear here.

✳ THE GREEN SALAD

The green salad is the best-liked, most-eaten salad of France, and it deserves to be made with great care. It is eaten as a separate course, served after the main course and before the cheese or the dessert. In addition to being delicious in itself, its strategic location in the meal ensures that the salad performs two important functions. It refreshes the mouth to conclude cleanly what has gone on before. And it clears the taste for new surprises to come.

In America the green salad is served before the main course or with it. Served alone before the main course, the salad becomes an hors d'oeuvre. Delicious, but that is all. Eaten as a first course, the salad cannot provide the refreshing respite that is its special forte.

When it is served with the main course, the role the salad plays is at the discretion of the diner. If it is eaten in snatches between bites of beef and forkfuls of peas, the green salad becomes little more than an extra vegetable. Also, the flavor of any wine served with the main course will be thoroughly mauled by the vinegar in the salad dressing. Only if the salad is eaten after the main course is its important role fulfilled.

The simplest green salad is a single "green" tossed with oil, vinegar, salt, and pepper until it is thoroughly coated. A salad "green" is any green vegetable or leafy portion of a vegetable that can be eaten raw. Lettuce, watercress, Belgian endive, spinach, cabbage, celery, sorrel, tender young dandelion shoots, scallions, all are salad greens.

The green (let us say it is Bibb lettuce) is carefully washed in volumes of cold water and the leaves carefully removed one at a time. Shake the leaves to remove excess water without breaking them, drain them on a towel, and carefully pat them dry. Or you may dry them in a wire salad basket powered by a child. The child takes the basket of greens outside and whirls it about his head, thereby expelling the water by centrifugal force. It is important that the greens be dry so that they will not dilute the dressing. Roll the dried greens in a towel, and chill them in the refrigerator.

A more complex green salad is the mixed green salad, consisting of several greens combined. This is a more interesting salad than one dressed green served alone. When mixing greens, my only caution to you is to avoid mixing very soft, tender greens like Boston lettuce with heavy greens like escarole. Short of this extreme, strive for varying textures and tastes. For example, you may choose a soft, buttery Boston lettuce; a crisp Bibb; peppery watercress; and the somewhat bitter chicory. Or, for a heftier, more bite-y salad, choose crisp Bibb; crunchy romaine; and bitter, chewy escarole. You will find all these greens described in Chapter 11.

The salads should be assembled just before serving. The vinegar in the dressing will attack the greens, so there is more than just show in the tradition of tossing salads at the table.

Tear the greens in bite-size pieces. (Do not cut greens with a knife—a dull knife bruises the greens; an iron knife discolors the cut edges. If you must shred greens, do it with a silver knife.) Put the torn greens into a bowl and pour the dressing over them. Toss lightly but thoroughly until the bottom of the bowl is dry.

✳ SALAD DRESSINGS

Before proceeding to the other kinds of salads, let us review their cold sauces or dressings. These include Vinaigrette Sauce and its variations, Mayonnaise and its variations, and a few simple preparations that are neither vinaigrette nor mayonnaise.

The usual dressing for green salads is vinaigrette, and I will repeat its recipe here. To 2 tablespoons wine vinegar, add ¼ to ½ teaspoon salt and a sprinkling of fresh-ground pepper. Allow the salt to dissolve in the vinegar, add 8 tablespoons olive oil, and beat with a fork or a wire whisk to blend the dressing. This 4-to-1 ratio of oil to vinegar differs from the traditional 3-to-1 ratio to make allowance for American vinegars, which are frequently more acrid than the French. Perhaps it should be 5-to-1. Consult your taste.

This amount of dressing, a little over ½ cup, should suffice for 2 to 3 quarts of salad greens. Salads should be only lightly dressed. The flavor of the dressing must not be allowed to blot out the fresh taste of the greens. Also, a salad should not be too oily. Dressing a salad is a matter of great delicacy.

There are many ways you can vary basic vinaigrette to add interest to the plain green and vegetable salads. Following are a few of these additions and substitutions; others you can invent for yourself. The quantities given should be applied to ½ cup of basic vinaigrette, but this is a delicate business and you must adjust the flavoring to your taste.

Vinaigrette with Mustard. Add 1 teaspoon prepared mustard or ½ teaspoon dry mustard. Use mustard, rather than more vinegar, to make the dressing stronger.

Vinaigrette with Garlic. It is important that the garlic flavor be very subtle. You may rub the bottom of the salad bowl with a cut clove of garlic. Or follow the traditional French method of rubbing a large piece or several cubes of hard bread with cut garlic (these are called *chapons*) and tossing the pieces with the salad. The bread is removed before the salad is served, providing a tidbit for the cook.

Vinaigrette with Lemon Juice. Substitute fresh-squeezed lemon juice for half of the vinegar.

Vinaigrette with Curry. Add ½ teaspoon curry powder and 2 teaspoons minced shallots. Especially good for the stronger-flavored greens.

Vinaigrette with Roquefort. Add 2 tablespoons crumbled Roquefort or other blue cheese.

Vinaigrette with Wine. Substitute dry red or white wine or champagne for ½ of the vinegar.

Vinaigrette with Anchovy. Add 2 filets of anchovy that you have rubbed through a fine sieve. Omit the salt in the basic dressing and salt to taste.

Vinaigrette with Bacon Fat. Substitute hot bacon fat for the olive oil. Omit the salt and heat the vinegar. For wilted green salads.

Vinaigrette with Egg Yolk. Add 2 hard-cooked egg yolks that you have rubbed through a sieve. Beat well into the dressing.

Vinaigrette with Malt. Make the dressing with malt vinegar.

Vinaigrette with Tarragon. Add 2 teaspoons fresh chopped tarragon, or make the dressing with tarragon vinegar.

Vinaigrette with Herbs. Add 1 teaspoon each of finely chopped fresh parsley, chives, chervil, and tarragon. (You may sprinkle the herbs into the greens instead.) When added to mixed greens, this gives you *salade aux fines herbes*.

Vinaigrette with Cream. Substitute rich heavy cream for the olive oil and use about one tablespoon vinegar to taste.

Vinaigrette with Watercress. To ½ cup vinaigrette add 2 tablespoons finely chopped cooked egg yolks and 2 tablespoons finely chopped watercress. (This concoction is also known as *sauce cressonière*.)

Mayonnaise is also a frequently used dressing for salads, particularly combination salads. You will find the recipe for Mayonnaise in Chapter 4. Mayonnaise is very rich and should be used discretely or thinned with cream. You may flavor the mayonnaise by adding to it, to taste: prepared mustard; a pinch of cayenne; chopped chives; mixed chopped green herbs such as parsley, chives, tarragon, chervil, watercress, and spinach, bottled Worcestershire sauce; vinaigrette; Robert Sauce; lemon juice; and Tomato Purée. Following are some specific recipes:

Mayonnaise with Anchovy. To 1 cup mayonnaise, add 1 or 2 mashed anchovy filets.

Mayonnaise with Curry. To 1 cup mayonnaise, add 1 teaspoon curry powder and 2 teaspoons chopped chives.

Mayonnaise with Watercress. To 1 cup mayonnaise add ¼ cup chopped watercress.

Mayonnaise with Tarragon. To 1 cup mayonnaise add ¼ cup chopped tarragon.

Mayonnaise with Herbs. To 1 cup mayonnaise add 1 teaspoon each of chopped parsley, chives, chervil, and tarragon.

Mayonnaise with Roquefort. To 1 cup mayonnaise add 1 cup sour cream, 1 cup mashed Roquefort cheese, and 4 drops Tabasco.

Also made with or made similarly to mayonnaise are the following cold sauces:

NIÇOISE SAUCE (*Sauce Niçoise*). To 1 cup Mayonnaise add 2 tablespoons Tomato Purée, 2 tablespoons chopped pimentos, and a few leaves of fresh tarragon.

COLLIOURE SAUCE (*Sauce Collioure*). To 1 cup mayonnaise add 1 teaspoon anchovy paste, ¼ chopped parsley, and a pinch of finely minced garlic.

DIJONNAISE SAUCE (*Sauce Dijonnaise*). Blend until smooth 4 mashed hard-cooked egg yolks, 1 tablespoon prepared Dijon Mustard, and ¼ cup wine vinegar. Beat into this mixture, a little at a time, 1 cup olive oil.

PARISIAN SAUCE (*Sauce Parisienne*). Blend until smooth 4 tablespoons fresh Gervaise cheese or cream cheese and ¼ cup wine vinegar, ¾ teaspoon salt, and ½ teaspoon paprika. Beat into this mixture, little by little, 1 cup olive oil. (This sauce is especially suited to cold asparagus.)

For other cold mayonnaise-type sauces used for dressing salads, see Chapter 4 for Gribiche, La Varenne, Mousquetaire, Rémoulade, Russian, and Tartar sauces.

In addition to dressings based on vinaigrette and mayonnaise, there are a few simple preparations based on cream.

Using fresh cream as the fat, and seasoning it with salt and white pepper, you may make a kind of vinaigrette by adding vinegar, or lemon juice or tomato sauce, as the acid. You may also add grated horseradish, curry powder, or chopped fresh herbs. A frequently used cream-based dressing is Mustard Cream.

MUSTARD CREAM SAUCE (*Sauce Moutarde à la Crème*). To 2 tablespoons prepared mustard, add a good squeeze of lemon juice. Beat in, little by little, 4 to 6 tablespoons heavy cream. Season to taste with salt and white pepper.

Sour cream, which carries its own acid flavor, is also used as a foundation for salad dressings. Add salt and white pepper, vinegar or lemon juice, and such flavorings as chopped chives or other herbs, finely chopped onion or garlic, grated horseradish, or crumbled Roquefort.

Having familiarized ourselves with some of the available dressings, let us proceed with the salads.

✳ RAW VEGETABLE SALADS

TOMATO SALADS

These delightful, simple salads are frequently served as hors d'oeuvres, although they may take the place of the green salad in the course of a meal as well. They are easy to make, but their success depends entirely on the quality of the tomatoes (see Tomatoes in Chapter 11).

Select firm, red, ripe tomatoes and peel them without heating them. (Scalding tomatoes or holding them over a flame slightly cooks the flesh beneath the skin, making it soft and mushy.) To peel without heating, scrape the entire surface of the tomato with a knife without breaking the skin. This loosens the bond between skin and flesh, and the tomato may then be peeled.

Cut the peeled tomatoes in half, horizontally, and squeeze out the seeds and the jelly. Slice the tomatoes in thin strips, arrange them on a serving dish, and sprinkle with Vinaigrette Sauce.

To serve tomato slices or quarters, cut the peeled tomatoes in half and carefully scoop out the seeds and jelly. Slice or quarter the tomatoes, lay them on a dish, sprinkle with salt, and allow them to stand for 30 minutes to extract their excess liquid. Dry the tomatoes, arrange on a serving dish, and sprinkle with vinaigrette.

In addition to vinaigrette, you may sprinkle a tomato salad with chopped fresh herbs such as parsley, basil, fennel, and tarragon. Or you may sprinkle it with finely chopped shallots, or cover with thinly sliced onions. Also, a curried vinaigrette is excellent with tomatoes.

CUCUMBER SALAD

Peel cucumbers and slice them thinly. Sprinkle them with salt and allow them to stand for 2 hours to release their excess liquid. Dry the cucumbers, arrange them on a serving dish, and sprinkle with 4 parts oil and 1 part vinegar. Do not salt or pepper the cucumbers. Sprinkle with chopped fresh chervil, parsley, or chives.

Old, large, end-of-season cucumbers should first be cut in half lengthwise and their seeds scooped out. The slices will then be "C"-shaped.

Instead of oil and vinegar, you may dress the cucumbers with 8 tablespoons heavy cream mixed with a scant 1 tablespoon vinegar. Or you may dress the cucumbers with 8 tablespoons sour cream mixed with 1 teaspoon horseradish, and sprinkle them with chopped fresh dill.

CABBAGE SALAD

Strip the tender, inner leaves of firm cabbage from the ribs and slice thinly in fine julienne.* Dress red cabbage with Vinaigrette Sauce, or with the variations of vinaigrette made with bacon fat or hard-cooked egg yolks. Dress green cabbage with 8 tablespoons cream and 1 scant tablespoon vinegar, salt, and pepper.

For a delicate warm salad, choose hearts of tender Boston or other butterhead lettuces, one for each person. Bring the lettuce hearts to room temperature, or steam them, tops down, over boiling water for one minute. Just before serving, season lightly with salt and pepper. To melted butter add a small squeeze of garlic and lemon juice, and pour the warm butter into the lettuces.

For a heftier warm salad, choose a robust flavorful lettuce such as romaine, chicory, escarole, Belgian endive, or spinach. Prepare the greens and bring them to room temperature. Sauté 6 to 8 slices of bacon until their fat is rendered and they are crisp. Crumble the bacon into the greens and season with pepper. Pour enough of the hot bacon fat onto the greens to coat them lightly when tossed. In the pan in which you sautéed the bacon, heat 1 or 2 tablespoons vinegar. Finish dressing the salad with vinegar and salt to taste.

❋ COOKED VEGETABLE SALADS

SIMPLE COOKED VEGETABLE SALADS

A number of vegetables are simply boiled in water, chilled, and served with a dressing. Leftover vegetables, which would be ruined by reheating, frequently end up this way. Cooked vegetable salads are usually served on beds of lettuce leaves as hors d'oeuvres.

Among the cooked vegetables served cold with Vinaigrette Sauce are artichokes, beans of various kinds, broccoli, Brussels sprouts, cabbage cut in julienne,* eggplant, green beans, lentils, hearts of lettuce, potatoes, and sweet potatoes. Artichokes, potatoes, and leeks are frequently served with Mayonnaise. Eggplant and beets are frequently served with Mustard Cream Sauce.

VEGETABLES À LA GRECQUE

Cooking *à la grecque* is a method of cooking and seasoning vegetables in a flavorful liquid that is a kind of Vinaigrette Sauce diluted with water. The liquid may then be reduced and used to dress the vegetables, which are frequently served as an hors d'oeuvre.

Vegetables that lend themselves to cooking à la grecque include asparagus, cauliflower separated into knobs, hearts of celery, carrots cut in olive shapes, tiny white onions, mushrooms, eggplant cut in sticks, and zucchini cut in rounds.

Clean the vegetable, cut it in the proper size or shape, and blanch it for 1 or 2 minutes in boiling water. Drain the vegetable, put it into an enameled pan, and add ½ cup olive oil, 2 tablespoons wine vinegar or the juice of 2 lemons, ½ teaspoon salt, 6 peppercorns, 3 sprigs of parsley, 1 bay leaf, and 1 sprig or pinch of thyme. You may also add other seasonings of your choice, such as tarragon, chervil, or a clove of garlic. Pour boiling water over the vegetables to just cover them, and boil until they are just tender.

Allow the vegetable to cool in the liquid and drain. Reduce the liquid in the pan by ½ or more, strain it, and season it to taste. It may require more vinegar. Pour the liquid over the vegetable, and chill.

POTATO SALAD

Potato salad is an American favorite, and I have tasted many delightful variations in every part of the country. French potato salad differs from the American in that the potato slices are dressed while they are still warm so that they may absorb the dressing. The salad is served warm, or at least at room temperature.

Choose 6 firm, waxy, medium potatoes (about 1½ pounds). Boil them in salted water until they are just tender. Peel and slice them thinly while they are still warm. Pack the slices in layers in a warm serving dish, sprinkling them with salt, pepper, and one teaspoon each of chopped parsley, chives, tarragon, and chervil. Sprinkle with 4 to 6 tablespoons hot water, or hot stock, or hot dry white wine; 1½ tablespoons wine vinegar; and 6 tablespoons olive oil. Allow the salad to stand until the dressing is absorbed, occasionally tipping the dish and spooning the dressing over the potato slices. Sprinkle with a little chopped parsley and serve at room temperature.

You may also sprinkle or garnish the potato salad with chopped shallots, onions, scallions, or pickles; diced cucumbers or beets; capers; anchovies; slices of hard-cooked egg; or green pepper rings.

ASPARAGUS SALAD

Boil asparagus in salted water until barely tender, and plunge it into cold water. Drain the asparagus and chill it. Chop 2 hard-cooked eggs and add 2 teaspoons finely chopped parsley. Arrange the asparagus on a bed of lettuce leaves, sprinkle with Vinaigrette Sauce and the chopped egg and parsley mixture.

MIXED COOKED VEGETABLE SALADS

These are endless. Vegetables chosen for their affinity of taste, texture, and color are cooked, chilled, combined with other vegetables, and dressed with a Vinaigrette Sauce or Mayonnaise dressing. They are sometimes garnished with greens, hard-cooked eggs, or something else. Following is a short selection of these salads which are served as hors d'oeuvres.

POTATO AND TOMATO SALAD (*Salade Américaine*). Combine cooked potato slices; raw, pressed tomato slices; and raw celery cut in julienne.* Garnish with thin slices of raw onion and hard-cooked eggs, and dress with Vinaigrette Sauce.

POTATO AND WATERCRESS SALAD (*Salade Cressonière*). Combine Potato Salad and watercress. Sprinkle with chopped parsley, chopped chervil, and chopped hard-cooked egg.

LETTUCE AND ARTICHOKE SALAD (*Salade Eléonora*). Surround hearts of lettuce with artichoke bottoms. Garnish with poached eggs and asparagus tips, and dress with Mayonnaise.

GREEN BEAN, POTATO, AND CELERY SALAD (*Salade Grande Duchesse*). Combine green beans with potatoes and celery, both cut in julienne.* Dress with Mayonnaise.

ARTICHOKE AND TOMATO SALAD (*Salade Provençale*). Combine artichoke bottoms and tomatoes, both cut in quarters, and sprinkle with chopped basil. Dress with Vinaigrette Sauce with Anchovy to which you have added a little finely minced garlic.

GREEN BEAN, CAULIFLOWER, AND WATERCRESS SALAD (*Salade Jeannette*). Combine green beans, cooked cauliflowerets, and watercress. Sprinkle with parsley and dress with Vinaigrette Sauce.

GREEN BEAN, TOMATO, AND CUCUMBER SALAD (*Salade Nantaise*). Combine green beans, quartered tomatoes, sliced cucumbers, and watercress. Sprinkle with chopped scallions and dress with Tartar Sauce.

CAULIFLOWER SALAD (*Salade Du Barry*). Garnish cooked cauliflowerets with chopped watercress and radishes. Dress with Vinaigrette Sauce with chopped chives.

BEET SALAD (*Salade de Betteraves*). Cut baked beets in thin slices or in julienne.* Sprinkle with finely chopped baked onion or chopped fresh scallions. Dress with Vinaigrette or Mustard Cream Sauce.

CELERY, POTATO, BEET, AND GREEN PEPPER SALAD (*Salade Belle-Fermière*). Combine equal amounts of potatoes, beets, and green peppers with half as much celery, all cut in julienne.* Dress with Vinaigrette Sauce, and sprinkle with chopped chervil.

❊ COMBINATION SALADS

SEAFOOD SALAD

Fill the bottom of a salad bowl with shredded greens, dressed with Vinaigrette Sauce and arranged in a dome. On top of the dome, heap cooked lobster, crab, or shrimp meat, or a combination of these, which you have sliced or diced and tossed in vinaigrette. Decorate the salad with quarters of hard-cooked eggs and hearts of lettuce. Sprinkle with chopped parsley and chervil or tarragon.

CHEF'S SALAD

Fill the bottom of a salad bowl with shredded greens. On top of these greens, with an eye to decoration, heap equal quantities of cooked breast of chicken, smoked tongue, smoked ham, and Swiss cheese, all cut in julienne.* Decorate the salad with watercress and halves of hard-cooked eggs. Toss the salad at the table with Vinaigrette Sauce.

RUSSIAN SALAD
(*Salade Russ*)

Make a mixed vegetable salad with potatoes, carrots, beets, and green beans, all cubed, and peas. Add cooked ham and pickled tongue, both cut in julienne,* and lobster meat. Toss lightly with Mayonnaise, heap the salad into a dome, and decorate with capers, gherkins, truffles, sliced beets, filets of anchovy, pickled tongue, sliced mushrooms, and truffles cut in julienne.

NIÇOISE SALAD

Make a mixed vegetable salad with equal amounts of cooked, diced potatoes and green beans. With an eye to decoration, garnish the salad with quarters of raw tomato; small, pitted ripe olives; capers; and anchovy filets. Toss at the table with Vinaigrette Sauce with Garlic, and sprinkle with chopped chervil and tarragon.

🌿 13   *Cheese*

Cheese may be the substance of a dish, such as a fondue. Or it may be the seasoning, as when grated into a bowl of hot onion soup. But the true measure of cheese in gastronomy is best realized when it is eaten as wine is drunk, for the wonder of its taste.

Cheese is the coagulated solids of milk; 5 quarts of milk make about 1 pound of cheese. It may be eaten fresh, as is cottage cheese. More often cheese is ripened by molds or bacteria to become the wine of food. Like wine in its bottle, a ripening cheese in its rind is a living thing that matures more or less slowly. Some cheeses reach their peak in a few weeks. Others improve for a hundred years. In Switzerland it is not unusual, when a baby is born, to set aside a large cheese. On every important occasion throughout life, the cheese is ceremoniously served. The cheese, which outlives the man, is finished by his descendants.

In the well-ordered French dinner, cheese commands a course of its own. This course follows the salad, when the taste is refreshed, and it precedes the dessert. Usually several kinds of cheese are served with chilled tart apples, pears, and other fruits, unsalted nuts, bread or biscuits, and sometimes sweet butter. At a less formal meal cheese may become the dessert, and some cheeses are served with sugar and cream, fresh berries, or jam. Cheese is always served at room temperature.

The French make about 400 different cheeses to provide variety for this course. About 100 French cheese are sold in the United States. We import many other cheeses, especially from Denmark, Holland, and Italy. Also, we produce many fine cheeses of our own. From this bounty I will try to select the most notable cheeses you are likely to find at your supermarket or cheese store.

I will discuss only natural cheese. Process cheese, which is identified as such on the label, is a mixture of natural cheeses that have been ground and heated to sterility. It is dead cheese, and of no gastronomic interest.

However, even if a package is marked natural cheese, the pleasure it will give you is doubtful if the cheese has been made by the rindless process. Rindless cheeses are cured in their plastic wrapper, instead of being freely exposed to the air. They lose less weight, but the curing process is inhibited and no rind or crust develops. There is no way to tell if a block of cheese wrapped in plastic has been made by the rindless process; large natural rind cheeses may be cut up and similarly wrapped before sale. Rindless cheeses may be aged and more or less sharp, but they are characterized by an incompleteness of flavor which is frustrating to the palate.

When buying imported cheese, always make certain as to where the cheese is imported from. Swiss cheese is imported from Argentina. Camembert is imported from Denmark. Although these imported cheeses may be quite good in themselves, they are not the cheeses they purport to be.

Classifying cheeses is somewhat of a problem. They are usually classified as to whether they are fresh or ripened, and the ripened cheeses are further classified into soft, semisoft, firm, and hard (grating) cheeses. But this tells you nothing about their taste. If, however, I try to rank the cheeses on their strength of flavor, I am confounded by the fact that many cheeses that are quite mild when young develop a formidable taste when aged. Consequently I will present the cheeses in an order of increasing firmness, and among cheeses of similar firmness I will present the most delicate first.

Finally, to enjoy a cheese, be certain to bring it to room temperature first. This may take 30 minutes for a small, soft cheese or 4 hours for a large, firm one.

This is not a book of cheese, and many fine cheeses have been left out of it, but I hope it should adequately survey the range of tastes and textures cheese has to offer. Do not fail to give special attention to the American originals—Liederkranz, Brick, and American Munster—cheeses we have given to the world and can be justly proud of.

COTTAGE CHEESE

This is the simplest cheese to make, but one of the most difficult to make right. One of the best milk companies I know, in the Middle West, using only the finest skim milk and with decades of experience behind it, is still sometimes humbled by a batch of cottage cheese that doesn't come up to standard.

So much cottage cheese is eaten in America I need say little about it here. Probably all of it is eaten chilled, but in order to enjoy the delicate, tangy flavor of cottage cheese it should, like all cheese, be brought to room temperature.

Most cottage cheese is creamed, that is, at least 4 percent butterfat is mixed into the curds. Uncreamed cottage cheese is called pot cheese and is noticeably dryer.

You can make your own cottage cheese. Add 1 teaspoon of rennet to 1 quart of milk and allow it to stand in a warm place for 8 hours or until it sets. Put the set milk in cheesecloth, hang it over a bowl or the sink, and allow the whey to drain until the remaining curd is thick and firm. Season with salt and moisten with thick cream.

FRESH CREAM CHEESE

American cream cheese is a smooth, soft, high-fat cheese with a fresh cream taste and a mild acid tang. It is rather like a smooth, rich, cottage cheese with a spreadable consistency. It is available everywhere and it is very good. In New York City, cream cheese on a bagel with smoked salmon (lox) is practically required eating.

French cream cheeses range from the leaner *carré frais* to the very rich triple-cream cheeses containing 75 percent butterfat. Cream cheeses are very perishable, and you are likely to find fresh ones only in stores with a large cheese clientele. Closest to American cream cheese are Petit-Suisse and Gervais. These contain about the same amount of butterfat, but they are more sour-tasting.

RIPENED CREAM CHEESE

Fresh cream cheese is ready for eating just as soon as it is made. If, however, you spray the fresh cheese with an appropriate mold, it will begin to ripen and become another cheese with a flavor reminiscent of the freshness of the original and with a new, delicate flavor of its own. This ripening takes 4 to 6 weeks, allowing the cheese to be shipped across the Atlantic, and it is in this ripened form that we receive most of our double-cream and triple-cream cheeses from abroad.

Double-cream cheeses contain 60 percent butterfat. Available here are Une Gourmandise and Fromage de Monsieur Fromage from France, and Hablé Crème Chantilly from Sweden. Triple-cream cheeses contain 75 percent butterfat, and you are most likely to find Boursault, Boursin, Triple Crème Parfait, and Le Roi, all imported from France.

These cheeses pass quickly through their prime of life, so you must buy them with care. Choose a plump cheese with a mild odor and a clean, dry surface rind, and prepare for an incredible experience. Some people are known to have framed the fork with which they ate their first triple-cream.

BRIE

Brie is a rich, soft, creamy yellow cheese encased in a thin, edible crust. The crust is usually golden-white or brownish-white, and sometimes reddish. I do not wish to allow myself to be carried away, but this is a great cheese.

Brie has a taste both new and old, the fresh taste of milk in earthen crocks, the hoary taste of benign molds. There is a hint of old wine in it, and deep woods. It exudes a fragrance you'd expect to find inside a fine old wooden butter churn. It is perhaps the greatest cheese in the world.

Brie comes only from France. The true Brie is Brie de Meaux, and it can be found in America from October to April. It comes in 16-inch and 12-inch discs a little over 1 inch thick and weighing 6 pounds and 3½ pounds respectively. Brie is copied even in France, and although the results are more or less enjoyable, they are not Brie de Meaux. Brie de Melun, made throughout the year, is a firmer, sharper cheese and less dependable in flavor. Neither is Brie de Coulommiers, a small 1-pound cheese sometimes called Petit Brie, a true Brie de Meaux.

Brie is a very active cheese. Like a butterfly it fleets from youth to old age. You should eat it during the 3 or 4 days it is at its prime. Deciding which 3 or 4 days are the correct ones has reduced many a gourmet to tears. Bries ripen from the outside in, and are very secretive about what's happening in their heart of hearts.

You can tell when a Brie has begun to ripen by pressing it with your fingertips; it will feel soft. But is it soft enough? Has it ripened to the core and matured in flavor? Or is it too soft? Has it begun to liquefy and become musty to the taste? The only foolproof way to tell when a Brie is perfectly ripened is to cut it open. But once you cut it open, normal ripening will cease. "Hah!" says the young Brie, revealing a hard-caked center, "take this for your impatience." Or "Ho, ho, ho," roars the old Brie, its crust collapsing with laughter as its odorous, overrunny insides spill out onto the plate.

There are ways to get a perfect Brie. Find a store where the Brie is displayed on the open counter, and wait at least 2 hours after the store has opened so that the cheese may come to room temperature. Look at the box label for the words Brie de Meaux. Then look at the cheese.

A whole Brie is sold only for parties; it is too perishable to buy for the family. Consequently, chances are good the cheese will have been cut into and the halves or wedges wrapped in plastic film. Look at the face of the cut. Between the two crusts the cheese should be a perfectly uniform creamy-yellow color. Now feel the face of the cut. It should have the same smooth, lumpless texture from top to bottom. If the cheese exhibits a crusty white layer in the center, or if in running your finger down the face of the cut you can feel a hardness in the center, the cheese is too young and may never ripen. If, on the other hand, the interior of the cheese is soft and runny and contained only by the plastic wrapping, and the crust is nearing a state of collapse, the cheese is too old.

A perfect Brie, then, is softhearted and uniformly colored throughout. The interior will bulge slightly against the plastic wrapping, the crust will be just barely depressed, and its fresh dairy and old fungi taste will utterly delight you. Eat it on crisp slices of apple, or with pears, or on crisp, unsalted biscuits.

CREMA DANIA

This is a new cheese, invented (or perhaps discovered) in Denmark in 1957. It has quickly, and justifiably, become popular in the United States and can be found at many supermarkets in prime condition. It is a soft cheese, with the incredibly smooth texture of a fine Brie. Unlike Brie, it ripens evenly throughout and remains at its prime for several weeks. It has a milder flavor than Brie, with a fine, dry taste that is all its own. Crema Dania is rather like a richly seasoned butter that has somehow aged without spoiling. It comes in 6-ounce rectangular blocks wrapped in gold foil, sold separately or 2 to a box. The cheese is ready to eat when it softens, and while the crust is still white and its odor still delicate.

CAMEMBERT

Except for its taste, Camembert is very much like Brie. True Camembert comes only from France. Its season runs from October through May, and it is at its best from January through March. It ripens from the outside in. And its great moment is very fleeting, allowing you only 2 or 3 days to seize the opportunity of enjoying it at its prime.

Camembert has a stronger, more authoritative flavor than Brie. Brie you eat with your eyes closed, your mind filled with visions of happy calico cows munching long, sweet, green meadow grasses, your palate searching out and savoring its delicate, new-old flavor. Camembert is more aromatic, more redolent, more tangy. Camembert you eat with your eyes wide open. You know you are eating a cheese.

Camembert comes in a little cake about 4½ inches in diameter, 1¼ inches thick, weighing about 8 ounces. The crust is rough-textured, beautifully golden with a sprinkling of white freckles when ripe, and eminently edible. It is packed in a thin wood box shaped to fit the cheese.

Choosing a Camembert is more difficult than choosing a Brie because you are not likely to find a half cheese you can peer into. As it ripens inward from the surface, the young Camembert softens and becomes tender. You can feel that ripening has begun, but you cannot be sure that it has penetrated to dissolve the last caked layer in the center. If you open the cheese and its center is white and hard, all you can do is put the pieces back together, wrap the cheese in a damp cloth, put it into the refrigerator, and hopefully sacrifice a goat.

An old Camembert is more revealing. Even when wrapped and chilled you may detect a certain odor ranging from the somewhat feisty to the strong smell of ammonia. (A slight ammonia odor is normal and will disappear in a few minutes after the cheese is opened.) Also, if the surface of the cheese has sunk leaving a raised rim around the sides, the cheese must be drying out. Pass it up for a plumper, fresher-smelling cheese.

America, Denmark, and other countries also make a cheese called Camembert. Some of these are very pleasant cheeses, but they are not really Camembert. American Camembert is ripened with an entirely different mold, and its taste is milder. It is, however, good to eat the year round.

BEL PAESE

This soft, sweet, mild-tasting import from Italy can be found in most supermarkets. It comes in wheels about 6 inches in diameter, weighing about 4½ pounds, and in wedges cut from these wheels. It has a delightful dairy taste with a delicate tang that rings a tinkling bell in your mouth. Excellent Bel Paese is also made in Wisconsin. To detect the difference, you should taste them both, the original Italian and the American version, one after the other.

LIEDERKRANZ

In 1882 a New York cheesemaker, Emil Frey, sought to duplicate a German cheese that could not survive the Atlantic voyage. He failed, but in failing he created a new kind of cheese. He named it Liederkranz in honor of the singing society of which he was a member.

Today Liederkranz is recognized as one of the great cheeses of the world. Like Brie, it has not been duplicated anywhere. There is only one Liederkranz, American Liederkranz, and this name is both the brand name and the name of the cheese itself. It is made in Ohio.

Liederkranz comes in ¼-pound blocks packed in dated cardboard boxes. Like Brie and Camembert it ripens from the surface inward. A too young Liederkranz will have a pale yellow crust and a caked center. The partially ripened cheese is pale yellow in color, with a slightly bitter, yeasty taste and an inconclusive flavor. A too old Liederkranz has a sticky brown crust and a runny center, butterscotch in color, with a strong odor and a salty, smoky taste that scratches in your throat. I am writing all this so you will be sure to persevere in your search for a perfect cheese.

A perfect Liederkranz is a wondrous cheese. The crust is a rich yellow color. When brought to room temperature and cut, a glossy cheese, the color of old gold, will flow out like heavy molasses. It has an authoritative Cambertish-Limburgerish taste that is somewhat milder than its odor, and altogether delicious. Buy Liederkranz cheese two weeks before the date stamped on the box and cut it when the cheese is soft and the crust is a good yellow color. It is not as short-lived as Camembert, and in my experience Liederkranz achieves its peak about one week before the date on the box.

LIMBURGER

Limburger, which originated in Belgium, is the strongest-tasting cheese that has any following in America. A natural Limburger is shaped in long blocks. It is a soft cheese, very smooth when ripened, and containing tiny holes. The surface mold is reddish-yellow and the interior is creamy white. Flavor and odor are powerful. It is made mostly in Wisconsin and New York. Imported Limburger cheeses are even stronger.

ROQUEFORT AND OTHER BLUE-GREEN CHEESES

The mold *Penicillium roquefortii* is used to inoculate a number of cheeses throughout the world. As this mold grows and ripens the cheeses, a characteristic blue to blue-green to green veining develops in the body of the cheeses and a similar pungency of flavor develops. The most famous and finest of these blue-green cheeses are French Roquefort, English Stilton, and Italian Gorgonzola. All are imported into the United States, and a quantity of Gorgonzola is made here. Other "bleu" cheeses ripened by the same mold are imported from France, Denmark, and Norway, and domestic "blue" cheeses using this mold are made in quantity here.

Roquefort is made exclusively from ewe's milk, and every Roquefort cheese is ripened in the limestone caves in the vicinity of Roquefort, France. It is said these caves are patrolled by squads of cats in search of the fortunate mice who prey upon the ripening cheeses. No nibbled cheeses are ever imported into the United States, however; these, it is said, are reserved for certain gourmets who pay a premium price for cheeses so painstakingly selected by the little four-footed connoisseurs.

Roquefort is a semisoft to crumbly white cheese with diffuse splotches of green throughout its body. It is made in small cakes, 8 inches in diameter and 3½ inches thick. It has a pungent taste with a delicate bite to it that leaves your mouth tingling.

English Stilton is firmer, with a flakier texture and a cream-colored body laced with thin blue-green veins. Its taste is less pungent, more mellow than Roquefort, with a suggestion of Cheddar cheese flavor. It comes in tall wheels, 8 inches in diameter and 8 to 12 inches thick.

Italian Gorgonzola is the softest of these cheeses, rich and creamy in texture, more yellow in color, with green veins of mold. It is more pungent than Roquefort. It comes in wheels 8 to 11 inches in diameter, 6½ to 8 inches thick.

Danish blue cheese is richer and softer than any of the above, and it is highly flavored. You can easily identify a Danish blue by the very fine marbling of blue-green mold throughout. The blue veins are not diffuse, but look like they had been inked on the surface of the cheese with a fine pen.

American blue cheeses, like the Danish, are good, but they are not on a par with Roquefort, Stilton, or Gorgonzola. Minnesota blue is ripened in caves, like Roquefort, but the caves are sandstone, not limestone, and the milk is cow's milk.

All these cheeses are excellent dessert cheeses, and they frequently add their piquancy to salads.

PORT-SALUT

This French cheese was first made by Trappist monks in the Abbey of Notre Dame de Port du Salut. It is now made commercially by agreement with the monks, and is imported into the United States under the Abbey brand. This is the true Port-Salut (or Port-du-Salut, as it is sometimes called).

Port-Salut is sold in small wheels weighing about 6 ounces and in larger wheels weighing about 6 pounds, as well as in wedges cut from these wheels. It is a semisoft cheese that ripens slowly and evenly both from the inside out and the outside in. Its prime of life is long, and it is practically always in fine condition.

The taste of Port-Salut ranges from very mild, when it is young, to very powerful when it is old. The Port-Salut you buy will almost invariably be young and mild. It is an excellent cheese as it is, but if you want to develop its full flavor you must age it for a number of months.

Oka is a Canadian Port-Salut made by the Trappists at Oka, Canada, by the same secret process as the original. You may sometimes find a French cheese in the market, similar in size and shape to Port-Salut, but labeled simply "Salut." This cheese is not Port-Salut but a more or less inferior copy.

Danish Port-Salut is a somewhat different cheese with a richer, stronger flavor. American Port-Salut, a very fine cheese, is similar to the Danish but milder.

PONT-L'ÉVÊQUE

This ancient cheese can be traced back to the Middle Ages. It is about 4 inches square and 1 to 1½ inches thick and weighs 10 ounces. It is mold-ripened like Camembert, from the outside in, and its striated soft crust is yellow-gold when ripe.

Pont l'Évêque is allied to the Limburger family, but it is not as strong as Liederkranz. It is a soft cheese but not runny, and it is a pale butter color. Its aroma is milder than Camembert, but its taste is definitely more flavorful. The ready-to-eat cheese is plump and its crust is soft and golden. Trouville, a similar cheese of excellent quality, is made in the same area of Normandy.

MUNSTER

The original Munster is a French cheese, made in the Münster Valley in Alsace. It is a strong cheese, frequently flavored with caraway or anise.

American Munster or Muenster is completely unlike its French namesake. It is very young and mild, with a refreshing, slightly tangy dairy taste that makes you want to slice it thickly. Taste many different Munsters. Some are excellent, some flavorless and bitter.

The cheese is semisoft, creamy in color, and it contains numerous tiny holes. It comes in wheels or blocks. High-quality milk is required for the making of Munster.

BRICK

Brick cheese is a nineteenth-century American invention, actually a variation of Limburger. It was originally shaped like a brick, and is made mostly in Wisconsin and the Middle West.

Brick is creamy colored, semisoft, and easy to slice. The cheese is perforated with numerous tiny holes. Young Brick is mild-tasting. Aged Brick develops formidable flavor, similar to but not quite as strong as Limburger. The rind is bitter and should be cut away.

EDAM AND GOUDA

These Holland cheeses are similar, the major difference being that Gouda contains a little more butterfat and is therefore a softer cheese. Edam is shaped like a cannon ball and is coated with red wax. Gouda is more oval shaped, like a flattened cannon ball; it is also available in wheels. It may or may not be coated with red wax.

Both cheeses are firm (Edam may be crumbly), with a creamy yellow to yellow-orange interior. The young cheeses are mild, mellow, and nutty with a hint of sweetness. They may be kept for a very long time and develop a greatness of flavor in about 2 years time.

CHEDDAR AND CHEDDARLIKE CHEESES

Cheddar cheese is named for the English village of Cheddar, where the process of Cheddaring cheese was developed in the sixteenth century. Cheddar and cheeses similar to it are so well liked in America that they have come to be called American cheese. It was homemade here in colonial times, and the first cheese factory in the United States, which opened in New York State in 1851, made only Cheddar cheese.

Cheddars are firm-textured cheeses. They may be from 2 months to 2 or more years old. The younger cheeses are quite mild in flavor and their body is pliant and waxy. The aged cheeses are intensely flavored and sharp with a texture that is outright crumbly. They range in color from near white to violent orange. The color, which comes from a vegetable dye, has no effect on flavor or texture.

Cheddars come in different shapes and sizes, giving rise to names that might perplex you. Variously sized wheels of Cheddar are called Cheddar, Daisy, Flat, Young American, and Picnic. Longhorn cheese is simply Cheddar formed into a cylinder 6 inches in diameter. Cheddar is also sold in rectangular blocks. There is no way of telling without tasting whether the cheese in any of these sizes is worth while.

Tasting, as with any cheese, is the best way to test a Cheddar. Whether you prefer a Cheddar that's young and mild or old and sharp, it should have a full, round flavor free of soapiness or bitterness. Notable American Cheddars include very sharp, white, aged Vermont Cheddar; New York's dry, brittle, lively Herkimer County Cheddar; and Oregon's Tillamook Cheddar, which gives you a full Cheddar flavor ranging from very, very mild to very, very sharp.

An unusual Cheddar, originating in Connecticut in 1845, is Pineapple cheese. Although no pineapples ever come near it, it is pineapple-shaped, with a diamond pattern resembling pineapple scales covering its surface. It is rubbed with oil and sometimes shellacked to make it bright yellow and glossy on the outside. Another unusual cheese is Vermont Sage cheese, a young, pale white Cheddar or Cheddarlike cheese that is given a sage flavoring and mottled green coloration.

Coon Cheddar, which is a high quality Cheddar cured in a special way, has a dark surface rind, a pale butter color, a crumbly body, and a deliciously sharp Cheddar taste when fully aged.

Canada sends us an excellent Cheddar. It is white, crumbly, and very like English Cheddar.

Colby cheese, made in the Middle West, is similar to Cheddar but softer, moister, and more open in texture.

From California comes the Cheddarlike cheese variously called Monterey or Jack or Monterey Jack. It is made three ways. Dry Monterey (or dry Jack) is made with skim milk. It is a firm cheese used for grating, and may be rubbed with oil and pepper. Whole-milk Monterey is a semisoft cheese, softer than Colby. High-moisture Jack, also made with whole milk, is even softer than Monterey. The cheeses are pale and very mild when young, gaining flavor as they age.

THE SWISSES

The true Swiss cheeses are Emmentaler and Gruyère, although Gruyère is also made on the French side of the border as well. They are important cheeses in French cooking, and you should know the differences between them and order them by name.

Emmentaler is imported in large wheels weighing from 160 to 230 pounds. It is a firm cheese, with a pale orange rind and a pale yellow interior, containing numerous holes ½ to 1 inch in diameter and spaced from 1 to 3 inches apart. In good quality cheese, the inside of these holes is glistening in appearance. Its flavor is mild, sweet, and nutty.

Gruyère cheese comes to us in small wheels weighing from 55 to 110 pounds. It is like Emmentaler in firmness and interior color, but it has a browning, wrinkled rind. Also, the holes in Gruyère are smaller, about the size of a pea. Its flavor is similar to that of Emmentaler, but it is sharper and has more tang.

Even more tangy than Gruyère is Appenzell. In the early stages of curing, Appenzell is steeped in brine with white wine and pepper. It has the dry, nutty Swiss cheese taste underlying an exciting sharpness of flavor, and it has a rich, ripe aroma. It is similar in appearance to Gruyère although smaller, with a thick rind resembling the crust of well-baked homemade bread.

Raclette is the most formidable of the Swisses, being exceedingly ripe and authoritative in both taste and aroma. Anyone with a tongue in his head cannot but envy the Swiss for the way in which they enjoy this cheese in Switzerland. A large chunk is impaled on a fork and held over a smoky fire until it becomes runny and molten. The molten mass is then scraped off with a knife and eaten in great cheesy, smoke-flavored mouthfuls with boiled potatoes, washed down with cold white wine.

A great volume of Swiss cheese is made in the United States, mainly in Wisconsin, and more is imported from countries other than Switzerland. Natural Wisconsin Swiss can be a very fine cheese. Unfortunately, many of these cheeses, especially those made by the "natural rindless" process, are bitter and unpleasant, and it is no wonder that children, with their delicate sense of taste, tend to reject what they think is "Swiss" cheese. Taste one of these cheeses and a Switzerland Swiss in succession, and you will understand my meaning. A Swiss Swiss is never bitter.

Swiss cheese will keep for a hundred years, so there is no excuse for not having it on hand. To keep the cheese moist, do as the Swiss do: wrap it in a cloth soaked in white wine and store it covered in the refrigerator.

PARMESAN AND ROMANO

Although eaten as a table cheese when young, aged Parmesan is best known as a seasoning cheese. In this capacity it has become indispensable in French cooking.

Aged Parmesan is not cut, it is broken. The broken edges, rough with crystals, look like rough, pale yellow granite. The full and proper name for the true Italian Parmesan is Parmigiano-Reggiano. There is no substitute for the real thing.

Only prime quality Parmesan is exported from Italy and it must be at least 2 years old. You will find the name Parmigiano-Reggiano stenciled on the rind. Another Parmesan cheese, Grana Padano, aged from 1 to 2 years, is less dependable in quality.

A young cheese for table use will be near white in color. As the cheese ages it becomes more yellow, increases in flavor, and is more suitable for grating and seasoning. It should not be too salty; it should have a sweet aftertaste. Look for a good grain, which is also available in a domestic Parmesan made in Fond du Lac, Wisconsin.

Another Italian grating cheese, Romano, is preferred in Southern Italy. Pecorino Romano, the most common type, is made from ewe's milk. Like Parmesan it is brittle and tangy, off-white when well aged, but it has a stronger flavor. Those who prefer Romano think Parmesan eaters are thin-blooded. Those who prefer Parmesan think Romano eaters are a common lot.

Pregrated cheese, even good imported Parmesan, is on its way to becoming sawdust.

✂ 14   *Desserts*

This heady realm of pastries and creams and chocolate, of glacéed fruits, sugared almonds, tarts and *petits fours,* is far too vast and complicated for me to attempt to describe here. Just as we must have a special pastry chef to create the sweet dishes of France, we would need a special book to describe them and teach their cooking. Someday, perhaps, but not now. In this chapter I will describe just a few of the French desserts that are favorites of mine.

CRÉMETS
(*Crémets*)

Some of the best desserts are the simplest. Whip 1 cup heavy cream. Beat 2 egg whites until they form peaks but are still moist. Then combine the cream and egg white and beat them together until they are well mixed. Pack the mixture into *coeur à la crème* molds, little heart-shaped molds with perforated bottoms that allow their contents to drain (these molds are now available at many kitchen specialty shops). Place the molds in a pan, cover them with a damp cloth, and put them in the refrigerator overnight to drain. To serve, unmold the *crémets,* and cover them all over with fresh heavy cream. Serve with powdered sugar. You may also serve fresh berries.

BANANAS À LA MALTAISE
(*Bananes à la Maltaise*)

This dessert takes only minutes to make, and may be flamed at the table. Peel the bananas and slice them in half lengthwise. In a skillet, melt 1 tablespoon butter for each banana and cook the banana halves for 2 minutes on each side. Sprinkle with 1 tablespoon sugar for each banana and cook for a few minutes more to lightly caramelize the sugar. Grate fresh orange peel over the banana halves, cut the end from the orange, wrap in cheesecloth, and squeeze the orange juice onto the bananas. Cook for a few minutes more until the juice is reduced to a syrup. Off the fire, swirl in* a few tablespoons of Grand Marnier or orange liqueur, set aflame, and serve.

CHERRIES DU BARRY
(*Cerises Du Barry*)

Butter a 7- or 8-inch spring mold and line it with *Pâte Sucrée*. Sprinkle the pastry dough lining with powdered sugar and prick the bottom of the dough all over with a fork. Pack the shell with pitted cherries, place it on a baking sheet, and bake in a 375° oven for about 40 minutes. Allow the tart to cool, chill it, and unmold it. Cover the surface and sides with whipped cream into which you have mixed crushed macaroons, and coat it all over with more crushed macaroons. Decorate the top with pink and white whipped cream piped through a pastry bag.

APPLE TART
(*Tarte Tatin*)

Heat 1 tablespoon butter in an ovenproof skillet about 8½ inches in diameter. Add ½ cup sugar and stir constantly over low heat until the sugar melts and turns a light caramel color. Peel, core, and slice 5 tart green apples, and arrange the slices in concentric rings to cover entirely the bottom of the skillet. Roll out Puff Paste ¼ inch thick and cut out a round 10 inches in diameter. Arrange the dough over the apples, tucking the rim of the dough down between the apple slices and the skillet until the rim is flush with the bottom of the skillet. Prick the top of the dough in several places with a knife, and bake in a 400° oven for 10 minutes or until the crust is browned and puffed (by cooking the tart upside down, the weight of the apples does not discourage the puffing of the dough). Place a flat lid or plate on top of the skillet and flip over quickly to unmold the tart.

APRICOT ICE
(*Glace à l'Abricot*)

Apricot is a favorite French fruit, and this simple dessert forthrightly presents apricots refreshing flavor. Pit 1 pound fresh apricots, put them in a pan with ½ cup water and 3 tablespoons sugar, cover and cook gently until they are soft. Put the cooked apricot through a food mill or sieve, or Purée in the blender, and chill it. Heat 1 cup light cream containing 1 strip lemon peel and 3 tablespoons sugar until the cream reaches the boiling point, and discard the peel. Beat 2 egg yolks in a bowl and, little by little, beat the hot cream into the eggs. Cool this custard and mix it with the puréed apricot. Whip ½ cup heavy cream and fold it into the custard and apricot mixture, pour the mixture into ice cube trays or similar dishes, and cover with foil. Chill in the freezer, stirring occasionally, for 2 to 3 hours, until the mixture achieves the consistency of soft sherbet.

CARAMEL CUSTARD WITH FLAMING PEACHES
(*Crème Caramel Flambé aux Pêches*)

In a heavy saucepan, caramelize* 3 tablespoons sugar with 1 tablespoon water. Pour the caramelized sugar into a 1-quart mold or bowl, swirling it to evenly coat the bottom with the caramel syrup. Heat 2 cups milk containing 2 strips orange peel and 1 strip lemon peel until the milk reaches the boiling point, and discard the strips. Beat 3 whole eggs with 5 tablespoons sugar and 1 teaspoon vanilla. Little by little, beat the hot milk into the eggs. Pour this mixture into the mold, and remove any foam from the top with a paper towel. In a baking pan large enough to hold the mold, place a paper towel and fill with 1 inch of boiling water. Place the mold on the towel (which helps prevent the custard from splitting) and bake in a 375° oven for about 1 hour, or until the custard has set. Chill the custard for 24 hours before serving. To serve, unmold on a large platter and surround with a ring of peach halves, hollowed side up. In a small pan, warm 3 tablespoons brandy with 3 tablespoons Grand Marnier liqueur, light it, and pour the flaming liquid into the centers of the peach halves.

PEARS IMPÉRATRICE
(*Poires Impératrice*)

Put ½ cup raw white rice, preferably short-grained, in 4 cups cold water and bring just to the boiling point. Drain the blanched rice and put it into a heavy saucepan with 4 cups hot milk, 2 tablespoons sugar, ¼ teaspoon vanilla extract. Bring to a gentle boil, stirring occasionally to prevent the rice from sticking and the milk from filming on the surface. Cook for 25 to 30 minutes, or until the rice is very soft and tender. Drain the rice, reserving the milk, and spread the rice on a plate to cool.

Dissolve 2½ teaspoons powdered gelatin in 2 tablespoons cold water, add this to the reserved milk (you should have about 1 cup), and bring just to the simmering point. In a bowl, lightly beat 2 egg yolks. Little by little, add the milk to the yolks, and then return milk and yolks to the pan. Cook this custard over very low heat without allowing the mixture to boil, until it is thick enough to coat a spoon. Pour the custard into a bowl, mix in the rice, and allow to cool.

Dissolve 1 teaspoon and a scant ½ teaspoon powdered gelatin in ¼ cup white wine. Pour this mixture into a 4-cup ring (Savarin) mold, tilt the mold to coat the curved bottom evenly, and chill in the refrigerator.

Whip ½ cup heavy cream and fold it into the rice mixture, taking care to achieve a good blend. (At this time, you may also fold in ¼ cup chopped candied fruit that you have washed clean in water and soaked in 2 table-spoons cognac for ½ hour.) Gently pour the cold mixture into the mold on top of the gelatin, and chill thoroughly.

Loosen the rice ring by dipping the mold briefly into warm water, or by covering the back of the mold with a hot towel. Unmold onto a serving platter at least 3 inches larger in diameter than the rice ring.

Combine canned pear halves to form whole pears, and arrange the pears in the center of the rice ring. Strain the syrup from a 10-ounce jar of apricot jam and heat it slowly until it coats a spoon thickly. Brush the syrup on the pears to glaze them all over. To the remaining syrup add 2 to 3 tablespoons rum or pear alcohol and a little syrup from the canned pears, and mix to make a smooth, light sauce. Pour a thin layer of this sauce around the rice ring, and serve the remaining sauce in a sauceboat.

✣ 15   *The Pastry Doughs*

The mastery of just a few pastry doughs, plus an understanding of *Salpicons* and Purées, will put you in command of literally hundreds of French entrees, luncheon dishes, hors d'oeuvres, and garnishes that are rarely enjoyed in America. These dishes range from simple but delicious preparations, made from leftover foods, to very elegant presentation dishes that few people have ever seen. The pastry doughs given here are the key to *Timbales, Vol-au-Vents, Bouchées,* Tartlets and *Barquettes, Croustades, Pâtés, Rissoles, Choux, Profiteroles,* and Éclairs. All of these can be made with one or more of three basic pastry doughs—a short, tender pie pastry, flaky pastry, and cream puff pastry.

THE PASTES
(*Les Pâtes*)

The French word for pastry is *pâtisserie,* and it includes pies, tarts, cakes, and cookies. The dough from which these pastries are made is called *pâte* or paste. The word *pâté,* with an accent on the *e,* means something else again

—namely, a smooth savory paste of meat, as in *pâté de foie gras.* Thus, we can have such a thing as *pâte à pâté,* which is a dough paste especially made to enclose a meat paste.

As you might expect, the French have a specific paste for everything. But these are nothing more than refinements on the basic pastes I will give you here. I will also tell you what happens when you add a little of this or take away a little of that. By understanding the interaction of the basic ingredients you will soon be doing the adding and subtracting yourself without the benefit of recipes. We will begin with the short pastes.

✳ SHORT PASTE
(*Pâte Brisée*)

Basic short paste is a mixture of flour and fat moistened with water. A good pastry crust must be tender, flaky, and flavorsome.

When flour is mixed with water and kneaded, the proteins in the flour are changed to gluten. Gluten forms an elastic, weblike framework that holds the flour, starch, and water together in an elastic mass. If rolled out and baked, the resulting crust would hold its shape but it would be dense and hard as plaster. To tenderize the crust, we add fat to it. The fat interferes with the gluten, getting between the individual particles and preventing them from linking up in long strands. This is called shortening. The more fat that is added, the shorter and more tender the crust will be. Too much fat, however, will interrupt the gluten to such an extent that the crust will crumble and fall apart.

Thus, within the crusts of our pies, a desperate silent battle is waged between the shortening and the gluten. You must referee this battle to achieve the crust you desire.

On the side of gluten are water and kneading. The more water you use, and the more you knead the resulting dough, the stronger the gluten becomes and the tougher the crust. On the side of shortening are warmth and intermixing. The warmer the shortening, and the more thoroughly it infiltrates between the strands of gluten, the stronger the shortening power and the weaker and more crumbly the crust.

With very little experience you can predict the quality of a pastry crust when you are rolling out and shaping the dough. If it tends to be short, it will be crumbly when too cold, greasy when too warm, and very difficult to handle without tearing even when it is at the proper temperature. If it tends to be too glutinous, which it will be if it is too floury or watery, it will stubbornly resist rolling out and it will shrink from the shape you form it in even before it is baked. We must compromise, as we must so often in cooking, between these extremes to achieve the tenderness of crust we desire.

But a pastry crust should be more than just optimally tender. It should be flaky, too. This flakiness is a joyful sight and it feels delightfully crisp on the teeth. A crust is flaky when its surface is delicately blistered and when small flakes chip away when the crust is broken. This is evidence that it is layered throughout with delicate leaves of crisp baked flour, separately basted with rich fat, preferably butter.

Flakiness of crust is achieved by keeping the fat and the flour distinct from one another. They must be intermixed but separate. You accomplish this by "cutting in," cutting the fat up in the dry flour with a pastry blender, two knives, or your fingertips. The fat must be cold, for if it is meltingly soft it will blend with the dry flour to form a paste.

When you add water and the dough is formed, distinct bits of fat are contained in it. When you roll out the dough, you flatten these fat bits and the moistened flour into separate but interlocking sheets. When you bake the rolled dough, the sheets of moistened flour harden into small, crisp flakes. These flakes are tough, but they are so small their toughness goes unnoticed. The crust is shortened by the fat, but it holds together. And for a bonus you have a flaky lightness because air, which you have inadvertently trapped in the dough, expands in the heat and forces the flakes apart.

If the fat in the dough is in pieces the size of a rice grain, your crust will be finer-flaked than it would be if the fat is in pieces the size of a pea. But the important thing to remember is that in order to get flakiness at all, the dough must be cold when it is formed and when it is rolled out. It must also be cold when baked, and it must be baked in a hot oven so that the flakes of flour may form before the fat can dissolve them. The oven may be turned down later, but initially it must be at 425°.

Our third concern is flavor. The only seasonings usual for pastry crusts are salt and sugar. If the crust is for a savory filling, we add 2 teaspoons salt for each pound of flour and ¼ teaspoon sugar. The salt contributes to the good taste of baked flour; the sugar, which is undetectable, adds roundness to the total flavor. If the crust is for a sweet filling, we add 5 tablespoons sugar for each pound flour, and ¼ teaspoon salt to add roundness to the total flavor. Given these ingredients, they will taste their best when the fat is good fresh butter. For savory fillings you may use either sweet or salted butter. If you use salted butter, allow for the fact that it contains approximately 1 teaspoon salt per pound; deduct the butter's salt from the amount of salt given in the recipe. For sweet fillings you should use sweet (unsalted) butter. Lard has a sweet flavor that many like. Margarines vary in flavor. Vegetable shortenings are tasteless. Butter, as usual, is favored by the French.

There is yet another ingredient we may add to the mixture. We may add the busy egg. Its major function, when used, is to help the gluten form a framework of crust. The egg does this by virtue of its own protein, which congeals and forms a supplementary framework. In addition, if well beaten, it incorporates air into the dough. To add the egg, beat it, mix it with the ice water, and count it as part of the liquid. The egg will also add color and flavor. But the use of egg is only supplementary. The real contest is between the moistened gluten and the fat, the starch being an interested bystander, and the properties of the crust being the prize. Let us make this crust to suit ourselves.

PÂTE ORDINAIRE
(General purpose short pastry dough for pies,
tarts, patty shells, and pastry cases)

Flour, 3½ cups sifted flour, or 1 pound	Butter, chilled, salted or sweet, 1 cup or 8 ounces
Salt, 1½ or 2 teaspoons	Ice water, ½ to ¾ cup as needed
Sugar, ¼ teaspoon	

The first step is to mix the dry ingredients with the butter. This must be done with a nice restraint. If the butter is not sufficiently intermixed, the crust will be like a hard Swiss cheese. If the butter is too thoroughly intermixed, the crust will crumble like a butter cooky.

Sift the flour and salt into a chilled bowl. Use 1½ teaspoons salt if your butter is salted, 2 teaspoons salt if your butter is sweet. Cut the chilled butter into ½-inch pieces and put them in the flour. Cut the pieces of butter with a pastry blender or rub flour and butter together with your fingertips. Use only your fingertips; your warm palms will melt the butter and create a flour-butter paste that will resist the absorption of water and refuse to form a dough. Continue blending until you have achieved the consistency of dry oatmeal, the small aggregates of butter being coated with flour.

Holding a receptacle of ice water in one hand, add ¼ cup and work the dough with your other hand or with a fork until it begins to hold together. As more water is needed, sprinkle it on the dry portions of the dough. Add only a few drops at a time for fear that you might add too much. As soon as the dough forms a ball, it has taken in enough water.

Rely on the look and feel of the dough to tell you how much water to use. Flour proportions, dry ingredients, and fats differ and require varying amounts of water. You need only enough water to make the dough workable. Too much water will make the dough sticky. It will also overencourage the gluten, and your crust will be tough.

Place the ball of dough on a lightly floured board or marble top and flatten it. Now knead the dough by capturing small, 2-tablespoon-size quantities under the heel of your hand and smearing it in a 6-inch streak across the board. Treat the entire ball of dough in this manner. This blends the flour, starch, and the activated gluten more thoroughly. The smearing action also serves to create sheets of butter in the dough, resulting in a flakier crust.

Scrape and gather the dough up in a ball, work it briefly to smooth and pack it together, and wrap it in wax paper or plastic. Chill in the refrigerator for at least 2 hours, and at best 24 hours, before using it. This allows the gluten to relax and become more tractable under your rolling pin. You may keep the dough in the refrigerator for 3 or 4 days.

When the gluten has rested, you are ready to shape the dough. This amount of dough is more than you can conveniently roll out at once, so cut the ball in two. Place one of the halves on a lightly floured board or marble top. If it is very stiff, beat it briefly with your rolling pin to flatten it and make the butter more plastic. Roll outward from the middle toward the edges, easing up on the pressure as you reach the edge. If the dough shatters at the edges, press it back together. Work quickly to keep the dough from becoming too warm; if it shows a hint of squishiness or greasiness, chill it in the refrigerator.

Also, roll the dough as little as possible to keep from overexciting the gluten. This would make the dough too elastic and cause it to shrink in the pie pan or mold.

Finally, shape the dough to fit your pie plate, or any of the patty shell or pastry case molds described in Chapter 4. Allow the shaped dough to rest again before baking, for 1 to 2 hours.

Knead scraps of leftover dough in a ball and store it wrapped, in the refrigerator. This dough may be kept for 3 or 4 days and be rolled out again after resting for a few hours. It will never be as good as the original dough, however.

When your crust is baked, analyze it. If it is too short—brittle and crumbly—perhaps you mixed the butter and flour too thoroughly, or the dough became too warm. If it is flaky but tough, perhaps you failed to mix the butter and flour sufficiently, or used too much water, or rolled the dough too much, or failed to rest it for a long enough time.

Both tenderness and flakiness can be increased by substituting lard for all or part of the butter at the expense of the butter flavor. A good compromise is to use 1 part lard to 3 parts butter. In this recipe, you would therefore use ¼ cup lard and ¾ cup butter, cutting them both into the flour at the same time. If you go beyond this proportion, to maintain the same degree of shortening you should allow for the increased shortening power of the 100 percent-fat lard versus the 80 percent-fat butter. Consequently, for a half lard, half butter mixture use 3½ ounces or 7 tablespoons lard and 4 ounces or 8 tablespoons or ½ cup butter. For an all lard shortening, use 7 ounces or ⅞ cup lard.

PÂTE À FONCER FINE
(Especially fine short pastry dough for elegant tarts, shells, and cases)

Flour, 3½ cups sifted flour, or 1 pound
Salt, 1 or 2 teaspoons
Sugar, ¼ teaspoon

Butter, chilled, salted or sweet, 1½ cups or 12 ounces
Egg, 1
Ice water, ½ to ¾ cup

This dough forms a richer, more fragile crust than the preceding one. Because of its higher fat content, it is a little trickier to handle. Just keep the ingredients cold, and prepare the dough as for the preceding *Pâte Ordinaire*.

If you use salted butter, use only 1 teaspoon salt. Beat the egg with ½ cup ice water, add it, and count it as part of the liquid measure. Use only as much as is required to form a dough. If more liquid is needed, add ice water.

PÂTE SUCRÉE
(Sweetened short pastry dough)

Patty shells and tart shells that contain sweet fillings may themselves be sweetened. Use either of the two preceding recipes with unsalted butter, substituting 5 tablespoons sugar and a pinch of salt for the amounts of salt and sugar given. (The salt enhances the taste of the sugar.)

PÂTE À PÂTÉ
(Short pastry dough for enclosing *pâtés* and meats that are baked in the shell)

Flour, 3½ cups sifted or 1 pound
Butter, chilled, salted or sweet, ½ cup or 4 ounces
Salt, 2 teaspoons

Sugar, ¼ teaspoon
Egg, 1
Ice water, ½ to ¾ cup

This dough provides a sturdier crust to contain *pâté* mixtures and meat juices. It is baked along with its contents, either in a mold or wrapped around a piece of meat. It is assembled exactly as the preceding dough, *Pâte à Foncer Fine*. And it is fun to say, *Pâte à Pâté*.

✳ PUFF PASTE
(*Pâte Feuilletée*)

This is the famous "thousand-leaved" pastry dough for incredibly light tart-lets, tarts, and pastry cases ranging from the tiny *petite bouchée* to the com-manding *vol-au-vent*. It comprises over 700 layers of dough and butter. It is really quite easy to make if you observe two important rules. The dough and the butter must be of the same consistency. And the ingredients must be kept cold.

Flour, 3½ cups sifted flour or 1 pound
Salt, 1 or 2 teaspoons
Ice water, about 1 cup
Butter, chilled, salted or sweet, 1 pound

Sift the flour and salt into a chilled bowl. Use 1 teaspoon salt if your butter is salted, 2 teaspoons of salt if your butter is sweet. Holding a recepta-cle of ice water in one hand, add ¼ cup and work the dough with your other hand or with a fork until it begins to hold together. As more water is needed, sprinkle it on the dry portions of the dough. As soon as the dough forms a ball, knead it briefly to make certain it will hold together. If it is too brittle, flatten it and sprinkle on a few drops of water. Do not knead the dough too much or your crust will be tough. Shape it in a ball, wrap it in wax paper or plastic, and chill it in the refrigerator.

Now you must bring the chilled butter to the right consistency. Place the butter on a lightly floured board, or between 2 pieces of wax paper, and pound it with your rolling pin to make it more plastic. Now knead the cold, plastic butter with your hands, working and squeezing it to "wring out" the almost 20 percent of water that it contains. If the butter becomes warm or greasy, plunge it in a bowl of cold water and continue kneading in the water until it is quite plastic and waxy, and has about the same consistency as the dough. The butter will give up its water as readily in the ice water as it will in the open air.

Take the chilled dough and roll it out on a floured board to form a rough circle about 14 inches across. Take the butter from the ice water, dry it, and form it into a rough 6-inch square. Place the butter in the center of the dough, and fold the dough up and over the butter on all 4 sides. Pinch the dough to completely enclose the butter, but do not stretch the dough. This package of dough and butter will look rough and untidy, but that is perfectly all right. Wrap it well in wax paper or plastic, and chill it in the refrigerator for at least 30 minutes.

Now you are ready to start doing your "turns." Place the chilled dough and butter package on a lightly floured board or marble top. Beat it a little with your rolling pin to make it more malleable. Roll it out to form a rectangle 8 inches wide and 16 inches long. Then, as you would fold a business letter, fold the bottom ⅓ of the dough (facing you) up over the middle ⅓, and fold the top ⅓ down over the bottom ⅓. This folding, which gives you 3 layers of butter, constitutes your first turn.

Now turn the dough so that the short, open end is facing you and roll it out again to form a rectangle about 8 inches across and 16 inches long. Again fold the rectangle into thirds. This folding, which gives you 9 layers of butter, constitutes your second turn. Give the dough a poke with your 2 fingers, leaving 2 impressions that indicate how many turns the dough has been given. This is traditional. Then wrap the dough in wax paper or plastic and chill it in the refrigerator for 30 minutes.

After the dough is chilled, beat it again with the rolling pin to make it plastic and make 2 more turns. These will give you 81 layers of butter. Poke the dough with 4 fingers, indicating 4 turns, wrap it, and chill it again.

You must give the dough 2 more turns, and these should be made just before it is baked. All told, you will have 1,459 layers of butter and of dough. Until you are ready to bake, keep the puff paste tightly wrapped in the refrigerator, where it may be kept for 3 or 4 days, or freeze it.

✳ CREAM PUFF PASTE
(Pâte à Chou)

This pastry puffs up by virtue of the large amount of eggs it contains, leaving a hollow center that can be gainfully occupied by a sweet or savory filling. The following recipe is for puffs to which a savory filling is added. If the puffs are to receive a sweet dessert filling, use just a pinch of salt and add 1 teaspoon sugar.

Water, 1 cup	Pepper, ⅛ teaspoon
Butter, 8 tablespoons	Flour, 1¼ cups
Salt, ½ teaspoon	Eggs, 4

Combine water, butter, salt, and pepper and bring to a boil. Remove from the fire and stir in the flour all at once. Beat to blend thoroughly, return to the fire, and stir with a wooden spoon for a few minutes until the mixture leaves the sides of the pan and forms a ball. Remove from the heat, make a depression in the center of the dough ball, add 1 whole egg, and beat vigorously until the egg is absorbed by the dough. Add 3 more whole eggs, one by one, beating each one into the dough until it is completely absorbed.

Cream puff paste is usually made just before it is used. It is at its best when fresh and warm. If some is left over, brush it with butter, wrap it securely in foil or plastic, and store in the refrigerator or freezer. Before using, heat the pastry in a saucepan, beating constantly, until it is barely lukewarm.

Depending upon their size, shape, and filling, cream puff pastries are given different names. Round puffs are called *choux,* small round puffs are called *profiteroles,* and elongated puffs are called *éclairs.*

To make small puffs or profiteroles: spoon half-walnut-sized gobs of paste onto a buttered baking sheet, allowing enough room between puffs for them to double in size. Or fill a pastry bag with the cream puff paste and squeeze onto the baking sheet through a ½-inch nozzle. Brush the tops of the puffs with 1 egg beaten with 1 teaspoon water and bake in a 425° oven for 20 minutes or until the puffs have risen and are brown and crispy. Remove them from the oven, pierce each of them on one side with a knife so that the moist centers can dry out, and return them to the turned-off oven for about 5 minutes.

To make large puffs or choux: spoon patties measuring 2 inches in diameter and 1 inch high onto a buttered baking sheet, allowing room enough between puffs for them to double in size, or fill a pastry bag with the cream puff paste and squeeze onto the baking sheet through a ¾-inch nozzle. Brush with 1 egg beaten with 1 tablespoon water, bake at 425° for 20 minutes, and at 375° for 15 to 20 minutes more or until the puffs have risen, are brown and crisp, and feel light for their size. Remove from the oven, make a slit on one side of each puff, and return to the turned off oven for 5 to 10 minutes. If the centers are still moist and uncooked, return them to the oven for 5 minutes more.

To make éclairs: for small éclairs, use a pastry bag to squeeze 2-inch by ½-inch strips of paste onto a buttered baking sheet. To make large éclairs, squeeze 3½-inch by 1-inch strips onto the sheet. Proceed as for small or large puffs, above.

Small savory puffs can be filled by piping various hot Purées into them through a pastry bag and then heating them in the oven for a few minutes.

Small dessert puffs can be filled in the same way with cream, ice cream, or custard fillings, topped with a chocolate or vanilla sauce, and chilled.

Large puffs can be filled with Purées, *Salpicons*, or other creamed preparations as hors d'oeuvres or small entrees.

Leftover puffs can be frozen and reheated in the oven just before serving.

Small appetizer cheese puffs, called *gougères*, are made by mixing ½ cup grated Swiss cheese or half Swiss and half Parmesan with 1 cup warm cream puff paste.

INDEX

Haddock, 230–31
  au Gratin, Creamed (Subst.), 243
  Hot Boiled (Subst.), 243
Hake, 231, 238
  au Gratin, Creamed (Subst.), 243
  Hot Boiled (Subst.), 243
Halibut, 231
  Fermière (Subst.), 247–48
  au Gratin, Creamed (Subst.), 243
  Hot Boiled (Subst.), 243
  à la Niçoise (Subst.), 260–61
Ham (Jambon),
  Calf's Liver à la Bordelaise with, 441
  Cold Appetizer, 160
  Eggs (Oeufs) with,
    à l'Alsacienne, 210
    à l'Italienne, 207
    Omelette au, 216
  Fresh. *See* Pork: Roast
  Garbure Soup with, 184–85
  Little Quiches with, 165
  Salads with, 562
  Soufflé, 220
    à la Strasbourgeoise, 220
Harvest Fish, 229
Herb Bunch, 113, 118
Herbs, 138–39
  Aromatics, 113–14
  Fines Herbes, 130
  Pluches, 55, 146
  in Sauces, 94
Herring (Herengs), 231
  Lake, 239
  à la Lyonnaise, Sautéed, 263
Hors d'Oeuvres, 157–66. *See also* Appetizers
Horseradish (Raifort) Sauce,
  Cold, 104
  Hot (Albert Sauce), 95

Ice, Apricot, 578

Jack Cheese, 573
Jellies. *See* Aspic Jellies
Jewfish, 235
Julienne, 51
Jus, au, 52

Kidneys (Rognons), 443–45
  Brochettes of, 445
  Broiled, 445
    au Vert-Pré, 445
  Fat, 130
  Sautéed, 444–45
    Bercy, 445
    à la Bordelaise, 444
    Chasseur, 445

à l'Indienne, 444–45
  with Mushrooms, 444
  with Wine, 444
Kingfish, 231
  California, 229
Kneading, 52
Kromeskies (Cromesquis), 139
  Appetizer, 165
  Batter for Deep-Frying, 116
  Egg (Oeufs), 203

Lamb (Agneau), 351, 423–33
  Braised, 27–28, 428–30
    en Ballon, Shoulder of, 430
    à la Bourgeoise, Shoulder of, 429
    en Daube à la Bourguignonne, Stuffed
      Shoulder of, 430
    à la Soubise, 429
    with a Spoon, 429
  Chops, 432–33
    à l'Anglaise, 432
    Barman, 432
    Du Barry, 432
    Maréchale, 433
    à la Minute, 433
    Montrouge, 433
    Navarraise, 432
    à la Parisienne, 433
  Cooking, 424
  Cuts of, 423–24
  Grilled or Broiled, 39, 432
  Kidneys. *See* Kidneys
  Liver, 440
  Pot-Roasted, 427–28
    à la Bonne Femme, Loin of, 428
    à la Bordelaise, Leg of, 427
    à la Niçoise, Loin of, 427
    with Noodles, Loin of, 428
  Roast, 424–27
    à la Boulangère, Leg of, 426
    à la Bouquetière, Loin of, 427
    à la Bruxelloise, Leg of, 426
    à la Clamart, Loin of, 427
    à la Dauphine, Leg of, 426
    à la Jardinière, Shoulder of, 426
    Leg of, 425–26
    Marie-Louise, Loin of, 427
    à la Parisienne, Shoulder of, 426
    Parslied Leg of, 425–26
    à la Renaissance, Leg of, 426
  Sautéed, 41, 432–33
  Stews, 430–32
    à l'Anglaise (Irish Stew), 430
    Curry of, 431
    Old-Fashioned Blanquette, 430
    Old-Fashioned Fricassee, 430

Pilaf of, 431–32
Printanier, 431
Langouste, 274
Lard, 130
Larding, 52
Lardoons, 139
Lasagna, Roast Chicken à la Sicilienne
Stuffed with, 323
Leaf Lard, 130
Leeks, 510–11
Boiled, 513–14
Braised, 514
in Cream, 514
au Gratin, 514
Mornay, 514
and Potato Soup, 182
Lemons (Limons), 139–40
Lettuce (Laitue), 498–501
Artichokes Clamart with Peas and, 457
Braised, 500–1
in Brown Butter, 501
in Cream, 501
au Gratin, 501
Peas, French Style with, 516–17
Purée of, 501
Salad. *See also* Salads, Artichoke and, 561
Warm, 559
Soaking, 22
Soufflé, 219
Soup, Cream of, 180
Starches in, 16–17
Liederkranz Cheese, 569
Limburger Cheese, 569
Liver (Foie), 440–43. *See also* Foie Gras
Braised Calf's, 442–43
Broiled Calf's, 442
en Brochette, 442
à l'Espagnole, 442
Sautéed Calf's, 441–42
à l'Anglaise, 441
à la Bordelaise, 441
à la Bourguignonne, 442
à l'Italienne, 441
à la Lyonnaise, 441
à la Provençale, 441–42
Lobster (Homard), 274–79
American, 277
Appetizer, Cold, 161
to Bake, 277
Bisque, 176
to Boil, 276
Bouillabaisse with, 187
to Broil, 277
Butter, 104
to Clean, 276
Cooking, 275–77

in Cream, 278
to Cut Up, 276
Eggs à la Americaine with, 204
à la Française, 278
to Kill, 276
à la Nage, 278
to Poach, 277
Russian Salad with, 562
Sauce, 104
to Sauté, 277
Seafood Salad, 562
Soufflé, 220
Soup, Velouté, 179
on the Spit, 279
Thermidor, 278–79
Longhorn Cheese, 573

Macédoine, 140
Macerating, 52
Mackerel (Maquereau), 231, 232
à la Boulonnaise, 246
with Gooseberry Sauce, Boiled, 244
à la Venetian, Filets of, 246
Madeira (Madère) Sauce, 105
Marinade; Marinating, 52–53, 140
Marrow (Moelle), 141
Sauce, 105
Masking, 53
Matelote à la Bourguignonne, 269
Matelote à la Marinière, 269
Matelote à la Normande, 269–70
Matignon, 141
Matjes, 231
Mayonnaise, 86–87, 556
with Anchovy, 556
Blender, 86–87
with Curry, 556
with Herbs, 556
with Roquefort, 556
with Tarragon, 556
with Watercress, 556
Mazagrans, 141–42
Meat (Viandes), 351–449. *See also* Force-
meats; Stocks; etc.; specific meats
Aspic, 63, 73–74
Braising, 27–28
Browning, 46
Cabbage Stuffed with, 476–77
Cold Appetizer, Smoked, 160
Cooking, 14–16
with Dry Heat. *See* specific methods
with Moist Heat, 17–18. *See also* spe-
cific methods
Croquettes, 125
Deep-Frying, 43, 116
Galantines, 137

Purée of, 542
Sautéed, 540
Stuffed, 441–42
Winter (Courges), 538–39, 540, 542–43
  Baked, 542
    Stuffed, 543
  Glazed, 542
    Purée of, 543
Starches, Cooking, 16–17
Steaming, 25–26
Stewing, 29–30
Stilton Cheese, 570
Stirring, 56
Stock Fat, 130
Stocks, 59–74
  Aspic, 62–63, 72–74
  Beef Consommé, 60, 64–66
  Brown, 61, 67–69
  Chicken, 60, 71
    Aspic, 63, 74
    Consommé, 61, 67
  Consommé, 59–61, 64–67
  Court Bouillon, 62, 71–72
  Estouffade, 61, 67–68
  Fish, 62, 70–71
    Aspic, 63, 74
  Giblet, 70
  Meat. *See also* specific meats
    Aspic, 63, 73–74
  Starch-Thickened, 92–93
  Veal, 61, 68–69
  White, 61, 69–70
    Court Bouillon, 62, 71
    Fish, 62, 70–71
Straining, 65
Striped Bass. *See* Bass
Studding, 56
Sturgeon, 236–37
Subrics, 151–52, 166
  Beef, à la Ménagère, 166
  Spinach, 166
Sucker, White. *See* Mullet
Suet, 130
Sweetbreads (Ris), 434–39
  Braised, 437–39
    Clamart, 437
    à la Crème, 438–39
    au Gratin, 439
    à la Jardinière, 438
    à la Périgourdine, 438
    à la Princesse, 438
    Talleyrand, 438
  Broiled, 436–37
    Jocelyne, 436–37
    St. Germain, 437
  Sautéed, 435–36
    à l'Allemande, Cutlets, 436

Florentine, Cutlets, 436
Grand Duke, Cutlets, 435
à l'Italienne, Cutlets, 436
à la Maréchale, Cutlets, 436
Rossini, Cutlets, 436
Sweet Flavors, 10, 11
Sweet Peppers. *See* Pepper(s)
Sweet Potato(es) (Patates), 543–44
  à la Lavigerie, 544
  Soufflé, 219
Swirling in, 56
Swiss Cheese, 573–74
Swordfish, 237

Tapioca, 152
Terragon (Estragon),
  Butter, 111
  Mayonnaise with, 556
  Sauce, 111
  Steak with, 396
Tartlets (Tartelettes), 152
  Appetizer, 162
    Hot, 164
  Fish, 266
Tarts (Tartes), 152
  Apple (Tatin), 577
Taste, 9–10
Tautog, 237
Terrines, 152–53
Thermometer, Meat, 34
Thickening, 56
Timbales, 153–54
Tomatoed Soubise Sauce, 111
Tomatoing, 56
Tomatoes (Tomates), 544–49. *As ingredient, see* specific dishes, *esp.* Espagnole, Provençale styles
  à l'Américaine, 159
  Deep-Fried, 548
  Fondue, 548
    à la Grecque, 548
    à la Niçoise, 548
  Grilled, 547
  au Naturel, 160
  Purée, 83
  Salads, 558–59
    Artichoke and, 561
    Green Bean, Cucumber, and, 561
    Potato and, 561
  Sauce, 82–83
  Sautéed, 547
    à la Lyonnaise, 547
    à la Provençale, 547
  Soufflé, 219
  Soup, Cream of, 179
  Soup, Purée of, 175
  Soup, Velouté, 177–78